Traveling Companions

Walking with the Saints of the Orthodox Church

Chris Moorey

ANCIENT FAITH PUBLISHING ✢ CHESTERTON, INDIANA

Scripture quotations are taken from the New King James Version, © 1979, 1980, 1982 by Thomas Nelson, Inc. Used by permission.

Published by:
   Ancient Faith Publishing
   A division of Ancient Faith Ministries
   P.O. Box 748
   Chesterton, IN 46304

Printed in the United States of America

ISBN: 978-1-936270-47-7

Cover design by Mark Wainwright, symbologycreative.com
Icon of All Saints (on cover) by Erin Kimmett, Annunciation Press, www.apicons.com

Library of Congress Cataloging-in-Publication Data

Moorey, Chris, 1948-
Traveling companions : walking with the saints of the Orthodox Church /
by Chris Moorey.
   pages cm
ISBN 978-1-936270-47-7 (alk. paper) -- ISBN 1-936270-47-1 (alk. paper)
1. Christian saints--Biography. 2. Orthodox Eastern Church--Biography.
I. Title.

BX393.M66 2013
281.9092'2--dc23

[B]

Dedicated to all those nameless saints "whose deeds are known only to God."

For all the saints, who from their labors rest,
Who Thee by faith before the world confessed,
Thy Name, O Jesus, be forever blessed.
Alleluia, Alleluia!
(Anglican Hymn by William Walsham How, 1864)

Contents

Why Yet Another Book of Saints?

When I see a film like *Hotel Rwanda* or *Schindler's List*, I am astounded by the way ordinary people with no pretensions to heroism can be catapulted by circumstances into heroic deeds. In much the same way, when I read the stories of the saints, it is apparent to me that God sometimes chooses the most unlikely people to proclaim His name, often unto the ultimate sacrifice.

In the Orthodox Church, we rightly venerate the saints as holy men and women who have heroically proclaimed the Faith and now have their place with God in heaven. However, before they were saints, they were people like us with human strengths and weaknesses. Even in the Gospels, it is the human fallibility of the apostles—their confusion and fear after the Crucifixion, Peter's impetuosity and short temper, Thomas's doubts—that gives the Gospel story a conviction of truth that would be absent from a mere myth or philosophical allegory. Going further back, what more reluctant hero could one find than Jonah, who did everything he could to avoid doing God's will until he was convinced by a large fish (Jonah 1)? Even the greatest patriarch, Moses, asked, "Why me?" and tried to wriggle out of his destiny when God gave him his mission (Exodus 3—4).

I believe that in a secular and skeptical age, it is not enough to speak in pompous prose or hushed and solemn whispers of the saints' invariable piety, their continual miracles, their unfailing courage. If we look behind the halo and see the human faces of these wonderful men and women, we may see them as living guides and companions who travel with us through life. Even if we are not Christians, we can see how ordinary people can sometimes make a big difference. It is with this in mind that I thought it worth making a contribution to the extensive literature on saints.

In the following pages, I have tried to give some idea of the wide variation in background and character of the men and women we call saints. They range from the world-renowned to the obscure, from saints venerated for centuries to those who are still awaiting official glorification. In addition, I'm a sucker for a good story and have therefore invoked author's privilege to include a number of saints I have a particular liking for or just find interesting.

However, the Orthodox calendar includes thousands of saints, and since this is not an encyclopedia, I have been forced to be selective. Wherever possible, feast days have been cross-checked, but regional differences exist, especially among the minor saints' days, and I cannot guarantee total accuracy. Some confusion may also occur with the dates of some of the Serbian and Russian saints due to the thirteen-day difference between the Julian and Gregorian calendars (see Appendix B).

By its nature, this book only scratches the surface of these extraordinary stories. These pen-pictures of the saints, although thoroughly researched, are very much written from a personal point of view. They constitute neither hagiography nor history, and I strongly recommend you have a look at some of the books and websites listed in Further Reading. If your appetite is whetted and you are tempted to read more, my work is done!

General Notes

All biblical references are taken from the New King James Version of the Bible. This is an excellent fusion of accuracy, clarity, and beauty and, at least in the quotations I have used, does not conflict with Orthodox belief.

The main feast day of saints in the Orthodox Church is usually their repose (martyrdom or death). Other dates celebrated include the transfer of their relics or the date of their glorification as saints (especially in the Russian Church).

You will also find the term *Synaxis* used to describe some of the feast days. This literally means "assembly" or "congregation" and is used in two ways. It can describe the feast for a group of similar saints—for example, the Synaxis of the Apostles of the Seventy. It can also relate to a general veneration and celebration of a saint associated with the previous day's feast. For example, the Synaxis of the Archangel Gabriel is celebrated the day after the Annunciation.

The main feast day of each saint mentioned is shown in brackets after the name. Where additional feast days exist, these are shown at the end of the article. The names of saints mentioned in the text who are also treated in this volume are shown in bold type.

Generally, I have used the word *Pascha* to describe the Feast of the Resurrection of Christ. Most languages use derivations of this Greek word meaning "Passover," and it is widely used in the Orthodox Church. Although the word "Easter" is almost universally used in the English language, its derivation from pagan roots makes many Orthodox uncomfortable with it.

Our Traveling Companions

The Unseen Congregation

Go into any Orthodox church and you will find the walls (and sometimes the ceiling) covered with icons of the saints. Although these are often of great beauty, they are not merely intended as decoration. They represent the unseen congregation that accompanies the living congregation in its worship.

Christ, the Lord of all, presides, and the **Blessed Virgin Mary**, first among the saints, watches over us. When celebrating the Holy Eucharist, we are "invisibly escorted by the angelic hosts," surrounded by "those who have fallen asleep in the Faith, forefathers, fathers, patriarchs, prophets, apostles, preachers, evangelists, martyrs, confessors, ascetics, and every righteous spirit made perfect in the Faith" (Divine Liturgy of **St. John Chrysostom**). In every aspect of an Orthodox Christian's life, the saints are our traveling companions, walking alongside us through the good times and the bad.

So what is it that makes a saint? Throughout the history of the Church, certain men and women have stood out in their devotion to God—sometimes through the holiness of their lives; sometimes through their work in proclaiming the Faith; often by the supreme sacrifice of martyrdom. This doesn't necessarily mean that everything they did was good, or even that they were all "nice" people.

In fact, as you will see, the saints are a somewhat mixed bunch. However, all stand as examples and guides to the faithful as having heroically proclaimed the Faith, even if only by a single act.

Indeed, it can be said that the very first "canonization" in the Christian Church was Jesus' promise to the penitent thief on the Cross: "Assuredly, I say to you, today you will be with Me in Paradise" (Luke 23:39–43). This was certainly a dramatic example of last-minute repentance, and its importance is recognized in Orthodox iconography by the inclusion of the thief at the foot of icons of All Saints.

The procedure whereby a person is glorified as a saint varies between different traditions of the Orthodox Church. Although the procedure has become more formalized in recent years, it is a relatively "democratic" process whereby a saint is generally recognized "without a prior initiative or intervention by a Church authority but rather by the voice and conscience of the entire body of the Church." In practice, this means that if veneration of a saintly person becomes widespread and/or continues for many years, the local bishop or Holy Synod will investigate the claims and eventually make a decision on whether or not formally to declare the person to be a saint. This can take anything from a few months (**Myron of Crete, New Martyr**) to more than a hundred years (**Cosmas of Aetolia**).

Once the bishops agree to the glorification, a special memorial service is held at which icons of the new saint are unveiled and new hymns to the saint are chanted. The feast day is established, the life of the saint is published, and other Orthodox Churches are notified of the glorification. To be recognized as a saint, the person must be a baptized member of the Orthodox Church and fulfill one or more of the following conditions: martyrdom for the Orthodox Christian Faith, a holy life, exceptional service to the Church, miracles performed by God through the saint (not a necessary condition), and sometimes the preservation of the body intact, "though this is not always a sign of sainthood."[1]

Both similarities and differences exist between the saints of the Eastern and Western Churches. The apostles and the martyrs of the early Church are, of course, venerated by both Orthodox and Roman Catholic, even if many of the feast days differ. Moreover, most of the Fathers of the Church, whether from the Greek East or the Latin West, are revered throughout the Christian world. Many of the early popes are honored as saints in the Orthodox Church, while prayers of **St. John Chrysostom** and the creed attributed to **St. Athanasius** are still used in Anglican and Roman Catholic services, and both saints are venerated in the West.

Generally, however, after the Great Schism of 1054, the paths of Eastern and Western Churches diverged, and they venerate few of the later saints in common. In fact, the bitter doctrinal disputes of the eleventh century mean, sadly, that a saint of one Church may be regarded as a schismatic or even a heretic by the other. One rather touching exception to this can be seen in a rare fresco of St. Francis in the Panagia Kera Church near Kritsa, Crete. During the Venetian occupation of Crete, this Roman Catholic saint became much loved and revered among the local Orthodox Greeks.

Even within the Orthodox Church, some saints are venerated only in a particular area or diocese. For example, the early saints and martyrs of the British Isles, especially those of the Celtic Church such as **St. David** and **St. Patrick,** are widely venerated by Orthodox in England while being virtually unknown in Greece or Russia.

For all Orthodox, the saints are not merely historical characters or even moral examples from the past; they are a living presence in our lives. The icons in the churches (and in our houses) certainly bring the saints closer to us as "family portraits" of our brothers and sisters in Christ. However, their presence is made explicit in many other aspects of our lives.

In every church service, the saints are commemorated in our prayers, often by name, while during the celebration of Holy Communion a portion of the consecrated bread is set aside to represent the saints who are joining in the Divine Liturgy in heaven. A service celebrating all the saints, known and unknown, is held on the first Sunday after Pentecost. Even in the home, when the traditional Greek cake (*vasilopita*) is cut at New Year, a slice is left to one side for **St. Basil the Great**. Outside the rituals of the Church, Orthodox will often ask a saint for help, guidance, or healing. As a teacher in Greece, I sometimes have to remind students that although prayers to the saints before exams are of value, they are not a complete substitute for study!*

The most direct link with a saint is, of course, one's personal name, given at baptism. In the Orthodox Church, this is always the name of a saint or related to a

---

* In fact, in spite of their deep reverence for the saints, most Greeks are essentially practical. There is a popular saying in the form of a dialogue: "Help me, St. George." "Yes, I will, but you must use your own hands."

major feast of the Church.* In Greece, names associated with ancient Greek history or even with mythology are also popular, but in most cases, they are also the names of saints, usually from the early days of Christianity. Names such as Leonidas, Socrates, or Dionysius thus have a double resonance, since they commemorate a saint but also recall the "glory days" of Greece. The Holy Forty Women Martyrs of Heraclea in Thrace (September 1) and St. Terence and forty martyrs beheaded at Carthage (April 10) included many with classical names.

1. Angels

The idea of a host of heavenly beings doing the work of God first appears in the Old Testament, where the angels (from the Greek for "messenger") appear frequently as messengers and protectors. Angels are only one category of immaterial beings (*asomatos* in Greek, meaning "nonbodily"), but together with the archangels, they are the only ones who interact with humans. The most dramatic image of the heavenly beings is given by Isaiah, who relates a vision of God sitting on a throne, protected by six-winged seraphim, flying high above Him and singing, "Holy, holy, holy *is* the LORD of hosts; / The whole earth *is* full of His glory!" (Isaiah 6:2–3). This "angelic hymn" still forms part of the Holy Liturgy, while the six-winged (*exapteryga*) angels are represented in Orthodox churches on two golden banners that usually stand behind the altar.

Angels also appear often in the New Testament, particularly at the time of the Nativity, when the importance of the occasion kept them particularly busy. Jesus Himself mentions the angels on many occasions, including His beautiful words about children: "Take heed that you do not despise one of these little ones, for I say to you that in heaven their angels always see the face of My Father who is in heaven" (Matthew 18:10). Later, two angels watched over Christ's empty tomb at the Resurrection, while at least one of **Peter**'s escapes from prison is attributed to angelic help (Acts 12:1–10).

For most Orthodox Christians, the angels are a real, albeit invisible, presence in human life; "they fence us around with their intercession, and shelter us under their protecting wings of immaterial glory" (Dismissal Hymn for the Feast of the Archangels). Throughout the churches, they can be seen in human form in

---

* An interesting exception to the general rule in Greece is the name *Vyron*, which became popular after 1821 in honor of the contribution made by the English poet Lord Byron to the cause of Greek independence.

icons, acting out their role of protectors or messengers. In many churches, the archangels **Michael** and **Gabriel** are depicted on the doors to the right and left of the altar screen, on guard, as it were, at the entrance to the Holy of Holies. A feast day for all the angels is held on November 8, but individual feasts are also kept for Michael and Gabriel.

Most of the names associated with the angels (Angela, Seraphim, etc.) are self-explanatory, but the Greek name *Stamatios* has an interesting and not so well-known origin. According to Christian tradition, the angel Lucifer (Satan) rebelled against God and tried to lead the other angels in his rebellion (dramatically described in John Milton's epic poem *Paradise Lost*). Although he took some with him, most remained loyal after the Archangel Michael had cried out in a great voice, "Stand firm!" (*Stomen kalos* in Greek). It is from the word *stomen* that the name *Stamatios* is derived. The words of Michael are repeated in the Divine Liturgy as a command to all of us to stand firm in our faith.

2. Prophets and Holy Fathers of the Old Testament

"The divinely inspired prophets preached Thee in word and honored Thee in works, and they received as their reward life without end" (Vespers for Orthodox Sunday). Although the Gospel of Jesus Christ represented a new beginning, the Old Testament has always played a pivotal role in Christianity. In the Orthodox Church, all the Holy Fathers and prophets of the Old Testament are venerated as being among the saints. Indeed, according to biblical texts backed up by ancient tradition, between His Crucifixion and Resurrection, Christ descended into hell and offered His message of salvation to the inhabitants.[2] Thus, the righteous Jews of the Old Testament were able to take their place in heaven along with the Christian saints.* One of the icons of the Resurrection, often called "The Harrowing of Hell," shows the Savior leading Adam and Eve out of hell, along with Moses, King David, **John the Baptist**, and others.

The Old Testament Fathers and prophets often feature in hymns and prayers as well as appearing in many icons. The Tree of Jesse shows the spiritual lineage of Jesus with Jesse, father of King David and Jesus' maternal ancestor, at the base

---

* Several Fathers of the Church and eminent theologians have even argued that it is not impossible for some of the righteous pagans to have joined them. In Romanian Orthodox churches, Greek philosophers such as Plato and Socrates are often depicted in the narthex, the area traditionally reserved for the nonbaptized believers.

of the tree and twelve of the prophets as the branches. Some of the prophets who foretold the coming of Christ form the first tier of frescoes in the dome of the church, while in the sanctuary we can see paintings of the Old Testament high priests such as Aaron and Melchizedek.

Abraham and all the Holy Fathers are celebrated on the Sunday between December 11 and 17, but many of the more important also have their own feast days, including **Elijah**. In the Orthodox Church, the Old Testament prophets are categorized as "major" and "minor," based on the length of their books, not on their importance. The five major prophets are Isaiah (September 9), Jeremiah (May 1), Baruch (September 28), Ezekiel (July 23), and **Daniel** (December 17). The twelve minor prophets are Hosea (October 17), Amos (June 15), Micah (August 14), Joel (October 19), Obadiah (November 19), Jonah (September 21), Nahum (December 1), Habakkuk (December 2), Zephaniah (December 3), Haggai (December 16), Zacharias (February 8, not to be confused with the father of John the Baptist), and Malachi (January 3).

3. Apostles, Evangelists, and Disciples

The twelve apostles and other disciples of Jesus hold a special place in the Christian Church as eyewitnesses to His life and direct recipients of His teachings. Each of them has an individual feast day, but all the apostles are celebrated as a group on June 30. Every Thursday's Daily Office is also dedicated to the apostles. In addition, the four evangelists **Matthew**, **Mark**, **Luke**, and **John**, writers of the Gospels, are, of course, particularly venerated. All four are depicted in icons on the cover of the Holy Gospel and often on the royal doors or at the base of the dome.

Strangely, there seem to be thirteen apostles commemorated in the Orthodox Church rather than the "usual" twelve. This is because the details of the names of the apostles are not entirely clear in the Gospels. Thus, it is not certain if **James, Son of Alphaeus**, was the same person as **James, Brother of the Lord**. The Orthodox Church, with typical pragmatism, doesn't worry too much and venerates both separately. All thirteen are included in the biographies below.

Although not one of the original Twelve, **Paul** is usually counted among the apostles. Indeed, so dramatic was his conversion on the road to Damascus that he includes himself among those who had actually seen Jesus after the Resurrection (1 Corinthians 15:8–11). For the same reason, Paul, the "Apostle to the Nations," is depicted on icons of Pentecost, although he was not actually present.

There were, of course, many other followers of Jesus, and all those named in the Gospels are venerated as saints, including **Joseph of Arimathea, Mary Magdalene,** and **Mary and Martha**, the sisters of Lazarus. The raising of **Lazarus** is commemorated on the day before Palm Sunday, while the second Sunday after Pascha is dedicated to the **Myrrh-bearing Women** who went to the tomb of Jesus to embalm the body. These include Mary and Martha of Bethany, Salome, Susanna, Joanna, and Mary Magdalene, plus **Joseph of Arimathea** and Nicodemus, who supplied herbs and ointments for the embalming. Interestingly, the Orthodox Church also venerates Procla, the wife of Pontius Pilate, on October 27 for her attempt to persuade her husband to release Jesus (Matthew 27:19).

In addition to the above, a wider group of early Christians named in the Acts of the Apostles or the letters of Paul were instrumental in spreading the Word of Christ in the early years after the Resurrection. These are all venerated in the Orthodox Church as the "Apostles of the Seventy" (see Luke 10:1). A feast day on January 4 commemorates the whole group, but they all have their own feast days, either individually or in small groups. Some of the better known are included in the biographies below.

In the Orthodox Church, a special category of saint is highly honored as "Equal to the Apostles" (Greek: *Isapostolos*), a title reserved for those who played a major role in the spread of Christianity in the years after the first apostolic missions. They range from the **Emperor Constantine** to the humble **Nino** to the wandering preacher **Cosmas of Aetolia**.

4. The Holy Martyrs

During the three centuries from the Crucifixion until the legalization of Christianity, the early Christians suffered severe persecution—sometimes systematic, more often sporadic. These persecutions were rarely based on religious intolerance as such, since the Roman authorities generally accepted a wide range of philosophies and religions within the empire. However, they did expect that, whatever their personal faith, all citizens should also acknowledge the state religion and take part in rituals relating to the divinity of the emperor.

The Christians, on the other hand, while usually loyal to the imperial government, refused to join in worship of other gods, including the emperor. It was this refusal that the authorities considered totally unacceptable. Moreover, as a minority sect with apparently bizarre and rigid beliefs, the Christians were perfect scapegoats for disasters, both natural and man-made. As the early Christian apologist Tertullian put it succinctly and wittily, "If the Tiber rises too high or the Nile too low, if the sky remains closed or the earth moves, if plague or famine come, the cry is 'The Christians to the lion.' All of them to a single lion?" Thus, the horrendous massacres under Nero in 64 were sparked off by the Christians being blamed for the great fire of Rome, a frame-up if ever there was one!

Other systematic persecutions occurred under Decius, Valerian, and massively under Diocletian,* but even the "good" emperors such as Trajan and Marcus Aurelius could not accept the "disloyalty" of the Christians and ordered their imprisonment and execution, albeit under the rule of law. For example, a letter from Trajan to one of his provincial governors in AD 112 notes: "They [Christians] are not to be sought out. If they are denounced and proved guilty, they are to be punished, with this reservation, that anyone who denies he is a Christian and really proves it—that is, by worshiping our gods—even though he was under suspicion in the past, shall obtain pardon through repentance. But accusations published anonymously should never be admitted in evidence. For this is both a dangerous kind of precedent and out of keeping with the spirit of our age" (Letter to Pliny the Younger).

Human nature being what it is, there were, no doubt, many who recanted to escape death. Indeed, the vigorous debate at the time about whether such apostates should be readmitted to the Church is clear evidence that not all the early Christians stuck to their faith. For example, St. Nicephorus of Antioch (February 9) went to his death voluntarily in place of a Christian priest who offered to sacrifice to the pagan gods to save his life.

Nevertheless, it is certain that during these times there must have been

---

* Diocletian was the "senior emperor" under his complex constitution and thus usually gets the blame for the horrendous persecutions of his rule. However, he himself was relatively tolerant towards the Christians, and it is likely that his wife and daughters were Christian. The "junior emperor," Galerius, was a fanatical opponent of Christianity and was largely responsible for the bloodbath when, as Eusebius says, "So many suffered that the murderous axe was dulled, and the executioners grew weary."

thousands of martyrs for the Faith, most of whom are unknown to us. Where documentary evidence does exist from court records or contemporary letters, a clear picture emerges of men and women (and even children) who were prepared to confront the most savage punishment rather than abandon their faith. Some of the information we have comes from the persecutors themselves, who very often expressed admiration for the courage of their victims in the face of death, sometimes even leading to atypical acts of mercy (see **Acacius**, for example).

So how authentic are the early martyrs and the stories about them? With the exception of the apostles and a few other leading churchmen, there is very little hard documentary evidence for many of the saints up to about the fourth century. It is also true that stories and legends grew up around even those who can be verified historically, many of which stretch the bounds of credibility somewhat.* Most of the lives of the saints were not written down until the Middle Ages, and in a more credulous age it may have seemed necessary to give the stories authenticity by piling up the details, often from the writer's imagination.

Unfortunately, nowadays, stories of martyrs picking up their severed heads or surviving impossible tortures can have the opposite effect, making us doubt the very existence of the saints. However, the stories for which we do have reliable historical documentation are often no less extraordinary than those that may have grown up later. Moreover, there is all too much evidence from the twentieth century of the extent to which people can willingly suffer the most barbaric acts of persecution for the sake of their faith. If we suspect that the savagery and demonic subtlety of some of the tortures devised by the persecutors are exaggerated, we don't have to look far to find modern equivalents.

It is worth noting here that some of the stories of the early saints exist in different versions, sometimes even contradictory ones. I have tried as far as possible to cross-reference the various sources to obtain the most authentic version and have told the stories according to the traditions of the Church, while trying to avoid the more outrageous legends.

One punishment that is found frequently in the stories of the younger female martyrs is their exposure in a brothel. So frequently does this barbarity

* As a teacher, I am particularly fond of the story of St. Cassian of Imola (not an Orthodox saint, I believe), which I came across in my research. He was a Christian schoolmaster who was intensely disliked by his pupils. When he refused to sacrifice to the gods, the authorities handed him over to the students, who stabbed him to death with their iron pens!

appear that it is tempting to think it a typical embellishment to make the story more interesting. However, it is quite possible that these stories are authentic, as historical precedents exist. Certainly, Emperor Caligula set up compulsory brothels for the wives of senators he disapproved of, but there was also a "legal" angle. Since Roman law forbade the execution of underage virgins, there are documented cases of young girls being raped before execution so that they would no longer be virgins! Moreover, from the viewpoint of the Roman authorities, there was a sort of logic to the idea. By being corrupted, the girls were either turned away from Christianity or suffered great spiritual torture.

Among the martyrs of the Orthodox Church, there are several different categories, some of which need explanation:

> » *Protomartyr*: This means "first martyr." Used on its own, the term refers to **Stephen**, the first male martyr, and **Thecla**, the first female martyr. It is also used to denote the first martyr of a particular area, as in "**St. Alban**, Protomartyr of England."
> » *Great Martyr*: Those martyrs held in the highest respect from the earliest days of the Church. Their feast days are celebrated throughout the Orthodox Church.
> » *Virgin Martyr, Monk Martyr, Nun Martyr*: These speak for themselves.
> » *Hieromartyr*: Bishops and priests who were also martyrs.
> » *New Martyr*: Martyrs from the later history of the Church, after about the fifth century.
> » *Martyr*: All the rest.

Although the majority of martyrs venerated in the Christian Church died during the early years of Christianity, the era of martyrdom didn't end in 313. Even after Constantine's conversion, many Christians were put to death by his co-emperor and rival, Licinius, and by one of his successors, Julian the Apostate, who briefly tried to restore paganism. It was not until 364 that the Roman Empire was relatively safe for Christians. As missionaries spread out into the pagan lands surrounding the empire, martyrs continued to be added to the list.

Even within Byzantium, the iconoclast controversy brought fresh waves of persecution, and every century since has had its share of martyrs for the Faith. Many Christians went to their deaths with courage and commitment under Ottoman rule in Greece (usually called the "New Martyrs of Greece"), while communist rule in Eastern Europe gave rise to a systematic persecution of all religious beliefs that was probably more far-reaching and effective than that of the Roman emperors. Although the intensity of this persecution varied from country to country and from decade to decade, in the Soviet Union there were tens of thousands of martyr priests in the 1920s and 1930s (often called "New Martyrs of the Communist Yoke").* During the Second World War, thousands of Orthodox Christians went to their deaths in the Nazi concentration camps. In Albania, after a mere twenty years of repression of all religions, not a single Orthodox bishop and fewer than twenty Orthodox priests remained alive in the country when the communist government fell in 1990.

The spirit and faith that have moved the martyrs from Roman times to the twenty-first century are vividly and movingly expressed in this extract from a letter written from a Soviet concentration camp:

> *On Easter Day, all of us who were imprisoned for religious convictions were united in the one joy of Christ. We were all taken into one spiritual triumph, glorifying the one eternal God. There was no solemn Paschal service with the ringing of church bells, no possibility in our camp to gather for worship, to dress up for the festival, to prepare Easter dishes. On the contrary, there was even more work and more interference than usual. All the prisoners here for religious convictions, whatever their denominations, were surrounded by more spying, by more threats from the secret police. Yet Easter was there: great, holy, spiritual, unforgettable. It was blessed by the presence of our risen God among us— blessed by the silent Siberian stars and by our sorrows. How our hearts beat joyfully in communion with the great Resurrection! Death is conquered, fear no more, an eternal Easter is given to us! Full of this marvelous Easter, we send you from our prison camp the victorious and joyful tidings: Christ is risen![3]*

5. Men and Women of God

It has been said that, in the spiritual realm, the Christian Church thrives under persecution. Certainly, when one is faced with torture and death for one's faith, there isn't a lot of mileage in being a Christian in name only. Conversely, in all eras when the Church has been powerful or an established body of the state, it

---

* An intriguing and ironic footnote to history is that Joseph Stalin was training for the priesthood as a young man but changed career before he was ordained. The what-ifs are mind-blowing!

has had a tendency to attract men of ambition or seekers of wealth and influence. Examples are, alas, too numerous to mention, but just consider nineteenth-century England, fifteenth-century Spain, or even the financial scandals that came to light in Greece in 2005.

Fortunately, at all such times, there have been men and women around to remind the world of what Christ's teaching was all about. Although not called upon to give their lives for Christ, they "heroically proclaimed the Faith" in many ways, always at the expense of their own comfort and often at the expense of their health. Among these men and women of God are some of the most revered and popular of the saints. They include the great Fathers of the Church who formulated the details of Orthodox belief and worship; ascetics and penitents who lived humble lives devoted to Christ and to others; wise bishops and teachers who cared for their flocks with love and compassion; missionaries who fearlessly traveled to wild and unexplored lands to carry the message of salvation. We know a lot more about most of these than we do of the martyrs, and their characters range from the gentle to the fierce and fiery, from the reclusive to the sociable. All of them, however, acted and still act as beacons to lead the Church back to the true message of Christ. All are members of the "hidden congregation" that joins us in worship and guides us in our lives.

Many of the early Church Fathers mentioned below were heavily involved in combating various heresies, mostly relating to the precise balance between Christ's humanity and His divinity. To avoid repetition, here is a very brief summary of the main controversies.

» *Arianism*: Arius was an Alexandrian priest who argued that Jesus was not truly divine or eternal by nature. This went against the basic beliefs of the Christian Church as still expressed by all the main denominations. However, the doctrine appealed to many, including some of the emperors, and continued to exert an influence for several centuries after Arius's death in 336. The First Ecumenical Council at Nicaea in 325 condemned the heresy and formulated the Nicene Creed, which is still the central statement of faith for Orthodox, Roman Catholic, and Anglican alike. The Second Ecumenical Council, held in Constantinople in 381, reaffirmed and extended the definitions set out in the First.

» *Nestorianism*: Nestorius, Bishop of Constantinople, argued that Christ was not one Person combining a divine and a human nature but two persons, God the Son and the man Jesus. At the Third Ecumenical Council at

Ephesus in 431, the Orthodox position was made clear by, among other things, the designation of Mary as *Theotokos* ("Bearer of God"). Some churches in Iran and Iraq still follow Nestorianism (usually called the Church of the East), but in recent years there has been a movement towards reconciliation with the general Orthodox Church.

» *Monophysitism* ("One Nature"): This argued that Christ was not really a man and that His human nature was fully absorbed in His divinity. If, however, Christ was not wholly human, He could not have redeemed mankind, and the heresy was therefore roundly condemned at the Fourth Ecumenical Council at Chalcedon in 451. A few churches in Egypt and Syria rejected the decision of Chalcedon and still exist. The Fifth Ecumenical Council at Constantinople in 553 reaffirmed and clarified the doctrine agreed at Chalcedon.

» *Monothelitism* ("One Will"): This was an attempt at compromise between Monophysitism and Orthodoxy but was not substantially different from the former. It gained widespread support, especially from Emperor Constans II (642–668), and for a time the patriarchs of Constantinople, Antioch, and Alexandria were all monothelites. The heresy was finally condemned at the Sixth Ecumenical Council, again at Constantinople, in 680–681.

» *Iconoclasm*: Between 726 and 843, several Byzantine emperors and bishops attempted to stamp out the use of icons in the churches. The reasons for this policy were complex, a mixture of politics, early puritanism, and even the influence of Islamic theology. A detailed discussion is outside the scope of this book, but the resulting persecutions were as bad as those of the worst of the Roman emperors. Patriarchs and bishops were deposed and exiled; priests were imprisoned; thousands of ordinary Christians were tortured, executed, or branded on the face with red-hot irons; monks had their heads shattered against icons or were sewn into sacks and drowned. Nobody would see such savagery of Christian against Christian again until the Reformation in Western Europe. The heresy was condemned at the Seventh (and final to date) Ecumenical Council at Nicaea in 787. However, it re-emerged in 814 and was not finally defeated until 843, when the Empress St. Theodora (February 11) restored the holy icons to the churches: "Adorned with her royal crown, the Empress, out of love for the true Kingdom of Christ, has restored in all the churches His most pure icon and the pictures of the saints. . . . The Orthodox people has regained the light and glory which it had of old" (Matins for Orthodox Sunday). This event is commemorated on Orthodox Sunday (also called "The Triumph of Orthodoxy"), a feast celebrated on the first Sunday of Great Lent.

The Seven Ecumenical Councils which, along with the Scriptures, form the foundations of the Orthodox Faith are commemorated in several special feast days throughout the church year.

The Holy Saints
from A to Z

In Orthodox services, when the priest censes the icons on the altar screen, a strict order is followed. First, of course, the icon of Christ is censed, then that of the Blessed Virgin Mary, and thirdly that of John the Baptist. Because of the importance of the Mother of God and of John the Forerunner in the Orthodox Church, I have followed the same order of precedence. After these two, the rest are in alphabetical order.

The Blessed Virgin Mary, Mother of God

Among all the saints in the Orthodox Church, a special position belongs to the Blessed Virgin Mary, who is honored and revered as "our All Holy, immaculate and most blessed and glorified Lady, Mother of God (Greek: *Theotokos*)* and Ever Virgin Mary." Icons of Mary are second only to those of Christ, both in number and in veneration, and act as a sort of mirror image. The icons of Christ represent God who became man, while those of Mary represent "the first human being who realized the goal of the Incarnation: the deification of Man."[4]

Interestingly, the colors of Mary's robes in traditional icons capture this mirror image. Whereas Christ's garments show divinity (red) covered by

---

* *Theotokos* literally means "Birth-giver of God," a term which more accurately reflects Orthodox doctrine. The term "Mother of God" is, however, more familiar to English-speaking readers, and I have used it throughout.

humanity (blue), Mary's garments show her humanity in the blue undergarment now veiled by the red of her glorification. Similarly, just as Christ is often referred to as the "New Adam," so Mary, in her complete submission to God's will, represents the "New Eve." However, for all the reverence shown to her, "we honor Mary because she is the Mother of God. We do not venerate her in isolation but because of her relation to Christ."[5] It has been said that while the Roman Catholics sometimes venerate Mary to excess, the Protestant churches tend to understate her importance. Orthodoxy strikes a balance between the two extremes and probably gets it about right.

The Gospels include few facts about Mary's life, and the later narratives are of doubtful provenance. However, various facts have been incorporated into Orthodox Tradition from the earliest days of the Church.* It is certainly clear from the Gospels that she was chosen by God to bear the Savior and that she accepted her destiny with joy:

> *My soul magnifies the Lord,*
> *And my spirit has rejoiced in God my Savior.*
> *For He has regarded the lowly state of His maidservant;*
> *For behold, henceforth all generations will call me blessed.*
> (Luke 1:46–48)

After Jesus began His ministry, Mary is mentioned only three more times in the Bible, but at significant moments. She was present at the marriage feast in Cana (John 2:1–12), where Jesus performed His first miracle of turning water into wine, and again at the Crucifixion, when Jesus gives her into the care of the **Apostle John** (John 19:25–27). She appears once more, in the Acts of the Apostles, as being among those who received the Holy Spirit on the Day of Pentecost (Acts 1:14).

The Church celebrates various feasts associated with the Mother of God.

CONCEPTION (DECEMBER 9)

In the Orthodox Church, the Conception of the Blessed Virgin Mary is, in fact, not counted strictly as a feast of the Mother of God but is one of the feast days for her mother, **Anna**. (See **Joachim**.) The feast is celebrated in the Roman

---

* The main source for these traditions is *The Protevangelion of the Apostle James*, widely accepted as genuine by many of the early Church Fathers.

Catholic Church on December 8 as the Feast of the Immaculate Conception. However, the doctrine that Mary was conceived without the taint of original sin is not widely accepted in the Orthodox Church (which does not view original sin in the same light).

NATIVITY OF THE VIRGIN MARY (SEPTEMBER 8)

This is the first major feast of the Orthodox ecclesiastical calendar, which begins on September 1. Interestingly, Mary's father, Joachim, was descended from David and her mother, Anna, from Aaron, the brother of Moses. Thus, Mary was of royal birth by her father and of priestly birth by her mother, prefiguring her Son's role as King and High Priest.

ENTRY INTO THE TEMPLE (NOVEMBER 21)

This feast celebrates a very ancient tradition that at the age of three, Mary was taken by her parents, Joachim and Anna, to the temple in Jerusalem so that she might be consecrated to the service of God. The feast day symbolizes the fact that Mary the Virgin herself became the temple of the living God. This day is kept by many Greeks, especially in Crete, as the name day for unmarried girls called Maria, although some in the Church do not officially sanction this.

ANNUNCIATION (MARCH 25)

The Annunciation (Greek: *Evangelismos* or "Good Tidings") to the Virgin Mary by the **Archangel Gabriel** of the forthcoming birth of the Savior (Luke 1:26–56) is one of the earliest Christian feasts, already being celebrated in the fourth century, while paintings of the Annunciation exist in the catacombs dating from the second century. In 1821, Annunciation Day was the day chosen for the raising of the flag of revolt against Ottoman rule in Greece. The feast thus has a double significance to the Greeks and is a public holiday. The feast day is always celebrated on its correct day, even if it falls on Good Friday or the Sunday of Pascha itself.

SYNAXIS OF THE MOTHER OF GOD (DECEMBER 26)

This feast continues the themes of Christmas Day. It combines the hymns of the Nativity with those celebrating the Mother of God, and honors Mary as the one through whom the Incarnation was made possible. "His humanity—concretely and historically—is the humanity He received from Mary. His body is, first of all, her body. His life is her life."[6] It is probably the most ancient feast of Mary in the Christian tradition, the very beginning of her veneration by the Church.

DORMITION (AUGUST 15)

By far the most important of the feast days dedicated to the Mother of God is her "falling asleep" or Dormition (Greek: *Kimisis*; Russian: *Ouspenye*). This is equivalent to the Roman Catholic Feast of the Assumption and is celebrated on the same day. However, although belief in the bodily assumption of the Virgin Mary into heaven is widely accepted in the Orthodox Church, it has never been officially proclaimed as an article of faith. In most Orthodox countries, major celebrations and festivals take place on August 15, which is often also a public holiday. Icons of the Dormition show many of the traditions associated with the falling asleep of Mary. The event is watched over by cherubim and seraphim, while the **Archangel Michael** in the foreground threatens the nonbeliever Jephonias, who dared to touch the holy bier. The apostles and four early Christian writers witness the scene, and a group of mourning women stands in the background. Christ carries the soul of the Virgin to heaven in a mirror image of the Odigitria icon of the Virgin Mary and Child.

LIFE-GIVING SPRING (FRIDAY AFTER SUNDAY OF PASCHA, "BRIGHT FRIDAY")

Shortly after Pascha comes the celebration of the Life-Giving Spring. The feast developed in Constantinople in the fourth century at a church dedicated to the Mother of God, where there was a well with miraculous and healing powers. The feast honors the Virgin Mary as the source or spring from which Christ, the Water of Life, entered the world: "I will give of the fountain of the water of life freely to him who thirsts" (Revelation 21:6).[7]

PROTECTION AND HELP

Throughout the history of the Church, the Mother of God has been regarded as a special protector for those in need of help. Stories of miracles abound, and even today you will meet many Orthodox who have a personal experience of her intervention for good. This role is celebrated in the Orthodox Church in three special feasts:

THE ROBE OF THE MOTHER OF GOD (JULY 2)

In the fifth century, two relatives of Emperor Leo the Great traveling in the Holy Land discovered part of the robe of the Virgin Mary. It had been bequeathed by Mary to a devout Jewish maiden and handed down through the family over the years. It was housed in a church near Constantinople, and many miracles of healing and protection from enemies are ascribed to the Mother of God acting through her precious relic. The feast day commemorates the protection of the Mother of God during a fierce Russian attack on Constantinople in 860. Ironically, in the fourteenth century part of the robe was transferred to Russia, where many other miracles are reported.

THE SASH OF THE MOTHER OF GOD (AUGUST 31)

By tradition, the sash of the Virgin Mary was entrusted to **St. Thomas** and kept by pious Christians in Jerusalem. It was later placed in a church in Constantinople. Parts of the belt now remain in the Vatopedi Monastery on Mount Athos, in the Trier Monastery, and in Georgia. The feast was established after the healing of the wife of Emperor Leo the Wise in the tenth century.

THE PROTECTION OF THE MOTHER OF GOD (OCTOBER 1)

In the middle of the tenth century, on October 1, an all-night vigil was held in the church where the robe and sash of the Mother of God were preserved. The Fool for Christ St. Andrew and his disciple St. Epiphanius had a vision of the Blessed Virgin, accompanied by many saints, praying for the entire world. She implored the Lord Jesus Christ to accept the prayers of all the people calling on His Most Holy Name and to respond speedily to her intercession: "O heavenly King, accept all those who pray to You and call on my name for help. Let them not go away from my icon unheard." The feast was probably established sometime in the twelfth century in both Greek and Russian areas. In 1952, the Holy Synod of the Church of Greece moved the date of this feast to October 28 to coincide with Ochi Day, the national holiday commemorating Greek resistance in the Second World War. This was in recognition of the part played by the Virgin Mary in protecting and inspiring the people of Greece during the bitter years of occupation.

John the Forerunner and Baptist

Among the icons on the altar screen (iconostasis), it is John the Baptist who comes third in honor of place, positioned to the left of Jesus Christ. This is because of the major role he plays as a link between the Old and New Testaments and as our intercessor. He was the last of the prophets to foretell the coming of the Messiah, but also the first person to recognize Jesus as that same Messiah. He is thus regarded as the forerunner of Christ (*Prodromos* in Greek).

John was related to Jesus through **Mary** and was born six months before Him. In about AD 27, at the age of thirty, John emerged from a period of prayer and fasting in the desert to preach his message: "Repent, for the Kingdom of heaven is at hand." As a symbol of repentance, he baptized people in the river Jordan, and it was here that Jesus came to him asking to be baptized. Although reluctant at first, considering himself unworthy, John consented, and it is from this point that the ministry of Jesus can be said to have begun (Matthew 3:13–17). Like the Old Testament prophets, John was uncompromising in his denunciation of sin, whatever the status of the sinner, and soon fell afoul of King Herod, eventually being beheaded.

John can be seen as a one-man composite of "All Saints." Christ Himself said of him, "there is not a greater prophet" (Luke 7:28), while the Prophet Malachi foretold his mission as a messenger (angel) of God (Malachi 3:1). In icons he is therefore sometimes depicted as an angel with wings, and his martyrdom is indicated by showing his severed head on a platter beside him. One of the hymns refers to him as "terrestrial angel and celestial man" (Vespers for the Birth of John the Baptist). His multiple and pivotal role is proclaimed in another: "How shall we call thee, O prophet? Angel, apostle, or martyr?" (Vespers for the Beheading of John the Baptist).

Appropriately, the number of feasts consecrated to John the Forerunner and Baptist is third only to Christ and the Theotokos, and every Tuesday is dedicated to his memory.

SYNAXIS OF JOHN THE FORERUNNER AND BAPTIST (JANUARY 7)

The Synaxis of John the Baptist is the most important of his feasts, celebrated on the day after the Baptism of Christ is commemorated at Theophany. It is usually celebrated as the nameday for those named after him.

Conception (September 23)

This might seem an odd occasion for a religious feast day but, as with the Virgin Mary, it proclaims that God's hand was involved in John's life even from the beginning. In John's case, his very existence originated in a miracle, since his parents were both old and had given up all hope of a child when he was conceived. (See **Zachariah and Elizabeth**.)

Birth (June 24)

For details, see **Zachariah and Elizabeth**.

Beheading (August 29, celebrated as a strict fast)

The story of John's execution is probably too well known to need repetition in detail. The prophet's continuous denunciation of Herod's sins, which included marriage to his brother's widow and an extravagant and licentious lifestyle, irritated the king but also pricked his conscience a little. Although he had John imprisoned, he was reluctant to take stronger action against a holy prophet. His wife Herodias, however, had no such qualms. She hated John and used the seductive charms of her daughter Salome to fool Herod into offering her John's head as a reward for her dancing (Mark 6:17–29). John's story doesn't end with his death, however. As early as the third century, Origen of Alexandria was writing that John continued his role as forerunner after his death by descending into hell to preach the coming of the Messiah and to prepare the way for Christ's later descent. In a similar way, according to some Orthodox traditions, John also appears to those who have not heard the Gospel at the time of their death and preaches Christ's message to them, so that everyone may have at least the chance of salvation.

First and Second Findings of the Head of John the Baptist (February 24)

According to ancient tradition, the severed head of John the Baptist had a very chequered history. It was found by two monks exploring the palace of King Herod, and was taken as a precious relic to the town of Emesa. Sometime later, it came into the possession of another monk, a hermit called Eustathius, who lived in a cave. He was a follower of the Arian heresy, but this was not known to the local people. He became well known for performing miracles but claimed the credit for himself instead of acknowledging the intercession of John the Baptist. When the locals found out his fraud and his heretical views, they chased him from the cave. There the head was left until it was discovered a second time and transferred to a monastery in Emesa in about 452.

THIRD FINDING OF THE HEAD OF JOHN THE BAPTIST (MAY 25)

Many years later, about 850, the head was rediscovered in the monastery and taken to Constantinople, where it remained as a precious relic of the Forerunner. It seems the relic was finally lost or destroyed either in 1204, when Constantinople was sacked by the Crusaders, or in 1453, when the city fell to the Ottoman Turks. However, John the Baptist is also revered by the Muslims as a "righteous prophet." According to their tradition, after the fall of Constantinople the head was taken to Damascus, where it is believed still to rest in a mosque.

Acacius the Confessor, Bishop of Melitene (March 31)

A cacius is possibly unique in the history of the early Church as a reprieved martyr. Not much is known of his early life until he was made Bishop of Melitene in Armenia, but he proved to be an energetic leader and an eminent scholar. He was much loved and revered by his flock, who nicknamed him Agathangelus ("Good Angel"). It is said that under the persecutions of Decius, not a single member of his diocese recanted or denied the Faith.

Around 251, on the orders of Decius, Acacius was arrested and charged with offenses against the state. He was put to the usual tortures over a period of six months, but in the intervals between tortures he was able to write an eloquent account of his faith, which was later read by the emperor himself. Eventually, he was called before the governor, Marcianus. He insisted that, although the members of his flock were Christian, they were all completely loyal to the emperor. However, when the governor argued that if that were the case, they should prove it by making sacrifices to the emperor as a god, Acacius, of course, refused.

The story then takes an extraordinary turn, though it is well documented. Marcianus continued the cross-examination, which turned into a philosophical debate, ranging widely over the myths of the Romans and Greeks, the existence of God, and the nature of angels. When Marcianus finally returned the discussion to the point and ordered Acacius to give him the names of other Christians, he gave him just two names: Acacius and Agathangelus.

The governor sent the entire transcript of the trial, together with Acacius's writings, to the emperor. Decius was so impressed by the wit and erudition of Acacius's arguments that he signed the order for his pardon and promoted Marcianus to a higher post. Acacius was freed and lived for many more years helping his flock to cope with the continuing persecution.

Additional Feast Day: September 15 (Uncovering of Relics)

Acacius the Centurion (May 7) was a martyr beheaded in Byzantium in 303, and another Acacius (April 17) was Bishop of Melitene in the fifth century.

Adrian and Natalia, Martyrs (August 26)

In 304, twenty-three Christians were being flogged in front of Emperor Maximian at Nicomedia. One of the imperial officers, Adrian, was so moved by their courage that he cried out, "Let me be counted as one of these, for I too am a Christian." In fact, although his wife of thirteen months, Natalia, was a Christian, Adrian himself had not yet felt ready for baptism. He was thrown into prison, where Natalia visited him and arranged for his instruction in the Faith. After sentence of death had been passed, visitors were forbidden, but she disguised herself as a boy and bribed her way in to pray with him and ask for his prayers in heaven. Later, she accompanied her husband to the execution block, where he was cut to pieces and burned. She had to be restrained from throwing herself into the flames, but before the body was consumed, a rainstorm put out the fire, and local Christians were able to gather up the remains. Natalia retrieved one of Adrian's hands and kept it with her as a relic. The body was taken to Argyropolis for burial, and Natalia went to live there until her death. Although she was not executed for her faith, Natalia's resolution and faithfulness both to her husband and to her Lord remain as an inspiration, and she was buried among the martyrs alongside Adrian.

Agatha, Virgin Martyr (February 5)

Agatha was the fifteen-year-old daughter of an aristocratic family in Catania, Sicily. In spite of her youth, she involved herself deeply in the affairs of the Church, at that time tolerated by Emperor Philip. Under his successor, Decius, however, things were very different, and the governor of Sicily was replaced by a fanatical anti-Christian called Quintian.

Attracted by her beauty and wealth, the new governor tried to persuade Agatha to marry him, but she refused, saying she would only marry him if he converted to Christianity. He, of course, would not consider such a move and, enraged by her refusal, had her installed in a brothel run by a woman called Frontisia with her nine daughters. Agatha resisted all attempts to shame or corrupt her, and eventually Frontisia returned her to the governor, claiming that Agatha was not only intractable but was turning away customers and ruining her business.

Agatha was then taken away for the usual tortures, which, in her case, were particularly horrible. Her breasts were cut off, the wounds being left untreated; she was stretched on a rack and then thrown naked onto burning coals. Although she never wavered in her faith, she did pray for release from her agony: "Lord Jesus Christ, You know what is in my heart and mind. Take me and all that I am and make me Your own." When her shattered body was returned to prison, her prayers were answered, and she died of her wounds.

Agnes, Virgin Martyr (January 21, or January 14 in some calendars)

Agnes lived in Rome in the early fourth century. She was only a child when she decided to dedicate her life to God. Unfortunately in the circumstances, she was extremely beautiful and was always surrounded by admiring young men. After her continuous refusal to accept any of them, a group of disappointed suitors denounced her as a Christian in the hope that fear of torture and death would make her more amenable. Agnes remained unmoved by threats of savage punishment and, like Agatha, was put into a brothel. However, even the customers were moved by her obvious innocence and meekness, and refused to touch her.

The governor flew into a temper and ordered her immediate execution. She still showed no fear, simply telling the executioner, "Do not delay. This body seems to cause admiration from some. Let it perish." Without further delay, she was stabbed in the throat. A church was later built over her grave in Rome. Her remains, recently examined by forensic archaeologists, confirm that this courageous girl was just twelve or thirteen years old.

Agrippina of Rome, Martyr (June 23)

Next to nothing is known about Agrippina, but she seems to have been a Roman from an aristocratic and wealthy family. During the reign of Valerian (or possibly Diocletian), she was tried as a Christian and, after being nearly beaten to death, was beheaded. Three devout Christian women, Bassa, Paula, and Agathonica, took her body to Mineo in Sicily, where her tomb became a popular place of pilgrimage, and many miracles of healing were reported at the site. In the eleventh century her remains are believed to have been moved to Constantinople.

There is a Roman Catholic church dedicated to Agrippina in Boston, Massachusetts, founded by Sicilian emigrants from Mineo. Since 1914, Agrippina's feast day has been honored here with a popular and lively celebration that includes, as well as a religious parade and high mass, concerts, dancing, and a tug-of-war!

Aidan of Lindisfarne, Missionary (August 31)

Born in Ireland, Aidan was a monk in the monastery founded by **St. Columba** in Iona. When the Christian king of Northumbria, Oswald (August 5), was seeking a missionary to spread Christianity through his largely pagan kingdom, he turned to Iona, having spent nearly twenty years in exile there. The first missionary sent was a bishop called Corman. An extremely abrasive man, Corman had little success and returned to Iona reporting that the Northumbrians were too stubborn to be converted. Aidan pointed out that simple and unlearned people should be handled gently, reminding Corman of St. Paul's advice to feed them milk rather than solid food (1 Corinthians 3:2). These wise words persuaded the abbot to have Aidan consecrated bishop and sent to replace Corman in 635.

This was an excellent move because Aidan proved to be one of the great missionaries of all time. With the island of Lindisfarne as a base, he traveled throughout the kingdom, always on foot, talking quietly and politely with the people on their own level, and gently leading them towards Christianity by example as well as words. Since he was not fluent in the Northumbrian language, King Oswald himself often acted as interpreter. The historian **Bede** writes, "It was a fair sight to see the king himself interpreting the Word of God to his elders and thanes for he had thoroughly learned the language of the Scots during his long banishment."

Aidan's insistence on walking everywhere was not just humility but practical missionary technique, as he could much more easily stop and chat to people, or turn aside to enter homes. On one occasion, the king gave Aidan a horse and cart to make his traveling easier, but Aidan gave them away to the first beggar he met. In his personal life he was austere, and he set an example of frugality and charity to all who met him, rich or poor. Any gifts he received were either immediately passed on to the poor or used to buy the freedom of slaves, many of whom became Christians and joined him in his work. It is a measure of the respect and reverence in which Aidan was (and is) held that the historian Bede wrote a beautiful and fulsome tribute to him, in spite of their being on opposite sides in the controversy over the date of Easter.[8]

The death of Oswald in battle in 642 deeply grieved Aidan, but the king's successor Oswin (August 20) was equally supportive and became a close friend of the monk. Aidan died at Bamburgh in 651, just two weeks after the murder of his friend Oswin. As he was dying, he leaned against a wooden beam in the west wall of the church. In spite of the church later being twice gutted by fire, the beam was never burned. When the church was rebuilt for the third time, the beam was set into the ceiling above the baptismal font, where it can still be seen. Aidan was buried at Lindisfarne, but after the Synod of Whitby in 664, St. Colman (February 18), who disagreed with its decision, took the remains back with him to Iona.

Alban, Protomartyr of England (June 22)

Alban (Albanus) was a Roman citizen living in Verulamium (modern St. Albans), northwest of London. He was a pagan, but when a Christian priest called Amphibalus asked him for help, he gave him shelter in his house. Alban was impressed by the priest's prayers and asked him about his beliefs. As a result, he became a Christian and was baptized. When Amphibalus decided to move on, Alban exchanged clothes with him to help him escape. Shortly afterwards, soldiers heard that a priest was hiding in Alban's house and, assuming Alban was the priest, arrested him. The magistrate was furious but offered not to execute Alban for assisting a fugitive if he would recant. Alban simply said, "I am also a Christian and worship the true God."

He was taken to a nearby hill for execution, and it is reported that there were so many people on the bridge over the river that the execution party couldn't get through. Alban prayed and made the sign of the Cross, and the water parted, allowing them to pass over. This miracle so astounded the executioner that he threw down his sword and refused to continue. He was arrested and was himself executed after Alban. Climbing the hill, Alban became thirsty, and it is said a small spring appeared allowing him to drink. St. Alban's well was used by pilgrims for many years afterward but is now dry. A second executioner was found, and Alban was beheaded. Estimates of the date of Alban's martyrdom vary from 209, when Emperor Septimus Severus was visiting Britain, to 251 under Decius or 257 under Valerian.

During the seventh century, a church was built on Holmhurst Hill, the site of the martyrdom, together with a shrine containing the relics of the saint. Later, the great Abbey of St. Albans was erected on the same site, but the shrine was destroyed during Henry VIII's dissolution of the monasteries. Although the shrine was later reassembled, the relics were lost. However, in 2002, some of St. Alban's relics were located in the church of St. Panteleimon in Cologne, Germany, where they had been preserved for many centuries, and were returned to the martyr's shrine. The Anglican and Orthodox ecumenical group, the Fellowship of St. Alban and **St. Sergius**, is named after the English martyr and Sergius of Radonezh.

Alexander, Patriarch of Constantinople (August 30)

Born between 237 and 244, Alexander was a priest in Constantinople at the time of Emperor Constantine. When the First Ecumenical Council assembled at Nicaea (325), the first Patriarch of Constantinople, St. Metrophanes (June 4), was too old and ill to travel, so Alexander was sent in his place. Obviously the right man at the right time, he argued cogently against the Arian heresy and helped to formulate the Nicene Creed, which remains the basis of the Christian Faith.

On the death of Metrophanes, Alexander was unanimously elected patriarch. He proved to be a wise and strong leader, essential qualities in that turbulent period. Constantine's successor, his son Constantius, attempted, largely for political reasons, to reinstate Arius in the Church, but Alexander refused to obey the emperor's command, thus helping to establish the boundaries between

Church and state. This particular issue was resolved by the sudden death of Arius shortly afterwards. Alexander died in 340 at the age of ninety-eight.

Alexander Nevsky, Holy Prince (November 23)

Best known in the West from the superb 1938 film by Sergei Eisenstein, Alexander Nevsky is the great warrior saint of Russia, often compared with his Catholic contemporary, St. Louis King of France. Alexander was born in 1220 during a period of great turmoil in the princedoms of Russia, which were under attack from north, west, and east. By 1237, the whole Russian territory had been overrun by the Tatars of the Golden Horde, except for the far north around Novgorod. At the same time, the Swedes were threatening from the north and the German Teutonic Knights from the west.

Although the Tatars demanded tribute from their conquered lands, they didn't generally interfere with religious life, whereas the others, especially the Teutonic Knights, were set on bringing the Orthodox "schismatics" under papal rule. Alexander, therefore, submitted to Tatar overlordship and payment of tribute in order to concentrate on the greater threat from the west. In 1240, not yet twenty years old and inspired by a vision of the **Passion Bearers Boris** and **Gleb**, he defeated the Swedes at the great battle of Neva, from which he earned his name. He then turned to the Teutonic Knights, who were openly boasting of "subjugating all the Slavic nations." On April 5, 1242, the two armies met in the great Battle of the Ice on a frozen lake near Pskov, where Alexander achieved a spectacular and decisive victory.

Alexander's dealings with the Tatars were complex and required, as he said, "the meekness of an angel and the wisdom of a snake," but relations with the Tatar Khan were generally cordial and mutually supportive. Alexander's policy culminated in the Golden Horde becoming strong enough to proclaim its independence from Mongolia, thus forming a protective shield to Russia's east. Some of the Russian princes and nobility mistrusted Alexander's eastern policy, however, and worked for an alliance with the pope, but Alexander rejected all approaches by the Roman ambassadors: "Our doctrines are those preached by the apostles. . . . The Tradition of the Holy Fathers of the Seven Councils we scrupulously keep."

When a rebellion against the Tatars led by his brother Andrew failed, Alexander became Great Prince of All Russia (Vladimir, Kiev, and Novgorod).

With the western borders secured and an alliance in place with the Tatars in the east, the shape of the future multinational Russian state began to emerge. On his return from a diplomatic mission to the Khan, Alexander fell ill and was taken to a monastery. There he took monastic vows under the name of Alexis before passing away in 1263.

Certainly a great leader, Alexander is also venerated as a saint for his unstinting service to his people, his religious integrity, and his protection of the Orthodox Faith. Interestingly, early icons of Alexander show him as a monk and penitent. It was only during the reign of Tsar Peter the Great that icons began to show him dressed as a warrior. Many scholars and theologians regard this as placing a completely wrong emphasis on the saint's life. He is, however, revered as a patron of soldiers, and his importance is recognized outside Russia, where churches dedicated to him exist in Sofia (Bulgaria), Tallinn (Estonia), and Tbilisi (Georgia).

Additional Feast Days: August 30 (Translation of Relics)

May 23 (Synaxis of the Rostov and Yaroslav Saints)

Alexander of Munich, Holy New Martyr (July 13)

On a freezing day in February, 2012, a moving ceremony was held in Munich in the Cathedral of the New Martyrs and Confessors of Russia. It was the beginning of two days of services held to recognize the glorification as a saint of a young German student who was beheaded by the Nazis in 1943.* Venerated locally for many years as a Passion Bearer, Alexander Schmorell stands out as a shining example of someone who put his Christian beliefs into practice even amid the horrors and complexities of modern totalitarianism.

Alexander was a mild-mannered and peaceable character, handsome and popular with the girls, and it is highly likely that, in a different age or country, he would have lived out an unexceptional life as a doctor in Munich. However, a man called Hitler changed all that. Alexander was born in 1917 in Orenburg, Russia, of Russian and German parents, and was brought up Orthodox. In 1921, the family fled the Bolsheviks and settled in Munich. While studying medicine in Munich in 1940, Alex joined two other students, Hans Scholl and Willi Graf,

---

* A full and very evocative description of the service can be found on http://www.jimandnancyforest.com.

to form the White Rose resistance group. The main activity of the group was the production and distribution of anti-Nazi leaflets.

Although these were joint efforts, it is almost certainly Alexander who was responsible for the moving outburst against the Holocaust in the second leaflet: "Here we see the most frightful crime against human dignity, a crime that is unparalleled in the whole of history. For Jews, too, are human beings."[9] The leaflets generally reject Prussian militarism and quote widely from the Bible, classical philosophy, and the giants of German literature. They are deeply imbued with Christian belief, and some of the language is clearly stamped with Orthodox theology.

In the summer of 1942, the three medical students were drafted as combat medics to the Eastern Front, where Alexander was appalled at the treatment of enemy soldiers and civilians. Remembering his mixed background, he declared that there was no way he could ever kill either a Russian or a German. While in the East, he was able to meet Orthodox priests and attend the Holy Liturgy with his friends. It must have been a bizarre sight to see Alexander, Hans, and Willi joining the Orthodox church services dressed in their Nazi uniforms!

Distribution of the White Rose leaflets was extended throughout Germany and Austria, and the group also began painting slogans around Munich. While the slogan "Freedom" was treasonous in itself, there can't have been many places in Germany where the graffiti "Down with Hitler" could be seen in 1942! At the beginning of 1943, however, several members of the group were arrested, and their trial and execution marked the beginning of the end of the White Rose.

Alex was arrested in February 1943. After interrogation by the Gestapo, he was tried on a charge of high treason, sentenced to death, and guillotined on July 13, at the age of twenty-five. His letters from prison to his family, especially the final one, are very moving, accepting his fate and restating firmly his religious faith: "By the will of God, today I shall have my earthly life come to a close in order to go into another, which will never end and in which all of us will again meet."[10] He was buried in the cemetery behind Stadelheim Prison. Along with the other members of the White Rose, he is, of course, respected and honored throughout contemporary Germany for his heroic stand against Nazism.*

---

* A German film about another member of the group, called *Sophie Scholl—The Final Days,* is still, at the time of writing, available on DVD with English subtitles.

Alexis, Man of God (March 17)

According to an almost contemporary account, in the year 440 in a hospital in Edessa, Mesopotamia, a nameless old man died. He had lived by begging, sharing whatever alms he got with other poor people. After the death of this "John Doe," a parchment was found hidden in his rags that revealed the remarkable truth about his life.

Born into a distinguished Roman family, Alexis at an early age became determined to devote his life to God, but out of respect for his parents' wishes suppressed his feelings. His parents arranged a highly advantageous marriage for him, but on his wedding day, he fled from Rome. Eventually turning up in Edessa, he took literally the words of Jesus, "Do not lay up for yourselves treasures on earth" (Matthew 6:19), and lived anonymously and in poverty until his death. A later story states that, after seventeen years, he returned to his parents' house as a beggar and worked there, humbly and unrecognized, as a servant for a further seventeen years, sharing his meager food with others and sleeping in a corner under the staircase of his own sumptuous home. The letter he had written was given to his family and read by the Bishop of Rome, who had Alexis buried in state in the chapel of St. Peter's, his coffin being carried by the pope and the emperor. Whatever the full truth about this extraordinary man may be, Alexis stands out as a saint who represents all the dispossessed and unwanted of society.

Alexis of Wilkes-Barre (May 7)

Alexis Toth was born in Slovakia in 1853. His father was a priest of the Eastern Rite Catholic Church,* and Alexis followed him into the priesthood, being ordained in 1878. After the death of his wife and child shortly afterwards, he threw himself into his work, holding several important posts in the Greek Catholic diocese.

In 1889, responding to a petition from the Ruthenian Catholic Church in the USA, his bishop sent him to serve as priest to St. Mary's Greek Catholic Church in Minneapolis, Minnesota. He found the church in a state of disrepair, with little

---

* Eastern Rite Catholics or Greek Catholics accept the authority of the pope but retain many of the liturgical and organizational traditions of the Orthodox Church, including married clergy.

furniture and no vestments. What it did have was a large debt. For a year, Father Alexis worked indefatigably, preaching, fundraising, and organizing, until the parish was on a sound financial basis, all without receiving a salary.

So why is Alexis an Orthodox and not a Catholic saint?

Etiquette demanded that Alexis pay his respects to the Roman Catholic archbishop of the area, so he duly visited Archbishop John Ireland. Unfortunately, the archbishop was a strong supporter of the "Americanization" movement in the Catholic Church in the USA. With so many immigrants arriving in America, large numbers of whom were Catholics from Italy, Germany, and Ireland, it was felt that future integration depended on common forms of worship and customs and the widest possible use of the English language.

There was a lot to be said for this argument, but unfortunately it left no room for ethnic parishes such as the one Father Alexis served, and Eastern Rite Catholicism certainly did not fit in with the archbishop's vision. Coupled with this was a definite clash of personalities between the two men. According to Alexis, both ended up losing their tempers, with the archbishop refusing to recognize Alexis as a Catholic priest and ordering his diocese to have nothing to do with either Alexis or his parishioners. Things came to a head when other Eastern Rite priests reported they had had similar confrontations. All of them were to be recalled to Europe and their parishes integrated into the existing Roman Catholic organization.

Receiving no guidance from his own bishop in Slovakia, Alexis and his parishioners looked for a way out of the impasse. Eventually, after discussions with the Russian Orthodox bishop of San Francisco, Father Alexis and 361 of his parishioners were received into the Orthodox Church in March 1892.

The disagreements between Eastern Rite Catholics and the Roman Catholic hierarchy continued to fester. Having made the break himself, Alexis worked tirelessly to advise and guide those who wished to reunite with Orthodoxy. It is estimated that, by the time of his death, he had been responsible for the reception of over twenty thousand into the Orthodox Church. A man of great humility, he firmly refused the offer of a bishopric as more suitable for a younger and healthier man. He died on May 7, 1909, and was buried at St. Tikhon's Monastery in Pennsylvania. On May 29, 1994, he was formally glorified as St. Alexis of Wilkes-Barre by the Orthodox Church in America, whose foundation and growth are largely traceable to his efforts.

Traveling Companions

Ambrose, Bishop of Milan (December 7)

Born in about 334, Ambrose was elected Bishop of Milan by popular acclaim in 374, while still undergoing instruction prior to baptism! This was a very responsible position for such a relatively young man, as Milan was the administrative capital of the Western Empire. Moreover, it was a time of great turmoil and change, as people flocked to be baptized into the recently legalized Church, while at the same time others were trying to restore paganism or spread the Arian doctrine.

Ambrose threw himself into the fray with vigor, fighting on both fronts. He was successful in preventing the restoration of the statue of the pagan goddess of victory to the senate house in Rome, and he later refused an order from the empress regent to hand over a building to the Arians for use as a church. He was equally stern in his reaction to Emperor Theodosius I's savage massacre of citizens in reprisal for riots in Salonika. "The emperor is within the Church; he is not above it," he said, and demanded that Theodosius do public penance for his brutality. The emperor, ashamed of his action, meekly complied.

In spite of such public and political events, Ambrose for the most part concerned himself more with his flock than with emperors and theologians, and set out, quite consciously, to be an exemplary bishop. His personal life was one of poverty and simplicity, and he instituted a custom of kneeling down to wash the feet of Christians he was baptizing. His sermons are full of practical advice and love for his fellows, and he is rightly honored as one of the four great Latin doctors of the Church. Among his most lasting achievements was his introduction into the Western Church of antiphonal singing (Ambrosian Chant). He composed twelve hymns, one of which, "Thee, O God, We Praise," is still used in the Orthodox Church. It is quite possible that he was also the author of the Athanasian Creed. He died, deeply loved by all who knew him, both great and humble, in 397.

Ambrose of Optina, Venerable (October 10)

Ambrose was born Alexander Grenkov in 1812, in a village near Tambov (southeast of Moscow). He came from a pious and strict family and was sent to theological college, where he did very well. During a severe illness just before graduation, he made a promise that, if he recovered, he would become a monk. However, as many of us have done, he forgot his promise as soon as he got better, and became a teacher. When he was twenty-seven, he was reminded of his promise when he visited a famous hermit, Father Hilarion, and was told he was needed at the monastery of Optina Pustin. Once again, however, he ignored the call and returned to teaching. God finally caught up with Alexander when, at a party, he felt a sudden revulsion at the frivolity of his life. With the recollection of his promise and the advice of Father Hilarion, he finally decided to become a monk. In 1839, he entered the Optina Monastery where, after a probationary period, he was tonsured in 1842 with the name Ambrose.

For the rest of his life, Ambrose served the monastery, first under the spiritual direction of Elder Macarius and, after 1860, as superior of the monastery. He became famous throughout Russia as a spiritual adviser and guide, and was visited by crowds of people, including Tolstoy and Dostoyevsky. As a result, he followed an incredibly punishing schedule that would have exhausted a far stronger man. A normal day would begin with prayers and tea at four AM. He would then answer letters until breakfast, after which he received visitors until lunch at noon. Then there would be more visitors, sometimes alone, sometimes in groups, until he had dinner at eight PM, only taking a short rest at three. After dinner, he would receive more visitors until eleven PM. After evening prayers, he would sleep for three or four hours and a new day would begin.

When asked for his advice, Ambrose rarely gave his personal opinion but referred the petitioner to the writings of the Church Fathers, perhaps explaining difficult passages in simple words. In spite of his own asceticism, he was gentle with others: "Moderation in all things is good. There is a spiritual age just as there is an outward age. Just as nine-year-olds cannot grasp what is proper for twenty-year-olds, so also in the spiritual life: with zeal that is foolish and beyond your strength, you can spiritually hurt yourself. . . . Go slowly and you'll go farther, as the experienced say. It is harmful not to take care of what is necessary, but it is dangerous to strive for what is beyond your limit."

As well as supervising the monastery, Ambrose founded a convent in nearby Shamordino in 1884. Through the support of Optina, the convent was able to open its doors to any woman who wished to become a nun, and did not have to rely on dowries or rich patronesses. Thus, poor women and those in poor health or blind could follow the religious life. On a pastoral visit to Shamordino Ambrose became ill but, forced by the weather to remain there, he continued to receive visitors until he passed away in 1891. As was the custom, he was buried in the nearby wilderness. In 1998, his relics, along with those of the other elders of Optina, were uncovered and now rest in the Church of the Vladimir Icon of the Theotokos. Ambrose was glorified in 1988, and a feast for all the Optina elders was initiated in 2000.

Additional Feast Days: June 27 (Uncovering of Relics)
August 7 (Elders of Optina)

Amphilochios Makris of Patmos, Elder

I don't think I'm stretching the rules too much by including this "saint in waiting," who is deeply revered by many people although he has yet to be formally glorified. Born in 1889 into a large rural family on Patmos, Athanasios Makris showed early signs of piety, observing at his own request the full rules of Great Lent even as an infant. In 1909, he entered the Monastery of St. John the Theologian on Patmos, taking the name Amphilochios. Ordained a priest, he was sent to the island of Kos, serving as confessor throughout the Dodecanese. In 1926, he was assigned back to his home island of Patmos, serving in the Cave of the Apocalypse and in the Ecclesiastical Academy. He was elected abbot in 1935, at a time when the Italian rulers of the Dodecanese were trying to interfere in Church organization. At one point, he used weaving and knitting classes as a cover for secret Greek lessons, which resulted in his exile to the mainland. Returning in 1939, he did not resume the abbacy but worked with the newly founded Convent of the Annunciation, establishing an orphanage in Rhodes and founding a hostel for pregnant women. He died after a severe bout of flu in 1970.

This outline of a largely uneventful life does not do justice to a man loved and revered for his deep spirituality, gentleness, and compassion. Although he was a passionate promoter of the value of monasticism, he was able to understand human weakness: "When you see a person who is spiritually tired, do not burden him any further, because his knees won't be able to bear it."[11] At the same time, he believed that anything was possible with the love and strength of God behind us. In particular, the Jesus Prayer could be a source of infinite spiritual power: "Cultivate love towards the Person of Christ to such an extent that, when you pronounce His name, tears fall from your eyes. Your heart must really burn.

Then He will become your teacher. He will be your Guide, your Brother, your Father, and your Elder."

Long before it became fashionable, Amphilochios had great concern for the environment. In this, of course, he was following Orthodox teaching on the responsibility of all of us to act as stewards of God's creation, but a comment like, "Whoever does not love trees, does not love Christ," certainly makes the point succinctly and bluntly. Putting thought into action, "if imposing a penance on the farmers who came to him for confession, he would tell them to plant two or three trees."[12] Deeply loved by all who knew him, Fr. Amphilochios cannot be far from formal canonization.

Anastasia, Great Martyr (December 22)

The daughter of an aristocratic Roman family, Anastasia was brought up a Christian. Widowed early, she devoted her life to helping victims of Diocletian's persecution. Under the influence of her Christian mentor, St. Chrysogonus (December 23), she opened her home to the poor and especially those who had suffered imprisonment and torture, treating their wounds and offering whatever help she could. She also visited prisoners, praying with them and giving them comfort and support. These prisoners, it is believed, include **Irene, Agape, and Chionia.**

It wasn't long, of course, before she was discovered and summoned to the tribunal of the prefect of Illyricum (modern Yugoslavia). She absolutely refused to abandon Christianity and was sentenced to death. She was put on board an unseaworthy ship along with a group of pagan criminals, and they were set adrift to sink, a very economical form of execution. However, a local Christian sailor managed to smuggle himself on board and steered them to safety. After their lucky escape, many of the criminals joyfully embraced Christianity. Anastasia's escape was, however, short-lived. She was recaptured, staked to the ground, and set alight. She was then buried alive in about 290. One of the epithets applied to Anastasia is "Deliverer from Potions," and in modern times, she has become the saint to whom people addicted to drugs most often turn for help. A gentle and loving lady, Anastasia remains a much-loved saint in the Orthodox Church.

Andrew, Holy Apostle and First-Called (November 30)

Andrew was a fisherman from Galilee and a follower of **John the Baptist**. After John's imprisonment, he was invited by Jesus to follow Him, and in one of history's more dramatic career moves, Andrew became a "fisher of men" (Matthew 4:18–20). He was Jesus' first disciple and is thus named the "First-called" in the Orthodox Church. Not long after his call, he introduced his brother Simon (**Peter**) to the Lord.

Andrew is mentioned several times in the Gospels. Unlike his brother, he seems to have been a quiet man but a deep thinker with a strong faith. Little is known of his later life, but traditions associate him with widespread missions in Greece, Scythia, and Asia Minor, where he established the Church in Byzantium. Some accounts claim that he even reached as far as Scotland and, in some traditions, Russia, in both of which countries he is revered as the patron saint. Certainly, Andrew has strong associations with Greece; he is believed to have been crucified at Patras in Achaea in AD 60. Like **St. Peter**, he felt he was not worthy to be crucified in the same way as his Savior and, at his request, was hung on an X-shaped cross, from which he continued to preach the Gospel message for two days until he died. His relics were lovingly preserved and taken to Constantinople, where they remained until the city fell to the Ottoman Turks, when they were taken to Rome. In 1964, the head of St. Andrew was returned to Patras, where it is preserved in the Church of Agios Andreas.

Andrew, Archbishop of Crete, Preacher and Hymnographer (July 4)

Born in about 660 in Damascus, Andrew, sometimes called Andrew of Jerusalem, studied the Scriptures and theology from an early age and was tonsured as a monk in St. Sava's Monastery in Jerusalem at the age of fourteen. He was mute until he was seven years old but, having miraculously found his voice while taking Holy Communion, used it to good effect, becoming an exceptionally eloquent preacher. He worked in several important church posts in Jerusalem and Constantinople and was present at the Sixth Ecumenical Council, where he spoke against the Monothelite heresy. In about 700 he was made Archbishop of Gortyna in Crete. He died on the island of Mytiline while returning from a journey to Constantinople, but the date is not certain. Various suggestions have been made, including 712, 726, and 740.

Revered in his lifetime for his piety, erudition, and preaching, Andrew is now best known for his hymns, many of which are still used in the worship of the Orthodox Church. In particular, he is said to have invented the type of hymn called the canon. The most famous of these is the Great Penitential Canon, sometimes simply called the Great Canon, which is read in sections on the first four evenings of Great Lent and in its entirety on the Thursday of the fifth week. It goes chronologically through the whole of the Old and New Testaments, taking examples relating to the theme of repentance. What makes it unusual and very moving is that it is largely written in the first person, so that the whole hymn becomes a personal quest for repentance and forgiveness. "It is steeped in biblical imagery, yet it is not simply a condensation of biblical themes. In the Canon, all the human events of scripture—creation, fall, exile, return, longing, redemption—all are made personal. They become *my* events: *my* creation, *my* fall, *my* redemption. Their story is *my* story, and I am made intensely aware of all its depth." In this context, the extreme length of the Canon becomes almost cathartic. From the story of Adam and Eve at the beginning to the Crucifixion at the end, it "brings each of us into the story of scripture; stirs us with moving imagery to realize the depths of our sin. We begin to see our exile, our distance from Christ; and from that distance, we begin to repent."

Where shall I begin to lament the deeds of my wretched life? What first-fruit shall I offer, O Christ, for my present lamentation? But in Thy compassion grant me release from my falls.

Come, wretched soul, with your flesh, confess to the Creator of all. In future refrain from your former brutishness, and offer to God tears in repentance.

Having rivaled the first-created Adam by my transgression, I realize that I am stripped naked of God and of the everlasting kingdom and bliss through my sins.

Alas, wretched soul! Why are you like the first Eve? For you have wickedly looked and been bitterly wounded, and you have touched the tree and rashly tasted the forbidden food.

A robber accused Thee, and a robber confessed Thee to be God, for both were hanging on a cross with Thee. But open even to me, O most compassionate Savior, the door of Thy glorious Kingdom as to Thy faithful robber who acknowledged Thee to be God.[13]

A further twenty-four canons are attributed to Andrew, along with 111 short hymns.

Anthony the Great, Venerable (January 17)

Anthony is paradoxically regarded as both the epitome of the saintly hermit and the founder of cenobitic (communal) monasticism. He was born near Memphis in Egypt in 251, and in about 276 his parents died, leaving him a very wealthy young man. Shortly afterwards, he heard the story of Jesus telling the rich young man that, if he wanted to enter the Kingdom of heaven, he should sell all he had and give the money to the poor (Matthew 19:21). Unlike the young man in the Bible, Anthony took the lesson to heart, did what Jesus said, and went to live alone in the desert, spending his time in prayer and study and doing manual work to earn his living. In about 312, seeking further solitude, he went to live in a cave by the Red Sea, where he remained until he died quietly in 356. At over a hundred years old, he had witnessed both the persecutions of Diocletian and the triumph of Christianity under Constantine.

In spite of his desire for solitude, Anthony couldn't avoid disciples collecting around him, and he eventually gathered the hermits into loose-knit communities over which he exercised a certain authority, giving guidance which set the standards for early monastic life. We know a fair bit about him from a biography by **St. Athanasius**, who knew him personally. In this he emerges as the opposite of the popular image of the wild, fanatical desert hermit. He was wise and level-headed, and his austerity was always consciously directed towards the better service of God: "Know yourselves. He who knows himself knows God."

In spite of his solitude, he was a practical man, giving help to the Christians persecuted under Maximian and traveling to Alexandria in 335 to help combat the Arian heresy. His advice was often practical, concerning our relations with others as well as our relations with God: "From our neighbor is life and from our neighbor is death. If we win our neighbor, we win God, but if we cause our neighbor to stumble, we sin against Christ." Of tremendous influence during his life, the "physician to all Egypt," as St. Athanasius described him, still serves as a model for the ascetic Christian life.

Aristobolus, Apostle of the 70 (March 15)

Born in Cyprus and brother of **St. Barnabas**, Aristobolus was one of the seventy apostles chosen by Christ to spread the Gospel throughout the world. He accompanied his brother and **St. Paul** on their journeys and is mentioned by Paul in his epistle to the Romans (Romans 16:10). He is of particular interest to British readers as he is believed to have preached in the Roman province of Britain, probably being martyred there. According to tradition, he was the first Bishop of Britannia and was particularly popular among the Brythonic Celts, who named the still extant district of Arwystli in Powys, Wales, after him.

Arsenius the Great, Venerable (May 8)

Arsenius was born in about 354 in Rome. He became a renowned teacher, eventually being recommended by the pope to tutor the sons of Emperor Theodosius I in Constantinople. After about ten years, however, he began to tire of the life of luxury in the imperial court and prayed, "O God, teach me how to be saved." He found his answer in the Gospels: "For what profit is it to a man if he gains the whole world, and loses his own soul?" (Matthew 16:26). So, in about 400, he retired to join the desert monks of Egypt.

An austere man, Arsenius subjected himself to strict self-discipline and expected others to do the same. However, he was capable of great compassion and was easily moved to tears; contemporaries wrote that his handkerchief was never far away. He wasn't a man to waste words and once said, "I have often been sorry for having spoken, but never for having held my tongue." Arsenius, in spite of the austerity of his life, was often tormented by a sense of his own failings and feared that his former self-centered life could still lead him to damnation: "I know a great deal of Greek and Latin learnings. I have still to learn even the alphabet of how to be a saint." At other times, he felt that he was truly dead to his previous life and, when a relative died and left him most of his wealth, Arsenius reacted in a typically brusque way: "I died before he did," he said, tearing up the will. A somewhat contradictory figure, in his lifetime Arsenius was admired rather than loved, but by the time of his death in about 449, he seems to have found spiritual peace. He left to a fellow monk all his possessions: a skin coat, a pair of sandals made of palm leaves, and a goatskin shirt.

Athanasius the Great, Patriarch of Alexandria (May 2)

Born in Alexandria in about 296, Athanasius was only a young deacon when he attended the Council of Nicaea. He impressed the delegates with his clear exposition of doctrine and was consecrated Bishop of Alexandria in 328. These were turbulent times, with the recently legalized Church split almost to breaking point by the ideas of Arius. Athanasius's vigorous opposition to Arianism led him into conflict with the emperor and resulted in his spending over seventeen of his forty-five years as bishop in exile. He was finally allowed to rule his church in peace from 366 until his death in 373.

A small man in stature but a spiritual giant, Athanasius wrote brilliantly in defense of the doctrine, established at the Council of Nicaea, that Jesus was both truly God and fully man, and defining the place of the Holy Spirit in the Trinity. Although he probably didn't write the Athanasian Creed, it was almost certainly compiled using his ideas and writings. As Bishop of Alexandria, he was responsible for the welfare of the desert monks. As well as writing a life of **St. Anthony**, he introduced the idea of monasticism to the West. An eighth-century monk wrote, "If you find a book by Athanasius and have no paper on which to copy it, write it on your shirt," while the great nineteenth-century Roman Catholic churchman Cardinal Newman called him "that extraordinary man . . . a principal instrument after the apostles by which the sacred truths of Christianity have been conveyed and secured to the world."

Even the somewhat cynical historian Gibbon said that Athanasius "displayed a superiority of character and abilities, which would have qualified him, far better than the degenerate sons of Constantine, for the government of a great monarchy."[14] The core of his faith is best expressed in his own words: "All of us are naturally frightened of dying and the dissolution of our bodies, but remember this most startling fact: that those who accept the faith of the Cross despise even what is normally terrifying, and for the sake of Christ, cease to fear even death. When he became a man, the Savior's love put away death from us and renewed us again; for Christ became man that we might become God."

Additional Feast Day: January 18 (together with Cyril of Alexandria)

Augustine of Canterbury, Evangelist of England (May 26)

Before he became pope, Gregory the Great (March 12) was walking through Rome when he passed a market where he saw a group of boys being sold as slaves. Struck by their fair complexion and blond hair, he asked where they were from. He was told they were from the British tribe of Angles, who were still pagan. "Alas! What a pity," said Gregory, "that the author of darkness should own men of such fair countenances; and that with such grace of outward form, their minds should be void of inward grace . . . It is right that they be called Angles for they truly look like angels." He went to the pope to seek permission to go on a mission to convert the people of Britain but was refused. However, he never forgot his "angels" and, when he himself became pope, thought again of sending a mission to their remote land. This lovely story, recorded in **Bede's** *Ecclesiastical History* but quite probably apocryphal, sets the scene for the real story of the first mission to England from Rome.

In 596, King Ethelbert of Kent (February 25), himself a pagan but with a Christian wife, asked Pope Gregory to send missionaries to evangelize England. Augustine and forty other Benedictine monks set out, but on the way, the party began to lose heart at the prospect of meeting such fierce and barbarous pagans, whose language they didn't understand. Augustine was sent back to Rome to ask the pope to abandon the mission, but Gregory's response was firm: "It is better not to begin a good work than to think of desisting from one which has been begun. Be assured that great labor is followed by the greater glory of an eternal reward."[15] The mission duly continued, landing at Thanet in Kent in the spring of 597. In spite of the monks' fears, Ethelbert allowed Augustine complete freedom to preach in his kingdom, and he himself was converted before the end of the year. At Christmas, he and 10,000 of his subjects were baptized.

Augustine and his mission quickly set about organizing an ecclesiastical structure, and when he was consecrated archbishop, he chose Canterbury as his seat, with two of his colleagues, Mellitus (April 24) and Justus (November 10), as bishops of London and Rochester respectively. He also founded a monastery and a school and built Christ Church, the predecessor of Canterbury Cathedral. Under instructions from Pope Gregory, he initiated the practice of consecrating former pagan temples as churches and of turning animal sacrifices into feasts to celebrate the saints. This was a wise and practical policy, helping to gain acceptance of the new faith among the people, for, as Gregory wrote in a letter to Mellitus, "there is no doubt that it is impossible to cut off everything at once from their rude natures; because he who endeavors to ascend to the highest place rises by degrees or steps, and not by leaps."

Augustine was equally active in secular affairs, helping the king draft some of the Roman code of law into English. Of a somewhat tactless and haughty nature, however, he was less successful in his negotiations with the existing Christian communities in the north who followed the Celtic tradition. In spite of his efforts to gain the support of the northern bishops in evangelizing the country, he failed to extend Roman practices outside his own sphere of influence.

Augustine died in 604 and was buried at the entrance of his unfinished Monastery of St. Peter and St. Paul. When the monastery was completed in 613, his remains were moved inside under a memorial which reads in part, "Here lies the Lord Augustine, first Archbishop of Canterbury, sent here by blessed Gregory, bishop of the city of Rome, who with the help of God, and aided by miracles, guided King Ethelbert and his people from the worship of idols to the Faith of Christ."

B

Barbara, Great Martyr (December 4)

There are many variations on the story of Barbara, and the place and date of her martyrdom are by no means certain. According to the most common tradition in the Orthodox Church, she lived in Nicomedia during the reign of Maximinus (235–238). Her father, a fanatical pagan called Dioscoros, found out that she was consorting with Christians and had her locked up in a tower. However, by various stratagems, she maintained contact with her Christian friends and, after a time, became a Christian herself.

Her father was furious and denounced her to the authorities. After torture, she refused to renounce her faith and, being underage, was returned to her father with orders that he himself should execute her. He took her into the mountains and beheaded her with his sword, but on the way back, he was struck by lightning and burned to death. Whether this was divine retribution or coincidence, it certainly seems a just reward for a vicious and unnatural father. The manner of his death led, by somewhat convoluted reasoning, to St. Barbara being regarded as the patron saint of artillery regiments in the armies of many countries, including the USA, Great Britain, Greece, and Cyprus.

In the sixth century, Barbara's relics were transferred to Constantinople. Six hundred years later they were moved again to Kiev, where they remain in the Cathedral of St. Vladimir.

Barlaam of Antioch, Martyr (November 19)

Although he is a little-known saint, Barlaam's story is a dramatic illustration of how even the poor and uneducated could hold their own in the face of persecution. He was an illiterate laborer who, having been converted to Christianity, took every opportunity to spread his new faith boldly. He was soon arrested and was whipped and stretched on a rack until his bones were dislocated. He still refused to recant, and the judge devised a plan that would easily fool an ignorant peasant. An altar was set up to one of the pagan gods and a fire lit on it. Incense was placed on Barlaam's hand, which was then forced into the flames on the altar. The idea was that Barlaam would pull his hand away in pain, thus dropping the incense onto the altar and "making a sacrifice" to the god. Though illiterate, Barlaam was no fool and, with great courage, held his hand steady in the flames until it was completely burned away. He was then executed in about 304.

Barnabas, Apostle of the Seventy (June 11, together with Bartholomew)

"A good man, full of the Holy Spirit and of faith" (Acts 11:24), Barnabas was a Jew from a wealthy Cypriot family, originally called Joseph. When the apostles in Jerusalem began to live a communal life, sharing all their possessions, Joseph was among the first to sell his possessions and hand the money over. For this they gave him the name Barnabas ("Son of Encouragement," Acts 4:32–37).

According to some traditions, he was educated in Jerusalem, where he was a student friend of Saul, later **Paul**. It was certainly Barnabas who persuaded the doubtful Christians of Jerusalem to believe in Paul's conversion and accept him as a true follower of Christ (Acts 9:26–28). He accompanied Paul on his first missionary journey and is regarded as the founder of the church in Cyprus. Later, he is believed to have been the first Christian to preach in Rome and may have founded the church in Milan. He seems to have been a man of great determination and courage, preaching with Paul to non-Jews for the first time and facing the opposition and violence of those Jews who rejected their message. In Lystra, they were faced with an almost comic situation when, after Paul healed a lame man, the locals decided they were pagan gods, Barnabas Zeus and Paul Hermes! It was all the apostles could do to prevent the crowd from offering sacrifices to them (Acts 14:8–18).

Perhaps it took even more courage for Barnabas to stand up to Paul's extremely forceful character and side with Mark in their later dispute. As a result of this, he accompanied **Mark** to Cyprus, where he was martyred at Salamis in about 62. Mark buried Barnabas's body at the western gate of the city with a copy of the Gospel of Matthew in his hands. Although the area near the grave became known as a place of healing, for centuries nobody knew why, and the location of the grave was forgotten. During the reign of Emperor Zeno, the Patriarch of Antioch was trying to extend his rule to include Cyprus. Three nights in a row, the Apostle Barnabas appeared to the Archbishop of Cyprus in a dream, revealing the location of the grave. The finding of Barnabas's relics proved the apostolic foundation of the church in Cyprus, and its independence from Antioch was assured.

Bartholomew, Holy Apostle (June 11, together with Barnabas)

Almost certainly the same person as Nathaniel, Bartholomew came from Cana in Galilee.[16] The story of Nathaniel's call is intriguing. Told by his friend **Philip** that the new preacher Jesus was truly the prophesied Savior, Nathaniel was doubtful that Galilee, known then as a backward, rural area, could produce the Messiah. He went to see for himself, however, and was convinced when Jesus told him that He had known him even before Philip had called him (John 1:45–51).

Nathaniel accompanied Philip and his sister to Phrygia and, after Philip's crucifixion, went on to India, where he translated the Gospel of Matthew. He then moved to Armenia, where he cured the king's daughter of insanity, an act which caused the king and most of his family to seek baptism. The king's brother, however, conspired with a group of pagan priests to have Nathaniel captured and crucified. Half dead, he was flayed and finally beheaded. There is reference to a Gospel of Bartholomew in early writings, but nothing survives.

Basil the Great, Archbishop of Caesarea (January 1)

Saint Amphilochius (November 23), a contemporary of Basil, said of him, "He belongs not to the Church of Caesarea alone, nor merely to his own time, nor was he of benefit only to his own kinsmen, but rather to all lands and cities worldwide, and to all people he brought and still brings benefit." These words are as true today as they were in the fourth century.

Basil was born in Caesarea in about 330 into a remarkable family: his grandmother, father, mother, two sisters, and two younger brothers are all saints in their own right. (See **Macrina the Elder.**) Basil studied at the University of Athens, where he met and became close friends with **Gregory the Theologian**. Interestingly, another close friend was Julian, who would later become emperor and attempt to re-establish paganism in the empire (Julian the Apostate). All three of the friends were baptized together.

In spite of having a brilliant mind, Basil tired of university life, writing in a letter, "I had wasted much time on follies and spent nearly all of my youth in vain labors, and devotion to the teachings of a wisdom that God had made foolish. Suddenly, I awoke as out of a deep sleep. I beheld the wonderful light of the Gospel truth, and I recognized the nothingness of the wisdom of the princes of this world." He left the university and became a monk, living for five years as a hermit on the banks of the River Iris in Pontus. Basil found, however that the solitary life wasn't for him, and since he had accumulated a large number of disciples, he turned to a communal religious life. The rules he formulated for the regulation of the monastic life still form the basis for Eastern Christian monasticism and were influential on the Rule of **St. Benedict** in the Western Church. These rules have a strong social emphasis, including care for the sick and poor, maintenance of hospitals and orphanages, and working directly for the benefit of society at large.

In 370, Basil was consecrated Archbishop of Caesarea. He was able to use his position to practical effect by building an estate that included houses for the poor, a church, a hospital, a hospice for travelers, and a staff of doctors and artisans. His strong practical sympathy with the poor and downtrodden, and his merciless preaching against the misdeeds and indulgence of the wealthy, set him at odds with many of the local bigwigs. Along with the other Cappadocian

Fathers (**St. Gregory of Nyssa** and St. Gregory the Theologian), Basil was also active in condemning Arianism and helped to formulate the ideas expressed in the Nicene Creed.

Eventually, Emperor Valens (a supporter of Arius) sent a prefect to threaten Basil with deprivation, exile, and death. Basil's response shows both his deep faith and his headstrong and often tactless nature: "If you take away my possessions, you will not enrich yourself, nor will you make me a pauper. You have no need of my old worn-out clothing, nor of my few books, of which the entirety of my wealth is comprised. Exile means nothing to me, since I am bound to no particular place. This place in which I now dwell is not mine, and any place you send me shall be mine. Better to say: every place is God's. Where would I be neither a stranger nor sojourner? Who can torture me? I am so weak, that the very first blow would render me insensible. Death would be a kindness to me, for it will bring me all the sooner to God, for Whom I live and labor, and to Whom I hasten."

When the prefect expressed astonishment at his temerity, Basil replied sharply, "Perhaps you've never before had to deal with a proper bishop." After that, he was left alone.

Basil had never been physically strong even in childhood. A life of strict asceticism and the heavy duties of office took their toll, and he died in 379 at only forty-nine years of age. In services, Basil is called, "a bee of the Church of Christ bringing the honey of divinely inspired wisdom to the faithful, stinging the uprising of heresy." He is the author of one of the three liturgies used in the Orthodox Church and is revered as one of the four great Greek Fathers of the Church and one of the **Three Hierarchs**. His head rests in the Great Lavra on Mount Athos.

Additional Feast Day: January 30 (Three Hierarchs)

Basil the Blessed, Wonder-worker of Moscow (August 2)

One of the more difficult categories of saint for the modern mind to understand is the "fool for the sake of Christ." These were men and women who took the virtue of humility to an extreme degree, behaving generally in such an eccentric way that they courted humiliation and the ridicule of the more "normal" population. They followed the words of **St. Paul** that "God has chosen the foolish things of the world to put to shame the wise" (1 Corinthians 1:27). One of the most revered of these was Basil of Moscow.

Basil was born near Moscow in about 1468. One could say his life exhibited a degree of eccentricity even from the beginning, as his mother gave birth to him in the portico of a church. Apprenticed as a child to a cobbler, he also showed an early aptitude for prophecy. He told a customer who had ordered a special and expensive pair of boots to save his money and cancel the order since he would never wear the boots. A few days later the man died.

At sixteen, Basil began to follow the difficult and dangerous path of deliberate eccentricity in the name of Christ. He walked barefoot through the harsh frosts of winter or when the heat of summer was burning his feet. At his most extreme, he would walk about naked, weighed down with heavy chains. Often, he would walk through the market, overturning the stalls of merchants selling shoddy or badly cooked goods, and when attacked by angry traders, would endure the beatings with joyful thanks to God.

Gradually, people began to see him as a "holy fool," a man of God, and a denouncer of wrong. He had a knack of looking beyond outward appearances and made a special point of helping those who were in great need but were ashamed to ask for alms. He once spotted a foreign merchant who, in spite of his fine clothes, was penniless and hadn't eaten for three days, and he gave him an expensive gift. Like his Lord, Basil had no time for hypocrites who made a great show of giving alms in the hope of attracting God's blessing, but he would always try to see a grain of goodness even in the most desperate sinners.

Basil's gift of prophecy never left him. In 1547, he predicted the great fire of Moscow. As a "holy fool," he seemed exempt even from Ivan the Terrible's cruelty, and when he berated the Tsar for thinking about building a new palace when he should have been concentrating on the Divine Liturgy, he was not punished. Indeed, when he died in 1557, not only did the Metropolitan of Moscow conduct the funeral, but Tsar Ivan acted as a pallbearer. Basil was buried in a chapel of the Cathedral of the Intercession of the Virgin by the Moat in Moscow (the famous "gateau" in Red Square). Because of the love felt for the saint by the people of Moscow, the Cathedral has for many years been almost universally, if inaccurately, known as St. Basil's. His chains are still preserved at the Moscow Spiritual Academy.

Bede, Venerable (May 27)

R enowned as a historian, Bede, the "Father of English History," is also venerated as a saint for his piety, scholarship, and influence on the early English Church. Born in about 672, near Jarrow in the northeast of England, he probably came from a noble family. He was placed in the monastery at Wearmouth at the age of seven, ordained a deacon at nineteen and a priest at thirty. Apart from occasional trips to York and Lindisfarne, he spent his whole life in the monastery, and in his own words, "I wholly applied myself to the study of Scripture; and amidst the observance of monastic rule, and the daily charge of singing in the church, I always took delight in learning, or teaching, or writing."

A sort of renaissance man about nine hundred years before the Renaissance, Bede had interests ranging from theology and scriptural commentary to music, history, grammar, and science. Among the many achievements attributed to him were a recalculation of the age of the earth, the popularization of the division of history into BC and AD, and the invention of the footnote. Though he was not a particularly original thinker, his commentaries on the Scriptures were of great value in synthesizing the writings of the early Church Fathers and, through his skill as a linguist and translator, making them accessible to Anglo-Saxon readers. It is mainly for this work and his considerable influence on early English church history that he is venerated as a Doctor of the Church and as a saint. He is the only Englishman to be mentioned in Dante's *Paradiso*, appearing among the Doctors of the Church.

Although we know little of Bede's life, we can piece together from his writing a picture of a devout and kindly man with a deep love of the truth, coupled with great common sense. Despite his erudition and probable noble birth, he seems to have had an essentially humble view of his talents when compared with spirituality: "Better a stupid and unlettered brother who, working the good things he knows, merits life in Heaven than one who though being distinguished for his learning in the Scriptures, or even holding the place of a doctor, lacks the bread of love." He saw all his work, including the study of science and history, as devoted to the glory of God and always put his church duties before other things. He once made the point that, since the angels were present with the monks during worship, he must not skip the services: "What if they [the angels] do not find me among the brethren when they assemble? Will they not say, 'Where is Bede?'"

The final days of his life, described in a letter from his disciple Cuthbert, create a moving picture of a man ready to meet his Maker. About two weeks before Pascha 735, he fell ill with frequent attacks of breathlessness but continued to teach, sing psalms, and dictate his last work, a translation of St. John's Gospel into Anglo-Saxon. Shortly before Ascension Day, his breathing deteriorated and his feet swelled, and he warned his pupils, "Learn quickly, for I do not know how long I can continue. The Lord may call me in a short while."

After a sleepless night, he continued dictating, but at three o'clock paused to distribute "a few treasures" among the priests of the monastery, "some pepper, and napkins, and some incense." He asked for their prayers and said, "The time of my departure is at hand, and my soul longs to see Christ my King in His beauty." That evening, his scribe Wilbert, writing down the last sentence of his work, said, "It is finished now." "You have spoken truly," said Bede, "it is well finished." He asked Wilbert to lift his head so that he could see the church he loved, sang the Doxology, and passed away.

The poem called "Bede's Death Song," although not definitely written by Bede, certainly relates to a theme often dealt with in his other writing:

> *Before the unavoidable journey there, no one becomes*
> *wiser in thought than him who, by need,*
> *ponders, before his going hence,*
> *what good and evil within his soul,*
> *after his day of death, will be judged.*[17]

Bede was buried at Jarrow, but in 1020 his remains were transferred to Durham Cathedral, where they still lie alongside those of St. Cuthbert of Lindisfarne.

Benedict of Nursia (March 14)

Considering the fame of St. Benedict, surprisingly few details are known about his life. He was born in about 470 or 480 in the Umbrian town of Nursia and was educated in Rome. He found the riotous and dissolute life of the city too much for his retiring and devout nature. He left to find solitude in the wilderness, living in a cave in the mountains of Subiaco, about forty miles east of Rome. A few years later, he was asked by a small community of monks to be their abbot, but it wasn't long before the level of asceticism he expected from them caused a rebellion and an attempt to poison him. He returned to Subiaco and, over the next few years, organized twelve small monastic communities, each consisting of twelve monks. In about 529, he established the monastery of Monte Cassino, where he remained as abbot for the rest of his life. Revered as a miracle worker even during his own life, he died in 543 or 547, his arms raised in prayer after receiving the Eucharist. Benedict's sister, Scholastica, was a strict ascetic nun in one of Benedict's communities and is venerated as a saint on February 10.

It was at Monte Cassino that Benedict wrote the monastic rule that has had such an influence on Western monasticism. Based on earlier work by St. John Cassian and **St. Basil the Great**, it calls for the renunciation of all personal possessions, unconditional obedience to one's abbot, and constant work.* It is also full of common sense and moderates the strict discipline with gentleness and an understanding of human weakness. He himself described it as a rule for beginners, "a school of the Lord's service, in which we hope to introduce nothing harsh or burdensome.... If you are really a servant of Jesus Christ, let the chain of love hold you firm in your resolve, not a chain of iron."

The Rule covers both the spiritual life and the administration of the monastery, and its seventy-three short chapters (little more than a paragraph each) still resonate** after over fourteen centuries. Recently, Pope Benedict XVI said that "with his life and work St Benedict exercised a fundamental influence on the development of European civilization and culture" and helped Europe to emerge from the "dark night of history" that followed the fall of the Roman Empire. Together with **Saints Cyril and Methodius,** Benedict was declared co-patron of Europe by Pope John Paul II in 1980.

---

* One of the main jobs in Benedictine monasteries until the advent of printing was the copying of manuscripts, and it is to thousands of nameless monks that we owe the preservation of many writings from antiquity and the early years of Christianity.

** The Benedictine Rule is still the most commonly used in Roman Catholic and Anglican monasteries and convents throughout the world and forms the basis for many other monastic rules in the Western Church.

Benjamin, Metropolitan of Petrograd, New Hieromartyr (August 13)

Benjamin was born in about 1872 in a village east of St. Petersburg, the son of a priest. He later wrote, "In my childhood and adolescence I immersed myself in reading the lives of the saints, and was enraptured by their heroism and their holy inspiration. With all my heart I sorrowed over the fact that times had changed and one no longer had to suffer what they suffered. Times have changed again, and the opportunity has been opened to suffer for Christ both from one's own people and from strangers!"

Benjamin was ordained a priest in 1896 and rose rapidly through the church hierarchy, becoming Bishop of Gdov in 1910. He spoke out openly against Rasputin, and after the February revolution of 1917, a majority of the people of Petrograd elected him archbishop to replace Rasputin's appointee. In March 1922, the Soviet government began a process of confiscating church valuables, ostensibly to relieve the famine victims of the Volga area. Benjamin was favorable towards the famine relief and was willing to donate much of the church property, but objected strongly to forced confiscation. The local soviet accepted the compromise but was overruled by the central soviet in Moscow, which insisted on confiscation. In spite of further attempts at compromise by Benjamin, there were demonstrations and violent clashes between Orthodox believers and the authorities, resulting in brutal repression. Charged with "resisting the requisitioning of church valuables," Benjamin was imprisoned and brought to trial on May 28, together with eighty-seven others, including bishops, priests, professors of theology, and ordinary Christians arrested during the street disturbances.

Three witnesses appeared for the defense but were immediately arrested, and no one else came forward. Benjamin's defense lawyer spoke eloquently on his behalf but to little avail, although there was loud applause in the courtroom: "If the metropolitan perishes for his faith, for his limitless devotion to the believing masses, he will become more dangerous for Soviet power than now. . . . The unfailing historical law warns us that faith grows, strengthens, and increases on the blood of martyrs."

Convicted of "organizing a counter-revolutionary group," Benjamin was sentenced to be shot along with nine others, although, on appeal, six had their sentences commuted to long terms of imprisonment. The rest of the defendants were also found guilty and sentenced to varying terms of imprisonment. In a letter from prison, Metropolitan Benjamin wrote, "Now is the time of trial. People are sacrificing everything for the sake of political convictions. . . . Cannot we Christians display a similar courage even unto death, if we have some faith in Christ and the life of the age to come?"

On the night of August 13, 1922, he and three others were shaved and dressed in rags so that the firing squad wouldn't know they were executing clergymen. They were then shot.

Bessarion the Wonderworker, Venerable (June 6, or February 20)

I cannot resist the delightful story of Bessarion, a hermit and disciple of St. Anthony. He lived in the desert, sleeping under the stars and often losing himself in the wilderness. His only possession was a copy of the Holy Gospel that he always carried with him. One day, he met a naked beggar and gladly gave him the only clothes he had, what he was wearing. He went on his way, naked, still carrying the Gospel. He was spotted by an officer of the watch, who thought he had been robbed and asked, "Who stripped you?" Bessarion held up his Gospel and replied, "He did." On another occasion, having nothing to give a beggar, he went to the nearest market and sold his beloved Gospel. When asked by a disciple where it was, he cheerfully replied, "I have sold it in obedience to the words which I never cease to hear—'Go, sell what you possess and give to the poor.'"

Some calendars show a feast day for Bessarion on February 20, but I have been unable to establish the reason for this variation.

Blaise, Bishop of Sebastea, Hieromartyr (February 11)

A physician by profession, Blaise was a kind and Christian man whose qualities caused him to be elected Bishop of Sebastea. During the persecutions of Diocletian, he worked tirelessly to encourage his flock, giving them both spiritual and practical support. However, the persecution in that area was so successful that eventually Blaise was the only Christian left alive. He retired to a cave in the mountains, where his peaceful nature even succeeded in taming many of the wild animals, which he cured when they were sick or injured.

It wasn't long before Blaise was captured and marched back to the city in chains. It is reported that he carried such an aura of gentleness and sanctity that many were converted just by his presence as he passed. Sentenced to death by drowning, he walked out across the surface of the water. Turning, he invited any pagans who had faith in their own gods to join him. Sixty-eight took up the challenge and drowned. He was then beheaded in 316. Blaise is venerated as a protector against wild beasts and a guardian of the health of domestic animals.

Brendan the Voyager, Missionary (May 16)

Born in about 484 in Tralee on the west coast of Ireland, Brendan was brought up in the school run by St. Ita (January 15), where she taught him the three things God loves:* "Faith in God with purity of heart; simplicity of life with religion; generosity with love." Few definite details exist about his life, but it is known that he became a monk and a priest. About 560, he founded the monastery at Clonfert, famous for its missionary work, where it is said that Brendan supervised three thousand monks. He certainly traveled to western Scotland and Iona, and may have preached in Wales and Brittany. He died in about 577 at the age of 93.

That is about all we know with any degree of certainty, but the early-ninth-century Latin chronicle *Navigatio Brendani (The Voyage of Brendan)* relates how he led a mission west across the Atlantic in search of the Garden of Eden, eventually reaching Newfoundland. This would have made him the first European to set foot on Canadian soil, many years before the Vikings. Historians have always doubted the truth of the narrative, mainly because of the seeming impossibility of making such a journey in a flimsy curragh** of the type available to Brendan. Moreover, the story contains unlikely descriptions of fabulous sea monsters and mountains of fire.

However, the story took an interesting turn in 1976, when Irish explorer Tim Severin built an ox-leather curragh, an exact replica of the one described in the *Navigatio,* and sailed it over two summers to Newfoundland, by way of the Hebrides, Faroe Islands, Iceland, and Greenland. On the way he saw whales and

---

* Ita also used to list the three things God hates: "a scowling face, an obstinate wrongdoing, and too much confidence in money."
** A small, square-rigged boat made of leather over a basketwork frame.

volcanoes not dissimilar to the wonders allegedly seen by Brendan. While this doesn't prove that Brendan made the journey, it does show that he *could* have.[18] There is no rancor in heaven, but perhaps Brendan is having a quiet smile at the confounding of the "experts."

Brigid of Kildare, Venerable (February 1)

B orn about 450 near Dundalk in Ireland, Brigid was the daughter of a pagan chieftain and a Christian slave. It is not clear whether she was brought up a Christian, but she was certainly inspired by the preaching of **St. Patrick** and was of a pious disposition from an early age. Although she felt called to enter a religious life, her father refused to give his consent. However, she had a generous heart and could never refuse to help people in need. This irritated her father since it was largely his butter, flour, milk, and even clothes that she was distributing to the poor.

When she gave away his jeweled sword to a leper, he seems to have finally accepted the inevitable and allowed her to enter a convent. Over the next few years, Brigid is believed to have founded several convents around the area, but her most famous foundation was a double monastery for monks and nuns, built in 470 at Kildare. She remained there as abbess until her death in 525. A wise and holy superior, she seems to have also had a great deal of common sense, and tried to improve the material as well as the spiritual lives of those around her. The monastery became a powerhouse of learning and culture, producing beautiful paintings and illuminated manuscripts.

A lovely story relates how, during a synod of the Irish Church, one of the priests dreamed that the Blessed Virgin Mary would appear among the assembled delegates. The next day, Brigid joined the assembly, and the priest recognized her as the lady from his dream. Thus, she became known as "the Mary of Gael," a name by which she is still known in Ireland. Interestingly, Brigid was named after the Celtic goddess of fire, and this saintly and loving lady sanctified the pagan name to become deeply loved and venerated throughout Ireland and in many parts of Europe. She was buried near the altar of her abbey church, but during the Viking raids her remains were transferred to Downpatrick and reburied alongside St. Patrick and **St. Columba**.

C

Caedmon, Hymnographer (February 11)

Having struggled to translate Caedmon's hymn at university, I regard him as an old friend (or adversary) and was delighted to find that he is venerated as a saint in the Orthodox Church. Author of the first recorded poem in the Anglo-Saxon language, he is known as the "Father of English Poetry," but his veneration as a saint stems from the content of the poem, which makes him, in fact, the "Father of English Hymnography."

All we know about Caedmon comes from **Bede**'s *Ecclesiastical History*. For most of his seventh-century life, he was a cowherd at the Yorkshire monastery of Whitby. When the lay workers ate together in the hall, they would entertain themselves by singing songs of battles and myths, passing the harp to each other in turn. Caedmon had no talent for singing, so when the harp was getting close, he would make some excuse and go off home or to feed the animals.

One night, he had a strange dream. A man appeared before him, called him by name, and told him to sing. Caedmon explained that he never sang to the others, but the man replied, "Nevertheless, you must sing to me." When Caedmon asked what he should sing about, the stranger said, "Sing the beginning of creation." Caedmon began to sing, and when he woke, not only did he remember the words, but he felt confident enough to add more lines. He told his supervisor what had happened and was taken to the abbey authorities, including Abbess **St. Hilda**. They were so impressed that St. Hilda asked Caedmon to be tonsured as a monk and work for the glory of God. This he did, and as he began to learn the Scriptures, he turned the stories from the Old Testament and the Gospels into song.

According to Bede, Caedmon wrote a vast number of hymns, but only the first has survived, although some scholars contend that the wonderful, anonymous Anglo-Saxon poem *The Dream of the Rood* may have been his work. He died peacefully after a short illness. Having made sure there were no outstanding grudges between him and the other brothers, "he prepared for the entrance into another life, and asked how near the time was when the brothers should be awakened to sing the nightly praises of the Lord? They answered, 'It is not far off.' Then he said, 'It is well, let us await that hour'; and signing himself with the sign of the Holy Cross, he laid his head on the pillow, and falling into a slumber for a little while, so ended his life in silence." Caedmon's Hymn, in translation (not mine, alas), is as follows:

> *Now we should praise the heaven-kingdom's guardian,*
> *the measurer's might and his mind-conception,*
> *work of the glorious father, as he each wonder,*
> *eternal Lord, instilled at the origin.*
> *He first created for men's sons*
> *heaven as a roof, holy creator;*
> *then, middle-earth, mankind's guardian,*
> *eternal Lord, afterward made*
> *the earth for men, father almighty.*[19]

Calliope, Martyr (June 8)

Calliope was a real beauty, living in the reign of Decius about 249–251. A Christian, she was a friendly and lively young woman who immersed herself in social and religious activities. At the age of twenty-one, she was besieged by suitors, including a young pagan who became enraged at her rejection of his advances. When he threatened to report her to the authorities as a Christian, she made him even angrier by declaring that she wouldn't marry him even if he were a Christian! He then paid informers to bring false accusations against her, ranging from mockery of the gods to treason against the state. She was publicly flogged and then branded on the face. Afterwards, salt was poured on the wounds, and she died soon after, although according to some accounts, she was beheaded.

Cassiane, Hymnographer (September 7)

A beautiful and feisty woman, and one of the great poets and composers of Byzantium, Cassiane* is certainly one of the more intriguing saints of the Orthodox Church. Add to that a romantic ending, and we have a story worthy of Hollywood.

She was born into a wealthy family in Constantinople in about 810. She grew up to be a beautiful young woman and was eventually chosen to participate in the "bride show," where Emperor Theophilos was to choose his wife from a group of eligible girls. Theophilos was left with a final choice between Cassiane and an equally beautiful girl called Theodora. By tradition, he was to give a golden apple to the girl of his choice.

Looking at the apple, he said to Cassiane, "From woman came the worst in the world" (referring to Eve). Cassiane looked at him calmly and replied, "From woman also came the best" (referring to the **Virgin Mary**). Not liking to be upstaged by a woman, Theophilos gave the apple to Theodora. In fact, this was no great hardship for Cassiane, as she had for a long time decided to devote her life to the Lord. In 843, she founded a convent on the outskirts of Constantinople and became its first abbess. She was a fierce and outspoken opponent of iconoclasm, a heresy Theophilos supported, and she was severely punished, including being flogged. After the restoration of the icons, she was left in peace until her death in 865.

Cassiane further demonstrated her determination and single-mindedness in the field for which she is mainly remembered today: hymnography. This was regarded very much as a male preserve at that time, and she was subject to much scorn for her efforts in writing hymns. Nevertheless, she persevered, and her critics were confounded when she began to produce some of the most sublime works of the period. With the encouragement of **Theodore of Studion** and most of the leading churchmen of Constantinople, she wrote a great number of hymns, of which about fifty survive and twenty-three are still used in Orthodox services. She also wrote many aphorisms and epigrams which give further insight into her character, for example, "I hate the rich man moaning as if he were poor."

Her hymns are of great spiritual beauty, both in the words and the music.**

---

* There are many variations of her name, including Kassia, Kassiane, Ikasia, and Cassia.
** Several CDs of Cassiane's hymns are available.

George Poulos makes the point that "from Mozart to the present day, it is difficult to recall a single classical composer on the distaff side, but hidden among the great hymnographers of all time is the exceptional female creator of church music whose creations have been heard for centuries in Orthodox churches, where the members are unaware that a woman wrote the inspirational melody."[20] Cassiane's greatest creation is *The Hymn of Cassiane*, which is sung every Holy Tuesday:

> *Sensing Thy divinity, O Lord, a woman of many sins*
> *takes it upon herself to become a myrrh-bearer,*
> *And in deep mourning brings before Thee fragrant oil*
> *in anticipation of Thy burial, crying:*
> *"Woe to me! For night surrounds me, dark and moonless,*
> *and stings my lustful passion with the love of sin.*
> *Receive the wellsprings of my tears,*
> *O Thou who gatherest the waters of the oceans into clouds."*

And the romantic story? It is said that Theophilus, towards the end of his life, still felt love for Cassiane and wanted to see her once more before he died. He rode to the monastery where Cassiane was writing her hymn, but because she still felt some love for him and feared this would distract her from her vows, she hid, leaving the hymn on the table. Theophilus found her cell empty, but noticed the unfinished hymn. He read through it to the end, where Cassiane had written: "I will kiss Thine immaculate feet / and dry them with the locks of my hair." Remembering her beauty and intelligence and his youthful arrogance, he cried and added the line, "Those very feet whose sound Eve heard at dusk in Paradise / and hid herself in fear." He left, and Cassiane returned to finish the hymn.

Catherine of Alexandria: See Katherine.

Charalambus, Hieromartyr (February 10)

A priest in Magnesia in Asia Minor, Charalambus was martyred in the reign of Severus in 202 at the age of 113. Although the area he worked in was fiercely anti-Christian, he was able to bring large numbers to Christ simply by the love he showed to all, Christian and pagan alike. He turned away nobody in need and, as a result, when he was arrested and tortured as a very old man, even the local pagans opposed his execution. He was therefore transferred to Antioch in Syria, where he suffered brutal tortures. After being flayed cruelly, he said, "Thank you, my brethren, for scraping off the old body and renewing my soul for new and eternal life." The courage of this centenarian converted many onlookers to Christianity, including possibly the emperor's daughter, Gallina. Sentenced to execution, he prayed, "Lord, Thou knowest that men are flesh and blood; forgive them their sins and pour out Thy blessing on all." He died just before he was beheaded.

On Russian icons, Charalambus is often depicted as a bishop, but there is no evidence that he was more than a priest. Many miracles of healing through his intercession have been reported, and he is especially loved in Greece. His skull is preserved in the Monastery of St. Stephen in Meteora.

Chinese Holy Martyrs of the Boxer Rebellion (June 11)

The twentieth century was barely six months old when one of the worst massacres of Christians since Roman times occurred. The Boxer Rebellion, like many similar movements before and since, was a mixture of genuine grievance, fanaticism, mass hysteria, and a large element of government manipulation for political ends, but its effects on the Christian community in China were devastating.

The Society of Righteous and Harmonious Fists (known in the West as the Boxers) was a secret society founded in the north of China in the 1890s. It was initially suppressed by the government, but a succession of events in 1898–99 changed the whole situation. In 1898, the Chinese government attempted to carry out a series of reforms, broadly attempting to Westernize the country. However, the main result was a financial crisis, not helped by disastrous floods in some parts of the country and drought in others.

As dissatisfaction grew, there was an increasing feeling that the (largely imagined) imperialist ambitions of the Christian missionaries were mostly responsible, and the Boxers blamed "foreign devils" for all the ills, real and imagined. By the autumn of 1899, the Boxers had begun to persecute the native Chinese Christians, and after attempts by the European powers to build up their troops in Beijing, the empress ordered all foreigners killed. Thus given their heads, and with the slogan, "Protect the country, destroy the foreigners," the Righteous Fists of Harmony, joined by some elements of the imperial army, began to attack foreign compounds in Tianjin and Beijing. In their attacks on the "foreign devils," the Boxers made no distinction between Western missionaries and Chinese Christians, or between different types of Christian. Between June and July 1900, the death toll was:

Chinese Orthodox	222 (+ nearly 800 who abandoned their Faith)
Protestant missionaries	182
Chinese Protestants	500
Catholic missionaries	48
Chinese Catholics	18,000

Archimandrite Innocent, head of the Russian mission in Beijing, described the events of June 1900 in graphic detail: "The day of reckoning for most Orthodox Chinese was June 11 1900. The evening before, leaflets were posted in the streets, calling for the massacre of the Christians, and threatening anyone who dared to shelter them with certain death. In the middle of the night, gangs of Boxers with blazing torches spread through Beijing, attacking Christian houses, seizing Christians and forcing them to deny Christ. Some, terrified of torture and death, indeed renounced the Faith in exchange for life, and burned incense before idols. Others, undaunted, confessed Christ. Their fate was horrible. They were ripped open, beheaded, and burned alive in their homes. Throughout the next few days, the search for Christians and the killings continued: Christian houses were destroyed, and the people taken out of town to temples set up by the Boxers, where they were interrogated and burned at the stake."[21] The martyrs of 1900 began to be revered as saints almost immediately afterward, and veneration was approved in 1902 by the Holy Synod of the Russian Church.

Christina of Tyre, Great Martyr (July 24)

The story of this third-century martyr is difficult to piece together due to the many variations. However, what seems reasonably clear is that she was the daughter of the governor of Tyre, a man called Urban. By the age of eleven, she was growing into an extremely beautiful girl, and Urban decided that, to protect her from the many suitors already wanting to marry her, she should be trained to become a pagan priestess. He built a special apartment, where Christina lived with two servants, performing rites and burning incense before the many gold and silver idols.

She spent a lot of time in quiet contemplation, especially looking out of the window at the lovely landscape and the beauty of the night sky. Gradually she began to doubt how the idols, inanimate objects made by the hand of man, could have been involved in the creation of such a wonderful universe. She started saying her prayers not to the idols, but to the unknown god that her simple logic convinced her must exist.

One night, an angel visited her and taught her the truth of the Gospel that she had been reaching towards. She smashed the idols and threw them out of the window, and now began to pray to the known God. When Christina told her father about her new faith and what she had done, he flew into a rage, had the servants killed, and threw his daughter into prison. After trial, she survived many tortures but refused to give up her faith. Three attempts were made to execute her, but each time she was saved through a miracle, the details of her sufferings varying according to different versions of the story. Eventually, she was beheaded in about 300 at the age of thirteen or fourteen.

Christodoulos of Patmos, Venerable (March 16)

A man of restless nature and abundant energy, Christodoulos, whose name means "Slave of God," traveled the length and breadth of the eleventh-century Byzantine Empire attempting to combat minor heresies and backsliding in the monasteries, especially in the remote regions. A deeply spiritual man himself, his aim was to encourage a more spiritual and right-thinking attitude by example rather than by ranting denunciation; no Torquemada he!

In about 1088, his journeys eventually took him to the island of Patmos, where the **Apostle John** had written the Book of Revelation. He found John's sanctuary in ruins and, with his usual energy, appealed for funds from the emperor and built a monastery on the sacred spot. The Monastery of St. John still exists, a splendid monument both to the beloved apostle and to its remark-able builder. The work involved in founding the monastery seems to have finally satisfied Christodoulos's wanderlust, and he remained on Patmos for the rest of his days. His holy remains are still enshrined there.

Christopher of Lycia, Martyr (May 9)

Little is known about Christopher's life, but a church dedicated to him existed in Chalcedon as early as 450. The well-known story about him is almost certainly a later parable based on the meaning of his name, but it is no less delightful for that.

In the third century, a very big man (some say a giant*) called Reprobus earned a meager living carrying travelers over a deep and dangerous river. His ambition was one day to serve the greatest king in the world, but in the remote area where he lived, this seemed little more than a pipe dream. One day, he was sleeping in his hut when he heard a child calling, "Christopher, come and carry me over the river." In spite of the odd name the child had called him, Reprobus lifted the boy onto his shoulders and set off. The swollen river rose higher and higher, and at the same time, the child seemed to grow heavier and heavier. Almost stumbling, Reprobus cried out, "Child, I am in great danger. You weigh almost as if the whole world were on my shoulders."

The child answered, "Christopher, do not be surprised. I am Jesus Christ, the King you already serve in this good work. You carry the weight of people, but on my shoulders I carry the burdens of the whole world." The Child told him to plant his staff in the ground, and as he did so, the staff sprouted into a tree. Reprobus had found his king and shortly afterward was baptized, taking the name *Christophoros* (Bearer of Christ). When he was later martyred for his faith in Lycia under Decius in about 250, he submitted willingly to his fate, although with his great strength he could easily have overcome his murderers—a "gentle giant" to the end.

In the Middle Ages, a tradition grew up that whoever looked on an image of St. Christopher would suffer no harm that day. This led to his reputation as a protector of travelers and, later, motorists in many countries.

---

* He was 7.5 feet tall and very ugly. An early description of him as "having the face of a dog" led to some Byzantine icons depicting him literally with a dog's head. The most well-known example of this oddity is in the Byzantine Museum of Athens.

Chrysanthus and Daria of Rome, Martyrs (March 19)

The tomb of these two martyrs still exists on the Salerian Way outside Rome. Chrysanthus was a young Alexandrian Christian whose father, a senator, was desperate to turn him away from his faith. Although he admired the courage of his son in choosing the dangerous path of Christianity, he feared for Chrysanthus's safety. He tried imprisoning him for a period to make him come to his senses, but when that didn't work, he had an inspired idea. He arranged for friends in Athens to send a beautiful and educated girl called Daria to Alexandria to marry the boy. He hoped that Daria, a priestess of Minerva, would tempt Chrysanthus away from Christianity—after the stick, the carrot.

Unfortunately, the plan backfired somewhat, since although Chrysanthus did indeed fall for Daria, he also converted her to Christianity. They married but lived together in a celibate relationship, using their influence and popularity to convert many others, especially among the aristocracy. Eventually, a Roman tribune called Claudius became suspicious and went to investigate them in their own home. In discussing their activities with Claudius, they succeeded in converting him and, through him, his whole family. Finally, they were denounced, arrested, and taken to Rome, where they were tried by Emperor Numerian himself. Claudius, meanwhile, was handed over to a military court, but his fate is unknown.

Chrysanthus and Daria were buried alive in 284, but their story doesn't end there. Their tomb became a place of prayer for other Christians until a later emperor had all those praying at the tomb walled up in it and left to die.

Clement, Bishop of Rome (November 25)

Clement was the third successor to the **Apostle Peter** as bishop of Rome, after Linus and Anacletus.[22] Little detail is known about his life, but it is possible that he was the same Clement who was a companion of **Paul** (Philippians 4:3), and it is quite likely that he was ordained a priest by Peter. Even the dates of his rule as bishop are uncertain, but Eusebius writes that "in the third year of the reign of [Trajan], Clement committed the episcopal government of the church of Rome to Evarestus, and departed this life after he had superintended the teaching of the divine word nine years in all." This places his rule between about 92 and 101.

According to another tradition, Clement was exiled to the Crimea, where he was forced to do hard labor in a stone quarry. While working, he continued to preach the Gospel and had great success in gaining converts. He was then martyred in about 102 by being thrown from a ship with an anchor tied around his neck. **Saints Cyril and Methodius** are believed to have retrieved the relics of Clement from the sea and taken them to Constantinople. Later some of the remains were taken to Rome, where they are still enshrined in the Basilica di San Clemente. Other relics, including his head, are believed to be in the Monastery of the Caves in Kiev.

What is known for certain is that Clement was the author of a letter to the church at Corinth, which was in a state of turmoil after a violent revolt in which the church leaders had been deposed. Using examples from the Old Testament to demonstrate the evils resulting from jealousy, Clement calls for the restoration of the presbyters and respect for those set in authority. Not only was the Church structure established by the apostles, but Jesus Himself called for tolerance and love between the disciples: "O God," Clement writes, "make us children of quietness and heirs of peace."

Although somewhat longwinded for modern readers, the epistle—the oldest outside of the New Testament—is "a model of pastoral solicitude and firm paternal admonition."[23] "Let not the strong man despise the weak; and let the weak see that he reverence the strong. Let the rich give enough to supply all the needs of the poor and let the poor thank God for supplying their needs. . . . We all need each other: the great need the small, the small need the great. In our body, the head is useless without the feet and the feet without the head. The tiniest limbs of our body are useful and necessary to the whole" (1 Clement 17:30–35).

What Eusebius calls "the wonderful Epistle of St. Clement" was well received by the Corinthians and was for many years read regularly at services, especially in Corinth. It also contains many valuable historical references relating to the early Church, and is the earliest extant statement of the apostolic authority of the clergy. A second letter and several other writings attributed to Clement are now generally believed not to be by him.

Counted as one of the "Apostolic Fathers," Clement is venerated throughout the Christian world and is particularly honored in Russia, where churches dedicated to him are widespread.

Clement of Ochrid, Equal to the Apostles (July 27 and November 25)

Of major importance to the early Church in Bulgaria and Macedonia, Clement was a Macedonian Slav born in about 840. Little is known about his early life, but he was one of the five disciples of **Saints Cyril and Methodius** who accompanied them on their mission to Moravia. After the death of Methodius, Clement took over the leadership of the mission along with Gorazd, later to become the first bishop of Moravia. A continuing dispute with the German princes, who favored the Latin form of worship (see Cyril and Methodius), led to his imprisonment, followed by his expulsion from Moravia, together with fellow missionaries Gorazd, Naum, Sava, and Angelar.

In about 885, Clement, Naum, and Angelar were invited by the Tsar of Bulgaria, Boris I, to conduct services in Slavonic and to instruct future clergy in that language. Since Bulgaria had become Christian in 865, services had been conducted in Greek by clergy sent from Byzantium. Now, however, Boris was hoping to reduce Byzantine influence and strengthen the independence of the Bulgarian state by the use of the Slavonic language and by the ordination of native-born clergy.

Angelar died shortly after their arrival, but Naum was appointed to found an academy in Pliska, while Clement was sent to Kutmicevica in what is now southwestern Macedonia, where he founded the academy of Ochrid. From 886 to 893 Clement taught theology in Old Church Slavonic to about 3,500 students, developing further the Glagolitic (Cyrillic) alphabet created by St. Cyril. In 893, Clement was appointed Archbishop of Drembica in the same area, the first hierarch in Bulgaria to conduct services, preach, teach, and write in Slavonic. He died in 916 and was buried in the famous Monastery of St. Panteleimon in Ochrid, which he had founded. In 2008, the Macedonian Orthodox Church donated some of the relics of St. Clement to the Bulgarian Orthodox Church as a goodwill gesture. All five of the missionaries to the Slavs are celebrated together on July 27 and November 25.

Clement was a prolific translator and writer. Many of his works became very popular in Russia and are still widely read. He is, of course, deeply revered in Bulgaria and Macedonia, where universities and libraries have been named in his honor. More exotically, the Bulgarian scientific base in Antarctica is called St. Kliment Ochridski.

Columba of Iona, Enlightener of Scotland (June 9)

Also known as the Apostle to the Picts, Columba (Columcille, or "Dove of the Church," in Irish) was born in Donegal, Ireland, in about 521. He was a direct descendant of the fourth-century Irish king Niall but seems to have decided on a monastic life at an early age. He became a pupil at the renowned monastic school of Clonard Abbey,* became a monk, and was eventually ordained a priest.

Columba rose in the church hierarchy and founded a number of monasteries, but sometime around 560 he became involved in a very unpriestly quarrel with St. Finian (December 12) over the copyright of a psalter. The argument ended in a pitched battle in which many men were killed. Threatened with excommunication, Columba was allowed to go into exile instead and offered to go to Scotland as a missionary, promising that he would convert as many people as had been killed in the battle. According to tradition, he first landed at the southern tip of the Kintyre peninsula, but since Ireland was still visible on the horizon, he moved on northwards, eventually settling on the island of Iona off Mull.

Having established a base on Iona, Columba traveled throughout Scotland, preaching to the Picts and converting many. He gained a reputation as a miracle worker and respect as a holy man and diplomat, even among the tribes that remained pagan. According to one story, he once met a group of Picts burying a man killed by a water monster. Seeing another swimmer being chased by the monster, he made the sign of the cross and cried out, "Thou shalt go no further, nor touch the man; go back with all speed!" whereupon the monster fled, causing the Picts to rejoice at the power of Columba's God. This happened on the shore of Loch Ness!

Columba's monastery on Iona became not only a school for missionaries but the only center of literacy in the region, and Columba alone is credited with transcribing three hundred books. He was a leading figure in the history of Western monasticism and central to the revival of Christianity in Western Europe after the fall of the Roman Empire. He seems to have had a pleasant personality, and Adomnán, a seventh-century abbot of Iona, describes him as "loving to everyone, happy faced, rejoicing in his inmost heart with the joy of the Holy Spirit." He would often escape the rigors of missionary life by retiring

---

* It is said that at its height, Clonard boasted about three thousand scholars studying under St. Finian, who became known as "the teacher of saints."

to the solitude of a small island, where he may well have written the lovely hymn attributed to him:

Alone with none but Thee, my God,
I journey on my way;
What need I fear when Thou art near,
O King of night and day?
More safe am I within Thy hand
Than if a host did round me stand.[24]

On June 8, 597, Columba was copying one of the psalms. At the verse, "But those who seek the LORD shall not lack any good *thing*" (Psalm 34:10), he stopped and asked a colleague to complete the psalm. He died the next day. His death is described by Adomnán: "After his soul had left the tabernacle of the body, his face still continued ruddy, and brightened in a wonderful way by his vision of the angels, and that to such a degree that he had the appearance, not so much of one dead, as of one alive and sleeping."

Columba was buried in his abbey, but during the Viking raids of the ninth century, his remains were removed, part to Ireland to be buried alongside **St. Patrick** and part to mainland Scotland, where his reliquary was often carried into battle by the Scots. Still venerated widely in the Orthodox Church in the West, Columba was the inspiration behind the founding of St. Columba of Iona Orthodox Monastery in Southbridge, Massachusetts, which aims to bring something of his missionary zeal to the American continent.

Constantine and Helen, Equal to the Apostles (May 21)

These are two of the most revered and loved saints in Greece, as well as being popular Christian names. Indeed, at the time I first started writing this book (2003), the president, prime minister, and leader of the opposition in Greece (not to mention the former king) were all called Konstantinos.

Constantine (274–337) was the Roman general in charge of the legions in Britain. In 313, he was marching his army to Rome to battle for the succession to the empire when he had a vision near York, where he saw a great cross in the sky and the words, *Hoc signo vince* ("By this sign, conquer"). He then ordered the Christian monogram *XP* ("CHR" in the Greek alphabet) to be emblazoned on his standards and went on to emerge victoriously as sole emperor.

As a brilliant general and astute politician, Constantine most likely recognized in Christianity a movement that could not be extinguished by persecution and might, perhaps, be the unifying force his empire desperately needed. Whatever his motivation, by the Edict of Milan in 313, he quickly legalized Christianity, bringing to an end nearly three centuries of persecution. He was deeply interested in theology and the organization of the Church and presided over the First Ecumenical Council at Nicaea. Later, he set about strengthening the Church so that Christianity became, to all intents and purposes, the state religion. Although he was only baptized on his deathbed, he took an active part in church affairs and is regarded as the first Christian emperor.

Helen (255–330) was Constantine's mother. Early records state that she came from a humble background, and according to some traditions, she was from a British tribe. It is not certain when she became a Christian, nor is the extent of her part in her son's conversion; but when he became emperor, Constantine treated her with the greatest honor, giving her the title Augusta. In spite of her wealth and position, she remained humble and unassuming in dress and character, and after toleration was extended to Christianity, she devoted all her influence to its promotion, to charitable works, and to the foundation of churches. When she was in her seventies, she visited the Holy Land on a well-documented pilgrimage, where she spent large sums on the relief of the poor. She tried to identify the location of all the important sites of Christ's life, founding churches at each site, many of which survive to this day. She is also believed to have found part of the Cross of Crucifixion.

Although not what we would regard as a devout man,* Constantine, by his actions and active interest in Christianity, laid the foundations of the modern Church, while Helen, by her goodness and influence, helped the spread of Christianity and was a true example of Christian charity and piety.

Cornelius the Centurion (September 13)

To a simple soldier goes the glory of being the first Gentile to be converted to Christianity by the apostles. Cornelius was a centurion in the Roman army, stationed in Caesarea, the administrative capital of Judea. According to

---

* Indeed, he is reputed to have had his wife Fausta and his son Crispus murdered!

Acts 10, he was "a devout *man* and one who feared God with all his household, who gave alms generously to the people, and prayed to God always." This rather enigmatic description seems to imply that he was certainly not a follower of the Roman gods and was a seeker after truth, possibly being influenced by local Judaism.[25]

One day, while at prayer, he had a vision of an angel who told him God was ready to give him answers to his prayers and questions. He was to send some men to Joppa, where they would find Simon **Peter**. Meanwhile, Peter, who was staying in Joppa, went up to the roof to pray. He suddenly saw a great sheet being lowered from heaven, containing all kinds of animals, reptiles, and birds, including those forbidden to be eaten according to Mosaic Law. He heard a voice saying, "Rise, Peter; kill and eat." Peter said he had never eaten anything ritually unclean or defiled ("common"), to which the voice replied, "What God has cleansed you must not call common." The vision was repeated three times, leaving Peter puzzled about its meaning. Just then, Cornelius's servants arrived, and when they explained why they had come, Peter began to get an inkling of what the vision had meant.

Taking some of the other Christians from Joppa with him, he went to Caesarea, where he broke an important rule of Judaism by entering the house of a Gentile. He said to Cornelius and his family, "You know how unlawful it is for a Jewish man to keep company with or go to one of another nation. But God has shown me that I should not call any man common or unclean." He didn't add, but surely must have felt, that of all Gentiles, the hated Roman conquerors were the last people a Jew would associate with.

After Peter had explained the message of Jesus to Cornelius, his family, and his close friends, the Jews from Joppa were amazed to hear the Gentiles begin to praise God and speak in tongues, just as the apostles had done at Pentecost. Peter immediately baptized the whole gathering. This dramatic event was pivotal in the expansion of the Gospel of Christ from an offshoot of Judaism into a universal faith, which would ultimately leave its homeland in Israel and spread throughout the world. The general conversion of Gentiles was formalized at the Council of Jerusalem a short time later (Acts 15).

According to tradition, Cornelius resigned from the army and joined Peter in missionary journeys. He may have become the first bishop of Caesarea, or of Skepsis in Asia Minor. The latter tradition tells of his destruction of the pagan temple, followed by his arrest and torture. After his miraculous rescue of the prince's wife and child from the rubble of the temple, Cornelius converted Prince Demetrius and nearly three hundred of his subjects, and went on to serve the city into old age.

Cosmas and Damian, Unmercenary Physicians (July 1, October 17, November 1)

These were two brothers born in Arabia. Their father was a pagan, but upon his death, their mother Theodotis (November 1) was free to give them a Christian education. They both studied medicine in Syria and set up practice together in Cilicia. There they treated anybody who needed them, including animals, for no payment, following the words of the Savior, "Heal the sick, cleanse the lepers, raise the dead, cast out demons. Freely you have received, freely give" (Matthew 10:8). All they asked was that those whom they had helped should confess their sins and believe in Christ. Because of their refusal to charge for their services, they became known as "Moneyless" or "Unmercenary" (*Anargyri* in Greek).

In spite of their good works, Cosmas and Damian were denounced as Christians during Diocletian's persecution, or perhaps earlier in the reign of Numerian. They were crucified together in about 303 (or 284). As they hung on their crosses, they were shot with arrows and pelted with stones by a mob, many of whom had probably been their patients. Their bodies were taken back to Syria and buried at Cyrrhus. They became revered as protectors of physicians, and over the years they continued their work of healing, teaching various remedies, and appearing to many sick people in dreams. Among these was Emperor Justinian I, who rebuilt a church in their honor in Constantinople.

Unusually for the early martyrs, they have three feast days. This is because veneration of the brothers was so widespread in the early years that the Byzantine compilers of the church calendars believed there were three separate pairs. Although this is now known to be mistaken, the three dates are still celebrated, although the relative importance of the three varies. The first Sunday in November (October 17 in some calendars) is also celebrated as the "Synaxis of all the Unmercenary Physicians."

Cosmas of Aetolia, Hieromartyr and Equal to the Apostles (August 24)

To be regarded as equal to the apostles is not the exclusive prerogative of saints of the early centuries of Christianity. The eighteenth-century monk Cosmas is generally revered both for his extensive missionary work and, in Greece, also for his contribution to the cause of Hellenic nationalism.

Born in Aetolia, central Greece, in 1714, Cosmas displayed an insatiable appetite for learning from an early age. Eventually, after many years of study, he became a monk on Mount Athos in 1759. At that time, most of the Balkans was under the rule of the Ottoman Empire, and ignorance of the Gospels among the Orthodox Christians was widespread. Deeply concerned about this, Cosmas traveled to Constantinople for further studies in the arts of preaching and rhetoric. Then, with the blessing of the patriarch, he set out in 1760 on a mission to combat this ignorance.

Over the next eighteen years, he traveled throughout Greece, Macedonia, Serbia, and Albania, preaching in every town, often in fields and city squares to accommodate the crowds—a sort of Orthodox John Wesley. His charismatic personality, reputation for holiness, and powerful preaching drew enormous numbers, not only of Christians but of Muslims as well, and he had considerable success in leading people back to their faith. He was not, however, universally popular. His outspoken attacks on the sins of the wealthy and his relentless condemnation of dishonesty in business stirred up enmity among the merchants, whether Christian, Jewish, or Muslim. At the same time, his passionate espousal of Greek nationalism caused the Turkish authorities to suspect him of being a Russian spy. Ironically, it was a gang of Christian businessmen who laid false charges of sedition and conspiracy to rebellion against him, charges which were readily believed by the authorities. He was arrested, hanged from a tree, and his body was thrown into a river in Albania in 1779 when he was sixty-five.

Cosmas was a writer and preacher of tremendous influence and, in many respects, way ahead of his time. For example, he was the first Greek of modern times to actively call for free education for all, putting his theory into practice by founding schools—possibly as many as two hundred—wherever he traveled. Similarly, his respect for women and espousal of equality of the sexes predate even the writings of the Enlightenment: "Oh man, you must not treat woman as a slave because she also is a creature of God. . . . God has her no lower than you. He did not make her of your head so that she be superior, nor from your feet so that she may be inferior, but from your side. And indeed from your left side, where your heart lies, in order to teach you that you must love her and not hold her in contempt." Cosmas's gift of prophecy could also be extraordinary at times: "The cause of the General War will come from Dalmatia. First Austria will be dismembered and then Turkey." This was nearly 150 years before the assassination of Archduke Franz Ferdinand in Sarajevo sparked off the First World War, which saw the destruction of the Austro-Hungarian and Ottoman empires.

Cosmas was declared a saint by the ecumenical patriarch in 1961. In June 2007, his holy relics were returned by Archbishop Anastasios of Albania to the monastery founded in his name at his birthplace in Aetolia.

Cuthman of Steyning, Venerable (February 8)

Cuthman is not widely known in the Orthodox Church, and even in the Roman Catholic and Anglican Churches, his veneration is mainly limited to the area around the village of Steyning in Sussex. However, he was a saint of the "undivided Church," his story is intriguing, and he lived only ten miles from my birthplace!

Although some traditions claim he came originally from Devon or Cornwall, it is more likely that Cuthman was born in Chidham, Sussex, in about 681. If this is the case, it was probably St. Wilfrid (October 12) who converted his parents to Christianity and baptized the family. Cuthman was a shepherd, and after his father died and his mother became paralyzed, he was forced to beg from door to door. He built a wheelbarrow to carry his mother, using a rope over his shoulders to help take the weight. He set out towards the east, begging on the way, and decided that wherever the rope broke, he would stop, settle, and build a church.

The rope broke near a village, now called Steyning, where Cuthman put up a small shack and began to build his church. He prayed, "Father Almighty, you have brought my wanderings to an end; now enable me to begin this work. For who am I, Lord, that I should build a house to your name? If I rely on myself, it will be of no avail, but it is you who will assist me. You have given me the desire to be a builder; make up for my lack of skill, and bring the work of building this holy house to its completion." The story goes that he did indeed receive help from the local people, and that those who refused received divine punishment. It is said that some farmers cutting hay in a nearby field laughed at him, whereupon a sudden heavy rainstorm ruined the hay.

As the building work was nearing completion, Cuthman was having great problems fitting a roof beam. A stranger appeared and showed him how to do the job, obviously a skilled carpenter. When Cuthman asked his name, he said, "I am he in whose name you are building this church." Various legendary stories exist about the saint, but it seems that he lived out his life quietly in his shack, preaching the Gospel to any who came to see him and leading a simple life of prayer and meditation.

Although St. Cuthman was venerated widely in England and France in the Middle Ages, after the Reformation he seems to have largely dropped out of sight. In 1938, however, Christopher Fry wrote a play based on one version of Cuthman's life called *The Boy with a Cart*. When it was performed in London, directed by John Geilgud and with Richard Burton as Cuthman, the saint became better known. The little stone church still exists and, in 2009, was rededicated to St. Andrew and St. Cuthman.

Cyprian, Hieromartyr, and Justina, Virgin Martyr of Antioch (October 2)

Cyprian was a sorcerer living in Antioch reputed to have extensive magical powers. He fell in love with a young girl called Justina, who had dedicated her life to Christ. In spite of using all his magical powers to win her, he failed, and was instead converted by the girl. He burned all his magic books and asked for baptism. He became as fervent in his Christianity as he had been in his magic and was ordained, eventually becoming a bishop. Both he and Justina were beheaded in Nicomedia in 304.

Cyprian, Bishop of Carthage, Hieromartyr (August 31)

The life of Cyprian is well documented in his own writings and other contemporary accounts. Born in about 200 in Carthage, North Africa, he became a popular and respected teacher of rhetoric and philosophy, as well as a leading lawyer. Through his studies in philosophy, he gradually became convinced of the truth of Christianity and was eventually baptized at the age of forty-six. He immediately devoted his considerable talents to his new faith, becoming a priest after two years, and was unanimously elected Bishop of Carthage in 248.

Almost immediately, Decius began a savage persecution of Christians, aiming to exterminate all bishops and leave the Church leaderless. In the circumstances, Cyprian considered it wise to go into hiding and continue to guide his community by letters, most of which survive. Although he was accused by some of cowardice at the time, his decision was sensible since the Church was in great need of strong leadership, being split to the point of schism by a very practical problem: should those who had recanted their Christian Faith under torture or to save their lives be readmitted to the Church? Cyprian sided with the more merciful view that, after a period of penance of varying severity, even the most serious lapses could be forgiven. When the dispute became bitter, with two rival popes contesting the See of Rome, Cyprian supported the moderate (and ultimately successful) Pope Cornelius, writing a book entitled *On the Unity of the Church*, which remains a classic exposition of the subject. In it he sums up the traditional creed of the Church: "He can no longer have God for his Father who has not the Church for his mother."

No sooner had this controversy died down than Cyprian was called upon to demonstrate the more practical and pastoral duties of a bishop. In 252, a devastating plague struck Carthage and hundreds fled the city, leaving the sick without help and the dead unburied. Cyprian remained, personally taking over the care of the sick and burial of the dead, Christian and pagan alike. He also browbeat the wealthier citizens into providing food for the starving. In 253, yet another wave of persecutions started under Emperor Valerian. This time, in contrast to his earlier caution, Cyprian was first to refuse to sacrifice to the Roman gods and, having refused to reveal the names of the other priests in Carthage, was exiled. After a short time, he made his way back to Carthage, where he was sentenced to death in 258.

The official records of his trial and execution still exist and paint a moving and vivid picture of calm and firm courage. At the place of execution, he knelt for a while in prayer, gave a generous gift (twenty-five gold pieces) to the executioner, blindfolded himself, and lowered his head for the sword. A towering figure from the early Church, Cyprian left writings that are models of clear and wise theology, rightly esteemed to this day. However, it is the common sense, love, and courage he demonstrated in his life (and death) that make him stand out: "Love is the foundation of all the virtues, and it continues with us eternally in the heavenly Kingdom."

Cyriacus the Recluse, Venerable (September 29)

The life of Cyriacus was written by a contemporary, Cyril of Scythopolis. Cyriacus was born in Corinth in 300 and, while still a young man, emigrated to Palestine to become a monk. He was tonsured as a monk by **St. Euthymius** and for a time was under the spiritual guidance of **St. Gerasimus of the Jordan**. He lived at several hermitages and monasteries in the Holy Land, including St. Chariton's Cave near Bethlehem, an immense complex of natural caves. It was here that he died peacefully in 408. At a time when tremendous events were shaking both the political and religious worlds, Cyriacus lived a completely uneventful life of prayer and the daily singing of psalms, but his gentleness and prophetic spirit have served as an inspiration to many down the centuries. It is said that for thirty years, Cyriacus never ate before sundown and was never known to be angry; perhaps this is the secret of a long life.

Cyril, Archbishop of Jerusalem (March 18)

Born in Jerusalem in 315, Cyril was ordained a priest in 346 and appointed Archbishop of Jerusalem four years later. As a strong opponent of Arianism, he was exiled three times, a total of about sixteen years out of his thirty-five years as bishop. On the first occasion, the Arian Bishop of Caesarea, Acacius, called a council that had him deposed on various slanderous charges, including the extraordinary charge of selling church property to help the poor. What actually happened was that during a severe famine in Jerusalem, Cyril used all his personal wealth to feed the starving, and, when that was used up, pawned some of the church plate to buy more wheat for the hungry.

He was reinstated shortly afterward, but in 362 he was banished again for a further year, this time by the apostate Emperor Julian, for preaching against the rebuilding of the Jewish temple in Jerusalem. In 367, the Arian Emperor Valens sent him into exile again, but after Valens's death in 378 he was allowed to spend the remainder of his life in peace. On his return from his final exile, he found Jerusalem in a state of disorder, with widespread corruption, and he spent most of his remaining eight years reclaiming and "cleaning up" the city. He died in 386.

In spite of his opposition to Arianism, Cyril was of a peaceful and conciliatory nature and generally took a moderate position on the debates about the Trinity. His most famous writings are the eighteen lectures to candidates for baptism and the five for the newly baptized which he wrote while still a priest. Full of warmth and pastoral love, they give instruction on the fundamental truths of Christianity in a very practical way. Cyril has been called a first grade teacher for new Christians, and he leads us by the hand into the most profound truths: "The Spirit comes gently and makes himself known by his fragrance. He is not felt as a burden for God is light, very light. Rays of light and knowledge stream before him as the Spirit approaches. The Spirit comes with the tenderness of a true friend to save, to heal, to teach, to counsel, to strengthen, and to console."

Cyril speaks directly to ordinary people, relating spiritual truths to the realities of life, as in this discussion of faith: "It is not only among us, who are marked with the name of Christ, that the dignity of faith is great; all the business of the world, even those outside the church, is accomplished by faith. By faith, marriage laws join in union persons who were strangers to one another. By faith, agriculture is sustained; for a man does not endure the toil involved unless he believes he will reap a harvest. By faith, seafaring men, entrusting themselves to a tiny wooden craft, exchange the solid element of the land for the unstable motion of the waves."

For all their practicality, however, Cyril's lectures are based firmly on the creed as it existed at that time, and which he puts at the center of his discourse: "The articles of the Faith were not written through human cleverness, but they contain everything that is most important in all the Scriptures, in a single teaching of faith. Just as the mustard seed contains all its plethora of branches within its small kernel, so also does the Faith in its several declarations combine all the pious teachings of the Old and the New Testaments."

Cyril, Archbishop of Alexandria (June 9)

A somewhat contradictory character, Cyril is more revered as a theologian and defender of the integrity of the Orthodox Faith than loved as a bishop, and his writings remain central to Orthodox theology. Born in Alexandria in 380, he succeeded his uncle to the archbishopric in 412, having already taken an active part in the deposing of **John Chrysostom**. In his early days as archbishop, he displayed an abrasive, even at times harsh, nature. Often hasty in his judgments, his attacks on schismatics, Jews, and non-Christians indicated a touch of the fanatic.

Nevertheless, at a time when many were attempting to water down the Christian doctrine, he was instrumental in maintaining its integrity, and his contribution to the early Church is undeniable. Specifically, the teaching of Nestorius, Archbishop of Constantinople, sought to draw a distinction between the human Jesus and the divine Word of God. Cyril took the lead in combating these ideas, using his considerable learning in an energetic defense of the unity of Christ's Person. He fought vehemently to give the **Virgin Mary** the title Theotokos, and his vigorous polemics convinced the Council of Ephesus, which in 431 condemned Nestorianism and removed Nestorius from the see of Constantinople.

Having succeeded in removing this threat, Cyril became more moderate and conciliatory, even attempting to reconcile the less extreme Nestorians to the Church. For a long time he maintained his dislike of St. John Chrysostom, refusing to include him in prayers, but as he grew older, he relented and convened all the Egyptian bishops to celebrate a solemn feast in honor of the saint. He died in 444.

Additional Feast Day: January 18 (together with **St. Athanasius**)

Cyril and Methodius, Equal to the Apostles (May 11)

Cyril (c. 827–869) and Methodius (c. 815–885) were brothers and both eminent citizens of Thessalonica, the former being a leading philosopher at the university and the latter governor of a province. At about the same time, they both decided to enter the priesthood, and in 863 were sent by the Patriarch of Constantinople to undertake missionary work among the Slavs of Moravia (roughly equivalent to modern Czechoslovakia). At the request of the local prince, they were to preach the Gospel in Slavonic, which was no problem as they were both fluent in the dialect of the Macedonian Slavs who lived in the area around Thessalonica. The Bible and church services, however, were another matter because there was no written Slavonic language. The brothers therefore set out to invent an alphabet suitable for the language, using Greek letters as the basis and inventing others for sounds not found in Greek. This Cyrillic alphabet is the one still used in Russia, Serbia, and Bulgaria.

Unfortunately, their mission fell afoul of some of the German princes who were trying to spread the Latin form of worship. The brothers appealed to Rome and received the pope's support. However, Cyril fell ill in Rome and died there at the age of forty-two. Methodius returned to Moravia and was consecrated bishop, but had little further success against the German princes. Indeed, he was imprisoned in Germany for two and a half years. After his release, he returned to Moravia, where he died at age sixty. At his funeral, as a brief but touching symbol of reconciliation and unity, the service was chanted in Latin, Greek, and Slavonic.

After his death, his disciples were exiled from Moravia and fled to Bulgaria, where they continued the expansion of the Church. Thus, Cyril and Methodius's mission to Moravia was largely unsuccessful, but it laid the foundations for the spread of Christianity to Bulgaria, Serbia, and indirectly Russia. The brothers' work of translation and the invention of the alphabet also had a major influence on the development of Slavonic literature. Without Cyril and Methodius, would we have Tolstoy?

The two saints are especially revered in Serbia and Bulgaria, but their work as apostles to the Slavs and their contribution to the Christian history of Eastern Europe transcend national and religious boundaries. This was recognized in 1981 when Pope John Paul II declared them joint patrons of Europe, along with **St. Benedict**. There are public holidays commemorating the saints in Bulgaria and Russia (May 24) and in Macedonia, the Czech Republic, and Slovakia (July 5).

Additional Feast Days: February 14 (Repose of Cyril)

April 6 (Repose of Methodius)

Cyrus and John, Unmercenary Physicians (January 31)

Cyrus was a Christian doctor in Alexandria in the third century. He often refused to accept payment for his services, healing in the name of Jesus Christ, but always advised his patients that to stay healthy they should not sin, because it was sin that often caused illness. The people of the city built a hospital for him to work in, and he became a popular and successful doctor. He made no secret of his Christian faith and would often preach the Gospel.

When Diocletian's persecution began, Cyrus narrowly escaped arrest and went into hiding in Arabia. There he joined a monastery near the Persian Gulf, continuing his medical activities and performing many miracles of healing. At about the same time, in Edessa, there was an army doctor called John, who was also a Christian. Cyrus's reputation as a healer reached John while he was in Jerusalem, and he traveled to the monastery to join Cyrus as a disciple.

As the persecution in Egypt continued, the two doctors heard news that an old friend of Cyrus, a pious Christian woman called Athanasia, had been arrested together with her three young daughters, Theoctista, Theodota, and Eudoxia. Fearing that torture would cause the four to abandon their faith, Cyrus and John hurried to the prison in Canopis to give support and encouragement to the women. They were, of course, arrested themselves, and their courage under the inevitable horrendous tortures did indeed give Athanasia and her daughters the resolution to stay true to their faith. All four were also tortured and then beheaded, and are commemorated as saints on the same day as Cyrus and John. The doctors were beheaded in about 311 and buried in the Church of St. Mark.

In 412, **Cyril, Patriarch of Alexandria,** transferred the relics of the saints to the village of Menuthis* to act as a counter-attraction to the still lingering worship of Isis at a local temple. It became a popular and much-visited shrine for many years, and many miracles of healing were reported. Later, the relics were transported to Rome and from there to Munich. Cyrus and John are invoked in the services of the Blessing of the Waters (January 6) and the Anointing of the Sick. Their help is also sought by those suffering from lack of sleep.

---

* Now known as Abukir ("Father Cyrus"), this village was the scene of Nelson's naval victory in 1798.

D

Daniel, Holy Prophet, and the Three Holy Youths (December 17)

As a kid in Baptist Sunday school, I loved the story of Daniel. I think I believed him to be a sort of religious Buck Rogers. I would join in with gusto as we sang the lovely old Baptist song, "Dare to be a Daniel, / Dare to stand alone! / Dare to have a purpose firm! / Dare to make it known," and held my breath in suspense as the three boys were thrown into the fiery furnace. Now, as an adult Orthodox Christian, although I realize we shouldn't forget the profundity of Daniel's prophecy, I still find his story to be a great yarn!

In about 606 BC, after the conquest of Jerusalem by the Babylonians, many of the Israelites were taken as prisoners to Babylon. Among them were Daniel and three other young men: Ananias, Misael, and Azarias. Although captives, the young men were treated well, taught the Chaldean language, given fine clothes, and trained to be pages in the court of King Nebuchadnezzar. They were also given Chaldean names, Daniel being called Baltasar and the other three being given the names by which they are generally known in the West: Shadrach, Meshach, and Abednego.

All four remained true to their faith in the One God and, with the connivance of their Babylonian instructor, avoided the ritually unclean food and wine of the court, keeping to a diet of vegetables and water. At the end of their three years' probation, they were presented to the king, and "in all matters of wisdom *and* understanding about which the king examined them, he found them ten times better than all the magicians *and* astrologers who *were* in all his realm"

(Daniel 1:19–20). After being the only one able to interpret a terrifying dream for Nebuchadnezzar, Daniel was made head of all the royal advisors and governor of the whole province of Babylon. At his request, Shadrach, Meshach, and Abednego were also appointed to high positions. Nebuchadnezzar even acknowledged that Daniel's God was the greatest (though not the only) god.

All was going well for the four Jews, but their success made many Babylonians jealous. The king erected a massive gold statue and commanded that people bow down to worship it. Shadrach, Meshach, and Abednego, of course, refused to bow down to the idol, and some of their enemies took the opportunity to denounce them to the king. Sentenced to death, the three were thrown into a furnace so incredibly hot that the guards who threw them in were themselves burnt to a cinder. The king suddenly saw that not only were the three young men walking about in the flames, but there seemed to be a fourth figure. He cried out, "Look! I see four men loose, walking in the midst of the fire; and they are not hurt, and the form of the fourth is like the Son of God" (Daniel 3:25). He called the three youths out of the fire, and they emerged unharmed. Nebuchadnezzar promoted them further and, in a beautiful hymn, seems to have accepted the God of Israel as the one true God: "How great *are* His signs, / And how mighty His wonders! / His kingdom *is* an everlasting kingdom, / And His dominion *is* from generation to generation" (Daniel 4:3).

Daniel was an extremely able administrator and continued in high office after the fall of Babylon to the Persians. Under Darius the Mede, he was appointed one of three chief governors, and the king was considering putting him in complete charge of the empire as a sort of prime minister. The other governors, however, tried to find ways to discredit him but failed because he carried out all his duties in exemplary fashion. They therefore persuaded Darius to issue a decree banning all prayers to anyone but the king for thirty days, knowing that Daniel openly prayed three times a day.

Daniel was duly arrested, and the king, bound by his own law, was reluctantly forced to have him thrown into a pit full of lions. The pit was sealed, and after a sleepless night, Darius hurried to the pit at dawn to find Daniel still alive. Daniel said to the king, "My God sent His angel and shut the lions' mouths, so that they have not hurt me, because I was found innocent before Him; and also, O king, I have done no wrong before you" (Daniel 6:22). He was released, and his accusers were thrown into the pit instead, where they were quickly killed.

Traveling Companions

Darius then issued a new decree commanding that the God of Daniel be respected and revered throughout the empire.

Daniel continued to prosper under Darius and his successor Cyrus the Great, and it was probably under his influence that Cyrus ended the Jewish captivity in 536 BC. In later life, Daniel was responsible for several profound apocalyptic prophecies relating to the future of the Israelites and the coming of the Messiah. According to tradition, he remained in Babylon even after the captivity ended and was about one hundred years old when he died. No fewer than six places in Iraq, Iran, and Uzbekistan claim to be the burial place of the prophet.

Additional Feast Day: Sunday of the Holy Fathers

David of Wales, Venerable Bishop (March 1)

David (Dewi in Welsh) was born in about 500 in southwest Wales, near the present-day city of St. David's. Although two extensive biographies of the saint were written in the eleventh and twelfth centuries, details of his early life are contradictory and confusing. His father was probably a chieftain from Cardigan who, according to some versions, raped David's mother, who is venerated by Welsh Christians as St. Non. What is more clearly established is that Non gave birth to her son on a cliff top during a violent storm—a dramatic arrival suitable for the opening of a film about the saint! The ruins of a medieval chapel dedicated to St. Non can still be seen nearby. Educated by St. Paulinus of Wales (November 23), David was ordained a priest and, while on a pilgrimage to Jerusalem, consecrated as a bishop by the patriarch. Renowned as a teacher and preacher, he founded twelve monasteries in Wales alone as well as several in Cornwall and Brittany.

The monastic rule David established was so strict it might have made even some of the Desert Fathers think twice. He encouraged all his followers to avoid meat and beer, while his monks could only drink water and eat bread with a little salt and herbs. Days in the monasteries were spent in hard manual labor, the monks pulling the ploughs by hand without the help of oxen, while evenings were spent in prayer, reading the Scriptures, and writing. The monks stayed awake in prayer from dusk on Friday until dawn on Sunday. Silence was observed at all times except under extreme necessity, and personal possessions were completely banned; even to use the words "*my* book" was an offense requiring penance.

David presided over two synods at Brefi in Cardigan, where he was confirmed as bishop, and at Caerleon. It was also at Brefi that his most famous miracle occurred. The synod was held in the open, and when people at the back complained they couldn't see or hear David, the ground rose up under his feet to form a small hill.* It is also reported that a white dove landed on his shoulder as a sign that he was speaking with the authority of the Holy Spirit.

David died in about 590, his final words being, "Be steadfast, brothers, and do the little things," a saying still popular in Wales. He was buried in the monastery he had founded and ruled as abbot, now St. David's Cathedral in Pembrokeshire. He is the patron saint of Wales and, appropriately, special protector of vegetarians.

Demetrius of Thessalonica, Great Martyr (October 26)

One of the most popular and revered of the "warrior saints," Demetrius was a soldier from a Christian family who never missed an opportunity to preach the Faith among his colleagues. When promoted to the rank of proconsul, he refused to obey Emperor Maximian's order to exterminate all Christians in the area. Instead, he continued to preach the Gospel and inspired many pupils and disciples to face their martyrdom with courage. As a result, he was thrown into prison.

On a visit to Thessalonica, Maximian held celebratory games, and his favorite gladiator, Lyaeus, a renowned wrestler, challenged all comers to a fight to the death. A young Christian soldier called Nestor (October 27) took up the challenge, but first visited Demetrius in prison to ask for his blessing. Then, in a scene reminiscent of the film *Gladiator*, he presented himself in the stadium, and crying out, "God of Demetrius, help me," he struck Lyaeus a mortal blow in the chest. Enraged at the death of his favorite, Maximian ordered Demetrius to be stabbed to death in prison, while he personally took a sword and killed Nestor on the spot.

Demetrius's remains are believed to be kept on Mount Athos, and he is credited with many miracles. The most famous is from 586, when Thessalonica

---

* Another version of the story is that he simply moved the meeting to higher ground. The historian John Davies[26] makes the point that, in a part of Wales noted for its mountains, one can scarcely conceive of any miracle more superfluous than the creation of a new hill!

was being attacked by Slavs, who greatly outnumbered the defending Greeks. St. Demetrius is said to have helped the Greeks repulse the Slavs, whose own records describe a great force opposed to them, led by a commander dressed in dazzling armor and a white cloak and riding a white stallion. Not surprisingly, Demetrius is the special protector of Thessalonica and also of young people. Perhaps a little ironically, he has been particularly revered by the Slavs since they were converted to Christianity. The additional feast on October 22 is in memory of those slain in the great battle of Kulidovo, when Prince St. Demetrius of the Don defeated the Golden Horde in 1380, with the assistance of the great martyr.

Demetrius is called "Myrrh-Gusher" because, ever since the seventh century, a miraculous flow of sweet-smelling myrrh has been found beneath the crypt where his relics lie. Demetrius and its variations continue to be popular names in Bulgaria, Russia, and Greece.

Additional Feast Day: October 22 (in Russia only)

Dionysius the Areopagite, Hieromartyr (October 3)

Dionysius was a learned Athenian and judge. After hearing **St. Paul** preach his famous sermon at the Areopagus (forum) on Mars Hill, he became a Christian and later the first, or perhaps the second, Bishop of Athens (Acts 17:34). He is believed to have been present at the repose of the **Blessed Virgin Mary** in about AD 57. According to some traditions, he traveled as a missionary to Rome, Germany, Spain, and Gaul and was the same St. Dionysius (Denys) who became the patron saint of Paris. This is not impossible, but it is more likely that he was beheaded in Athens at the age of ninety-six. Several works of mystical theology written under the name Dionysius the Areopagite have been of tremendous importance in the development of Christian thought. However, it is now believed they are the work of a fifth-century Syrian writer.

Dionysius of Zakynthos, Venerable (December 17)

Born in 1546 on the island of Zakynthos, Dionysius was descended from a noble Venetian family. He was a deeply spiritual man with a genuine gift of healing, and after being consecrated Archbishop of Aegina, he attracted enormous numbers of people seeking his help. He was overwhelmed by this popularity and, fearing that he would fall into the sin of pride or vanity, he eventually resigned his office and retired to a monastery in the mountains of his home island. There he became well known for many miracles of healing and for his mild and loving nature.

The latter was severely put to the test when a murderer on the run sought sanctuary at the monastery. The fugitive didn't know that Dionysius was the brother of the man he had murdered, although Dionysius himself was aware of the fact. Nevertheless, the monk accepted the murderer into his cell and gave him food as well as spiritual guidance, begging him to repent of his sin and turn to God. When the search party was near, Dionysius revealed who he was and sent the fugitive on his way with food and money for the journey. Few are given the chance to live so dramatically the words of Christ, "Judge not, that you be not judged" (Matthew 7:1–2).

Dionysius died in 1622 at the age of seventy-five after a long and painful illness. He is loved and revered by the people of Zakynthos as their special protector. Dionysius is one of Greece's three "walking saints," along with **Saints Spyridon** and **Gerasimus of Kephalonia**. These are believed to occasionally walk the earth in their bodies. The slippers on their feet seem to wear out and need replacing from time to time.

Additional Feast Day: August 24 (Transfer of Relics)

Dorotheus of Gaza, Venerable (June 5)

Dorotheus of Gaza (sometimes called Dorotheus of Palestine) was born in Antioch in about 500. Well-educated, with a passion for books, he studied at the school of rhetoric in Gaza, but left it to become a monk and disciple of St. Barsanuphius and St. John the Prophet (both February 6). His main duties seem to have been the care of Abba John, the running of the infirmary, and instruction of the younger monks, work for which his training in rhetoric fitted him well. In about 540, he left to set up his own monastery nearby and became abbot there.

We know little more about his life except that he died in about 560, but we do have a large body of his writings, which give fascinating insights into monastic life during the sixth century, as well as revealing something of Dorotheus's character. His was a mild asceticism, and his instructions to the monks are full of gentle admonition rather than severity. When talking of humility, for example, he used examples from his own life to show how he had learned the virtue, stories that are often to his own detriment. His mild and nonjudgmental nature is described by his disciple, St. Dositheus (February 19): "Towards the brethren laboring with him he responded with modesty, with humility, and was gracious without arrogance or audacity. He was good-natured and direct, he would engage in a dispute, but always preserved the principle of respect, of good will, and that which is sweeter than honey, oneness of soul, the mother of all virtues."

In all his writing, perhaps influenced by his philosophical studies at the School of Rhetoric, Dorotheus emphasized moderation.[27] He regarded pride as the cause of all sin, and its opposite, humility, as the chief virtue. Nevertheless, even humility must be "in the middle between arrogance and obsequiousness." He took the same middle road in monastic organization, recognizing the importance of solitude but also stressing the need for community and the interdependence of the brothers.

Dorotheus's refusal to judge others is beautifully illustrated by his description of a friend who, when he visited a house that was untidy and dirty, would bless the owner who must obviously spend his time in prayer, leaving no time for household chores. If he visited a neat and tidy house, he would bless the owner because he must have a neat and clean soul. Dorotheus writes, "May the good Lord grant us the same kind disposition, so that we too may receive benefits from everyone, and so that we never notice the failings of others." Much of Dorotheus's work is preserved in the writings of **St. Theodore of Studion,** who was greatly influenced by Dorotheus. These remain widely read today, not just by monks.

Dorotheus of Gaza should not be confused with Dorotheus of Egypt (September 16), a sixth-century hermit who lived an extremely austere life in the Skete Desert, west of the Nile.

D

Traveling Companions

Є

Eleutherius, Bishop of Illyricum, Hieromartyr (December 15)

Eleutherius was a Roman who lost his father at an early age. His mother, St. Anthia (beheaded with her son and celebrated on the same day), sent him to the Bishop of Rome for his education and spiritual supervision. He was an able student and of a pious nature, and these qualities caused him to be ordained at seventeen and consecrated as Bishop of Illyricum at twenty.

The life of a bishop in the third-century Roman Empire was not one of prestige and pomp and, indeed, tended to be somewhat short. Worshipping and preaching in secret, the bishop was not only pastor of his flock but very often the first to be identified and executed by the authorities. Nevertheless, Eleutherius succeeded in converting many to Christianity through his preaching and by example. He was eventually captured during the persecution by Severus Alexander (or Hadrian, by some accounts). During the journey to Rome, he converted the captain of the guard, Felix, who accompanied him to the trial and died with him. In spite of creating a good impression on his interrogators with his courageous and rational answers, he was tortured and eventually murdered in prison in about 226. One of his torturers was converted and also executed. Traditionally, his name is invoked by pregnant women praying for a safe delivery.

In Greece, the name Eleutherios, as well as being associated with the martyr, has a special resonance. The word *eleutheria* means "freedom." During the struggle for independence from the Ottoman Turks, the battle cry of the freedom fighters was *Eleutheria i Thanatos*—"Freedom or Death."

Elijah, Holy Prophet (July 20)

One of the most charismatic and awe-inspiring of the Old Testament prophets, Elijah ("Strength of the Lord") was a strict ascetic and a daring preacher, full of zeal and "aflame with the fire of love for God." He lived in the tenth century BC, and his life is well documented in the Books of Kings, a gripping read for anyone who likes a good story (1 Kings 17—19, 2 Kings 1—2).[28] In bearing witness of the power of God to the people of Israel, Elijah was granted power over the elements, ending a drought that had laid waste the land and, on more than one occasion, bringing down fire from heaven by the force of his prayer. His end was possibly one of the most dramatic in the Old Testament, as he was carried directly to heaven in a chariot of fire, leaving only his coat to his disciple Elisha (June 14) (2 Kings 2:11).

Paradoxically, in spite of all the drama of his life and the "fire and brimstone" of his preaching,* icons of Elijah usually depict him in quiet contemplation in a cave, where, the story goes, ravens brought him bread to keep him from starvation. Furthermore, his story includes one of the most tender and beautiful images of God: "And behold, the LORD passed by, and a great and strong wind tore into the mountains and broke the rocks in pieces before the LORD, *but* the LORD *was* not in the wind; and after the wind an earthquake, *but* the LORD *was* not in the earthquake; and after the earthquake a fire, *but* the LORD *was* not in the fire; and after the fire a still small voice" (1 Kings 19:11–12).

Elijah's connection with the forces of nature makes him especially venerated by men close to the earth, such as fishermen and farmers. He is also regarded as a protector against fire and a guardian of firemen, and his assistance is prayed for in times of drought.

Elizabeth, Grand Duchess of Russia, New Martyr (July 18)

Born in 1864, Princess Elizabeth of Hesse was the elder sister of Alexandra, later the wife of Tsar Nicholas II. In 1884, she married Grand Duke Sergei, a member of the royal family but not in line for the throne. Because of this, unlike her sister, she wasn't obliged to become Orthodox, but nevertheless she felt more and more drawn to Russian Orthodoxy, and much against the wishes of

---

* In Romania he is nicknamed "Elijah the Thunderer."

her family,* she was received into the Church by chrismation in 1891. "I am sure God's blessing will accompany my act which I do with such fervent belief, with the feeling that I may become a better Christian and be one step nearer to God," she wrote. The extent and depth of Elizabeth's faith was demonstrated when, during the civil unrest of 1905, Grand Duke Sergei was assassinated with a bomb. She was close to the explosion and witnessed the terrible results, not only helping to collect the remains but comforting the mortally injured coachman and arranging his transport to the hospital. She even visited the assassin in prison, where she spent some time talking to him and reading the Gospel.

After the loss of her husband, the luxury of the imperial court began to irk Elizabeth more and more, and she eventually sold most of her possessions, using the proceeds to open a convent in Moscow. There she gathered a group of like-minded women, including her former maid, Barbara Yakovleva. She said to her colleagues, "I am leaving a glittering world where I had a glittering position but, with all of you, I am descending into a *greater* world—the world of the poor and suffering." The nuns combined a life of prayer with practical charitable activities among the poor and orphans. They later expanded their work by opening an orphanage and a hospital, along with homes for tuberculosis victims, the physically disabled, pregnant women, and the elderly.

Even after the revolution of 1917, the work of the convent continued for a time. Elizabeth, in spite of her aristocratic background, felt she could understand the motivation behind the revolution, while condemning the methods, and refused an offer of refuge in the Kremlin made by the Provisional Government. Because of her simplicity, love of the people, and refusal to attack the revolutionaries, many of the Bolsheviks grew to admire and respect her. For a while, the Soviet government even supported the convent and gave the residents a considerable degree of freedom.

By 1918, however, opinion was shifting against the royal family, and pressure grew from the more hard-line Bolsheviks to move against all those connected with the tsar. At Pascha, Elizabeth was arrested along with several other grand dukes and princes and exiled to Ekaterinburg. Barbara Yakovleva voluntarily accompanied her. They were later moved to Alapaevsk, where they were murdered on July 18. All the prisoners were taken at gunpoint to an abandoned mineshaft, clubbed on the head, and pushed in. Most survived the fall, and even

---

* But with the support of her grandmother, Queen Victoria of Great Britain.

after grenades were thrown in after them, eyewitnesses still heard hymns being sung for some time. Soon after, the area was briefly recaptured by the White Army and the bodies were taken out. They found evidence that Elizabeth had bandaged the wounds of one of the young princes with her handkerchief and held him in her arms until they died. Elizabeth's relics were recovered and taken to Beijing, then later (according to her wish) to Jerusalem.

Elizabeth, together with Barbara, was glorified by the Russian Orthodox Church Outside Russia in 1981 and by the Russian Orthodox Church as a whole in 1992. Her main shrine is in the Saints Mary and Martha Convent she founded in Moscow, and some of her relics now lie there. She is also one of the ten twentieth-century martyrs depicted above the West Door of Westminster Abbey in London.

Additional Feast Day: Sunday nearest January 25 (New Martyrs and Confessors of Russia)

Ephraim the Syrian, Venerable (January 28)

Ephraim, sometimes called "the Harp of the Spirit," was born in about 306 in Nisibis, Mesopotamia, at that time under Roman rule. As a child he was impetuous and had a quick temper, but under the influence of St. James, Bishop of Nisibis (January 13), he moderated his temper and learned the virtues of humility and submission to God's will. St. James recognized the talents of his young disciple and allowed him, young as he was, to preach sermons and teach in the school. To help in his educational work, Ephraim began to write biblical commentaries, as well as composing hymns.

After the death of Constantine I in 337, Nisibis, as a border town, was three times besieged by the Persian army. It was eventually ceded back to Persia in 363, on condition that the Christian population be allowed to leave. Ephraim settled in Edessa, where he continued his educational work. At that time, Edessa was a hotbed of competing philosophies, religions, and sects, and it was here that he wrote many of his greatest hymns in defense of Orthodoxy. At some point, he was ordained a deacon and remained one all his life, believing he was unworthy of higher office. **Basil the Great**, no less, tried to persuade him to be ordained a priest, but he refused, and when Basil later offered him a bishopric, he even feigned madness to avoid the honor. He died peacefully in 373, or possibly 379.

Over four hundred of Ephraim's lyric hymns still exist, so it is quite likely that he wrote many more. Written in a somewhat flowery style, they are full of rich imagery drawn not only from the Bible but from Syriac folk tradition, Greek philosophy, and even other religions. It is only possible to give a brief taste of the work of one who has been called "the greatest poet of the patristic age and, perhaps, the only theologian-poet to rank beside Dante," but I love the powerful and dramatic use of paradox in this sample:

Whom have we, Lord, like you—
The Great One who became small, the Wakeful who slept,
The Pure One who was baptized, the Living One who died,
The King who abased himself to ensure honor for all.
Blessed is your honor!

It is right that man should acknowledge your divinity,
It is right for heavenly beings to worship your humanity.
The heavenly beings were amazed to see how small you became,
And earthly ones to see how exalted.[29]

He also wrote many sermons in poetry, biblical commentaries, refutations against various heresies, and prayers. His great prayer of repentance is used in the services of Great Lent: "O Lord and Master of my life, take from me the spirit of sloth, meddling, lust of power, and idle talk. But give rather the spirit of chastity, humility, patience, and love to thy servant. Yea, O Lord and King, grant me to see my own sins, and not to judge my brother, for thou art blessed unto ages of ages."

Eudokia (Eudoxia) of Heliopolis, Martyr (March 1)

Eudokia lived in Samaria during the reign of Trajan (98–117). She was one of those fortunate (if infuriating) people who have everything—beauty, intelligence, and wealth, the latter stemming from an incredible talent for making money. By the age of twenty-four she had amassed a considerable fortune, and then she proceeded to use her money and her beauty to gain political influence—a real Roman yuppie! She was, of course, surrounded by young men and thoroughly enjoyed their adulation, while keeping them at arm's length as serious suitors. She became quite notorious for her lavish parties, which seem to have often ended up as orgies.

One day, a monk called Germanus visited Eudokia, and always on the lookout for novelty, she listened to him while he explained the Gospel of Christ. She was enthralled by what he had to say and asked him to remain in her palace, converting the room where she held her "raves" into a chapel for him to hold services. After a lengthy apprenticeship in the Faith, Eudokia was baptized at the age of thirty and began dispensing her wealth for the needs of the Church and the poor. She had a monastery built, and her good works, coupled with her vivacious personality, converted many to Christianity until her activities were reported to the authorities, and she was beheaded in about 107.

A fourth-century martyr, Eudokia of Persia, is commemorated on August 4.

Eugenia of Rome, Nun Martyr (December 24)

Eugenia was the daughter of a Roman prefect of Alexandria called Philip. She was a Christian, and feeling the call to escape the worldly life, she left home with two servants, Protus and Hyacinth. She disguised herself as a man and entered a monastery, where she stayed undiscovered for some time. However, a woman called Melanthia fell in love with "Eugenius," and when her advances were rejected, charged the monk with rape! Eugenia was brought up before the magistrate, her father, and was forced to reveal her true identity. Thereupon, Philip converted to Christianity and later became Bishop of Alexandria, where he was beheaded. Eugenia moved to Rome with her two servants, but Protus and Hyacinth were burned and Eugenia was beheaded shortly afterwards, on the day of the Nativity.

There are several variations in the dates of the martyrdom, some setting it in about 190 in the reign of Commodus (180–192) and others in 258 in the reign of Valerian. Eugenia's mother Claudia, her father Philip, and Protus and Hyacinth are all celebrated on the same day. In 1845, a wall tomb was excavated on the Salerian Way in Rome. It contained a piece of cloth wrapped around human ashes and charred bones which bore the inscription, "Burned on 11 September the martyr Hyacinth." Close by was another inscription which read, "The tomb of the martyr Protus."

Euphemia, Great Martyr (September 16)

Euphemia is among those saints revered more for their reputation after death than for their lives. In fact, little is known about this martyr except that she was born in Chalcedon and burned at the stake in about 308. A chapel was later built on the site of her burial, and the many miracles of healing attributed to the saint caused it to become a place of pilgrimage from all over the Byzantine Empire. Chalcedon became so well known as a holy place that it was chosen as the meeting place for the Fourth Ecumenical Council, called in 451.

This council had been convened to debate the growing heretical notion that Christ only had a single divine nature. This contradicted the traditional doctrine of two natures, human and divine, and reduced the significance of Christ's humanity. However, the theology of the argument was (and still is) extremely complex, and even the assembled bishops found it impossible to come to a decision. Eventually, the patriarch proposed a solution to the impasse. They would seek God's judgment through the help of his servant, the holy Euphemia. The supporters of each doctrine wrote out their arguments, and the manuscripts were both placed in the tomb of the saint. The assembly then spent the next three days in prayer, asking God to help resolve this problem. When the tomb was opened again, the book proclaiming the single nature lay at the saint's feet, while the book of the traditional dogma was clutched in her hands. This miracle seems to have clinched the matter, and little more was heard of the "single nature" heresy. Euphemia has continued to be revered, and her remains have rested in the patriarchate Church of St. George since 750.

Additional Feast Day: July 11 (The Miracle at Chalcedon)

Eustathius Placidas (Eustace), Great Martyr (September 20)

Placidas was a Roman general who served under three emperors—Titus, Trajan, and Hadrian. He was a virtuous and charitable man, always prepared to help those in need. One day, he was out hunting when he had a vision of a beautiful stag with a shining crucifix set between its antlers. He heard a voice calling him to follow the crucified Lord. As a result of this vision, Placidas was converted to Christianity, taking the name Eustathius. He continued to serve his Emperor Hadrian loyally, leading his legions in a brilliant and victorious campaign. However, on his return to Rome, he refused to make sacrifices to the gods as part of the victory celebrations. His wife, Theopista, and his two sons, Agapius and Theopistus, joined him in his defiance, and all four were sentenced to death. They were taken to the Colosseum, locked inside a bronze statue of a bull, and roasted to death. Eustathius is venerated as a great martyr, while his family members are also venerated as saints on the same day.

Eustratius and his companions, Martyrs (December 13)

Eustratius is venerated along with his four companions, Auxentius, Eugenius, Orestes, and Mardarius. Eustratius was a highly educated official in the government of Armenia under Diocletian, an orator and archivist for the proconsul of the province. When the persecutions began, all five turned themselves in to the proconsul, declaring their Christianity. They were, of course, tortured, to such an extent that Auxentius, Eugenius, and Mardarius died. Eustratius and Orestes survived and were sent to Sebastea, where they were burned to death in 296. While in prison, they were visited and given Communion by **St. Blaise**.

The relics of the martyrs were taken to Constantinople and are preserved in the Church of the Holy Five Companions. One of the prayers still read in the Orthodox Church is ascribed to Eustratius: "I magnify Thee exceedingly, O Lord, for Thou hast regarded my lowliness and hast not shut me up in the hands of my enemies but hast saved my soul from want." A prayer by St. Mardarius is also read regularly.

Euthymius the Great, Venerable (January 20)

Born in Melitene, Armenia, in 377, Euthymius was born late to his parents, who gave him the name "Good Cheer." He became a priest at a young age and quickly became drawn to the monastic life. He spent five years in prayer and meditation, serving humbly in a monastery in Palestine making baskets. Through this he developed an inward spiritual strength and a mystical insight, which stood him in good stead for his return to the world. He traveled widely in Palestine, preaching and healing the sick, and became much loved and revered by all who met him, even those who had few or no religious convictions. After healing a young Arab, paralyzed in an accident, he gained great influence among the Arabs of the area, gaining many converts. Interestingly, according to tradition, the Arab boy was the son of a local Saracen chieftain called Aspebetus, who was himself converted, was later ordained, and eventually became a bishop, attending the Council of Ephesus in 431. Euthymius was visited by many for spiritual guidance, including the Empress Eudokia. He died in 473 at the age of ninety-six in the company of his disciple Sabbas.

F–G

Forty Martyrs of Sebastea (March 9)

Tragically, this mass murder occurred after Constantine had extended toleration to Christians in 313. In 320, his co-emperor and brother, Licinius, suddenly reversed the decision in the eastern part of the empire which he controlled and ordered every Christian to renounce his faith. Forty soldiers of the twelfth legion, stationed in Sebastea, Armenia, were among those who refused. The governor of the province could ill afford to lose forty trained soldiers and tried to persuade them, but when that failed, he worked out a plan he was sure would make them recant and save their lives. He ordered the soldiers to strip naked and lie on the ice of a frozen lake. To help break their resistance, a fire was lit on the shore and hot baths prepared in full view of the freezing soldiers. Only one of them broke, however. He jumped into the hot bath, but the contrast between the intense cold and the heat killed him. A soldier who was observing the massacre was so impressed by the faith and courage of the thirty-nine that he declared himself a Christian, stripped off, and joined them to make up the fortieth place. By the next morning, nearly all were dead and the survivors were executed, including the youngest, a boy called Meliton, whose widowed mother was watching from the shore, encouraging him to the last.

Gabriel, Archangel (March 26)

Gabriel means "Light of God," and the most well-known of the archangels appears frequently in both the Old and New Testaments as the bringer of (usually good) news. He announced the births of Samson, **John the Baptist,** and, of course, Jesus, as well as, according to tradition, that of the **Virgin Mary**. He is regarded as chief among the angels, the "great captain of the heavenly host," and three feast days are devoted to his veneration. In addition to the Synaxis of the Archangels on November 8, he is venerated on the day after the Annunciation, while the feast day on July 13 was initiated in the ninth century. It commemorates the revelation of the words of the hymn *Axion Esti* by Gabriel to a monk on Mount Athos. Whether or not Gabriel was involved, this beautiful hymn was certainly divinely inspired:

> *It is truly right to bless thee, O Theotokos,*
> *Ever blessed and most pure, and the Mother of our God.*
> *More honorable than the cherubim,*
> *And beyond compare more glorious than the seraphim,*
> *Without corruption thou gavest birth to God the Word.*
> *True Theotokos, we magnify thee.*

Additional Feast Days: July 13 (Axion Esti)
November 8 (Synaxis of the Archangels)

Geneviève of Paris, Venerable (January 3)

Geneviève was born to wealthy parents in Nanterre, Gaul (modern France) in about 422. At the age of seven, she caught the attention of St. Germanus of Auxerre (July 31) as he passed through the town on his way to England. She told him she wanted to live only for God, whereupon the bishop blessed her, foretelling that she would become great in the sight of God and would lead many to Christ. He gave her a brass medallion of the Cross, which she wore as her only adornment from then on.

At fifteen, Geneviève entered a convent in Paris, where she remained for the rest of her life. She devoted her life to prayer and charitable work, and gradually gained a reputation for prophecy and miracle-working. In the beginning, her visions and prophecies actually made her very unpopular with the people of Paris, but with the help of Germanus, she gradually won them over. Her asceticism was legendary, and she kept to a strictly vegetarian diet, eating only twice a week. She continued to fast rigorously for over thirty years, until her bishop insisted that she diminish her austerities.

In 451, when the Huns under Attila were advancing towards Paris, she begged the people not to flee, and instead organized a "prayer marathon" which is believed to have caused Attila's army to turn off towards Orleans, leaving Paris safe. Later, in 464, she used less spiritual ways to help her city, leading a convoy along the Seine that broke through a Frankish blockade to bring back food to the starving citizens. When the Franks finally captured the city, Geneviève used her influence successfully to obtain lenient treatment for the prisoners of war and their eventual release by King Clovis.

Geneviève died in about 512 at the age of eighty-nine and was buried in the church of Saints Peter and Paul, which she had encouraged King Clovis to build some years earlier. Her relics were later moved to the church of St. Etienne du Mont. Along with the relics of many other saints, they were dumped in the River Seine during the French Revolution, but in the nineteenth century, relics of Geneviève were collected from various churches in other parts of France and returned to Paris.

She continued to protect Paris after her death; in 1129 a serious epidemic was halted when her relics were carried around the city. At her grave, now in the church dedicated to her, there is a plaque that movingly shows the respect accorded to Geneviève by the refugees from the Russian revolution who found sanctuary in her city: "Consolation of exiles, you have manifested yourself to the Russian Orthodox émigrés. In all times, at your tomb, they venerate you. O Holy Geneviève, pray for us, Apostle of Unity." Geneviève is, of course, one of the patrons of Paris, along with St. Denis (October 9).

George, Great Martyr, Victory Bearer and Wonderworker (April 23)

George is one of the most popular and well-known saints throughout the Christian world, but little is known of his life. He was probably from Palestine, and it is very likely that he was a soldier in the imperial guard—a tribune in charge of one thousand men.

Emperor Diocletian was present at a ceremony when pagan priests were consulting the entrails of animals to foretell the future. Some Christians among the guards were spotted making the sign of the Cross, which enraged the emperor, who had them flogged and dismissed from the army. He then published an edict ordering all Christian clergy to make sacrifices to the gods. Seeing a copy of the edict posted on the door of the emperor's palace, George tore it down.

He then went to the senate and declared his Christianity openly, whereupon he was imprisoned, tortured, and beheaded in about 303. His remains were taken to Lydda in Palestine, where his parents still lived, and when Christianity was legalized in 313, a church was built on the site of his burial.

Most of the stories about St. George did not appear until the Middle Ages, including the famous story of the slaying of the dragon. However, veneration of George existed from very early times, and by the end of the fifth century, Pope Gelasius was including him among those "whose names are justly reverenced among men, but whose deeds are known only to God." It is not certain how he came to be the patron saint of England, but it is likely that his veneration was taken back there by Crusaders returning from the Holy Land. He is also the patron saint of Georgia, Bulgaria, Serbia, and Russia and is one of the protectors of Moscow. In Greece, George is the protector of the army and Boy Scouts, as well as of agriculture and shepherds. He is also known as "the deliverer of prisoners and protector of the poor," a busy saint indeed.

On icons, St. George is sometimes depicted on horseback striking down the dragon, sometimes as a soldier on foot or as a military tribune. In spite of the military imagery, however, his title "Victory Bearer" doesn't refer to his prowess as a soldier but to his "conquest" of his tormentors through his martyrdom. Even the story of the dragon represents victory over evil and ignorance rather than a fairy tale of a knight in shining armor rescuing a damsel in distress. In one version of the story, the dragon is not killed but led away by the princess, using her girdle as a leash. This represents the defeat of evil by conversion rather than killing.

St. George and the stories about him epitomize the "warrior saint," courageous both in the battle against evil and in the willing surrender of his life for his faith. "As is the case with any icon, the Saint George icon is not a decoration, but is intended to be a place of prayer. It belongs in the icon corner of any home where courage is sought—courage to be a faithful disciple of Christ; courage to fight rather than flee from whatever dragons we meet in life; courage to prefer the conversion rather than the death of our adversaries; courage to live in such a way that others may be made more aware of Christ and the life he offers to us."[30]

Additional Feast Days: Monday after Pascha (if April 23 falls during Lent)
November 3 (Transfer of Relics to Lydda)
November 26 (Dedication of Kiev church, Russian Church only)

Gerasimus of the Jordan, Venerable (March 4)

As a young man, Gerasimus visited the desert monks in Egypt and Palestine, eventually settling near the Dead Sea in about 450. He flirted with the Monophysite heresy for a while, but was convinced of the truth of the Orthodox doctrine by **St. Euthymius the Great** and spoke against the heresy at the Fourth Ecumenical Council at Chalcedon. Near Jericho, Gerasimus founded a semi-hermit community (*lavra*) that was noted for its strict austerity. The monks ate only a little dry bread and some dates on weekdays, while on Saturdays and Sundays, they gorged themselves on a few boiled vegetables and a little wine! Each monk's entire possessions amounted to a single garment.

Gerasimus exceeded even this austerity and, during Great Lent, only ate what he received at Communion. It is said that he was surrounded by an aura of sanctity that affected all those who met him. This even seems to have extended to wildlife. He once found a lion in the desert in great pain from a thorn in its paw. Making the sign of the Cross, he removed the thorn, whereupon the lion followed him back to the monastery and stayed with him as a "pet" called Jordanes. On Gerasimus's death in 475, the lion lay down on his grave and pined to death a few days later.

FG

Gerasimus the New of Kephalonia, Venerable (August 16)

Familiar to those who have read *Captain Corelli's Mandolin*, Gerasimus became a monk as a young man. After a time on the island of Zakynthos, he studied with the ascetics of Mount Athos and then traveled to Jerusalem. There he was given the post of lamplighter in the Sepulcher of the Lord, and was ordained a deacon and then a priest. He then spent some time in solitude near the river Jordan. Returning to Zakynthos, he continued to lead a life of solitude and extreme abstinence but, after five years, was inspired to go to Kephalonia, where he lived in a cave.

Although he remained a hermit, Gerasimus was responsible for the restoration of a church at Omalia and the foundation of a convent. He also had a gift of healing both the physically sick and the mentally afflicted. He died, much loved by all the inhabitants of the island, in 1579 at the age of seventy-one. After two years, his grave was opened and his relics were found uncorrupted and sweet-smelling, as they remain to this day. Many miracles of healing have been ascribed to Gerasimus, and he remains one of the most revered saints in the Ionian Islands. In the early twentieth century, a church was dedicated to him in New York, built by émigrés from Kephalonia. After the Kephalonia earthquake of 1953, there were many reported sightings of him comforting the trapped and injured.

Additional Feast Day: October 20 (Uncovering of Relics)

Gregory of Neocaesarea, Wonderworker (November 17)

Gregory was born the son of pagan parents in about 213 in Neocaesarea, northern Asia Minor. He received a good education, including eight years in Alexandria, where he studied under the great teacher and theologian Origen, who baptized him. Returning to his hometown, he spent some time in solitude in the desert, but sometime around 238, in spite of his youth, he was made bishop of Neocaesarea. At first this was done in his absence as, hearing of the proposal, Gregory went into hiding. Eventually, he accepted that his elevation was the will of God and returned to be formally consecrated.

As a bishop, Gregory was practical and down-to-earth, with a lively preaching style and some ability as a miracle-worker. During the persecution by Decius, he led his entire flock into the mountains, where, through his prayers, they became invisible to the searching soldiers. On another occasion, he solved a bitter land dispute between two brothers who were on the point of outright violence. The focus of the argument about their inheritance was a large lake which they both claimed. Gregory spent the night in prayer by the side of the lake, and in the morning, the lake had dried up completely, leaving only a small stream that marked the disputed border.

Gregory is the first missionary known to have used secular attractions to popularize religious festivals, another reason for his success. Thus, through a mixture of common sense, a warm personality, and dramatic miracles, he succeeded in converting large numbers to Christianity, in spite of the difficult times of war and persecution. It is said that, when he became bishop, there were only seventeen Christians in the city, but when he died in about 270, there were only seventeen pagans.

Gregory is perhaps now known best in the Orthodox Church for his influence on early doctrine. His theological writings were greatly admired by **Basil the Great** and **Gregory the Theologian**, to whom we owe most of the scant details about his life. When he first became bishop, one of the many early heresies, that of the renegade priest Sabellius, was prevalent in the area. This belief was extremely complex but, in essence, taught that the Heavenly Father, the Resurrected Son, and the Holy Spirit are merely different facets of a single God, as perceived by the believer, rather than three distinct Persons in God Himself. Following a vision of the **Virgin Mary** and **St. John the Theologian**, Gregory wrote a careful analysis of the correct doctrine, which formed the foundation for the Orthodox teaching about the Trinity as expressed in the First Ecumenical Council nearly a century later: "There is therefore nothing created, nothing greater or less in the Trinity, nothing superadded, as though it had not existed before, but never been without the Son, nor the Son without the Spirit; and this same Trinity is immutable and unalterable forever."

Gregory the Enlightener of Armenia, Equal to the Apostles (September 30)

Armenia was the first nation to be wholly converted to Christianity, in about 301,* and Gregory was the missionary responsible. At that time, Armenia was an independent state bordering the eastern edge of the Roman Empire. Gregory was the son of the Parthian prince Anak, born in about 257. When he was still an infant, his father was executed for the assassination of the Armenian king Khosrov, and according to the norms of the time, the whole family was now in danger of execution. Gregory's nurse took him to Cappadocia, where he was raised as a Christian.

By the time he was in his early twenties, he was married with two sons. After his wife's death, he decided to return to Armenia, and in 280 entered the service of Khosrov's son Tiridates III. Partly as atonement for his father's crime, he served Tiridates faithfully, and the two became friends. Unfortunately, the king had no tolerance for Christians and in spite of their friendship, eventually insisted that Gregory renounce his faith. When Gregory refused, he was imprisoned for fourteen years and subjected to many tortures, including being thrown into a pit of venomous snakes, which he survived. Tiridates began a campaign of persecution against the Christians in his country, culminating in the murder of St. Rhipsime, the abbess Gaiana, and thirty-five nuns (September 30). Shortly afterwards, he suffered a serious illness that left him with a badly disfigured face.

---

* Some historians suggest other dates, but the conversion was certainly no later than 314.

Fearing the disfigurement was some kind of judgment, Tiridates had Gregory released from prison and allowed him some freedom to preach. Gregory gave the murdered nuns a proper funeral and later transferred their relics to a new church he had built, inviting the king to the interment. When he saw the bodies of the martyrs, Tiridates repented his action, and at that moment his face was healed. He was baptized by Gregory and in 301 declared his country to be Christian, destroying the pagan temples and building churches throughout his kingdom. The next year, Gregory was consecrated the first archbishop (*katholikos*) of Armenia, and he devoted the next sixteen years to preaching the Gospel, training priests, and organizing the new Church. In 318, he appointed one of his sons, Aristakes, as katholikos and retired to a remote monastery, where he died in about 331.

Gregory, Bishop of Nyssa (January 10)

Somewhat overshadowed by his older brother **Basil the Great** and his friend **Gregory the Theologian**, Gregory was nonetheless one of the great theologians of the fourth century. Born in about 335, the son of **Basil the Elder** and **Emmelia** received, like his brothers and sisters, an excellent education. Appointed Bishop of Nyssa in Cappadocia, he became embroiled in the controversy with the Arians and was twice deposed, finally being restored in 378. The early death of his brother Basil in 379 and of his sister Macrina shortly after grieved him greatly, and his moving funeral oration for Basil and his biography of Macrina still exist. He devoted much of the rest of his life to writing books and attending councils to combat various heresies. At the local Council of Antioch, he successfully defended the doctrine of the perpetual virginity of the **Mother of God**, and in 381 was among those who finally defeated the ideas of Arius at the Second Ecumenical Council. Gregory died sometime after 394.

Gregory of Nyssa, Basil the Great, and Gregory the Theologian are collectively known as the Cappadocian Fathers. These three, together with **Athanasius,** played a pivotal role in the formulation of the doctrine of the Holy Trinity that remains at the heart of the Nicene Creed: "three Persons but one Substance." He was also one of the earliest exponents of the "unknowability" of God, an idea which was developed further by **John of Damascus** and **Maximus the Confessor** and became a major theme in Orthodox theology: "The true knowledge and vision of God consist in this—in seeing that He is invisible, because what we seek lies beyond all knowledge, being wholly separated by the darkness of incomprehensibility."

One thing we cannot know about God is how people will be treated at the Last Judgment, and here Gregory takes a much milder and more hopeful view than theologians such as Augustine who state that some people *must* be condemned to everlasting hell. Since one of the things we do know about God is His love, Gregory's view was that, although it would be heresy to believe that all *must* be saved in the end, it is perfectly permissible to hope and pray that all *may* be saved.

While his theological writings were of great profundity, Gregory also had his feet firmly on the ground. He wrote a witty summary of the extraordinary extent of the interest in theology among all classes in fourth-century Byzantium: "The whole city is full of [theological argument], the squares, the market place, the crossroads, the alleyways; old-clothes men, money changers, food sellers; they are all busy arguing. If you ask someone to give you change, he philosophizes about the Begotten and the Unbegotten; if you enquire about the price of a loaf, you are told by way of reply that the Father is greater and the Son inferior; if you ask 'Is my bath ready?' the attendant answers that the Son was made out of nothing."[31]

Nor did he forget the social aspect of the Christian Gospel. Taking as his starting point the fact that man is made in the image and likeness of God, he goes on to make a passionate attack on slavery, still practiced in Byzantium: "If [man] is in the likeness of God, and rules the whole earth, and has been granted authority over everything on earth from God, who is his buyer, tell me? Who is his seller? To God alone belongs this power; or, rather, not even to God himself. For his gracious gifts, [Scripture] says, are irrevocable. God would not therefore reduce the human race to slavery, since He himself, when we had been enslaved to sin, spontaneously recalled us to freedom. But if God does not enslave what is free, who is he that sets his own power above God's?" The Christian case against slavery has never been expressed more clearly or succinctly.

Gregory the Theologian, Archbishop of Constantinople (January 25)

Born in Arianzus in 329, Gregory was the son of St. Gregory, Bishop of Nazianzus (January 1), and St. Nonna (August 5) and a close friend of

123

St. Basil the Great, whom he met at university in Athens. He studied rhetoric, poetry, geometry, and astronomy and later taught rhetoric at the university. He was also well read in pagan literature and philosophy. In spite of his erudition, all he really wanted to do was become a monk, but much against his will, he was ordained a priest in 362. It was about this time that he wrote his *Invective Against Julian,* a homily against the paganism of his old college friend, in which he says, "Christianity will overcome imperfect rulers through love and patience."

Ten years later, again unwillingly, Gregory was consecrated bishop by St. Basil but did not take up his diocese, preferring to act as auxiliary to his father in his hometown. For some years, he found the seclusion he yearned for in a monastery but, in 379, accepted charge of the Orthodox community in Constantinople, which at that time was ravaged by heresies and in a state of turmoil. He wrote and preached cogently against the various misinterpretations of the Gospel and was elected bishop by popular acclaim. However, there were still opposing groups, and his election caused great controversy. An attempt was even made to assassinate him. Eventually he resigned to keep the peace, and soon after withdrew to end his days near his birthplace in the solitude he had always desired. In his letter of resignation he wrote, "Let me be as the Prophet Jonah! I was responsible for the storm but I would sacrifice myself for the salvation of the ship. Seize me and throw me overboard. . . . I was not happy when I ascended the throne and gladly would I descend it." He died in 389. Along with **St. John Chrysostom** and St. Basil the Great, he is one of the **Three Hierarchs** celebrated in a feast on January 30.

Gregory was a sensitive and retiring man, little suited to public life, which he loathed. As a bishop, he refused all pomp and ceremony. Nevertheless, he was one of the finest orators of the time, as well as an accomplished poet. He preached eloquently against the Arian heresy at the Council of Nicaea, and it was his attendance at these deliberations that prompted his endearing and characteristic comment: "Synods and Councils I salute from a distance for I know how troublesome they are. . . . Never again will I sit in those gatherings of cranes and geese." He is acknowledged as one of the great Fathers of the Church, and his writings still strike a chord: "Let it be assured that to do no wrong is really superhuman and belongs to God alone."

After the sack of Constantinople in 1204, Gregory's relics were taken to Rome. After negotiations between His All Holiness Ecumenical Patriarch Bartholomew and Pope John Paul II, the relics, together with those of St. John Chrysostom, were returned to Constantinople on November 27, 2004. The pope agreed to the return "with joy as a sign of brotherhood and of a complete union to which we are called constantly more and more. . . . The return of the relics to their home country . . . will become a new bridge between us."

Additional Feast Day: January 30 (Three Hierarchs)

Gregory Palamas, Archbishop of Thessalonica (November 14)

B orn probably in Constantinople in 1296, Gregory was attracted to monasticism from an early age and, in fact, persuaded his two brothers, his sisters, and his widowed mother to take up a monastic life. At the age of about twenty, he went with his brothers to Mount Athos, but in 1326, Turkish incursions forced him to flee to Thessalonica, where he was ordained a priest, returning to Athos five years later. For most of the rest of his life, he was involved in the bitter hesychast controversy, one of the most significant developments in Orthodox theology after the Ecumenical Councils.

In essence, hesychasm (from the Greek *hesychia*, "inner stillness") developed from the mystical theology of people like **Gregory of Nyssa**. Accepting the "unknowability" of God, the hesychasts believed that, by the perfect quieting of the body and mind through asceticism, bodily exercises, and constant prayer, it was possible to achieve a kind of mystical state in which a vision of God's Uncreated Light was possible.* This doctrine had gained wide support among the monks of the Holy Mountain, and when it was attacked by Barlaam, a learned Greek monk from southern Italy, they asked Gregory to prepare a defense. Again in simplistic terms, Barlaam's argument was that the hesychasts were violating the transcendence of God by claiming a direct experience of Him. The Uncreated Light that surrounded Jesus at His Transfiguration was part of God's essential unity and could not be experienced by a human.

Gregory wrote his brilliant *Triads in Defense of the Holy Hesychasts* in 1338, a work which drew a distinction between God's unknowable essence and His energies—what He does and His relationship with His creation and with man. The apostles had seen the Uncreated Light of the Transfiguration, but it was

---

* This is an extreme oversimplification of some complex and deep theological ideas. For a lucid and comprehensive explanation of hesychasm, see *The Orthodox Church* by Kallistos Ware.

part of God's energies, not His essence. It was therefore possible for others to do the same, but only through repentance and prayer and under strict spiritual discipline. Central to this discipline was the Jesus Prayer, "Lord Jesus Christ, Son of God, have mercy on me." However, the value of this prayer goes far beyond its use in meditation. It is of value to all Christians: "The prayer of the heart is the source of all good, which refreshes the soul as if it were a garden."

Gregory's support, together with a statement from a council of all the monks of the Holy Mountain, was enough to persuade a synod held in Constantinople to accept hesychasm. However, a few years later, Barlaam managed to have the decision reversed by the patriarch, and Gregory was excommunicated and imprisoned for heresy. He was reinstated by a further synod in 1347 and appointed Archbishop of Thessalonica, but the controversy was not finally resolved until a third synod in 1351, at which Gregory's teaching was declared orthodox once and for all. By this time, however, his health was beginning to suffer, and it was made worse by a year's imprisonment after capture by Turkish pirates. He died in 1359 and was canonized within nine years.

The three synods of Constantinople that brought hesychasm into the mainstream of Orthodox doctrine have been considered by many Orthodox theologians to have had collectively the authority of an eighth Ecumenical Council. Although Western Christendom does not recognize these synods, many Western Christians accept the theology of Gregory Palamas, and in recent years there has been a revival of interest in hesychasm in both East and West. Gregory wrote, "When we strive with diligent sobriety to keep watch over our rational faculties, to control and correct them, how else can we succeed in this task except by collecting our mind, which is dispersed abroad through the senses, and bringing it back into the world within, into the heart itself, which is the storehouse of all our thoughts?" Statements such as this should appeal to the yearning for spirituality in the developed world, apparent in the popularity of Eastern religions and New Age mysticism.

Additional Feast Day: Second Sunday of Lent

H

Haritini, Martyr (October 5)

Either the servant or the adopted daughter of Roman citizen Claudius, Haritini was a pretty and sensible girl who converted many by her kindness and strong faith. She was arrested and brutally tortured in the reign of Diocletian in about 304. Among other things, her teeth and nails were pulled out. The governor of the prison then sent a gang of youths to rape her. She prayed to be spared this disgrace and mercifully died of her wounds before the youths could molest her.

Herman of Alaska, Venerable Wonderworker of All America (November 15)

The history of the Russian missions to the Far East, the Aleutian Islands, and, eventually, to Alaska is an adventure story that, if it has not already been filmed, ought to be. Among the greatest and most loved of these missionaries was Herman, the "North Star of Christ's Holy Church," as he has been called. Born near Moscow in about 1756 (1760 by some accounts), Herman was tonsured a monk at the age of sixteen and, a few years later, entered the Valaam Monastery on Lake Ladoga. He loved the life there and the beauty of the area, and was very fond of his abbot, but his time there was brief.

At that time, the Russians were exploring and trading in the Aleutian Islands and Alaska, more or less colonizing the area in the process. When one of the fur-trading companies asked for monks to set up a mission in Alaska, Herman was one of the eight selected. Arriving on Kodiak Island in September 1794, the monks set about educating and converting the natives with considerable success. However, they suffered great hardship, not only from the harsh physical conditions but also from ill-treatment by the Russian-American Company. Feeling it their duty to defend their Alaskan flock from exploitation, they conceived the imaginative idea of administering to the natives an oath of allegiance to the tsar, thus placing them under imperial protection. For this "interference," the monks were met with physical violence and placed under house arrest by the company. Within five years, hardship and accident had claimed the lives of seven of the original mission.

Now alone, Herman settled on the nearby forest-covered Spruce Island, which he renamed New Valaam after the monastery he loved. There he lived for the rest of his life in a cave during the summer and a small wooden hut in the winter. He also built a wooden chapel, an orphanage, a school, and a guest house. He was largely self-sufficient, living on the vegetables from his garden and fish from the sea, and kept himself busy in prayer, caring for the orphans, teaching, and missionary work. He could always find time, however, to bake cookies for the children.

Herman followed an ascetic life, severe even by the standards of other Orthodox hermits, sleeping on a wooden bench with two bricks as pillows and a wooden board as a "blanket." It was typical of Herman, however, that when visitors entered the cell, he was careful to cover the bricks with a shirt to avoid being ostentatiously ascetic. As well as maintaining a very strict diet, he often wore heavy chains, which are still kept in the chapel he built. He continued to help and protect the natives, defending them before the governors and giving his advice, not only on spiritual matters but on practical problems such as marital relations. The natives called him *Apa* ("Elder" or "Grandfather"), a title of both honor and affection. They regarded him as their intercessor before God, a belief apparently vindicated when he used an icon of the **Virgin Mary** to protect the island from a tidal wave.

Simon Yanusky, an administrator of the colony and friend of Herman, wrote the following description of the Hermit of Spruce Island: "I have a vivid memory of all the features of the Elder's face reflecting goodness; his pleasant smile, his meek and attractive mien, his humble and quiet behavior, and his gracious word. He was short of stature. His face was pale and covered with wrinkles. His eyes were grayish-blue, full of sparkle, and on his head there were a few gray hairs. His voice was not powerful, but it was very pleasant."[32]

Before his death in 1837, Herman predicted that there would be no priest to bury him and that he would be forgotten for thirty years, a prophecy sadly fulfilled. It wasn't until 1867 that Bishop Peter of Alaska investigated his life, and after a hundred more years, he was finally recognized as a saint in the Orthodox Church of America on August 9, 1970. He is also honored in the Episcopal Church of the USA.

Additional Feast Days: December 13 (Date of burial; through a clerical error, originally thought to be the date of his repose)

August 9 (Glorification)

Hilarion the Great, Venerable (October 21)

Most of what we know about the first recorded hermit in Palestine comes from a life written by St. Jerome. Hilarion was born in 292 in Gaza, Palestine. His parents were pagan, but he became a Christian and was baptized while he was a student in Alexandria. He stayed for a while with **St. Anthony the Great** and decided to emulate him in following the ascetic life of a hermit. After his parents died, he returned to Palestine, sold all his possessions, and settled in a reed hut in the desert near Maium, the port of Gaza.

Here, for over fifty years, Hilarion lived a life of extreme austerity, eating little, doing manual labor to support himself, and devoting his time to prayer. He became known throughout Palestine for his holiness and his gift of healing, especially those with mental afflictions, and both of these characteristics drew many people to the Gospel message. Intriguingly, according to Jerome, he also performed a miracle that enabled a young man to win a chariot race, a somewhat unconventional but successful way of gaining converts!

Under Hilarion's influence, many monasteries were founded in Palestine, all of which he took under his spiritual direction, instituting rules for the ascetic life. In about 360, he became weary of the constant stream of visitors and the need to supervise the monasteries and embarked on a quest for solitude. In Egypt, he was threatened with arrest by Julian the Apostate and had to flee to the Libyan desert. From there, he moved on to Sicily, Dalmatia, and finally Cyprus, where he lived a completely solitary life for a few years until his death in 372. A disciple took his body back to Maium for burial.

Hilary of Poitiers, Venerable (January 13)

Born in Poitiers, Gaul, in about 320, Hilary came from a wealthy pagan family. A cultivated and educated man, he was led by his extensive studies in the Old and New Testaments from Greek philosophy to Christianity. He was baptized along with his wife and daughter, and such was his popularity in his native town that, although he was married, he was elected bishop at the age of about thirty-five.

Often called "the Athanasius of the West" and "the Hammer of the Arians," Hilary vigorously opposed the Arians and spoke out strongly against Constantius II's attempts to impose Arianism on the Western Church. After his attempts to have the Arian bishop of Arles excommunicated, he was exiled to Phrygia. In exile, however, he continued his campaigning until, after four years, it was the Arians who had him sent back to Gaul, where they thought the "mischief-maker" could do them less harm. He did not hurry on his return to Poitiers, stopping at every opportunity to preach against the errors of Arius, and he never ceased in his aim of defeating Arianism and establishing the full Nicene definition of the Trinity.

In spite of his single-mindedness, Hilary was no fanatic and seems to have been a sympathetic and friendly man, devoting as much energy to his diocese as to controversy. He made use, like **St. Ambrose**, of metrical hymns to teach doctrine, although his efforts were not so successful, and he wrote commentaries on the Psalms and St. Matthew's Gospel. During his exile, he had studied the Eastern Fathers, and his greatest work, *On the Trinity*, was one of the first successful attempts to translate the subtleties of the Greek theological definitions into Latin. He died in 367, highly respected in his own time, and his work has been influential ever since. Augustine of Hippo called him "the illustrious doctor of the churches."

Hilda of Whitby, Venerable (November 17)

Born in 614 and related to the king of Northumbria, Hilda was christened at the age of thirteen by St. Paulinus (October 10) at York. Tonsured a nun some twenty years later, she at first went to East Anglia in preparation for missionary work in Gaul (France), but was recalled by **St. Aidan** and made abbess of a small convent in Hartlepool. Some years later, she founded a double monastery for men and women at Whitby.

Hilda was a skilled and energetic administrator, and under her rule the monastery became famous for its learning, producing no fewer than five bishops, of whom two became saints. Because of its fame, Whitby was chosen as the location of the important Synod of 664, in which the conflict between the Celtic and Roman Churches over the calculation of the date of Pascha and other disputes were resolved.

According to **Bede**, Hilda developed a strict rule for her abbey, including justice, chastity, and the study of the Scriptures, at the same time laying particular emphasis on the need for peace and charity. Everything in the monastery was held in common "so that, after the example of the primitive Church, no one there was rich, and none poor." From far and wide, both ordinary people and kings and princes came to her for advice, and she seems to have been one of the most respected figures of the time, "whom all that knew her called Mother, for her singular piety and grace." In 673, she developed a serious fever, but in spite of her sufferings, she continued to rule her abbey with love and wisdom until her death seven years later. After taking Communion, she called the nuns together and "admonished them to preserve the peace of the Gospel among themselves, and with all others; and even as she spoke her words of exhortation, she joyfully saw death come, or, in the words of our Lord, passed from death unto life." There is a tradition that, at the moment of her death, the bells at a sister monastery thirteen miles away began to toll, and one of the nuns saw her soul being carried to heaven by angels.

The location of Hilda's relics is unknown, both Glastonbury and Gloucester laying claim to their possession. Whitby Abbey was destroyed by Danish raiders in 867; the ruins still visible are mainly from a later Benedictine monastery built on the same site and destroyed in the Dissolution of the Monasteries by Henry VIII in 1539. The saint is widely respected and loved locally, and the people of Whitby still say that seabirds flying over the abbey dip their wings in honor of St. Hilda. Somewhat more fanciful is the belief that the large number of ammonites found in the area is the result of a plague of snakes which Hilda turned to stone.

I

Ignatius of Antioch, Hieromartyr (December 20)

Although little is known of Ignatius's life, we know a great deal more about the man himself than about most of the early martyrs through the letters he wrote to various Christian communities on his way to execution in Rome. He was a disciple of the **Apostle John** and probably of Syrian origin. A lovely tradition suggests he may have been the child hugged by Jesus when He said, "Unless you are converted and become as little children, you will by no means enter the kingdom of heaven" (Matthew 18:2–3). He became the second or third Bishop of Antioch in about AD 68, and was quite old when he was sentenced to death and sent to Rome to be thrown to the wild beasts at the public games in about 108, during the reign of Trajan.

His seven letters, one to **Polycarp**, then a young bishop, offering guidance and encouragement, are full of good advice and show a keen interest in holding the fledgling Christian community together. They have been invaluable to church historians for the light they shed on Christian practices and belief only about seventy years after the Ascension of Christ. Central to Ignatius's advice was that, in the face of persecution, the Christians should maintain their unity, especially by meeting together with their bishop to celebrate the Eucharist, "the medicine of immortality, our antidote that we should not die, but live forever in Christ Jesus" (Ignatius's Epistle to the Ephesians 4:16).

Ignatius's letters reveal a patient, gentle man with immense humanity and not a little humor. Aware of the fate that awaits him in Rome, he writes of the hardships of the journey, "From Syria to Rome I seem to be fighting with wild beasts, night and day, on land and sea, bound to ten leopards. I mean a bunch of soldiers whose treatment of me grows harsher the kinder I am to them" (Ignatius's Epistle to the Romans 2:8). He was quite prepared for death and wrote of the beasts that awaited him in the arena, "I pray that they will be prompt with me; I shall entice them to eat me speedily."

In the Orthodox Church, Ignatius is called "God-Bearer" (*Theophoros* in Greek) because of the intensity of his love for God and his continuing belief that, in spite of all his sufferings, he remained a sinner who would ultimately be saved only through following "the example of the suffering of my God." "I am the wheat of God," he wrote, "and, ground by the teeth of the beasts, I will find myself to be pure new bread" (Ignatius's Epistle to the Romans 2:3). It is reported that Trajan was so impressed by his courage that he suspended his persecution of Christians (at least for a time). After his death, Ignatius's bones were gathered up and returned to Antioch, where they were interred, an event commemorated on January 29. In 637 the relics were transferred to Rome, where they remain in the Church of St. Clement.

Additional Feast Day: January 29 (Transfer of Relics)

Innocent of Alaska, Equal to the Apostles and Enlightener of America (March 31)

Innocent was born Ivan Veniaminov in 1797 in the Irkutsk area of Russia. After graduating from the Irkutsk Theological Seminary in 1817, he married and was ordained a priest in 1821. After a short period as a parish priest, he volunteered to serve as priest on the island of Unalaska in the Aleutians. He took his whole family with him—his aging mother, his pregnant wife, his young son, and his brother—arriving in July 1824.

This was the beginning of an extraordinary story of courage and indefatigable missionary work that set the Orthodox Church in Alaska on a solid foundation. For the next fourteen years, he not only worked in his parish, which comprised Unalaska itself, the Fox Islands, and the remote Pribilof Islands,* but traveled

---

* You only have to glance at an atlas to see the extent of his parish!

widely to the Bering Sea coast of the Alaskan mainland and south to Fort Ross.*
Here, he conducted services for the Russian settlers, visited some of the Spanish
missions of northern California, and caught his first cold. All his Alaskan
journeys were carried out in a flimsy native kayak in stormy seas, with, in his
own words, "not a single plank to save you from death—just skins."

Ivan became proficient in six of the native dialects and, having invented an
alphabet based on Cyrillic letters, translated the Gospel of St. Matthew and the
Divine Liturgy into Unagan, the most widespread of the Aleutian dialects. He
was also keen to build up a native priesthood, and when he was transferred to
Sitka Island in 1834, he set up a seminary in New Archangel (modern Sitka).
From his new base, he continued to study the local languages and culture and,
in addition to his missionary work, produced several scholarly works about the
natives and their languages, which became primary source material for modern
anthropological studies of the region.

In 1838, while he was on a trip to St. Petersburg, Kiev, and Moscow to report
on his activities, his wife died. He was persuaded reluctantly to accept tonsure
as a monk, taking the name Innocent. Consecrated as bishop of Kamchatka and
the Aleutian Islands, he returned to New Archangel in 1841. He continued to
travel widely and conduct missionary work throughout his enormous diocese,
work that did not diminish when he was elevated to archbishop and the
province of Yakutsk was added to his diocese. From his new base in Yakutsk, he
administered his archdiocese with energy and skill, traveled on missions, and
set about translating the Scriptures and service books into the Yakut language.
Where did he get the energy?

After forty-three years of constant labor under the most difficult of conditions,
Innocent was appointed Metropolitan of Moscow. Here he turned his academic
skills to revising church texts and his pastoral efforts to improving the living
conditions of the poorer clergy and founding a retirement home for priests.
Innocent died in March 1879 and was buried in the Trinity-Sergius Monastery.
In 1977, at the request of the Orthodox Church in America, he was glorified as a
saint by the Russian Orthodox Church.

Additional Feast Days: October 6 (Glorification)
October 5 (Synaxis of the Moscow Hierarchs)

---

* In what is now Sonoma County, California, Fort Ross was the southernmost Russian
  settlement in North America from 1812 to 1841. It is now a state park, and services
  are held in its chapel every year on July 4 to commemorate St. Innocent's visit.

Irenaeus of Lyons, Hieromartyr (August 23)

A disciple of **Polycarp**,* who in turn was a disciple of the apostle **John the Theologian**, Irenaeus was one of the most important theologians of the second century. Little is known about his life, but he is believed to have been born in about 130 and was probably a native of Smyrna in Asia Minor. He was sent as a priest to Lugdunum in Gaul (modern Lyons, France) to serve the bishop, Pothinus. Around 177, Pothinus was martyred, and Irenaeus was appointed bishop. According to St. Gregory of Tours (November 17), "During this time, by his preaching he transformed all Lugdunum into a Christian city!"[33]

When the persecutions of Christians became less severe, he had leisure to write *Against Heresies*, a careful and comprehensive refutation of various Gnostic beliefs. Sometime later, Irenaeus was involved as a peacemaker in a bitter dispute between the Bishop of Rome and the churches of Asia Minor over the date on which Pascha should be celebrated. The date and details of his death are unknown, but Gregory of Tours suggests he was beheaded in the reign of Severus in about 202. He was buried in the Church of St. John in Lyons (later renamed in his honor), but the tomb and his remains were destroyed by Huguenots in 1562.

Although written against the Gnostics, the five-volume *Against Heresies* is of great historical interest for its clear and comprehensive description of Gnostic beliefs. More important from an Orthodox point of view is that, in refuting these beliefs, Irenaeus was one of the first Christian writers to define some of the fundamentals of Orthodoxy. This is not the place to dive into the complexities of Gnostic philosophy, but two of its main concepts were the division of God into a number of entities and the belief that matter was intrinsically evil. In combating this, Irenaeus emphasized the unity of God and made an early attempt to define the Trinity, calling the Son and the Holy Spirit the "hands of God." He was one of the earliest writers to propose that God would have sent Christ into the world even if humanity had never sinned, but that the Fall made the Incarnation more urgent and added the element of salvation to Christ's role. Irenaeus followed

---

* In later life, according to Eusebius, Irenaeus recalled that he had learned and treasured the teaching of Polycarp and his memories of John and others who had seen the Lord. "I listened eagerly to these things, by the mercy of God, and wrote them, not on paper, but in my heart, for the things we learnt in childhood are part of our soul."

earlier writers in seeing Christ as the new Adam, undoing the sin of the Fall, but was probably the first to go further and contrast the **Virgin Mary**'s submission to God's will with Eve's rebelliousness, making Mary the new Eve.

Irene, Great Martyr (May 5)

Irene was a Persian princess, daughter of King Licinius and originally called Penelope. She was converted and baptized possibly by the **Apostle Timothy**, taking the name Irene ("Peace"). She enraged her father by smashing the household idols and refusing to marry the suitor he had arranged for her, and he tried to have her put to death. Instead, however, she succeeded in converting him, and together they spread the Gospel throughout Persia. Irene traveled widely throughout the Middle East, suffering many punishments and tortures but also converting thousands of people to Christianity. She ended up in Ephesus, where some accounts say she was beheaded and others that she died of natural causes. The latter story relates that, two days after her death, her grave was opened and found to be empty. Many churches were dedicated to this tireless preacher from the earliest times, including two in Constantinople. Her aid is invoked by those seeking a swift and happy marriage. She is also the patron of policemen and of the Greek island of Santorini.

Irene, Agape, and Chionia of Thessalonica, Virgin Martyrs (April 16)

Unusually among the early martyrs, the story of these three brave women is fully documented in genuine court records. They were arrested in Salonika (Thessalonica) in about 304. Brought before the governor of Macedonia, they were charged with refusing to eat food that had been offered in sacrifice to the gods. When asked where they had got such strange ideas, Chionia replied, "From our Lord Jesus Christ." She and Agape continued to refuse to eat the impure food, and both were burned alive.

Irene was kept in prison for further questioning about allegations that she had kept Christian books in defiance of the law. In her testimony she said that when the emperor's decree against Christians was published, she and others had fled to the mountains. She carefully avoided implicating those who had helped them and declared that nobody else knew of the existence of the books. "We feared our own people as much as anybody," she said, a simple statement that sums up the pervasive atmosphere of fear and suspicion in which the early Christians lived, reminiscent of life under the totalitarian regimes of the twentieth century. When it seemed safe, Irene and her companions had returned to the city but hidden the books, a great sacrifice as they could no longer study the Scriptures.

Irene was ordered to be stripped naked and exposed in a brothel, but she remained unmolested, and after being given a last chance to conform, she was sentenced to death. The books were found and publicly burned. Three other women and a man were tried at the same time as Irene, of whom one woman was remanded because she was pregnant. The sentence and fate of the others is not recorded, but we can make a reasonable guess.

Irene Chrysovalantou, Venerable (July 28)

Irene was the very beautiful daughter of aristocratic parents in ninth-century Byzantium. She caught the attention of the Empress Theodora, who chose her to be the wife of her son Michael, for whom she was acting as regent. On her way to Constantinople for the wedding, Irene visited a holy hermit called Ioannikius (November 4) to get his blessing. He told her that her future lay not with the royal court but as a nun in the monastery of Chrysovalantou.

When she reached the city, Irene found that Michael had already married another girl, so the way was clear for her to follow the advice of Ioannikius. She gave everything she owned to the poor (including her dowry and the gifts from the empress) and entered the monastery. There she cheerfully carried out even the most menial tasks and began a life of prayer and fasting. For the rest of her long life, she would spend whole nights standing motionless in prayer. During fasts, she would eat only a few greens once a week and drink only a little water. In spite of her privations (or perhaps because of them!) she is said to have retained her youthful beauty until her death in 912 at the age of ninety-seven.

Irene was eventually elected abbess unanimously and with the blessing of **Patriarch St. Methodius** (June 14), but she continued to work as an ordinary nun as well as giving spiritual guidance to her sisters. During her life, Irene was credited with many miracles of healing, and she had a strong gift of prophecy, although she tried to keep both secret to avoid becoming famous. She remains one of the most dearly loved saints in Greece, and reports of miracles of healing in her name have continued to the present day. In 1930, a monastery dedicated to her was built at Lykovrysi in Attica, which has become a major place of pilgrimage in Greece.

Ivan (John) of Rila, Venerable (August 18)

R eminiscent of the early Desert Fathers, the patron saint of Bulgaria was a great spiritual guide, ascetic, and hermit, widely recognized as a saint even in his lifetime. Born in 876 in a village near Sofia, he was a solitary child and, when orphaned at an early age, took a job as a cowherd to keep away from people. At the age of twenty-five he entered a monastery, but then left to find a life of solitude and prayer. He tried several locations, including a cave in the Rila Mountains and the hollow of a tree in the wilderness.

His life was hard and, in his own words, "when I came into this wilderness of Rila, I found no man over here, but only wild animals and impenetrable thickets. I settled alone in it among the wild animals, without food nor shelter, but the sky was my shelter and the earth my bed and the herbs my food."[34]

He quickly became known as a healer of both physical and spiritual ailments, and unfortunately (for him), his reputation as a holy man and miracle-worker brought him great fame. Many disciples settled in the area, causing him to flee to an almost inaccessible crag high up in the mountain, where he lived in the open for the rest of his life. Eventually, he did allow his disciples to build a monastery in the cave which had been his home* and continued to guide his "flock" from the cliff top.

On one occasion, Tsar Peter I of Bulgaria braved the seventy-five-mile trip into the mountains to meet Ivan and seek spiritual advice. On his arrival, however, he was daunted by the inaccessibility of the cave, while Ivan refused to go down to meet him for fear that being greeted by such an important visitor would tempt him to pride and vanity. In the end, they just bowed to each other from a distance. The tsar sent gifts up to the hermit, but Ivan only kept the food, returning the gold and other precious gifts on the grounds that the tsar needed them more than he did, for protecting the country and helping the poor.

Five years before he died in 946, Ivan wrote one of the great treasures of Old Bulgarian literature, *A Testament to Disciples,* full of spiritual and practical advice for the running of the monastery: "Do not amass wealth, keep yourselves away

---

* The Rila Monastery is still one of the main cultural, historical, and architectural monuments in Bulgaria and is a UNESCO World Heritage Site.

from the avaricious snake. For gold and silver are great enemies of the monk and bite those who have them like a snake."

Shortly after his death, his remains were transferred to Sofia. After several other moves, the holy relics were finally returned to Rila Monastery in 1469, where they still remain. He is deeply revered in Bulgaria, where his icons appear on coins and banknotes. His veneration has been carried to the USA, where the Bulgarian Orthodox Church of St. Ivan of Rila in Chicago is dedicated to him. Even more remote from his homeland, the St. Ivan Rilski Chapel built in 2003 at the Bulgarian Antarctic base on Livingston Island is the first Eastern Orthodox church in Antarctica and the southernmost Eastern Orthodox building of worship in the world. For a man who loved solitude, this must be a fitting tribute.

Additional Feast Day: October 19 (Transfer of Relics)

J

Jacob Netsvetov, Enlightener of Alaska (July 26)

Jacob was born in 1802 on Atka Island in the Aleutians. His father was Russian and his mother Aleut, and he was brought up fluent in both languages and familiar with both cultures. When the family moved to Irkutsk, he enrolled in the seminary, graduating in 1826. Having married in 1825, he was ordained to the priesthood in 1828 and immediately resolved to serve in his native islands. He set out on the perilous journey back to Atka, accompanied by his wife Anna and his father Yegor, who had recently been ordained a church reader.

The parish was, to say the least, challenging, as it covered an enormous number of islands and stretched nearly two thousand miles, but Jacob traveled widely on his missions, carrying with him a large tent in which to hold services. Within six months of his arrival, he had conducted 16 baptisms, 442 chrismations, 53 weddings, and 8 funerals. With the completion of the new church on Atka, he turned his attention to education, teaching the children in both Russian and the local Aleut dialect. In his "spare time," Jacob collected marine specimens for the Russian museums and, in cooperation with **St. Innocent**, worked on a new Aleutian alphabet and translations of the Bible and service books. Tragedy struck in 1836 when the death of his beloved wife Anna was followed almost immediately by the destruction of his home by fire. When his father also died the next year, he petitioned to be allowed to return to Irkutsk and enter a monastery. Bishop Innocent, however, persuaded him that his vocation was elsewhere, leading a mission into deepest Alaska.

At the end of 1844, Jacob was appointed head of a mission to the Yukon River, and for the next twenty years he worked indefatigably to spread the Gospel to the tribes living along the Yukon, Kuskokwim, and Innoko rivers. He learned many of the languages of the tribes, invented another alphabet, and built many churches. By bringing the Gospel to the native villages, he was able to act as peacemaker between tribes previously hostile to each other. According to his own records, on his last journey along the rivers, he baptized 1320 people.

The story of this courageous and holy missionary ends rather sadly. In 1863, one of his assistants laid malicious and false accusations against him, and he was summoned to Sitka to answer them. Although Jacob was completely exonerated, his health was deteriorating, and he remained in Sitka for the last year of his life, serving as priest at a native Tlingit chapel. He died in 1864 at the age of sixty and was buried at the entrance to the chapel.

James, Brother of the Lord, Holy Apostle (October 23)

Sometimes given the wonderful title James, Brother of God (*Adelphotheos* in Greek), James was one of the sons of **Joseph** by his earlier marriage. Although many scholars identify him with **James the Younger**, the Orthodox Church makes a clear distinction between the two. According to tradition, he accompanied the Holy Family in their flight into Egypt and lived there with the Mother of God, Joseph, and the infant Jesus. After Herod's death, he returned to Israel with them.

Even as a Jew, James had a reputation for holiness and purity and may have been a Nazarene, a member of a strict sect of Judaism. He was described by an early writer as "holy from his mother's womb. He drank neither wine nor strong drink, ate no flesh, never shaved or anointed himself with ointment or bathed. He alone had the privilege of entering the Holy of Holies, since indeed he did not use woolen vestments but linen, and went alone into the temple and prayed in behalf of the people, insomuch that his knees were reputed to have acquired the hardness of camels' knees."

As soon as Christ began his preaching, James became a loyal follower and was regarded, along with **Peter** and **John**, as one of the three pillars of the Church (Galatians 2:9). After the Ascension, he was elected the first Bishop of Jerusalem and was highly respected as a leader. One of the earliest controversies in the infant Church was whether Gentile converts to Christianity should follow the Law of Moses and be circumcised. James presided over the Council of Jerusalem and spoke firmly but tactfully in support of the Gentiles, and his view was decisive. He proposed that Gentile converts should follow the Law of Moses by not eating any food offered to idols, nor any animal that had been strangled, nor any blood, and that they should keep away from sexual immorality. However, no further burden, such as circumcision, should be imposed on them (Acts 15).

From his early days as a Nazarene, James was often called "the Just" because of his integrity, and even as a Christian, he was respected by the Jewish authorities as an honest man. According to an almost contemporary source, this prompted a group of Pharisees and scribes to try to persuade him to preach against Christ to the crowds assembled for the Passover. In AD 63, they led him up to the roof of the temple and asked him to declare whether Jesus was in fact the Messiah. Their plan backfired somewhat as he declared, "Why do you ask me concerning Jesus, the Son of Man? He himself sits in heaven at the right hand of the great Power, and is about to come upon the clouds of heaven." They threw him off the roof and, when they realized he had survived the fall, stoned him to death.

According to the historian Josephus, the high priest Ananus took the opportunity of a gap between the death of the Roman procurator and the arrival of his replacement to try James and execute him by stoning. This act, little more than judicial murder, offended many of those Jews "who were considered the most fair-minded people in the City, and strict in their observance of the Law." They petitioned the new procurator to have Ananus dismissed, which he was after only three months as high priest.

The Epistle of James is considered to be authored by James the Brother of the Lord, and the Liturgies of **St. Basil the Great** and **St. John Chrysostom** are believed to be based on an earlier Divine Liturgy composed by James. The Protevangelion of James is also attributed to the apostle, although this is more doubtful.

James the Elder, Holy Apostle (April 30)

The son of Zebedee and **Salome** (one of the myrrh-bearing women) and brother of the **Apostle John**, James was born in Bethsaida but later lived in Capernaum, working as a fisherman. He seems to have been one of the "senior" apostles and, together with John and **Peter**, was chosen to witness the raising of Jairus's daughter (Mark 5:21–43), the Transfiguration (Matthew 17:1–9), and Jesus' agony in the Garden of Gethsemane (Matthew 26:36–46).

J

Traveling Companions

After Pentecost, he preached widely in Judea, but there is little evidence that he ventured as far as Spain, a tradition that only appeared about the seventh century. He was beheaded by Herod Agrippa in about AD 44 (Acts 12:1–2).

Eusebius, writing in the fourth century but quoting a much earlier source, describes how James listened calmly to his sentence of death and continued to preach the Gospel. One of his accusers, Josiah, was so struck by his courage that, as the apostle was led to execution, he fell at his feet and begged forgiveness. James embraced him and said, "Peace and forgiveness to you," whereupon Josiah openly confessed his faith in Christ and was beheaded along with James. In the Western Church, he is referred to as James the Greater.

James the Younger, Holy Apostle (October 9)

James the Younger is sometimes referred to in the West as James the Lesser to distinguish him from James the Greater. He was the son of Alphaeus and, like many of the disciples, from Galilee. He may well have been the brother of the **Evangelist Matthew**, whose father is also named as Alphaeus. There is little reference to him in the Gospels or Acts, but early tradition reports him preaching in Judea and accompanying **Andrew** on missions to Edessa, Gaza, and Eleutheropolis. He is believed to have been crucified in Egypt.

Joachim and Anna, Righteous Parents of the Mother of God (September 9)

Joachim and Anna were the parents of the **Blessed Virgin Mary**. They were a devout couple and led a quiet life together. However, Anna was barren, and after fifty years of marriage, they had despaired of having children. Joachim especially felt deep shame at the scorn of those who had children. Even when he went to the temple, the high priest deemed him unworthy to make a sacrifice because he was childless. Joachim went off into the mountains to pray. The **Archangel Gabriel**, however, appeared to both Anna and Joachim separately, telling them that Anna was to conceive a child. When Anna was told this, she said, "As my God lives, if I conceive either a boy or a girl, the child shall be a gift to my God, serving Him in holiness throughout the whole of its life" (Protevangelion 4:2).

When Mary was three years old, her parents took her to the temple to be dedicated to the service of God. They visited her often, until Joachim died at the age of eighty, and Anna a few years later aged seventy-nine.

There is a feast day dedicated to both Joachim and Anna on the day after the nativity of the Virgin Mary. In addition, Anna is celebrated on the feast of the Conception of the Virgin Mary and on the Dormition of the Righteous Anna. People called Anna can celebrate their name day on either (or both!). The names of both saints are often invoked by couples trying to have children. The image of the two parents embracing in joy is one of the most endearing in iconography. A hymn describes the scene: "Joachim rejoices, Anna celebrates. She cries out: 'The barren gives birth to the Mother of God and our life's sustenance'" (Vespers, Forefeast of the Nativity).

Additional Feast Days: December 9 (Conception of the Virgin Mary)
July 25 (Dormition of the Righteous Anna)

Job of Pochaev, Venerable (October 28)

Born Ivan Zhelezo in 1551 in the Polish province of Galicia, Job, at his own request, was tonsured a monk at the age of twelve. For nearly twenty years, he fulfilled his monastic duties conscientiously, and at the age of thirty-one, he was ordained a priest. Shortly afterwards, he was appointed abbot of the Exaltation of the Cross Monastery in Dubno. In accepting this post, he was thrown into the increasingly bitter disputes with the Eastern Rite Catholics following the Council of Brest-Litovsk, where six out of the eight Orthodox bishops of the Ukraine voted for union with Rome.

For twenty years, Job wrote and preached extensively, expressing the Orthodox doctrine clearly and cogently. He argued convincingly against both the errors of Roman Catholicism and the new doctrines being expounded by Protestant missionaries from northern Europe. He was also responsible for the first printed edition of the complete Orthodox Bible in 1581. Job's activities brought him considerable attention and some fame, which he feared would distract him from his spiritual progress. Therefore, in about 1604, he retired to a cave in the mountains of Pochaev. Even here, he could not find complete seclusion, as the monks of the nearby Lavra of the Dormition asked him to become their abbot.

For fifty years, Job combined periods of seclusion and prayer in his cave with governing the monastery with a firm but kind and gentle hand. He would spend a lot of time in the manual labor of the monastery, planting trees and improving the drainage and irrigation systems. He continued to take an active part in the defense of Orthodoxy, using the printing press of the lavra to disseminate articles and books. Job died in 1651 and was almost immediately glorified as a saint in 1659. At the same time, his remains were uncovered and found to be incorrupt. The relics were moved twice and now rest in a church dedicated to St. Job in the Pochaev Lavra, the site of an annual pilgrimage on August 28.

Additional Feast Day: August 28 (Transfer of Relics)

John the Theologian, Holy Apostle and Evangelist (September 26)

Known in the Western Church as "John the Divine," the writer of the fourth Gospel appears often in the Gospels as one of the leading disciples. As a young man, he was of an excitable and quick-tempered nature, and Jesus nicknamed him and his brother **James** "Sons of Thunder." Nevertheless, he is believed by scholars to have been "the disciple whom Jesus loved," and it was to him that Jesus, on the Cross, entrusted the care of His mother, **Mary** (John 19:26–27).

John's Gospel, the last of the four, written in about AD 85–90, is obviously the product of deep and mature reflection. It is also a work of considerable literary genius, both in the original Greek and in the King James translation. John's Gospel is the most "philosophical" of the four, concentrating largely on the spiritual meaning of Christ's Incarnation and teaching. The word "love" appears frequently, and John can be said to have summed up the entire message of Christianity in one powerful sentence: "For God so loved the world that He gave His only begotten Son, that whoever believes in Him should not perish but have everlasting life" (John 3:16).

John was the author of three epistles as well, which are also full of the message of love, and of the Book of Revelation (the Apocalypse). The latter was written on the island of Patmos, to which he had been exiled "for the word of God and for the testimony of Jesus Christ" (Revelation 1:9). It is a vision of our restoration to Paradise, forming a fitting antithesis to the first book of the Bible, which tells of the expulsion from Eden. Full of complex symbolism and mysticism and, alas, a goldmine for cranky beliefs and weird sects, it nonetheless includes passages of great beauty and simplicity, such as the compassionate words of Jesus to the world: "Behold, I stand at the door and knock. If anyone hears My voice and opens the door, I will come in to him and dine with him, and he with Me" (Revelation 3:20).

John died at Ephesus at a great age, possibly around 100. St. Jerome wrote that "when he was too old to preach, John would simply say to the assembled people: 'Love one another. That is the Lord's command, and if you keep it, that by itself is enough.'" The feast day on May 8 commemorates an annual pilgrimage to the grave of the saint that dates from very soon after his death.

Additional Feast Day: May 8

John Chrysostom, Archbishop of Constantinople (November 13)

B orn in Antioch about 344, John was the only son of a general in the imperial army. Although brought up a Christian by his mother, he was not baptized until adulthood, as was the custom in the early Church. He began studying the law, but was drawn more and more to the ascetic life and went to live alone in the mountains for several years. In 383, he became a priest in Antioch and quickly gained the nickname *Chrysostomos* ("Golden Mouth") for the power and beauty of his preaching. In 397, much against his will, he was elected Archbishop of Constantinople.

As archbishop, he still led a strict and austere life, inspired by a burning zeal for social justice and a concern for the poor and oppressed. He was also outspoken to the point of tactlessness, and these qualities quickly earned him powerful enemies, including the wife of the emperor and the Archbishop of Alexandria (uncle of **St. Cyril**). These joined forces with other enemies, and in 403 he was deposed for a variety of mostly frivolous charges. He was sent into exile in Armenia, where he suffered great hardship for three years. For security reasons, he was then ordered to be moved further away, but on the journey, his health, impaired by his early privations in the mountains and worsened by his exile, gave out, and he died of exhaustion in 407. His last words were, "Glory to God for everything."

Physically, John was not an inspiring figure; his long limbs and short thin body caused him to describe himself as a spider. But once he opened his mouth, he filled the church with his presence. "When I begin to speak," he said, "weariness disappears." A large body of his sermons (1447) and letters (240) remain and are still popular reading among Christians of all denominations. They are eloquent, if somewhat lengthy, and always straightforward and practical.

He tried always to explain the Bible in a way ordinary people could understand, using concrete examples rather than vague abstractions wherever possible. "What good is it if the eucharistic table is overloaded with golden chalices when your brother is dying of hunger? Start by satisfying his hunger and then with what is left you may adorn the altar as well." "It is not possible for one to be wealthy and just at the same time. Do you pay such honor to your excrements as to receive them into a silver chamber-pot when another man made in the image of God is perishing in the cold?" Who could fail to sit up and take notice of vivid language like this?

John still remains a model of good sermon writing (apart from the lack of brevity!), and his famous Pascha sermon is still learned by heart by many of the faithful.[35] Cardinal Newman spoke of his "intimate sympathy and compassionateness for the whole world, not only in its strength but in its weakness." The shorter form of the Divine Liturgy, the most commonly celebrated in the Orthodox Church, is ascribed to his authorship, as indeed is one of the prayers still used in the Anglican Communion Service. John is one of the **Three Hierarchs** together with **St. Basil** and **St. Gregory**.

John was not without support in his troubles. Among his defenders was St. John Cassian (February 28), a deacon who traveled to Rome to plead his cause and went on to become the founder of two monasteries and an influential writer on monastic life. Another supporter was the deaconess **St. Olympia**, an amazing woman who worked tirelessly to clear John's name and get him reinstated at the expense of her own comfort and health.

John's remains were eventually brought back to Constantinople with great honor by the next emperor, Theodosius II, in 438, largely under the influence of his extraordinary elder sister Empress St. Pulcheria (February 17).* This event is commemorated in a feast day on January 27. In 1204, John's relics were taken to Rome, to be returned eight hundred years later along with those of **Gregory the Theologian**.

Additional Feast Days: January 27 (Transfer of Relics)
January 30 (Three Hierarchs)

---

* Gibbon says of Empress Pulcheria that "she alone among all the descendants of the great Theodosius [I] appears to have inherited any share of his manly spirit and abilities."

John of Damascus, Venerable (December 4)

John was born in about 676 in Damascus, at that time under Muslim rule. Although a Christian, his father held the hereditary post of chief treasurer to the caliph. John was educated by Cosmas of Calabria, an extremely erudite monk who had been taken prisoner in a raid on Italy and released by John's father. Under his guidance, John became proficient in music, theology, astronomy, and mathematics, and on his father's death, John succeeded him as treasurer and chief councilor of Damascus.

In 726, the Byzantine Emperor Leo the Isaurian issued the first edict against the holy icons, initiating the persecutions of the iconoclast period. Secure from attack in Damascus, John was able to write a clearly argued and passionate defense of icons, which was of tremendous influence in the fight against iconoclasm as well as giving morale-boosting support to the defenders of icons suffering in Byzantium. Unfortunately, John was not entirely safe from Leo, who had a letter forged that purported to be from John to the emperor, offering to deliver Damascus into the hands of Byzantium. The caliph dismissed John from his post and had his writing hand cut off. According to a tenth-century biography of the saint, John's hand was miraculously restored overnight by the intercession of the **Virgin Mary**.

What happened next is an intriguing piece of the history of iconography. As a thanks offering, John had a silver model of his hand made and attached it to an icon of the Mother of God. In later years, icon painters making copies of the icon forgot the origin of the hand and painted the icon as if Mary had three hands! This "Icon of the Theotokos with Three Hands" is commemorated on June 28 and July 12.

Although the caliph realized that John was innocent and wanted to restore him to his post, John preferred to retire to the Monastery of St. Sabbas near Jerusalem, where he wrote a large quantity of hymns, treatises, and works of dogma. He died there in 749.

John's two most important works are *An Exact Exposition of the Orthodox Faith* and *On the Holy Icons*. The former, the third part of his *Fount of Knowledge*, is a summary of Christian doctrine as expounded by the early Church Fathers and is still of great interest. John's simple and clear language means that, even in translation, his work can appeal to those of us who find deep theology incomprehensible. What could be more comforting to the ordinary Christian than to read, "The manner of the generation [of the Son] and the manner of the procession [of the Holy Spirit] are incomprehensible. We have been told that there is a difference between generation and procession, but what is the nature of this difference, we do not understand at all." As Metropolitan Kallistos says, "If St. John of Damascus confessed himself baffled, then so may we."[36]

As for John's defense of the holy icons, the case against the iconoclasts has probably never been more clearly or succinctly expressed:* "Of old, God the incorporeal and uncircumscribed was never depicted. Now, however, when God has appeared in the flesh, and conversed with men, I make an image of the God who can be seen. I do not worship matter, but I worship the Creator of matter, who for my sake became matter, and deigned to inhabit matter, who through matter effected my salvation. I will not cease from honoring that matter through which my salvation has been effected." John also wrote a large number of hymns, many of which are still used in the Orthodox Church. Two of them in English translation are also used in Protestant churches.[37]

John of Kronstadt, Righteous Wonderworker (December 20)

"The purer the heart becomes, the larger it becomes." So said John of Kronstadt, the epitome of the loving parish priest and proof that you don't have to be a monk to be a saint. The only married priest in the Russian calendar of saints was born in 1829 in Archangel province to poor but devout parents. A compassionate and thoughtful child, he felt drawn to the Church from an early age, his dream being to become a missionary to China or Siberia. He eventually realized, however, that there was equally important pastoral work closer to home. He married a girl from the suburb of Kronstadt, and was ordained deacon in 1855 and priest two days later. Assigned to St. Andrew's Cathedral in Kronstadt, he worked there as a parish priest for the rest of his life.

Like his namesake **St. John the Theologian**, John's single and overriding motivation was love. He believed that forgiveness, meekness, and love were the very center and power of Christianity and the only path to God: "Do not

---

* The same arguments are, of course, equally valid in discussions with the Protestant denominations today.

confuse man—this image of God—with the evil which is in him, because evil is only his accidental misfortune, a sickness, a devil's dream; but man's essence—the image of God—is always there." As parish priest, he considered no one a stranger; everyone who came for help became a friend and relative.

Kronstadt at that time was a naval base and also a place of exile for many hardened criminals. It was a nightmare world of unspeakable squalor and misery, disease and starvation, crime and alcoholism. John would visit the hovels of his parishioners, not just as a priest but as a "brother," staying sometimes for hours at a time talking with them. Nor did he forget the material needs of his flock, shopping for food, seeking out doctors, and giving money, often his last few coins. His parishioners got used to seeing him walking home barefoot, having given his shoes to a beggar. He set up a charitable foundation to provide more help to the needy, including a "House of Industry" that provided jobs and training as well as food, shelter, and medical care. His greatest pleasure was teaching in the local schools, always aiming to fill the students' souls with the joy of living Christ's will, rather than with dry repetition and dusty theology.

In church, too, John's motivation was joy and love. He tried to reintroduce the practice of frequent Holy Communion, which had lapsed in Russia at that time, and he is usually depicted in icons holding a chalice. Coupled with this was the need for more frequent confession. Since the numbers involved left him with no time to hear these individually, he established a form of public confession, with everyone shouting out their sins simultaneously. He also reverted to the more ancient form of the iconostasis, a low screen that made altar and celebrant visible to the congregation throughout the service.

As for his prayers, they sound closer to those of the Roman Catholic Charismatic Movement or even the Pentecostalists than to traditional Orthodox services. Entirely carried away by the power of the Liturgy, "he could not keep the prescribed measure of liturgical intonation; he called out to God; he shouted; he wept in the face of the visions of Golgotha and the Resurrection which presented themselves to him with such shattering immediacy."[38] Matins and the Divine Liturgy would often last from four AM till noon, with up to five thousand people filling the cathedral to take Communion.

Father John fell ill and died in 1908. Many miracles of healing have been attributed to his intercession (almost as many as to St. Nicholas!), and his burial place in the crypt of the St. John of Rila Convent has become a major place of pilgrimage. Even during the Soviet era, flowers were regularly placed on the street closest to his grave. He was glorified by the Russian Orthodox Church Outside Russia in 1964 and by the Russian Orthodox Church in 1990.

Additional Feast Days: June 8 (Glorification)

October 19 (Birth)

John, Archbishop of Shanghai and San Francisco, Wonderworker (Saturday nearest to July 2)

One of the most recent saints of the Orthodox Church was born Michael Maximovitch in southern Russia (now Ukraine) in 1896. He gained a degree in law at Kharkov University, followed by a degree in theology from the University of Belgrade, to which the family had fled to escape the Bolsheviks. Tonsured a monk with the name of John in 1926, he was later ordained and, in 1934, appointed Bishop of Shanghai.

"Blessed are the peacemakers," said Jesus, and it was in Shanghai that John showed his ability to bring harmony to feuding factions. The diocese was in something of a mess, with an uncompleted cathedral and an Orthodox community split into several ethnic groups. By the force of his personality, John brought the groups together to work as one congregation. Under his leadership, the cathedral was completed, and orphanages, hospitals, and churches were built.

John himself followed a strictly ascetic lifestyle, sleeping little, praying much, and eating sparingly. Although he tried to hide this by often playing the fool, he soon began to get a reputation as an extremely holy man. It was in Shanghai that he also became known for miracles performed through his prayers. He was tireless in his pastoral work, making a point of visiting hospitals, prisons, and mental hospitals to give Holy Communion. It is said that even hardened criminals behaved themselves in his presence, and seriously mentally ill patients became calm.

He continued his pastoral activities throughout the Japanese occupation, ignoring the curfew to attend the sick. With the end of the war, John was appointed Archbishop of China in 1946, but within three years, the coming of the Communist government caused a mass exodus of Orthodox Christians from China. Demonstrating that spirituality doesn't preclude practicality, he organized the safe evacuation of five thousand of his flock to the Philippines, including the 1500 orphans under his care, and then went to Washington, DC, to lobby successfully for their acceptance into the USA.

J

Traveling Companions

Now without a diocese, John was assigned to the Orthodox Archdiocese of Western Europe, centered in Paris and later Brussels. It was a difficult post because the Orthodox congregation was widely dispersed, but he continued his pastoral work as devotedly as he had done in Shanghai. He accepted under his jurisdiction the scattered French and Dutch Orthodox communities, and celebrated the Divine Liturgy for them in their own languages. John had been fascinated by the saints of the Church from an early age and at university had sometimes spent more time reading their lives than going to classes. Now he began to take an interest in the lives of the Western saints from before the schism, many of whom were not known or venerated in the Orthodox Church. He compiled a substantial collection of their lives and submitted a list to the synod of bishops for inclusion in the Church calendar.*

In 1962, he was appointed Archbishop of San Francisco, where he found a second opportunity to act as a peacemaker. Here, too, the cathedral was only half completed, and the Orthodox community was deeply divided. Although John was able to get the cathedral finished and restored a certain amount of peace, a lot of ill will towards him remained. The result was that a malicious court action was initiated against him, falsely accusing him of financial irregularities in the building work on the cathedral. He was completely exonerated, but for the rest of his life felt a deep sadness that such malice could be found among his own Christian brethren. John died in 1966, while on a visit to Seattle, and is buried under the altar in the crypt of his cathedral. He was glorified in the Russian Orthodox Church Abroad in 1994 and by the Patriarchate of Moscow in 2008.

It would be difficult to exaggerate the love and respect that people around the world have for John the Wonderworker, and thousands of miracles have been attributed to him, both in his life and since his death. Portions of his relics are now located in Serbia, Russia, Mount Athos, Bulgaria, Canada, and the USA.

Physically frail, he was of immense spiritual strength and was generally non-judgmental. Some of his flock once complained about a priest who rushed the Vespers service, leaving out parts so that it was all over in less than half the usual time. John just smiled and said, "How difficult it is to please you people. I celebrate too long and he too short!" When necessary, however, he could be full of righteous anger, and I doubt if anybody present ever forgot his wrath when

Traveling Companions

---

* Perhaps without St. John's work, this book would be a lot thinner!

many of the Russian Orthodox in San Francisco attended a Halloween Ball instead of an important church service.

However, his predominant characteristics were joy and gentleness. His sense of fun on occasions reached the level of a "fool for Christ." For example, when blessing people with holy water, he would not sprinkle the top of the head but splash them liberally in the face. He was especially fond of children, and although strict when he needed to be, he could be completely relaxed with them. Outside the sanctuary, he would joke with the altar boys and even play with the little ones during the service while not "on duty."

John's holiness was recognized even among the non-Orthodox. A Roman Catholic priest in Paris once said to his congregation, "You demand proofs. You say that now there are neither miracles nor saints. Why should I give you theoretical proofs, when today there walks in the streets of Paris a Saint—Saint John the Barefoot."* In writing of his beloved saints, John once said, "Sanctity is not just a virtue. It is an attainment of such spiritual height, that the abundance of God's grace which fills the saint overflows on all who associate with him. Great is the saint's state of bliss in which they dwell contemplating the Glory of God. Being filled with love for God and man, they are responsive to man's needs, interceding before God and helping those who turn to them."[39] Although he would never have done such a thing, he could have been writing of himself.

Joseph the Betrothed (Sunday after the Nativity, or December 26 if Christmas Day is a Sunday)

The husband of the **Virgin Mary** plays an important part in the Incarnation as the foster father of Jesus. He acts as a representative of and model for all of us ordinary people who have doubts in the face of miraculous events, but nonetheless accept God's purpose and obey His will. He comes across as a just and kind man, dignified and self-effacing in his secondary role but prepared to take prompt action when necessary.

The Gospels give few details about Joseph's life, but we know he was a carpenter of the lineage of King David. He was either from Nazareth (Luke 2:4) or moved there with the family after the return from Egypt (Matthew 2:23). When told by Mary that she was going to have a child, Joseph was not

---

* From his first tonsure as a monk, John had always gone barefoot, even in the winter.

unnaturally upset and started making plans to break off the engagement, quietly to avoid a scandal. In icons of the Nativity, Joseph's confused and troubled mind is dramatically portrayed in a vignette of his temptation by the devil. After a vision of the **Archangel Gabriel**, however, he accepted that he was involved in an event that would change the world.

He seems to have been a caring and model father to Jesus. His concern for Mary during the lead-up to the birth is movingly described in the *Protevangelion*, and he acted promptly to protect the Holy Family by fleeing to Egypt to escape King Herod. Although Joseph was alive when Jesus was twelve years old (Luke 2:41–52), it is reasonable to assume that he died before the Crucifixion, when Jesus gave Mary into the care of **John**, and **Joseph of Arimathea** arranged for the funeral, usually the responsibility of the father.

Considerable time and effort* has been spent over the years on the question of Jesus' brothers and sisters (Mark 6:3). The Orthodox Church holds to a tradition dating from as early as the second century that Joseph was a widower with several children from his first wife, at least three of whom, **James**, **Jude**, and **Salome**, were followers of Jesus. This fact is linked with the important doctrine of the perpetual virginity of Mary. The Church teaches that Joseph had no sexual relations with Mary either before *or after* the birth of Jesus. As **John of Damascus** put it in the eighth century, "How would it be possible for her to give birth to God, and with the experience of all that accompanied the miracle, condescend to enter into ordinary marriage relations with a man! Impossible!" Given the character of Joseph as we infer it from the Gospels, a celibate relationship of love between the two is totally believable.

Additional Feast Day: Sunday of the Forefathers (between December 11 and 17)

Joseph of Arimathea, Righteous (July 31)

A wealthy man and a member of the Jewish Council of Elders (Sanhedrin), Joseph was "a good and just man . . . who himself was also waiting for the Kingdom of God" (Luke 23:50–51). He and another member of the Sanhedrin, Nicodemus, were secret disciples of Christ, but his only appearance in the Gospels is when he provided the tomb for Jesus' body.[40] Since he was not a

---

* Not to mention hot air!

Traveling Companions

J

known Christian, he was able to go to Pilate and ask permission to bury the body of Jesus because it was almost the Sabbath. Together with Nicodemus, he took down the body, anointed it with aromatic oils, and wrapped it in a linen cloth. He then placed the body in his own tomb, which he had recently had cut out of solid rock, and rolled a large stone across the entrance.

According to tradition, after the Resurrection, Joseph was sent as a missionary by the Apostle Philip to Gaul and then to Britain, where he founded a church at Glastonbury. A whole body of tradition and legend associates Joseph with the Holy Grail and King Arthur, but these stories date from the late twelfth century and are more related to the world of literature than to Christian history.

Jude, Holy Apostle (June 19)

As with many of the apostles, there is much confusion over Jude's name. He is also described as "Judas (not Iscariot)" (John 14:22) and "Lebbaeus, whose surname was Thaddaeus" (Matthew 10:3). Another of Jesus' stepbrothers, Jude, unlike **James**, did not immediately believe in His divine nature. According to tradition, when **Joseph** brought the family back from Egypt, he wanted to divide his possessions among his sons, but with the exception of James, the brothers were against giving a share to Jesus because he was from a different mother.

After he became a follower of Jesus, Jude never forgot his earlier unpleasantness. In the Epistle of Jude, he feels unworthy to be called "brother of the Lord" and refers to himself merely as "brother of James." Jude preached widely in Judea, Samaria, and Galilee, and later traveled further afield to Arabia, Syria, Mesopotamia, Persia, and Armenia, where he was crucified and shot with arrows near Mt. Ararat in about AD 80. His epistle, possibly written from Persia, shows a passionate concern for the purity of the Faith and the good reputation of Christian people.[41]

Jude's journey to Mesopotamia was made, by tradition, at the direct request of Jesus. A delightful story, recounted by Eusebius, explains the origin of the oldest known type of icon of Christ, the "Holy Face," or the image "not made by the hand of man" as it is known in the Orthodox Church. It seems that Abgar, king of Edessa, a small state in what is now Iraq, was a leper. Hearing of Christ's miracles, he sent his secretary, a painter called Hannan, to ask the Lord to go to Edessa to heal him. When Hannan finally found Jesus, He was, as always, surrounded by

J

Traveling Companions

155

crowds, and the secretary was not able to get near Him. He tried at least to paint His portrait but failed to capture "the indescribable glory of His face."

Seeing his attempts, Jesus called for water and a towel, washed Himself, and wiped His face. His features remained imprinted on the linen, which He gave to Hannan. He sent the painter back to Abgar with a letter promising to send one of His disciples after He had completed His mission. On receiving the "portrait," Abgar was healed but was left with scars on his face. On his missionary journeys, Jude went to Edessa, Abgar converted to Christianity, and at his baptism, the scars were healed. Certainly, it is a fact that Edessa was the first state, albeit small, to become Christian in about 170.

Juliana of Lazarevo, Righteous (January 2)

"Truly God does not look to see who is a virgin or who is married, who is a monastic or who is in the lay state, but only looks for the inclination of the heart toward good deeds." **Macarius the Great** made this comment in the fourth century, but it could well be applied to the sixteenth-century saint Juliana. This lovely lady gives hope to us all that we can lead a good and holy life even as ordinary family men and women.

Juliana was born into a wealthy Moscow family in about 1530. From a very early age, she followed a devout way of life, following the fasts and spending a lot of time in prayer. Orphaned at the age of six, she was looked after by relations who found her piety very strange in one so young. They insulted and laughed at her, but she still kept to her principles, and instead of playing games with her young relatives, she spent her free time making clothes for the poor.

When she was sixteen, Juliana married a local landowner, George Ossorgin, and moved to his estate in Lazarevo. Her gentle and loving nature quickly won over her husband's parents, who entrusted the running of the house to the young girl. Unusually in the Russian culture of the time, she even got along well with her sisters-in-law! Her household duties did not divert her either from prayer or from charitable work; she simply got up earlier and went to bed later. She took especial care of the village of Lazarevo, giving food to the peasants during a famine and helping them during a plague.

Juliana had ten sons, one of whom later wrote a biography of his mother, and three daughters. She was heartbroken when her eldest son was murdered by a servant and her second was killed in the army, and she begged George to allow her to retire to a convent. However, he convinced her that her vocation was to serve God in the family, and she continued to combine her duties as a wife and mother with an almost monastic lifestyle. She and George now lived together in a celibate relationship, and she would only sleep for two hours a night, eating only once a day and fasting completely on Fridays.

After her husband's death, she turned her room into a sort of monastic cell, gave away most of her possessions, and lived in complete poverty, devoting herself to caring for the sick and poor. Through all this, Juliana never became gloomy or complaining but was always full of life, with a happy disposition. She passed away after a brief illness in 1604, at the age of about seventy-four.

In 1614, her coffin was uncovered and found to be full of a sweet smell of myrrh. Many reports of healing miracles followed over subsequent years. During the Russian Revolution, a descendant of Juliana obtained permission from the bishop to remove a small portion of the relics, which he placed in an icon and took with him when he fled Russia. The icon containing the relics now rests in the church dedicated to St. Juliana of Lazarevo in Santa Fe, New Mexico.[42]

Justin, Philosopher and Martyr (June 1)

A Greek living in Samaria, Justin is interesting for his attempt to reconcile the ancient philosophies with Christianity. A philosopher himself, born about 114, he actually came to Christianity through a long study of a whole range of philosophers, especially Plato. Impressed by the courage of Christians facing execution, he finally became a Christian at the age of thirty-three. He became a bold preacher and defender of Christianity, both against pagan philosophy and against Gnosticism.

Justin was the author of three open letters that still exist, the first to Emperor Antoninus Pius, which resulted in a temporary cessation of persecution; the second to the Roman senate; and the third to the Jewish authorities. In these, he attempted to demonstrate that faith and rational thought were not incompatible, and even went so far as to wish to embrace Socrates and Plato into the Christian fold, as well as the Jewish patriarchs: "Those who have been inspired by the creative Word of God see through this a measure of the truth. We are taught that Christ, the First-born of God, is the Word of which the whole human race partakes, so that those who before Him lived according to reason may be called Christians, even though accounted atheists."

His writing alone would probably have secured Justin a place among the Fathers of the Church and probably sainthood. But in addition, on a visit to Rome, he was denounced by a rival philosopher and, along with five others, was beheaded in about 167, in the reign of Marcus Aurelius. From the official report of the trial, we know of the courage of all six. A man of letters with the courage of his convictions, when ordered to sacrifice to the gods Justin replied simply, "No right-minded man forsakes truth for falsehood." Justin deserves to be much more widely known as a saint suited to the "rational" twenty-first century.

Juvenaly of Alaska, Protomartyr of America (July 2)

Juvenaly (Juvenal) was born in Ekaterinburg, Russia, in 1761. After being tonsured a monk and later ordained, he spent some years in northern Russia at the Konyaevsky and Valaam Monasteries. He was selected as one of the eight monks sent as missionaries to Alaska in 1794, a group which also included **St. Herman**. The monks settled on Kodiak Island and, in spite of difficulties with the Russian colonists and extremely harsh conditions, still managed to convert a great number of the natives. Part of their success lay in not attacking the shamanism of the tribes but showing how the Gospel of Christ actually fulfilled the ancient traditions. The monks' activities gradually spread further afield, and by 1796, Juvenaly was preaching on the mainland of Alaska. However, as he moved into the remote northwest region towards the Bering Sea, he disappeared.

All we know of Fr. Juvenaly's death comes from the oral traditions of the local tribes, and the stories are confused and contradictory. Some say the native Eskimos misunderstood the sign of the Cross and a shaman ordered an attack. Another story maintains Juvenaly had upset some of the chiefs by ordering that new converts immediately give up polygamy. It is also possible that he gained the agreement of some of the chiefs to allow him to take their children to Kodiak for education. As he set out with the children, the tribesmen changed their minds, chased after him, and killed him.

All of these are feasible, but what seems to be certain is that Juvenaly offered no resistance to his killers, although he had a gun with him, merely begging them to spare the converts who were with him. This they appear to have done, although some say that his guide, a native convert, was killed with him. Many years later, some of the witnesses told **St. Innocent of Alaska** that after he was killed, Juvenaly got up several times and followed his murderers, begging them to repent. Eventually, they hacked the body to pieces.

Perhaps we are not meant to know the exact details of Juvenaly's death. What is certain is that this tireless and courageous missionary converted many thousands of natives to Christianity and gave his life in the process.

Additional Feast Days: September 24 (All Saints of Alaska)

December 12 (with St. Peter the Aleut)

K-L

Katherine of Alexandria, Great Martyr (November 25)

In 305, Katherine was a beautiful and educated girl of eighteen, daughter of the governor of Egypt and possibly a member of the imperial family. When she publicly protested to Emperor Maxentius against the worship of idols, he set a team of fifty philosophers to debate the issue with her. Unfortunately for him, she demolished their arguments so effectively that all fifty were converted to Christianity.

Maxentius had them all put to death for their "failure," but was nevertheless so impressed by Katherine's intelligence and beauty that he wanted to marry her. She refused both to deny her Faith and to accept his proposal, and was beaten for two hours and then imprisoned. An attempt to break her on a spiked wheel failed when it fell to pieces, killing some of the spectators with flying splinters, while Katherine remained unharmed. Her courage and faith converted many prominent people, including the emperor's wife and an officer of the imperial guard, who, in turn, converted two hundred of his soldiers. All were beheaded by Maxentius.

Finally Katherine, too, was beheaded, calling down blessings on all who should remember her. It is said that milk rather than blood flowed from her severed head. Her body was carried to Mount Sinai, tradition claims, by angels. Her shrine still exists in the Monastery of St. Katherine, the oldest continuously occupied monastery in the Christian world. Pilgrims to the monastery still receive a commemorative ring as a souvenir.

In Russian churches, the feast day is held on November 24. This resulted from a decision by the Empress Catherine the Great, who did not wish to share her name day with the important feast of the Leavetaking of the Presentation of the Theotokos on November 25.

Kyriaki of Nicomedia, Great Martyr (July 7)

The daughter of Christian parents, Kyriaki was named after the day of her birth, the "Lord's Day" (*Kyriaki* in Greek). During the reign of Diocletian in about 282, her parents were betrayed to the authorities, tortured, and exiled. The girl was also sent for trial and subjected to such horrific tortures that many of the onlookers were overcome with pity and were converted by her courage. Her words to the general in charge sum up the way in which the martyrs found inspiration from their predecessors: "There is no way you can turn me from my Faith. Throw me into the fire—I have the example of the Three Children.* Throw me to the wild beasts—I have the example of Daniel. Throw me into the sea—I have the example of Jonah the Prophet. Put me to the sword—I will remember the honored Forerunner.** For me, to die is life in Christ." When she was ordered to be beheaded, tradition says Kyriaki prayed that her blood would not be on the hands of the executioners. She stretched out her hands in prayer, and her broken body gave up the ghost before the sword struck.

KL

Lawrence, Archdeacon of Rome and Martyr (August 10)

Sometimes described as the epitome of the martyr, Lawrence was one of seven deacons in Rome serving Pope Sixtus II. In 258, under the reign of Valerian, Sixtus was martyred (August 10). Lawrence was devoted to his bishop and accompanied him to his execution. He asked why he could not share his bishop's martyrdom. Sixtus replied, "My son, I am not leaving you. In three days you will follow me."

Thus prepared, Lawrence was not surprised to be summoned before the prefect of Rome, who ordered him to hand over all the wealth of the Church to the authorities. Lawrence asked for three days to collect everything together and immediately proceeded to give away all his possessions, including most of

---

* Shadrach, Meshach, and Abednego.
** John the Baptist.

the church gold and silver, to the poor. He then brought together all the lepers, blind, sick, poor, old, widows, and orphans he could find and led them to the prefect. "Here is the Church's treasure," he said. "The Church is truly rich, far richer than your emperor."

For this "insolence," the prefect arranged a particularly slow and painful death for Lawrence, having him roasted to death on a huge gridiron. He maintained his good humor to the last, quipping after the roasting had gone on some time, "Turn him over, he's done on this side."

Lazarus of the Four Days, Righteous (Saturday before Palm Sunday)

Unusually, Lazarus is venerated not so much for what he did as for what was done to him. His resurrection from the dead by Jesus was certainly the most dramatic and important of all the miracles in the Gospels and was a pivotal event in the lead-up to the Crucifixion and Resurrection.

Lazarus was a friend of Jesus who lived with his sisters, **Martha and Mary**, in Bethany, not far from Jerusalem. On His way to Jerusalem for the Passover, Jesus received a message from the sisters that Lazarus was ill, but rather than hurrying to help him, Jesus deliberately stayed where He was for two days. By the time He and the disciples finally got to Bethany, Lazarus was dead and had been buried for four days. While the onlookers were muttering about how He could have prevented Lazarus's death if He had arrived in time, Jesus went to the tomb. He cried out in a loud voice, "Lazarus, come out," whereupon Lazarus emerged from the tomb, still wrapped in his grave clothes.

This miracle, described in John 11, not only converted many more people to believe in Christ's message but was also a direct challenge to the Jewish authorities, as the hierarchy was, at that time, largely under the control of the Sadducees, a group who did not believe in the resurrection of the dead. It was from this point that serious plans were made to arrest Jesus. Thus, the miracle can be seen on many levels: it was a dramatic proof of Christ's divinity, the catalyst for His arrest and death, and a "preview" of Christ's own Resurrection and conquest of death. Lazarus proved that not only the Son of God could rise from the dead but all of humanity: "By raising Lazarus from the dead before Thy Passion, Thou didst confirm the universal resurrection" (Hymn for Lazarus Saturday).

On a personal level, Lazarus was now in some danger: "the chief priests plotted to put Lazarus to death also, because on account of him many of the Jews went away and believed in Jesus" (John 12:10–11). According to tradition, he left Judea and sought refuge in Kittium (modern Larnaca) in Cyprus. It is believed that when **Paul** and **Barnabas** visited Cyprus, they appointed Lazarus as the first bishop of Kittium. To this day, all episcopal thrones in the Larnaca diocese have an icon of Lazarus instead of the usual icon of Christ the Great High Priest. His tomb was found in Kittium in 890 with the inscription, "Lazarus of the Four Days, the friend of Christ," and a church dedicated to the saint was built on the site. His relics were transferred to Constantinople in 898. Lazarus's first tomb in Bethany is still a place of pilgrimage.

Additional Feast Day: October 17 (Transfer of Relics)

Lazarus the Painter (November 17)

Picture the scene: the place, Constantinople; the year, 837. A monk called Lazarus crawls on all fours towards the Church of St. John the Baptist. Every movement is agony to a body beaten to a pulp by imperial guards. His hands are burned to the bone after being forcibly held in a fire. What horrendous crime has this monk committed to deserve such torture? Is he a thief, a murderer, a heretic? No, he is guilty of painting icons!

KL

We know next to nothing about Lazarus apart from this event, but his story is a dramatic illustration both of the savagery of the iconoclast persecution and of the heroism of those who supported the holy icons. Lazarus struggles into the church on his knees and, ignoring the pain of third-degree burns, grasps a brush in black and blistered hands. Quietly and reverently, he continues to work on the icon he has just been punished for starting.

Leo the Great, Bishop of Rome (February 18)

Elected in 440, Leo I is one of several popes venerated as saints in the Orthodox Church, in spite of his strong belief in the primacy of the See of Rome—which was later to be one of the causes of the Great Schism. This is because of his other great contribution to the Church: his staunch upholding of the Orthodox Faith against various heresies prevalent at the time. Leo summed up the orthodox view succinctly with the words, "Jesus Christ was born true God in the entire and perfect nature of true man."

He is also something of a hero in the history of Europe, having twice saved the city of Rome from complete devastation by barbarian invaders. In 452, Attila the Hun and his army were poised ready for their assault on the city when Leo, accompanied only by a few churchmen and two civic dignitaries, went out to meet them. Leo convinced Attila that nothing was to be gained by looting and destroying the city, and actually persuaded him to turn back. Attila in fact withdrew beyond the Danube, albeit with a promise from the Romans to pay tribute.

Leo was a little less successful three years later, when the Vandal leader, Gaeseric, insisted on entering the city and seizing booty; but, like Attila, he agreed not to destroy the city or massacre the inhabitants. A man of great nobility and strength of character, not to mention courage, Leo is rightly respected throughout the Christian world. He died in 461, leaving behind 96 sermons and 143 letters.

Longinus the Centurion (October 16)

Another background but significant figure from the New Testament, Longinus is the name traditionally associated with one of the Roman guards at the Crucifixion. Although his name is not given in the Gospels and was probably derived from Latinizing the Greek word for "lance," the facts are clear (John 19:31–37). The crucifixions took place on a Friday, and it would not be right to have the bodies remaining on the crosses on the Sabbath. The Jewish authorities therefore asked the soldiers to hasten the deaths of the three who were being crucified by breaking their legs. This was done to the two thieves, but when Longinus came to Jesus, he realized that He was already dead, so he thrust a spear into His side. This could well have been an act of mercy to ensure that Jesus was truly dead and would not suffer any further agony, but the true significance of the act was its fulfillment of two Old Testament prophecies about the Messiah: "Not one of His bones shall be broken," and, "They shall look on Him whom they pierced."[43]

According to tradition, Longinus was cured of an eye ailment as the mixed water and blood flowed from the wound. Longinus is also usually assumed to be the same soldier who, seeing the darkened sky, the earthquake, and other portents

KL

as Christ died, cried out, "Truly this was the Son of God!" (Matthew 27:54).

In the Eastern Church tradition, Longinus was also on duty guarding Christ's tomb and was therefore a witness of the stone being rolled away, although the guards passed out in fear when the angel appeared. He and two companions refused to accept the money offered by the Jewish authorities to lie about the event and say that the disciples had stolen the body. Instead, he confirmed the truth of the Resurrection, was baptized by the apostles, and later went to preach the Gospel in his native Cappadocia. He is believed to have been martyred there by soldiers acting on the instructions of the Jewish Sanhedrin.

Lucian of Antioch, Hieromartyr (October 15)

The martyrdom of Lucian illustrates how many great minds were lost to the early Church through persecution. Head of the theological school in Antioch, he was responsible for a major revision of the Greek version of the Old Testament and of the four Gospels. However, he was imprisoned for nine years in Nicomedia at the time of Diocletian's persecution. After twice defending himself in court, he was finally sentenced to death by starvation in about 312. Bound in chains in his dungeon, Lucian celebrated the Eucharist lying on his back, but nevertheless managed to offer Holy Communion to all the Christian prisoners. As his life ebbed away, he said three times, "I am a Christian," and died. Who knows what works of scholarship he might have completed in happier times?

Lucy (Lucia) of Syracuse, Virgin Martyr (December 13)

The story of St. Lucy is almost identical to that of St. Agatha, and many historians have dismissed her story as a legend. However, a fourth-century marble inscription in the catacombs of St. John in Syracuse attests to the genuineness of at least part of the story. As a young girl, Lucy dedicated herself to a life of chastity and poverty in the service of Christ. During the reign of Diocletian, she was denounced as a Christian by a rejected suitor. After exposure in a brothel, she was burned alive, finally being stabbed in the throat in about 304. She is believed to have been about twenty-one years old. Veneration of the martyr began soon after her death, and many churches and monasteries were dedicated to her, including the sixth-century Monastery of Santa Lucia in Syracuse. A tradition that she was blinded by her torturers probably stems from

KL

her name (*Lux* is Latin for "Light"), but nevertheless, her name is often invoked for eye problems.

Although she was Sicilian, St. Lucy is best known in Northern Europe and the USA through the Swedish traditions surrounding her. A legend states that she brought a ship full of wheat to Sweden during a famine in the Middle Ages, thus saving the people from starvation. She has been honored as the patron saint of Sweden ever since, and her feast day is kept as a national holiday.

Ludmilla (September 16) and Wenceslaus (September 28), Holy Martyrs

B orn about 860, Ludmilla, together with her husband Prince Borivoy, was converted by **Ss. Cyril and Methodius** and baptized in about 873. Both worked hard to spread Christianity throughout the princedom of Bohemia, but their efforts were initially not well received by the pagan nobility, and for a short time they were exiled. On their return, they continued their work, and when Borivoy died at the age of thirty-six, Ludmilla continued to support the Church during the thirty-three year reign of her son Bratislav.

After Bratislav's death in 920, his wife Dragomira, mother of Wenceslaus, acted as regent and began to reintroduce pagan beliefs and customs. Ludmilla vigorously opposed her daughter-in-law, and in 921 pagan nobles loyal to Dragomira strangled her while she was at prayer. Her body was buried in St. Michael's Church, Techin, and many miracles of healing were reported. Sometime before 1100, possibly during the reign of Wenceslaus, her remains were transferred to St. George's Church in Prague. She is revered by both Orthodox and Catholics and is patroness of Bohemia, the Czech Republic, converts, duchesses, and widows. Charmingly, her help is also sought for problems with in-laws.

Ludmilla's grandson Wenceslaus was born about 907. Widely educated in Latin and Greek and brought up as a Christian by his grandmother, he came to the throne at the age of eight, on the death of his father Bratislav. On reaching his majority, he began to rule in his own right, reversing Dragomira's paganizing policies and sending her into exile. He set out to promote Christianity and the rule of law among his subjects, building and embellishing many churches, including the Church of St. Vitus, which still exists in Prague.

Much of Bohemia was still pagan, however, including many of the nobility and Wenceslaus's own younger brother Boleslav, and there was much bitterness against the spread of Christianity. In 935* Wenceslaus accepted an invitation to his brother's estate for the Feast of **Ss. Cosmas and Damian**. Boleslav engineered a quarrel with his brother, and in the ensuing ruckus Wenceslaus was stabbed to death at the door of the church by Boleslav's supporters. His body was left unburied, but later Boleslav relented and Wenceslaus's relics were transferred to the Church of St. Vitus.

Although his murder was as much political as religious, the peace-loving prince was soon acclaimed a martyr and became patron saint of the Czech people. Since 2000, his feast day has been a public holiday in the Czech Republic. The famous Christmas song, "Good King Wenceslaus," written in the nineteenth century by J. M. Neale, relates a purely imaginary story.

Luke, Apostle of the Seventy and Evangelist (October 18)

The third Gospel was written in about AD 60 by Luke, a Greek physician from Antioch. He also wrote possibly the greatest sequel of all time, the Acts of the Apostles, an invaluable account of the early Church after Christ's Ascension. Luke mentions himself from time to time in Acts but not in his Gospel, and few details are known about his life. He probably accompanied **Paul** on parts of the latter's second and third missionary journeys and on the voyage to Italy when their ship was wrecked. He was certainly with Paul in Rome, where he may well have acted as Paul's secretary and where he probably wrote his Gospel. Some traditions say he was martyred in Thebes, but it is more likely that he died at the age of 84 in Boeotia in Greece.

Also according to tradition, Luke was a talented painter and is believed to have painted early portraits of the **Virgin Mary**, **Peter**, and Paul. Luke's Gospel is a deliberately historical and chronological account of the life of Jesus. As a non-Jew, he places great emphasis in his Gospel on Christ's mission to the whole world and not just to the people of Israel. He also highlights more than the other evangelists how Jesus cared for the poor and outcasts in society as well as for the status and salvation of women.

Luke's relics were taken from Constantinople to Padua, possibly after the 1204 Crusade. In 1992, the Metropolitan of Thebes asked the Roman Catholic

---

* There is some discrepancy in the dates (and many other details) of Wenceslaus's story, but most scholars now favor 935 rather than 929 as the date of his death.

bishop to obtain some part of the relics for the saint's empty sepulcher in Thebes Cathedral. The request was approved, and at the exhumation, analysis of the skeleton found it to be of an elderly man of strong build.

Lydia, the Seller of Purple (May 20)

O n St. Paul's second missionary journey, he stopped in Philippi, Macedonia, where he and Silas went down to the riverside on the Sabbath to talk to the many Jews who met there for prayer. They caught the attention of Lydia, the first of Paul's converts known to us by name. She was a Jewish businesswoman from Thyatira in Asia Minor. As a dealer in purple cloth, the most expensive material in the first-century Middle East, she was almost certainly a wealthy woman, and her conversion must have been of immense help to Paul in spreading the Gospel. She was baptized along with her entire household and opened her house to the apostles (Acts 16:13–15). Nothing else is known of her, but we can surmise that her house became a center for Christian worship and meetings, because after a period in prison, Paul and Silas went to Lydia's house, "and when they had seen the brethren, they encouraged them and departed" (Acts 16:40).

Lydia of Illyria, Martyr (March 27)

A nother Lydia venerated in the Orthodox Church was the wife of Philetus, an official in the court of Emperor Hadrian (117–138). Philetus openly confessed his faith in Christ and refused to pay homage to the Roman gods. He, Lydia, and their sons, Macedonius and Theoprepius, were brought to trial and, after savage torture, all four were executed. The four are all venerated together as saints.

Lydia, New Martyr of the Communist Rule (July 20 in the Russian Orthodox Church)

A third Lydia is not a widely known saint, but her story gives me the opportunity to briefly honor the countless ordinary Christians who suffered hardship and martyrdom under Soviet rule in Russia. Born in 1901, she was a sensitive girl and became a devout member of the "Catacomb" Church (secret Christians). Arrested by the GPU Secret Police, she was interrogated and tortured for ten days. Her courage and sanctity actually so moved one of the guards that he attempted to rescue her, but he was shot by two GPU interrogators, one of whom later became a Christian himself and was martyred. Lydia was shot in 1928, and she is commemorated together with the guard, Kyril Ataev, and the GPU interrogator, Alexei Ikonnikov.

KL

M

Macarius the Great of Egypt, Venerable (January 19)

Sometimes called "The Lamp of the Desert," Macarius was one of the most influential of the early Desert Fathers. He was born in Upper Egypt about 300, after his parents had waited a long time for a son, which is why they named him Macarius, or "Blessed." According to some writers, he spent some time as a young man smuggling in the desert, thus learning valuable survival techniques. Married against his will, he ran away into the desert for a time and returned to find his new wife had died. He continued to support his parents until they, too, died a short time later. With no further family ties, he was free to follow his desire to seek a life of solitude in the desert, giving away all his property to the poor.

An early incident illustrates Macarius's character. Accused falsely of seducing a village girl and making her pregnant, he accepted the sneers and attacks of the villagers, even working to support the girl. When, however, the truth was discovered, and the people wanted to praise him for his goodness, he fled. For a time he was a disciple of **St. Anthony**, from whom he learned the rules of monastic life and gained much spiritual advice. In about 330, he settled in the desert of Sketis in the northwest of Egypt, where he spent most of the rest of his life. Within a short time, Macarius became the acknowledged leader of the loose community of monks and hermits in the area and received the nickname "the Young Elder" from his colleagues, because of the wisdom of such a relatively young man. In 360, he founded the monastery* now

---

* The word *skete* to describe a monastery based on a loose confederation of individual monks derives from Macarius's monastery at Sketis.

called St. Macarius's Monastery, and over the years became spiritual father of over four thousand monks and hermits from all over the Christian world of the time.

For a short time, Macarius was banished to a small island in the Nile Delta by the Arian Emperor Valens for his support of the Nicene Creed. Since the island was entirely inhabited by pagans, this was designed to be a punishment for the devout ascetic, but the plan backfired somewhat when he converted all the islanders to Christianity. He was immediately released and returned to Sketis, where he lived until his death in 391. He had instructed his disciples to bury him in secret, but local villagers, who were already venerating him as a saint, stole the body and placed it in a specially built church. Towards the end of the tenth century, the head of the Coptic Church had the body removed back to his monastery in Sketis.

Macarius remains deeply venerated in the Coptic Church of Egypt, as well as being honored by all Christian denominations. Stories of him abound, depicting a man of deep spirituality but also profound common sense. His advice to one novice monk is typical. He told the young man to go to the cemetery and spend some time mocking the dead, followed by an equal time praising them. The young man, somewhat baffled, did as he was told and returned to Macarius. "What did they say?" asked the saint, to which the monk replied, "They were silent to both praise and reproach." Macarius said, "If you wish to be saved, be as one dead. Do not become angry when insulted, nor puffed up when praised. If slander is like praise for you, poverty like riches, insufficiency like abundance, then you shall not perish."

Most of the stories of Macarius and many of his sayings are to be found in almost contemporaneous documents by a priest named Rufinus and by St. Serapion (April 7). Fifty Spiritual Homilies, which have been of immense influence on Christian mysticism, were ascribed to Macarius but were almost certainly written in the sixth century. Several of the prayers of Macarius are still used in the Orthodox Church, especially those before sleep and in the morning: "Having risen from sleep I hasten to Thee, O Lord, Lover of men, and by Thy loving-kindness I strive to do Thy work, and I pray to Thee: help me at all times, in everything, and deliver me from every evil thing of the world and every attack of the devil, and lead me into Thine eternal Kingdom."

Confusingly, Macarius of Alexandria (January 19), a contemporary and friend of Macarius, is also venerated as a saint. He is sometimes called Macarius the

M

Younger. A third Macarius, the Martyr and Bishop of Edkao, is commemorated on September 6.

Macrina the Elder and Her Extraordinary Family

It is not unknown in Christian history for a family to produce more than one saint, but the family of Macrina the Elder must be unusual if not unique. Herself a saint, she was the mother of one saint, the mother-in-law of another, and the grandmother of no fewer than five, two of whom were major figures among the Church Fathers. Quite a family!

MACRINA THE ELDER (JANUARY 14, RUSSIAN TRADITION; MAY 8, GREEK TRADITION)

Macrina was born sometime before 270. She lived in Neocaesarea in Pontus and was a devout Christian under the spiritual supervision of **Gregory the Wonderworker**. Little is known of her life, but it seems that she and her husband suffered under the persecutions of Galerius and Diocletian, spending over six years in hiding by the Black Sea. A woman of strong faith, she had enormous influence on the spiritual lives of her children and grandchildren. She died in about 340, living to see the legalization of Christianity in the Empire and the First Ecumenical Council.

BASIL THE ELDER (JANUARY 1)

The son of Macrina, Basil was raised in Neocaesarea and was a respected lawyer and orator. On his marriage to Emmelia, he settled in Caesarea, where they produced ten children. With the help of Macrina, all the children were brought up to be good Christians, to the extent that five of them became saints. Little more is known about this "father of saints."

EMMELIA (JANUARY 1, RUSSIAN TRADITION; MAY 8 OR MAY 30, GREEK TRADITION)

Also known as Emilia or Emily, the wife of Basil the Elder was from a wealthy family, and one of her parents is believed to have been a martyr. She had a tremendous influence on the spiritual development of her children, and it was largely through her encouragement that all of them became deeply involved in religious life. Once the children had grown up and left home, her eldest daughter,

Macrina, suggested the two of them retire from the world. Emmelia divided most of her possessions between the children and founded a convent in one of the more secluded of the family estates, a beautiful location on the bank of the River Iris at Annesi. She had already liberated all the family slaves, and many of the freed women joined Macrina in the convent. The nuns lived a life of prayer and work in peace and, according to reports, in complete harmony. She died in old age with her eldest child, Macrina, and her youngest, Peter, at her side. She was buried in the chapel of Annesi beside her husband Basil and her beloved son Naucratius, who had died suddenly at the age of twenty-seven.

MACRINA THE YOUNGER (JULY 19)

Educated by her mother and grandmother, Macrina grew up to be a devout young lady, widely read in the Scriptures and a regular churchgoer. She was betrothed to a pious young man, but when he died before the wedding, her thoughts turned more and more towards a monastic life. She rejected many potential suitors and devoted herself to helping in the house and looking after her younger brothers and sisters. She was particularly fond of her youngest brother, Peter, guiding him in his spiritual development and encouraging him in his leanings towards an ascetic life. It was largely under her influence that her mother set up her convent, and she was active in its organization, taking over the administration after Emmelia's death. She followed a strict ascetic program of prayer and fasting, gaining great respect for her temperance and self-discipline. She had the gift of healing, and many miracles were reported by the nuns after her death. Her brother, Gregory of Nyssa, wrote a biography of Macrina in which these reports are documented as well as details of the sanctity of her life. Macrina died in 379 or 380 and was buried with her parents at Annesi. Gregory wrote his *Dialogue on the Soul and Resurrection* in her memory.

BASIL THE GREAT (JANUARY 1). SEE MAIN ARTICLE.

GREGORY OF NYSSA (JANUARY 10). SEE MAIN ARTICLE.

THEOSEBIA (JANUARY 10)

The younger sister of Macrina devoted herself from an early age to a life of chastity and, although not formally tonsured, remained celibate for the whole of her life. She became a deaconess and took care of the practical and charitable activities

M

of the Church, looking after the sick, distributing food to the homeless, caring for orphans, and preparing women for baptism. When her brother Gregory was exiled for three years, she shared his exile as a companion and helper. A quiet and loving woman of God, when she died in 385, **Gregory the Theologian** spoke the eulogy.

Peter of Sebastea (January 9)

Born in about 340, Peter was the youngest of the family. Unlike Basil, he was drawn to the life of an ascetic hermit and, even after his ordination as a priest, still preferred to continue his solitary life. He remained close to his mother and sister Macrina, however, and was of great help to them in the founding of their convent. Around 380, he was consecrated Bishop of Sebastea in Armenia, and in spite of his love of solitude, he seems to have fulfilled his duties conscientiously. He supported his brothers in their fight against heresy and was present at the Second Ecumenical Council. He is also believed to have inspired Gregory to write some of his works, but typically he worked mainly in the background, shunning the limelight. He died in 391 and began to be honored as a saint very shortly afterwards.

Mamas of Caesarea, Great Martyr (September 2)

Mamas was born in about 260 in prison, where his parents were awaiting execution as Christians. After their deaths, he was released and adopted by a patrician lady, Ammia, who brought him up as a Christian. He was so traumatized by his experience that he didn't speak until he was five. His first word was "Mama," from which Ammia gave him his name.

When he was fifteen, Ammia died and Mamas began working as a shepherd. Shortly afterwards, he was arrested for refusing to obey Emperor Aurelian's decree that everybody in the empire, whatever their own religion, should sacrifice to the Roman gods. He was sentenced to death by drowning but escaped and went to live in the mountains of Caesarea. There he built a small chapel, where he lived alone, becoming so friendly with the wild animals that they allowed him to milk them. He used the milk to make cheese, which he lived on, giving the surplus to the surrounding poor people. Mamas was recaptured and thrown into the arena to be eaten by the wild beasts. However, the animals refused to attack him, merely sniffing him or licking his hand. Eventually, he was stoned to death.

Mamas is now regarded as a special protector of animals and is a favorite saint of veterinarians, a sort of Orthodox St. Francis. Shepherds also look to him to protect their flocks. A church was built at the place of his death, where a memorial service was held every spring from very early times. Services there were attended by both **St. Gregory the Theologian** and **St. Basil the Great**, both of whom wrote about his life. Mamas's parents, Theodotus and Rufina, are also saints, celebrated on the same day as their son.

Maria Methymopoula of Fourni, New Martyr (May 1)

I sneaked in an almost unknown saint from my birthplace (Cuthman), so I don't see why I shouldn't pay my respects to an equally unknown saint from my adopted home in Crete. In any case, hers is a simple and sad story that illustrates the fact that not all martyrdoms are dramatic.

Born in the early nineteenth century, when Crete was still under the rule of the Ottoman Empire, Maria was the daughter of the baker in the small village of Fourni, a few miles from Elounda. In 1826, she caught the eye of a Turkish-Albanian policeman, who fell in love with her. He asked her to marry him, but this would mean her converting to Islam, which she totally refused to do. The policeman tried every way to persuade her, but she was adamant. Eventually, while she was out picking mulberry leaves to feed the silkworms, he shot her in the chest, killing her instantly. There was no attempt to investigate the crime.

Although it could be argued that Maria's murder was as much a crime of passion as martyrdom, it was undoubtedly her firm Christian resolve that led to her death. A church dedicated to Maria was built in Fourni, and she has been commemorated as a martyr locally for many years.

Maria Skobtsova (Mother Maria of Paris), Righteous Martyr (July 20)

The story of Maria Skobtsova reminds us that the Second World War saw the martyrdom of many Christians, including Orthodox, who in one way or another fought against Nazi oppression. However, as a twice-married former socialist politician, intellectual, and poet, she is certainly not a typical Orthodox saint! Born Elizaveta Pilenko into an aristocratic Latvian family in 1891, she became involved in the turmoil of radical politics in the lead-up to the 1917 revolution. Her exploits, from her marriage to a Bolshevik in 1910 to her flight from Russia with her second husband and family in about 1919, read like an adventure story.[44] However, we will take up the story in 1923, when the family arrived in Paris and was at last able to settle down.

By 1926, Elizaveta's marriage had broken down, and after the death from influenza of her youngest daughter, she went through a period of deep spiritual anguish. As she emerged from the double trauma, she found "a new road before me and a new meaning in life, to be a mother for all, for all who need maternal care, assistance, or protection." She set about helping the many destitute Russian refugees in Paris. Granted an ecclesiastical divorce, she took monastic vows in 1932 with the name Maria. She rented a house which she turned into a shelter for the refugees, complete with a chapel and soup kitchen. Her "cell" was a bed behind the boiler in the basement. Maria's aim was to build a new kind of "monasticism in the world." Together with Fr. Dimitry Klepinin and Ilya Fondaminsky (both also martyred by the Nazis), she formed the Orthodox Action movement, committed to putting into action the social implications of the Gospel message. Maria's work among the poor and her writings, full of practical and compassionate theology, might alone have put her among the revered and blessed. But then the Germans invaded France and occupied Paris.

Although she continued her work with the poor, Maria now found a new cause: helping the Jews. Along with Fr. Dimitry and her son Yuri, she organized forged documents and escape routes to the unoccupied south of France, helped hide Jews from the Nazis, and smuggled food into the camps for those already rounded up. Well aware that she was under Gestapo surveillance, Maria continued her activities until, on February 8, 1943, she was arrested, together with Yuri and Fr. Dimitry.

Maria was taken to the women's concentration camp at Ravensbrück, where she did her best to continue her work of looking after the "less fortunate," maintaining her spiritual life by reciting passages from the New Testament and some of the services from memory. Her earlier ascetic lifestyle and her spiritual strength helped her cope with the terrible privations of the camp, and she survived almost to the end of the war. Eventually, however, she became so ill that she could no longer pass the roll call for work. As the Russian troops were approaching Berlin and gunfire could be heard in the distance, she was sent to the gas chamber on Holy Saturday 1945. "At the Last Judgment," she wrote, "I shall not be asked whether I was successful in my ascetic exercises, nor how many

M

bows and prostrations I made. Instead I shall be asked, 'Did I feed the hungry, clothe the naked, visit the sick and the prisoners?' That is all I shall be asked."[45]

On February 11, 2004, Maria was formally added to the Synaxarion of saints, along with her son Yuri, Fr. Dimitry Klepinin, and Ilia Fondaminsky. She is also honored by the state of Israel as one of the "Righteous among the nations." Metropolitan Anthony Bloom called her "a saint of our day and for our day, a woman of flesh and blood, possessed by the love of God who stands face to face with the problems of this century."

Marina of Antioch, Great Martyr (July 17)

Marina lived in Antioch during Diocletian's reign and, although the daughter of a pagan priest, was herself a Christian. When she was fifteen, her father discovered this and threw her out of the house. During Diocletian's persecutions, she was denounced as a Christian and arrested. A prefect called Olybrius was charmed by her and offered her marriage, but when she rejected him, he had her tortured and thrown into prison. Although a Christian, she had not yet been baptized, and after a particularly horrible torture by fire, she prayed, "Lord, You have granted me to go through fire for Your Name; grant me also to go through the water of Holy Baptism." She was then partially drowned in a cauldron of water, which became the font of baptism for this courageous girl. Finally, she was beheaded.

According to an old legend, while in prison she fought against a dragon, which almost swallowed her until the cross she carried caught in its throat and it had to disgorge her. This fanciful story is a colorful metaphor for the spiritual torment she (and all like her) faced in the temptation to save her life by recanting, strengthened only by her faith in the Cross. St. Marina is known in the Western Church as Margaret and is invoked for deliverance from demonic possession.

Mark, Evangelist and Apostle of the Seventy (April 25)

The second Gospel, written by Mark in Greek, is believed by many scholars to have been the first written, in the mid-fifties AD. It is certainly the most straightforward, concentrating on the simple narrative of Christ's life, and it is a model of clear storytelling. For this reason, Mark's Gospel has always been a favorite among missionaries for introducing people to the Christian message.

M

Mark himself was probably one of Jesus' younger disciples and may have been the young man who fled from the Garden of Gethsemane when Jesus was arrested.* There is some debate among historians and biblical scholars about whether the Evangelist Mark, John Mark of Acts, and Mark the cousin of **Barnabas** were the same person, but the Orthodox Church generally assumes this to be the case. Mark accompanied **Paul** and Barnabas on their first missionary journey, but perhaps because of his relative youth and inexperience, he upset Paul, who considered him somewhat impetuous and unreliable and refused to accept him on his second mission (Acts 15:36–41). Instead, Mark went with Barnabas to Cyprus, but was later reconciled to Paul and supported him while he was a prisoner in Rome.

It was also in Rome that he acted for a time as **Peter's** secretary, and it is probably there that he wrote his Gospel, based largely on Peter's recollections. After the deaths of Peter and Paul, Mark went to Egypt to continue preaching and is believed to have founded the first Christian church in Alexandria. He was probably martyred there during the reign of Trajan (98–117). In 828, his remains were taken to Venice, where they were interred in the cathedral that bears his name. Accounts vary, some saying the relics were abducted by Venetian merchants and others that they were moved to safety after the Arab conquest of Egypt. Mark is deeply loved and venerated by the Coptic Church, and in 1968 his relics were returned to Egypt.

Martha and Mary of Bethany, Righteous Disciples (June 4)

Sisters of **Lazarus**, these two friends of Jesus come across as real people, giving us a rare insight into Jesus' daily life. On a visit to Bethany, Jesus called on the sisters. While Martha busied herself preparing a meal and generally tidying the house for their visitor, Mary sat quietly listening to Jesus as he taught His message. Martha, not unnaturally, was a bit harassed and complained that she had been left to do all the work. Jesus gently replied, "Martha, Martha, you are worried and troubled about many things. But one thing is needed, and Mary has chosen that good part, which will not be taken away from her" (Luke 10:41–42). This incident has often been used in discussions of the relative importance of faith and works on the road to salvation.

---

* Certainly, the incident is only mentioned in Mark's Gospel (Mark 14:51).

On another occasion, Martha berated Jesus for his delay in coming too late to save Lazarus, at the same time showing her deep faith in the Lord: "Lord, if You had been here, my brother would not have died. But even now I know that whatever You ask of God, God will give You." When Jesus replied that her brother would rise to life, she thought he meant the general resurrection, which many Jews believed in. This gave Jesus the opportunity to explain His meaning in the world-shattering words with which all Christians are familiar: "I am the resurrection and the life. He who believes in Me, though he may die, he shall live. And whoever lives and believes in Me shall never die. Do you believe this?" Martha replied, "Yes, Lord, I believe that You are the Christ, the Son of God, who is to come into the world" (John 11:20–27).

Mary also demonstrated her simple faith shortly after the raising of her brother when at dinner she anointed Jesus' feet* with very expensive ointment. The disciples were outraged at the waste, saying the money would have been better used to help the poor. Jesus supported Mary, however, and gently rebuked the critics: "Why do you trouble the woman? For she has done a good work for Me. For you have the poor with you always, but Me you do not have always. For in pouring this fragrant oil on My body, she did it for My burial. Assuredly, I say to you, wherever this gospel is preached in the whole world, what this woman has done will also be told as a memorial to her" (Matthew 26:10–13).

Although they are not mentioned by name, it is believed that Martha and Mary were among those who went to Christ's tomb on the day of Resurrection, and they are venerated on the Sunday of the **Myrrh-Bearers**. There is no mention of their later life, but according to tradition they went with their brother to Cyprus, where they helped him with his work for the rest of their lives.

Additional Feast Day: Sunday of the Myrrh-Bearers

Martin the Confessor, Bishop of Rome (April 13)

Martin I was the last pope to date to be martyred. His veneration in the Orthodox Church is not without irony in view of the later schism between Orthodoxy and the Roman Catholic Church, since his death in 656 was brought about by a Byzantine emperor, Constans II. At that time, monothelitism, a heresy which, in essence, was inconsistent with belief in the full humanity of

---

* The story as reported by Matthew (26:6–13) and Mark (14:3–9) varies a little from John's Gospel (12:1–8) and does not mention Mary by name.

Jesus, was gaining ground in the Church, and was supported by the Patriarch of Constantinople and the emperor. Martin's first act as pope was to call a council, which condemned these ideas and the imperial proclamation that supported them. This brought him into direct conflict with Constans, who ordered him to be brought to Constantinople as a prisoner.

After a period in prison on the island of Naxos, where his treatment was extremely harsh, he arrived in Constantinople already a sick man. "For forty-seven days," he wrote, "I have not been given water to wash in. I am frozen through and wasting away with dysentery. The food I get makes me vomit. But God sees all things and I trust Him." He said to his guards, "The Lord knows what a great kindness you would show me if you would deliver me quickly over to death." He was not allowed to defend himself at his trial and was sentenced to deposition and death. After pleas from the patriarch, Constans commuted the sentence to banishment to the Crimea, but, broken in body and spirit, Martin died soon afterwards.

Mary of Egypt, Venerable Ascetic (April 1)

Perhaps the most famous of the penitential saints, Mary of Egypt was born in Alexandria in the fifth century.* At the age of twelve, she ran away from her parents and began to live a life of such extreme sexual promiscuity that, in modern terms, she would be called a nymphomaniac. Her desires were solely for sexual gratification, and she would refuse payment when it was offered. She continued this life for seventeen years, but one day she saw a crowd of people heading for the docks. She asked where they were heading and found that they were sailing to Jerusalem to visit the holy sites. Out of curiosity, she decided to join them, paying for the passage with her body.

In Jerusalem, she tried to enter the Church of the Holy Sepulcher but found something holding her back. Realizing it was her sinful life that was denying her entrance, she wept and vowed to God that, if she were allowed to enter and venerate the Holy Cross, she would abandon her old ways. "O Lady, Mother of God, who gave birth in the flesh to God the Word," she prayed, "I know, O how well I know, that it is no honour or praise to thee when one so impure and depraved as I look up to thy icon, O ever-virgin, who didst keep thy body and

---

* There are many discrepancies in the dates of her life, but I have used those generally adopted by the Orthodox Church.

soul in purity. Rightly do I inspire hatred and disgust before thy virginal purity. But I have heard that God Who was born of thee became man on purpose to call sinners to repentance. Then help me, for I have no other help."*

After her repentance, she went to live across the river Jordan in the desert, where she remained for forty-seven years, living only on the few herbs and vegetables she could find in the desert. She would be unknown to us if a venerable monk called Zosimas hadn't met her in his wanderings in the desert during Great Lent. She told him her story, and the next year he took her Holy Communion during Holy Week. The following year, 522, he again went to find her, but she had died.

Mary is revered in all the Christian churches as the epitome of the penitent hermit, and her life is celebrated on the fifth Sunday of Great Lent as well as on her feast day.

Additional Feast Day: Fifth Sunday of Great Lent

Mary Magdalene, Holy Myrrh-bearer, Equal to the Apostles (July 22)

Mary of Magdala was a devoted disciple of Jesus from the time He cured her of severe mental illness, or as the Gospels describe it, "out of whom He had cast seven demons" (Mark 16:9). She was present at the Crucifixion and was one of the women who went to Jesus' Tomb and found it empty. They had gone as soon as the Sabbath was over to anoint the body, and Mary is therefore described in the Orthodox Church as a "myrrh-bearer." She was also blessed as the first person to whom the Risen Christ appeared, as related in all four Gospels but most movingly in the Gospel of John (John 20:1–2, 11–18).

M

According to tradition, Mary traveled widely, preaching the Gospel, and was the first to bring the message of Christ to the island of Zakynthos, where she preached on her way to Rome in about AD 34. On reaching Rome, she reported Christ's death and Resurrection to Emperor Tiberius, presenting him with a red egg as a symbol of new life. This has remained a symbol of Pascha in the Orthodox Church to this day. From Rome, she is believed to have gone to Ephesus, where she died peacefully. Notwithstanding *The Da Vinci Code*, there is no real evidence that Mary was anything more than a loyal follower of Jesus, nor

---

* *The Life of St. Mary of Egypt*, St. Sophronius of Jerusalem. www.monachos.net

does the Orthodox Church identify her with the "sinful woman" of the Gospels, as some biblical scholars do.

Additional Feast Day: Second Sunday after Pascha (Sunday of the Myrrh-bearers)

Matthew, Holy Apostle and Evangelist (November 16)

Little is known of the life of the writer of the first Gospel, but he was certainly a Jew and probably the same Matthew (originally called Levi) who was a tax collector called by Jesus to be a disciple (Matthew 9:9–13). If so, his change of career was even more dramatic than **Andrew's**. The emphasis of his Gospel, written in Hebrew in the sixties AD, is to show his fellow Jews how Jesus fulfilled all the prophecies of the Old Testament concerning the Messiah and how He met all the deepest hopes of the Jewish people. However, Matthew also looks forward to the salvation of all, ending his Gospel with Jesus' command to His followers to baptize disciples from all mankind and with His final promise: "Lo, I am with you always, *even* to the end of the age" (Matthew 28:20). Matthew faithfully recorded the words of Jesus which we know as the Sermon on the Mount (Matthew 5:3—7:27), but which were probably a collection of teachings from many different occasions. Nothing is known for certain of Matthew's later life, but according to tradition, after preaching in Syria, Media, Persia, and Parthia, he was finally martyred in Ethiopia.

Matthias, Holy Apostle (August 9)

Born in Bethlehem, Matthias studied the Law of God from early childhood, possibly under the guidance of **Simeon the God-Receiver**. He was a disciple of Jesus from the beginning, as testified by Peter when organizing a replacement for Judas Iscariot: "Therefore, of these men who have accompanied us all the time that the Lord Jesus went in and out among us, beginning from the baptism of John to that day when He was taken up from us, one of these must become a witness with us of His resurrection." After prayer, the apostles drew lots and Matthias was chosen (Acts 1:21–26).

Along with the other apostles, he preached widely in Judea and the surrounding countries. He may have traveled with **Andrew** and was, in fact, rescued from prison in Sinope by Andrew. The time and place of his death are

Traveling Companions

M

unknown, and several different traditions exist. By some accounts, after the execution of **James, Brother of the Lord**, the Jewish high priest Ananus ordered Matthias to be arrested and brought to trial by the Sanhedrin in Jerusalem. After an impassioned defense of the truth that Christ was the Messiah, he was found guilty of blasphemy and stoned to death in AD 63. Other historians believe he was crucified in Colchis in what is now western Georgia in about 80. A Gospel said to be written by Matthias circulated in the early years of the Church, but only a few sentences remain as quotations in the works of other writers, and as early as Eusebius, it was generally regarded as fictitious and heretical.

Maxim (Maximus) Sandovich, New Hieromartyr (August 6)

Galicia in southern Poland and the area west of the Carpathian Mountains formed for many centuries the frontier between Roman Catholicism and Orthodoxy in Eastern Europe. This was complicated by the existence of an Eastern Rite Catholic (Uniate*) Church that recognized the supremacy of the pope while adhering to much of the Orthodox tradition, such as married clergy and much of the liturgy. In the late nineteenth century, Galicia and a portion of the Ukraine were part of the predominantly Roman Catholic Austro-Hungarian Empire, and because Orthodoxy was closely linked in the government's mind with pan-Slavism and rebellion against Austrian rule, a fierce persecution of Orthodox in this area was instituted.** Even the Uniate clergy were expelled if they had been educated in Russia and were replaced by newly ordained priests from the Jesuit seminary in Krakow. For the Orthodox clergy and their families, the situation was far worse, as they were regarded as Russophiles and traitors.

Maxim Sandovich was born in 1886 into the family of a prosperous farmer in Zhdynia, a village in Galicia. He was a gifted student and began to study for the priesthood in the Krakow seminary. Not satisfied with the theology taught there, he crossed the border into the Russian area of Poland to attend an Orthodox seminary. After six years he graduated and, in 1910, returned home,

M

---

* The term "Uniate" is not used by the Eastern Rite Catholics themselves, being regarded by them as somewhat contemptuous.

** Although there was a grain of truth in the association of Orthodoxy and pan-Slavism, the persecution was largely a typical example of a warped syllogism: "Since most anti-government rebels are Orthodox, most Orthodox must be anti-government rebels."

where the villagers begged him to be ordained so they could have an Orthodox priest in the area. This he did. He married a young Orthodox woman called Pelagia, then became a deacon and later a priest. He returned home again in 1911, where, as an Orthodox priest, he suffered continual harassment from the authorities. Forbidden to hold services, he was several times fined and arrested for disobeying the law.

Things became much more serious in 1912, when together with another priest, Maxim was arrested on charges of espionage. The two priests were held in appalling conditions for two years until the case finally came to trial in March 1914. In spite of the testimony of many false witnesses, the priests were cleared of all charges and released in June. Barely two months later, however, on August 1, 1914, war was declared between Austria-Hungary and Russia, and a new wave of anti-Russian hysteria and repression began. All openly Orthodox people in the region were arrested as Russian sympathizers, including Maxim, his father, and his pregnant wife, all of whom were marched to prison in Gorlice.

At dawn on August 6, Maxim was aroused from his prayers and led to the place of execution. His execution was witnessed by many prisoners from their cells, so we have a detailed description of the events. The militia captain ripped the cross from Maxim's neck and marked a white chalk line on his cassock as a target. His hands were tied behind his back, he was blindfolded, the death sentence was read out, and the firing squad opened fire. Although only two bullets hit him, he fell dying, but was able to cry out in an increasingly weak voice: "Long live the Russian people, long live the holy Orthodox Faith, long live Slavdom." The captain then fired three more shots into his head. Maxim was buried quickly and without ceremony in the Gorlice cemetery.

Pelagia was eventually released, but then rearrested and sent to the infamous Talerhoff concentration camp, where she gave birth to a son, whom she named Maximus after his father. They survived the horrors of the camp, and many years later in happier times, Maximus was also ordained and returned to his home area as a priest. In 1922, Maxim's father was given permission by the newly independent Polish Republic to transfer his son's remains to a cemetery in Zhdynia. Maxim was glorified as a martyr by the Polish Orthodox Church in 1994.

Additional Feast Day: September 6 (Glorification)

M

Maximus the Confessor, Venerable (January 21)

Maximus was born in about 580 near Constantinople and started his working life as chief secretary to Emperor Heraclius. In his early thirties, however, he became a monk in the monastery of Chrysopolis (modern Skutari), where he eventually became abbot. When the Persians invaded the Byzantine Empire, the monastery broke up, and Maximus fled to Alexandria. He later moved to Carthage and finally to Rome.

It was while he was in Rome that the controversy over the Monothelite heresy broke out, and he actively supported **Pope St. Martin** in his opposition to Emperor Constans. "I have the faith of the Latins," he said, "but the language of the Greeks." He was taken to Constantinople with Martin, where he was subjected to savage punishments for defying the emperor. He was flogged, his tongue and right hand were cut off, and at the age of about eighty-two he was imprisoned in a remote fortress on the Black Sea. There he died shortly afterwards in 662. He was exonerated by the Sixth Ecumenical Council in 680–681 and recognized as a Father of the Church. Sometime later his remains were taken back to Constantinople and then interred in the Chrysopolis monastery.

Apart from his courageous stand against heresy, Maximus is revered as a great theologian, in particular for his mystical and ascetical writings. One of his books, *Four Centuries of Charity,* has been called "one of the most profound and beautiful works in all Christian writing."[46] For Maximus, God is "unknowable" and we can only approach Him indirectly: "We do not know God in His essence. We know Him rather from the grandeur of His creation, and from His providential care for all creatures. For by this means, as if using a mirror, we attain insight into His infinite goodness, wisdom and Power."[47]

Additional Feast Day: August 13 (Transfer of Relics)

Melania the Younger, Venerable (December 31)

A lady of extraordinary charity and devotion to God, Melania was born into a wealthy patrician family in Rome in about 383. From an early age, she wanted to devote herself to a life of virginity, but against her will, she was married at the age of fourteen to a young relative, Valerius Pinianus. Her new husband had sympathy with her desire for a celibate marriage, but begged her to give him two children to ensure the inheritance, after which they would both remain celibate.

A daughter and son were born to the couple, but both died in infancy. From then on, Pinianus honored his promise, and he and Melania set out on a strange new life together, he only twenty-four years old and she twenty. They moved to a small farm outside Rome, where Melania cared for the sick, helped the poor, and visited convicts in the mines and debtors in prison. They sold most of their property and distributed the proceeds, about 120,000 gold pieces, to the Church and the poor, and emancipated all their 8,000 slaves. This caused their relatives to appeal to Emperor Honorius, but he supported their action.

In 408, the Visigoths invaded Italy, and the pair fled to their remaining estates in Thagaste in North Africa, where they established two monasteries and continued their charitable activities. After seven years, they went to Alexandria, where they were welcomed by **St. Cyril**, and then, in 417, moved on to Jerusalem. After Pinianus's death in 432, Melania founded a convent on the Mount of Olives, but she refused to become abbess, contenting herself with living an ordinary nun's life of prayer, charitable work, and the copying of manuscripts. She also founded a men's monastery on the Mount of the Ascension. After a short illness, Melania died peacefully in 439. Her final words were those of Job: "As the Lord wishes, so let it be."

Melania's paternal grandmother, Melania the Elder, is also commemorated as a saint (June 8). She lived from 325 to 410 and was very influential in the ascetic movement of the Desert Fathers (and Mothers) of the fourth and fifth centuries.

Menas of Egypt, Great Martyr (November 11)

Born in Egypt, Menas was a camel driver in the Roman army. He was a Christian, and while his legion was stationed in Phrygia, the persecution of Diocletian began. Not all the early martyrs were brave all the time, and Menas deserted the army to escape death, hiding in a cave in the mountains. However, as more and more Christians were put to death, his conscience was aroused, and he came to feel that he must make a public profession of his faith. He did this in dramatic fashion by marching into the arena where the annual games were being held. There he announced to the spectators that he was a Christian and was immediately arrested. In spite of beatings and torture, he refused to recant and was finally beheaded in about 303.

His body was taken back to Egypt and buried southwest of Alexandria. His shrine became a major place of pilgrimage, and the ruins of the church built on the spot still exist. The village nearby was named after him—El Alamein. Many people believe that, at the defense of El Alamein in June 1942, the victory of the Allies over a superior German force was assisted by the intervention of Menas. Shortly after the war, the church was restored by Greek soldiers of the Eighth Army, and a monastery was built on the site as a thanksgiving. St. Menas also became the patron saint of Iraklion in Crete following a widely reported miracle on the Sunday of Pascha, 1826, when the saint protected worshippers from an attempted massacre by the Ottoman Turks.

Michael, Archangel (November 8, Synaxis of the Archangels)

By far the most revered of the angels, Michael, whose name means "He who resembles God," has been honored from the beginning of Christianity as well as in Jewish and Islamic tradition. A church bearing his name existed outside Constantinople from the time of the city's foundation. Michael has always been regarded as God's warrior. In the Epistle of Jude, we read of him fighting with the devil over the body of Moses (Jude 9), and in the Apocalypse (Revelation) he is seen leading the host of heaven in the last great battle against the powers of evil (Revelation 12:7–9). Less dramatically, he is honored as our helper and protector in our own personal battle with sin. In the Orthodox Church, Michael is regarded as the special guardian of the sick and the protector of airmen. A second feast day for Michael in September commemorates a miracle at Colossae when a church dedicated to the archangel was saved from destruction. A flooded river heading towards the church was miraculously diverted by Michael's intervention.

Additional Feast Day: September 6 (Miracle at Colossae)

Mitrophan Tsi-Chung and Family, Holy Martyrs (June 11)

The most famous of the martyrs of the **Boxer Rebellion**, Fr. Mitrophan was the first Chinese to be ordained a priest. Born in 1855, he was an unassuming young man, quiet and gentle and rarely moved to anger. Initially, he was reluctant to be ordained, because in his words, "How can a person with insufficient abilities and charity dare to accept this great rank?" Eventually he

Traveling Companions

M

was persuaded and was ordained by Nicholas, Bishop of Japan, in 1880. For the next fifteen years he worked quietly in the mission, mainly on translating and editing work. Although he cared deeply for his flock, his reserve could easily be mistaken for coldness, and he was not a particularly popular priest. He had to endure quite a lot of abuse and malice both from outsiders and from his own people, which led eventually to a mild nervous breakdown. After that, he spent the next three years living outside the mission on half-pay.

On the evening of June 1, 1900, Boxers burned down the mission buildings, and many Christians sought refuge in Fr. Mitrophan's house. He welcomed all, including some of his erstwhile detractors, and busied himself trying to keep their spirits up. In all, about seventy found shelter in the house. On the evening of June 10, the house was surrounded by soldiers and Boxers. Although a few of the inhabitants managed to escape, Fr. Mitrophan and the rest, mostly women and children, were attacked and tortured. Fr. Mitrophan was stabbed repeatedly with swords and spears until he died.

His wife Tatiana, aged forty-four, escaped the massacre with the help of her daughter-in-law Maria, but was captured the next morning and beheaded, along with nineteen others. Their eldest son, Isaiah, had already been beheaded in the street on June 7, in spite of being a distinguished soldier. His young wife Maria, only nineteen, helped several escape from Fr. Mitrophan's house by climbing the wall. She herself, however, refused to leave, in spite of being urged by Mitrophan's son Sergei. "I was born near the Church of the Most Holy Mother of God," she said, "and here I will die." She was wounded in the Boxers' first attack but was not killed until a second one.

John, Mitrophan's youngest son, aged eight, also showed immense courage in spite of his youth. In the first attack, he received a deep wound in the shoulder, and his ears, nose, and toes were cut off, but Maria saved him from death by hiding him in a cesspit. One can hardly imagine what he suffered during that long night. In the morning, he went out to try to get water but was chased away by the neighbors as a "devil's disciple." He was seized again by the Boxers, and although some of the onlookers made fun of him, others were moved by the young boy's courage. As he was finally killed, one old man asked, "What is this boy guilty of? It is his parents' fault that he became a devil's disciple."

In 1903, the bodies of St. Mitrophan and others were placed under the altar of the new Church of the All Holy Orthodox Martyrs, built between 1900 and

M

1916. The church was destroyed by the communists in 1954, and the where-abouts of the relics are unknown. A cross was also erected on the site of St. Mitrophan's martyrdom, but this also disappeared.

Moses the Ethiopian, Venerable (August 28)

Born in about 330, Moses was an Ethiopian* of immense physical strength. He worked as a servant in an Egyptian household, but was dismissed for theft and suspected murder, whereupon he formed a gang of robbers. They preyed on travelers over a wide area and were certainly no Robin Hoods but merciless cutthroats. At some stage, however, in hiding from the authorities, Moses took refuge with some monks in the desert west of Alexandria. The peace of the monastery and the quiet contentment of the monks deeply affected him, and after some time, he joined them.

His conversion was by no means instantaneous; he fought long and valiantly to suppress the darker side of his nature. On one occasion, he was attacked in his cell by four robbers, whom he fought and overpowered, tying them together and dragging them to the chapel. There he dumped them in front of the other monks and asked what he should do with them, as he thought it might not be "Christian" to hurt them. He remained conscious of his own shortcomings, and when invited to sit in judgment on a brother monk who had committed a fault, he turned up at the meeting carrying a leaking jug full of water on his shoulder. When asked what he was doing, he said, "My sins run out behind me, and I do not see them, but today I am coming to judge the errors of another." The monks said no more but forgave the wrongdoing brother.

Moses eventually became the leader of a colony of hermit monks and was at some time ordained a priest. In spite of his strength and early violence, when the monastery was raided by Berbers in about 407, he forbade any resistance, telling the monks to retreat. He himself, with seven others, stayed to greet the attackers with smiles and open arms. He was killed. The monastery where his body was buried, Dair al-Baramus in the Wadi Natrun, is still inhabited by monks. Moses is honored in modern times as an apostle of non-violence and is particularly revered by African-American Orthodox.

---

* Traditionally called "Moses the Black," but this usage has largely disappeared.

M

Myron, Bishop of Crete, Wonderworker (August 8)

Myron was a farmer in Raucia, Crete, known and respected for his goodness. He never refused help to anyone who asked. On one occasion, finding a group of thieves stealing his grain, he helped them fill their sacks and sent them on their way. It is said the thieves were shamed by his generosity and went straight from then on. After his wife died, the people of the area urged Myron to accept ordination into the priesthood and later chose him to be their bishop. He was a wise and loving ruler, beloved by all and having a gift for miracles. As well as performing miracles of healing, he once prevented the river Triton from flooding by his prayers. He died at the age of one hundred in about 350.

Myron of Crete, New Martyr (March 20)

The story of Myron illustrates vividly the conditions under which Christians lived in Greece under the Ottoman Empire. Born into a devout Christian family in 1775, Myron was a tailor who served as a cantor in the church and spent his free time helping the priest. He was a young man of a peaceful disposition and posed no threat to the authorities. However, some of the local Turks took exception to his quiet faith, friendly nature, and good looks, and began a campaign of harassment designed to provoke him into retaliation, which would bring about immediate punishment. When this failed, they bribed a twelve-year-old Turkish boy to accuse him of sexual molestation, for which the sentence was death. He was formally charged and found guilty, but the magistrate, in an effort to keep the peace, offered to pardon him if he converted to Islam. He refused and was sentenced to be hanged, as an example to others and to frighten the local Christians into a more compliant frame of mind. After a second refusal to convert, Myron was hanged in the square. He was just twenty years old. Afterwards, the Turkish boy was filled with remorse and confessed his perjury. Only a few months after Myron's death, people began to venerate him as a martyr and saint, and it was not long before he was officially recognised.

Myrrhbearers, Holy (Second Sunday after Pascha, Sunday of the Myrrhbearers)

Although the twelve main disciples of Jesus were all men, there is evidence from the New Testament that women played an important role in His

M

ministry. They certainly seem to have been involved to a greater extent than would be expected, given the norms of Jewish society at that time, and it is significant that a group of women were the first witnesses of the Resurrection.*

After **Joseph of Arimathea** had been allowed to take the body of Jesus from the Cross, the women who had followed Jesus from Galilee prepared spices and perfumes to anoint the body. When they arrived at the Tomb, they found the stone rolled away and the Tomb empty. "And it happened, as they were greatly perplexed about this, that behold, two men stood by them in shining garments. Then, as they were afraid and bowed *their* faces to the earth, they said to them, 'Why do you seek the living among the dead? He is not here, but is risen!'" (Luke 24:4–6). They ran back to the disciples with the news, thus becoming, as someone once said, "apostles to the Apostles." These women, together with Nicodemus, who had paid for the myrrh and other expensive spices, are commemorated on the Sunday of the Myrrhbearers. Besides **Mary Magdalene**, four others are known by name.

JOANNA (JUNE 27)

The wife of Chuza, a senior administrator in the court of King Herod, Joanna was in a good position to help the ministry of Jesus. According to one tradition, it was Joanna who discovered the head of **John the Baptist** in Herod's palace and gave it to two monks for safekeeping. It has been argued that she is the same person as Junia, mentioned by **Paul** in Romans 16:7 as being "of note among the apostles," who had been in prison with him and had become a Christian before he did.

SALOME (AUGUST 3)

According to tradition, Salome was the daughter of **Joseph the Betrothed** by his first marriage and thus the stepdaughter of the Theotokos. Married to Zebedee, she was also the mother of the apostles **James and John**. There is a touching scene in the Gospel of Matthew (20:20) when, as a typical devoted mother, she asks Jesus to allow her sons to sit on His right and left in Paradise. She is named

M

---

* It has been suggested with some logic that this is yet another piece of internal evidence for the truth of the Gospel story. In Jewish, Greek, and Roman societies of the time, the testimony of women counted for little. Thus, if the story were a fabrication, the writers would have used "more convincing" witnesses than a group of grieving women!

in Mark as being present at the Crucifixion and as one of the myrrhbearing women. In the Protevangelion of James, a woman called Salome was also one of the first witnesses of the miraculous birth of Jesus, which would fit in with her kinship with Mary and her later following of Jesus.

MARY, THE MOTHER OF JAMES

Matthew describes one of the women who went to the tomb as "the other Mary," but **Luke** and **Mark** both describe her as the mother of James, presumably **James the Younger**. As is often the case, there is little certainty about who exactly this Mary is, but it is likely she is the same Mary mentioned by **John** (19:25) as the wife of Clopas who was with the Mother of Jesus at the Crucifixion. If that is the case, she was either the Virgin Mary's cousin or her sister-in-law.

SUSANNA

Nothing is known of Susanna except that she was one of the women "who provided for Him from their substance" (Luke 8:3). Although not named in the Gospels as one of the women who went to the Tomb, she is traditionally included among the Myrrhbearing Women.

Traveling Companions

M

N–O

Nektarios Kephalas of Aegina (November 9)

As evidence that sanctity is not the exclusive preserve of the early Church, Nektarios (1846–1920) is a fine example of a "kenotic" saint, one who "empties himself" for the love of God. His life, resembling in some ways that of one of his own favorite saints, **St. John Chrysostom**, reads something like a novel, and I can only touch on it here. He came from a very poor family, and the story of his early struggle to gain an education and become a priest would itself form the subject of a good book. However, our story begins when, at a relatively young age, he was appointed Metropolitan of Pentapolis in Egypt. He was respected and powerful, and with the backing of the Patriarch of Alexandria, his career in the hierarchy of the Church seemed assured. However, his honesty, simplicity, and outspokenness in support of the poor caused jealousy among his colleagues, and a variety of false accusations were leveled against him, resulting in his being anathematized and dismissed from his post. He made no attempt to defend himself or to reply to his slanderers, preferring to slip away to Athens.

After a period of great poverty, Nektarios was appointed Dean of the Rizarios Ecclesiastical School in Athens. There, he became much loved by students and staff alike, although his financial affairs didn't improve as he was in the habit of giving most of what he earned to those "who need it more." His help and guidance to those around him were not just spiritual and financial but eminently practical as well. On one occasion, the school janitor fell ill and couldn't work, which meant, in those days, that he would probably lose his job. Nektarios secretly took on his duties, scrubbing floors and cleaning toilets at night, until the janitor was fit to return.

In spite of his humble and loving nature, he continued to attract ill will from some in the church hierarchy, and the slanders from Egypt continued to dog his career. Eventually, he retired to the Monastery of the Holy Trinity, a convent he had helped to found on the island of Aegina. He spent his final years there, again in great poverty, acting as chaplain to the nuns and doing manual work around the buildings and garden. He remained full of patience and love for all, even those who had maliciously accused him. He died of prostate cancer in 1920.

Both before and after his death, many miracles of healing attributed to Nektarios were reported, although ironically he rather deplored the emphasis among the people on miracle-working saints at the expense of the great teachers. When his body was exhumed on the third anniversary of his death, the usual practice in Greece, it was found to be still intact and smelling sweetly of myrrh, the face calm as if sleeping peacefully. It was the same on the tenth anniversary, and it was not until twenty years after his death that the body finally disintegrated, the sweet smell remaining in the bones. Nektarios's tomb at the convent has become a major place of pilgrimage since 1953. He was officially recognized as being among the saints in 1961, although in the Patriarchate of Alexandria the anathema was not finally lifted until 1998, when the current patriarch made a moving statement of humility and repentance recognizing the error of his predecessor.

Nicephorus Phocas, Emperor of Byzantium (December 11)

Of particular interest in Greece and especially Crete is Nicephorus Phocas. Born in 912, he was an able soldier and in 960 was entrusted by the Byzantine emperor with the recapture of Crete from the Saracen Arabs, who had held the island for 140 years. His campaign was successful, and in 963, he himself became emperor.

Nicephorus ("Bringer of Victory") was a contradictory character. As a general he was ruthless, and as a ruler severe to the point of harshness. Yet, in his personal life, he was deeply religious and noted for his asceticism. Together with St. Athanasius the Athonite (July 5), he had the first monastery built on Mount Athos, the Great Lavra, but he also tried to limit the growth of ecclesiastical property and wealth as not being appropriate to the spiritual nature of the

Church. As a result of the severity of his rule, he was murdered in 969. He is venerated as a saint in Greece because of his role in re-establishing the Church in Crete, his founding of the first monastery on the Holy Mountain, and his personal spirituality.

Nicholas of Myra, Wonderworker (December 6)

One of the most popular saints throughout the Christian world,* Nicholas was born of a wealthy family in Patara, Asia Minor, in about 260 and was Bishop of Myra in Lycia in the fourth century. Aside from this, little is known about his life except that he may have been one of the delegates at the Council of Nicaea and probably died about 343.

However, there are numerous stories and traditions associated with him, and although many of these tales may be later creations, they point to a kind and loving man, always ready to come to the aid of people in trouble. The consistency of this theme indicates that the stories could well be oral tradition, based on popular memories of the real man. Nicholas's compassion coupled with a down-to-earth practicality is illustrated by his saving of three girls from prostitution by throwing three bags of gold through their window at night to provide them with dowries. This event may be the origin of the Santa Claus legend.

He was no softy, however, and was stern in his denunciation of injustice and heresy. At the Council of Nicaea, for example, he became so incensed with Arius that he attacked him with his bishop's staff and had to be restrained by his fellow bishops. On another occasion, he bravely halted the execution of three men unjustly condemned to death by a governor who had taken bribes. Having saved the lives of the prisoners, he went to the governor and was so uncompromising and severe in his denunciation of this unjust act that the governor confessed his crime and begged forgiveness. Also, at great risk to his life, Nicholas once cut down a tree dedicated to a pagan cult, but although he may well have been imprisoned under Diocletian, there is no evidence that he was martyred. Because of another miracle attributed to him, Nicholas is revered in Greece as the special protector of sailors.

Nicholas, whose name means "Victory of the People," is the personification of the bishop as both loving shepherd of his flock and fierce defender of the

NO

---

* There is an old Russian saying: "If anything happens to God, we've always got St. Nicholas." Nicholas is also venerated by many Muslims.

Faith. Canon Jim Rosenthal, founder of the St. Nicholas Society in England, writes, "He's the quintessential Christian. There's a little bit of St. Nicholas in all of us. We like to think we're generous and kind . . . firm in our faith and firm in our commitment to other people. He's not a wimp. He really exemplifies the best way to live."[48]

In 1087, Nicholas's remains were taken to Bari in Italy, where they lie to this day. It is not certain whether they were moved to protect them from the ravages of the Ottoman Turks or stolen by Italian merchants. Relics of the saints were big business in the Middle Ages, so the latter is not impossible. During the restoration of the chapel in Bari, permission was granted for a select group of scientists to photograph and measure the bones. In 2005, a forensic laboratory in England analyzed the data and found that Nicholas was barely five feet tall and had a broken nose—a rare glimpse of the appearance of an early saint.

Nikolai of Zhicha (March 18)

Even in this secular age, there are still men and women who live a life of Christian duty with courage and love, and Nikolai is one such person. Born in Lelich, Serbia, in 1881, he was never physically strong, and having failed his army medical exam, he entered the St. Sava Seminary in Belgrade at an early age. After graduation in 1905, he studied for doctorates at Berne and King's College, Oxford.* On his return to Serbia, he entered the monastery of Rakovica and was ordained a priest in 1909.

Nikolai's deepest desire was to teach: "I wanted to be a shepherd. As a child, I tended my father's sheep. Now that I am a man, I wish to tend the rational flock of my heavenly Father." He taught philosophy, logic, history, and foreign languages at the seminary, speaking seven languages himself. He also used his excellent communication skills in his sermons, which dealt with no more than three main points, never lasted more than twenty minutes, and used language people could understand. This led to his being nicknamed "the Serbian Chrysostom." You can see evidence of his skill as a writer and communicator in the books by him mentioned in Further Reading.

At the outbreak of the First World War, Nikolai traveled to England to seek support and help for Serbia, speaking in Westminster Abbey and leaving a lasting impression on many in the Anglican Church. After a longer lecture tour

NO

---

* Is Nikolai the only Orthodox saint with a PhD from Oxford?

of the USA, he returned to Serbia in 1919. Consecrated Bishop of Zhicha, he spent a tremendous amount of time and energy helping those ravaged by the war, building orphanages, and raising funds for the destitute. He also helped lead a spiritual revival among the laity as well as renewing monastic life in Serbia.

A fearless critic of the Nazis, he was interned in a monastery after the German invasion in 1941 and three years later was transferred to Dachau concentration camp. In spite of suffering terrible privation and torture, he survived to be liberated in May 1945. He went to England, and when the communists came to power, he decided it was better not to return to Serbia but to serve his people from outside the country. He spent the remainder of his life in the USA, teaching, writing, preaching, and speaking in support of the Serbian Church.

Never physically strong, his health problems were made worse by his time in Dachau, but he continued to travel and work indefatigably. On March 17, 1958, after serving the Liturgy, he gave a short sermon, bowed, and said, "Forgive me, brothers." On the following day, he passed away. He was buried at St. Sava's Monastery, Libertyville, Illinois, but in 1991 his relics were transferred to his hometown of Lelich. In 2003, the Serbian Church recognized him as a saint, but the respect for this gentle and loving man of God has spread much more widely. He is venerated especially in the USA, where his *Prayers by the Lake* are perennially popular.

Nikon and 199 Companions, Martyrs (March 23)

The martyrdom of Nikon is one of the most savage acts in a savage age. Born in Neapolis, Italy, Nikon served with distinction in the Roman army. On leave in Chios, he was converted to Christianity by a holy man of the island. He progressed rapidly in the Church, becoming bishop in charge of a large monastery in Sicily, with spiritual oversight of 199 monks. Although this was during the time of Decius's persecutions, the authorities on the mainland regarded the monks as a relatively harmless group of eccentric recluses, and they were left to themselves for quite a time. However, their success in converting people to Christianity and the influence Nikon and his monks had over growing numbers even on the mainland stirred the governor to take action. He felt that the monks' activities were undermining his own authority. He called on Nikon to abandon the monastery and leave the island or be executed. Nikon refused point-blank, and the governor sent a lieutenant to the monastery with carte

NO

blanche to do whatever was necessary. The monks were again asked to leave, and when they refused, they were beheaded one by one in front of Nikon. Finally, Nikon himself was tortured and executed in about 251.

Nino, Enlightener of Georgia and Equal to the Apostles (January 14)

Nino (also called Nina) was a Christian girl from Cappadocia, born in about 280. She came from an eminent Christian family.* According to Orthodox tradition, she was quite young when she felt the call to spread the Gospel in the Caucasus and set out to take Christianity to the region. Roman Catholic tradition says she was captured and taken to Georgia as a slave, but whichever version is true, she became well known for her goodness and her ability in healing the sick, which she always did in the name of Christ.

Eventually, the king and queen summoned her to tell them about this new religion. Her testimony so impressed them that the king sent to Constantinople for clergy to come to Georgia and spread the Gospel. The missionaries were received warmly, and Christianity quickly spread through the country. So through this humble missionary, the Christian Church took root. Nino is numbered among those equal to the apostles, along with emperors and princes. She died in about 347 and is, of course, the patron of Georgia. Her relics still lie in the Bodbe Monastery in East Georgia.

Olga (July 11) and Vladimir (July 15), Equal to the Apostles, and Boris and Gleb (July 24), Holy Passion Bearers

Olga, widow of Prince Igor (of opera fame), was an early convert to Christianity in Kiev, at that time the main princedom in Russia. She received baptism in about 957 at the age of seventy and was influential in spreading the Faith in the princedom. She asked for missionaries to be sent to convert her subjects, but they had scarcely begun their work when her son Svyatoslav, who was a pagan, deposed his mother and killed the missionaries. She died in 969, but her influence continued.

Her grandson, Prince Vladimir (reigned 980–1015), led a brutal, blood-

---

* Her father was related to **St. George** and her mother was sister of the Patriarch of Jerusalem.

thirsty, and dissolute life until he was eventually converted and baptized in about 989. Like **Constantine**, he saw in Christianity a powerful unifying force for his attempt to weld together a kingdom, but he also took his new faith seriously. Although he could be forceful, even harsh, in imposing Christianity on a sometimes unwilling people, he made genuine attempts to establish the rule of Christ in his realm. He organized a highly efficient system of social welfare, and the distribution of food to the poor and sick was a standard feature of all state banquets. He introduced the Byzantine Code of Laws but took it much further, and it is here that I find his story extraordinary. He abolished not only the death penalty but mutilation and torture as well. Even corporal punishment was rarely used. And this in the tenth century! Although Kiev reverted to more "normal" medieval regimes after Vladimir's death, it took most European countries another thousand years to match the gentleness and Christian compassion of his penal code. Some Christian countries are still waiting.

To complete the story, Vladimir's two youngest sons, Boris and Gleb, are also saints in the Orthodox Church and deeply revered in Russia. On Vladimir's death, their older half-brother had them murdered in order to consolidate his position as prince. What makes the two boys stand out from other political victims was their refusal to fight back or to allow their supporters to defend them. As Christians and true sons of their father, they took the Gospel commands literally and would not use force, especially against an older brother. Although not martyrs for the Faith, they represent another category of saint—"Passion Bearers"—because, by their innocent and voluntary suffering, they shared in the Passion of Christ. Ironically, the way in which they met their deaths so inspired and enraged the people that they quickly overthrew the murderer.

NO

Olympia, Deaconess (July 25)

One of the most extraordinary women of the fourth century, Olympia (or Olympias) was the principal supporter of **John Chrysostom** after his banishment. Born in Nicomedia in about 366, she was the daughter of a rich senator. She was married to the city prefect at the age of eighteen but widowed two years later. This, together with the death of her parents, left her an extremely wealthy young woman. As well as money, she had great personal charm and experienced some difficulties fighting off suitors, but she was determined to devote her abilities to God.

By 391, she had established a reputation as a strong-willed and generous benefactress, donating huge sums to the poor and to the Church. Having been ordained a deaconess, she worked tirelessly to assist the church hierarchy in Constantinople and became friends with many of them. She became especially close to John Chrysostom, and when he was sent into exile, she and the other deaconesses bade a tearful farewell to him. She continued to be vocal in her support of John.

When a large church in Constantinople was burned down, Olympia was arrested, although there was no evidence she had anything to do with it. At her trial, she answered the prefect with irony and boldness, continuing to refuse to acknowledge John's successor. She was fined heavily and from then on was harried and persecuted for the rest of her life, including a spell in prison in 405. She died in exile, somewhere in Nicomedia, in about 408.

Shortly before her death, she left instructions that her coffin be thrown into the sea, leaving her final resting place to divine Providence. Her request was carried out, and the coffin washed up near Constantinople, where it was buried in a nearby church. In the seventh century the church was burned by invading Persians and the relics were moved to Constantinople, where they were buried in the monastery Olympia had founded.

Seventeen of John Chrysostom's surviving letters are written to Olympia. They are full of sympathy for her difficulties and praise for her patience and dignity: "Be not therefore dismayed or troubled but continue to give thanks to God for all things, praising, and invoking Him. . . . For not only to bear misfortunes bravely but to be actually insensible to them, to overlook them, and with such little exertion to wreathe your brows with the garland prize of patience, . . . this is indeed a proof of the most finished philosophy. Therefore I rejoice, and leap for joy; I am in a flutter of delight, I am insensible to my present loneliness, and the other troubles which surround me, being cheered, and brightened, and not a little proud on account of your greatness of soul, and the repeated victories which you have won." Her courage and faith, together with her charity towards those who were oppressing her, "have won a glory and reward which later on will make your sufferings seem light and passing, when you are confronted with unending happiness."

NO

P

Paisius Velichkovsky, Venerable (November 15)

Paisius (or Paissy) was born Peter in 1722 in what is now the Ukraine. He was sent to study at the Kiev Theological School at the age of thirteen, but by 1739 he had decided on a monastic life. At that time, Russian monasticism was going through something of a decline, and Peter, repelled by the secularism he found in the Kiev theological schools, went on a six-year quest to find a suitable monastery and spiritual father. After a year in Romania, he arrived on Mount Athos in 1746, finally being tonsured a monk four years later.

Still searching for a spiritual guide, he made friends with a young monk called Bessarion who was on a similar quest. When he started to talk to Bessarion about the qualities needed by an elder and to explain the Jesus Prayer, the young man realized that Paisius himself was the guide he needed! Although Paisius did not consider himself worthy to teach and refused to accept Bessarion as a disciple, he eventually consented to becoming his friend, and the two monks worked together on their spiritual development for the next four years.

As people began to realize Paisius's spiritual gifts, a group of disciples did begin to gather around him, and he was eventually persuaded to accept ordination so that his supervision and guidance of the other monks could be regularized. Paisius spent seventeen years on Athos before moving back to Romania. Here, the original sixty-four monks who accompanied him grew to three hundred fifty. After being forced to leave the area by war and plague in 1779, Paisius spent the last fifteen years of his life as abbot of the monastery of Niamets with over five hundred brothers under his guidance.

He died in 1794 after a brief illness. It is likely that he was aware of his impending death, because some time prior to it he stopped his translation work and just corrected work he had already done. His relics, buried in the monastery, were found to be still uncorrupted as late as 1872, the last time they were uncovered. Elder Paisius was glorified on July 20, 1982, at the Prophet Elias Skete, which he had founded on Mount Athos.

Paisius had tremendous influence not only on Romanian monasticism but on the great Russian religious renewal and monastic revival of the nineteenth century. Although he never returned to Russia, many of his disciples traveled there, carrying his ideas with them. His influence was twofold. His translation of the *Philokalia*[49] into Slavonic brought the wisdom of a thousand years of Orthodox ascetic and mystical texts to the whole Slavic Orthodox world. Moreover, through his time on Mount Athos, Paisius became familiar with the hesychast tradition (see **Gregory Palamas**), which he passed on to his disciples together with emphasis on continual prayer, especially the Jesus Prayer, and the need for obedience to an elder or spiritual guide.

Recognition of his importance continues to grow. Fr. Seraphim Rose wrote, "[For] Orthodox Christians of the 20th century there is no more important Holy Father of recent times than Blessed Paisius Velichkovsky . . . he redirected the attention of Orthodox Christians to the sources of Holy Orthodoxy, which are the only foundation of true Orthodox life and thought whether of the past or of the present, whether of monks or of laymen."[50]

Panteleimon, Great Martyr and Healer (July 27)

Panteleimon was a native of Nicomedia whose father was pagan but whose mother, Eubola (March 30), came from an old Christian family. He was trained as a doctor and became court physician to Emperor Maximian. In spite of his Christian upbringing, the fanatically anti-Christian and dissolute court led him to abandon his faith and lead a life of self-indulgence. Eventually, a friend and priest called Hermolaus, later himself martyred (July 26), brought Panteleimon back to Christianity, gave him instruction in the Faith, and baptized him.

Panteleimon's life changed, and although he continued in his career, whatever he earned he now gave away. He put his skills at the disposal of the poor, showing as much concern for the souls of his patients as for their bodies. He continued to be a successful physician under Diocletian, and it was probably the jealousy of his colleagues that caused him to be denounced to the emperor as a Christian. He underwent repeated beatings and tortures, eventually being beheaded in about 305.

In the Orthodox Church, he is regarded as the protector of the sick and of soldiers, and many miracles of healing are attributed to him. He is also regarded as a healer of spiritual wounds in our warfare against sin. Panteleimon is invoked in the prayers for the sick, the Sacrament of Anointing the sick, and the Blessing of the Waters. His name, taken at baptism, means appropriately "all-compassionate," although his given name "Panteleon" ("a lion in all things") is probably just as apt. It is under the name Panteleon that he is venerated in the Roman Catholic Church.

Paraskeva of Rome, Great Martyr (July 26)

Two saints called Paraskeva are honored in the Orthodox Church— Paraskeva, Great Martyr of Rome (July 26), and Paraskeva of Iconium (October 28)—and there seems to be some confusion between the two stories. To simplify matters, I have followed the most common version of the story of Paraskeva of Rome, but you may well find variations.

Paraskeva was the daughter of Christian parents, being named after the day of her birth (Friday, *Paraskevi* in Greek). She was taught the Holy Scriptures from childhood and, as she grew older, preached the Faith openly and with great courage. She was eventually arrested in the time of Antoninus Pius. When urged to worship idols, she replied in the words of Jeremiah: "The gods that have not made the heavens and the earth shall perish from the earth and from under these heavens" (Jeremiah 10:11).

During questioning, she was asked her name but would only reply, "I believe in the Lord Jesus Christ." When asked why she wouldn't give her name, she replied, "It was necessary first to give the name of eternal life and only then the name of temporary existence." The daring and unyielding firmness with which she preached and endured torture have given Paraskeva a special place among the martyrs. She is deeply revered in Greece and Russia, where she is regarded as the special protector of the work of women and market traders and also as a helper with eye problems. After many tortures, she was finally beheaded in 140.

P

Parthenius of Lampsacus (February 7)

Parthenius was the son of a deacon, born in the reign of Constantine when Christianity had just been legalized. Although his father was well educated, Parthenius preferred from an early age to go fishing rather than study, a trait that should endear the saint to many young people. As a result, he was virtually illiterate when his father gave up the struggle to educate him and apprenticed him to a fishing captain. Eventually, Parthenius took over the boat as captain and continued to ply his trade, giving away most of his catch to the poor.

While still a young man, he began to show signs of having a gift of healing, and although he tried to play it down, increasing numbers sought him out. The local bishop investigated the matter and not only concluded that the gift of healing was genuine and from God, but discovered that, illiterate though he was, Parthenius could quote the Scriptures at great length from memory. The bishop persuaded the young man to become a priest, and eventually he was made Bishop of Lampsacus. Among the tasks assigned to him was the destruction of pagan temples and their replacement with Christian churches, a task he completed in his diocese, winning many converts in the process. The purity and gentleness of his character, coupled with his healing power, made this unlettered fisherman so deeply loved by all who knew him (including the emperor) that, on his death, he was given a state funeral, usually reserved for emperors and patriarchs—a worthy successor to those earlier fishermen called by Jesus.

Patrick, Enlightener of Ireland (March 17)

Patrick (Pádraig in Irish) was a Romano-Briton, probably born between 385 and 390. Although he was certainly from the west coast of Britain, the exact location of his birth is not known, and there is considerable rivalry among locations claiming the honor. He was from a Christian family, his father a deacon and his grandfather a priest, but as a youth he did not yet follow their faith. Captured by pirates at the age of sixteen, he was taken as a slave to Ireland, where he worked as a shepherd for six years, probably in Antrim.

During his enslavement, he found great solace in the faith of his family and in prayer: "More and more did the love of God, and my fear of him and faith increase, and my spirit was moved so that in a day I said from one up to a hundred prayers, and in the night a like number; besides I used to stay out in the forests and on the mountain and I would wake up before daylight to pray in the snow, in icy coldness, in rain, and I used to feel neither ill nor any slothfulness, because, as I now see, the Spirit was burning in me at that time."[51] He eventually escaped and, after a two-hundred mile walk to the east coast, found a ship to return him to England. When, a little later, he had a dream in which he saw the people of Ireland calling him to come back to them, he decided to train for the priesthood. He was ordained in Gaul by St. Germanus (July 31) and eventually consecrated bishop in 430. He returned to Ireland as a missionary two years later.

There were already some Christians in Ireland, but their bishop, St. Palladius (July 7), had had little success and had returned to Scotland. Missionaries were also active on the southeast coast, but it was Patrick who established Christianity on a firm base throughout the island. At Tara in Meath, he bravely defied the king on the eve of Pascha and lit a paschal fire which could not be extinguished except by him. He went on to explain the Gospel, using the three-leafed shamrock to illustrate the Holy Trinity. His courage, together with the miracle, silenced the druids and made the king take him seriously so that he was allowed to preach freely in the area, converting the king's three daughters in the process.

All was not smooth sailing, however. Patrick was constantly aware of the danger that he would be killed or enslaved by the pagans. On top of this, he had to battle against criticism from other clergy, some of whom had been his friends, who accused him of being an ambitious ignoramus and unsuitable to be a bishop. In his *Confession,* he refutes some of the slanders against him of receiving payment for baptisms and ordinations, and of general financial corruption. Ironically, one of the criticisms was that he received many gifts from kings and wealthy women, which was actually the reverse of the truth. His refusal to accept such gifts went against the traditions of hospitality among the Celts and actually placed him in some danger. Being a foreigner, outside the normal ties of kinship and patronage, he had little protection, and on one occasion he was attacked, beaten, and put in chains, expecting at any moment to be executed.

A popular legend associated with Patrick is his expulsion of all snakes from Ireland. Since there is no fossil evidence that snakes ever existed in Ireland, this may well be an allegory of his conversion of the druids, who used the symbol of a serpent extensively in their worship.

In 444 Patrick established the bishopric of Armagh, which became the base from which he was able to organize the administration of the Irish Church and set it on a firm foundation. It remains the primary seat of both Roman Catholic and

P

Protestant churches in Ireland, and both cathedrals are dedicated to St. Patrick. He died at Saul in County Down, Ireland, on March 17, 461. He is believed to be buried in the cathedral at Downpatrick alongside **St. Brigid** and **St. Columba**, but this has never been established for certain.

In character Patrick was, in spite of his undoubted courage and ability as a preacher, an essentially humble man, very conscious of his lack of education and his sinfulness. In one sense he agreed with his critics about his unworthiness, but he asserted forcefully that his work was the will of God and that whatever he achieved was through the Holy Spirit: "I, Patrick, am a sinner, a most simple countryman, the least of all the faithful and most contemptible to many . . . I am greatly God's debtor, because he granted me so much grace, that through me many people would be reborn in God."

The prayer called "St. Patrick's Breastplate" is attributed to Patrick and certainly expresses both his belief and something of his character. Many translations exist, and it is used by Christians of all denominations as a prayer. The most well-known version is the beautiful hymn written by C. F. Alexander in 1889, of which this is a brief extract:

I bind unto myself this day
The strong name of the Trinity,
By invocation of the same,
The three in one and one in three . . .
Christ be with me, Christ within me,
Christ behind me, Christ before me,
Christ beside me, Christ to win me,
Christ to comfort and restore me.
Christ beneath me, Christ above me,
Christ in quiet, Christ in danger,
Christ in hearts of all that love me,
Christ in mouth of friend and stranger.

Paul, Leader of the Apostles (June 29, together with Peter)

O riginally called Saul, Paul was a strict Pharisee and a fanatical opponent of the new "sect" of Christians. In his own words, he "made havoc of the Church" until his conversion following a dramatic vision on the road to

Damascus. He was the prime instigator of the mission to take Christ's teaching to the non-Jews, and from about AD 45, he went on missionary journeys to Cyprus, Asia Minor, Syria, Macedonia, Greece, and Rome. He never wavered in his faith in spite of a life full of hardship. In one letter, he shows a very human touch of pride in cataloguing his sufferings for the Lord: he was prosecuted, flogged, imprisoned, stoned, and shipwrecked (2 Corinthians 11:23–28). Paul was eventually executed in Rome in about 68, on the orders of Nero, probably beheaded with a sword since he was a Roman citizen.

Paul was a tireless letter writer, and his letters are full of common sense and practical advice to the fledgling Church as well as love and spiritual depth: "Though I speak with the tongues of men and of angels, but have not love, I have become sounding brass or a clanging cymbal. . . . And though I bestow all my goods to feed *the poor,* and though I give my body to be burned, but have not love, it profits me nothing" (1 Corinthians 13:1–3). A small man, bald and slightly bow-legged, Paul must nevertheless have been a powerful and charismatic speaker.* His letters were not only of enormous importance in the early development of the Church but have continued to exert a profound and enduring influence to this day.

In recent years, there has been much criticism of his "misogynism" based on some of his comments about women, but while his letters reveal some of the male assumptions of the society in which he lived, there is no evidence of any antagonism towards women. For every comment such as, "Wives, submit to your own husbands, as is fitting in the Lord" (Colossians 3:18), there are many others like, "There is neither Jew nor Greek, there is neither slave nor free, there is neither male nor female; for you are all one in Christ Jesus" (Galatians 3:28).

Pelagia of Tarsus, Virgin Martyr (May 4)

Pelagia was the fifteen-year-old daughter of pagan parents. She was apparently very beautiful and caught the eye of Emperor Diocletian's son, who wanted to marry her. Having no particular desire to marry and needing someone to turn to for advice, she went to a Christian bishop, Linus, well known for his common

---

* A medallion showing the faces of St. Peter and St. Paul dating from the second or third century exists in the Vatican library. There is some evidence that this is a copy of an earlier original, and it is therefore not impossible that the images of the two saints in icons are true representations.

sense and insight. During their conversations, his compassion and helpful guidance converted the girl to his faith. She was baptized a Christian, but her mother found out and reported her to the emperor, hoping the threat of torture would cause her to give up her "crazy" new ideas. However, in spite of the pleas of her parents and of the emperor's son, she refused to recant. Even the emperor was captivated by her and offered her anything she wanted if she would become his wife. She replied simply, "I have Christ, the King of heaven, as my bridegroom." She was roasted to death in a hollow bronze bull in 288. Her remains were buried by the bishop who had converted her, and a church was built over the relics.

Pelagia the Penitent, Venerable (October 8)

Pelagia was a notoriously licentious pagan dancing girl in Antioch. One day she caught the attention of Bishop Nonnus of Edessa (November 10), who commented, "This girl is a lesson to us bishops. She takes more trouble over her beauty and her dancing than we do about our souls and our flocks!" It may have been this non-judgmental attitude of the bishop that caused Pelagia to listen a little more carefully to his sermons, because a little later, she was moved to repentance and was baptized a Christian by Nonnus. Seeking a quiet life of penitence, she went to Jerusalem, where she lived as a solitary in a cave on the Mount of Olives, disguised as a man under the name of Pelagius. She died there some fifty-eight years later in about 284 and is revered as an example of true penitence. It is possible that Pelagia's story originated as an edifying parable, but in one of his sermons, **St. John Chrysostom** does refer to a real woman of Antioch who led a life very similar to Pelagia's, although he does not name her.

Peter, Leader of the Apostles (June 29, together with Paul)

Perhaps more than any of the other apostles, Peter emerges in the Gospels and Acts as a well-rounded person and stands out as a saint we can relate to on a human level. For a start, he was far from perfect: impetuous and occasionally short-tempered, he was often obstinate and several times showed great timidity. On one notable occasion after the arrest of Jesus, he denied all knowledge of his Master three times for fear of arrest. And yet, it was to him that Christ entrusted "the keys of the Kingdom."

His original name was Simon, but Jesus gave him the Aramaic name Cephas

("Rock," John 1:42), Petros in Greek, telling him, "On this rock I will build my Church, and the gates of Hades shall not prevail against it" (Matthew 16:18–19). In spite of his occasionally shaky start, he did indeed become the undoubted leader of the apostles and was instrumental in moving the early Church away from the strict dietary laws of Judaism. Despite early reluctance, he joined **Paul** enthusiastically in leading the mission to the Gentiles, thus laying the foundation for a universal Church rather than a sect of Judaism.

He was imprisoned several times, and a feast called "The Chains of St. Peter" is celebrated on January 16, commemorating one miraculous escape from prison (Acts 12:6–11). He was eventually martyred in Rome about AD 64 by Nero. When sent for crucifixion, he declared that he was unworthy to suffer the same death as Jesus and was crucified upside down. Traditionally, his burial place is under the altar of the Vatican basilica which bears his name. He is, of course, the patron of St. Petersburg, Russia.

Additional Feast Day: January 16 (Chains of St. Peter)

Peter the Aleut, Martyr of San Francisco (December 12, with St. Juvenaly)

It has been one of the great tragedies of Christian history that fanaticism and violence have existed among those purporting to teach Christ's Gospel of love. No church or denomination can claim completely clean hands, but the story of Peter is a tragic example of the workings of the "worship God my way or die" creed, more reminiscent of the Reformation than the nineteenth century.

A native of Kodiak Island, Cungagnaq was baptized with the name Peter by monks of the Alaskan mission led by **St. Herman**. In 1815, he was on a seal hunt with thirteen others from his tribe when the group was captured by Spanish sailors and taken to San Francisco, then still ruled by Spain. There, they were interrogated by Franciscan priests and found to be Orthodox. They were threatened with torture if they did not convert. When they refused, the priests made an example of Peter by cutting off one toe from each foot. Since the Aleuts still refused to give up their Orthodox faith, a group of Californian Indians was ordered to torture Peter further in a particularly grisly way. Each finger was cut off one joint at a time, then his hands and feet were cut off and he was left to bleed to death.*

---

* Some reports say he was also disemboweled.

Traveling Companions

P

Mercifully, before they could start on the next prisoner, they received orders to send the Aleuts under escort to the monastery at Monterey, where they were to be imprisoned. One of them later escaped and reported the incident to Simon Yanusky, an administrator of the Russian colony of Alaska. When St. Herman heard from Yanusky of Peter's death, he crossed himself and cried out, "Holy newly-martyred Peter, pray to God for us!" Peter was formally glorified by the Orthodox Church in America in 1980. "Today Alaska rejoices and America celebrates, / For the new world has been sanctified by martyrdom" (Hymn for Feast of All Saints of Alaska).

Additional Feast Day: September 24 (All Saints of Alaska)

Philip, Holy Apostle (November 4)

B orn in Bethsaida, Philip was well acquainted with the Holy Scriptures, and when called by Jesus to follow Him, he immediately recognized Jesus as the Messiah. He rushed off excitedly to find his friend Nathaniel (**Bartholomew**) and tell him that "we have found Him of whom Moses in the law, and also the prophets, wrote—Jesus of Nazareth, the son of Joseph." To this, Nathaniel replied with the classic put-down, "Can anything good come out of Nazareth?" "Come and see," said Philip (John 1:43–46).

By nature, Philip seems to have been a bit of a worrier, and John reports a lovely scene before the miracle of the feeding of the multitude when Jesus gently pulls his leg. Already knowing exactly what He intends to do, Jesus asks, "Where shall we buy bread, that these may eat?" We can almost see the concern on Philip's face as he replies, "Two hundred denarii worth of bread is not sufficient for them, that every one of them may have a little." The miracle of the loaves and fishes, of course, followed (John 6:5–8). Philip again gave Jesus an opportunity to demonstrate a profound truth when, at the Last Supper, he requested, "Lord, show us the Father," to which Jesus replied with the wonderful words, "He who has seen Me has seen the Father" (John 14:8–9).

After Pentecost, Philip preached in Greece, Phrygia, and Syria, accompanied by his sister Mariamne (February 17) and the Apostle Bartholomew. In Greece, the Jewish chief priest became enraged at his preaching and, along with his companions, attacked him with a club. They were suddenly struck blind. When Philip prayed and restored their sight, many new converts were made.

According to some accounts, while preaching in the city of Hierapolis,

P

Philip converted the wife of the proconsul, who was outraged and had the three missionaries tortured. The two apostles were then crucified upside down, Philip continuing to preach the Gospel. Moved by his courage, the onlookers rushed to release them, but although Bartholomew was rescued, Philip refused and remained to die on the cross. Another tradition reports that they were arrested for killing a giant serpent worshipped by the pagans. As they were being crucified, there was an earthquake that killed the procurator, the pagan priests, and many of the officials. Believing it to be a judgment from the gods, the people rushed to rescue the apostles, but Philip was already dead. Mariamne went on to Lykaonia, where she died shortly afterwards.

In July 2011, it was announced that during excavations in Hierapolis, Italian archaeologists had unearthed the tomb of the Apostle Philip. At the time of writing, however, there is no definitive evidence for the identification.

Philip the Deacon, Apostle of the Seventy (October 11)

Not to be confused with the Apostle, this Philip was one of the seven deacons appointed by the apostles in Jerusalem to deal with the finances of the early Church and take care of the widows, orphans, and needy (Acts 6:1–7). After the martyrdom of **Stephen**, he settled in Samaria, where he was responsible for the dramatic conversion of the magician Simon Magus, who, "when he was baptized . . . continued with Philip, and was amazed, seeing the miracles and signs which were done" (Acts 8:13).

Another of Philip's conversions used to charm me at Sunday school because of its simplicity. On a journey from Jerusalem to Gaza, he came across an Ethiopian official traveling in his carriage. The official was returning home from a trip to Jerusalem and, as he traveled, was reading one of Isaiah's prophesies (Isaiah 53:7–8). He was having great trouble understanding it and invited Philip to join him and help. Philip explained to him that the passage referred to the Messiah and that Jesus was the One spoken of. He went on to speak of the Gospel of Jesus, and as they passed a pool of water, the official, obviously a man of quick and decisive action, said, "See, *here is* water. What hinders me from being baptized?" He stopped the carriage, the two of them went into the water, and Philip baptized him. "Now when they came up out of the water, the Spirit of the Lord caught Philip away, so that the eunuch saw him no more; and he went on his way rejoicing" (Acts 8:36–39).

P

A few years later, Philip seems to have settled in Caesarea with his family, four daughters who had the gift of prophecy. It was here that Paul and his companions stayed with him on one of their journeys (Acts 21:8–9). According to tradition, the apostles at Jerusalem later appointed Philip Bishop of Tralles in Asia Minor, where he died at a great age.

Philip II, Metropolitan of Moscow, Hieromartyr (January 9)

Born in 1507, Theodore Kolychev came from a wealthy aristocratic family. He became a soldier and served with distinction against the Lithuanians and Crimean Tatars. He was brought into the court of the Prince of Moscow, where he became a close friend of the future Tsar Ivan IV ("the Terrible"). As a deeply committed Christian, however, he decided at the age of thirty that he could no longer serve two masters (Matthew 6:24), resigned his commission, and went to live a solitary life as a shepherd in a remote village.* In 1538, he fulfilled his longstanding ambition and entered the Solovetsky Monastery on the White Sea, where he was tonsured with the name Philip.

As a novice and even later as an abbot, in spite of his aristocratic background, Philip was quite happy to work as a gardener and woodcutter. After less than ten years, he was elected abbot and proved himself not only a conscientious spiritual leader but an able practical engineer, devising a network of canals linking seventy-two lakes to produce a more efficient irrigation and drainage system for the region. He was also responsible for the building of two cathedrals, a brick factory, water mills, and storehouses, joining in much of the physical labor himself. Most of these buildings still survive. Whenever he felt the need to renew his spiritual strength, he would retire for prayer and meditation to a desolate area, later nicknamed "the Philippov Wilderness."

Meanwhile, Ivan IV had begun his reign in 1547 with peaceful reforms, modernization, and good relations with the Church. As he became more and more paranoid, however, he created a personal bodyguard called the *Oprichniki*—in his eyes a sort of devout monastic brotherhood, but in reality a totally ruthless

P

---

* Some historians believe he was involved in a court conspiracy and escaped to a monastery when the plot was discovered. If this was the case, it was probably a wise move in the political climate of the time and certainly doesn't detract from Philip's later achievements and courage.

and efficient secret police force. In 1566, hearing of the repute and sanctity of Philip and with fond memories of his childhood friend, he appointed Philip Metropolitan of Moscow. After refusing the appointment for a long time, Philip eventually accepted the "poisoned chalice" on condition that Ivan disband the Oprichniki. In return, Philip undertook not to interfere in the tsar's political affairs.

The truce was short-lived, however. Within two years, the Oprichniki were active again, massacring political opponents in Novgorod, including many innocent people. Philip felt forced to remonstrate with Ivan privately, but this only enraged the tsar further. When he continued the barbarities, Philip decided to go public. During the Divine Liturgy in the Moscow Cathedral, he addressed Ivan directly: "At the altar, we are offering a pure and bloodless sacrifice for men's salvation. Outside this holy temple, the blood of innocent Christians is being shed. God rejects him who does not love his neighbor. I have to tell you this, though I die for it." Philip continued to speak out until Ivan engineered his deposition on the absurd charges of "sorcery and corrupt living." He was dragged in chains from prison to prison until eventually he was choked to death by a servant of the tsar in 1569.

Twenty-one years after his death, the body was disinterred and found to be intact. In 1652, Philip's holy relics were transferred to the Cathedral of the Assumption in Moscow, where they remain. His feast day was celebrated at first on the day of his death, December 23, but the commemoration was transferred to January 9 in 1660. In a bizarre twist of fate, a vociferous movement has recently arisen in Russia calling for the glorification of Ivan IV as a saint. This idea has received short shrift from Patriarch Alexei of Moscow and the Orthodox Church in general.

Additional Feast Days: July 3 (Translation of Relics)

October 5 (Synaxis of the Hierarchs of Moscow)

Philothea of Athens, Nun Martyr (February 19)

The rule of the Ottoman Turks in Greece was a period of great suffering and renewed persecution of the Orthodox Christian Greeks. Although in theory the Greeks were free to follow their own faith, in practice many of the rulers attempted to undermine and subvert the Church, both by political controls and harsh taxation. They also turned a blind eye to the spasmodic pogroms carried out by the more fanatical Muslims. Philothea was the victim of one such outburst.

Born into an affluent Athens family in 1528, she was widowed at the age of sixteen and, with the death of her parents a few years later, found herself a very wealthy woman. Having always been of a spiritual and retiring nature, she felt little desire for the life of a woman of affairs and entered a convent. She used her wealth for the relief of poverty and the building of several churches and convents around Athens, most of which still exist. She also founded a hospital, a hospice for the poor, boys' and girls' schools, and a refuge for Christian slaves who had fled their masters.

Some of the local Turks were enraged by her resolute propagation of the Faith, and in 1589, they attacked her and some of her friends during a service in the Church of St. Andrew (built by her and still in existence). The women were clubbed and stoned, then dragged into the street, where they were beaten to death. Philothea's remains were enshrined in St. Andrew's Church, and her relics remain incorrupt to this day. A number of miracles have been attributed to her since her death. She is deeply revered in Greece, and a number of women's organizations bear her name in honor of this sincere and courageous woman of God.

Phocas the Gardener, Martyr (September 22)

Phocas is not a widely known saint but one whose story delights with its simple dignity. Phocas was a market gardener living at Sinope in Pontus on the southern shore of the Black Sea. He led a quiet, simple life as a Christian until, during one of the more systematic persecutions, his name became known to the authorities. Soldiers were dispatched, and late one night they arrived at his house asking where a Christian called Phocas lived, as they had orders to kill him. Phocas invited them to stay the night, as he would be able to direct them better in the light of day. He gave them a meal, and after they were asleep, he spent the night quietly digging his own grave in the garden. In the morning, he told his guests who he was. The soldiers were moved by his cool and quiet courage, but this didn't prevent them from carrying out their orders, albeit reluctantly.

Phocas, Bishop of Sinope, Hieromartyr (September 22)

A second saint by the name of Phocas* was Bishop of Sinope, martyred in 117 under Trajan by being scalded to death in a bathhouse. Along with his ecclesiastical office, he continued his trade as a shipbuilder, a not uncommon practice in the early Church, and soon after his death was honored as the protector of sailors and defender against fires. His relics were transferred to Constantinople in 404, an event commemorated on July 23.

Additional Feast Day: July 23 (Transfer of Relics)

Photina (Svetlana in Russian), Holy Martyr (February 26 in Greece, May 22 in Russia)

A lthough she is not named in the Gospels, an ancient tradition identifies the Samaritan woman Jesus met at Jacob's Well as Photina, one of the early martyrs. Her story illustrates the message of reconciliation Jesus brought to the world. At that time, for historical reasons, the Jews regarded the Samaritans as "untouchables" although they shared belief in the same God and looked forward to the same Messiah. The enmity was so great that the Jews would have nothing at all to do with the Samaritans and would not even use the same cups to drink from. Nevertheless, Jesus, resting by a well in Samaria, asked the woman for a drink and then sat with her for a long time, discussing the beliefs of the two groups and allowing her some unique insights into His mission. Through her, many of the Samaritans in the town came to hear Jesus speak and accepted Him as the Messiah (John 4:5–42). According to tradition, Photina and her entire family became tireless missionaries, all of them being martyred by Nero in about 66.

Additional Feast Day: Fourth Sunday after Pascha (Sunday of the Samaritan Woman)

P

Polycarp, Bishop of Smyrna, Hieromartyr (February 23)

P olycarp, a disciple of **St. John the Theologian**, was Bishop of Smyrna in Asia Minor and an important figure in the early Church. **St. Ignatius** wrote to him, "This age is in need of you if it is to reach God, just as pilots need winds

---

* Recent research has indicated that Phocas the Bishop and Phocas the Gardener may well have been the same person, whose stories became confused with the passage of time.

and as a storm-tossed sailor needs a port" (Letter to Polycarp 1:11). After Polycarp's martyrdom, the church at Smyrna wrote a long account of his death, which Eusebius copied into his *History of the Church*. We thus have an authentic narrative of an act of martyrdom, the first after **St. Stephen**.

In 155, in the reign of Marcus Aurelius, when Polycarp was an old man, he was betrayed by a servant and arrested. He refused to take an oath by the emperor's guardian spirit, declaring, "Fourscore and six years have I served Christ and He has done me no wrong. How then can I blaspheme my King and Savior now?" The proconsul threatened to have him thrown into a fire, to which he replied, "You threaten me with a fire that will certainly die out. You know nothing of the eternal fire that is reserved for the wicked."

He refused to be nailed to the stake and stood erect on the pyre. After he had prayed and praised God, the fire was lit. Then, according to an eyewitness, "the flames made a sort of arch, like a ship's sail filled with the wind and they were like a wall round the martyr's body; and he looked not like burning flesh but like bread in the oven or gold and silver being refined in a furnace." The executioner was ordered to stab him to hasten his end. The feast day of St. Polycarp is the oldest regular commemoration for which we have records and has, of course, continued to the present day.

Polychronius the Presbyter, Martyr (October 7)

A later martyr, Polychronius was the son of peasants, noted from an early age for his piety and asceticism. As a child, his prayers helped save the village from drought through the miraculous appearance of a spring. He worked in the vineyards near Constantinople for some years, maintaining a strict and prayerful way of life. His master was so impressed that he released the boy from service, gave him a large sum of money, and asked him to go home and lead a life of prayer. Polychronius built a church with the money and settled nearby. After a few years he was ordained a priest and would have lived out his life in peace and prayer. However, he was present at the Council of Nicaea, where he defended Orthodoxy so fervently that, after the death of Emperor **Constantine**, a gang of Arian supporters attacked and killed him while he was celebrating the Divine Liturgy.

P

Procopius, Great Martyr (July 8)

Procopius was a soldier in the army of Diocletian by the name of Neanius. Sent as proconsul to Alexandria to persecute the Christians there, he had a vision of Christ that caused him to become a believer. His mother denounced him to the emperor, but when called before the procurator, he tore up the emperor's decree against the Christians. While in prison, he was baptized, taking the name Procopius. His courage in the face of torture converted many, including his mother, who was executed. He was beheaded in about 303. His story is often confused with some of the details of **Procopius the Reader**.

Procopius the Reader, Martyr (November 22)

Another Procopius is well documented through the writings of Eusebius, the church historian, who was a contemporary. He was born in Jerusalem but moved to Scythopolis, where he worked for the Church in various lowly but very useful ways. He was a gentle, humble man, willing to do whatever tasks were assigned to him and living mostly on bread and water. Eusebius tells us that "he had reduced his body until it looked like a corpse, but his soul drew from the Word of God such strength that the body was refreshed too."

At the beginning of Diocletian's persecution (about 303), Procopius was sent on a mission to Caesarea, where he was arrested and ordered to sacrifice to the gods. When he refused, the magistrate tried to persuade him at least to sacrifice to the emperor, but he again refused, surprisingly quoting Homer's *Iliad*: "A multitude of rulers is not a good thing. Let there be one ruler, one king."[52] He was at once beheaded. Eusebius wrote in his *Martyrs of Palestine*, "He passed happily to eternal life by the shortest road, in the first year of our persecution."

P

R

Raphael, Archangel (November 8, Synaxis of the Archangels)

Although not so well known as **Gabriel** and **Michael**, the Archangel Raphael is mentioned by name in the delightful Old Testament Book of Tobit. He is one of the seven archangels who hear the prayers of godly men and bring them before the Almighty. His name means "God heals," and elsewhere he is spoken of as healing the earth, defiled by the fallen angels. With the environmental problems in the world today, we could certainly do with some help from Raphael. Perhaps the Green Movement should adopt him as their patron. The healing aspects of Raphael's powers are recalled in the New Testament, where he is generally assumed to be the angel associated with the healing pool in the temple of Jerusalem (John 5:2–7).

Raphael, Bishop of Brooklyn (February 27, OCA; First Saturday in November, AOCA)

Raphael (Rafla) Hawaweeny was born in Syria in 1860 to pious Orthodox parents. At that time there were violent attacks on Christians in the area. The parish priest, St. Joseph of Damascus (July 10), and more than three thousand Orthodox Christians were martyred. The family fled to Beirut, where Raphael was born. As a young man, he proved to be an able student. After studies in Damascus, Constantinople, and Kiev, he was ordained a priest in 1889 and appointed head of the Antiochian Church in Moscow.

Raphael was an efficient and successful administrator, but soon became involved in church politics with unfortunate results. There was a growing movement in Syria for the Patriarch of Antioch to be appointed from the Syrian clergy rather than from outside the country. Raphael conducted a vigorous campaign for an Arab patriarch, and when Metropolitan Spyridon, a Greek Cypriot, was elected, he refused to commemorate the new patriarch in services. He also continued to write articles in support of the Arab cause. As a result he was suspended from his post and his duties as priest. The whole thing was getting out of hand until a hierarch of the Russian Church, a friend of Raphael's, persuaded him to seek forgiveness from the patriarch. The suspension was lifted, and he was allowed to transfer to the jurisdiction of the Russian Church, taking up a post as teacher of Arabic studies at the Kazan theological academy.

In 1895, Raphael was invited to become pastor of the Arab Orthodox community in New York. He quickly realized there were small communities of Arab Christians scattered across North America who had no spiritual guidance and were often forced either to neglect their religious duties completely or to attend churches of other denominations. From then until his death twenty years later, he worked tirelessly to organize these communities and bring them back into the Church fold.

In three long and exhausting pastoral tours across the continent, he visited cities, towns, and remote farms and villages, performing weddings and baptisms, hearing confessions, and celebrating the Divine Liturgy, often in someone's home. He regularized weddings of Orthodox married by non-Orthodox clergy and chrismated children baptized by Catholic priests. He established twenty-nine parishes. With the support of his bishop, he brought qualified priests from Syria and began to select suitable local candidates for ordination.

Before the turn of the century, one of Raphael's dreams came true when a Syrian Arab, Metropolitan Meletios Doumani, was elected Patriarch of Antioch, the first native-born primate for 168 years. In spite of several offers of promotion by the new patriarch, Raphael remained committed to his pastoral work in the USA, and in 1904 became the first Orthodox bishop to be consecrated in North America.

An indefatigable administrator, Raphael was also an accomplished scholar and author. Among his works is a service book in Arabic called *The Book of True Consolation in the Divine Prayer*, which, in English translation, is still in use today. Although his first concern was work among the Arab Orthodox, he also reached out to Orthodox from the Greek and Russian traditions, being fluent in

R

both languages. He was also fluent in English, and as Orthodoxy developed in America, was among the first to encourage its use in services to make them more meaningful to the younger generation, who were mainly born in the USA.

Raphael died in 1915 and was buried in New York. In 1989, his remains were transferred to the Antiochian Village Camp in Ligonier, Pennsylvania. Bishop Raphael was glorified by the Holy Synod of the Orthodox Church in America (OCA) in its March 2000 session.

Raphael, Nicholas, and Irene, New Martyrs of Lesbos (April 9, but usually held on Bright Tuesday, the Tuesday after Pascha)

Although martyred in 1463, these three New Martyrs of Greece were only recently canonized after the discovery of their bodies in 1959. A great deal of mystery surrounds this discovery, as after the first body was uncovered by archaeologists, many different people had dreams in which St. Raphael identified himself, told his story, and pointed out the locations of the other bodies—as well as of his head, which was buried separately. In every case, the remains were found exactly where he said they would be. Much of his story was later authenticated by scholars.

Raphael was the abbot of a small community at Thermi, about nine miles from Mytilene on the island of Lesbos. Nicholas was his deacon. In 1462, Lesbos was captured by the Turks, and during Holy Week 1463, they moved against Thermi. The local people fled to the mountains, but the community chief and his family remained hidden in the monastery. When the monastery was captured, the prisoners were tortured to make them reveal the whereabouts of the rest of the villagers. Among the victims was Irene, the twelve-year-old daughter of the community chief, who refused to talk in spite of having her hand cut off in front of her parents. She was then put in a large earthenware pot and burned to death. Raphael was also tortured, being beaten, stabbed with bayonets, and hung upside down from a tree. Then his jaw was cut off and he bled to death. The deacon, Nicholas, was also tied to a tree but mercifully died of a heart attack as he watched the torture of his beloved abbot.

Since 1963, when a convent was built on the site of the martyrdom, many miracles of healing have been reported, and the convent has become a major place of pilgrimage. It is certainly well worth a visit.

Romanos the Melodist (October 1)

The sixth century has been described as the golden age of Byzantine hymnography. Among many great hymn writers, Romanos was probably the greatest and certainly the most original. He was born in Emesa, Syria, in about 490 to Jewish parents, and was baptized a Christian as a young boy. Almost immediately he became deeply immersed in church life, and after moving to Beirut he became a deacon. Sometime later he moved to Constantinople, where he acted as sacristan at the Church of the Holy Wisdom, living in the monastery of Kyros. He remained there until his death in about 556.

Apparently, Romanos was a pretty hopeless reader and chanter but was highly respected by the patriarch (among others) for his piety, humility, and conscientiousness. He was therefore assigned an important reading from the Psalms at the Christmas Eve service one year. He made such a mess of it that another reader had to take his place, and many of the other clergy sneered at him. Utterly humiliated, he spent the night in tearful prayer before an icon of the **Mother of God**. During the night, he had a vision of the Virgin, who handed him a scroll, telling him to eat it. Romanos did so, and at the next morning's Nativity service he went straight to the pulpit and began singing, in a clear and tuneful voice, the hymn we now know as the Kontakion of the Nativity.

Romanos is reputed to have composed over one thousand hymns for various feasts, of which about eighty survive, although some of these may not be by him. The form that he more or less invented is the kontakion,* a long hymn that is a sort of sermon in verse accompanied by music. Although the music that originally accompanied the hymns has now been lost, we know that after the sermon, the preacher would recite the main body of the hymn, probably in some sort of recitative, while the choir and congregation would join in the chorus. The kontakia written by Romanos are vivid and dramatic, full of rich imagery and complex wordplay, a combination of dignity, drama, and liveliness. Although the full hymns are somewhat lengthy for modern tastes, the prologue and first verse of many are still used in Orthodox services, especially the wonderful Nativity Kontakion:

Today the Virgin gives birth to him who is above all being,
and the earth offers a cave to him whom no one can approach.

---

* The term, first used in the ninth century, derives from the word *kontos*, which was the shaft on which a scroll was wound.

Angels with shepherds give glory,
and magi journey with a star,
for to us there has been born
a little Child, God before the ages.

Bethlehem has opened Eden, come, let us see;
we have found delight in secret, come, let us receive
the joys of Paradise within the cave.
There the unwatered root whose blossom is forgiveness has appeared.
There has been found the undug well
from which David once longed to drink.
There a virgin has borne a babe
and has quenched at once Adam's and David's thirst.
For this, let us hasten to this place where there has been born
a little Child, God before the ages.[53]

S

Sabbas the Sanctified, Venerable (December 5)

An outstanding figure among the early monks and an important influence on Eastern monasticism, Sabbas entered a monastery as a child under the spiritual guidance of **St. Euthymius the Great**. At eighteen, he asked permission to become a hermit, but Euthymius told him he wasn't yet ready and should ask again when he was thirty. In the meantime, he was sent to a nearby monastery, where he trained himself rigorously for the life of a desert father. When he was thirty, Euthymius gave him permission to live for five days a week in a cave, but he had to return to the monastery each weekend. Nor was he allowed to devote himself entirely to prayer; he had to do practical labor, making ten wicker baskets a day for the monastery. The whole episode illustrates the sensible guidance of Euthymius and the lack of fanaticism and "other-worldliness" of the desert hermits.

After Euthymius's death, Sabbas spent four years alone in the desert before founding a loose community of hermits (a *lavra*) in about 478. He remained in the desert, founding other monasteries and building hospitals. He gained a reputation for great wisdom and was eventually given spiritual oversight of all the hermit monks in Palestine. He died at the age of ninety-four in 533, but the St. Sabbas Monastery (now called Mar Saba) is still in existence.

Sava (Sabas), First Archbishop of Serbia (January 14)

Born in about 1175, Sava was the third son of King Stephen I of Serbia. In 1191, having talked to some visiting monks from Mount Athos, he secretly left with them and became a monk. Four years later, his father, worn out with the duties and troubles of kingship, abdicated the throne in favor of his two older sons and joined Sava on the Holy Mountain, taking the monastic name Simeon. Together, father and son set up the Monastery of Hilandari for Serbian monks. This still exists as one of the seventeen ruling monasteries of Mount Athos, ranked fourth in the hierarchy. Simeon died in 1199 and is also a saint in the Orthodox Church (February 13).

By 1208, infighting and rivalry between Sava's two brothers had reduced Serbia to a state of near-anarchy, and Sava was asked to return to the country to help restore order. This he did, attacking on two fronts. With help from a group of monks who accompanied him, he reorganized the Church and set it on solid foundations, based on canon law and the rulings of the Ecumenical Councils. So successful were his efforts that Sava was able to seek and obtain emancipation for the Serbian Church from the Greek Archbishopric, and in 1219 he was consecrated as the first Archbishop of Serbia.

At the same time, he used his considerable diplomatic and organizational skills in the secular reorganization and integration of the Serbian kingdom, writing Serbia's first constitution. He founded schools throughout the country and generally brought stability to an often lawless land—even, it is said, involving himself in the improvement of agricultural methods to increase productivity. To Sava, the secular and spiritual were two sides of the same coin. "If you listen to me," he said, "and if God enables me to do good among you, if you become holy and one in God, there will be twofold gain and salvation will be ours." In spite of his hectic life, Sava remained at heart a monk. He would often retire from public life to a remote hermitage to gain strength and recharge his spiritual batteries. Active to the last, he died of pneumonia in 1235 at Trnovo in Bulgaria on the way back from Jerusalem, where he had gone to found a hospice for Serbian pilgrims.

Sava was buried in the Cathedral of Trnovo, but on May 6, 1237, his relics were transferred to the Monastery of Mileseva in Serbia. Many miracles of healing were reported at Sava's grave, and by the sixteenth century, not only Serbs but Turks and Jews were visiting the monastery in search of healing. In 1594, however, as punishment for an uprising, the Turks dug up Sava's remains and burned them. The Cathedral of St. Sava in Belgrade was built on the site of the desecration. Begun in 1939 but not completed until 2004, it is the largest Orthodox church in the world at the time of writing.

St. Sava is, of course, the patron saint of Serbia and in particular the protector of Serb schools and schoolchildren. Under the influence of St. Sava the Enlightener, Serbs, Greeks, and Latin speakers began to live together in peace, and he is still loved and revered as a saint by Orthodox and honored by Roman Catholics in Serbia. There are discrepancies in the date of St. Sava's passing away, but at present in the Serbian Orthodox Church the official date is January 14.

Additional Feast Day: May 6 (Transfer of Relics)

Seraphim the Wonderworker of Sarov, Venerable (January 2)

From the earliest times, spiritual fathers (and mothers) have withdrawn from the world for a period of prayer and solitary contemplation in order to return to the world as advisers and healers, both spiritual and physical. From **St. Anthony** onwards, such elders, in Russian called *starets* (Greek *geron*), have had a tremendous influence on the development of Christianity.

The greatest of the nineteenth-century elders was St. Seraphim, who, along with **Theodosius of the Caves** and **Sergius of Radonezh**, is one of the three great Russian saints. Born in Kursk in 1759, the son of a builder, Seraphim became a monk at nineteen. He began by spending sixteen years in the ordinary daily life of the community and was ordained a priest in 1793. For the next twenty years, he withdrew to live in seclusion in the forest, once emulating **St. Simon the Stylite** by taking up residence on a stone slab, where he remained for one thousand days and nights, only leaving it for the essentials of life. He then moved into the "luxury" of a wooden shack in the forest, growing vegetables, felling trees, keeping bees, studying, and praying.

He carried the Holy Gospels with him, reading the whole of the New Testament each week, and regularly studied the writings of the Holy Fathers. While at work he either sang hymns or practiced the Jesus Prayer: "Lord Jesus Christ, Son of God, have mercy on me." He maintained a strict fast, eating only once a day with nothing at all on Wednesdays and Fridays, and had frequent visions in which he met and talked with **Peter** and **John** and sometimes the **Virgin Mary**. However, he never considered himself anything special: "The Kingdom of God

Traveling Companions

S

is within us all," he wrote, "and only through the Holy Spirit can come the joy of complete tranquility and the inner peace which comes with faith."

In 1804, he was badly beaten up by robbers who mistakenly believed he had treasure hidden in his shack. Close to death and suffering severely from shock, he was cared for in the monastery for five months but then returned to his solitude, begging that the robbers not be punished. However, the injuries he had suffered meant that he could never stand up straight again. By 1810, his strength was failing and he was no longer able to walk to the monastery for Sunday services. He returned to the monastery but, with the abbot's permission, lived in an enclosed cell, even eating his meals and receiving Holy Communion alone. In 1815, he opened the door but continued in silence, teaching by example only until, in 1825, following a vision of the Mother of God, he ended his seclusion to devote himself to others.

From then until his death, he received all who came for help, healing the sick and giving spiritual advice, often giving the answer before the question was asked. Although severely ascetic himself, Seraphim was always gentle and kind to others and always full of joy. At all times of the year, he would greet people cheerfully with the Paschal words, "Christ is Risen, my joy." He especially loved children and delighted in their company. One young girl perceptively remarked, "Father Seraphim only looks like an old man. He is really a child like us." Sometimes the joy of the Holy Spirit took visible form, transfiguring his body as if it were full of light. The most well-known of these manifestations has been described fully by Nicholas Motovilov, one of his spiritual children: "I glanced at his face and there came over me an even greater reverent awe. Imagine in the center of the sun, in the dazzling light of its midday rays, the face of a man talking to you."[54] Seraphim died peacefully at prayer in 1833, having already prepared his coffin and decided on his burial place.

Seraphim was glorified in 1903 at a special church service during which his relics were exposed for public veneration. After the revolution, the relics disappeared but were rediscovered in 1991 in a Soviet museum, where they had been hidden for seventy years. Although he is only formally revered as a saint in the Orthodox Church, Christians of all denominations honor him, and Pope John Paul II refers to him as a saint in his book, *Crossing the Threshold of Hope*.

Additional Feast Day: July 19 (Uncovering of Relics)

Sergius, Abbot and Wonderworker of Radonezh
(September 25)

Sergius holds a special place both in the history of Russian monasticism and, surprisingly, in the political development of the Russian Empire. He was born near Rostov in 1314 (or 1319 or 1322—accounts differ) into a wealthy landowning family and given the name Bartholomew. In about 1328, the family lost all its property and was forced to move to Radonezh, northeast of Moscow. After the death of his parents about nine years later, Bartholomew was tonsured a monk with the name Sergius and ordained a priest. Together with his widowed brother Stephen, he went off to lead a secluded life deep in the nearby forest.

It wasn't long before Stephen found the harsh Russian winter, the lack of food, and the marauding wild animals too much to handle and returned to Moscow to join a regular monastery. Sergius remained on his own in his cell, where he befriended the wild animals, even, it is reported, feeding wolves and bears from his meager supplies. As people heard of him, disciples began to gather, and eventually the hermitage and the chapel of the Holy Trinity developed into a regular lavra.

The Monastery of the Holy Trinity marked a new beginning for Russian monasticism, which had almost disappeared during the Tatar invasions, and it became a model for northern Russian monastic life, just as the Kiev Caves had been a model in the south (see **Theodosius**). Sergius continued to live a very simple life even as abbot, one visitor complaining bitterly, "I came to see a prophet and you show me a beggar." By most, however, he was deeply loved as "one of the people." "In character, if not by origin, he was a 'peasant soul': simple, humble, grave and gentle, neighborly."[55] Sergius's influence was such that, in 1378, he was offered the Patriarchate of Moscow, but he refused: "Since the days of my youth," he said, "I have never worn gold. Now that I am an old man, more than ever I adhere to my poverty." However, he did use his influence to keep the peace between the princes. He encouraged the expansion of Moscow and resistance to the Tatars.

Sergius has been called a "Builder of Russia," and it is certainly true that he was indirectly responsible for the expansion of Russian boundaries further and further to the north and northeast. The process was as follows: Having looked for solitude in the wilderness, Sergius ended up founding a monastery, around which a small town developed. Some of his disciples, in turn, wanting to escape the town, moved further away into more distant forests. New communities would form, fresh land would be cleared, and soon new towns would grow up. And so on. It has been said that the British Empire was largely acquired "in a fit of absence of mind," and it certainly seems that large parts of the Russian Empire developed in much the same way. At least fifty communities were founded by disciples of Sergius in his own lifetime and forty more by the next generation of hermit missionaries.

Together with his practical influence, Sergius also gave to the Russian Church a new dimension of spirituality. He often had visions of the **Virgin Mary** and sometimes exhibited the transfiguration noted in other mystics. "Better perhaps than any other Russian saint, he succeeded in balancing the social and mystical aspects of monasticism. Under his influence and that of his followers, the two centuries from 1350 to 1550 proved a golden age in Russian spirituality."[56] In 1382, Sergius resigned as abbot to live the rest of his life in peace. He died in 1392, by which time the Holy Trinity Monastery had become the most renowned in Russia. In honor of this deeply loved saint, the monastery was renamed the Trinity-Sergius Lavra. His shrine in the monastery is still a place of pilgrimage.

Additional Feast Day: July 5 (Finding of Relics)

Sergius of Valaam, Enlightener of Karelia (June 28, with St. Herman)

Although he was a major figure in the history of Orthodoxy in northern Russia and Finland, there is no certainty about when Sergius lived. We can be reasonably sure that he was sent by the Byzantine emperor to convert the Karelian tribes around Lake Ladoga and that he settled on Valaam Island, an area sacred to the pagan tribes. However, whether this was in 992 or as late as 1329 is by no means clear. Together with Herman, a Karelian who may have been one of his converts, he is believed to have founded the famous Valaam Monastery which later played such an important part in Russian monasticism and missionary work. According to one tradition, Sergius died in 1353 and was buried in his monastery. Another story, however, states that his relics were taken to Novgorod in about 1162 to protect them from the invading Swedes and were

S

returned to Valaam in about 1180. So it is a confusing and incomplete story, but it is probably enough to know that Sergius bravely settled in hostile lands and successfully preached the Gospel, beginning the Christianization of Karelia and Finland.

Additional Feast Days: September 11 (Translation of Relics)

Saturday between October 31 and November 6 (All Enlighteners of Karelia)

Seven Sleepers of Ephesus (August 4, Falling Asleep; October 22, Awakening)

One of the most mysterious stories from the early days of Christianity, the story of the Seven Sleepers has links with both mythology and Islam and has appeared in the literature of many countries. However, the Seven are widely venerated in the Orthodox Church, and their adventure has been of immense importance in the debate about the physical resurrection of the body.

During the reign of Decius, there were seven young men of Ephesus: Maximilian, Iamblicus, Martinian, John, Dionysius, Constantine, and Antoninus. All were from prominent families and were friends from childhood, eventually serving as soldiers together. They were all Christians, and when Decius's persecution began, they were denounced, arrested, and stripped of their military rank. The emperor, however, allowed them to be freed while he went on a campaign, hoping they would "see reason" by the time he returned. Although the seven friends knew their time was limited, they hid out in a cave, where they spent their time in prayer, awaiting their fate. The youngest, Iamblicus, was sent into the town to buy bread and found out that the emperor had returned. But before they could give themselves up, Decius ordered the cave to be sealed, leaving the seven to starve to death. However, two secret Christians hid a brass plaque in the mouth of the cave, inscribed with the names of the martyrs and the story of their death.

Two hundred years passed, and Christianity became the state religion of the Byzantine Empire. During the reign of Theodosius the Younger (408–450), a dispute arose in the Church about the resurrection of the dead. All Christians, of course, believed in life after death, but some argued that the physical body could not be resurrected because it would eventually decay into dust.

At about this time, some workmen found the entrance to the cave and opened it up. The seven awoke from their "sleep," thinking they had only been asleep one

Traveling Companions

S

day. Not realizing what had happened, they sent Iamblicus into town, where he was astounded to see a cross on the gates and to hear the name of Jesus spoken openly in the street. He tried to buy bread with a coin of the time of Decius and was taken to the Bishop of Ephesus to explain how he had come by such a coin. When the bishop went with him to the cave, he saw that the others were all in good health and their clothing intact. He read the plaque and realized that a miracle had occurred which demonstrated the power of God and the possibility of the bodily resurrection of the dead. The seven then lay down on the ground and fell asleep again, this time to await the general resurrection.

As well as the two feast days, the Seven are also commemorated in prayers on September 1, the beginning of the church year.

Silas, Apostle of the Seventy (July 30)

Silas, sometimes referred to by the Latin name Silvanus, was a highly respected member of the early Church in Jerusalem, one of the "leading men among the brethren" (Acts 15:22). He was present at the Council of Jerusalem, where the question of whether Gentiles needed to be circumcised to become Christians was settled. Along with **Jude**, he was then given the sensitive task of delivering the conclusion of the council to Antioch so that it could be explained in more detail (Acts 15:22–33).

Silas remained in Antioch for a time and then joined **Paul** on his missionary journeys to Syria, Cilicia, and Macedonia. In Philippi, Macedonia, the two apostles had one of their more dramatic adventures. Accused of inciting unrest, they were arrested, flogged, and thrown into prison. While they were at prayer at midnight, a powerful earthquake caused their chains to be loosened and the doors to be destroyed. When things calmed down, the guard assumed the prisoners had escaped and was about to kill himself. Paul shouted out, "Don't harm yourself! We are all here," and indeed Paul and Silas were still sitting quietly in their cell. The guard took them back to his house, where they spent some time preaching the Gospel to him and his family, with the result that the whole household sought baptism (Acts 16:19–40). Silas was later consecrated Bishop of Corinth, where he died in about 50.

S

Silouan the Athonite, Venerable (September 24)

Sometimes called Silouan of Mount Athos, this modern saint was born Simeon Antonov in 1866 in Russia. He became a monk at the Monastery of St. Panteleimon on Mount Athos at the age of twenty-seven, taking the name Silouan, the Russian version of the biblical name Silvanus. He spent the rest of his life in the monastery, remaining an ordinary monk and never being ordained a priest. He died in 1938. This completely uneventful outer life hides the extraordinary inner life of a deeply loved and loving man of God who, in spite of being almost illiterate, "left behind him some deeply moving meditations, poetic in style, and profound in their theological vision."[57] Much of his spiritual wisdom was edited and published by his disciple, Archimandrite Sophrony.[58]

Elders and spiritual fathers are not made overnight, however, and Silouan spent many years in heartbreaking spiritual struggles against pride as well as doubt in the effectiveness and value of his prayers. When quite a young monk, he became popular among the brothers for his patience and mild nature, and among his superiors for his hard work and obedience. This, however, caused him to feel in danger of the sin of pride. He began a vicious circle of repentance, prayer, and feeling that his sins were forgiven, followed by a feeling of pride in leading a saintly life. Eventually, he reached the edge of despair, feeling that it was impossible to reach God through prayer. At this point he had a vision of the Living Christ, which set him once more on the right path.

Out of his continuing struggles, Silouan gradually developed the three great themes of his faith: humility, love for all mankind, and the absolute necessity of continuous prayer. "It is through prayer that we feel the grace of the Holy Spirit. Prayer saves man from sin, for a praying mind is busy with God and stands in humility before the Lord." Conscious of his own sin, he could feel nothing but pity for other sinners, which for him meant everyone in the world. He pointed out that true inner peace can only be attained through humility and love: "If we adapt to diligent prayer for our enemies and love for them, then peace will ever be in our souls; and if we should hate and condemn our brethren, then our minds shall become clouded and they will both lose inner peace. . . . The heart that has learned to love has pity for all creation."

Silouan summed up the shortest and easiest path to salvation in a simple but powerful sentence: "Be obedient and temperate, do not judge, and keep your mind and heart free of evil thoughts; believe instead that all people are kind and

S

that God loves them. For these humble thoughts the grace of the Holy Spirit will live within you." Silouan was regarded in his lifetime as a great spiritual guide and elder, and even the famous Roman Catholic monk Thomas Merton called him "the most authentic monk of the twentieth century." He was glorified by the Ecumenical Patriarch in 1987.

Simeon "Salus" of Emesa, Venerable (July 21)

Another fool for Christ like **Basil the Blessed**, Simeon was a monk and hermit living in Syria in the late sixth century. After twenty-nine years of ascetic isolation, he decided he had reached a level of detachment from the world that would enable him to rejoin it and help others. He devoted his life to caring for the most wretched outcasts of society, especially prostitutes. Rather than being a "do-gooder," however, he identified completely with the most despised, dressing in rags and stealing from shops to give food to the destitute. He was also gifted with considerable spiritual insight and had the rather disconcerting habit of prancing up to strangers in the street and whispering the sins they had committed in their ears, always with an uncanny accuracy. However, whatever good works he did were hidden under a cloak of utterly outrageous behavior that earned him the nickname *Salus* ("crazy"). He would sit at the back of the church during services and throw nuts at the priest, or run up and blow out the candles. On solemn fast days, he would eat vast quantities of beans with predictably noisy results.

Although to most people he was a scandalous eccentric, to many others he was a holy and prophetic figure, whose "insanity" lay merely in his complete rejection of polite behavior for the sake of Christian charity and love and to make people repent of their sins. He died when nearly seventy in 590, and it was only after his death that his deep spirituality and the true extent of his good works gradually came to light. Even some of his ways of helping, however, showed Simeon's characteristic oddity. He miraculously turned a poor mule driver's vinegar stock into wine, enabling him to start a successful tavern; he saved a rich man from death by throwing a lucky triple six at dice; to save a young man from an affair with a married woman, he punched him on the jaw and knocked him out. Recently, the eccentric English preacher Philip Howard was given an Antisocial Behavior Order (ASBO)* for reading the Bible through a loudspeaker to

---

* A legal penalty in Britain designed to cut down on hooliganism.

S

passers-by in Oxford Circus, London. I wonder what the present-day authorities would make of Simeon.*

Simeon, the God-Receiver, and Anna, Righteous Prophetess (February 3, the day after the Presentation of Christ in the Temple)

Forty days after His birth, Jesus was presented in the temple at Jerusalem, in accordance with Jewish custom. Here two aging prophets, Simeon and Anna, recognized the baby as the longed-for Messiah. In fact, Simeon, a just and devout man, had been promised by the Holy Spirit that he would not see death until he had seen the Messiah. Taking the Babe in his arms, he spoke the beautiful words still used in Evening Prayers in the Orthodox, Roman Catholic, and Anglican Churches:

> Lord, now You are letting Your servant depart in peace,
> According to Your Word;
> For my eyes have seen Your salvation
> Which You have prepared before the face of all peoples,
> A light to bring revelation to the Gentiles,
> And the glory of Your people Israel.

Anna, a widow of eighty-four years, lived in the temple, fasting and praying day and night. Seeing the baby Jesus, she also thanked God and prophesied the redemption of Jerusalem (Luke 2:22–39).

Simon the Zealot, Holy Apostle (May 10)

Since Simon is only mentioned as a name in the New Testament, a host of stories and legends have grown up about him. I have tried to piece together the main beliefs about the "mystery apostle" as taught in the Orthodox Church, but even these accounts vary.

Born in Cana, Galilee, Simon was in his youth a Zealot, a radical nationalist,

Traveling Companions

S

---

* I do sometimes think that if Our Lord returned to earth today in the Western world, preaching that we should give away all our possessions to the poor and love our enemies, He would very soon find Himself placed in psychiatric care.

possibly a member of a group seeking the liberation of Palestine from the Romans. He was an acquaintance of Jesus and **His Mother** and may have been the bridegroom at the wedding feast in Cana where Christ performed His first miracle. It could well have been this dramatic miracle of turning water into wine that persuaded him to follow Jesus. Having realized that the Messiah was not seeking a political revolution but a spiritual one, he became a zealous supporter of the Lord, a zealot in a new way.

Little is known of his later life, but he may have preached the Gospel in Mauretania and in the region of the Black Sea. One tradition even claims that he was martyred in Britain at Caistor in Norfolk, but there is absolutely no evidence for this. He is generally believed to have ended his mission in Georgia and been martyred by crucifixion in Abkhazia.

Simon (or Simeon) Stylites the Elder (September 1)

Born in Cilicia about 390, Simon was the first and most famous of the "pillar ascetics" (*stylos* means "pillar" in Greek). He was the son of a shepherd and, from an early age, practiced fasting and bodily austerity. He spent some time staying in various monasteries, working as the lowest of servants and deeply loved by all he came into contact with. All the time he sought a stricter and more rigorous life. At one point, he decided to eat nothing at all during Lent, but fortunately a priest found out and wisely kept watch to make sure he didn't starve himself to death.

This somewhat fanatical asceticism mellowed with age, but his search for seclusion continued. In 423, "despairing of escaping the world horizontally, he tried to escape it vertically," and took to living on a low pillar at Telamissus in Syria. Over the years, he increased the height of the pillar to about 60 feet, with a twelve-foot-square platform at the top surrounded by a balustrade. He spent the remaining thirty-six years of his life on the pillar. After his death in 461, a monastery and sanctuary were built over the spot, and the base of Simon's column can still be seen in the ruins.

Simon built his pillar to avoid the crowds of people who came to him for his prayers and advice, but in fact it attracted more and more people, including the emperor, either as pilgrims or as sightseers. Every afternoon he put himself at their disposal, teaching, preaching, and giving advice. He was a kind man, full of sympathy for human failings, and in spite of his eccentric mode of living, he was entirely free of fanaticism and full of practical common sense. When a pilgrim couldn't believe he was human and thought he must be an angelic spirit, Simon invited him to climb the pillar and examine the sores on his feet. He brought about many conversions, especially among the Bedouin Arabs, and his fame spread far beyond Syria. People who couldn't make the long journey consulted him by letter. "In an age and land of license and luxury, Simon bore witness to the claims of virtue and selflessness in so striking a fashion that no one could fail to see it."[59]

Simon had several later imitators, including Daniel (December 11) and another Simon, the Younger (May 24). The former, a disciple of Simon, lived on his pillar for thirty-three years. He refused to come down even for his ordination as a priest, and the Patriarch of Constantinople was forced to climb up the pillar for the laying on of hands. He was the trusted advisor of two emperors, and the only occasion on which he ever descended from the pillar was to reprove one of them for his sins.

Sophia, Pistis, Elpis, and Agape, Martyrs (September 17)

Few details are known about these martyrs, but their names are popular in Greece because of their meanings. Sophia ("Wisdom") was a widow in Rome in the time of Hadrian and a respected and popular figure in the clandestine Christian community. She was the mother of three daughters: Pistis ("Faith"), aged twelve, Elpis ("Hope"), aged ten, and Agape ("Love"), aged nine. In about 126, she was arrested together with her daughters. The authorities hoped the mother would recant in order to save her children. However, young as they were, they stood by her in refusing to reject their faith. In spite of Sophia's pleas to the authorities, the girls were tortured and executed in front of their mother. She was allowed to take the bodies for burial, and overcome with grief, she sat by the grave for three days and then died herself. Although Sophia was not executed, she is counted among the martyrs because of the torment she endured watching her little girls die.

Sozon of Cilicia, Martyr (September 7)

The bravery of youth in the face of persecution is charmingly illustrated by the story of Sozon, a lesser-known saint and contemporary of **Agnes**. He was a young shepherd boy in Cilicia who, following a dream, marched to the main town of the area and into the pagan temple. There, he used his crook to smash an enormous golden idol and, breaking off one of its hands, gave the pieces of gold to the poor in the town. When some other Christians were arrested for the offense, he turned himself in and confessed. The magistrate ordered nails to be driven up through the soles of his shoes, and he was forced to walk to the amphitheater. His courage impressed the magistrate, who, looking for an excuse to release him, asked him to play his pipe for the audience. Sozon's reply was brief and cheeky: "I used to play for the sheep. Now I will play only for God." For this "impudence," he was burned to death.

Spyridon of Corfu (Kerkyra), Wonderworker (December 12)

Spyridon was a Cypriot shepherd, humble but of deep faith. Although not ordained, he preached the Gospel widely and became so admired by his fellow Christians that they elected him Bishop of Tremithus in Cyprus. Despite being uneducated and rough in manner, Spyridon was also shrewd and straightforward, embodying a sort of "no-nonsense" Christianity with no frills, in contrast to the subtlety and pomp of the imperial court.

At the Council of Nicaea, the assembled bishops were astonished by his peasant dress, but even more by his simple but cogent statement of the Orthodox doctrine. At one point, he used a broken piece of pottery to illustrate the doctrine of the Holy Trinity, showing how a single entity, pottery, could be composed of three unique entities, fire, water, and clay. In icons, he is depicted in his bishop's regalia but wearing a simple peasant's straw hat. Spyridon was the epitome of the bishop as pastor* rather than ruler and was greatly loved by his flock until his death in about 348 at the age of seventy-eight.

One revealing story about him is that he was once celebrating the Divine Liturgy in a remote and empty church, accompanied only by a deacon. He nevertheless followed the complete service, and when he turned to the nonexistent congregation to say, "Peace be unto all," the deacon clearly heard a choir of angels respond, "And with thy spirit"—surely a vivid example of the unseen congregation. On another occasion, a band of robbers broke into his sheepfold one night but found they couldn't get out. When Spyridon found

---

* Literally. He continued to tend his sheep, even as a bishop!

them in the morning, he freed them, told them to live honestly in future, and gave them two sheep as compensation for keeping "an all-night vigil."

Spyridon's remains were removed to Constantinople in the sixth century as a result of barbarian raids, but when the city fell in 1453, they were taken to Corfu in the Ionian Islands. They remain there to this day, and his body is said to be uncorrupted still after 1600 years. He is revered as the special protector of Corfu and is called the "Keeper of the City."

Additional Feast Day: Cheesefare Sunday (Sunday before Lent)

Stephen, Protomartyr and Apostle of the Seventy (December 27)

The story of the first Christian martyr is well documented in Acts 6—7. Stephen was a Greek-speaking Jew appointed by the apostles to be one of seven deacons with special responsibility for the care of widows. He was also a fearless preacher and was eventually charged with blasphemy by the Jewish council of elders. At his trial, he made a powerful speech in defense of the truth of Christ's teaching, quoting at length from the Hebrew Scriptures and pulling no punches: "Which of the prophets did your fathers not persecute? And they killed those who foretold the coming of the Just One, of whom you now have become the betrayers and murderers."

His outspokenness did not go down well with the elders, and he was dragged outside the city, where he was stoned to death. As the stones rained down, he prayed, "Lord Jesus, receive my spirit," and just as he died, he echoed the words of his Savior: "Lord, do not charge them with this sin." Stephen's nobility in the face of death was the inspiration of the thousands of martyrs who came after him. Among the bystanders at his death, looking after the clothes, was Saul of Tarsus, a fanatical persecutor of Christians, later to be converted himself under the name of **Paul**. Stephen's relics were preserved, and a feast honoring their interment is kept on August 2. Another feast on September 15 commemorates the uncovering of his relics in 415.

Additional Feast Day: August 2 (Interment of Relics)
September 15 (Uncovering of Relics)

Traveling Companions

S

237

Stephen the Confessor, Monk-martyr (November 28)

The story of Stephen the Confessor is a vivid illustration of the bitterness surrounding the iconoclast controversy. In 761, Emperor Constantine V revived the iconoclast laws. Stephen, a hermit living near Constantinople, was one of the staunchest defenders of the holy images. He spoke out against the edicts of the emperor and for this was banished to a tiny island in the Sea of Marmara for three years. Eventually brought before the emperor for interrogation, he took out a coin and asked, "Is it not wrong to show disrespect to the image of the emperor shown here? How much more, then, does he deserve punishment who stamps on an image of Christ or his mother and burns it?" (a common practice among the iconoclasts). He threw the coin on the floor and trampled on it. He was then thrown into jail, where he remained for eleven months with over three hundred other monks, leading a kind of monastic life together. The emperor was unwilling to order his execution outright, but as with Henry II and Thomas à Becket in England, he dropped such strong hints about the "troublesome monk" that some of his followers battered Stephen to death in his cell in 767.

Stephen, Bishop of Perm, Venerable (April 26)

One of the great missionaries of Russia, Stephen was born in about 1340 in Ustiug. As a boy, he would often meet with Zyrians from the pagan area to the northeast and developed a strong ambition to convert these tribes. He entered a monastery in Rostov in 1365 and spent the next seventeen years preparing for a missionary life. The library at the monastery was famous throughout the Russian lands, and Stephen, having studied Greek, was able to immerse himself in the writings of the Holy Fathers of Orthodoxy. He also studied the local dialects of the tribes and set about translating the church books and Gospels. He first had to create a Zyrian alphabet, which he based on native runes, traditional carvings, and designs from embroidery.

Having been ordained a priest in 1379, he set off on his mission. His journey into Zyrian lands was arduous and dangerous, but he eventually settled in a cell and began to preach the Gospel. Among the idols worshipped by the Zyrians was an enormous birch tree growing on top of a hill. Stephen took his courage in both hands and set fire to the tree, considering that he would either quickly find a martyr's death or make a dramatic impact on the pagans. "Judge for yourselves,"

S

he said, "whether or not your gods have any power, since they are not able to defend themselves from the fire. Can they be gods when they are so powerless? ... The Christian God is not like this."

His courage and the logic of his words began to convince many of the tribesmen, and he converted and baptized quite a number. He felt confident enough to build a church on the site of the birch tree, dedicated to the **Archangel Michael**, "vanquisher of the spirits of darkness." All was not smooth sailing, however, and one of the shamans, Pama, tried to halt the spread of Christianity. He argued that, while the Christians had only one God, animists had spirits in every tree and river, ensuring good hunting and revealing magic mysteries inaccessible to Stephen. After a lengthy debate, Pama challenged Stephen to an ordeal by fire and water as a test of faith. To his surprise, Stephen accepted the challenge, whereupon Pama lost his nerve and backed out, leaving the field to the Christian. From then on, the Church spread rapidly, and in 1383, Stephen was consecrated Bishop of Perm.

He then set about vigorously consolidating the Christian Church in the area, opening schools where the Gospel was taught in the Zyrian language, training young men for the priesthood, and building churches for them. He also founded several monasteries. He was a firm believer that the Christian God is a God of beauty as well as truth and used his talents as an icon painter to beautify the churches. Like all good missionaries, he was a fearless defender of "his" people against oppression from Moscow and Novgorod, and often had to travel to these cities to protect local interests.

On one such trip in 1390, a strange and touching event occurred. Stephen, who was a fervent admirer of **Sergius of Radonezh**, was on his way to Moscow and wanted to visit Sergius. Since he had no time for the diversion, about four miles from Sergius's monastery, he turned in its direction, bowed, and said, "Peace to you, my spiritual brother." At the same time, Sergius, who was eating with his fellow monks, stood up, bowed in the direction Stephen was riding, and answered, "Hail also to you, pastor of the flock of Christ, may the peace of God be with you."

In 1395, Stephen was again on a visit to Moscow when he died. He was buried in the Church of the Transfiguration in the Kremlin, where he remained in spite of pleas by the Zyrians to transfer the relics of their "father" to the land he loved.

Traveling Companions

S

Stylianus of Paphlagonia, Venerable (November 26)

Born in Adrianopolis sometime in the fifth or sixth century, Stylianus was from a wealthy family.[60] When his parents died, he inherited a great deal of money but felt called upon to give it all away and become a hermit in the desert. He didn't cut himself off from the world, however, but would go out into society to help wherever and however he could, retreating to his cave from time to time to refresh himself spiritually. He possessed considerable healing powers, and his cave quickly became a magnet for those in need. He turned nobody away, but his first concern was always the spiritual and physical health of the children. He took the beautiful words of Jesus as his motto: "Let the little children come to Me, and do not forbid them; for of such is the kingdom of heaven" (Matthew 19:14). So many families entrusted their children to him for guidance and care that he had to enlist the help of his fellow hermits, forming what has been called "the first day-care center in the world."[61] His prayers also seemed effective in helping infertile women. As always, there were plenty of people around who tried to commercialize his gift, but he refused all attempts to make money, saying simply that he had already been paid in advance with the serenity the Holy Spirit had given him. He was never without a smile, and when he died, it is said that his face still bore a faint smile as they buried him. A loving and loved man of God, Stylianus is, of course, special protector of children.

T

Tabitha the Merciful (October 25)

When giving the apostles their commission to preach the Gospel, Jesus also gave them authority to perform miracles in His name: "Heal the sick, cleanse the lepers, raise the dead, cast out demons" (Matthew 10:8). Acts includes several examples of healing miracles, but the story of Tabitha is the only recorded case of one of the Twelve Apostles raising the dead (Acts 9:36–43).

Tabitha (called Dorcas in Greek) was a disciple living in Joppa (modern Jaffa). She seems to have been an important figure in the early Church in that area, well known for her charity and her habit of making clothes for the poor.* When she died, the **Apostle Peter** happened to be in Lydda, about ten miles away, and when he heard the news, he immediately hurried to Joppa. At Tabitha's house, he sent all the mourners from the room where she lay and then knelt and prayed. Then he turned to the body and simply said, "Tabitha, arise." Tabitha opened her eyes, sat up, and taking Peter's hand, got out of bed. In his typical understated manner, Luke concludes the story of this amazing miracle with the simple words, "When he had called the saints and widows, he presented her alive. And it became known throughout all Joppa, and many believed on the Lord."

---

* Groups of charitable women who do needlework and knitting are often known as Dorcas Circles in Protestant churches.

Tatiana of Rome, Martyr (January 12)

Tatiana's father was a member of the landed aristocracy of Rome and three times a consul. He had embraced Christianity but, like many others, kept his beliefs secret. He was a deacon of the secret Church, and his daughter grew up to help him in his work, eventually being made a deaconess herself at an early age. She became so familiar with the maze of catacombs under the streets of Rome that she became a living map of the secret meeting and hiding places used by the Christians.

When her father was betrayed to Emperor Severus Alexander, there was no real evidence against him, and he would probably have been released had he kept silent. However, he pleaded guilty "to love for my fellow man through Jesus Christ the Savior" and was executed. Tatiana was arrested a short time later. The emperor decided that the recantation of such a pretty, aristocratic girl would be more valuable than her execution and used all his considerable skills to convince her. Failing in this, he had the girl placed under armed guard in one of the temples, where she was ordered to bow to the statues. Still defiant, she was flogged to the point of collapse and fell to her knees begging God, not for help, but to demonstrate His strength. It is reported that the earth shook and all the statues crashed to the floor. When order was restored, Tatiana was taken into the street and executed. She was just nineteen.

In Russia, Belarus, and the Ukraine, Tatiana is the patron of students, and her feast day ("Students' Day") is a public holiday.

Thecla, Protomartyr and Equal to the Apostles (September 24)

Although Thecla certainly existed, many of the stories about her life are probably pious fables to illustrate the virtues of chastity in a later, somewhat licentious era. The main source of information about her life is the apocryphal *Acts of Paul and Thecla*, written in the second century, but there is also some circumstantial evidence from early tombs and inscriptions.

Thecla was a native of Iconium who, after hearing the preaching of **St. Paul** on the subject of chastity, decided to devote herself to Christ and the preaching of His Gospel. Her mother and fiancé complained to the city authorities that

Paul had turned her against her betrothed, and Paul was imprisoned. Thecla bribed her way into the prison, where she stayed for three days, receiving further counsel and teaching from Paul. When he was banished, she was again urged to consent to the marriage, but still refused and was sentenced to death by burning. However, a sudden violent thunderstorm extinguished the flames, and she was able to escape. She eventually joined Paul and **Barnabas**, accompanying them on their mission to Antioch. Here she was again arrested and sentenced to death in the arena. The animals, however, refused to attack her, and she again escaped death.

Through many persecutions, Thecla continued her mission among the pagans of Seleucia, where she lived for many years, preaching and healing the sick through prayer but frequently suffering imprisonment and torture. Nevertheless, she seems to have survived to a great age. Yet due to the extent of her suffering, she is counted as the first female martyr. At the age of ninety, she was again attacked, this time by pagan sorcerers angry at her gift of healing. According to tradition, she ran to a cliff face, which split open to hide her. Near the site in Maaloula, Syria, a Greek Orthodox convent was built that remains to this day. For her missionary work, she is also counted as "Equal to the Apostles." As "the glory of women and guide for the suffering, opening up the way through every torment," Thecla is also venerated as an intercessor for ascetics. Her name is invoked during the tonsure of women into monastic orders.

Theodora of Alexandria, Venerable (September 11)

Theodora lived in fifth-century Alexandria. As a young woman, she committed adultery, but was then so filled with remorse that she could no longer face her husband and ran away. Fearing her husband would be able to track her down in a convent, she dressed as a man and found refuge in a monastery under the name Theodore. There she spent nine years in fasting, prayer, and vigils in repentance for that one sin. Her secret was only discovered after her early death, and her husband attended the funeral. It may be that he felt he had played a part in Theodora's flight and felt remorse for her death, because he then entered the monastery himself and lived in his wife's former cell until his own death.

Traveling Companions

T

243

Theodore

Two great martyrs named Theodore are commemorated in the Orthodox Church, but there is considerable confusion about their stories. There was certainly a Theodore martyred in Pontus and venerated since the fourth century. His burial place in Euchaita was an important place of pilgrimage. However, it is possible that details of their stories got somewhat muddled over the course of time. The stories as presented below are an amalgamation of the best sources I could find, but you may well find different versions.

THEODORE TYRON (THE RECRUIT), GREAT MARTYR (FEBRUARY 17)

Even the name of this Theodore is confusing, as some sources call him *Tyron* ("The Recruit") and others *Teron* ("Chosen") because he served in the elite Terian legion. A soldier from a poor background during the reign of Maximian, he was a secret Christian and for a long time managed to attend services and prayers without arousing suspicion. However, after a victorious campaign in which Theodore distinguished himself, the legion was ordered to attend a ceremony at the temple of the goddess Cybele. There they would sacrifice to the goddess and to the emperor and be honored for their victory. Theodore held the place of honor, leading the legion to the temple carrying a flaming torch. Then, to the astonishment of everybody, he used the torch to set fire to the temple. He was immediately arrested and thrown into a furnace in about 305. His name means "Gift of God," and he is revered as one of the great soldier-saints of the Church.

In 361–363, the Byzantine emperor Julian the Apostate attempted to restore paganism to the empire and waged a campaign of intimidation against the Christians. One of his ploys was to defile observance of Lent by ordering that all food sold in the markets of Constantinople be sprinkled with blood from the sacrifices. St. Theodore appeared in a dream to Archbishop Eudoxius (September 6), ordering him to warn his flock not to buy food from the market but to boil wheat (*kolyva*) and eat that alone. For this reason, St. Theodore is venerated on the first Saturday of Lent as well as his own feast day. Kolyva is still eaten on certain days in Lent as well as after funerals and some memorial services.

Additional Feast Day: First Saturday of Lent

Theodore was a provincial governor and military commander under Licinius. On finding out that he was a Christian, Licinius tried to force him to sacrifice to the pagan gods. Theodore invited the emperor to send him a selection of idols so that he could worship them, but when this was done, he smashed the gold and silver statues and distributed the pieces among the poor. He was imprisoned and sentenced to death. Because of his popularity in the area, many people wanted to revolt and release him, but he firmly discouraged them: "Beloved, halt! My Lord Jesus Christ, hanging upon the Cross, restrained the angels and did not permit them to take revenge on the race of men." He was executed in 319.

Additional Feast Day: June 8 (Transfer of Relics)

Theodore of Studion, Venerable (November 11)

This Theodore, a much better documented saint, was abbot of Studion, a famous monastery in Constantinople. Born in that city in 758, he was son of the imperial tax collector and brought up as a devout Christian. In fact, his father resigned from government service when the iconoclast beliefs of the emperor conflicted with his Orthodox Faith, and together with his wife he took monastic vows.

Theodore was an accomplished orator and used his considerable skills to combat the arguments of the iconoclasts. After the Seventh Ecumenical Council put a temporary end to the dissension, Theodore, under the influence of his uncle St. Platon (April 5), went with his brothers Joseph and Euthymius to join the monks on Mount Olympus, eventually being elected abbot. His outspoken condemnation of the emperor for breaking church law, however, led to his exile. Freed by the empress Irene in 796, he was appointed abbot of the Studion Monastery, which he restored and expanded from the existing twelve monks to about one thousand. Here he composed the "Studite Rule" governing monastic life, which was of tremendous influence on the development of Orthodox monasticism.

However, he again fell foul of a new emperor and, after torture, was sent into exile again for two years. After a brief respite, the fanatical iconoclast Emperor Leo came to the throne, and Theodore was again at the forefront of opposition to the heresy. He was dragged from prison to prison and beaten to such an extent that his bruised flesh became gangrenous; it had to be cut away with a knife by

Traveling Companions

T

his companion and disciple St. Nicholas, later himself to become abbot of Studion (February 4).

Eventually, with the accession of a new emperor, an iconoclast but more tolerant than Leo, Theodore was released and settled in Bithynia, where, worn out and sick, he died in 826. In 845, after the final defeat of iconoclasm, Theodore's remains were transferred to Constantinople, an event celebrated on January 26. For his immense contribution to Byzantine monasticism and for his courageous stand against the iconoclasts, Theodore is deeply revered by the Orthodox Church.

Additional Feast Day: January 26 (Transfer of Relics)

Theodosia of Tyre, Virgin Martyr (May 29)

Two holy martyrs called Theodosia are venerated on the same day. The first, Theodosia of Tyre, was seventeen at the height of the persecutions under Diocletian. At Pascha, she visited some of the condemned Christian prisoners in Caesarea, Palestine, asking them to remember her before God when they stood before Him. She was spotted and arrested, but in spite of the pleas of her parents, she refused to sacrifice to the gods. After many days of horrendous torture, she was commanded again to make a sacrifice. She replied that it would be an honor to join in the suffering of God's martyrs and to be considered worthy to accompany the prisoners she had visited. She was thrown into the sea with a stone around her neck. Having miraculously escaped drowning, she was beheaded in about 308.

Additional Feast Day: April 3 (Transfer of Relics)

Theodosia of Constantinople, Virgin Martyr (May 29)

A later martyr called Theodosia illustrates dramatically the point I have made elsewhere that not all saints are peaceful contemplatives. She was a nun in Constantinople during the iconoclast period. Above the gates of the city was a beautiful bronze icon of the Savior, over four hundred years old, which Theodosia had a particular affection for. In 730, the iconoclast Patriarch Anastasius ordered the icon removed and destroyed, and a soldier was ordered to climb a ladder to take it down. Theodosia rushed to protect the icon, shaking the ladder so vigorously that the soldier fell off and was killed. She then led a group of women to attack Anastasius's palace and stone the heretical patriarch. The emperor ordered the other women to be beheaded, and Theodosia was imprisoned. She was flogged daily for a week and finally led around the city, being beaten all the way. She was then stabbed in the throat and died.

Theodosius the Great, Venerable (November 11)

B orn in 423, Theodosius left his home at the age of thirty and settled in Palestine, founding a small community of monks close to Bethlehem. The monks came from a variety of nationalities, and Greeks, Armenians, and Persians all worked and prayed happily together. They devoted their lives to working among the sick, aged, and mentally ill, and built three hospitals to care for them. However little the monks had to eat themselves, it is recorded that no one was ever turned away from their door without a meal.

Theodosius stands out as a shining example of Christianity in practical action, and his contribution was recognized when he was appointed head of all the monastic communities in Palestine at the same time as his friend **St. Sabbas** was given oversight of all the individual hermit monks. This is why he is often referred to as "the Cenobiarch," a cenobite monk being one who lives in a community. He spoke out courageously against the heretical Emperor Anastasius, who refused to recognize the sacraments or the clergy, and was banished for a short time. But on the death of the emperor, he returned to live out his life in his community. He died in 529 at the age of 105.

Theodosius of the Caves of Kiev, Venerable (May 3)

T heodosius was born near Kiev in about 1008. He was the son of a judge and was a devout youth with a yearning for the ascetic life. His family were Christians, but his mother considered his piety a bit extreme and his humility not fitting for his social position. A domineering woman, she even chained him up at one point to prevent his running away with a group of pilgrims headed for the Holy Land. While she was away in the country, however, Theodosius took note of the words of Jesus, "He who loves father or mother more than Me is not worthy of Me" (Matthew 10:37), and set out for the Kiev Caves. Here he was accepted by St. Anthony (July 10) as a disciple.

St. Anthony of Kiev, an austere ascetic, had gone to live as a hermit in a cave by

T

the River Dnieper in 1028. As more disciples joined him, the first purely Russian monastery began to develop, and it was this community that Theodosius joined in 1032 at the age of twenty-four. When Anthony left to seek greater solitude in about 1057, Theodosius was elected abbot. He set about reorganizing the community into a full communal life based on the rule of the Studion Monastery in Constantinople. He enlarged the buildings to provide food and shelter for the sick, poor, and travelers. Like St. Francis in the West, he identified closely with the poor, living a life of total poverty and "self-emptying" (*kenosis*).

Theodosius set out to make his monks living examples of love, unity, and harmony, but whatever austerity he demanded of his monks he imposed more severely on himself, eating only rye bread and boiled vegetables, and spending whole nights in prayer. Even as abbot, he wore the coarsest of patched clothes and would often work in the fields alongside the serfs, felling trees, carrying water, and grinding wheat. "Our Lord Jesus Christ became poor and humble Himself," he wrote, "offering Himself as an example, so that we should humble ourselves in His name." Although he rejected all outward signs of authority, he mixed freely with the outside world when necessary and was an honored friend and advisor of princes and nobles. Nor was he afraid to denounce the sins of the powerful. He was a ready defender of victims of injustice; even the judges would review decisions at his request. After forty years as a monk, Theodosius died peacefully in 1074 at the age of sixty-five, just a few months after St. Anthony.

Six of Theodosius's sermons, two pastoral letters to one of the Russian princes, and one of his prayers have survived. A life of Theodosius was written by a disciple, St. Nestor the Chronicler (October 27), sometime after his death; it still remains a popular book among the Orthodox in Russia. Through his life and writing, Theodosius set the standard for Russian monasticism. St. Nestor calls him and St. Anthony "the first great candles lighted in the name of Russia before the universal image of Christ."

Additional Feast Days: August 14 (Translation of Relics)
September 2 (together with St. Anthony)
August 28 (Synaxis of the Saints of the Kiev Caves)

Theophan the Recluse, Venerable (January 6)

Theophan was born George Govorov in 1815 in Chernavsk, Russia. He studied at the Kiev Theological Academy, where he was tonsured a monk while still a student, taking the name Theophan. He worked in various academic posts until, in 1859, he was consecrated Bishop of Tambov, then Bishop of Vladimir in 1863.

Although he fulfilled his pastoral duties conscientiously and with great love for all his flock, he yearned for a life of seclusion, and he was allowed to retire to the monastery of Vysha in 1866. For the first six years, he attended the services of the monastery, but from 1872 he retired to his cell, performing the services alone in his chapel. The only person he saw regularly was his confessor, and he would keep conversation with necessary visitors to an absolute minimum. He spent his time in prayer, writing, painting icons, and replying to every single letter he received asking for advice or spiritual guidance—between twenty and forty a day! In spite of deteriorating eyesight, this was his life for twenty-two years, until he died peacefully in 1894.

Theophan was a prolific writer whose books remain popular both in Russia and in English translation. He was able to present spiritual and theological truths in an approachable and understandable way, emphasizing at all times the wholeness of body and soul. His writing on prayer is not only full of spiritual depth but also gives practical advice on how to build up a fruitful life of prayer: "Not every act of prayer is prayer. Standing at home before your icons, or here in church, and venerating them is not yet prayer, but the 'equipment' of prayer. Reading prayers either by heart or from a book, or hearing someone else read them is not yet prayer, but only a tool or method for obtaining and awakening prayer. Prayer itself is the piercing of our hearts by pious feelings towards God, one after another—feelings of humility, submission, gratitude, doxology, forgiveness, heart-felt prostration, brokenness, conformity to the will of God."[62]

Theophan also translated two classics of Orthodox spirituality, the *Philokalia* and the *Sermons of St. Simeon the New Theologian*, into modern Russian. His "deep theological understanding of the Christian teaching, as well as its performance in practice . . . allow for his writings to be regarded as a development of the teaching of the Holy Fathers, preserving the same Orthodox purity and Divine enlightenment."[63] He was glorified by the Russian Orthodox Church in 1988, but his writing is respected throughout the Christian world. I will leave to Theophan the last word, a very simple and comforting comment: "God abandons no one. For Him all are children. None are stepchildren."

Additional Feast Day: January 10 (Birth)

T

Thomas, Holy Apostle (October 6)

I know one shouldn't show favoritism in the family, but although I venerate all the saints, there are some I love more than others. One of these is Thomas, truly an apostle for modern times. He was a genuine seeker after truth but at the same time skeptical, refusing to take things purely on trust. Often impetuous, he was always prepared to ask the questions that were probably in the other disciples' minds, but which they weren't brave enough to ask. Jesus once told His followers, "And if I go and prepare a place for you, I will come again and receive you to Myself; that where I am, *there* you may be also. And where I go you know, and the way you know." It was Thomas who asked the obvious question: "Lord, we do not know where You are going, and how can we know the way?" which prompted Jesus' wonderful words, familiar to us all: "I am the Way, the Truth, and the Life. No one comes to the Father except through Me" (John 14:3–6).

On another occasion, when Jesus told the apostles they were heading for Judea because **Lazarus** was dead, they protested that it would be too dangerous and He might be killed. Thomas leaped in, crying out, "Let us also go, that we may die with Him" (John 11: 16).

Thomas was not present when Jesus appeared to the other ten apostles after the Resurrection and refused to take their word for such an extraordinary occurrence: "Unless I see in His hands the print of the nails, and put my finger into the print of the nails, and put my hand into His side, I will not believe." Eight days later, Jesus appeared again to the apostles, with Thomas present. He touched Jesus' hands and side and cried out, "My Lord and my God." Although Jesus mildly rebuked him with the comment, "Thomas, because you have seen Me, you have believed. Blessed *are* those who have not seen and *yet* have believed," Thomas never again doubted but became wholehearted and triumphant in his belief (John 20:24–29).

In the Orthodox Church, Thomas's mixture of doubt and belief are important enough that we devote the Gospels for the Sunday of Pascha and the following Sunday to this story.* **St. John Chrysostom** wrote, "Thomas, being once weaker in faith than the other apostles, toiled through the grace of God more bravely, more zealously and tirelessly than all of them, so that he went preaching over

---

* The Gospel in the Paschal "Service of Love" (Agape Vespers) ends with a wonderful "cliffhanger," as Thomas cries out, "I will not believe."

nearly all the earth, not fearing to proclaim the Word of God to savage nations."

Most of Thomas's later life is uncertain, and the *Acts of Thomas*, written in the third or fourth century, is almost certainly apocryphal. There is, however, some evidence that he preached the Gospel in Parthia and probably in India as well. Certainly a Christian Church has existed in Kerala from very early times, and Indian Christians have called themselves "Christians of St. Thomas" for centuries. There is a sixth-century cross that mentions St. Thomas in its inscription in the church in Mylapore, and some traditions maintain he was martyred and buried in Madras, from whence his relics are said to have been transferred to Edessa in 232.

Additional Feast Day: Sunday after Pascha

Three Hierarchs (January 30)

All three of these saints are described elsewhere, but the existence of this feast has an interesting background. **St. Basil the Great**, **St. Gregory the Theologian**, and **St. John Chrysostom** are rightly regarded as three of the greatest Fathers of the early Orthodox Church. However, at the end of the eleventh century, a violent dispute erupted in Constantinople as to which of them was the greatest. It is difficult nowadays to imagine how seriously this dispute was taken by everyone from bishops to road sweepers. Each saint had his group of supporters, whose behavior was often similar to that of modern European football fans, including the hooliganism. Gangs of "Basilians" clashed with gangs of "Johnites" who fought mobs of "Gregorists," and the whole thing was getting out of hand.

Fortunately, a monk, St. John Mauropus (June 14), appeared on the scene. He announced that all three saints had appeared to him in a dream. They had declared that they were not in opposition to each other but stood "together in harmony and in equal glory before the heavenly throne." The dream was widely publicized, order was restored, and a feast was inaugurated in 1100 to venerate the three saints together. January 30 was chosen for a feast to set the seal on a month when each of the saints is commemorated individually. Thanks to this decision, Greek schoolchildren (and teachers!) now have a holiday on the feast day of the Three Hierarchs.

Traveling Companions

T

Tikhon, Patriarch of Moscow and Apostle to America (April 7)

From the beginning of Christianity, there have been periods when the Church needed careful guidance through stormy waters. There have been few times more dangerous than the early years of Soviet rule in Russia, and Patriarch Tikhon was the pilot who steered through the minefield of dealing with the Bolsheviks while attempting to preserve the liberty and integrity of the Church.

Born in 1865, he was a likeable and affectionate young man and a bright student, always ready to help his fellow students. Appointed Bishop of the Aleutians and Alaska in 1898, the young bishop found his enormous diocese badly in need of reorganization. Tikhon completely restructured the diocese, renaming it the "Diocese of the Aleutians and North America," a very important step for the future of Orthodoxy in the USA. In 1905, the diocese was made an archdiocese with Tikhon as its first archbishop. His popularity, even among non-Orthodox, led to his being made an honorary citizen of the USA. In 1907, he returned to Russia, where he continued to move up in the church hierarchy, not through ambition but because of his wise and kind nature. He always spoke simply and gently to subordinates, and if he did have to reprimand someone, he was good-natured, even making a joke out of the telling-off.

By August 1917, Tikhon was Metropolitan of Moscow. As the October Revolution raged, he was elected patriarch—not a very attractive post at that time! However, his mild nature, so often commented on, actually covered a considerable strength of character and firmness of mind, essential qualities in a time of revolution, famine, civil war, schisms, and the coming to power of an avowedly atheist and anti-Church regime. Tikhon began firmly by pronouncing anathema on the "enemies of Christ, open or disguised"; this was confirmed by the Russian Church Council and never revoked. He publicly denounced the murder of the royal family and was pretty well alone in speaking out against the government for abuses of justice and human rights. However, he maintained neutrality on purely political matters and probably saved thousands of lives by issuing a message to all clergy urging them to keep away from the political struggle during the civil war. For the same reason, he even refused to send his blessing to the White Army commander, although the Whites were fighting partly in support of the Church.

T

In 1921, Tikhon volunteered donations of church valuables to help with the severe famine in the Volga region, but when the government issued a decree confiscating all church valuables, he spoke out strongly against it. There were protests all over Russia, and after nearly two thousand trials, about ten thousand believers were shot, including **Metropolitan Benjamin of Petrograd**. Tikhon was imprisoned for just over a year. Nobody knows what he suffered in prison, but the subtleties of Soviet interrogation techniques are well known. When he was released in June 1923, he seemed to be more conciliatory towards the government and stronger in his opposition to political involvement: "The Russian Orthodox Church is non-political and henceforward does not want to be either a Red or a White Church; it should and will be One Catholic Apostolic Church and all attempts coming from any side to embroil the Church in the political struggle should be rejected and condemned." Nevertheless, he had lost little of his sharpness, and when in 1924 sewage leaked into the first, badly built, Lenin mausoleum, he quietly commented, "The balm is appropriate for the relics!"

Tikhon's sudden death in 1925 has never been fully explained, and "certainly a confessor for the Faith, very possibly he was also a martyr."[64] In defiance of the government, nearly a million people turned out for his funeral at the Donskoy Monastery Cathedral. In 1989, the Russian Orthodox Church glorified Patriarch Tikhon and numbered him among the saints. For seventy years, his remains were believed to be lost, but in February 1992 they were discovered hidden in the Donskoy Monastery.

Tikhon of Zadonsk, Bishop of Voronezh, Venerable (August 13)

In his relatively short life, Tikhon exemplified in turn both the active pastoral care of a good bishop and the quiet spirituality of an elder. He was born in 1724 in Novgorod into an impoverished family and entered into an ecclesiastical school at the age of fourteen. After receiving a state grant to attend the seminary, he became a monk in 1758 and was elected Bishop of Voronezh in 1763.

This was a difficult time for the Church because first Tsar Peter I "the Great" (who died the year after Tikhon was born) and then Tsarina Catherine II "the Great" were intent on westernizing Russia. The movement included secularization of church property and attacks on the influence of the monasteries and the

T

"ignorance" of the clergy. The latter criticism was not altogether unjustified, as there were few good seminaries and most of the poorer clergy were uneducated, merely going through the motions in their duties to make a meager living.

Tikhon worked tirelessly to improve the situation, writing books of pastoral guidance, restoring churches, and founding a seminary. He insisted that every priest, deacon, and monk keep a copy of the New Testament and follow a prescribed course of daily readings, and he imposed strict rules of conduct on all clergy, insisting that the Holy Sacraments be performed with due reverence and understanding. He was equally demanding with the laity, believing they should have the same standards of Christian behavior as the clergy. When people tried to excuse their shortcomings by pleading that they weren't monks, he would simply say, "My dears, all those words calling for love and poverty and service were spoken before there were such things as monasteries."

Tikhon's concern with spiritual education led him to write one of his first booklets, *The Duty of Christian Parents*, addressing the upper classes sternly: "God will not ask you whether you taught your children French, German, or Italian or the politics of society life—but you will not escape divine reprobation for not having instilled goodness into them." On the other hand, he had little patience with the complacency of many "pious" church people and would remind the teetotalers, "Satan too never drinks!" His enormous workload and the discouraging response he received from many of his flock caused Tikhon's physical health to suffer, and in 1767 he was allowed to resign and retire to the Monastery of Zadonsk, where he remained until his death.

A great preacher and a fluent popular writer, Tikhon exerted an influence that was quiet and unspectacular but enormous. His writings are still widely read, and although firmly rooted in Orthodox spirituality, they also draw inspiration from Lutheran, Anglican, and even Roman Catholic books of devotion and mysticism. He writes at the beginning of his most famous book, "As a merchant from various lands gathers various goods, and brings them into his house and treasures them there, likewise a Christian can collect from the world soul-saving thoughts, and by collecting them in the treasury of his heart can form his soul."[65]

Tikhon was never happier than when talking to ordinary people, peasants, beggars, and even criminals, and in spite of the austerity of his own life, he was gentle and moderate with others. Once, during Lent on a "no-fish day," he found one of his fellow monks preparing fish with a friend. They both jumped up in embarrassment and started to apologize, but Tikhon just said, "Sit down, for I know you. Love is higher than fasting," and ate a spoonful of fish with them. At the same time, he was strongly against any form of authoritarianism and could be quick-tempered when faced with hypocrisy or abuse of power. He often had mystical visions, and his fellow monks would find him in a state of rapture, his face transfigured and luminous, but he always begged them to keep this secret as he didn't want to draw attention to himself. His visions often had an element of prophecy, and he predicted the Russian victory over the French in 1812.

Aware of the date of his own death, he spent three years in spiritual (and practical) preparation for it. True to his prediction, he passed away after a stroke in 1783. His incorrupt remains were uncovered in 1846. His life inspired Dostoyevsky, who claimed to have based the wonderful character of the Elder Zossima in *The Brothers Karamazov* on Tikhon.

Additional Feast Day: May 14 (Uncovering of Relics)

Timothy, Apostle of the Seventy (January 22)

Born in about AD 17, Timothy, whose name means "honoring God" or "honored by God," was a native of Lystra in Asia Minor. His mother Eunice and his grandmother Lois are known to have been of "genuine faith" (2 Timothy 1:5), but nothing is known of his father except that he was a Greek. Timothy was converted by **Paul**, probably on the latter's first visit to Lystra in about 52, and quickly became Paul's close companion and helper. Paul thought very highly of him and wrote, "You have carefully followed my doctrine, manner of life, purpose, faith" (2 Timothy 3:10–11).

Timothy accompanied Paul on many of his journeys and was entrusted with a mission to Thessalonica "to establish you and encourage you concerning your faith" (1 Thessalonians 3:2). He was certainly with Paul in Rome during Paul's first imprisonment and may well have been in prison with him (Philemon 1:1 and Hebrews 13:23). Timothy was entrusted by Paul with the supervision of the Christians of Ephesus in about 65 and is regarded as the first bishop of that city. During Paul's second imprisonment prior to his martyrdom, he must have been feeling lonely and abandoned, as he wrote movingly to his faithful friend asking him to join him: "Be diligent to come to me quickly. . . . Only Luke is with me. . . . Bring the cloak that I left with Carpus at Troas when you come—and the books, especially the parchments" (2 Timothy 4:9–13).

T

According to tradition, Timothy was beaten to death in about 80 (some say 93 or 96) by a mob after he tried to stop a pagan festival. His relics were transferred to Constantinople in the fourth century and placed in the Church of the Holy Apostles near the tombs of **Andrew** and **Luke**.

Titus, Bishop of Crete, Apostle of the Seventy (August 25)

Titus was a Greek native of Crete and, according to an ancient tradition, descended from the royal house of Minoan Crete. A learned philosopher, he became a follower of Jesus and was later baptized by **St. Paul**. He accompanied Paul on some of his missionary journeys and for a time was given oversight of the church in Corinth, which was going through a difficult time (2 Corinthians 8:5–7). Titus was also with Paul when he preached in Crete and later founded the first Christian church there, becoming the island's first bishop, with his seat at Gortyn on the south coast.

One of Paul's epistles is written to Titus, giving his young helper advice on setting up the church, including some rather cutting words about the Cretan character: "A prophet of their own, said, 'Cretans *are* always liars, evil beasts, lazy gluttons.' This testimony is true. Therefore rebuke them sharply, that they may be sound in the faith" (Titus 1:12–13). Living in Crete, I believe things have improved somewhat in two thousand years! After ruling his flock with intelligence and compassion for many years, Titus died peacefully at the age of ninety-seven. His relics were removed to Venice during the Turkish occupation of Crete, but the skull was returned to St. Titus Church in Iraklion, Crete, in 1966.

Trophimus and Eucarpion, Martyrs (March 18)

They are not major saints, but the intriguing story of these two "Scarlet Pimpernels" deserves a wider audience. They were officers in the army of Maximian who, in 298, started a wave of persecution designed to stamp out the Christian religion once and for all. They were adept at tracking down Christians and were highly regarded by the emperor as his most successful "hunters." On their way to exterminate a Christian camp, they had a vision of Christ similar to that of St. Paul on the road to Damascus. They continued on their way and, although greeted with considerable suspicion at first, were eventually received into the Christian ranks. Remaining in full army uniform, they were able to visit the arenas and prisons and order the release of the Christians, successfully freeing a great number before being discovered by a superior officer. They fled to rejoin the Christians in hiding, but were able to use their extensive knowledge of army tactics to help the fugitives evade capture. They were eventually betrayed by a Roman spy and burned in 299.

Tryphon of Lampsacus, Martyr (February 1)

Although only a shepherd, Tryphon, a native of Phrygia in Asia Minor, seemed to have a genuine gift of healing and was visited by many sick and crippled, whom he healed in the name of Jesus Christ. He made no attempt to exploit his gift and continued quietly to tend his flocks, but his reputation grew, and word eventually reached the ear of Emperor Gordianus. He was one of the few emperors who showed tolerance towards the Christians, and he called Tryphon to Rome, hoping for a cure for his daughter, who was terminally ill. The boy knelt at her bedside in prayer for several days, and the girl was returned to health. Refusing all honors and rewards, Tryphon returned to his flocks in Phrygia, where he lived the ascetic life of a monk, although not formally tonsured.

Within a few years, however, Decius came to the throne. Tryphon was arrested and sent to Rome, where he again stood before an emperor, though in somewhat different circumstances. After interrogation and torture, he was beheaded in 251. He is considered a protector of workers in the field and is invoked for the protection of gardens and farmland against pests. In Russia, St. Tryphon is venerated as one of the special protectors of Moscow.

T

V

Veronica (Berenice) (July 12)

"**A** woman who had a flow of blood for twelve years came from behind and touched the hem of His garment. For she said to herself, 'If only I may touch His garment, I shall be made well.' But Jesus turned around, and when He saw her He said, 'Be of good cheer, daughter; your faith has made you well.' And the woman was made well from that hour" (Matthew 9:20-22).[66]

According to very old tradition, this woman healed by Jesus was called Veronica (or Berenice). Her miraculous cure led her to become a follower of Christ, and she is widely believed to have been an onlooker as Jesus was led to His Crucifixion. When He stumbled in exhaustion, she gave Him her veil to wipe His brow. He returned the veil to her, and she saw the image of Christ's face imprinted on it. Another story says that she later traveled widely with her husband, preaching the Gospel, and that she used the miraculous veil to cure Emperor Tiberius of a serious illness. The story of Veronica is a confusing mix of legend and tradition, but as the *Catholic Encyclopedia* puts it, when talking of the wiping of Christ's brow, "These pious traditions cannot be documented, but there is no reason why the belief that such an act of compassion did occur should not find expression in the veneration paid to one called Veronica."

While the Orthodox Church honors Veronica, greater emphasis is placed on the story of Abgar and the image of Christ "not made by the hand of man," celebrated on August 16 (see **Jude**). Interestingly, there exists a very early bas-relief of Jesus healing the woman with a hemorrhage, and it has been argued convincingly[67] that this may well be a copy of an earlier statue erected by the woman herself as a thank offering. If this is the case, this bas-relief may be the oldest extant portrayal of Jesus.

Victor of Marseilles, Martyr (July 21)

Victor was a Roman army officer stationed in Massilia, Gaul (modern Marseilles) during the reign of Maximian (286–305). After speaking out publicly against the worship of idols, he was arrested and taken before the emperor. After being beaten and stretched on a rack, he was dragged through the streets and then put in prison. There he converted three of his guards, Longinus, Alexander, and Felician, who were immediately beheaded. Victor himself was first crushed under a millstone and, as he still refused to burn incense to Jupiter, was also beheaded in about 290. The bodies of all four martyrs were buried in a cave, and in the fourth century, John Cassian built a monastery on the site, which became one of the most popular places of pilgrimage in Gaul. This later became the Benedictine Abbey of St. Victor. The three guards are venerated as martyrs on the same day as Victor.

Vincent of Lérins, Venerable (May 24)

Although not a major saint in the Orthodox Church, Vincent was of immense importance in the consolidation of Christian doctrine during the fifth century. We know next to nothing about his life, other than hints and references in his writing. He was a monk in the monastery of Lérins (modern Isle St. Honorat) off the south coast of France, where he wrote his famous *Commonitorium* ("Reminder"). This was intended to be a summary of "those things which I have truthfully received from the holy Fathers, which they have handed down to us and committed to our keeping."

Writing in about 434, shortly after the Third Ecumenical Council, he sets out to provide himself with a general yardstick by which to distinguish between Christian truth and heresy. The Holy Scriptures are not sufficient because they can often be interpreted in a variety of ways, as can be seen in the ideas of Arius, Nestorius, and other heretics.* It is the Church that ensures the continuity

---

* Not to mention the proliferation of denominations and sects following the Reformation.

of truth because, in Vincent's classic phrase, it is the guardian of beliefs held "everywhere, always, by everyone."[68] The aim of the Church is "to treat tradition faithfully and wisely; to nurse and polish what from old times may have remained unshaped and unfinished; to consolidate and to strengthen what already was clear and plain; and to guard what already was confirmed and defined." This does not mean, however, that everything remains the same or that there is no room for progress, but "it must be progress in the proper sense of the word, and not a change in faith. Progress means that each thing grows within itself, whereas change implies that one thing is transformed into another. . . . The growth of religion in the soul should be like the growth of the body, which in the course of years develops and unfolds, yet remains the same as it was." This clear statement of the relationship between stability and progress is still relevant even fifteen hundred years after Vincent's death, which came in about 445.

X-Z

Xenia of Rome, Venerable (January 24)

We have seen that it's not always necessary to be a "nice" person to be a saint, but Xenia was (and is) loved by all for her sweet and gentle disposition. She was born into an aristocratic Roman family in the fifth century and baptized with the name Eusebia. She was a serious child and a sincere Christian, but had an open nature, and her parents did not notice the depth of her spirituality. As she grew into her teens, Eusebia began to feel more and more isolated from the world around her. When her parents selected a suitable husband for her, she slipped away and, with the help of a servant, boarded a boat for the Holy Land.

After visiting the Tomb of Christ and spending considerable time in prayer, she left for the island of Kos. There she met a monk called Paul, who nicknamed her *Xeni* ("Stranger" in Greek), a name that she adopted from then on. She was given an isolated hut to live in where she had the solitude she yearned for, spending her time in prayer. After some time, she emerged from her retreat to work among the islanders, giving them not only spiritual guidance but healing and practical help. When the monk Paul was made a bishop, he persuaded Xenia to become his deacon. She continued to do her good work, now with the support of the bishop, until her death in 450. Although Xenia was not a martyr, like many of the ascetic saints, she is often shown in icons carrying a cross. This represents the sacrifices and privations she bore in the service of Christ: "If anyone desires to come after Me, let him deny himself, and take up his cross, and follow Me" (Matthew 16:24).

Xenia of St. Petersburg, Fool for Christ (January 24)

Like **Basil the Blessed**, Xenia was one who took on the life of a fool for the sake of Christ. But as a woman her life was, if anything, even more difficult and dangerous. The date of her birth is not known but may have been about 1731. She was married to an army officer, Colonel Andrei Feodorovich Petrov, and on his death when she was only twenty-six, she was overcome with grief. She gave away her house as a refuge for paupers and distributed all her possessions to the poor. Her relatives believed she had suffered some kind of mental breakdown and took her to court, complaining that the family wealth was being squandered as a result of insanity. After lengthy questioning, however, the judge concluded that she was in her right mind. He declared that she had made a perfectly rational, if unusual, decision to seek a life of Christian poverty and was entitled to dispose of her property in any way she wished.

Xenia dressed herself in her husband's old uniform and spent the remaining forty-five years of her life wandering the streets of St. Petersburg. She insisted that she be known as Andrei Feodorovich because, as she said, it was she who had died (to her old life), while her husband still lived (in heaven). She refused all offers of help from her relatives, who were probably as much motivated by embarrassment at her behavior as by altruism.

Living on the little food she was given, she roamed the poorest parts of the city, spending the nights in prayer in a quiet field. She was often mocked for her strange behavior, but gradually the people of the city began to see the sanctity behind her eccentricity. She was welcomed into their homes as a blessing. Shopkeepers who gave her food found their businesses improving, as people wanted to use the shops of those who helped their beloved Xenia. The small amount of money she accepted was immediately given away to the poor. While a new church was being built in the Smolensk Cemetery, she would secretly carry the next day's bricks up to the top of the building, an act of kindness only discovered when two of the workmen spent a night on watch. She had a gift of prophecy and foretold several events relating to the city and even the royal family.

The exact date and circumstances of her death are as unknown as her birth, but it occurred in the early years of the nineteenth century, possibly around 1803. She was buried in the Smolensk Cemetery, and her grave became a place of pilgrimage, so many people taking a piece of soil from it that the earth had to be topped up every year. Many miracles of healing are attributed to her prayers, and she has often appeared in visions to people in distress or despair. She is also regarded as a helper of the homeless and unemployed, and is still deeply loved by Orthodox throughout the world. During the Soviet era, the authorities locked the small chapel built over Xenia's grave, but people would still leave flowers outside, write their prayers on a piece of paper, and push them into the cracks in the wall.

Xenophon, Maria, John, and Arcadius, Venerable (January 26)

The extraordinary story of this family is well documented but still reads like a Shakespeare play. Xenophon was a wealthy senator in the court of the Byzantine Emperor Justinian (527–565). He and his wife Maria were intensely religious and brought up their two sons John and Arcadius to be the same. It was decided to send the two boys to school in Beirut to complete their education, but the ship on which they were traveling foundered in heavy seas. The two boys survived by clinging to pieces of timber but were washed ashore many miles apart. John was rescued and restored to health by some monks in the desert near Tyre.

After his recovery, believing his brother to be lost, John entered the monastery as a monk. Meanwhile, Arcadius had landed some miles south of Tyre, also believing his brother dead. He, too, became a monk in the Monastery of St. Sabbas in Jerusalem. Sometime later, an itinerant monk on a visit to Constantinople sought out Xenophon and Maria and told them he had met a shipwreck survivor called Arcadius, whom he believed to be their son. The parents immediately set out for the Holy Land, while at the same time John was on a pilgrimage to Jerusalem. There the family was reunited. Overwhelmed by the miraculous chain of events, Xenophon resigned from the senate and entered the Monastery of St. Sabbas, while Maria entered a nearby convent. All four of the family became respected and revered members of their communities and have been credited with many miracles.

Zachariah and Elizabeth, Righteous Parents of John the Forerunner (September 5)

According to St. Luke's Gospel, the parents of **John the Baptist** were both "righteous before God, walking in all the commandments and ordinances of the Lord blameless." Elizabeth was barren, and both she and her husband were old when Zachariah, a priest, was visited in the temple by the **Archangel Gabriel,** who told him that his wife would bear a child and they were to call him John. Not surprisingly, Zachariah was a bit skeptical about this, and Gabriel decreed that he would remain dumb until the prophecy was fulfilled.

When the child was born, the neighbors and relatives wanted to call him after his father, but Elizabeth declared, "He shall be called John," which Zachariah confirmed by writing the name on a clay tablet. He thereupon regained his voice and immediately used it to praise God, for "He has visited and redeemed His people" (Luke 1:60, 68). According to tradition, Zachariah was later murdered in the temple for refusing to tell Herod where his son was, Elizabeth surviving him for just forty days (Protevangelion 16:12–16). Zachariah and Elizabeth are two of the biblical couples mentioned in the service for the Sacrament of Marriage: "Bless them, O Lord our God, as Thou didst bless Zachariah and Elizabeth."

Additional Feast Day: June 24 (Nativity of John the Baptist)

Notes

1 Both quotations are from a statement by the Holy Synod of the Orthodox Archdiocese of Greece, April 4, 2006, as reported in the *Athens News*. As this book was being written, there was much debate in the Greek press concerning the body of a holy monk, Father Vyssarion of Agathon Monastery, which was found to be intact and in a mummified state 15 years after his death in 1991. Although official recognition of Fr. Vyssarion as a saint may well take decades, the Holy Synod of the Archdiocese of Greece has given its approval to informal veneration by the many pilgrims who have begun to visit his tomb.

2 Many scriptural references seem to imply the descent of Christ into hell, the most important being 1 Peter 3:19, where Peter writes that Christ "went and preached to the spirits in prison." Also, in Acts 2:31, Peter says somewhat cryptically that King David was prophesying the Resurrection when he wrote, "His soul was not left in Hades, nor did His flesh see corruption."

3 Quoted in Bishop Kallistos Ware, *The Orthodox Way* (St. Vladimir's Seminary Press, 1995), p. 87.

4 Ouspensky, *The Theology of the Icon* (St. Vladimir's Seminary Press, 1990), p. 72.

5 Bishop Kallistos Ware, *The Orthodox Church* (Penguin Books, 1993), p. 258.

6 Alexander Schmemann, *The Services of Christmas* (Unknown Edition, 1981).

7 See also John 4:13–14: "Whoever drinks of this water will thirst again, but whoever drinks of the water that I shall give him will never thirst. But the water that I shall give him will become in him a fountain of water springing up into everlasting life."

8 Bede's beautiful but slightly equivocal praise of Aidan is worth quoting in full: "I have written thus much concerning the character and works of the aforesaid Aidan, in no way commending or approving his lack of wisdom with regard to the observance of Easter . . . but, like an impartial historian, unreservedly relating what was done by or through him, and commending such things as are praiseworthy in his actions, and preserving the memory thereof for the benefit of the readers; to wit, his love of peace and charity; of continence and humility; his mind superior to anger and avarice, and despising pride and vainglory; his industry in keeping and teaching the Divine commandments, his power of study and keeping vigil; his priestly authority in reproving the haughty and powerful, and at the same time his tenderness in comforting the afflicted, and relieving or defending the poor. To be brief, so far as I have learnt from those that knew him, he took care to neglect none of those things which he found in the Gospels and the writings of Apostles and prophets, but to the utmost of his power endeavored to fulfill them all in his deeds."

9 Translation by the White Rose fellowship (www.weisse-rose-stiftung.de). Quoted with permission of Ursula Kaufmann.

10 Translation by Katja Yurschak (www.katjasdacha.com). Quoted with her permission.

11 All quotes from Father Amphilochios are translated by Marina M. Robb, copyright Evangelismos Monastery, Patmos (www.agrino.org/cyberdesert/makris).

12 Bishop Kallistos Ware, *The Orthodox Church*, p. 132.

13 Quotations and extracts from monachos.net, used with permission of Archimandrite Irenei.

14 Edward Gibbon, *History of the Decline and Fall of the Roman Empire.*

15 The Venerable Bede, *Ecclesiastical History of England.*

16 The evidence is circumstantial, but in the Gospels of Matthew, Mark and Luke, lists of the twelve apostles include Bartholomew, while the list of the Twelve in John 21:2 includes Nathaniel but not Bartholomew. Moreover, in John's Gospel, Bartholomew is not mentioned, but the calling of Nathaniel strongly implies that he was to be one of the Twelve. Many of the early Church Fathers, including John Chrysostom and Cyril of Alexandria, support this view, and it is generally accepted in the Orthodox Church.

17 Translation by Ian Lancashire, University of Toronto. Quoted with his permission.

18 Timothy Severin, *The Brendan Voyage* (Abacus, 1996).

19 Translation by Ian Lancashire, University of Toronto. Quoted with his permission.

20 George Poulos, *Orthodox Saints Vol. 3* (Holy Cross Orthodox Press, 1990). Quoted with permission.

21 From the Orthodox China website (http://www.orthodox.cn/saints/chinesemartyrs _en.htm). Quoted here with permission of Nelson Mitrofan Chin.

22 We know little about the exact organization of the early Church in Rome, and details are confused. Thus, some early writers call Clement the second after Peter, with Linus and Anacletus being "assistant bishops." This confusion is not helped by Clement using the terms "bishop" and "presbyter" apparently interchangeably.

23 Donald Attwater, *Penguin Book of Saints* (Penguin Books, 1983).

24 Anonymous translation, 1915.

25 This was not as unusual as it might seem. It has been estimated that a significant proportion of the population of the Roman Empire of that time were "God-fearers" who had rejected the pagan gods as not consistent with morality or logic and had embraced belief in one God who had created the world and instituted the moral law. It has been suggested that, since the description of Cornelius closely matches that of the centurion whose servant Jesus cured (Luke 7:1–10), they may have been the same person, and thus Cornelius already had some knowledge of Jesus. An intriguing idea.

26 John Davies, *A History of Wales* (Penguin 1994), p. 74.

27 An excellent summary of Dorotheus's work by Timothy W. Seid may be found on the website www2.evansville.edu/ecoleweb/articles/dorotheos.html.

28 This is the NKJV Bible numbering. Orthodox Study Bible: 3 Kingdoms 17—19, 4 Kingdoms 1—2.

29 Sebastian Brock (translator), *The Harp of the Spirit: Eighteen Poems of Saint Ephraim* (Fellowship of St. Alban and St. Sergius, 1983). Quoted in Ware, *The Orthodox Way,* p. 86.

30 Jim Forest, *The Real Saint George* (from *In Communion*, the magazine of the Orthodox Peace Fellowship, website http://www.incommunion.org).

31 Quoted in Bishop Kallistos Ware, *The Orthodox Church*, p. 35.

32 Quoted on Orthodox Church of America website: http://oca.org.

33 Writing in the sixth century in his *History of the Franks.*

34 Quotations from *A Testament to Disciples* by Ivan of Rila. Translation from Dumbarton Oaks Studies No. 35 (© 2000 Dumbarton Oaks). (www.doaks.org/etexts.html)

35 One of the most moving Paschal services in history was held by the surviving Orthodox Christian prisoners of Dachau after its liberation in 1945. With no service books, the liturgy was recited from memory, including John Chrysostom's sermon for Pascha.

36 John of Damascus, *On the Orthodox Faith.* Translation and comment from Kallistos Ware, *The Orthodox Way,* p. 34.

37 Both translated by John M. Neale, in 1859 and 1862 respectively:

a) Come, ye faithful, raise the strain of triumphant gladness;
God hath brought forth Israel into joy from sadness;
Loosed from Pharaoh's bitter yoke Jacob's sons and daughters,
Led them with unmoisted foot through the Red Sea waters.

b) The day of resurrection! Earth, tell it out abroad;
The Passover of gladness, the Passover of God.
From death to life eternal, from earth unto the sky,
Our Christ hath brought us over, with hymns of victory!

38 G. P. Fedotov, *A Treasury of Russian Spirituality* (Sheed and Ward, 1950), p. 348.

39 Quoted in Bishop Alexander Mileant, *Archbishop John the Wonderworker,* on website www.fatheralexander.org/.

40 The story of the burial of Jesus is told in Matt. 27:57–61; Mark 15:42–47; Luke 23:50–54; and John 19:38–42.

41 Some scholars believe verse 17 of the epistle seems to imply that the apostles have already died: "But you, beloved, remember the words which were spoken before by the apostles of our Lord Jesus Christ." However, this use of words is ambiguous and may simply be reminding the recipients of the letter of earlier visits by the apostles.

42 See website http://stjuliana.com/.

43 The first of these relates to Ex. 12:46 and actually refers to the rules for preparation of the lamb for the Passover meal. It is often taken to be a prophecy of the Paschal sacrifice of the Lamb of God. The second prophecy is from Zech. 12:10: "And I will pour on the house of David and on the inhabitants of Jerusalem the Spirit of grace and supplication; then they will look on Me whom they pierced. Yes, they will mourn for Him as one mourns for his only son, and grieve for Him as one grieves for a firstborn."

44 See Sergei Hackel, *Pearl of Great Price: The Life of Mother Maria Skobtsova* (St. Vladimir's Seminary Press, 2007).

45 Mother Maria Skobtsova, *Essential Writings* (Orbis Books, 2003).

46 Quoted in Donald Attwater, *Penguin Book of Saints.* Original source unknown.

47 *On Love,* included in *The Philokalia,* translated by G.E.H. Palmer, Philip Sherard, and Kallistos Ware (Faber & Faber, 1981), p. 64.

The great Protestant hymn, *How Great Thou Art,* inspired by Psalm 8, although not Orthodox, is a beautiful illustration of this approach:

O Lord my God, when I in awesome wonder
Consider all the worlds Thy hands have made;
I see the stars, I hear the rolling thunder,

Thy power throughout the universe displayed.
Then sings my soul, My Savior God, to Thee,
How great Thou art, How great Thou art.

48 *The Guardian*, 24.12.04.

49 An enormous collection of Greek texts from the fourth to the fifteenth century, compiled by St. Macarius, Metropolitan of Corinth (April 17) and St. Nicodemus of the Holy Mountain (July 14), and published in 1782. It is now available in English translation.

50 Fr. Seraphim Rose of Platina, *Introduction to Blessed Paisius Velichkovsky: The Man Behind the Philokalia.*

51 St. Patrick, *Confession* (http://www.WhatSaithTheScripture.com).

52 This tag was often quoted by the early Christians and may not be evidence that Procopius was actually acquainted with the works of Homer.

53 Translated by Archimandrite Ephrem Lash, *Romanus the Melodist, On the Life of Christ: Kontakia* (Harper, San Francisco, 1995). See http://jbburnett.com/resources/romanos_nativity.

54 G. P. Fedotov, *A Treasury of Russian Spirituality*, pp. 273–5.

55 Donald Attwater, *Penguin Book of Saints*, p. 296.

56 Bishop Kallistos Ware, *The Orthodox Church*, p. 86.

57 Bishop Kallistos Ware, *The Orthodox Church*, p. 130.

58 Archimandrite Sophrony, *Saint Silouan the Athonite* (St. Vladimir's Seminary, 1999). All quotations in this article are from this book.

59 Donald Attwater, *Penguin Book of Saints*, p. 300.

60 Some accounts, including that of George Poulos, say that his parents were very poor, but I have been unable to establish a definitive version.

61 George Poulos, *Orthodox Saints Vol. 3*. Quoted with permission.

62 Theophan the Recluse, *On Prayer, Homily 1* (translated by Rev. Michael van Opstall and published on www.monachos.net). Quoted by permission of Archimandrite Irenei.

63 The Act of Canonization of the Local Council of the Russian Orthodox Church, Trinity-Sergius Lavra, June 6–9, 1988.

64 Bishop Kallistos Ware, *The Orthodox Church*, p. 151.

65 St. Tikhon of Zadonsk, *A Spiritual Treasury Gathered from the World* (1776).

66 See also Mark 5:23–34; Luke 8:43–48.

67 By the theologian Leonid Ouspensky in *The Theology of the Icon.*

68 "*Quod ubique, quod semper, quod ab omnibus.*"

APPENDIX A

Spellings and Names

C orrectly spelling the names of saints from many different nationalities and languages is a bit of a nightmare. To make life simpler for the reader (not to mention the author!), I have generally used the English version, as in George, or the Latin spelling, as in Acacius. In a few cases, I have used the Greek spelling for later saints whose names were clearly Greek, such as Nektarios. I am sure I haven't always been consistent, but who said consistency was a virtue? Below is a partial cross-reference of English, Greek, and Russian versions of the names.

ENGLISH	GREEK	RUSSIAN
Acacius	Akakios	
Adrian (See **Natalia**)	Adrianos	Adrian
Agatha	Agathi	Agafya
Agnes	Agni	Agnessa
Alexander	Alexandros	Aleksandr
Alexis	Alexios	Aleksey
Ambrose	Amvrosios	Amvrosiy
Anastasia	Anastasia	Anastasiya
Anastasius	Anastasios	Anastas
Andrew	Andreas	Andrey
Anna (See **Joachim**)	Anna	Anna
Anthony	Antonios	Anton
Aristobolus	Aristovoulos	
Arsenius	Arsenios	Arseniy
Athanasius	Athanasios	Afanasiy
Barbara	Varvara	Varvara
Barlaam	Varlaam	Varlaam
Barnabas	Varnavas	Varnava
Bartholomew	Vartholomaios	Varfolomey
Basil	Vasileios	Vasiliy

Benjamin	Veniamin	Venyamin
Bessarion	Vissarion	Vissarion
Blaise	Vlassios	Vlasi
Boris (See **Olga**)	Boris	Boris
Calliope	Kalliopi	
Charalambus	Haralambos	
Charity (See **Sophia**)	Agape	Liubov
Christodoulos	Christodoulos	
Christopher	Christophoros	
Chrysanthus	Chrysanthos	
Constantine	Konstantinos	Konstantin
Cosmas	Kosmas	Kuzma
Cyprian	Kyprianos	Kyprian
Cyriaci	Kyriaki	
Cyriacus	Kyriakos	
Cyril	Kyrillos	Kirill
Damian (See **Cosmas**)	Damianos	Demyan
Daniel	Daniil	Daniil
Daria (See **Chrysanthus**)	Daria	Darya
Demetrius	Dimitrios	Dmitriy
Dionysius	Dionysios	Denis
Dorotheus	Dorotheos	Dorofei
Eleutherius	Eleftherios	
Elijah	Ilias	Ilya
Elizabeth (See **Zachariah**)	Elizabeth	Yelizaveta
Ephraim	Ephraim	Yefrem
Eucarpion	Evkarpion	
Eudokia	Evdokia	Yevdokiya
Eugenia	Evgenia	Yevgeniya
Euphemia	Efphemia	
Eustace	Efstathios	
Eustratius	Efstratios	
Euthymius	Efthymios	
Faith (See **Sophia**)	Pistis	Vera
Gabriel	Gavriil	Gavriil
George	Georgios	Georgiy

Gerasimus	Gerasimos	Gerasim
Gleb (See **Olga**)	Glev	Gleb
Gregory	Gregorios	Grigoriy
Haritini	Haritini	
Helen (See **Constantine**)	Eleni	Yelena
Hilarion	Ilarion	Illarion
Hope (See **Sophia**)	Elpis	Nadezhda
Ignatius	Ignatios	Ignatiy
Innocent		Innokenti
Irene	Eirini	Irina
James/Jacob	Iakovos	Yakov
Joachim	Ioachim	Yakim
John	Ioannis	Ivan
Joseph	Iosif	Iosif
Jude	Iudas	
Justin	Ioustinos	
Justina (See **Cyprian**)	Ioustina	Yustina
Katherine/Catherine	Ekaterini	Yekaterina
Lawrence	Lavrentios	Lavrentiy
Leo	Leo	Lev
Lucian	Loukianos	
Lucy	Loukia	
Ludmilla	Loudmilla	Lyudmila
Luke	Loukas	Luka
Lydia	Lydia	Lidiya
Mamas	Mamas	
Marina	Marina	Marina
Mark	Markos	Mark
Martin	Martinos	Martin
Mary	Maria	Mariya
Matthew	Mattheios	Matvey
Maximus	Maximos	Maksim
Menas	Menas	
Methodius (See **Cyril**)	Methodios	Mefodiy
Michael	Michael	Mikhail
Mitrophan	Metrophanes	Mitrofan

Moses	Moises	Moisey
Myron	Myron	Miron
Natalie	Natalia	Nataliya
Nectarius	Nektarios	Nektariy
Nicephorus	Nikephoras	Nikifor
Nikon	Nikon	Nikon
Nino	Nina	Nina
Olga	Olga	Olga
Panteleimon	Panteleimon	
Paraskeva	Paraskevi	Praskoviya
Parthenius	Parthenios	Parfeniy
Paul	Pavlos	Pavel
Pelagia	Pelagia	Pelageya
Peter	Petros	Pyotr
Philip	Philippos	Filipp
Philothea	Philothei	
Phocas	Phokas	Foka
Photina	Photeini	Svetlana
Polycarp	Polykarpos	
Polychronius	Polychronios	
Procopius	Prokopios	Prokopy
Raphael	Raphael	
Sabbas	Savvas	Savva
Seraphim	Serafeim	Serafim
Sergius	Sergios	Sergey
Silas/Silvanus	Silouanos	Silouan
Simon (Simeon)	Symeon	Semyon
Sophia	Sophia	Sofya
Sozon	Sozon	
Spyridon	Spyridon	Spyridon
Stephen	Stephanos	Stepan
Stylianus	Stylianos	
Tatiana	Tatiani	Tatiana
Thecla	Thekla	Tekla
Theodora	Theodora	Feodora
Theodore	Theodoros	Fyodor

Theodosia	Theodosia	
Theodosius	Theodosios	Feodosiy
Thomas	Thomas	Foma
Tichon	Tychon	Tikhon
Timothy	Timotheos	Timofey
Titus	Titos	Tit
Trophimus	Trophimos	Trofim
Tryphon	Tryphon	
Vladimir (See **Olga**)	Vladimiros	Vladimir
Wenceslaus (See **Ludmilla**)	Vyacheslav	
Xenia	Xeni	Kseniya
Xenophon	Xenophon	
Zachariah	Zacharias	Zakhar

APPENDIX B

Dates

As far as possible, I've cross-checked the dates of feast days thoroughly, but there may well be regional variations, especially for the minor saints. There is, however, also the problem of calendars.

Until the sixteenth century, the Julian calendar devised by the Romans was used throughout Europe. However, in 1582, Pope Gregory XIII authorized a revision to get rid of inaccuracies, leading to the New (Gregorian) Calendar. This resulted in dates shifting thirteen days forward—January 1, for example, becoming January 13. The new calendar was immediately adopted in all Roman Catholic countries, and the Protestant countries in Western Europe followed gradually, in spite of riots demanding the return of the thirteen lost days. This is the calendar with which we are all familiar.

In the Orthodox world, however, the Julian calendar continued to be used until 1924, when it was revised to correspond to the New Calendar. Most governments accepted the change, but its acceptance by the Orthodox Church was more complicated. The churches in Greece and Cyprus and the Ecumenical Patriarchate,* for example, implemented the change, while others, such as Russia and Serbia,** continued to use the Old Calendar. All religious festivals (except those in the Paschal cycle) in churches following the Julian calendar fall thirteen days after those using the Gregorian calendar. For example, Christmas Day in the Russian Church is January 7. To complicate matters still further, the whole Orthodox Church still sets the date of Pascha by calculations based on the Julian calendar. Thus, Orthodox Pascha falls between one and five weeks later than the Western Easter, the two corresponding about every four years.

---

* Together with the Patriarchates of Alexandria and Antioch, the Orthodox Church in America (with some exceptions in individual parishes) and the churches of Romania, Poland, and Bulgaria.

** Others included the Patriarchate of Jerusalem, the churches of Macedonia, Georgia, and the Ukraine, and the semi-autonomous community of Mount Athos. In Greece, a minority of monasteries and parishes adhere to the Old Calendar, although their influence is now very small.

For simplicity, I have used the Gregorian calendar for all feasts and saints' days in this book, but bear in mind that the dates for some of the Serbian and Russian saints may differ.

APPENDIX C

Emperors and Martyrs

This is a highly abridged list of the main Roman emperors, showing the extent of the persecutions and dates of martyrdoms mentioned in this book.

27 BC–AD 14 Augustus	Birth of Christ
14–37 Tiberius	John the Baptist beheaded, Crucifixion of Christ, Stephen martyred
37–54 Caligula, Claudius	Persecution had not yet got underway, even under the insane Caligula. The martyrdom of the apostle James in 44 was, like that of Stephen, perpetrated by the Jewish authorities.
54–68 Nero	The first systematic persecution, more for political ends than any religious intolerance. Andrew, James the Brother of the Lord, Peter, Paul, Dionysius, and Photina were martyred.
81–96 Domitian	St. Luke died.
96–180 Nerva, Trajan, Hadrian, Antoninus Pius, Marcus Aurelius	
	The "Five Good Emperors" were men of immense ability and great moral rectitude. However, they also insisted on adherence to the state religion and were responsible for many martyrdoms, including those of Eudokia, Eustathius, Ignatius, Justin, Mark, Paraskeva, Phocas, Polycarp, and Sophia.
180–182 Commodus	Eugenia
193–211 Septimus Severus	Charalambus
222–235 Severus Alexander	Eleutherius, Tatiana

235–238 Maximinus	Barbara

238–249 Gordianus, Philip the Arab These were two of the few emperors to show a high degree of tolerance towards the Christians.

249–251 Decius	Acacius (reprieved), Agatha, Christopher, Calliope, Nikon, Tryphon
253–260 Valerian	Lawrence and Sixtus, Cyprian of Carthage
260–268 Galienus	Issued a decree of toleration, soon to be reversed
270–275 Aurelian	Mamas

284–305 Numerian	From 284 to 312, the situation becomes far too
284–305 Diocletian	complex for a summary. Suffice it to say that
286–305 Maximian	various emperors either shared the empire or
284–311 Galerius	fought each other for control of it. Most of them
305–307 Constantius	systematically persecuted the Christians with
305–312 Maxentius	great savagery, in some cases in a conscious effort to exterminate the "sect." The martyrs from this period are too numerous to mention here.

307–324 Licinius	After 312, Constantine and Licinius became
307–337 Constantine	joint rulers. In 313, they jointly issued the Edict of Milan, legalizing Christianity. But Licinius later revoked it in the Eastern Empire and was responsible for many martyrdoms, including Blaise, Lucian, the Forty Martyrs of Sebastea, and Theodore Stratelates. In 324, Constantine emerged as sole emperor and Christianity became the de facto state religion.

360–363 Julian the Apostate	Attempt to restore paganism in the empire
364–378 Valens	Attempt to promote Arianism
378–395 Theodosius I	Christianity finally firmly established

Calendar of Saints & Feast Days

(Saints who are the subjects of full articles are shown in bold type.)

JANUARY

1   **Basil the Great**
    Basil the Elder (see **Macrina the Elder**)
    Emmelia (Russian Tradition)
    Gregory of Nazianzus
    Seraphim of Sarov
    Synaxis of the 70 Apostles
2   **Juliana of Lazarevo**
3   **Geneviève of Paris**
6   **Theophan the Recluse**
    Theophany (Baptism of Christ)
7   **Synaxis of John the Baptist**
9   **Philip of Moscow**
    Peter of Sebastea
10 **Theosebia**
    Gregory of Nyssa
    Theophan the Recluse
12 **Tatiana**
13 **Hilary of Poitiers**
    James of Nisibis
14 **Nino**
    Sava of Serbia
    Macrina the Elder (Russian Tradition)
15 Ita
16 Chains of St. Peter
17 **Anthony the Great**
18 **Athanasius and Cyril of Alexandria**
19 **Macarius the Great**
    Macarius of Alexandria
20 **Euthymius**
21 **Agnes**
22 **Timothy**
24 **Xenia of Rome**
    Xenia of St. Petersburg
25 **Gregory the Theologian**
26 **Xenophon & his Family**
    Relics of **Theodore of Studion**
27 Relics of **John Chrysostom**
28 **Ephraim the Syrian**
29 Relics of **Ignatius**
30 **Three Hierarchs**
31 **Cyrus and John**
    Athanasia and Her Daughters

FEBRUARY

1   **Tryphon**
    Brigid
2   Presentation of Christ in the Temple
3   **Simeon and Anna**
4   Nicholas of Studion
5   **Agatha**
6   Barsanuphius and John the Prophet
7   **Parthenius**
8   **Theodore Stratelates** (see **Theodore**)
    Cuthman
    Prophet Zachariah
9   Nicephorus of Antioch
10 **Charalambus**
    Scholastica
11 **Blaise**
    Caedmon
    Empress Theodora

13 Simeon of Serbia
14 Repose of **Cyril, Apostle to the Slavs**
17 Theodore Tyron
Empress Pulcheria
18 Leo of Rome
19 Philothea
Dositheus
20 **Bessarion**
23 **Polycarp**
24 1ˢᵗ & 2ⁿᵈ Findings of Head of **John the Baptist**
26 **Photina (Greece)**
27 **Raphael of Brooklyn (OCA)**
28 John Cassian

MARCH
1 **Eudokia of Heliopolis**
David of Wales
4 **Gerasimus of the Jordan**
9 **Forty Martyrs of Sebastea**
14 **Benedict of Nursia**
15 **Aristobolus**
16 **Christodoulos**
17 **Alexis**
Patrick
18 **Trophimus & Eucarpion**
Cyril of Jerusalem
Nikolai of Zhicha
19 **Chrysanthus & Daria**
20 **Myron, New Martyr**
23 **Nikon**
25 **Annunciation**
26 **Synaxis of the Archangel Gabriel**
27 **Lydia of Illyria**
30 Eubola
31 **Acacius**
Innocent of Alaska

APRIL
1 **Mary of Egypt**

3 Relics of **Theodosia of Tyre**
5 Platon
6 Repose of **Methodius, Apostle to the Slavs**
7 **Tikhon of Moscow**
Serapion
9 **Raphael, Nicholas & Irene**
10 Terence and the 40 martyrs of Carthage
13 **Martin**
16 **Irene, Agape & Chionia**
17 **Acacius, Bishop of Melitine**
Macarius of Corinth
22 **Nathaniel**
23 **George**
25 **Mark**
26 **Stephen of Perm**
30 **James, Brother of John**

MAY
1 **Maria of Fourni**
2 **Athanasius**
3 **Theodosius of the Caves of Kiev**
4 **Pelagia of Tarsus**
5 **Irene, Great Martyr**
6 Relics of **Sava of Serbia**
7 **Alexis of Wilkes-Barre**
Acacius the Centurion
8 **Arsenius**
Macrina the Elder (Greek Tradition)
Emmelia (Greek Tradition) (see **Macrina the Elder**)
Grave of **John the Theologian**
9 **Christopher**
10 **Simon the Zealot**
11 **Cyril & Methodius**
14 Relics of **Tikhon of Zadonsk**
16 **Brendan**
20 **Lydia the Seller of Purple**

21 Constantine & Helen
22 Svetlana (Russia) (see
   Photina)
23 Synaxis of the Rostov and
   Yaroslav Saints
24 Vincent of Lérins
   Simon Stylites the Younger
25 3rd Finding of the Head of John
   the Baptist
26 Augustine
27 Bede
29 Theodosia of Tyre
   Theodosia of Constantinople
30 Emmelia (Greek Tradition)
   (see Macrina the Elder)

JUNE
1 Justin
4 Martha and Mary of Bethany
   Metrophanes, Patriarch of
   Constantinople
5 Dorotheus of Gaza
8 Calliope
   Theodore Stratelates (see
      Theodore)
   Melania the Elder
   Glorification of John of
   Kronstadt
9 Cyril of Alexandria
   Columba
11 Mitrophan Tsi-Chung and the
   Boxer Martyrs
   Barnabas
   Bartholomew
13 Archangel Gabriel
14 Elisha
   John Mauropus
19 Jude
22 Alban
23 Agrippina of Rome
24 Birth of John the Baptist

27 Joanna
   Relics of Ambrose of Optina
28 Sergius of Valaam
   Icon of the Three Hands
29 Peter and Paul
30 Synaxis of the Holy Apostles

JULY
1 Cosmas & Damian of Rome
2 Robe of the Theotokos
   Juvenaly of Alaska
3 Relics of Philip of Moscow
4 Andrew of Crete
5 Athanasius the Athonite
   Relics of Sergius of Radonezh
7 Kyriaki
   Palladius
8 Procopius, Great Martyr
10 Anthony of the Caves of Kiev
11 Olga
   Miracle at Chalcedon
12 Veronica
   Icon of the Three Hands
13 Archangel Gabriel
14 Nicodemus of the Holy
   Mountain
15 Vladimir
17 Marina
18 Elizabeth New Martyr of
   Russia
19 Macrina the Younger (see
      Emmelia)
   Relics of Seraphim of Sarov
20 Elijah
   Mother Maria of Paris
   Lydia, New Martyr of Russia
21 Simeon Salus
   Victor of Marseilles
22 Mary Magdalene
23 Relics of Phocas
24 Boris & Gleb

Christina
25 Dormition of **Righteous Anna**
Olympia
26 **Paraskeva of Rome**
Jacob Netsvetov
Hermolaus
27 **Panteleimon**
28 **Irene Chrysovalantou**
30 **Silas**
31 **Joseph of Arimathea**
Germanus of Auxerre

AUGUST

2 **Basil the Blessed**
Relics of **St. Stephen**
3 **Salome** (see **Myrrhbearers**)
4 **Seven Sleepers of Ephesus**
Eudokia of Persia
5 Nonna
6 **Maxim Sandovich**
Transfiguration
Herman of Alaska
7 Elders of Optina
8 **Myron, Bishop of Crete**
9 **Matthias**
10 **Lawrence**
Sixtus
13 **Benjamin of Petrograd**
Tikhon of Zadonsk
14 Relics of Anthony of the Caves
15 Dormition of the **Theotokos**
16 **Gerasimus of Kephalonia**
Icon of Christ Not Made by
Hands
18 **Ivan of Rila**
20 Prophet Samuel
23 **Irenaeus of Lyons**
24 **Cosmas of Aetolia**
Relics of **Dionysius of**
Zakynthos
25 **Titus**

26 **Adrian & Natalia**
28 **Moses the Ethiopian**
Synaxis of Saints of the Kiev
Caves
Relics of **Job of Pochaev**
29 Beheading of **John the Baptist**
30 **Alexander, Patriarch of**
Constantinople
Relics of **Alexander Nevsky**
31 **Cyprian of Carthage**
Sash of the **Theotokos**
Aidan

SEPTEMBER

1 Beginning of Ecclesiastical Year
Simon Stylites the Elder
Forty Nun Martyrs of Heraclea
2 **Mamas**
Anthony and Theodosius of
the Caves of Kiev
Theodotus & Rufina
5 **Zachariah & Elizabeth**
6 **Archangel Michael** at Colossae
Glorification of **Maxim**
Sandovich
Macarius the Martyr
7 **Sozon**
Cassiane
8 Nativity of **Virgin Mary**
9 **Joachim & Anna**
11 **Theodora of Alexandria**
Relics of **Sergius of Valaam**
13 **Cornelius**
15 Relics of **Acacius**
Relics of **Stephen**
16 **Euphemia**
Ludmilla
Dorotheus of Egypt
17 **Sophia, Pistis, Elpis & Agape**
20 **Eustathius, Theopista, Agapius**
& Theopistus

22 Phocas the Gardener
    Phocas the Bishop
23 Conception of John the Baptist
24 Thecla
    Silouan the Athonite
    All Saints of Alaska
25 Sergius of Radonezh
28 Wenceslaus (see Ludmilla and Wenceslaus)
26 John the Theologian
29 Cyriacus
30 Gregory of Armenia

OCTOBER

1   Protection of the Theotokos (General in Orthodox Church)
    Romanus the Melodist
2   Cyprian & Justina
3   Dionysius the Areopagite
5   Haritini
    Synaxis of the Hierarchs of Moscow
6   Apostle Thomas
    Innocent of Alaska
7   Polychronius
8   Pelagia the Penitent
9   James, Son of Alphaeus
    Denis of Paris
10 Ambrose of Optina
11 Philip the Deacon
15 Lucian
16 Longinus the Centurion
17 Cosmas & Damian of Arabia
    Relics of Lazarus
18 Luke
19 Birth of John of Kronstadt
    Relics of Ivan of Rila
20 Andrew of Crete, Martyr
    Relics of Gerasimus of Kephalonia
21 Hilarion the Great

22 Seven Sleepers of Ephesus
    St. Demetrius Memorial Day
23 James, Brother of the Lord
25 Tabitha
26 Demetrius
27 Nestor
28 Protection of the Theotokos (in Greece)
    Job of Pochaev
    Paraskeva of Iconium

NOVEMBER

1   Cosmas & Damian of Asia Minor
3   Transfer of Relics of St. George
4   Ioannikios
8   Synaxis of the Archangels
9   Nektarios
10 Nonnus of Antioch
11 Menas
    Theodore of Studion
    Theodosius the Great
13 John Chrysostom
14 Philip the Apostle
    Gregory Palamas
15 Paisius Velichkovsky
    Herman of Alaska
16 Matthew
17 Gregory of Neocaesarea
    Hilda of Whitby
    Lazarus the Painter
19 Barlaam
21 Entry of Mary into the Temple
22 Procopius the Reader
23 Alexander Nevsky
    Paulinus of Wales
25 Katherine
    Clement of Rome
26 Stylianus
    Dedication of Church of St. George, Kiev

28	Stephen the Confessor		Eustratius, Eugenius,
30	Andrew, Holy Apostle		Auxentius, Orestes &
			Mardarius
	DECEMBER	15	Eleutherius
4	Barbara		Anthia
	John of Damascus	17	Dionysius of Zakynthos
5	Sabbas		Prophet Daniel
6	Nicholas	20	Ignatius
7	Ambrose, Bishop of Milan		John of Kronstadt
9	Conception of Mary	22	Anastasia
11	Nicephorus Phocas	23	Chrysogenus
	Daniel Stylites	24	Eugenia, Philip, Claudia, Protas
12	Spyridon		& Hyacinth
	Juvenaly of Alaska	25	Nativity of the Lord
	Peter the Aleut	26	Synaxis of the Theotokos
	Finian	27	Stephen, First Martyr
13	Lucy	31	Melania the Younger
	Herman of Alaska		

MOVABLE FEASTS

Sunday nearest January 25	New Martyrs and Confessors of Russia
Sunday before Lent	**Spyridon**
1st Saturday of Lent	**Theodore Tyron**
1st Sunday of Lent	Triumph of Orthodoxy
2nd Sunday of Lent	**Gregory Palamas**
3rd Sunday of Lent	Veneration of the Cross
4th Sunday of Lent	John Climacus
5th Sunday of Lent	**Mary of Egypt**
Saturday before Palm Sunday	Raising of **Lazarus**
Sunday before Easter	Palm Sunday
Easter Day	Resurrection
Tuesday after Easter	**Raphael, Nicholas & Irene**
Friday after Easter	Life-Giving Spring
Sunday after Easter	**Thomas**
2nd Sunday after Easter	**Myrrh-bearers**
4th Sunday after Easter	**Samaritan Woman**
40 Days after Easter	Ascension
Sunday before Pentecost	Fathers of 1st Ecumenical Council
50 Days after Easter	Pentecost
1st Sunday after Pentecost	All Saints

3rd Sunday in June	Fathers of 1st–6th Ecumenical Councils
Nearest Saturday to July 2	**John of San Francisco**
3rd Sunday in October	Fathers of 7th Ecumenical Council
Sat. between Oct. 31 & Nov. 6	Enlighteners of Karelia
1st Saturday in November	**Raphael of Brooklyn** (AOCA)
1st Sunday in November	Synaxis of the **Unmercenary Physicians**
Sunday between Dec. 11 & 17	Sunday of the Holy Fathers

Further Reading

I could not begin to list even a fraction of the books that cover the subjects I've introduced in this little offering, so this is not a bibliography. I have, however, found the following useful, and if you want to study further, they may be of interest.

Orthodoxy in General

Two excellent books by Metropolitan Kallistos Ware are certainly a good starting point. *The Orthodox Church* remains by far the best introduction to all aspects of Orthodoxy. *The Orthodox Way* is a bit more advanced but is highly recommended as a very clear introduction to Orthodox spirituality and theology.

There are also many Orthodox websites. The most useful I've found so far are:

www.patriarchate.org – The Ecumenical Patriarchate.

www.oca.org – The Orthodox Church of America.

www.goarch.org – Greek Orthodox Archdiocese of America.

www.goawa.orthodoxpages.com – The Greek Orthodox Church in Western Australia.

www.christopherklitou.com – Run by Fr. Christopher Klitou in Cyprus, this contains downloadable translations of many of the Orthodox services, a complete calendar of feast days, fasting rules, icons, and many stimulating articles and sermons.

www.incommunion.org – The website of the Orthodox Peace Fellowship is full of interesting and stimulating articles. It contains a great deal of information about Mother Maria of Paris.

You also may be interested in my blog at www.chrismoorey.blogspot.gr. For updated information on all my writings, see facebook.com/chrismooreybooks.

For information on Byzantium and the early Church, Edward Gibbon's *Decline and Fall of the Roman Empire* is still great fun, though somewhat biased. If you're put off by its size, it can now be downloaded in full from the Project Gutenberg website (www.gutenberg.org/catalog), and by judicious use of the chapter descriptions and the search facility, you can find what you want fairly easily.

Similarly, *The History of the Church, The Life of Constantine,* and *Martyrs of Palestine* by the fourth-century historian Eusebius are great sources of information about the early Church and the persecutions. Doubt has been cast by many scholars on Eusebius's reliability, but recently there has been something of a restoration of his reputation. The books can be found on www.newadvent. org and www.tertullian.org/fathers/eusebius.

For the early Church in Britain, Bede's *Ecclesiastical History of England* is still remarkably readable and is available in many translations. A public domain version can be found on http://www.ccel.org/ccel/bede/history.html.

Saints

Primary Sources

For the lives of the prophets and apostles, the Bible is, of course, *the* primary source. If you want to just enjoy the stories, any good modern translation will suffice, but you still can't beat the King James Version (Authorized Version) for beauty.

The Protevangelion of the Apostle James, although not included in the canonical New Testament, is the main source for the traditions relating to the Virgin Mary and her parents. It was certainly accepted as genuine by many of the early Church Fathers, including St. John Chrysostom.

The Protevangelion, together with *The Acts of Paul and Thecla, The Acts of Thomas,* the letters of Ignatius, *The Martyrdom of Polycarp,* and many other early writings are of great interest although excluded from the official New Testament. They can be read in the book *Forbidden Gospels and Epistles,* by Archbishop Wake, available on the Project Gutenberg website (www.gutenberg.org/catalog). These books, together with a fantastic library of translations of all the early Church Fathers (both Greek and Latin), are also available on the Roman Catholic website www.newadvent.org.

Secondary Sources

I have found the following of great help in the research for this book:

The Penguin Dictionary of Saints, by Donald Attwater, is a very readable alphabetical listing with an excellent introduction by the author. It is a bit more comprehensive on the Western Church and is somewhat dismissive of the wilder stories of the martyrs.

A Calendar of Saints, by James Bentley (Tiger Books International), contains brief biographies in calendar order of feast days. Mr. Bentley goes for a more personal approach with many quotations and illustrations which help to bring the saints to life.

Christ in His Saints, by Fr. Patrick Reardon (Conciliar Press), is brilliant on the saints of the Bible, including the Old Testament.

Orthodox Saints, by George Poulos (Holy Cross Orthodox Press), is a very useful guide, written in a lively style in four volumes. It lists the saints according to their feast days and includes many of the lesser known Orthodox saints. The emphasis is more on the spiritual value of the saints' lives than on detailed biography.

The Oxford Dictionary of Saints, by David Hugh Farmer (Oxford).

Lives of the Saints of the Orthodox Church (Ormylia). The Synaxarion translated into English is very comprehensive, covering the lives of the saints in six volumes (one for two months), but it is rather expensive.

The following websites are also a good source for the lives of saints:

www.oca.org – The Orthodox Church of America

www.abbamoses.com

www.westsrbdio.org/prolog/my.html – contains the *Prologue to Ochrid,* by St. Nicholas of Zhicha, which is mentioned in the text. You might also like to read his *Prayers by the Lake* (available in print or audio book from Conciliar Press).

SOURCES FOR INDIVIDUAL SAINTS

Saint Nektarios, a Saint for Our Times by Sotos Chondropoulos.

Saints Raphael, Nicholas, and Irene of Lesvos by Constantine Cavarnos.

For a comprehensive tribute to every one of the Chinese martyrs by name, see *Accounts of the Martyrs of the Chinese Orthodox Church* on www.orthodox.cn/history/martyrs/index.

There is a tremendous database of the new martyrs of the Soviet Union on the website www.orthodox.net/russianm/index. In addition, Vladimir Moss's encyclopedic five-volume *Martyrs and Confessors of the Soviet Union* is available for free download on his website (www.orthodoxchristianbooks.com).

Finally, if the story of Alexander Schmorell inspired you as much as it did me, there is an enormous amount of material about the White Rose group, including all the leaflets and all Alexander's letters from prison, on www.katjasdacha.com. The website of the White Rose Fellowship is also worth visiting (www.weisse-rose-stiftung.de).

Acknowledgments and Thanks

I have made every effort to follow the laws of copyright and the rules of good manners in acknowledging sources. Indeed, I sometimes feel I have spent more time and effort in tracking down sources and writing e-mails and letters than I did in writing the book! Nonetheless, one of the wonderful side effects of this project has been the kindness and helpfulness of people from all over the world whom I have contacted for copyright permission. With very few exceptions, this has been freely given, and in fact, some of the people concerned have since become "e-friends."

I would particularly like to thank Metropolitan Kallistos of Diokleia for his continuing support and encouragement.

The following people have been particularly helpful in giving permission to use their material and in offering friendly encouragement and advice:

Nelson Mitrofan Chin of Orthodoxy in China

Jim Forest of In Communion

Fr. Seraphim Holland of St. Nicholas Orthodox Church, McKinney, Texas

Archimandrite Irenei of monarchos.net

Ursula Kaufmann of the White Rose Fellowship

Ian Lancashire of the University of Toronto

Fr. John Matusiak of the OCA website

Dr. Vladimir Moss

Dr. George Poulos

Katja Yurschak

I would also like to thank:

Dimitri Kokkinos and all the staff at Akritas Books, Athens, for having enough faith in my original manuscript to have it translated into Greek and published.

Katherine Hyde and Conciliar Press for believing in my work and for their help and advice in preparing the manuscript for publication. It's a much better book for their efforts.

Last but not least, I thank my wife, Eleni, from the bottom of my heart for her unfailing support and love, and for keeping my feet firmly on the ground by her occasional gentle reminders that I was writing a book for the general reader and not an academic textbook of theology!

About the Author

B orn in Sussex, England, in 1948, Chris Moorey attended St. Catherine's College, Oxford, and Surrey University. Having worked for British Telecomm for about twenty years, he solved his midlife crisis in 1994 by moving with his wife to Greece. Here Chris found a new career teaching English and they both found a new spiritual home in the Orthodox Church, into which they were baptized in 2001. Chris is the author of an introduction to Greek Orthodox churches for visitors and a book of saints' lives, published in Greek translation. He lives with his wife Eleni in Elounda, Crete.

Ancient Faith Ministries hopes you have enjoyed and benefited from this book. The proceeds from the sales of our books only partially cover the costs of operating our nonprofit ministry—which includes both the work of **Ancient Faith Publishing** and the work of **Ancient Faith Radio.** Your financial support makes it possible to continue this ministry both in print and online. Donations are tax-deductible and can be made at www.ancientfaith.com.

To view our other publications,
please visit our website: store.ancientfaith.com

ANCIENT FAITH RADIO

Bringing you Orthodox Christian music,
readings, prayers, teaching, and podcasts
24 hours a day since 2004 at
www.ancientfaith.com

CPSIA information can be obtained
at www.ICGtesting.com
Printed in the USA
FSHW011709270321
79797FS

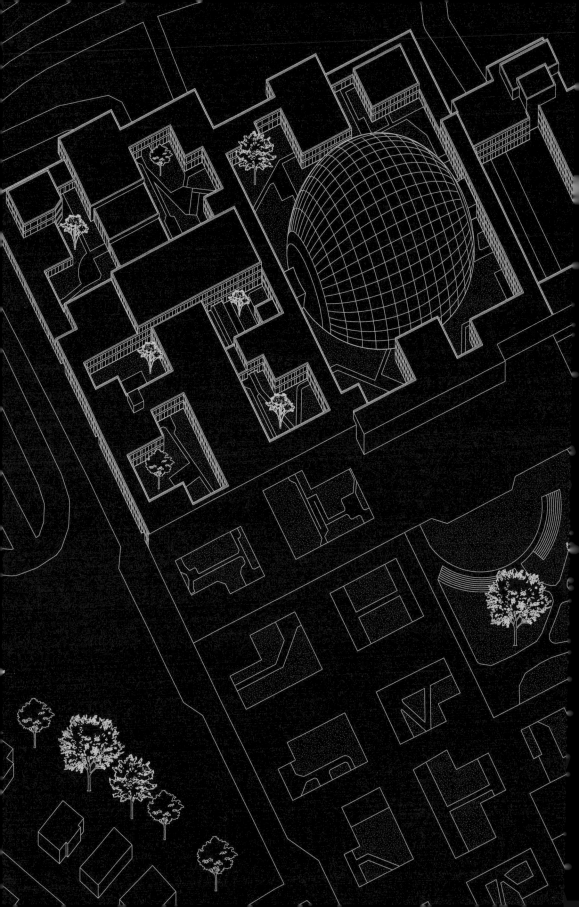

THE
ARCHITECTURE
OF
URBANITY

Vishaan
Chakrabarti

THE ARCHITECTURE OF URBANITY

Designing
for
Nature,
Culture,
and Joy

Princeton University Press

Princeton and Oxford

For Maria, Evan, and Avia,
without whom I am just an animal looking for a home.

Published by Princeton University Press,
41 William Street, Princeton, New Jersey 08540
In the United Kingdom: Princeton University Press,
99 Banbury Road, Oxford OX2 6JX
press.princeton.edu

Front and back cover design by
Michael Bierut, Britt Cobb, and Ethan Pidgeon, Pentagram.

All Rights Reserved
ISBN 978-0-691-20843-5
ISBN (ebook) 978-0-691-26152-2
British Library Cataloging-in-Publication Data is available

Design by Michael Bierut, Britt Cobb, and Ethan Pidgeon, Pentagram.
This book has been composed in Druk, Graphik, and Lyon.
Printed on acid-free paper.
Printed in China
10 9 8 7 6 5 4 3 2 1

CONTENTS

AUTHOR'S NOTE

I WROTE THIS BOOK IN THE YEARS SPANNING

2018 to 2023, a period that upended the life of nearly every person on earth. Humanity has endured past pandemics, but none before combined the need for strict physical isolation with the widespread availability of virtual telecommunications, forever altering our sense of ourselves, our relationships, and the places we inhabit. Space and time ruptured, leaving us with more questions than ever about the nature of our existence—questions no vaccines, however miraculous, could answer. Did solidarity formed around a shared global threat catalyze planetary consciousness, or did solitude from that threat calcify long-standing divisions? Will the challenges we understood before the pandemic, from global warming to social justice, be easier or harder to address in a post-pandemic reality? Is the mental health scourge the pandemic unleashed, or at least unearthed, inextricably tied to our segregated lives? How lonely are we? Are we now untethered from place, or do we appreciate our physical world even more dearly? Will the economic rationale for gathering in cities—which never really explained the desire for urban existence—remain as it was, unravel altogether, or be supplanted by a new logic?

Cities, regardless of size, are now for the people who love them. Collective and connected living, whether at the scale of the village or the metropolis, is sought primarily through choice more than at any point in human history, which presents an opportunity rather than a loss. Although most essential workers have less locational freedom, many others from paralegals to programmers can now decide how and where they live through the glory of agency rather than the grind of necessity. Geography has more significance than before the pandemic because at the individual level more of us can choose where we live and how we work. Yet at the societal scale our mutual decisions about the location of housing, infrastructure, and the nature that is subsequently left unbuilt impact the entire planet and all who call it home. We need to reconcile these individual and collective choices to ensure they are not working at cross-purposes. This book seeks to inform individuals and societies about such choices by asking us to consider the undeniable relationship between our sprawling built environment and our failing natural environment, the communal versus segregationist struggles in our past and present, and the delight of our face-to-face cultural bonds when they transcend the exigencies of work.

Might we choose to live in urbanity in part out of economic necessity, in greater measure out of a shared commitment to environmental stewardship, but most importantly, out of a joyous, devoted, pluralistic desire to unwind this mortal coil together?

Written in geographies both rural and urban, this book attempts to reconcile my two great professional passions, architecture and cities, by arguing for the critical relevance of both to the most pressing problems of our reeling world—

a world in which our societies have become further disconnected, segregated, and divisive at the precise moment when we need to build places of human connection to fix a climate and culture in crisis. This argument for the relevance of architecture and urbanism is as important, if not more, for those outside the design professions than those within because if we ignore the economic, ecological, and social impacts of our built environment, we do so at our mutual peril.

Social Connections Are Essential to Health, Happiness, and Longevity
Multiple research projects—including the world's longest scientific study of happiness at Harvard University—found that social connections are *essential* to human happiness and "increased the likelihood of surviving any given year by more than 50 percent across all age groups, genders, and ethnicities." This book examines how the design of our physical environment can foster these connections, and therefore our health and happiness.[1]

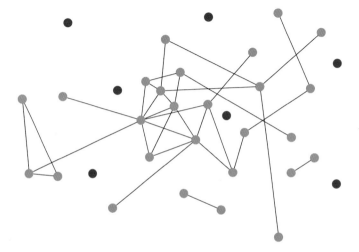

This endeavor is unusual for several reasons, largely because I am unabashed about weaving together seemingly disparate topics such as architecture, global warming, social and racial division, human happiness, the geography of rising fascism, neoliberal economics, the history and culture of urbanism, and the land-use battles taking place across our cities. Many consider these topics to be unrelated and may therefore find the simultaneous discussion of them to be too simplistic, ambitious, or discordant. Others will hopefully find in these pages a long-missing link between the professions of architecture and urbanism and the broad context in which their practice can serve civilization and its endangered home.

Consequently, this book is equally intended for the general public, decision makers, and those in the design professions, whether practitioners, students, or teachers. The public has a far better understanding of the other professions that deeply influence their lives—people know most politicians are lawyers, most health-care professionals study medicine, and farmers grow food. By contrast, how our world is built and who builds it is largely a mystery to the people who inhabit it despite the fact that shelter is among the most fundamental of human needs. Humanity is one with the architecture around us, and the work of those who construct our built environment should be more transparent to those who live in it. To provide this insight, this book asks readers to absorb and act upon the material here regardless of their relationship to the design disciplines because the form of our shared surroundings impacts not only all of our lives but those of every species on the planet.

Structurally, the book begins with an introduction about the broader relevance of the design professions to our world, which is followed by an initial section of five chapters that discuss architecture's relationship to our largest social challenges. The book closes with a set of chapters that suggest how design can deliver hope to all. Chapters 2, 6, and 9 are intended as graphic palette cleansers to help readers both digest the density of the material and contemplate the book's arguments through a plurality of media. In chapter 8, I have included the advocacy and professional work of my own architecture studio, PAU, after extensively discussing the precedents and practices that inspire us in the preceding chapters. I realize that the addition of these projects may feel promotional to some, but simply put, our studio's work is included because writing a book about the relevance and instrumentality of my profession demands that I present my own attempts at the same.

Can we solve the existential challenges we confront by designing communities for nature, culture, and joy, with the explicit aim of creating shared health and prosperity for every being on earth? I pose this audacious question because to do otherwise would lead to catastrophic failure for us all. The inexorable facts of global warming, income and racial inequity, political division, and population growth will not be alleviated only through good governance, redistributive capitalism, or technological panaceas like clean electricity or artificial intelligence if we don't simultaneously and proactively design for a better future. Design in this book is conceived as our shared intentionality about the environment we now choose to create and inhabit in the aftermath of the pandemic we all have navigated as a species. I invite you to believe that we can build a socially connected, pluralistic, place-specific, largely communal world in which everybody can responsibly share the treasures of this planet. I appreciate that such an invitation demands an immense leap of faith, and can only hope these pages reward your journey with luminosity, creativity, wit, abundant amounts of alliteration, and, yes, much-needed but rarely heeded doses of popular culture.

Vishaan Chakrabarti
New York City

THE EXCELLENCE OF RELEVANCE

THE UNITED NATIONS PROJECTS THAT THE

world's population will plateau at just over ten billion people by the close of this century, and while birth rates are declining in wealthy nations, most experts state that by 2100 we will share the planet with over two billion more neighbors than the eight billion we have today.[1] Despite significant reductions in global poverty and famine over the past several decades, too much of our existing population remains in precarious circumstances, while the rest of us consume far more resources than our environment can afford. Given the addition of two billion more individuals on the earth, the stakes seem clear, perilous, and, for many, hopeless. But rather than be fearful, imagine the overwhelming intellectual, artistic, social, and material bounty these billions of new hearts and minds would offer humanity if we could all live sustainably, in dignity, together. Imagine the discoveries made, the books written, the cures found, the music scored, the planets visited, the food grown, the plays produced, the intelligence created, and the peace established if we could form a healthy and harmonious world of ten billion. Given that most people worldwide already live in urbanized environments—including both cities and the suburban regions that surround them—the prospect of a sustainable planet of ten billion is only achievable if we intentionally design more ecological and equitable spaces of collective living, be they small villages or big cities.[2]

A city is a cultural, social, political, economic, and infrastructural construct, formed as much through people, policy, and advocacy as it is through its physicality. Cities have always been my fascination because they spatially mediate between people and the planet. The promise of the city is to be a beehive abuzz with multitudes who through their individual and collective agency produce culture and commerce, where the unexpected and iconoclastic are embraced, where politicians are directly accountable to their constituents, and where leaders and residents can innovate at scale. As we will see, new policies that address equitable housing, global warming, social infrastructure, or public space can be adopted en masse across a large city but also can be spread to other communities, large and small, around the world to great effect. Carbon negative urban buildings, groundbreaking cultural institutions, unique public spaces, streets closed to private cars, local manufacturing, new forms of supportive homeless housing—these are all initiatives mayors can enact and share. But beyond government, everyday people in cities regularly alter human history. Largely peaceful protests, be it those of Black Lives Matter, the Velvet Revolution, or the Arab Spring, almost always occur in cities because that is where the revolution gets televised; without cities, nations and the societies they house would rarely change.

Architecture, by contrast, has traditionally been a monastic practice limited to a handful of us absorbed in form, space, material, light, use, construction, and the theories that bind them. As architects we toil with the knowledge—and too often the resentment—that excellence is narrowly judged, rarely achieved, and poorly

A World of Ten Billion

The United Nations projects the global population to plateau at just over ten billion people by 2100 , with the vast majority living in cities and their suburbs. Two billion people are projected to be rural residents by 2100, which is similar to the number of rural inhabitants worldwide during the 1960s.

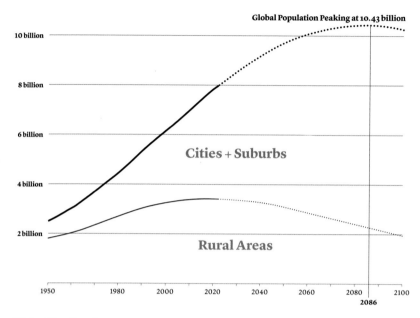

A Tale of Two Trends

Birth rates are declining—in some cases precipitously—in today's wealthy nations, but the overall global population is still projected to rise until the end of this century. It is clear to this author that the empowerment of women, sustainable urban and rural development, and sound immigration policies will stabilize population by equalizing opportunity in regions devastated by colonialism, slavery, and ongoing exploitation.

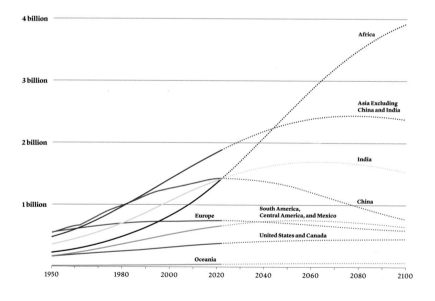

understood. For humanity, cities may be physically composed of architecture, yet this is taken for granted as much as the air we breathe or the sidewalks we traverse.

The nexus between cities and architecture has been written about extensively, especially in the twentieth century.[3] But ours is a new world, emerging from a global pandemic, embroiled in ongoing fundamentalist and increasingly violent challenges to democracies worldwide, and riddled with environmental, racial, political, economic, and technological challenges that few thinkers from centuries past could have anticipated much less addressed. Consequently, issues of racial equity and sustainable ecology permeate this book unlike the work of some canonical twentieth-century urbanists like Jane Jacobs and Rem Koolhaas.[4]

Despite the remarkable possibilities and challenges confronting the professions of the built environment, practitioners, rather than coalesce in response, have splintered over the last few decades in the wake of both global capitalism and social critique. As someone who alternately works among architects, planners, academics, journalists, policy wonks, community advocates, preservationists, environmentalists, political leaders, business executives, and entrepreneurs, I see the walls that divide the professions much more than the bridges that connect them, which frightens me considering the multiple planetary emergencies we collectively face.

Given this precarious state of the planet, why write a book about, of all things, architecture?

Most find architecture to be of little relevance to the pressing challenges of our time, including a climate in crisis, domestic terrorism, unprovoked wars, overdue racial reckoning, expanding social inequity, world-stopping global pandemics, the abrogation of established rights, and accelerating technological dislocations. (Instead of the tech-sector idea of "disruptions" I prefer the term "dislocations," which refers to a series of effects society experiences as a result of technological change, including jobs replaced by automation, remote and hybrid work, fraying political discourse fueled by social media, and the dissociative psychological impact of people absorbed more by the bubble of their smartphones than the world around them.)[5] Given that some of these challenges are truly existential—which together are culminating in a resurgence of fascism worldwide—shouldn't it be our leading policymakers, scientists, and social critics who address the pressing questions of our time? Given the enormity of these challenges, what relevance do architects and cities have? Reciprocally, perhaps we as practitioners need new standards for excellence in order to achieve relevance.

Practicing architects, urban planners, and engineers might balk at such questions by claiming their relevance based upon certain inarguable facts. For example, two of the leading sources of global carbon emissions are buildings and cars, topics about which the design disciplines have deep expertise. Affordable housing production and social infrastructure projects are intended, however unsuccessfully, to ameliorate inequity. Much of the racial and gender discrimination found globally is geographic and territorial, with urban renewal as envisioned by architects and perpetrated by planners having played a demonstrable role in racial segregation and heteronormative gender typecasting.[6] The ubiquitous problems created worldwide by the promulgation of highways and the incentivizing of segregated suburbs throughout the twentieth century are unquestionably central to today's issues of global warming and racial division.[7]

Theoreticians might go further still, arguing that all these problems stem from the means by which space itself is produced. Landscape architects and city planners, typically operating on broader territories than most architects, could claim more relevance to the problems of our epoch, given the larger-scale impacts their respective fields have on human habitation and land use. A communal finger from all these disciplines might point at neoliberal economics as the main culprit of our woes, bolstered by undeniable evidence that the religion of free markets and weak government has fueled many of our current societal, public health, environmental, and geopolitical failures.[8]

And while all these assertions ring true, and are indeed discussed in the pages that follow, there is at the heart of this book a more direct correlation between the problems of our world and the potentials of design, a correlation directly centered on the instrumentality of *connective design* and its ability to reknit the fragmented cultures of our ever more polarized world. Throughout this book I will use the term "connective design," whether at the scale of architecture or larger-scale urban strategies, to refer to something more comprehensive than socially responsible efforts at sustainability or affordability, both of which are necessary but not sufficient. Connective design as discussed here is an intentional method of practice, describing the conscious attempt of the designer to forge deeper physical bonds across society at every scale, whether it be the placement of a door, the creation of an arcade, the planning of public space, the place-based evolution of a skyline, or the deployment of materials or tectonics that reflect local narratives, all in the service of creating connections across the fractious human condition we must together reknit. This is not a Pollyannaish plea for a homogenized, gentrified, go-along-get-along world; to the contrary, it is a plea for embracing difference. Connective design, when successful, generates *positive social friction* across differing cultures, races, and classes, enabling through serendipitous physical encounters our ability to confront, understand, and bridge the differences among us, thereby generating *urbanity* as defined below. Cities are the starting point for this investigation but by no means the end. In the pages that follow, we will explore the idea of connective design as a prerequisite to the condition of urbanity, which can manifest in rural areas and walkable villages, as well as in cities.

Why focus so specifically on the design of cities and communal settings as a means for connection? Because to address our largest challenges like global warming, we must design more ecological communities—but such designs will never be adopted rapidly enough to be impactful when we have a society as disconnected as ours. Metropolitan regions are the primary form of habitation for our species today, and as such are fertile ground for cultural connection even though they, too, are polarized politically, economically, racially, and socially.

In 2013, I wrote a book, building upon the work of many, that extolled the environmental, economic, and social benefits of building dense, transit-based cities both in the United States and globally. *A Country of Cities: A Manifesto for an Urban America* was well received, but for its Achilles' heel.[9] Informed by exhaustively researched data and infographics, readers were open to the argument that dense urban life produces a lower carbon footprint per capita, creates more opportunities for shared health and prosperity, and improves social mobility when coupled with progressive policies that build affordability and infrastructure. But the dilemma of this argument is that it is largely quantitative without speaking to the qualitative aspects of city building. Many people, even if they are open to greater urban density, find most contemporary metropolitan growth to be soul crushing, especially when built by mainstream developers.

Of all the arguments that challenged my previous book, the one I could never address to my satisfaction is this: most people find new high-density districts to be formulaic and most new buildings to possess few praiseworthy qualities—most find the environment that run-of-the-mill development offers to be devoid of culture, history, texture, or humanity. Backed by solid evidence and popular opinion, critics point to the ubiquity of blue glass skyscrapers, historicized shopping streets, privatized public space, and repetitive chain stores, and can rightfully claim that our cities are oversaturated with these uninspired forms of urban growth, however transit-oriented they may be. The quotidian in our built environment used to be quaint and quirky—now it is mundane and monolithic. In a world of social media, the urban commons is increasingly the only thing we physically share, but its design has become so commonplace that a rare consensus among progressives and conservatives has emerged: the growing global metropolis is largely a banal physical future brimming with ennui.[10]

When we speak of a new, transit-based, denser world, to quote Peggy Lee, *is that all there is?*[11] And if all we can manage to build is a technocratically performative yet culturally repellent world, doesn't the entire urban project unravel? Even if—and it's a very big if—we could address all the concerns that come with new urban growth—gentrification, community agency, sustainability, congestion, traffic, diversity in representation, fair labor, data privacy, and so on—does any of it matter if humanity finds the new world we build to be experientially repugnant?

This predicament is precisely why the practice of architecture and its allied fields is so relevant today: because great design centers on lived experience. Empirical success without experiential uplift is a pyrrhic victory.

Is that all there is? —Homogeneous Suburbs across Six Continents

Outskirts of Rio de Janeiro, Brazil (*top left*); Bangalore, India (*top middle*); Cairo, Egypt (*top right*);
Paris, France (*bottom left*); Sydney, Australia (*bottom middle*); Toronto, Canada (*bottom right*).

Is that all there is? —Homogeneous Downtowns across Six Continents

Frankfurt, Germany (*top left*); Johannesburg, South Africa (*top middle*); Panama City, Panama (*top right*);
Sydney, Australia (*bottom left*); Ulaanbaatar, Mongolia (*bottom middle*); Calgary, Canada (*bottom right*).

Achieving important performance metrics such as transit-orientation and affordability is necessary but not sufficient to reach a world that meets our aspirations, a world in which experience matters as much as efficiency. In terms of both global warming and social inequity, most reasonable people agree that we must invest in our communities and their infrastructure. Among progressives and some centrists a consensus appears to be emerging that we must reconsider the way we live, the way we use land and other resources, the way we tax ourselves to equalize opportunity, the way we invest in social and physical infrastructure, and the means by which we invest in these changes in terms of labor rights, social mobility, and community input.[12] No matter what new technologies emerge, if we are to save the planet and the civilization that inhabits it, we need to adopt more compact lifestyles that are undergirded by social fairness, self-determination, and human agency. This last point demands particular emphasis if we are to focus on lived experience: one can imagine a sustainable and economically equalized society that is governed as a totalitarian state. Human agency, our freedom to realize our own aspirations—to be entrepreneurial, to be racially and sexually free, to be expressive without fear, to control our own bodies—must be part of any humanitarian vision for our collective future.

What is exciting is that we, as a society, are finally beginning to talk about all of these issues as an interrelated set of problems that could be addressed holistically. As a noted climate expert at the University of California, Berkeley, said to me in 2020, "It used to be that we felt it important to leave untouched nature alone, but it has become apparent that there is no such thing as untouched nature, therefore the entire environment is fundamentally a design problem."[13] This is not to suggest that holistic approaches equate to monocultures and groupthink. To the contrary, as we consider comprehensive approaches to our challenges, we must have a fuller understanding of the planet's diversity—not only in the cities and regions in which most of us will live but in the rural environments, oceans, and wilderness that sequester our carbon, shield us from zoonotic diseases, supply our food, give us solace, and house vibrant cultures that should remain distinct from urban and suburban life.

Given the emerging consensus around community investment and the need to rethink the design of our environment, what are our aspirations for how we live? If we were to design dense but humane new forms of habitation that accommodated our anticipated population growth, the palimpsest of our narratives, the rich biodiversity of our planet, and the needs of the species with which we share it, what would such a world look and feel like? What would its experiences be? Humility demands that the full resolution of that future is far too much to seek to envision, cognizant as we are of failing past attempts at the same. But can we at least imagine some immediate glimpses of a better horizon, of some pixels that hint at a hopeful vision as our lens hunts for clear focus?

I will attempt to address this dauntingly complex question through the inextricable relationships among architecture, cities, and our shared global ecology, drawing, in chapter 7, on the select efforts of a small group of practicing international architects who together are moving toward this asymptote and increasingly represent new forms of excellence that extend beyond singular notions of sustainability, affordability, or social responsibility. Implicit in this collective body of work is that this asymptote has a name, has a complex central and subtle aspiration, which is to nurture *urbanity* in projects across communities large and small as models of shared health and prosperity. As these examples will hopefully illustrate, connective design generates positive social friction in the service of nature, culture, and joy.

"Urbanity" is a common term, but what does it really mean?

The dictionary definitions of both "urbanity" and "urbane" have only a vague relationship to cities, referring instead to general notions of sophistication or snobbery.[14] Their formal meaning tends to be pejorative, with connotations of "city slickers" that I suspect have been biased by the anti-urbanism long embedded in Western culture. (Such bias dates back to the Bible—consider the Old Testament story of Sodom and Gomorrah, in which God destroys two cities in response to the sins of their citizens, or contemporary disaster and science fiction films like *Independence Day*, in which cities outside "the heartland" like New York and Los Angeles repeatedly get destroyed.) In more recent decades, the term "urban" has been used synonymously with inner-city culture, rarely in a positive manner, and often with a deeply racist subtext. This dovetails with the incendiary and retrograde anti-urbanism infamously conjured by the phrase "this American carnage,"

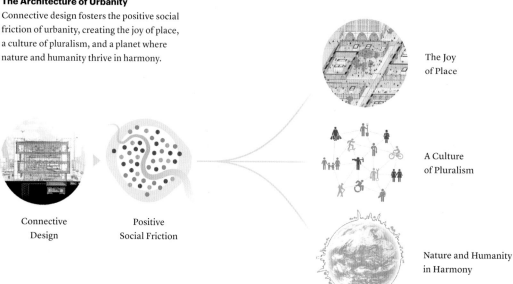

The Architecture of Urbanity
Connective design fosters the positive social friction of urbanity, creating the joy of place, a culture of pluralism, and a planet where nature and humanity thrive in harmony.

Connective
Design

Positive
Social Friction

The Joy
of Place

A Culture
of Pluralism

Nature and Humanity
in Harmony

Anti-Urbanism in Western Culture
Cities destroyed by God: *Sodom and Gomorrah* (1680). Cities destroyed by aliens: *Independence Day* (1996)

a craven political sensibility that is a cynically effective and highly profitable wedge in our long-standing, largely manufactured, and increasingly global urban-rural divide.[15]

We must bridge this division if we are to survive as a species. The urban and rural are inextricable—we need each other too much to withstand the animus that has been created between us. We must think of urbanity as a condition that transcends the physical and economic phenomenon of the metropolis: the condition of urbanity can be found or nurtured in tight-knit rural villages, interwoven academic campuses, international refugee settlements, and in some, but only some, of our big cities. All great cities should strive to be urban, but communities certainly can be urban without being cities.

Despite the stereotype of being elitist, urbanity speaks to the converse of elitism because it refers to the grittiness of the commons, a place where social, racial, and economic differences collide positively, if not always comfortably. For the purposes of this book, we will use the words "urban," "urbane," and "urbanity" in a positive, egalitarian, and expansive light, particularly given that most people worldwide live in metropolitan regions and, consequently, our future as a species is contingent upon successful policies and projects that have no implicit anti-urban bias.

In this book we will also use the word "urbanity" as it is linked to the lesser-known term "cosmopolis." Distinct from the elite connotations of the word "cosmopolitan," the term "cosmopolis" has been in widespread use since the mid-nineteenth century and is derived from the Greek *kosmos*, meaning world, and *polis*, or city, revealing a simple definition, "*a city inhabited by people from many different countries.*"[16]

A silver lining of both capitalism and colonialism, it is not a coincidence that the idea of the cosmopolis would emerge during the Industrial Revolution and the height of European colonial power when widespread global travel—whether by free will or enslavement—became possible.[17] As architectural historian Kathleen James-Chakraborty has noted, the suburbs may well have derived in part from the colonial cantonments designed to separate the colonizers from the colonized. As the colonized inevitably immigrated to the cities of their colonizers, those same overlords sought segregation in domestic cantonments, or suburbs, in an effort to escape a cosmopolis like London. Thus the diversity of the cosmopolis

The Urbanity of Rural Villages in India
In the Kakinada district of Andhra Pradesh, a tight-knit neighborhood of farmers is surrounded by paddy fields.

in its original incarnation was hardly seen as a good thing; it was simply an inevitable by-product of early globalization.[18]

Instead of focusing on city dwellers hailing from different *countries* per the original definition of cosmopolis, let's rethink the idea as a city inhabited by people from many different *cultures and classes* to be more expansive in terms of race, gender, and socioeconomics. Yet this too is insufficient because if such a city is sprawling and segregated like most metropoles today, the diverse populations they house will rarely meet face-to-face, which arguably is the requisite condition for generating the cultural exchanges that cause society to progress. When this criterion of physical proximity is introduced, we can retool the old idea of cosmopolis as *a city inhabited by people from many different cultures and classes who spatially interact.*

Some of the best examples of small but intensely urbane communities exist as two very different forms of human settlement: academic campuses and international refugee camps, both of which at times house people from a wide range of cultures and classes. In the formal economy, however, cities tend to have these urbane characteristics more than most rural areas, in part due to the vast expanse of agrarian geographies. Therefore, while this book will not participate in a faddy fetish for the rural—although in the last chapter we will discuss the tantalizing possibilities of "rurbanity" in the Garden of Urban—for our purposes and in the spirit of optimism, we establish here a renewed definition for the condition of urbanity: *a community inhabited by people from many different cultures and classes who spatially interact.*

The merits of aspiring toward pluralism in this definition of urbanity—as opposed to more technocratic goals like density for density's sake, metropolitanism, or smart growth—become evident upon further consideration. For example, if a municipality upzones a neighborhood for greater density without enacting protections for local tenants against harassment by landlords, displacement of existing residents can occur, which in turn erodes urbanity by erasing the cultural richness provided by the stable presence of a mixture of races and classes. A metropolitan region might include suburban sprawl, but an urbane region by definition would not, because the spatial segregation of sprawl would inhibit the positive social friction of different cultures and classes mixing together eye to eye. Even smart growth, or the more nefarious marketing of so-called smart cities, does not equate to urbanity in the sense that technology is never a silver bullet.

Technology has never neutrally promoted cultural exchange and must be held accountable to larger humanist goals. There is mounting evidence that technology

Big ≠ Urban and Urban ≠ Big

A segregated metropolis is not synonymous with urbanity, whereas a pluralistic village can be recognized as such.

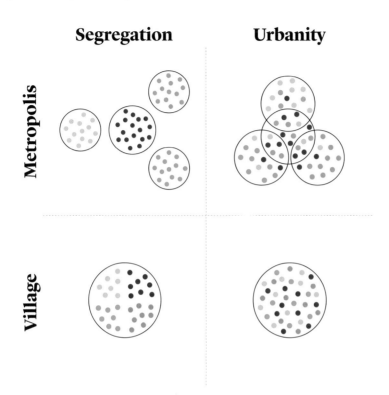

Urbanity Advances Culture

Urbanity engenders cultural progress by hosting face to face contact with people who differ from mainstream society. (See also page 87.)

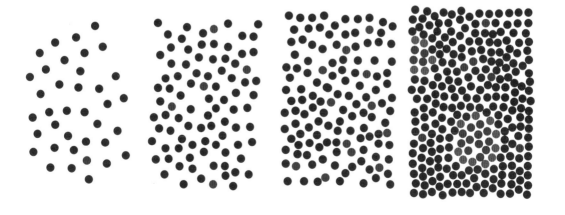

companies profit from anger-fueled rhetoric on their platforms.[19] Of course social media can peacefully connect people around the world, but it is also clear that it has become an organizing platform for rising global fundamentalism. These fascistic populists, fragile as they are in their delusions of being replaced, are terrified by the prospect of a world brimming with communities inhabited by people from many different cultures, all mixing, face-to-face. Such a multicultural vision is at the core of their worst fears, animating their desires for civil war. In this era of widening spatial, social, and technological tribalism, few ideas could be as important, as galvanizing, and as filled with civic delight as that of urbanity instilling a collective, pluralistic, and necessarily friction-filled sense of cultural belonging to a physical commons.

Small-Town Urbanity
Patchogue, New York (*top*); Goodwood, Ontario (*middle*, filming location for *Schitt's Creek*); and Columbus, Indiana (*bottom*).

If we are to avoid the civil unrest associated with our fractious global politics, we cannot focus on the urban to the exclusion of the rural. Urbanity is not dependent on cities: a pluralistic small town can have all the fixings of a big metropolis in terms of cultural exchange if it is truly diverse, truly inclusive, and in both its demography and geography it manifests a true sense of belonging for all who inhabit it. The fictional small town in *Schitt's Creek* embodies this spirit, as does the burgeoning village of Patchogue, New York, which has made a series of investments in denser housing, social infrastructure, and a broad range of restaurants, producing a quilt of small-town urbanity imbued with economic and racial diversity.[20] A famous example of modestly scaled urbanity, in this case surrounded by farmland, is Columbus, Indiana, where the Miller family hired famed global architects and landscape designers for public and private commissions, instilling within that small city a palpable sense of communal innovation that is lacking in many a large, immodest metropolis.

By this definition an urbane community is not elitist or metropolitan. It is a community that embraces and celebrates pluralism across race, class, and gender regardless of its size. It is a community that creates a sense of belonging for all. After all, for those of us who constantly bandy about and praise the idea of community, we would be wise to remember that communities are not intrinsically urbane—some nurture difference and change while others tacitly or explicitly revel in their stasis of social, class, or racial segregation.

As used in this book, the terms "urbanity" and "urbane" represent expansive, positive, and inclusive concepts that describe many of the greatest communities, large and small, on the planet. While these words might conjure a metropolis like New York City, we must think more broadly about the many places that fit this revised definition of urbanity, such as Rio de Janeiro, Kolkata, and Mexico City, in addition to the refugee settlements and academic campuses we will discuss in further detail.

Similarly, a city like Tokyo does not house vast numbers of people from many different nationalities, but it nonetheless feels urban because it is a hotbed of thriving subcultures. This is an important distinction that allows one to escape the tired focus on the polyglot nature of London and New York, as well as the rather demeaning Western view of the ever-expanding "third-world megalopolis," such as São Paulo or Mumbai, as problems to be solved rather than a condition to be celebrated, albeit critically so. (It is important to note here that the term "third world" was coined in the 1950s not to connote poverty but rather to identify those nations during the Cold War that were not aligned with either the Western or Soviet bloc.)[21]

Not every city fits this definition of urbanity because of the degree to which many cities value cultural conformity over pluralistic differences, regardless of how racially diverse yet segregated their populations may be. For example, we must question whether cities that are the vaunted paradise of planners, such as Copenhagen, actually represent heterogeneity as opposed to a fundamentally homogeneous vision of urban life.[22] Such places do not sufficiently value a mix of skin color, bank balances, and—perhaps most importantly—mindsets in a way that true urbanity must. In this sense, a city without social friction isn't really a city no matter how big, sustainable, wealthy, healthy, or self-important.

Thus defined, urbanity is identified in this book as one of the central goals to which mindful design practice should aspire if architecture and its allied arts—including landscape architecture, urban planning, historic preservation, engineering, and a host of other related disciplines—wish to be relevant to today's global challenges. (I say "one of the central goals" because I do not wish to be exclusionary to the efforts of others who are exploring mindful design practice for other arenas, such as the non-Anthropocene, the oceans, or outer space. Valuable as these investigations may be, they are not the focus of this book.) Despite the risk of being criticized as positivists, we must recognize that the means to promote urbanity are complex but clear.

AS ARCHITECTS, URBANISTS, POLICYMAKERS, AND ALL OTHERS WHO CARE ABOUT BETTERING OUR COMMUNITIES

WE MUST

DESIGN with dedication and impassioned skill that flow from talent and tenacity—our political, social, and environmental convictions are most impactful when they are grounded in, rather than substitutes for, our core aptitudes. The work of designing urbanity is extraordinarily difficult and must be undertaken with study, commitment, and rigor.

PREPARE our communities for global warming while reducing further catastrophic damage through intensified metropolitan land use coupled with the conservation of unbuilt territories, resilient infrastructure, green urban construction, and advocacy for environmental justice.

BUILD income-based multifamily and transitional social housing, not only because it is an ethical imperative that would generate far more equitable outcomes across many metrics from higher educational achievement to reduced incarceration to more resilient public health to less homelessness but also because urbanity requires the presence of the alternative cultures that affordable communities create.

CREATE a magnetic public realm for a multiplicity of cultures across myriad races, ages, abilities, and societal classes so that we can thrive together in the space of our communities, not merely to have "diversity" as a consumable good but for us to be challenged by face-to-face differences in an urbane society that values positive social friction and just public safety over the allure of working from home.

ADVANCE pluralistic cultural, educational, and social institutions in villages, campuses, and cities that celebrate diversity, justice, and urbanity.

REIMAGINE urban mobility by dispensing with daily private car trips in our metropolitan regions, regardless of the technology behind the drivetrain, in order to enhance commute times, safety, and experiences while saving our planet.

COLLABORATE with like-minded counterparts in the public, private, nonprofit, and community sectors to achieve our goals across multitudes.

RECOGNIZE the means of production, including the economic, environmental, and labor standards that undergird our efforts in and beyond our offices.

If architects ignore these broader imperatives and instead continue down the more-is-more irrational exuberance of the 1990s, fueled by an increasingly irrelevant and insular "starchitect" culture, the profession will never tackle the fundamental challenges of the human condition nor will it have the economic or societal value it claims to desire. Historicist architects, who differ in their style but not necessarily in their solipsism, may arbitrarily deploy Western symbols from eras past in an effort to humanize architecture, but they too must consider the degree to which producing such symbols are off-putting to those of us not from the dominant culture, which in turn degrades the pluralism demanded by urbanity. (A "New Urbanist" once white-mansplained to me that the colonial architecture in India was better than its modern architecture, oblivious to both the oppression such historic architecture represents and the pride with which many progressive Indians view their homegrown contemporary architecture, despite the efforts of the current conservative government to regress.) Similarly, the attempt in 2020 to adopt neoclassical architecture as the official government style of the United States was eerily reminiscent of both the aesthetic leanings of the Third Reich and the subsequent attacks on modern art and architecture as communist symbols during decades of McCarthyite Red Scare hysteria.[23] Lastly, in addition to both profligate starchitecture and retrograde historicism, architects must reject the twentieth-century, tabula-rasa urban renewal impulses that led society to tear down too much and preserve too little, which not only introduced far more embodied energy into our cities but erased the cultural narratives that generate a sense of cross-cultural neighborhood belonging, particularly in black and brown communities. As we go forward, it is paramount to implement historic preservation only when it is conceived with surgical justification, rather than when it is wielded as a cudgel to stop progressive high-density mixed-income development that sustains the cultures of our existing neighborhoods while meeting the needs of our growing population.

To have meaning to everyone beyond the profession, architectural practice must adopt broad approaches and strong guardrails with little regard for the self-referential paradigms and prerogatives of the twentieth century. Design can regain its societal relevance but to do so, architects cannot be the people who live off of gentrifying luxury condominium developments, who bankrupt cities with budget-busting "public" monuments, who shrug when indentured servants die on building sites, who sexually harass or don't pay employees, who blithely work for dictators and human rights abusers, and who visibly, recklessly, and to the detriment of us all fiddle while Rome burns. If architects do not strive toward a stronger, clearer sense of what they will and will not do as professionals, how can they avoid the adage that they represent "the second oldest profession in the world," and thereby relegate themselves to the dustbin of the irrelevant?

It is time—once and for all—to exterminate the idea of the starchitect, and from its ashes let the phoenix of a new definition of architectural excellence rise, one in which we act as design thought leaders, one in which we act as the honorable, impactful professionals the world actually needs.

This book, however, seeks to illuminate a different path forward not only for architects but for landscape architects, city planners, historic preservationists, cultural leaders, public officials, civic advocates, community activists, artists, engineers, technologists, educators, entrepreneurs, and builders dedicated to the art and science of creating urbanity. This path would lead to a sea change, recasting the significance of all urban professions that share the goal of creating climate-conscious communities of belonging, communities that are as experientially uplifting as they are empirically performative.

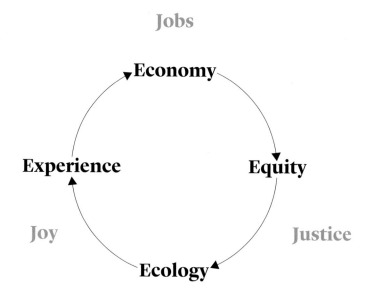

To better understand the broader path I am advocating, consider the fact that before the pandemic public officials commonly repeated the economic development refrain of "jobs, jobs, jobs" with the assumption that metropolitan regions would attract human capital, and therefore fiscally thrive, as long as their economies supplied employment for their residents. By contrast, today's public policy mantra may want to become "jobs, justice, and joy" to reflect two undeniable realities. First, many employers, though certainly not all, will for the foreseeable future offer their personnel some degree of flexibility to work from home, meaning that for cities to thrive they must now work harder to create better designed public experiences instead of lazily relying on the economic activity generated by frustrated commuters who, until recently, had few alternatives to ugly commutes on substandard infrastructure. Second, employment is a necessary but insufficient condition to attract and retain people because most forward-thinkers, be they fresh out of college, new immigrants and migrants, long-standing community residents, smart entrepreneurs, or empty nesters, want to know that their municipalities value justice and joy in equal measure to jobs. Whether it be the murder of George Floyd or the ravages to New Orleans's Lower Ninth Ward during Hurricane Katrina, most of us want to live in a community that practices racial and environmental justice, which by no means is a stand against first responders or law enforcement because what is the law enforcing if not justice? This leaves joy as the most ineffable of the triad, but who are we without it? What good are jobs and justice if we can't experience the collective joy of a playground brimming with kids from every walk and color of life, or a beautiful tree-lined urban streetscape composed of diverse architecture and uses, or an electrifying subway pole dance that evokes smiles between strangers? As a species we need more to satisfy us than good analytical outcomes, no matter how important they may be.

The promise of an architecture of urbanity is to deliver jobs, justice, and joy in the near term, and shared planetary prosperity in the far, forsaking forever the architecture of the star and the city of the car. This book centers on a call to redefine excellence within and beyond the design professions, not in an effort to jettison beauty and culture but rather to reimagine them for our pluralistic, resource-constrained age. Both Walt Whitman and Barack Obama declared that as humans we are multitudes, and it is this abundance of being that must be reflected in our collective design processes.[24] Unlike the singularity and segregation that defile our history and still dominate our world for reasons we will explore in the first half of this book, we must in lockstep with a much broader range of contributors embrace a multifaceted design approach, as described in the book's second half. The future architecture of our world will be relevant when it celebrates the communities, cultures, climates, and construction methods that together express the pressing narrative of our kaleidoscopic humanity.

DES

PAIR

FROM

HERE

TO

BANALITY

THE WORLD SEEMS TO BE DISINTEGRATING

into a series of warring binaries, with the rural and the urban pitted against each other politically, culturally, and economically. We are used to thinking of politics along the schism of left and right, but the more relevant binary today is inclusion versus exclusion—across our political spectrum many feel marginalized. In some cases this has dangerous implications from policy to public space. Exploiting an increased sense of social, physical, and technological isolation, fascistic political movements fighting for singular religious theocracies have gained power and popular support across Europe, the Middle East, and Latin America, as well as in the far right wing of our largest democracies, including India and the United States, nations that had promised us the exact opposite: pluralistic secularism.

There is little daylight between the fundamentalists in these democracies and the Taliban, who "told us who they were" to paraphrase Maya Angelou, when they destroyed the statues at Bamiyan at the outset of this century.[1] Art embodies the aspirations we hold, the perils we face, and the cultures we risk, which is why it is the target of testosterone. The airplane and the internet, with their physical and virtual promise to bind the world, have just as equally destabilized it. Globalization has wrought a fanatical populist backlash in which the urge to sift, separate, and segregate, both physically and online, has deepened to the point of contempt, violence, and sedition.

The Century Begins
In March 2001, the Buddha of Bamiyan was destroyed on orders from the Taliban.

While most leaders throughout the private, public, and nonprofit sectors understand this existentially challenging state of affairs, few consider its relationship to our built environment, which serves as both a mirror and a window into our fractured society. Fewer still consider the latent potential our built environment has to help bridge these fearsome divisions. To understand this possibility we first need to understand the road humanity has traversed to arrive at this segregated juncture—our physical world, brimming as it is with banality, both manifests and foments our divided society. Yes, we are growing economically, but we do so aimlessly, believing growth for growth's sake will somehow better the situation without acknowledging the obvious: a larger divided world is more dangerous than a smaller one simply because the divisions, too, grow bigger. Yet we hurtle on, if not forward. Today we build metropolis, not urbanity. In terms of most global metropolitan growth and the potential it has to heal our broken world, we are on a road to nowhere.

Well, how did we get here? Below please find a few thousand years of urbanism condensed into a single, admittedly simplified chapter, starting with the idea that as a species predominantly consisting of bipeds, we have throughout history built societies of streets for communal connection as well as transportation.[2] Streets and sidewalks are not functional mobility corridors to be planned by technocrats for the contradictory goals of speed and safety; they are fundamental to how we interact with different cultures eye to eye in the space of the city.

Streets Predate Cars
A raised sidewalk and crosswalk can be found on a paved street in the ruins of Pompeii, Italy.

Our city streets have played this connective role for millennia, with sidewalks alone dating back over four thousand years.[3] Entire metropolitan worlds are being built today predicated on the rejection of the street as anything more than a corridor for cars, the historical causes for which are unearthed below. Just one century of amnesia triggered by the internal combustion engine has fueled our current metropolitan malaise in terms of both global warming and racial segregation, a century that must now recede in the rearview mirror.

This Is Not a Street
State Highway 121 in Texas, from I-35E toward Grapevine.

Let's begin with the fact that the majority of humanity seems to believe that the image above is a picture of a street.

Most people operate under the misapprehension that streets were invented for cars. Nothing could be further from the truth. For thousands of years humans have used street grids to organize cities and connect communities for reasons as spiritual and societal as they were economic and functional. I begin with the public space of streets because they are the building block of the physical city and how we mix within it, an interaction that today is constantly obfuscated by the isolation of cars, the tribalism of social media, and an urbanism that has evolved since the Enlightenment, as we will see, with the explicit purpose of segregation and separation—an urbanism that has not always been thus.

Throughout the twentieth century, many economists tried to convince us that cities emerged from what they termed *material surplus*.[4] Essentially, their argument held that as Homo sapiens replaced Neanderthals and humanity became a species

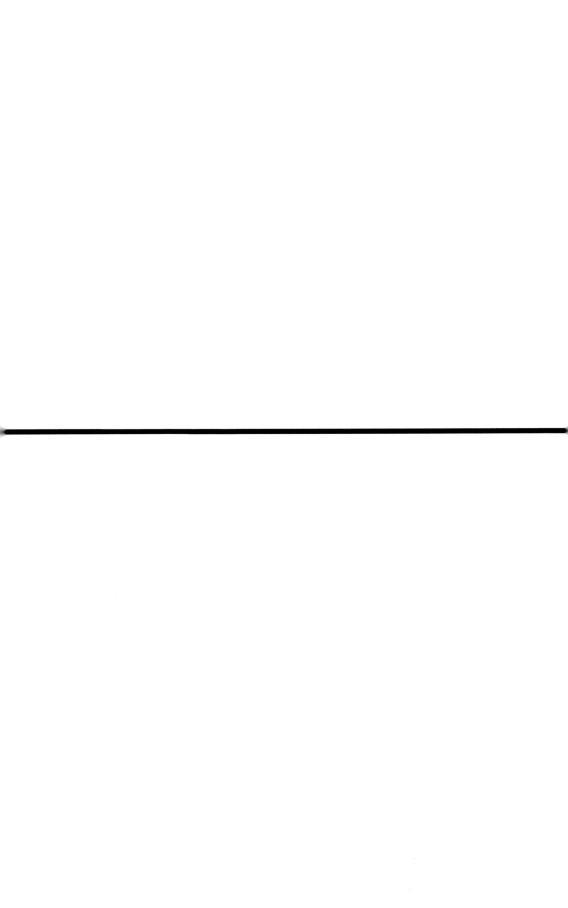

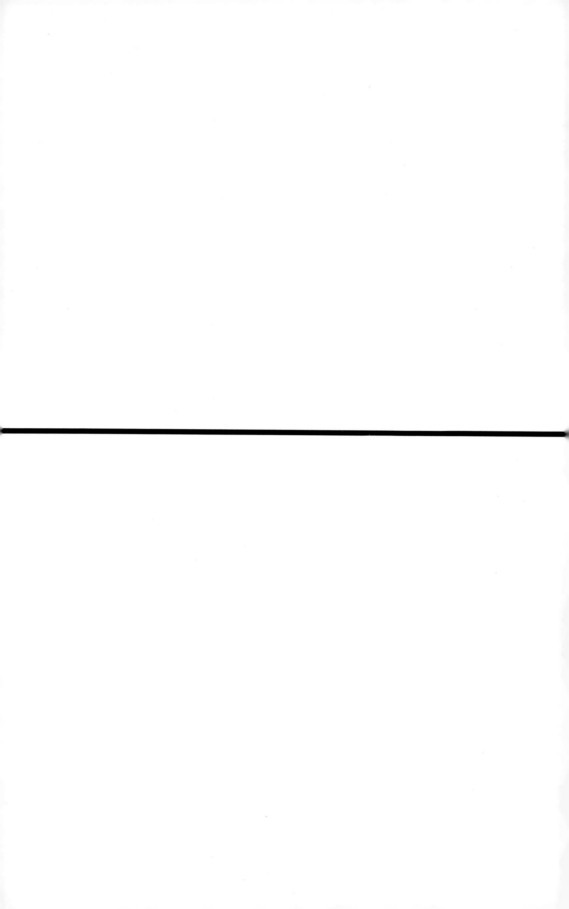

Homo Sapiens Generated Material Surplus
Agricultural societies were able to produce more food than hunter-gatherer communities, enabling them to sustain denser populations.

of farmers instead of hunter-gatherers, humans started generating more food than they could consume. This surplus in turn generated the incentive to barter for goods and services as people learned specialized skills; trade thus necessitated proximity, which therefore necessitated cities. The converse of this same theory is equally pernicious: people have predicted the fall of cities with the rise of telecommunications and electronic trade, particularly during the pandemic.[5] With the invention of the telephone and even the fax machine, people imagined the economic logic for cities would disappear despite the fact that cities have since burgeoned while the fax machine disappeared. Although the long-term impacts of remote work are yet to be known, global urban growth continues largely unabated, although we are witnessing a population shift from larger, expensive cities to smaller, less costly but still urban communities.[6]

Humans congregated into urban communities for social and spiritual needs, as well as reasons of material surplus, something we continue to do today in cities as diverse as New York, Paris, and Kolkata despite the changes brought by the pandemic. This is precisely why cities continue to thrive despite terrorist attacks, natural disasters, fires, plagues, and technologies that make them feel unsafe or anachronistic. Had early human settlements been built solely for farming and trade, their physical form, or *morphology*, would have been quite similar across the ancient world, accommodating largely for differences in climate. Some similarities certainly appear across antiquity, such as compression structures like the pyramids built throughout the ancient world, but again, these were constructed not for economic but spiritual and societal reasons, a way to get closer to the celestial world in a skyward quest that has always gripped the human imagination.

Morphological differences across ancient cities abound primarily due to cultural distinctions.[7] For instance, in historic Chinese cities the streets were organized into an orthogonal grid on the cardinal axes such that north represented an ascent to the heavens. By contrast, in ancient India the urban organizational tool of the mandala was based on a very different orthogonal nine-square grid in which circumambulation spiraling into the center represented a spiritual journey. The ancient North African capital of Memphis was built not only for trading reasons but also to unify the upper and lower kingdoms of Egypt. Centuries later Hippodamus would lay out the city of Miletus with its agora and acropolis surrounded by a relatively non-hierarchical grid that for the ancient Greeks represented democracy itself, at least for a certain class of men.

Even the Romans, considered by Enlightenment thinkers to represent the height of classical rationality, laid out their cities with spiritual ritual for symbolic

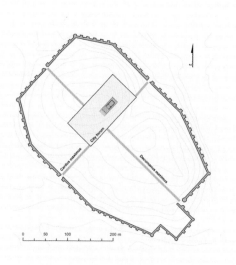

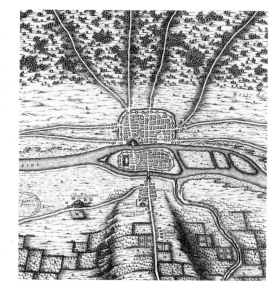

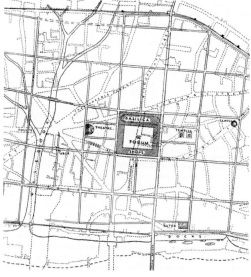

The Cardo and Decumanus Unify an Empire
"Wherever the Roman soldier was, he was in Rome"—the
standard Roman city plan, characterized by an orthogonal
grid, as implemented in Barcino (Barcelona), Lutece (Paris),
Timgad (Marciana Traiana Thamugadi) and Londinium
(London) (*clockwise from top left*).

reasons. The cardo and decumanus, which were the famed founding cross-shaped intersection of Roman cities built across the empire, were established using a tool dragged by oxen known as a gnomon under the *Ritus Etruscus*, a ritual that recalled the original founding of Rome supposedly after Romulus killed Remus—hardly a consequence of rational material surplus. So powerful was this grid that across the far-flung empire it was said, "Wherever the Roman soldier was, he was always in Rome." It is extraordinary to imagine that the symbolic potency of a street grid helped hold together the identity of a singular empire second in size throughout history only to the Mongolian empire under Genghis Khan. (It would be wonderful to include a discussion of the Mongols here, but Genghis Khan did not believe in the permanence of city building, nor did he seek the wealth and grandeur of physical trappings.)

Similar to the Romans, the Spanish Empire imposed across its colonies in Latin America and the Philippines the Laws of the Indies, morphological rules that among other things established a grid of streets, buildings, and open spaces in order to express the power of the crown and the Catholic Church.[8] Examples abound across the Americas, even in places like San Antonio, Texas, in which one can feel the scalar remnants of Spanish colonial power.

By the late seventeenth century, Greek and Roman influence inspired austere neoclassicist works such as the east facade of the Louvre, which presaged the Enlightenment's desire for order while shedding the specific spiritual aspects of either ancient civilization. René Descartes, based on the principles of Aristotle, devised the ultimate abstract grid in his coordinate system, laying the groundwork for the overtly rationalist worldview adopted by Enlightenment philosophers. The subsequent overthrow of the monarchy in the French Revolution of 1789, visually foreshadowed in Jacques-Louis David's painting *Oath of the Horatii* (1784), set the stage for the French Republic and the Beaux-Arts movement as expressed in architecture and city building.

East Facade of the Louvre (1667–74)
Austere neoclassical architecture with Greek and Roman influences, and the beginnings of modern architecture in the West.

Jacques-Louis David,
***Oath of the Horatii* (1784)**
The painting presages the French Revolution in 1789, as well as modernism in art history with the flattening of the picture plane.

French city planning principles manifested outside of the republic in the newly forming United States, where urban grids took on differing morphologies to express the contradictory values of a new slave-owning democracy. The hierarchical ethos of the French directly informed the design

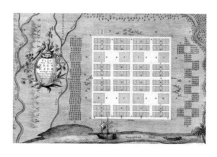

The Oglethorpe Plan for Savannah, Georgia (1733)
A rhythmic grid plan with the capacity to change over time.

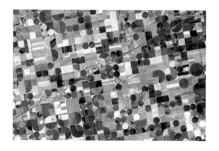

THEORETICAL
TOWNSHIP DIAGRAM
SHOWING
METHOD OF NUMBERING SECTIONS
WITH ADJOINING SECTIONS

36	31	32	33	34	35	36	31
	6	5	4	3	2	1	6
12	7	8	9	10	11	12	7
13	18	17	16	15	14	13	18
24	19	20	21	22	23	24	19
25	30	29	28	27	26	25	30
36	31	32	33	34	35	36	31
1	6	5	4	3	2	1	6

The Jeffersonian Grid Unifies a Nation
The one-square-mile grid, imposed across the United States by Thomas Jefferson, is evident in the current landscape of farmland in Kansas, organized into quarter sections.

of America's new capitol in 1791, for which George Washington commissioned the French architect and military officer Pierre Charles L'Enfant. L'Enfant purportedly used broad open spaces and axial city planning principles to be inclusive, but their expression of the symbolic power of the government, much like Edwin Lutyens's later axial plan of Imperial New Delhi, is much more palpable. Since Washington, D.C., was built by enslaved people, the egalitarian underpinnings of L'Enfant's plan are even more suspect, yet it is undeniable that its Mall would almost two centuries later provide the platform for Dr. Martin Luther King Jr.'s March on Washington speech that conveyed so powerfully, "I have a dream."

Less hierarchical grid plans in the United States, reminiscent of Hippodamus's Miletus, formed the basis for important North American cities like William Penn's plan for Philadelphia in 1682 and James Oglethorpe's plan for Savannah in 1733. Of Savannah's plan, MIT architectural theoretician Stanford Anderson wrote about the city's "possibilism," in that its design not only was economical but has the capacity to change with needs over time: "Savannah has shown a remarkable durability with concomitant benefits both in the efficient use of resources and in the cumulative reinforcement of certain increasingly valued environmental qualities."[9]

Perhaps the clearest manifestation of Cartesian rationality in the United States was the conception of a one-square-mile grid imposed across much of the United States by Thomas Jefferson. A Francophile and slave owner who completed the purchase of the Louisiana Territory from the French in 1803, he believed in an American agricultural hegemony that would come to be known as Manifest Destiny by the middle of the nineteenth century. This destiny was clearly intended for whites given that, as Mabel O. Wilson writes, "Jefferson held 'physical and moral' objections to Negroes based on a lifetime of observations of what he considered to be their comportment and character."[10]

It would take decades after the upheavals of the French Revolution for Enlightenment city planning principles to take hold in Paris under the virtually limitless powers of Georges-Eugène Haussmann. In his mid-1800s "renovation," Haussmann enabled the creative destruction of much of the city in order to create iconic focal points at the culmination of radiating axial boulevards, axes that also carried critical water and sewer infrastructure belowground.[11] Haussmann's planning, along with the concepts espoused by the English garden city planner Ebenezer Howard, in turn inspired the American City Beautiful Movement and its effort to not only beautify urban settings but instill "civic virtue" among the nation's burgeoning industrial population.

While Haussmann's wide boulevards served multiple purposes—from providing the newly minted bourgeoisie a stage, to accommodating the military overthrow of the Paris Commune—it was in Barcelona in 1859 that one of the first major urban grids emerged in the service of both faster-moving vehicles and real-estate speculation. Designed by Ildefons Cerdà I Sunyer, a Catalonian civil engineer, the famed *illes* blocks of the *Eixample*, or expansion district, that surrounded the city's historic Gothic quarter had chamfered corners for the specific utilitarian reason of allowing horse-drawn carriages to speed through turns without having to stop.[12] So empirical was Cerdà that he actually had an elaborate formula of unknown origin and suspect rationale with which he attempted to design modern Barcelona, in which "x is the side of the block, 2b is the width of the street, f is the depth of the building site, d is the height of the façade, v is the number of inhabitants per house, and p is the number of surface square meters per person."[13]

$$x = \frac{pv - 2bd}{d} \pm \sqrt{\frac{pv}{d^2 f}(pvf - 4bdf - 4b^2 d)}$$

In order to have his plans approved by area landowners, however, Cerdà had to agree to drop his initial ideas about development restrictions, hence the extraordinarily high-density, mixed-use nature of the city today. As an interesting consequence of greed overriding planning, 30 percent of Barcelonans walk to work, an enviable condition that has generated a plan to combine groups of blocks into car-free superblocks.[14]

Cerdà's Studies of Block Chamfers

Barcelona's octagonal block geometry was shaped by the streetcar's turning radius.

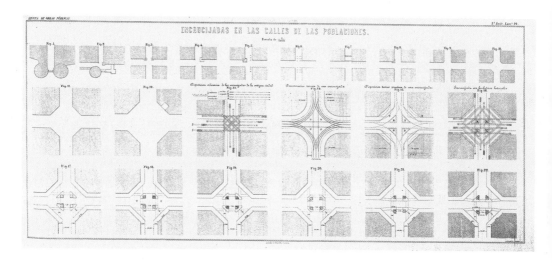

Barcelona's Superblocks (*Superilles*)

The city's initiative combined groups of blocks into car-free superblocks.

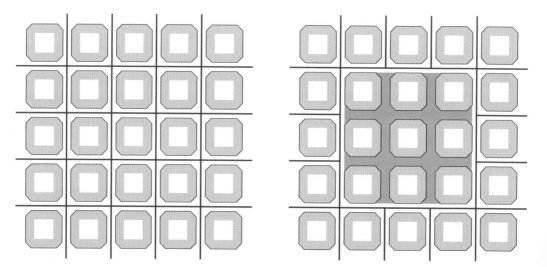

While there is no similarity in terms of morphology, the motivations behind Cerdà's *Eixample* share parallels with New York's early Commissioners Grid for Manhattan (1811), which was put in place to ease both real-estate development and the mobility of horse-drawn carriages as spectacularly depicted in Martin Scorsese's film *The Age of Innocence* (1993).[15] Vilified and valorized by Rem Koolhaas in his book *Delirious New York* (1978), Manhattan's grid is, in Koolhaas's telling, the modern apotheosis of control in two dimensions with chaos in the third, a condition he deemed "a culture of congestion."[16] While Koolhaas extolled the sectional programmatic freedoms offered by the Manhattan grid, the truth is that the major cities that adopted specific grids in the nineteenth century would fail to future-proof against the fin de siècle innovations that would soon transform the world.

The industrial inventions of the internal combustion engine, the elevator, and structural steel formed a trifecta that would forever alter cities as we know them by breaking the human-scaled parameters of Belle Époque city planning. In city after city, prior to these three inventions, blocks laid out in the nineteenth century comfortably accommodated the dimensional needs of brick row houses and horse-drawn carriages, creating a highly functional array of avenues and side streets north of the poorer parts of the city, with handsome brownstones ending in light-filled rear yards that fit seamlessly in the city's 200-by-800-foot blocks. That 200-foot dimension was likely determined based on the light penetration into a 60-foot-deep row house (ambient natural light penetrates 30 feet from the front and back), leaving room for north and south sidewalks and a generous rear yard between buildings that was proportionate to the height of the row houses, which were limited in scale not by zoning laws or preservation requirements but by the reasonable number of stairs that could be climbed daily by residents.[17] Similarly, streets and avenues that met at 90-degree angles worked well for pedestrian crosswalks and were sufficient for slow-moving horse-drawn carriages to turn.

The sunny relationship between city blocks and their buildings was transformed by the marriage of the elevator and structural steel. When paired, these led to a soaring new building typology, the skyscraper. These new high-rises, together with the third major invention of the late 1800s, the internal combustion engine, put tremendous pressure on the tight-knit streets of most established cities to be wider for the purposes of both speed and access to light and air.

Cities dating back to antiquity transformed radically as a result. When I first visited Beijing as an exchange student at Tsinghua University in the early 1990s, the ancient Chinese capital had resisted towers in favor of a series of ring roads that could help accommodate the city's burgeoning population. The prohibition against high-rises downtown was predicated on the desire to not see them from within the hallowed courtyards of the Imperial Palace. This preference ultimately gave way to Deng Xiaoping's sentiment that to get rich is glorious, alongside a realization that the horizontal growth was becoming unsustainable. The city transformed

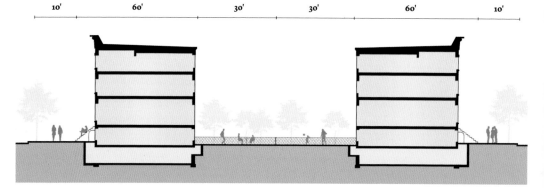

10' 60' 30' 30' 60' 10'

200'

The Logic of Nineteenth-Century New York City
Rowhouses were designed with a width optimized for
ambient light penetration, and their height was determined
by the number of stairs that residents could comfortably
climb daily (*above*). The Commissioner's Plan laid out
200-by-800-foot blocks that seamlessly accommodated
brownstones with light-filled rear yards (*right*).

The Industrial Era Trifecta
That Transformed the World
The internal combustion engine put
tremendous pressure on tight-knit streets,
while elevators and structural steel paved
the way for the first skyscrapers.

in tandem with the Chinese economy by replacing most of its historic downtown Hutong fabric with modern office towers and housing blocks. Among the saddest aspects of this transformation was the replacement of some of the world's most robust bicycle infrastructure—including enormous yet lyrical flyovers built expressly for cyclists—with large arterials intended primarily for cars and trucks. Once an ancient city with some of the most beautiful street sections in the world, with lush islands filled with tea and watermelon stalls that also protected bike lanes from vehicles, Beijing became in a few short decades a metropolis known globally for its traffic congestion and air pollution.

Most nineteenth-century cities also strained to accommodate this trifecta of technologies, with the notable exception of Chicago, which embraced them with a pragmatic immediacy that led to poetic consequences. Beyond the famed World's Columbian Exposition of 1893, two historical circumstances set the stage for the city's modern architectural splendor. In 1830, the surveyor James Thompson laid out an unusually capacious grid for cities of this era, with 350-by-400-foot blocks reflective of both the expansive horizontal plain and the commercial trading milieu in which the metropolis was founded.[18] These blocks were organized by a highly functional orthogonal network of wide streets and narrow service alleys. When coupled with the subsequent great fire of 1871, Chicago had a unique ability on its generous, well-proportioned blocks to rebuild in concert with this new technological triad. This convergence resulted in what would become known as the Chicago School of architecture, characterized by early skyscrapers clad with fire-resistant terra cotta and large tripartite "Chicago windows" that were made possible by the porosity of steel-frame construction. The city's bold spirit went on to inspire important urban design innovations, including a sectionally layered downtown loop of roads and rail; historically significant architecture

The Chicago School

Steel-frame construction liberated the exterior wall from load-bearing duties, allowing for terra-cotta cladding and large tripartite "Chicago windows."

Chicago's "Goldilocks" Block Size Compared to Those of Other Cities

Chicago's medium-sized and well-proportioned blocks set it apart from other cities with longer or narrower blocks, even those that were planned around the same time.

New York, NY
The Commissioner's Plan, 1811
800'
200'

Chicago, IL
James Thompson's Plat, 1830
350'
400'

Portland, OR
Platted in 1866
200'
200'

Glasgow, UK
James Gillespie's Layout, 1820
300'
130'

Beijing, China
Inherited from 13th Century
1,470'
200'

Johannesburg, South Africa
First Surveyed in 1886
250'
250'

0   500'   1,000'   2,000'

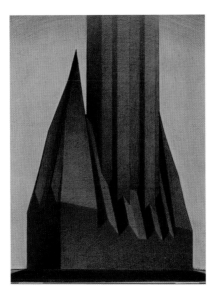

by Ludwig Mies van der Rohe, Wendell Campbell, Fazlur Khan, Edward Durell
Stone, Bertrand Goldberg, and Jeanne Gang; and landscape interventions ranging
from beautiful street trees to glorious public spaces such as Millennium Park
and the Riverwalk. As a deeply segregated city with ongoing pain resulting from
disinvestment in the West and South Sides, one can only hope, through projects like
the Obama Presidential Center in Jackson Park by Tod Williams and Billie Tsien,
and Theaster Gates's Stony Brook Bank and Rebuild Foundation, that Chicago is
able to better share its history of public largesse with its communities most in need.

Cities with smaller, narrower, and more historic European grids, like New
York's Lower Manhattan, adapted to the new technologies with less grace.
The Equitable Building in New York (1915), also made possible by steel and
elevators, rose straight for forty stories, denying light and air to the blocks
surrounding it. Its construction triggered New York's zoning resolution in 1916,
which called for a system of setbacks and other bulk controls to mitigate the
impacts of newly tall buildings.[19] From Portland to Barcelona to New York,
twentieth-century buildings were crowbarred into small historic blocks like ten
pounds of manure jammed into a five-pound bag. While some buildings achieved
brilliant success within this framework, such as the prewar setback spires of the
Empire State and Chrysler Buildings as well as the postwar sheer modernist forms
of Lever House and the Seagram Building, most of Gotham's blocks strained
under the weight of new construction and continue to be a battleground today as
community groups try to eke out public space, planners try to enforce continuous
streetwalls and setbacks, and developers try to maximize profit.

Cars, trucks, and rail traffic invaded and congested the streets of the
transforming nineteenth-century city. Famously, New York's High Line was built

**Twentieth-Century Buildings Crowbarred
into Small Nineteenth-Century Blocks**
Portland, OR (*top*), New York, NY (*middle*),
Barcelona, Spain (*bottom*).

in the 1930s to elevate freight trains because Tenth Avenue had been renamed "Death Avenue" due to pedestrian fatalities from the previous mix of on-grade rail with busy street traffic. The French architect Charles-Édouard Jeanneret, who reinvented himself as Le Corbusier, would later visit New York City and comment, "A hundred times have I thought New York is a catastrophe, and fifty times: It is a beautiful catastrophe."[20] For any true New Yorker, Corb had it spot on, but only half the time.

Over a decade earlier in Europe the blood, smoke, and ash of World War I and the Soviet Revolution would give brutal birth to the early modernists. Influenced by previous art movements like Fauvism and Cubism, Kazimir Malevich, Wassily Kandinsky, and particularly Vladimir Tatlin would form the Constructivist movement in the Soviet Union and deeply influence their German counterparts. Looking to remake the world and respond to a housing crisis across Germany, the architects of the Bauhaus led by Walter Gropius sponsored middle-class housing exhibitions like the 1927 Weissenhofsiedlung. While laudable in their social motivations, the early modernists were enamored of the new Machine Age, especially the automobile. Corb would issue plan after plan of a new urban order, heavily influenced by Tony Garnier's 1901 Cité Industrielle, in which uses such as housing, culture, hospitals, and industry were physically segregated into zoned areas. Corb's Athens Charter called for cities organized into four separate categories: housing, work, recreation, and traffic, which would go on to influence the planning of Brasília, the new capital of Brazil, designed by Lucio Costa and Oscar Niemeyer.[21]

The car had such an extraordinary hold over Corb's thinking that it warranted its own urban category, "Traffic," a classification of equal valence to how people would live, work, and play. In writing about his Plan Voisin—in which he called for the demolition of much of central Paris and replacing it with a series of towers, parks, and highways—Corb proposed *a final solution* for the conundrum of twentieth-century technologies having to be shoehorned into nineteenth-century urban fabric: Destroy the Street.[22]

"Death Avenue"

Long before the construction of the High Line, freight trains, horse-drawn carts, cars, and pedestrians all jostled for space on New York's Tenth Avenue (ca. 1920).

Le Corbusier on New York

"A hundred times have I thought New York is a catastrophe, and fifty times: It is a beautiful catastrophe" (1964).

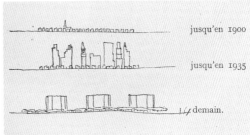

The Modernist Movement in the Machine Age

Weissenhofsiedlung (*top left*), Brasília (*top right*), and Cité Industrielle (*bottom*).

Le Corbusier, Plan Voisin
"We must kill the street."

Le Corbusier, Plan Obus
The segregation of the colonizers from the colonized.

Controversy rages round street-traffic, for the narrow, leisurely stream of horse-drawn vehicles has swollen into a broad estuary of rushing motor-cars. Therefore we must have roadways of ample dimensions and a proper division of their surface as between motor-transport and foot-passengers ... then the Street as we know it will cease to exist.[23]

Separation and segregation were at the heart of the early modern movement just as they were for earlier Enlightenment planners like Haussmann despite vast differences in architectural style. These objectives were rooted not only in the desires of well-intentioned planners and architects from the close of the nineteenth century—such as Ebenezer Howard and Tony Garnier, who understandably sought to separate residences from the noxious factories emerging from the

Gustav Klimt, Beethoven Frieze (1902)
A visual representation of Beethoven's Symphony No. 9, also known as the "Choral Symphony," particularly the final movement featuring the "Ode to Joy."

"Ornament Is Crime"
Otto Wagner and Adolf Loos
called for stripping ornament
from architecture. *Top*: Wagner's
Austrian Postal Savings Bank,
Vienna (1906); *Center*: Loos's
Steiner House, Vienna (1910);
Bottom: "Bedroom of my wife,"
Loos House, Vienna (1903).

Berlin of "Germania"
Albert Speer's hyper-scaled
neoclassical vision for a
fascist Berlin.

Industrial Revolution—but also in the racial segregation desired by colonial rulers. This propensity to segregate manifests not only with the British Raj but in the French colonial apparatus in northern Africa, where Le Corbusier as well as architects who had graduated from the École des Beaux-Arts sought work. Unable to realize his plans to demolish much of central Paris, Corb went on to propose one of the most sensual, beguiling, and racist urban plans ever conceived, his early 1930s Plan Obus for Algeria, in which he called for the segregation of the colonizers from the colonized at an extraordinary scale. It is undeniable that he was a prodigious and incomparable talent, but two things can be true at once: Le Corbusier was a brilliant architect but a horrifying urbanist—he saw in the modern project a chance to educate "the Arab":

> I believe that cities animated by the new spirit ... constructed of steel and glass, standing erect beside the sea, or standing erect in the valleys or on the plateau at the foot of the Atlas Mountains, would have created among the Arabs an atmosphere of enthusiasm, of admiration, of respect, through the remarkable means at the disposal of architecture and city planning.[24]

The European yearning for dominance, order, and its subsequent embrace of fascism reached its apotheosis in the failed Viennese art and architecture student Adolf Hitler, who ultimately rose to lead the Third Reich. It was in the aftermath of the early 1900s Vienna Secession arts movement that figures like Otto Wagner and Adolf Loos called for the stripping of ornament from architecture, while Gustav Klimt and contemporaries like Sigmund Freud explored the unleashing of sexual mores. Hitler was appalled by his perception of Viennese sexual and moral promiscuity, which he directly associated with Jews, and sought solace in Germany. In 1925, his supremacist manifesto *Mein Kampf* was published in the midst of the collapse of the German economy under the hyperinflation of the Weimar Republic. As the elected leader of a faltering government he would quickly remake as his murderous regime, Hitler turned to Albert Speer to translate his fascist worldview into a

Pierre Charles L'Enfant · Georges-Eugène Haussmann · Le Corbusier · Robert Moses · Jane Jacobs · Hannah Beachler

Urbanity Strikes Back (the inclusion of Hannah Beachler is explained in chapter 10)

dominating hyper-scaled neoclassical order. Aesthetic styles notwithstanding, the ordered axes of Speer's grandiose plan for Berlin fall well within the canon of modernist morphology, particularly along the through line from L'Enfant to Haussmann to Le Corbusier to Robert Moses. Whether for the symbol of order or the eventual invention of the automobile, almost all Western city planning over a span of more than three centuries called for eliminating the pedestrian-oriented, human-scaled cities that predated the Enlightenment.

The collapse of this through line is often credited to Jane Jacobs, who argued for the idiosyncratic city, mixed use, small blocks, and the power of street life in her writings. In the 1960s, Jacobs famously fought and won against Moses's plans for a Lower Manhattan Expressway, arguably ending three centuries of male-dominated Western planning centered upon ordering and partitioning the city.[25]

Jane Jacobs's confrontations with Robert Moses have been well-documented. More significant for our purposes in investigating today's urbanity is the fact that it would have been impossible for Jacobs or Moses to imagine the global urban

Saskia Sassen and the Global City
Canary Wharf, London (*left*); Roppongi Hills, Tokyo (*middle*); Hudson Yards, New York (*right*).

(Sub)urbanization
The global catastrophe of sprawl is too often conflated with "urbanization": Pflugerville, Texas (*top*); Dubai, United Arab Emirates (*middle*); São Paulo, Brazil (*bottom*).

growth we are now experiencing. Soon after their conflict—and particularly as a consequence of both deindustrialization and the urban renewal Moses would inspire nationwide—American cities became hotbeds of crime as well as wellsprings of culture. Cities in that era were affordable to low-income residents and artists because they were not in high demand by the wealthy, especially white upper-middle-class residents who feared what they saw and perceived on their screens and streets. By the 1970s, cities like New York continued to have pockets of affluence, but most who could afford it sped off to the suburbs, subsidized as they were by highway and housing policies such as redlining that heavily favored white people. But with the rapid and contentious decline in urban crime that would begin in the 1990s, combined with a shift from an industrial to a service economy that could more easily locate near residential neighborhoods, demand returned to cities in synchrony with the advent of our modern financial service economy, as Saskia Sassen documented in *The Global City*.[26]

Cities today remain the geographic epicenters of the global economy, with major financial hubs tied together via broadband. Since 2007, more people live in metropolitan areas than rural, a first in our history.[27] This oft-quoted statistic blankets over a number of more salient dynamics. For instance, much of what is touted as urban expansion is actually suburban, and it is this specific form of development—as opposed to general population growth—that is leading to catastrophic environmental consequences. And while many tout this as a new urban age globally, such a view also masks the enormous differences in what is driving urban growth in our developed versus our developing economies.

Despite some recent pandemic-related blips, metropoles like New York experienced a precipitous drop in crime over the last few decades, at times due to racially controversial policing practices.[28] Simultaneously, explosive and uneven economic growth associated primarily with the financial and technology sectors has created a class of professionals who earn dramatically outsized salaries compared to their cities' respective working classes. But unlike their upper-middle-class predecessors from generations past who chose to live in suburban enclaves and commute, much of the wealthy professional class of the new urban century has chosen to stay put and raise their families in the inner city. The demand for expensive private education has soared in cities like New York ever since. The real-estate industry also transformed for these families in an attempt to meet new

The Demand for Space

Choosing to remain in the city to raise their families, wealthy professionals now demand amenity-rich, three- to five-bedroom apartments.

One-Bedroom Apartment
Liberty View at Battery Park City
800 sq. ft.

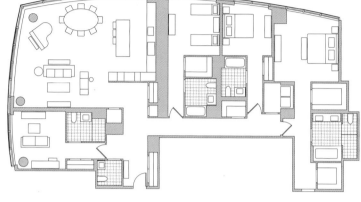

Four-Bedroom Apartment
Fifteen Hudson Yards
3,000 sq. ft.

demand for three- to five-bedroom condominiums with lavish amenities that well exceed the best that any gated suburban community could offer. The degree of this market transformation cannot be overstated: prior to this boom even into the tail end of the twentieth century, few developers built either condominiums or large apartments; theirs was a mundane industry of building studio and one-bedroom rental apartments for older middle-class singles or young college graduates who would typically move out of the city after marrying. While remote work may change urban demand once again, the desire to live in dense, walkable circumstances—even in smaller communities—has yet to abate.[29] Should some of the privileged decide to reside elsewhere in this new era, cities can catalyze new demand across a broader socioeconomic mix if they equitably invest in quality of life, affordable housing, transit infrastructure, and just forms of community policing.

Somewhat different dynamics are at play in the expanding cities of the Global South. A metropolis like Mumbai, while also home to extraordinary wealth, is experiencing explosive growth due to the enormous influx of rural migrants hoping to send earnings back to their home villages. A city of some 21 million, Mumbai is estimated to be gaining well over 1,000 residents per day.[30] Clearly, these are largely not software engineers and hedge fund managers, although these professionals are growing in number as well. Mumbai is filling with glistening new condo towers similar to those in New York and London, while the streets are teeming with the informal economies of everyday people.

The Wealth Gap of Mumbai
New luxury condominium towers juxtaposed with the informal economies of the streets.

Parasite
The film's protagonist serves as the disrespected chauffeur of a wealthy family while living in a congested semi-basement in Seoul with his wife and children.

Megacities in the developed and developing worlds are experiencing homogeneous, luxury condominium growth driven far more by capitalism than anything one could regard as good planning. From an environmental standpoint, as well as from a city budget perspective, this author would rather see this wealthy population housed in the inner city than in 10,000-square-foot suburban estates with five-car garages. But this bourgeois influx into our cities has become so overwhelming that one must address the cultural, aesthetic, and displacement impacts this population has wrought. For example, the streets of our dense inner cities are now clogged with the private vehicles of well-heeled residents, who demand not only overflowing amenities in their towers but also luxury trucks to escort their children to private schools. As mercilessly documented in the film *Parasite* (2019), with its protagonist cast as a driver for the elite, this is hardly a phenomenon limited to the United States.[31]

When one looks at new residential construction across six continents, be it urban or suburban, the results are strikingly similar, yielding the same urban condo tower or the same suburban subdivision in Shanghai, Dubai, Mumbai, Denver, Chicago, or London. In response to rapid urbanization, capitalism has brought about the homogenization of our building materials, such as glass exterior wall systems, concrete, and steel, and in the development industry itself. Historically, real estate was a local industry due to the complex knowledge required of local building systems, land markets, and regulatory hurdles. Today, we are seeing the rise of global real-estate conglomerates that build the same structures worldwide using the same physical and financial products—and employing the same corporate architects—to bring them into existence.

But beyond capitalism, our well-intentioned international building codes are also creating a soul-crushing physical homogeneity. Everything from the mandated turning radius required for a fire truck to the critically important standards for wheelchair access are leading most urban development worldwide to be hauntingly similar. For instance, one of our best urban building strategies in the early twentieth century was the single "cage" elevator wrapped by an open stairwell, around which pinwheeled some thirty apartments in a five-story structure; this configuration was deployed in cities worldwide with theme and variation, resulting in a magnificently

Homogenized Cities Formed by Well-Intentioned Codes

Cherished urban forms from the past, as in Rome (*upper left*), Beijing Hutong (*middle*), and Venice (*upper right*), are no longer code-compliant, and have been replaced by anonymous and banal global repetition.

**This Is Not the Density
We Are Looking For**
Madison Square Park Tower
in New York City.

communal urban density in which neighbors could know
and see each other. That configuration is illegal today because
it violates fire and wheelchair codes. Replacing it is the
requirement for multiple concrete fire stairs and elevators,
the enormous investments for which necessitate long
anonymous "double-loaded" hallways to connect the floors of
much larger buildings that can spread the fixed costs of these
pricey circulation elements across more units. Confronted
with both high-priced land and such expensive infrastructure
requirements, urban builders can only get a new apartment
complex to be economical—and then only for wealthier
residents—if the development is much larger, with, say, 150
to 250 repetitively stacked apartments, leaving little financial
room for varying unit types or facade treatments. Facades are
also heavily regulated in terms of international energy code,
which, when combined with user demand for floor-to-ceiling
glass, results in the preponderance of reflective blue glass
towers that we are all learning to hate as would have both
Le Corbusier and Jane Jacobs. Taken together, capitalism
and code have created the perfect storm for banal worldwide
urbanization, perpetuating the deafening thud of the same towers being erected
in city after city to the point where we can no longer differentiate our major cities
from one another.

At the scale of city streets, sidewalks, and public spaces, these homogenizing
factors are just as alarming as the architectural ramifications impacting our building
stock. Some of the most cherished destinations in the world, from the bridges of
Venice, to Rome's Spanish Steps, to the tight-knit streets of Tokyo and Shanghai and
Fez, to the rolling landscape of New York's Central Park, to the tiled steps of Rio's
favelas, are all illegal today because their streets, slopes, and stairs violate our codes.
Celebrating the *structure*, as opposed to the appearance, of historic environments
is not, however, a cry for pastiche; newly built, code-compliant, ersatz versions
of historical settings are as banal as their all-glass counterparts. To the contrary,
imagine a contemporary city with a public realm that is as radical and experimental
as Venice—nothing could be further from nostalgia.

With mostly good intentions, global society has inadvertently made the
emulation—not in terms of aesthetics but in terms of aspiration—of our most prized
historic urban environments illegal. Wheelchair access, fire safety, energy code,
and all of the other goals that drove twentieth-century regulations are enormously
important and a major step forward for the populations they safeguard, but we
should also recognize the unintended consequences of our well-intentioned rules
in order to achieve their original protective aims and the more nuanced but equally

Building Codes: The Wrong Tools for the Right Battles
Advancements in technology can now effectively address many of the safeguarding
objectives that building codes aim to achieve without homogenizing our environment.
The left is our current approach, while the right could represent our future.

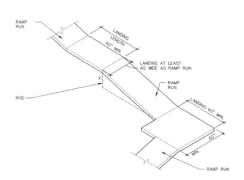

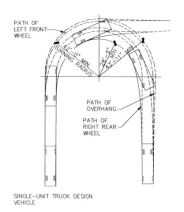

important objective of heterogeneous, urbane, and beloved cities. While Jacobs's
fight was largely with the failed expertise of public sector urban planning, today's
fight is in many ways the opposite. Government intervention is essential to plan
for more urban density near transit, but it must do so in a way that maintains
the culture and character of our cities by encouraging more connective design—
a goal that can be achieved only with the engagement of communities and
specialized thought partners including architects, landscape architects, urban
designers, and technologists.

Technology offers much promise in this regard not in terms of the smart
city movement but in terms of the "back to the future" possibilities offered by
innovations that could allow us to return to the original motivations for building cities
as interconnected social spaces. Imagine a world in which technologists reinvented

"For a city of immigrants, the public realm is more than ever now the street."
J. Max Bond Jr.

"History is an angel / being blown backwards into the future."
—Walter Benjamin/Laurie Anderson
Paul Klee, *Angelus Novus* (1920)

the wheelchair to climb stairs, or drones and robots for firefighting that could replace the enormous ladder trucks that demand so much asphalt, or 3D-printed solar wall systems that could create varied facades while still meeting energy codes and building budgets. Fanciful as all of this may sound, most of the technology already exists. Wheelchairs that climb stairs and steeper slopes have been around for some time and could be distributed to all in need for a fraction of the billions we invest to make spaces worldwide accessible for traditional wheelchairs. Drones and robots are already being used in emergency rescue. And digital fabrication of building and facade systems has existed for decades. In other words, our building codes are fighting the right battles but with the wrong tools.

We are at an inflection point in history, a crossroads where we can choose a different path that recognizes that the basic physical building blocks of our cities—streets, sidewalks, public spaces, buildings, and infrastructure—need not be the homogenizing, soul-crushing, mass-produced elements they became in the twentieth century. As the late, great architect J. Max Bond Jr. said of New York decades ago, and which holds just as true for any great urbane community well into the future, "For a city of immigrants, the public realm is more than ever now the street."[32]

Laurie Anderson quotes Walter Benjamin observing Paul Klee when she sings "History is an angel / being blown backwards into the future."[33] These lyrics echo the urban histories and futures we must layer to design connected, attractive, ecological cities where people want to be, grow, change, and exchange. This would represent a tomorrow that could return us to a road back to somewhere after the long noxious detour of segregation fueled by the automobile. The pandemic was a reminder of how much we need human interaction and the extent to which our communities could be designed to encourage human health, spatial equity, and social well-being. Scientists and scholars are documenting the physical and mental health benefits of walking in cities, like neuroscientist Shane O'Mara, who calls walking the "superpower" of our species in terms of brain and body health.[34] The possibilities of this urban paradigm could be joyful, ecological, and equitable. We must look more closely at problems like our deadly auto-centric landscape in order to imagine this better world.

THERE ARE MANY FORCES THAT MAKE OUR

cities banal, inequitable, and unsustainable, but none is as deleterious as our daily use of the private automobile, which threatens human health, community experience, and planetary well-being. As the direct cause of fatalities and injuries through accidents, airborne particulate matter, sedentary lifestyles that fuel an obesity crisis, isolation that reinforces loneliness and our sociopolitical bubbles, traffic congestion that creates psychological and societal harm, and the existential threat of global carbon emissions, daily car use—as opposed to the occasional road trip—has become a deadly addiction for which we must seek global rehabilitation. When considered in tandem with the historic wrongs perpetrated on neighborhoods of color when freeways were first built, to the continuing pulmonary hazards tailpipes impose on those same neighborhoods today, driving to satisfy everyday needs in our cities perpetuates environmental injustice as much as it does global warming. This collateral damage is compounded by the sheer amount of public space and dollars private cars demand of urban areas, regardless of their power source, at a time when so many other pressing needs in our cities require room and resources. Commuting by private car is damaging physically, fiscally, and socially, and the fact that entrenched special interests prioritize cars over urban density and the mass transit it enables is more than maddening. For these reasons global mobility advocacy doesn't just rage against these machines but rages, rages against the dying of the street. The following chapter highlights the myriad adverse impacts of private cars in our daily lives and how we might change this self-imposed reality by adaptively reusing our streets for people.

CAR COMMUTING KILLS.

Cars are a major cause of global fatalities annually

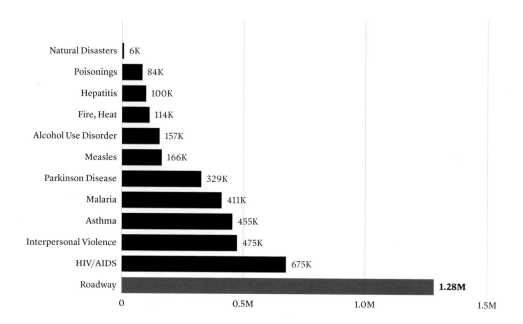

A global death toll close to 70 percent of 2020 Covid-19 deaths has resulted every year from roadway fatalities for the past two decades

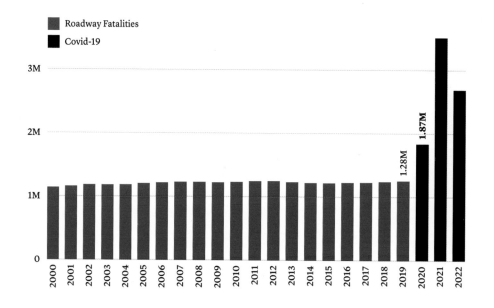

**Americans are up to 1.5 times more likely to be obese and
34 percent less physically active as a result of long commutes**

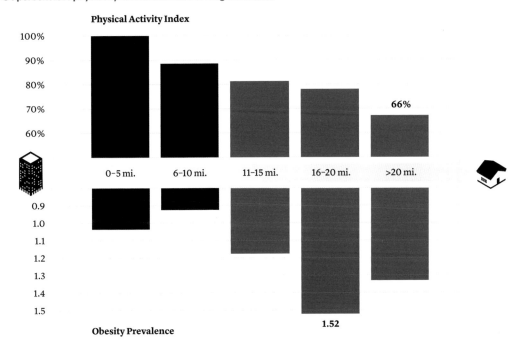

Physical Activity Index

0–5 mi.	6–10 mi.	11–15 mi.	16–20 mi.	>20 mi.

66%

Obesity Prevalence

1.52

**There is a 4 percent higher rate of separation or divorce for couples
with commute times over 45 minutes each way**

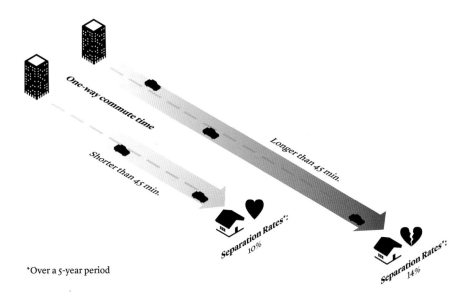

One-way commute time

Shorter than 45 min.

Longer than 45 min.

Separation Rates*:
10%

Separation Rates*:
14%

*Over a 5-year period

HEAVY TRAFFIC SPATIALLY CORRELATES WITH HEALTH HAZARDS ...

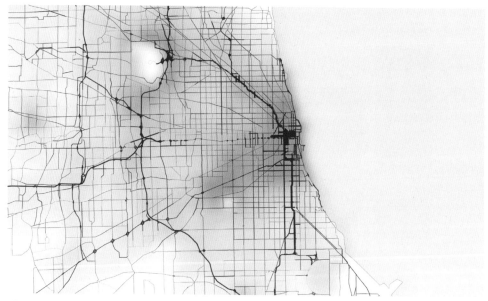

Chicago, Respiratory Hazard

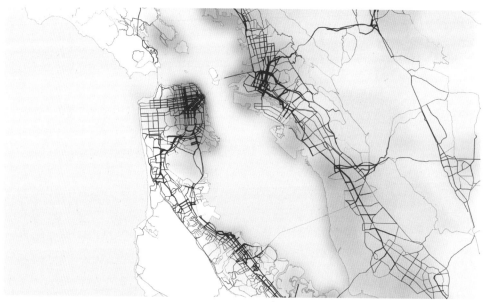

Bay Area, Respiratory Hazard

Road Traffic Volume (% compared to nation's highest)

0 ————————————— 100%

NATA Respitory Hazard Index (% compared to nation's highest)

0 ————————————— 100%

... COMPOUNDING HEALTH DISPARITIES AMONG MARGINALIZED POPULATIONS.

Chicago, Low-Income Populations

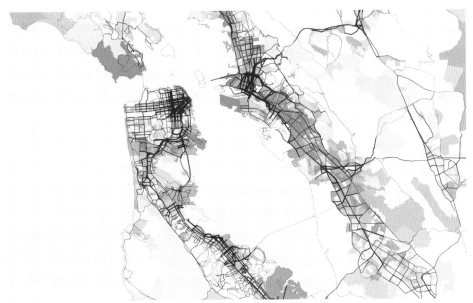

Bay Area, Low-Income Populations

Road Traffic Volume (% compared to nation's highest)

0 ⬛ 100%

Percentage of Low-Income Populations

0 ⬛ 100%

WHITE FLIGHT TO THE SUBURBS
TRIGGERED "FREEWAYS" ...

**Hastings Street/
Chrysler Freeway**
Detroit, MI

... THAT DECIMATED RACIALLY DIVERSE NEIGHBORHOODS STILL HEALING TODAY.

Cypress Street/
Cypress Freeway
West Oakland, CA

CARS ERASE OUR CITIES ...

1916

1950

1960

1969

1994

2004

Urban Fabric of Downtown
Detroit, MI

... EXACERBATED BY INDUCED DEMAND.

2004

8 Lanes, 52-minute Commute*

2014

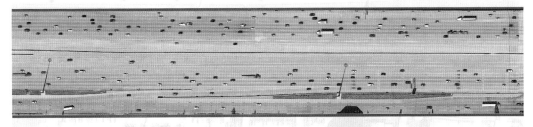

23 Lanes, 70-minute Commute*

Katy Freeway Expansion
Houston, TX

* Average rush-hour commute time, Pin Oak to Downtown Houston

TODAY, THE NEGATIVE IMPACTS OF DAILY CAR USE ARE GLOBAL.

Greenhouse Gas Emissions

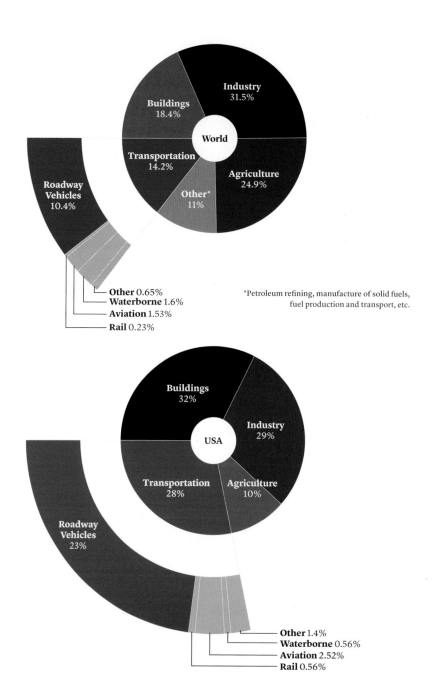

*Petroleum refining, manufacture of solid fuels, fuel production and transport, etc.

Carbon Footprints by Transportation Mode

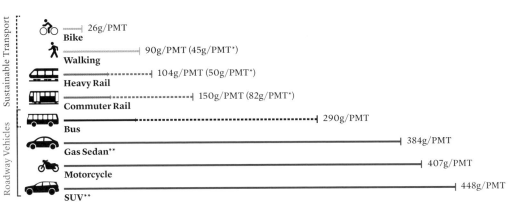

Sustainable Transport

- 🚲 **Bike** — 26g/PMT
- 🚶 **Walking** — 90g/PMT (45g/PMT*)
- 🚈 **Heavy Rail** — 104g/PMT (50g/PMT*)
- 🚃 **Commuter Rail** — 150g/PMT (82g/PMT*)

Roadway Vehicles

- 🚌 **Bus** — 290g/PMT
- 🚗 **Gas Sedan**** — 384g/PMT
- 🏍 **Motorcycle** — 407g/PMT
- 🚙 **SUV**** — 448g/PMT

*Full passenger occupancy as compared to average passenger occupancy
**With an average of 1.6 passengers
g/PMT: CO_2 grams per passenger-mile-traveled

Global Private Car Ownership and Greenhouse Gas Emission Growth

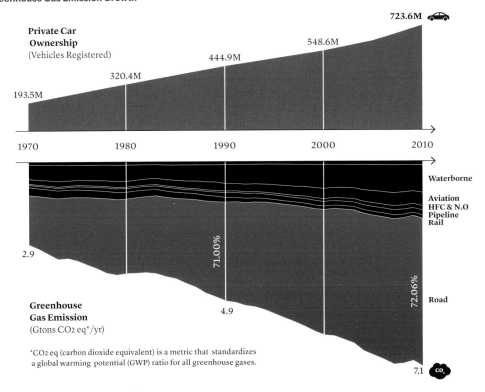

Private Car Ownership
(Vehicles Registered)

- 193.5M
- 320.4M
- 444.9M
- 548.6M
- 723.6M 🚗

1970 1980 1990 2000 2010

Greenhouse Gas Emission
(Gtons CO2 eq*/yr)

- 2.9
- 4.9
- 7.1 ☁

71.00% 72.06%

Waterborne
Aviation
HFC & N_2O
Pipeline
Rail
Road

*CO2 eq (carbon dioxide equivalent) is a metric that standardizes
a global warming potential (GWP) ratio for all greenhouse gases.

NEW MOBILITY TECHNOLOGIES OFFER PROMISE ...

Carbon Footprint by Vehicle Type

Ride-hailing

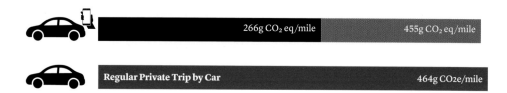

266g CO_2 eq/mile   455g CO_2 eq/mile

Regular Private Trip by Car   464g CO2e/mile

Autonomous vehicle

23–39% reduction
in CO_2 eq/mile

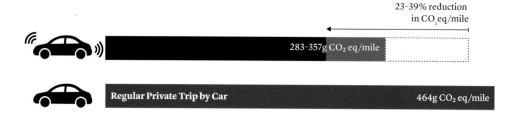

283–357g CO_2 eq/mile

Regular Private Trip by Car   464g CO_2 eq/mile

Electric vehicle

Based on average emissions needed
to generate the power to charge
vehicle; actual values vary
significantly with power source.

125g CO_2 eq/mile

Regular Private Trip by Car   464g CO_2 eq/mile

... BUT RAISE DIFFICULT NEW QUESTIONS.

Questions by Vehicle Type

Undermines public transit?

2012–2017 change of ridership type in New York City.

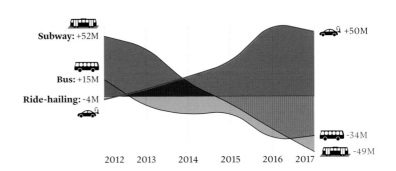

Subway: +52M

Bus: +15M

Ride-hailing: -4M

+50M

-34M

-49M

2012 2013 2014 2015 2016 2017

Ethical decision making?

Autonomous vehicles are challenged by the lack of clear, ethical decision-making guidelines.

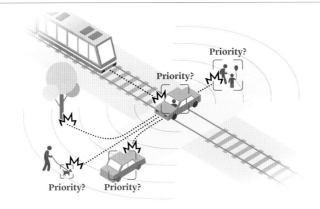

Priority?
Priority?
Priority?
Priority?

Power source?

Currently, electric vehicle deployment connects to the electrical grids, which predominantly rely on high-carbon power sources.

Environmental Impact

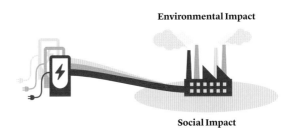

Social Impact

REGARDLESS OF THE TECHNOLOGY, WE NEED TO THINK ABOUT THE EMBODIED ENERGY ASSOCIATED WITH PRIVATE CARS AND THEIR INFRASTRUCTURE ...

Private Vehicle Life-Cycle CO_2 Emissions

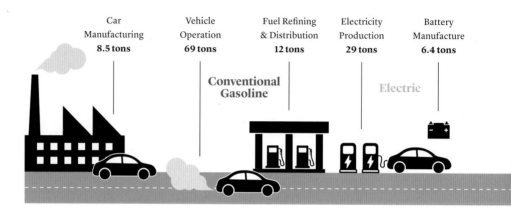

Car Manufacturing	Vehicle Operation	Fuel Refining & Distribution	Electricity Production	Battery Manufacture
8.5 tons	69 tons	12 tons	29 tons	6.4 tons

Conventional Gasoline

Electric

Average Occupancy per Vehicle: **1.6**
Life-Cycle Mile Traveled per Vehicle: **186,500 miles**
CO_2 Emisson per Passenger-Mile-Traveled:

384g/PMT (Gasoline)

231g/PMT (Electrical)

*Based on electricity source in the United States.

Subway Life-Cycle CO_2 Emissions

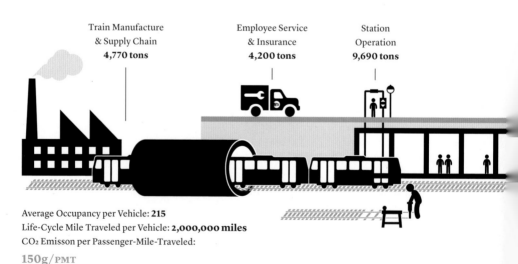

Train Manufacture & Supply Chain	Employee Service & Insurance	Station Operation
4,770 tons	4,200 tons	9,690 tons

Average Occupancy per Vehicle: **215**
Life-Cycle Mile Traveled per Vehicle: **2,000,000 miles**
CO_2 Emisson per Passenger-Mile-Traveled:

150g/PMT

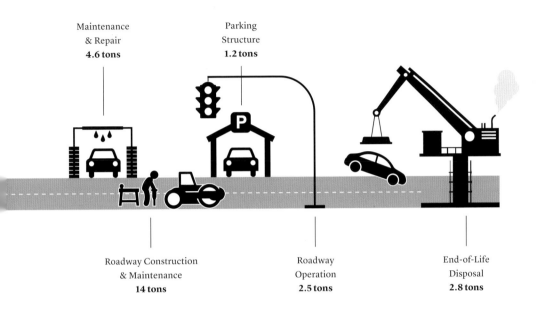

Maintenance
& Repair
4.6 tons

Parking
Structure
1.2 tons

Roadway Construction
& Maintenance
14 tons

Roadway
Operation
2.5 tons

End-of-Life
Disposal
2.8 tons

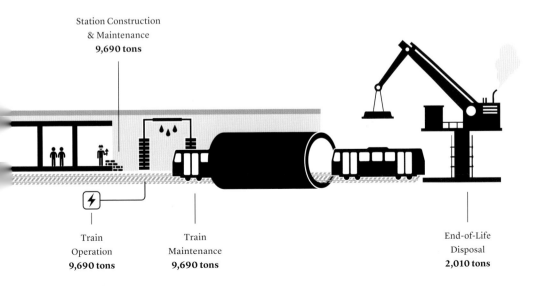

Station Construction
& Maintenance
9,690 tons

Train
Operation
9,690 tons

Train
Maintenance
9,690 tons

End-of-Life
Disposal
2,010 tons

... NOT TO MENTION THAT CARS USE A DISPROPORTIONATE AMOUNT OF SPACE PER PERSON ...

"Gehzeug" or "Walkmobile" Used at a Protest in Thailand

... REGARDLESS OF THEIR UNDERLYING TECHNOLOGIES.

Different Transportation Modes to Move 50 People

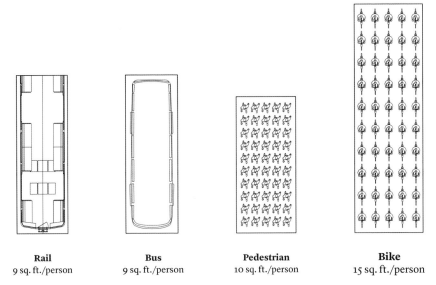

Rail
9 sq. ft./person

Bus
9 sq. ft./person

Pedestrian
10 sq. ft./person

Bike
15 sq. ft./person

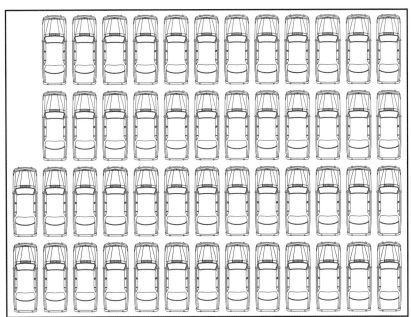

Car
55 sq. ft./person

THESE TWO IMAGES ARE ...

Pregerson Interchange
Los Angeles, CA
Idea Credit: Steve Mouzon on *The Original Green* blog post.

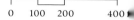

0   100   200   400

... AT THE SAME SCALE.

Centro Storico
Florence, Italy

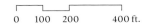

0   100   200   400 ft.

ONE THIRD OF MOST CITIES IS DEDICATED TO ROAD BED, SPACE THAT COULD BE PUT TO BETTER USE.

Central Park
843 acres

×2.9

Total Area of Roadbed
Space for Cars
2,450 acres

Roadbed Space
Car Lanes and
Street Parking

Empire State Building
2.7 million sq. ft.

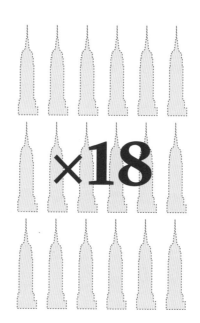

×18

Total Area of Car Facilities
48 million sq. ft.

Car Facilities
Repair Shops, Gas Stati
Parking Garages, et

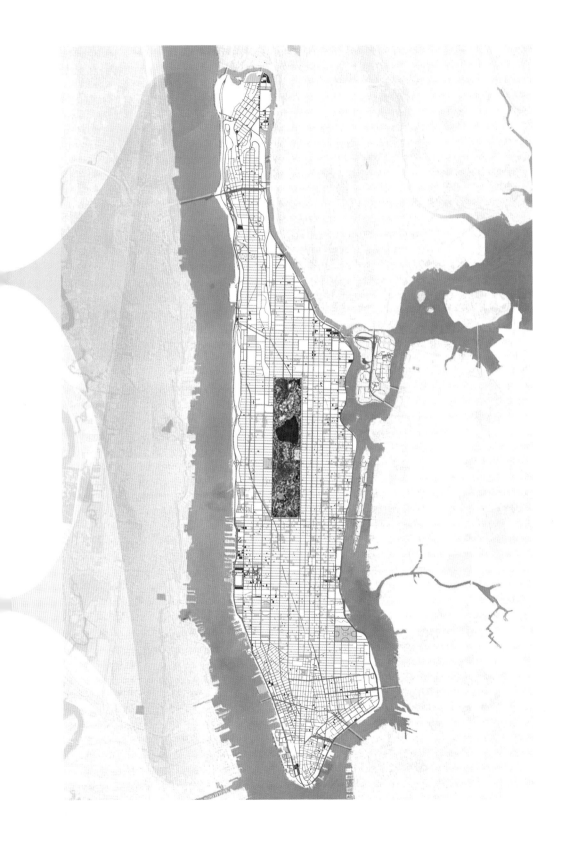

SO LET'S CORRECT PAST MISTAKES
BY ADAPTIVELY REUSING OUR CITY STREETS ...

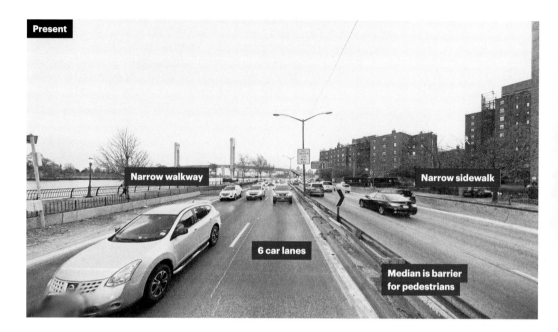

Present
Narrow walkway
Narrow sidewalk
6 car lanes
Median is barrier
for pedestrians

Future

Re-imagining FDR Dr. New York, USA
Source: PAU with the *New York Times* and Buro Happold,
N.Y.C.—*Not Your Car*

... AS PUBLIC SPACES THAT CONNECT PEOPLE OF ALL BACKGROUNDS, AGES, AND ABILITIES.

Re-imagining 46th St. New York, USA
Source: PAU with the *New York Times* and Buro Happold,
N.Y.C.—*Not Your Car*

AS THE WORLD BURNS BURNS BURNS BURNS BURNS BURNS BURNS BURNS

IT IS CLEAR THAT OUR PLANET IS IN EXTREME

jeopardy due to global warming caused by human activity, particularly the ways in which we have chosen to live and drive. But within the international environmentalist discourse, the larger role of cities is often misunderstood.

Without question, our urban regions contribute greatly to climate change. Our metropolitan areas, which include cities and their suburban surroundings, are heat islands that account for the majority of the world's carbon emissions, most of which are attributed to buildings and cars, as illustrated in the previous chapter. But the heat-island issue obscures the larger story—the planet's billions must live somewhere, and cities are by far our best bet.

As I argued extensively in *A Country of Cities*, dense, transit-based, urbane inner cities are humankind's greenest invention. On a per capita basis, the city centers of Hong Kong, Tokyo, London, and the island of Manhattan are some of the greenest places on earth because their inhabitants—rich and poor alike—walk, bike, and use mass transit, all while living and working in vertically stacked apartments and offices that efficiently heat and cool one another. The individual carbon footprints of most inner-city residents remain far smaller than those of people who commute long distances daily from suburban homes to office parks in a two-ton personal vehicle. Unlike suburbia, rural areas are justifiably car and truck dependent due to their agricultural and cultural significance; the needs of the countryside should not be conflated with the profligacy of sprawl, which is often the nemesis of the farming communities.

Recent data indicate that the carbon footprint per person in our inner cities is similar to that of our conservation-minded rural areas—it is the suburban zone between the two that is the problem, due to daily automobile commutation, high-emission landscaping equipment, and thermally inefficient single-family housing.[1] Unlike suburbs, villages, smaller cities, and even some academic campuses offer many of the same environmental benefits as big cities due to their mixed-use, walkable, tight-knit nature. A handful of older rail-based suburbs feature some of these attributes as well, but the more sprawling they become, the more dependent they are on driving, inefficient heating and cooling, and a host of other environmental maladies. While it is true that people are attracted to exurbs because they are cheaper than either inner-ring suburbs or big cities (the cities cited above are among the most expensive places to live in the world), suburban and exurban life has been made artificially inexpensive since the 1950s, particularly in the United States, through federally funded highways, absurdly low gasoline taxes, segregation of public school funding, and other subsidies that keep our sprawling subdivision, highway construction, and fossil fuel industries alive. As with factories that once polluted rivers without paying for cleanup, we have subsidized millions of people to live in large single-family homes that threaten our collective larger house.

Humankind's Greenest Invention
Dense, transit-oriented urban cores like Hong Kong, Tokyo, New York, and London are some of the greenest places on earth per capita, but also the most expensive (*clockwise from top left*).

Average Household Carbon Footprint in Eastern United States
Cities and rural areas share similarly low emissions per household, unlike the suburbs.
©CoolClimate Network

The Predicament of Suburban Living
The smoke and flames of California wildfires serve as a stark reminder that sprawl is not sustainable.

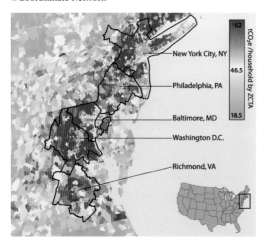

It astonishes me to this day the extent to which this set of facts needs to be reiterated again and again. What neither conservative nor liberal suburbanites want to believe is that they—and not the caricature of inner-city welfare recipients—are the Americans most bankrolled by the government due to their free highways, unjustifiable tax deductions, artificially uplifted public-school systems, and barely taxed gasoline. Gasoline prices spiked in the aftermath of Russia's invasion of Ukraine, yet they never reached the levels needed to sufficiently deter driving or pay for the impacts private auto use has had on the environment. More generally, we remain reluctant to acknowledge how vulnerable our fossil-fueled economy makes us to petro-dictators. Arguably, it is not the expansion of NATO that has enabled Putin's criminality; it is the subsidized expansion of our houses and cars.

But on the horizon we are seeing a more enlightened population, both younger and older, who are driving less, are attracted to apartment living, and are gravitating toward smaller cities with light rail or larger cities with extensive mass transit, all in an effort to diminish resource consumption and lead more communal lives. Yet it is clear to me that even smaller cities comprised largely of single-family homes have their environmental limitations. In 2020, my family moved from the expensive island of Manhattan to the expensive city of Berkeley, California, where we purposefully eschewed the fire-prone hills in favor of a neighborhood where we could walk or bike for daily needs (including commutes to work and school) and where we installed extensive rooftop solar panels to power weekend car trips and climate control our home. During this period I became convinced of the substantial growth of our family's energy usage regardless of these decisions, and despite the pandemic, mainly because the substantial solar power we were generating could have gone back into the grid rather than fuel a big house and an electric car. With a world in crisis, offsetting a profligate daily lifestyle with new technology is nowhere near as impactful as leading a more sustainable life by design. With our return to New York City, our California interlude has only confirmed my belief in urban density and mass transit as the most direct and enjoyable means to reduce carbon footprint per capita per day. This is a sustainable lifestyle that we must bring within the grasp of all incomes by redirecting suburban subsidies to our denser urban communities.

Regardless of how we live, human habitation has been, since the rise of Homo sapiens, resource intensive. As Yuval Noah Harari describes in his book *Sapiens* (2014), the emergence of our species gave way to the decimation of other species, to the clearing of land, and to a general manipulation of nature that was destructive and widespread.[2] Our willingness to abuse our environment dates back seventy thousand years, and then with a population that was minuscule compared to our now teeming planet of eight billion.

Today, from Australia and Bangladesh to the west coast of the United States, we are beginning to experience the full force of global warming, sea-level rise, ocean acidification, forest fires, and a torrent of other catastrophes brought about by our wasteful lifestyles. This is no longer an abstract argument, and the finger-pointing has begun to intensify. As the impacts of climate change worsen, one worries that something more harmful than fingers will get pointed at each other.

If you read a major newspaper article about climate change and scroll through the comments section, you will quickly find observers claiming that our burgeoning global population is the source of global warming. What makes this assertion absurd is that our fully developed nations, many of which have declining birth rates, are our planet's biggest polluters per capita—particularly the United States and the United Arab Emirates. The birth of an additional child in rural Africa will likely have minimal impact on the planet's resources. The birth of an additional child in suburban America, however, will have far greater impacts as that kid grows up learning that meals entail a massive wastage of food in the name of choices their parents wish to provide; that play requires intensive use of plastics and electronics; that getting to school or soccer practice demands a ride in a luxurious three-ton truck permitted by the government to masquerade as a car; and that future success as an adult means owning several of said trucks and a house sitting on a parcel larger than the African child's entire village. Beyond the handwringing that frames Africa as the source of climate change or stereotypes it as the place being victimized, some experts believe Africa may be the first continent to become net carbon negative.[3]

Furthermore, even if the assertion about population growth as the primary source of global warming held any truth, what are these commentators proposing as a solution? The human race has a dire history with forced birth control. As previously discussed, global population should plateau at just over ten billion people by 2100 as birth rates stabilize in the world's newly developing economies. (People have fewer kids in less agrarian economies because children live longer and are less useful as farm labor.) Worrying about the world's multitudes increasing, as happened in 2007 when the world hit seven billion, is dangerous when it reeks of xenophobia, particularly when it is accompanied by the craven sensibility that we who do the handwringing want to inhibit population increases so we can continue to use resources at our profligate rates. Obviously, we should not be fans of unbridled growth. As Jeffrey Sachs lays out in *The End of Poverty* (2005), everything from education to economic development is required in developing nations to curb population growth in accordance with free will.[4] It is particularly important for progressives to understand the role economic development plays in voluntary birth control, which is not to say that we should be fans of economic growth as it is defined today. Economists like Kate Raworth have envisioned circular forms of shared prosperity that are essential for us to understand as we imagine a more enlightened form of progress for the world's poor in which their

Stop the Subsidies

Federally funded highways, low gasoline taxes, and various other subsidies have collectively fueled the expansion of houses and cars since World War II.

Polluters vs. Population

The biggest polluters per capita are not located where the population is growing rapidly.

CO₂ Emission per Capita

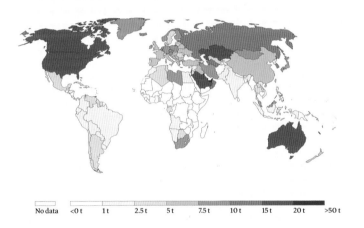

No data   <0 t   1 t   2.5 t   5 t   7.5 t   10 t   15 t   20 t   >50 t

Population Growth Rate

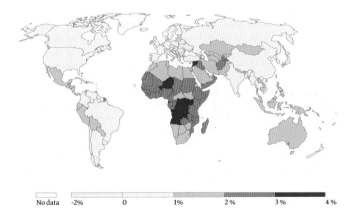

No data   -2%   0   1%   2%   3%   4%

A Suburban Lot Larger than an Entire African Village

6,000-sq.-ft. suburban lot

6,000-sq.-ft. village

```
0   10'    30'              60'
```

Africa Could Become the World's First Net Negative Continent
In the Sustainable Africa Scenario envisioned by the International Energy Agency (IEA),
 renewables, such as solar, wind, hydropower, and geothermal, could constitute over
80 percent of the power generation capacity by 2030.

Power Generation Capacity Additions in Africa
in IEA's Sustainable Africa Scenario

Renewables

Fossil Fuels

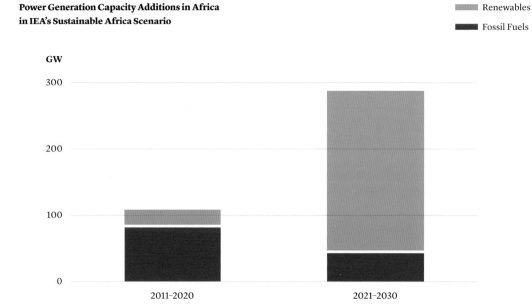

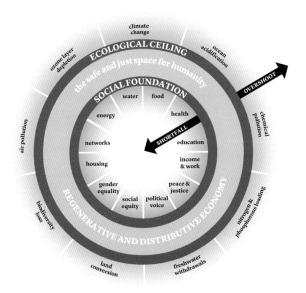

Raworth's Doughnut Economics
An economy is considered prosperous when all twelve social foundations are met without overshooting any of the nine ecological ceilings, as outlined in Kate Raworth's *Doughnut Economics*. Adapted by PAU with permission of author.

incentive to have large numbers of children diminishes.[5] The key to Raworth's conception is that we need to consider both the outer boundary above which we use more resources than we have, and an inner boundary below which our global standard of living is drastically unequal.

As Raworth's graphic indicates, for ten billion to inhabit the earth, renewable energy is necessary but not sufficient because of all the other metrics we will need to meet in order to live within the "donut" between a solid social foundation and our ecological ceiling. Solar and wind power are already cheaper than fossil fuels, and these and other renewable energy sources should play a significant role in urban sustainability, but these miracles of science should not lull us into a sense of complacency about suburban sustainability.

Former American vice president Al Gore said something similar in a 2018 talk he gave that was, much like this book, equal in pessimism and optimism.[6] On the pessimistic side, he delivered an appraisal of how much worse the environment has become since his landmark work *An Inconvenient Truth* (2006). An extraordinary *New York Times* story, which came out soon after his talk, corroborated the dangers faced by multiple coastal cities based on the most recent data.[7]

The source of Gore's optimism was equally clear. China and India have been adhering to the Paris Accord, which the United States rejoined under President Biden. Coal plants are being replaced by solar and wind farms at a substantial rate in the two most populous nations in the world, meaning that a third of humanity is lurching, however imperfectly, toward renewables. With air pollution in India's capital of New Delhi approaching uninhabitable levels, and with China facing a national security crisis around its lack of a lasting domestic energy supply,

Green Tech Cannot Solve Sprawl

Even with the adoption of electric cars and solar panels, sprawl continues to perpetuate the loss of natural habitat, farmland, and social interaction.

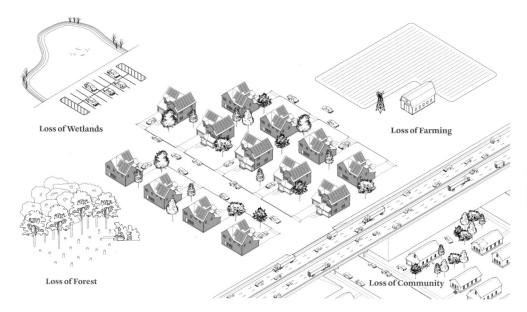

Loss of Wetlands

Loss of Farming

Loss of Forest

Loss of Community

the appeal of solar and wind has become evident to the citizens of these two notoriously science-oriented cultures. Furthermore, Gore spoke extensively about his excitement about electric cars and the advancement of battery technology in tandem with renewable electricity, despite concerns about the resource demands of new batteries. The audience clearly needed this boost of optimism, needed the sense that there is an achievable future for which we must fight.

After the talk I approached Gore about his thesis, with a sense of despondence about my life's work as an urbanist. "Mr. Vice President, if you are so optimistic about electric cars and renewable electricity, am I worrying about the wrong thing when I worry about sprawl?" He responded, "Not at all. Sprawl still creates innumerable other problems even if everyone had electric cars and solar panels. Problems like soil erosion, loss of natural habitat and farmland, irrigated lawns, subdivisions in flood and fire zones, the list goes on. Not to mention batteries for electric cars are expensive, energy intensive, require rare earths. Keep doing what you're doing."

The complexities of our burning house do not lend themselves to panaceas, especially technological ones. Of course we will need new technologies to combat global warming, including the promising but controversial possibilities of carbon capture and smaller-scale nuclear power, but we should keep in mind that decarbonization in the form of these new technologies will continue to come at a cost if we do not simultaneously reduce our voracious demand for energy. The rare earths and other minerals used in battery and other decarbonization technologies, which are mined across Africa and Latin America and largely processed in China, are already changing geopolitics. If past is prologue, excavation for concentrated energy resources, even with the purpose of clean energy, leads to wars, dictators, ecosystem damage, and other global imbalances.[8] Of course, we should decarbonize, but we must proceed cautiously with this history in mind, and we must reduce our energy demand even as we clean up our supply. As former president Jimmy Carter learned the hard way when he lost the election of 1980 in the aftermath of numerous crises, including an energy crisis that compelled him to ask Americans to reduce demand while wearing a cardigan, it is far better to present opportunity than sacrifice. How we can design better lifestyles by reducing consumption is a question we will consider more deeply in the book's second half.

In the last decades the middle class worldwide has almost tripled, and most are emulating a 1950s lifestyle we in the West invented with the single-family house, the lawn, and the car.[9] According to David Wallace-Wells, it is just in the last few decades, not the window of time dating back to the beginnings of the Industrial Revolution as many erroneously believe, that we have added the carbon to the atmosphere that has brought us to the brink of decimation.[10] We can all fantasize about a silver bullet with little required from us in terms of how we live together, but this is a fantasy that blinds us to our greater challenge: forging a society willing to fight for collective environmental action at scale and do so with joy. This is a significantly more difficult problem than scrutinizing our individual lightbulbs and diets.

No matter what changes we make at this late juncture, global warming will impact all of our communities but some worse than others, especially those that are both impoverished and imperiled. Already the differences in attitudes about this reality have emerged; if poor communities in Paradise, California, or the Lower Ninth Ward in New Orleans are decimated by environmental tragedies, the response of the general public seems to be that those communities shouldn't have built their homes in harm's way. If a similar circumstance befalls a wealthy community in the hills of California, in coastal Florida, or on the shores of the Hamptons, the response is notably different, with federal aid, insurance underwriting, and media sympathy often forthcoming. Globally, the repercussions of this disparity will become apparent as climate-change refugees become a new normal, generating more social unrest and directly linking environmental injustice with social injustice.

Making change will also be hard because we have powerful forces fighting for today's status quo. Just one hundred corporations around the world, particularly national fossil fuel companies, account for slightly more than 70 percent of global carbon emissions—the equivalent of what our cities generate as they accommodate the majority of the world's population![11] Consider it: eight billion people generate the same global emissions as one hundred companies. Certainly, each of us has an obligation to live less-consumptive lives that rely less on these corporations, but

Carbon Emissions Dominated by 100 Corporations

Approximately 70 percent of global industrial carbon emissions
can be attributed to just one hundred corporations worldwide,
with a notable contribution from nationalized fossil fuel companies.

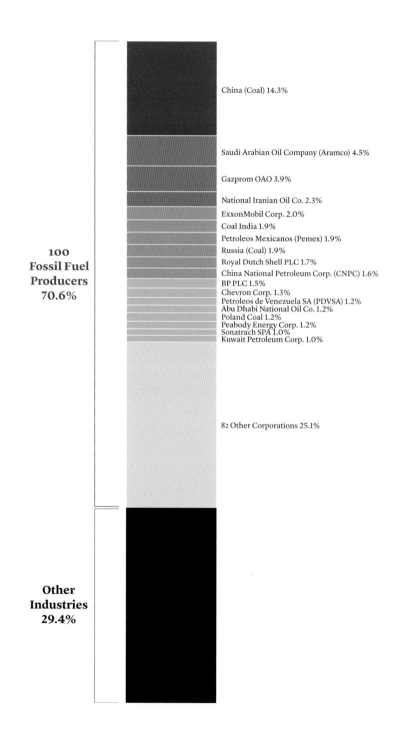

**Global Industrial
GHG Emission
1988–2015**

**100
Fossil Fuel
Producers
70.6%**

China (Coal) 14.3%

Saudi Arabian Oil Company (Aramco) 4.5%

Gazprom OAO 3.9%

National Iranian Oil Co. 2.3%
ExxonMobil Corp. 2.0%
Coal India 1.9%
Petroleos Mexicanos (Pemex) 1.9%
Russia (Coal) 1.9%
Royal Dutch Shell PLC 1.7%
China National Petroleum Corp. (CNPC) 1.6%
BP PLC 1.5%
Chevron Corp. 1.3%
Petroleos de Venezuela SA (PDVSA) 1.2%
Abu Dhabi National Oil Co. 1.2%
Poland Coal 1.2%
Peabody Energy Corp. 1.2%
Sonatrach SPA 1.0%
Kuwait Petroleum Corp. 1.0%

82 Other Corporations 25.1%

**Other
Industries
29.4%**

Disparity in Responses to Environmental Tragedies
Poor communities facing environmental tragedies (Santa Rosa, California [*top left*]; Lower Ninth Ward in New Orleans, Louisiana [*top right*]) are often blamed for residing in vulnerable areas, while affluent ones (Laguna Niguel, California [*bottom left*]; New Jersey Coast [*bottom right*]) receive federal aid, insurance support, and media sympathy despite their residents having more locational choice.

everyone driving a Tesla while using a stainless-steel straw won't make a dent in global warming unless and until these companies change not only what they do but how they do it. The outsize lobbying influence of the fossil fuel industry in particular led to the policies that have subsidized sprawl and spawned oil wars. It is this noxious industry that is the through line among many of the world's political strongmen today as they attempt to destabilize democracies, exploit social media, protect extractive economies, and foment our great urban-rural divide.

So, while we are all burning down the house, some of us are more responsible than others, and some will be feeling the heat far worse than those who fuel the conflagration. Without question the fossil fuel industry is the arsonist and their corporate greed has lit the match—they will protest in response that they are simply satisfying popular demand, but this rings hollow given that they have gleefully amplified that demand with decades of pro-suburban, pro-consumptive lobbying even though they were well aware of the damage their product was incurring.[12] That said, they know they are losing. They know fossil fuel is just that, a fossil. But they and their affiliated petro-states want to keep us addicted as long as they can, and while they need to be fought with every political weapon in our arsenal, we all need to go to rehab in ways that have global impact. We can recognize that they may be the arsonists, but the burning house is ours, and we need to redesign that house and what powers it. From this perspective, architects and urbanists are firefighters alongside climate scientists, politicians, activists, journalists, cleantech entrepreneurs, and all of us who view ourselves as stakeholders in this one planet we call home. We must use our skills as designers, researchers, practitioners, and advocates—our instrumentality—to help the world visualize and realize what it could experience, both environmentally and socially, as a stable, equitable, and prosperous planet of ten billion. But to do so, we must first consider the precarious circumstances in which billions of souls continue to find themselves.

MISTER ROBINSON'S NEIGHBORHOO

IN A TRIUMPHANT RETURN TO *Saturday Night Live* in late 2019, Eddie Murphy reprised some of his legendary early characters and skits, including "Gumby" and "Mister Robinson's Neighborhood," his deep, dark, delicious take on the children's classic *Mister Rogers' Neighborhood*. Reflecting the changes that have happened to our cities over the last several decades, the opening scene to "Mister Robinson's Neighborhood" is different from the original skit. Next to his older brick apartment building stands a newly erected architecturally self-important condominium with fancy cars parked out front. A now elderly Mr. Robinson explains:

> Hi, boys and girls, it's your old pal Mr. Robinson. So much has changed since we last spent some time together. My neighborhood has gone through so much. It's gone through something called *gentrification*. ... Can you say "gentrification," boys and girls? It's like a magic trick: white people pay a lot of money and then ... POOF ... all the black people are gone![1]

Murphy's blade is long, sharp, and poignant. Homelessness and displacement, often but not always caused by gentrification, have become rampant in cities like New York and San Francisco, particularly in the aftermath of the pandemic. About this much has been written, and I leave to better experts a fuller discussion of the underlying economic drivers of this social calamity.

Since the primary focus of this book is the culture of cities in terms of their lived experience, this chapter focuses on the negative cultural impacts when our cities become homogeneous and gated in terms of race, class, heritage, and, perhaps most elusively, mindset. This loss is in no way greater than the very real losses that the displaced experience; rather, it is to recognize that the losses of racial and economic diversity in our cities are manifold for both those who are displaced and those who are left behind, as Heather McGhee similarly argues in *The Sum of Us*.[2]

In the introduction to this book, we defined urbanity as a community inhabited by many different cultures and classes who spatially interact. This is reminiscent of the ideas of the Greek city planner Constantine Doxiades, who wrote about the city as a place where iconoclasts, or "blue people," would influence those of more orthodox mindsets, or "red people" (he wrote well before our current political

Doxiades: Cities as Catalysts for Social Change
Constantine Doxiades envisioned the city as a place where iconoclasts ("blue people") would influence those of more orthodox mindsets (or "red people"), thereby generating social change (in the form of "purple people"). Diagram concept credit: Charles Correa

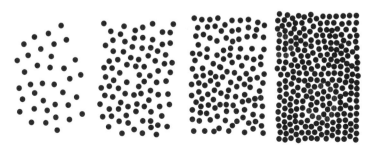

nomenclature of red and blue), thereby generating social change in the form of "purple people."[3] Somewhat implicit in Doxiades' construct is that iconoclasts tend to earn less because our economy is generally structured to reward orthodoxy. Of course, there is the occasional rebel who is a successful film star, tech genius, or financial whiz, but most unorthodox people are so because they view themselves, or more typically are viewed by others, as different and therefore less comfortable in the normative world. The striver, the dreamer, the artist, the vocalist, the poet: these people may change society, but rarely are they rewarded by it.

Similarly, because of institutionalized racism or implicit bias, entire cultures are often economically marginalized in our cities, yet the neighborhoods and communities these cultures form are often richer and more culturally saturated than a wealthy neighborhood composed of chain stores and overpriced pasta places. Much like its feminist predecessor *The Stepford Wives* (1975), Jordan Peele's cult classic *Get Out* (2017) crystallizes this dynamic by depicting an ostensibly liberal white community that steals, through murder and transfusion, the physical and cultural talents of African Americans in an effort to imbue themselves with the attributes they lack.[4] MIT's Julian Beinart, who while lecturing presented images of elderly San Diegans wearing tourist sombreros in Tijuana, referred to a

similar sensibility in cities as "bipolarity," in which wealthy people from dominant but staid cultures depend on economically poor but culturally vibrant neighborhoods for excitement, difference, art, music, and cuisine.[5]

This allure of "the other" is the cultural fountainhead of gentrification. It is the most pronounced not in the traditionally wealthy yet boring parts of our cities—where there are few left to gentrify—but in the cooler neighborhoods sought out by young professionals, hipsters, recent college grads, and cagey real-estate agents. It is ironic to watch first-wave gentrifiers, often oblivious to their role, fight subsequent waves of gentrification when it was actually their "pioneering" act of moving to lower-income communities that in turn attracted their less-intrepid followers. Some argue that for young people trying to make it in expensive cities, these choices flow out of economic necessity, but typically one can today find cheaper rents in less exciting neighborhoods that young people often eschew. For example, Manhattan's far Upper East Side, now accessible by subway, is actually cheaper

Upper East Side versus Williamsburg
Less popular but budget-friendly areas accessible by subway, like Manhattan's far Upper East Side, often offer cheaper rents compared to trendy parts of Brooklyn.

than many of the gentrifying parts of Brooklyn, but it is nowhere near as hip!

In addition to the tragedy of displacement and homelessness, the ugliness to which these dynamics have given birth across expensive left-leaning cities now includes the anti-growth liberal. Draped in the flag of Jane Jacobs, these self-appointed guardians will fight growth and change in the name of community, despite the fact that they benefit from gentrification themselves, particularly if they purchased their homes—but even if they didn't. By caricaturing developers as the bogeymen, anti-housing advocates refuse to acknowledge that for every proposed mixed-income apartment building near mass transit that they fight, the worse they are making the world in terms of both ecology and equity. This is not to let mainstream developers off the hook, given that most of them build the banal, but we now live in a time when entrenched liberal communities are regularly defeating projects that are 100 percent affordable housing, much to the detriment of our growing cities.

While some who fight development may have legitimate grievances, particularly those with deep local roots, many are organized anti-growth crusaders who operate across a metropolis with limited concern for the desires of the actual local community. Unfortunately, we have reached a point where too many residents in our most popular cities want to hang a "No Vacancy" sign at the city limits.

Shamefully, if extremists on the right want to build walls declaring the country is full, extremists on the left want to pass legislation that declares the city is full. Both groups smack of xenophobia. In the case of California, this vitriol has become statewide, to the point where special interests, particularly homeowners wanting to keep their equity levels high by keeping supply low, are celebrating the state's steady population loss to Texas, Idaho, Colorado, Arizona, Oregon, and Washington. In New York, we have witnessed politicians demand that newcomers return to the Midwest, whence they supposedly came, despite the lack of data to support such wild assertions. Some commentators have even gone so far as to suggest that the pandemic was good for our cities by driving out the bourgeoisie, a horrifying sentiment that resonates with those who pine for our cities of the 1970s, when bohemian white liberals got high while communities of color got assaulted.

Today, substandard infrastructure like a lack of classrooms, poor mass transit, or the dearth of water is often cited as the justification for fighting urban growth, as if we as a wealthy society don't have the means to build more schools, fix our subways, or retain our storm water. Creating equitable urban outcomes in response to population growth is a matter of finding the political will to support dense affordable housing in our cities that is calibrated to income, up-front public infrastructure investment, social services, and other community needs. This is a coordinated strategy we must deploy if we are to fight homelessness and displacement with equity, sustainability, and dignity—it is not enough just to build formulaic multifamily housing.

Extreme Right: "The Country Is Full"

Extreme Left: "The City Is Full"

The urban poor symbolized by Mr. Robinson bear the brunt of anti-housing policies, including wealthy conservative and liberal neighborhoods in which residents fight supportive and transitional housing for the unhoused, all as the supply of residential units dwindles, subsistence wages barely increase, and homelessness beckons.

My family's apartment in Manhattan is situated right next to a well-run food pantry that serves the unhoused and is utterly harmless. The left can rail on about neoliberalism—which without question has failed the poor, as we discuss extensively in the next chapter—but as liberals pass a person sleeping on the street they should take a hard look in the mirror at their own role in our collective national malaise. Instead, they tilt at the windmill of defeating capitalism, but one cannot wait for a national political revolution to solve immediate local housing and infrastructure needs; to do so is the ultimate in self-serving rationalization. Cities like Houston are proving to big blue cities like New York and San Francisco that homelessness is addressable within the confines of our economic system with the right public interventions.[6]

Culturally, our urban housing crisis has us careering toward monocultures, whether it be in our wealthy white enclaves or our bohemian white enclaves. Hipsters do not urbanity make; pluralism does, pluralism in terms of not only diverse skin colors and bank accounts but also diverse mindsets that avoid groupthink at all costs. True urbanity is filled with original thinkers, iconoclasts who promulgate change beyond the empty rhetoric of angry tweets.

It is challenging for design to impact this state of affairs, which is so driven by both our land economics and the self-serving choices made across generations in our dominant culture. Bringing down the cost of urban housing, working toward easier and cheaper options for commuting, and designing healthier communities are all impactful goals for the architecture, landscape architecture, and urban planning professions to pursue, but we remain today a far cry from early modern roots of architecture and urbanism, which espoused many of these same concepts after the housing crises brought on by both world wars.

To be fair to today's design professionals, they receive none of the partnership from government that their predecessors did under Roosevelt's New Deal, Tito's Yugoslavia, or the social expansiveness of the Weimar period. Common to each of these was a desire for collective housing action not only as a social good but also as an artistic one, in which different thinkers could flourish. As imperfect as the Works Progress Administration and the Bauhaus may have been, both were art and social movements buoyed by largely supportive societies. Perhaps we can form a truly progressive political movement that calls for more government and NGO partnerships, coupled with more inclusive representation in the public sector, to create social housing, climate projects, and public infrastructure, or as Ezra Klein calls it, "a liberalism that builds."[7]

Until then, our big progressive cities are sustained by a highly regulated capitalist real-estate system that is failing because of the combination of greed-driven market mechanisms and anti-housing regulatory regimes. Exclusionary regulations are the hammer and sickle of the anti-housing liberals who have learned to abuse the tactics of Jacobs to control weak local politicians and make new housing— including homeless shelters and affordable housing—nearly impossible to build. In response, capitalism seeks to squeeze more and more revenue out of the fewer and fewer housing units it can produce in such an environment, consequently veering toward the luxury resident who can afford the enormous underlying costs of regulated construction, artificially created land scarcity, and profit levels sufficient to incentivize a developer to undertake the risks of building. It's no wonder that the housing markets in many of our biggest cities primarily serve those in the well-compensated financial and technology industries, industries that despite their efforts remain insufficiently diverse, which in turn has an outsized homogenizing impact on the culture of our cities.

Nonetheless, it is important and laudable that a number of major technology companies as well as their smaller counterparts have evolved from their early Silicon Valley office park roots into the space of the city, driven by the knowledge that much of the talent they seek wants to live in urban environments even in the aftermath of the pandemic. In a number of cases the larger companies have actively sought to do more than occupy urban real estate, working to help revitalize waterfronts and historic structures as new urban magnets. This has been particularly critical for city officials who have wanted to diversify their economies and provide new employment opportunities for their citizenry.

For many but not all technologists, however, the tendency remains to look at the messy, democratic, untidy nature of cities as a problem to be solved rather than as a complex ecosystem to be celebrated. Much of that untidiness is the result of racial representation fought for in the wake of urban renewal, a history some from Silicon Valley don't sufficiently understand. For those who fought for democratic representation in urban governance, they cannot afford to view technological solutions as mere questions of efficiency but instead they must ask from experience, efficiency *for whom*?

Positive Social Friction versus Unsocial Frictionless Transactions
Street retail, a source of positive social friction, faces the looming threat of technological "optimization" through online shopping and delivery systems, ostensibly driven by the pursuit of efficiency.

It is this hopefully waning tech desire for "solving" the city and creating "frictionless" transactions that drives the so-called smart city movement, which seems to view human inefficiency as something to be minimized. And yet human inefficiency is what drives the arts, what drives urbane culture, what we have been calling positive social friction throughout these pages. Urban residents are not avatars to be optimized, they are people who pause, who question, who engage the differences within the communities that surround them. During the tremendous growth of Paris in the nineteenth century, the French created a literary figure known as the *flâneur*, a quintessential city dweller, who strolls the sidewalks without overt purpose, a wanderer who seeks the inefficient yet rich journey urban streets can provide. This is not to say that technology has no role—to the contrary. But in the quest to create smart cities, we must question the implication that all cities that came before, including the cultures and communities that made them, were somehow not "smart."

Over a century ago, robber barons created communities that they fully controlled, like Pullman, Illinois, often with enormous social and racial implications. Today's real-estate magnates continue to create homogeneous gated communities, both suburban and urban, respectively horizontal and vertical, with similar motivations that privilege segregation and predictability over inclusion and serendipity. And now some tech companies seek to do the same with sensors that monitor our every move. In all cases, one can surmise a distinct desire to exclude or extract, to create something that simulates a city but does not allow for the positive social friction of urbanity. We live in an era in which personal agency is increasingly sacrosanct, particularly in cities where individual freedoms are a primary draw. It is incumbent on large-scale urban companies to prove to us that they are on our side in a way that surpasses the saccharine entreaties of marketing campaigns. New urban industries are welcome to anchor our cities, but they simultaneously need to fight alongside us for our individual liberties at every turn, including enthusiasm for sound government regulation when needed.

For Mr. Robinson to have true autonomy, to live with dignity on a modest salary, public support and intervention are paramount. How, then, does this call for governmental action differ from the exclusionary regulatory regimes criticized above? This question—of public investment for all versus public protectionism for a few—is the topic of the next chapter and will help set the stage for the hope imagined in the chapters to follow.

FOR

WHOM

THE

DOLE

TOLLS

NO SOCIOECONOMIC SYSTEM HAS ACHIEVED

global dominance as profoundly as the ideology of unregulated markets known as neoliberalism, which was promulgated by the Chicago School of economics and made manifest by Ronald Reagan and Margaret Thatcher. In our deeply polarized times readers may forget that Reagan, who believed government and the taxes that funded it hurt the nation, in his landslide reelection victory of 1984 won every state in the union except his opponent Walter Mondale's home state of Minnesota. Well before today's divided states of blue and red, there was the United States of Tax Cuts.

Neoliberal Icons
Margaret Thatcher and Ronald Reagan; Milton Friedman with Augusto Pinochet (second and third from left, respectively).

The United States of Tax Cuts
Ronald Reagan's 1984 reelection marked a historic landslide with forty-nine states won and the highest-ever electoral vote count.

America, a country whose young history has included as much socialist fervor as it has capitalist fever, had by the mid-1980s become a deeply conservative nation steeped in an economic theory well to the right of Adam Smith's rulebound capitalism.[1] Nobel laureate Milton Friedman, the economist most closely associated with neoliberalism, preached it not only to Western leaders but also to dictators like Chile's Augusto Pinochet, fomenting a worldwide economic restructuring enforced by the World Bank and the International Monetary Fund. The Chernobyl nuclear disaster occurred simultaneous with this global restructuring, fully discrediting the statist worldview embodied by a crumbling, starving Soviet Union. By the fall of the Berlin Wall in 1989, a pan-global religion of unregulated free markets became dominant with its avatar in Gordon Gekko, the protagonist in *Wall Street* (1987).[2] More insidious, however, was the rarely discussed market alliance the Gekko character found with the cast of *The Big Chill* (1983), a generation who by the 1980s let their love of flowers and drugs transmogrify into a love of stock portfolios and lawns fueled by tax cuts and deficit spending.[3] Neoliberalism remains broadly popular not only because it serves the wealthy who mightily influence government but because of how well it serves the much larger number of voters known as the upper-middle class, often known today as the "suburban swing vote."

Reagan's presidency was a tsunami of historic proportion, decimating the country's two-century-old approach to and belief in public investment.

The Reagan Coalition
Gordon Gekko in *Wall Street* and the cast of *The Big Chill*.

This change was inevitable because by the 1970s, which was the decade that set the stage for the ascendance of Reagan and his neoliberal agenda, the definition of the term "public" now included more than white people for the first time in American history due to the victories of the civil rights movement in the years prior. For example, it is important and staggering to recall that black women did not fully have the right to vote across all fifty states, and therefore were not considered by those in power to be part of "the public" in the most expansive political sense, before 1965.[4]

Prior to the 1960s, the nation's history of federal investment was truly extraordinary, but there was an implicit understanding that these investments were made by the government on behalf of a largely white electorate even if others were beneficiaries on occasion. Republican Abraham Lincoln signed the Morrill Act, giving us the land grant colleges that form the basis of America's great public higher education institutions like the University of Michigan, the University of California system, and even some private institutions like the Massachusetts Institute of Technology.[5] Republican Theodore Roosevelt built our National Park System and broke up the railroad monopoly. Democrat Franklin Delano Roosevelt—in response to a rising socialist movement in the wake of the Depression—adopted Catherine Bauer's 1937 Housing Act, enabled the Tennessee Valley Authority, and created the Works Progress Administration, which led to extraordinary public infrastructure like the Hoover Dam.[6] Republican Dwight Eisenhower passed the 1956 National Interstate and Defense Highways Act, creating the largest public infrastructure the nation has ever built in the form of our interstate system.[7] While it is true that these historic investments helped Americans of every race to some degree, it is the nation's ascendant white middle class, which built much of its financial and social equity in the postwar era, that was the primary beneficiary. The highway system, in tandem with racist policies such as the redlining of mortgages, subsidized and enabled suburban flight for the white upper-middle and middle classes. Simultaneously, deindustrialization began to take its multidecade toll on inner-city America. Containerized shipping, born from the Suez Canal crisis of the 1950s, decimated the employment base for urban dock workers, black and white alike.

Not until Lyndon B. Johnson's Great Society and War on Poverty programs of the 1960s, which were clearly intended to be inclusive of black citizens due largely to the intense political pressure he received from Dr. Martin Luther King

The "Again" in MAGA:
1950s Welfare for Whites
Levittown, fueled by the GI Bill and federal
housing and highway subsidies, lowered
upfront housing costs for buyers but
implemented discriminatory practices by
restricting the sale of houses exclusively to
white families.

and other civil rights activists, did American
whites in reaction begin to reconsider government
spending as profligate waste.[8] During the Johnson
era—the period during which a younger Ronald
Reagan transformed from actor to politician and
declared that Medicare would be the "end of
freedom in America"—the nation transformed
socially and geographically. Johnson knew that the
black electorate would be key to the future of the
Democratic Party because it was losing its southern,
historically racist base known as "Dixiecrats" to
Richard Nixon's new "silent majority." By Reagan's
first presidential victory in 1980, the political
tables had fully turned, and the party of Lincoln
transformed into what would ultimately evolve
into today's GOP.

It is important to note that sweeping federal investments prior to Johnson's
programs in the 1960s were not characterized as welfare because their benefits
went largely to white people, but this changed after the civil rights movement
and into the Reagan era in terms of both structure and narrative.[9] Government
expenditures that served, and in many cases still serve, majority white populations,
such as agricultural and ethanol subsidies, highway construction, mortgage
interest deductions, the GI Bill, school investments, and other monies that
flowed to the segregated suburbs, went largely unquestioned, all while funds that
supported increasingly black urban life were demonized. For white middle-class
America, public expenditures that helped them were posited as unquestionable
entitlements or deductions, part of their Manifest Destiny, but public expenditures
on behalf of black America were purposefully framed and exaggerated as a socially
dysfunctional "beast" that must be "starved."[10]

Over just a few decades these sweeping changes in political and philosophical
approaches to governance and investment had manifold impacts on cities, on
suburbs, and more generally on the lifestyles Americans chose and the aspirations
those choices represented. "The American Dream," a phrase coined by James
Truslow Adams in the 1930s to capture an aspiration of equal opportunity for
every man and woman in the United States regardless of material possessions,
transfigured into the pursuit of private cars and single-family homes. As middle-
class families were incentivized to suburbanize in the 1950s and 1960s, the words
"public" and "urban" took on negative and synonymous connotations, which for
the ensuing decades despoiled urban life and the infrastructure that supported it.
For instance, in 1963, New York's Pennsylvania Station—which, ironically, was built
by the private sector as a beautiful fortress meant to serve well-heeled interstate

patrons and protect them from the largely African American neighborhood that surrounded the facility in the early 1900s—was torn down in favor of private real-estate development because the station's then-owner, Penn Central Railroad, faced bankruptcy in competition with federally subsidized highways. Following a substantial loss of rail ridership due to public funds that had been allocated to the highway system and favored automobile travel, the railroad could no longer maintain the enormous station and wanted the revenue from the sale of its land above the sidewalk level, with the achieved intention of creating a lightless subterranean station beneath, both literally and symbolically, private development above. New York's then-mayor, Robert Wagner, who signed the demolition order despite laudable but limited public protests, could have instead taken over the station as a municipal facility, but with the city in grave financial straits as a consequence of deindustrialization and white flight, there was an insufficient financial argument or electoral mandate to fight for a glorious but poorly maintained communal facility. While its demolition would go on to trigger the nation's landmark laws, the destruction at a larger level embodied an inflection point in U.S. and arguably world history, symbolizing as it did the death of public dignity in favor of private interests like real-estate developers and middle-class automobiles.

The contention that inner-city public investment was inherently foolhardy plays out most vividly in the arena of public housing. Pruitt-Igoe, the infamous St. Louis housing project designed by Minoru Yamasaki in 1954 and demolished in 1972, has become the poster child for the failures of federally sponsored public housing in the United States. The iconic photograph of its destruction has for detractors of public housing served to justify the full privatization of the housing market, including the provision of what we now call "affordable housing." For the left, the image is emblematic of the failures of modernism as both an architectural and philosophical enterprise; Pruitt-Igoe is still understood today by many liberals to be endemic of the failures of top-down planning, in which urban renewal cleared so-called slums and "warehoused the poor," particularly African Americans. For the right, the demolition of Pruitt-Igoe remains an easy punching bag for the follies of government investment and the naivete of modernist idealism.

Neoliberalism Made Manifest:
The Detritus of the
Historic Pennsylvania Station
Penn Station's demolition was fueled by competition from federally funded highways and commercial aviation, with the station's private owner unable to maintain the facility and a city and state government unwilling to take it over and reclaim it as a public facility.

The typical right and left viewpoints about the project quickly unravel upon closer inspection. When one watches the documentary *The Pruitt-Igoe Myth* (2011), made by a former resident who interviews other former residents, their stories reveal that Pruitt-Igoe and its architecture were, initially, a massive success.[11] When it opened the housing project served a mixed-income, mixed-race community and had indeed helped people move from substandard housing that lacked decent plumbing and other services to a glistening, bright, greenery-laced new community. Its failures only began as the larger forces of deindustrialization and white flight took hold in St. Louis. Steadily the housing complex became more impoverished as those who couldn't move to the suburbs also lost local manufacturing jobs. The St. Louis Housing Authority went on to make a number of ill-conceived, racist decisions that led to the downfall of the complex, including separating African American fathers from their families, and ultimately mismanaging the complex to the point that basic services like trash collection, elevators, and heating rarely functioned. Those who could, fled, predictably leaving behind crime and social dysfunction until the complex was deemed too dangerous to exist. What the documentary reveals, however, is that the simplistic bogeymen blamed for the project's downfall—public investment for the right, top-down urban renewal for the left, and modernist architecture for both—belie the more nuanced reasons behind the failure. To prove this one only needs to look at the innumerable "tower in the park" housing projects that have been successful, like New York's Penn South, Detroit's Lafayette Park, or other examples in Europe, where the same levels of mismanagement and disinvestment did not occur.[12]

But the die was cast. With the Watergate scandal of the early 1970s souring the American public on the integrity of government, Reagan swept into power in 1980 by openly mocking the idea that a civil servant could sincerely mean "I'm from the government and I'm here to help." Reelected by a baby boomer demographic that had been won over as "Reagan Democrats," the convivial conservative went on to pass sweeping tax legislation in 1986 that replaced federal funding for public housing with a developer tax credit system, a framework still in place to this day as our system for providing affordable housing. This framework did introduce the benefit of housing mixed-income individuals in the same building in most instances, which is a face-to-face level of interaction among races and classes still foreign to most European socialist settings. I have lived in rental buildings with low-income neighbors—it is wonderful to experience how seamlessly different socioeconomic groups can share not only the same lobbies and elevators but the same walkable neighborhoods, public school systems, and parks. As time has progressed with this system, through turbulent trial and error including a "poor door" moment when low-income residents were housed in adjacent but separate facilities, regulations now mandate that apartments for the poor be integrated and indistinguishable from market-rate units in terms of size, building location, and access to amenities. Nonetheless, many on the left criticize this form of affordable housing because it is developer driven, it often does not reach low enough income levels, and the symbol of public investment is not visible.

Private Defeats Public

The demolition of Pruitt-Igoe—primarily a result of racism, mismanagement, and the city's loss of tax base due to white flight, as depicted in the documentary *The Pruitt-Igoe Myth*—foreshadowed the shift from federal public housing funding to a developer tax credit system.

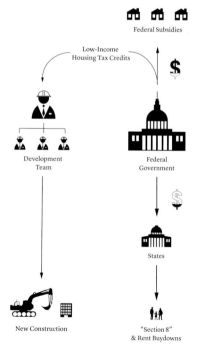

While these criticisms have merit in many instances, the true problem with this system is that it has insufficient public funding available to it in the wake of neoliberal tax cuts and rising land, financing, and construction costs. Furthermore, because it is largely reliant on developers employing private construction and land markets, we severely constrict society's ability to provide much-needed social housing at scale. By 1999, the Faircloth Amendment essentially made it illegal for the federal government to build or fund the development of public housing.[13] Is it any wonder, then, that we witness today a nationwide housing crisis in which supply cannot keep up with demand, while developers fight with suspect anti-housing crusaders and our homelessness crisis explodes?

Gentrification is not the cause of our housing shortage. Rather the housing crisis is a by-product of believing the government is inept; it is this widespread, bipartisan belief in government ineptitude that is the true victory of Reagan, Thatcher, and Friedman. When I worked nonstop through nights and weekends for New York City government in the years after 9/11, both conservative and liberal acquaintances would joke that, as a municipal employee, I was surely able to leave the office at 5:00 p.m. if not before. Convincing fellow Americans that government service was some of the most challenging, time-consuming, ennobling work that I have done remains an uphill battle, despite the fact that I'm usually surrounded by well-meaning people. This stands to reason in the sense that Milton Friedman and Jane Jacobs, who was a self-proclaimed neoliberal economist, were not that far apart in terms of their distrust of government. In either of their worlds, who is to build a subway line? For Friedman, it was the private sector, and only if it could turn a profit. For Jacobs, who needs a subway line and the top-down government required to plan, build, and manage it when you have the West Village?

The insidious nature of this anti-government sentiment is precisely what gives succor to those tech evangelists who want to "disrupt" municipal systems. Is it any wonder that Elon Musk, a man smart enough to help revolutionize the automobile industry, refers to critics of his ridiculous hyperloop subway-tunnels-for-private-cars fantasy as "subway Stalinists"?[14] The whole tendency toward disruption is too often a troubling desire to dismantle government oversight that might protect our data, worker rights, social equity, or public safety. It is libertarianism cloaked in a designer hoodie and we should be as wary of it as we should of Reagan's decimation of the idea that government can be a force for good.

Reconciling the critique of regulatory overreach in our cities with the critique of anti-government polemicists is difficult but vital if we are going to create urbanity, because urbanity is dependent on public infrastructure expenditure. With the reminder that we define urbanity as a community in which many different cultures and classes spatially interact, it is clear that without expanding what I defined in my first book as an *infrastructure of opportunity*—which includes streets, sidewalks,

An Infrastructure of Opportunity

As defined in the author's book *A Country of Cities*, it includes both infrastructure in its traditional sense and public goods that create urban social mobility.

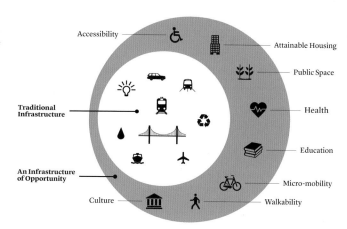

Polling in Online Public Meetings

Remote public meetings, with features like anonymous polling, are reshaping community engagement dynamics by allowing a wider constituency to participate.

The Fight over the 14th Street Bus Lanes

The closure of Manhattan's 14th Street to private vehicles transformed the city's slowest bus line into a high-speed route, yet it triggered outrage and legal challenges from nearby communities.

public parks, mass transportation, schools, social housing, cultural institutions, health care, clean water and power systems, community centers, and all of the other public goods that create urban social mobility—we cannot design for interaction among people across lines of differing race, class, gender, and mindset.[15]

Public infrastructure is the connective tissue of urbanity, and it cannot be turned over to the private sector or some DIY framework in which communities are left to fend for themselves. Yes, community guidance of public infrastructure is critically important, but several cautionary tales have emerged around full community control. We have seen communities across the political and geographic spectrum fight homeless shelters, bike lanes, affordable housing, mass transit lines, busways, and even some parks, sometimes due to legitimate concerns but often for extraordinarily selfish or even overtly racist or classist reasons. Furthermore, with the advent of social media, we have seen the amplification of non-representative voices, some fueled far more by national politic rhetoric or organized special interests than local community concerns. The idea that architects and planners in such a circumstance are simply supposed to be scribes at community board meetings, assiduously fulfilling every community desire no matter how parochial or rhetorical, is an absurdity that even Jane Jacobs would not have supported. Interestingly, the dynamics of community engagement may shift with the advent of remote public meetings in which a broader constituency can participate, including the use of new digital functionality such as anonymous online polling.

Unfortunately, most local politicians are too often rewarded with approval and reelection when they undermine the work of sound planning by succumbing to vocal constituents even when they don't represent the majority. Rare is the leader who instead agrees with these special interest groups when they are right but takes the risk of pointing it out when they are wrong.

The 2019 closure of Manhattan's 14th Street to private vehicles, which has successfully preserved the crosstown thoroughfare for high-speed buses, bicycles, freight delivery, and pedestrians, serves as a poignant illustration of why full community control is problematic. The proposal incited outrage at community board meetings despite the obvious environmental and social benefits.[16] It is not surprising that the same wealthy, white, car-owning Greenwich Village neighborhoods once valorized by Jane Jacobs filed lawsuits to fight the busway, lawsuits that failed in court due to their clearly specious and self-serving rationale. Similar land-use battles are playing out across the country as wealthy, often politically left communities are fighting much-needed transit-oriented affordable housing, particularly throughout California.

Yet to talk of such urban debates between liberals and progressives is at some level a deep distraction from the true battle at the heart of government, which was embodied by the seditious terrorist insurrection of January 6, 2021.[17] Romney Republicans may look aghast at the true American carnage of this deadly

**The Culture Wars of
"Guns, God, and Gays"
Now Includes Gas Guzzlers**
Supporters of Donald Trump
paraded in supersized cars and
trucks in Florida; during the
Covid-19 pandemic, health-care
workers counterprotested a truck
parade demanding an end to
Colorado's stay-at-home order;
a large pickup truck pulling a
trailer blocked multiple Tesla
Superchargers.

insurrection, but the roots of this movement have been fueled by the GOP since Richard Nixon's Southern Strategy in the 1960s and the subsequent rise of Pat Buchanan, Newt Gingrich, Michele Bachmann, and Sarah Palin.

The banner of the white supremacists, "Make America Great Again," is both a consequence of and departure from neoliberalism in the sense that their deep distrust of government was without question seeded by Reagan, but they do not share his goal of turning off the spigot of federal spending. Rather, they want that spigot redirected back to them and only them as the entitled white, as it was before the civil rights movement. This is precisely what is meant by the "Again" in MAGA. They want a return to a supremacy when whites were on the dole, while the rest of us knew our place, under their knee.

It is interesting to note that MAGA has strayed so far from its neoliberal origins and into more overt racism and anti-Semitism that corporate America and global capitalism are trying to shed their racist pasts, with many aligning publicly with the Black Lives Matter movement and disposing of toxic brand ambassadors, at least as of this writing. It is doubtful that much of this transformation is due to altruism or a sudden racial awakening; rather, it is likely because our majority minority demographics are where the markets are trending. But if demography is with urbanity and BLM, the geography of exurbia is firmly in the vice grip of MAGA, an exurbia that essentially says, "ask not for whom the dole tolls, it tolls for me."

As Matthew Desmond, author of the 2023 must-read book, *Poverty, by America*, puts it succinctly: "The American Government gives the most help to those who need it least."[18]

As I learned after publishing *A Country of Cities*, the issues of cities, suburbs, cars, highways, and white welfare are deeply related to the MAGA movement as cultural flashpoints that are as incendiary as reproductive rights, gender identity, and of course guns. My social media feed quickly revealed that people revere their $70,000 pickup trucks as much as they do their semi-automatic weaponry. After an op-ed I wrote for the *New York Times* titled "America's Urban Future" got republished in the *Dallas Morning News* along with my personal email address, I received many a colorful and threatening missive.[19] From iconic images of huge SUVs bearing down on health-care workers during the pandemic to large pickup trucks blocking Tesla charging stations, it is clear that the GOP's age-old fury around "Guns, God, and Gays" now includes Gas Guzzlers.

In the aftermath of the pandemic—which deeply increased homelessness and subsequent calls for government support—our need for policies that create urban public housing, social infrastructure, and forward-looking economic development policy is even more pronounced and will be for the foreseeable future, despite the dangers and delusions presented by fundamentalists.[20] The tensions of our land-use battles will likely persist as metropolitan economies rebuild and the necessity to live in denser circumstances in response to both climate change and public demand once again becomes clear, all of which will occur despite incessant worries about remote work supplanting the city.

As discussed in the previous chapter, for lower-income communities the fear of displacement from new development is real, but the answer cannot be to stop building in the face of a growing and aspirational population that desires face-to-face, car-free contact in our cities rather than on suburban Zoom calls. The NIMBY idea that people should "just live somewhere else" rather than find housing in our cities will only lead to more sprawl, social injustice, petro-dictators, and climate inequity. We are already witnessing an alarming amount of suburban poverty in the United States—akin to the peripheral areas of wealthy left-leaning European cities—as a consequence of this "let them live elsewhere" attitude.

Fundamentally, we must accept that if we are to build successful urbanity across big cities and small villages, we need smart, activist, fact-based, community-informed government at all levels in this nation. What happens in the United States, whether we like it or not, will continue to influence what the rest of the world does. We clearly experienced this with the ascension of Donald Trump and the concomitant rise in fascism globally. After all, if Reagan's conception of government was to "starve the beast" and reduce it to its least, the inevitable outcome for the detritus of the public sector is for it to devolve into a kleptocracy. Hopefully, with the Biden administration more prone to public investment, social mobility, and climate intelligence, we will see if a reimagined Keynesian view of government can now spread worldwide instead.

Yet the outlook for such a move away from fascism remains murky at best, particularly when facts are in free fall, and for this reason we need government policies that help bridge the widening global rural-urban divide. In the United States, the federal government, the electoral college, and our two-party system will be, and to some extent already are, enormously challenged by the fact that by mid-century, 70 percent of the nation's population will be represented by 30 senators and, conversely, 30 percent will be represented by 70 senators.[21] This vestigial construct of our founders must be addressed if we are ever to deliver both for the areas of the nation in decline and for the booming geographic regions that house the majority of the American populace throughout blue, purple, and red states. For example, the Texas Triangle and the "Charlanta Corridor" need infrastructure and affordable multifamily housing as badly as Cascadia,

Suburban Poverty on the Rise

Between 2000 and 2015, suburbs in the country's largest metro areas experienced a 57 percent increase in the number of residents living below the poverty line.

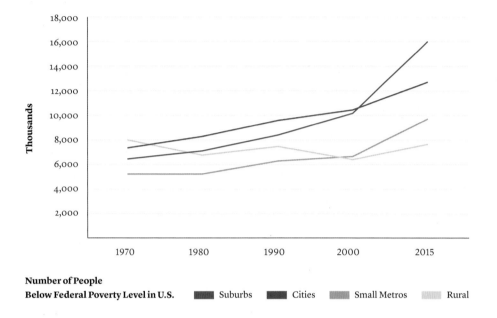

Number of People
Below Federal Poverty Level in U.S.   ▮ Suburbs   ▮ Cities   ▮ Small Metros   ▮ Rural

the Northeast Corridor, and the California coast. Internationally, this is precisely why we are seeing city-states with far less internal division such as Singapore, and the politically autonomous city of Vienna, build much more advanced infrastructure and social housing than the wealthiest nation on earth.

The necessary focus on these political, cultural, economic, and environmental divisions between urban and rural in the United States and their impact on governance leads to the inevitable and correct quandary about the fate of the huge geographic swaths of the nation that are losing their population, economic base, and social glue. While this includes parts of rural America, the decline is particularly acute in many faltering small cities that have suffered the most from deindustrialization and global free trade agreements enacted without strong labor and environmental standards.

The urban-rural divide that resulted from the widespread adoption of neoliberalism has manifested, albeit in differing forms, in many diverse nations across the world from India to China to Brazil. These countries, which in some cases benefited substantially from international free trade, adopted not only our economic philosophy but also our materialistic version of the American Dream with all its suburban trappings. There are many, like Steven Pinker in *Enlightenment Now* (2018), who have argued that global capitalism has drastically reduced poverty around the planet, and it is undeniable that free markets have freed millions if not

Population without Representation

By mid-century, 70 percent of the U.S. population will be represented by
30 senators, and 30 percent will be represented by 70 senators.

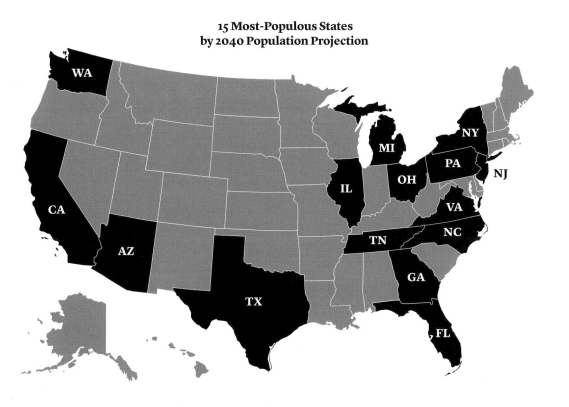

15 Most-Populous States by 2040 Population Projection

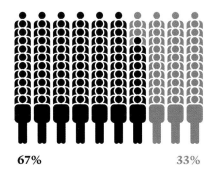

15 Most-Populous States   Rest of U.S.

67%   33%

Projected Population

15 Most-Populous States   Rest of U.S.

30 Seats   70 Seats

Projected Population

billions from subsistence living since the 1990s.[22] I have witnessed this firsthand with my own family in India as well as in my travels worldwide—Western progressives would be unwise to scoff at these extraordinary and very real gains out of a knee-jerk reaction against capitalism. But again, two things can be true at once. The fact that entrepreneurialism and reducing government red tape have unquestionably bettered the lot of the global poor on average does not negate the simultaneous damage to our global climate and our crassly commercialized culture, not to mention the rise of fascist leaders around the world who have thrived in the petri dish of anti-government rhetoric. The pandemic illustrated this duality in spades, showing us both the benefits of private sector ingenuity in terms of vaccine production as spurred on by the American government—particularly as compared to the lower-quality vaccines developed in state-run economies—as well as the highly inequitable failures of our privately run health-care system.

One senses that of the many victims of Covid, neoliberalism may have been one of them. A half century of disinvestment was laid bare in the years 2020 and 2021, a raw exposure few of us will soon forget as the disease ravaged the most vulnerable among us and fomented national rage. Despite the fundamentalists in our midst, a new attitude around public sector investment is distinctly emergent, particularly among our youth, with the recognition that the pandemic may well have been the appetizer for what is to come with climate change.

A true government investment strategy, which began to take hold under President Obama and accelerated dramatically under President Biden, as well as innumerable governors and mayors, could lift all boats, rural and urban, not only by investing in a robust social safety net in terms of universal health care, broadband, and education but also by encouraging economies through industrial policy in which both booming and declining geographies could benefit—a focus on "rurbanity," to which we will return in the last chapter. Such a strategy would stem the population losses in economically declining areas while depressurizing the demand that causes gentrification in economically ascendant areas. For example, cross-laminated timber, which is still not a legal building material in most parts of the United States for taller urban structures, could create more sustainable urban housing and fuel the growth of rural industry and forestry in a manner that is equally sustainable, due to the need to strategically thin our forests before they burn.[23] Similarly, at the regional level, both small-scale agriculture and big-scale logistics could help rural areas grow as cities grow. The key is to not view this as a zero-sum policy game that pits the urban versus the rural but instead to envision an activist, investment-forward federal government to enact win-win industrial policies, particularly given the pain still felt from the pandemic, the Great Recession, the Afghan and Iraq wars, and the opioid crisis that has decimated small-town America.

A Win-Win for Rural and Urban
Rural areas can prefabricate sustainable building materials for
urban social housing and share in the economic growth of cities.

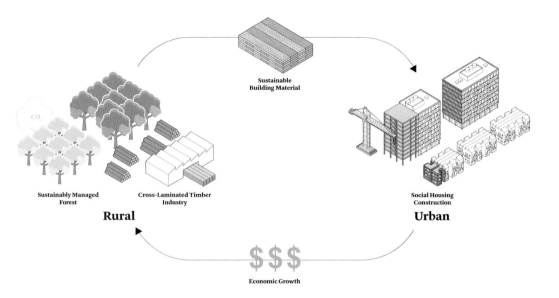

Sustainable
Building Material

Sustainably Managed
Forest

Cross-Laminated Timber
Industry

Rural

Social Housing
Construction

Urban

$$$
Economic Growth

It is in this context that two new progressive albeit distinct generations have
emerged—the Millennials and Generation Z—who will drive both markets and
policy, due to their size and voice. Global trends among these groups include
low levels of car ownership, a tendency toward choosing smaller living units,
and a general concern about climate change that leads these young people to
walk, bike, take mass transit, and seek urban density. These patterns seem
to be holding even as the Millennials age and have children. It is critical that
these cohorts do not fall into Reagan and Thatcher's neoliberal rhetorical trap
of eschewing all government. These generations should reject the fantasy that
small-scale initiatives fueled by individual actions will halt global warming or
social inequity. Furthermore, we are still in the midst of understanding the interest
technology companies have shown in urban markets as well as the potential
impacts public data sharing and artificial intelligence may have on urban society.
As a consequence our younger demographic waves, who represent the first digital
natives in human history, should be at the forefront of fighting for a well-regulated
and healthy urban tech industry as well as a strong public sector that smartly
invests in collective communities big and small.

Young people would be wise to form a new philosophical pact with government
if they are to achieve the connected, ecological, urbane, and just communities
they seem to desire. The pandemic, the insurrection, new global wars, and our

American Smart Infrastructure Act (from *A Country of Cities*, 2013)
Subsidies can be shifted from highways, suburbs, and fossil fuels
to invest in clean infrastructure, urban mass transit, rural broadband,
and nationwide affordable housing. Dollar amounts are from 2013.

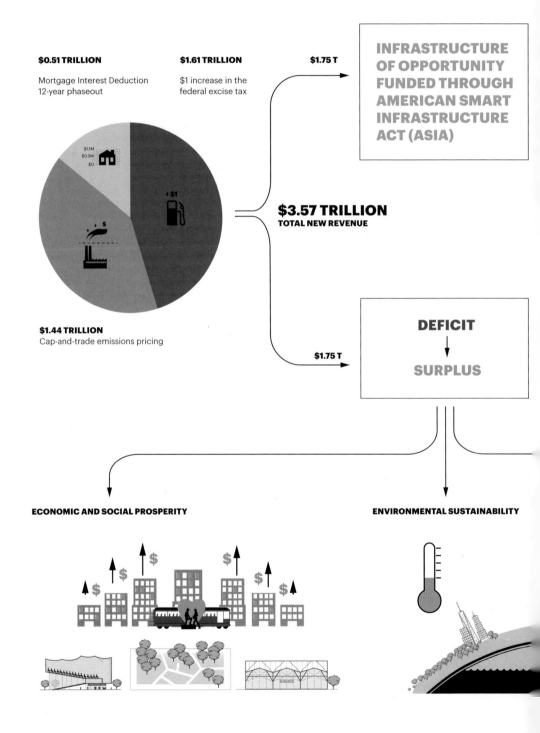

$0.51 TRILLION

Mortgage Interest Deduction
12-year phaseout

$1.61 TRILLION

$1 increase in the
federal excise tax

$1.75 T

INFRASTRUCTURE OF OPPORTUNITY FUNDED THROUGH AMERICAN SMART INFRASTRUCTURE ACT (ASIA)

$3.57 TRILLION
TOTAL NEW REVENUE

$1.44 TRILLION
Cap-and-trade emissions pricing

$1.75 T

DEFICIT
↓
SURPLUS

ECONOMIC AND SOCIAL PROSPERITY

ENVIRONMENTAL SUSTAINABILITY

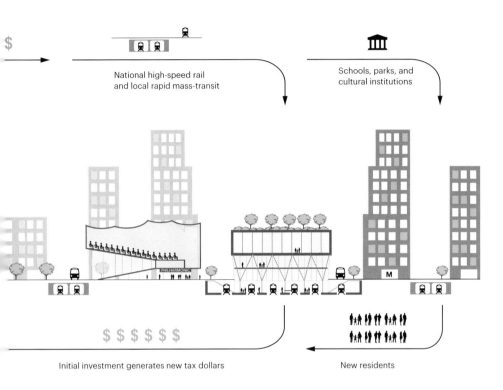

National high-speed rail
and local rapid mass-transit

Schools, parks, and
cultural institutions

Initial investment generates new tax dollars

New residents

EQUAL OPPORTUNITY OF THE AMERICAN DREAM

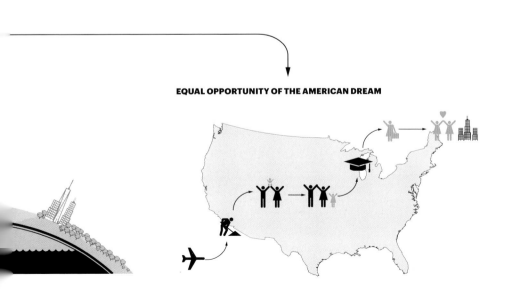

ongoing intellectual cold war with China all make crystal clear the need for effective, knowledge-based government in which expertise matters. The Biden administration, to its credit, has passed historic legislation that moves toward building an infrastructure of opportunity.

In *A Country of Cities*, I called for something similarly ambitious titled the American Smart Infrastructure Act (or ASIA for short, with every possible pun intended).[24] This plan would retool our periodic, pathetic, and pork-laden Intermodal Surface Transportation Efficiency Act (ISTEA) as legislation that would redirect the billions of dollars of subsidies that today go to highways, suburbs, and fossil fuels toward clean infrastructure, urban mass transportation, rural broadband, and nationwide affordable housing. But regardless of the specific legislative mechanism, we must at the federal, state, and municipal level refocus on large-scale public investments that go beyond our current infrastructure thinking if we are to build a cohesive platform for a connected urbanity. Beyond money, we have to dismantle—and in some cases forcefully override—local rules that require parking or prohibit multifamily housing, as well as federal rules that require endless environmental analysis for which the only use is to stop infrastructure projects and progressive policies like congestion pricing. In some cases such efforts have faltered, as with California's SB 50, but in others we have seen remarkable progress, such as the recent limitations passed or proposed on single-family housing in Minnesota, Oregon, Virginia, California (in the cities of Sacramento and Berkeley), and Washington.[25]

In most of these cases heroic elected officials and grassroots activists worked together to enact tremendously hard-fought advancements in local urbanism. A number of us in the design professions have had the privilege of collaborating directly with mayors from around the country representing municipalities big and small under the aegis of the National Endowment for the Arts Mayors' Institute on City Design on such efforts. To a person these women and men have proven themselves to be dedicated public servants who run the gamut of political beliefs but share a passion for smart governance. It is from these interactions and my own experiences working in the public sector that I know Reagan was wrong: sometimes people are from the government and they are here to help.

As the Talking Heads sang in 1977, some civil servants are just like our loved ones: they do work hard, and they try to be strong.[26] I know many who fit this description, and they are loved ones to boot. If we are to find our way from despair to hope, if we are to rescue the planet, if we are to fully recover from these tough past decades, if we are to create equal opportunity across race, class, and gender, if we are to reimagine not only the American Dream but a global aspiration for a healed and fair planet as well, we must rethink our relationship to government.

This means neither blind trust nor blind disgust. Perhaps it simply means *trust but verify*, with the hopes that a less market-driven, socially mediated press corps can deliver the facts to help us do so. It most definitely means we can't rip apart every public infrastructure or housing or health-care or educational project just because it goes a few percent over budget, or there is a minor scandal, or a website faltered, or if the project does not fulfill every community need or satisfy every voice or represent every constituency. As a society we should always strive for a better public sector, but anyone who has toiled in government knows that we constantly try but we often fail. Imperfection is endemic to the human condition, and government is nothing but a reflection into that imperfect condition. As my son commented to me years ago, perhaps people hate legislative bodies like Congress so much because legislatures are so much like those whom they serve. Neither our governments nor our planet will survive purity tests. I choose to place my faith in our impurity as a species, in our character with its warts and all, in our ability to cognitively connect and to solve problems big and small. Here, woven in with the tapestry of our imperfections, comes hope.

THIS CHAPTER SERVES AS PALETTE CLEANSER

and prologue, introducing readers to the splendor of an architecture of urbanity. Readers with little knowledge of architecture and urbanism should glean from these pages the desire on the part of great designers across the globe, be they formally trained or not, to create places of communal connection in our biggest cities or deep in the hinterland.

Gertrude Stein's oft-misquoted quip, "there is no there there," is shorthand to say that a place feels placeless, that it has little hold on one's attention, imagination, or memory.[1] But what gives a place the converse qualities—the ability to say unequivocally, "there is a here *here*"? Such places might be designed formally or informally, but what they share is the ability to connect humanity, hold our gaze, offer contemplation, and trigger recall in ensuing years. Such places are the platform for generating positive social friction through connective design.

We all carry examples. Our cognition might conjure a town square, a train station, a waterfront, or a bridge—all points of memory that variously have been understood as the "genius loci," as epicenters of "place and occasion," or for the ancient Greeks, as the "omphalos," which literally means the navel but actually connotes the center of the center. For several decades in academic architectural circles, such talk has been condemned, assailed for being nostalgic or even worse, *humanist*. Humanism, a liberal idea that originated in ancient Greece and was resuscitated by the Enlightenment, is often derided as elitist. But as these pages reflect, the ability to create places that draw together collective communities is by no means limited to the dominant cultures in power—even those on the margins of society yearn for centering, for a sense of belonging to something larger. Some of these examples are driven by informal local actors, while others show that they draw valence not just from the strength of their original design but from inhabitation by their users.

The examples that follow—while mainly from centuries past unlike the case studies in the subsequent chapters—speak to no specific architectural style, dominant culture, or particular moment in human history. What they do speak to is the capacity across our species to create connective tissue with civic joy, in places small and large, with methods grand and granular.

These places share the rigor of instrumentality, the discipline with which design is practiced. Great spaces don't simply emerge from debating architecture, as these pages so inarguably illustrate. These are places crafted by design, by communities, and by time—by the conception of form, its delivery through construction, and its inhabitation through use.

Lastly, a word on representation. Architecture is often discussed as an art, and at times rightfully so, yet we present these places more as *sampuru*, the Japanese craft of presenting food through the plasticity of replica. We hope you enjoy the taste of each delicious dimension, as we have in drawing them, with love for every measured morsel and colorful commons.

URBAN INFRASTRUCTURE

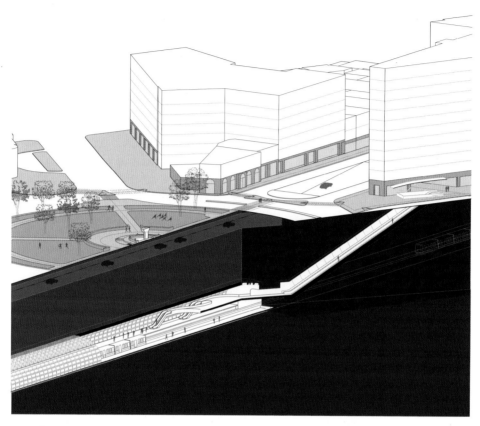

Dupont Circle Metro
Washington, D.C., USA (1977)

Mobility infrastructure, particularly when
it transcends the utilitarian, is the great
unifier of our cities, pulling together far-flung
neighborhoods and the city that binds them.
Designed by famed architect Harry Weese,
the D.C. Metro provides a continuous
experience throughout the city; most of the
original stations feature iconic coffered vaults
with dramatic uplighting. In deeper stations
like Dupont Circle, the descent into the system
from the capital's streets down long escalators
runs through distinctive concrete tubes,
reinforcing its futurist vibe.

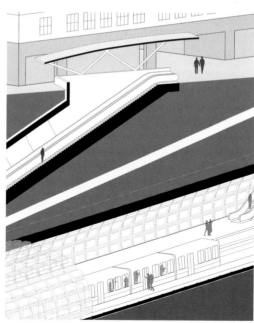

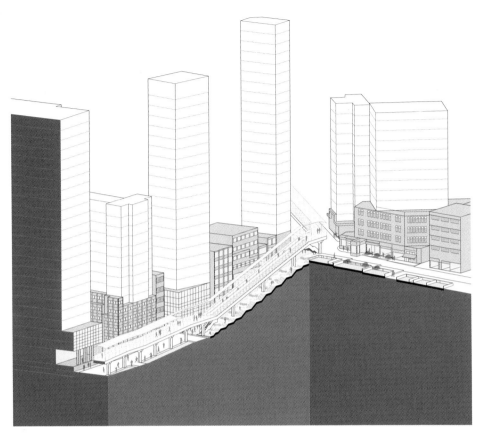

Central and Mid-Levels Escalator System Hong Kong (1993)

While less singular in its aesthetics, Hong Kong's Mid-Levels Escalator system is just as instantly recognizable. Connecting the Central and Mid-Levels Districts across steep topography that roads cannot easily traverse, the network provides an accessible route that climbs a daunting 443 feet along a run of 2,600 feet. Especially distinctive at the system's elevated portions, the escalators separate the circulation of speeding pedestrian through-traffic from the repose of those mingling on the terraced, bar, restaurant, and shop-lined street below. The continuous canopy provides shelter while acting as a holistic design gesture that unifies a diverse array of urban streetscapes.

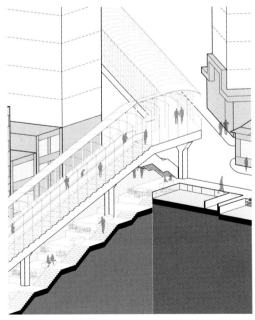

MEGA STRUCTURES

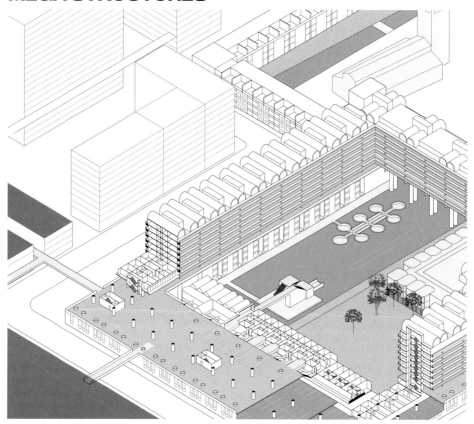

Barbican Estate
London, UK (1976)

Following the devastations of World War II
and into the period of late modernism, the
ambitions of the era grew such that the program
of single complexes came to encompass
those of a city. The Barbican Estate, designed
by Chamberlain, Powell and Bon, includes
the Barbican Centre (home to the London
Symphony Orchestra), the London Museum,
a conservatory, a public school for girls, a library,
and nearly 2,000 apartments, all connected
by a single parking plinth topped with plazas,
green squares, and a lake. The estate remains
a coveted address, with its variety of housing
scales and types, thoughtfully designed
common spaces, and well-appointed amenities.
While it is a world unto itself, with the plinth
and residential blocks acting as ramparts that
disconnect it from surrounding neighborhoods,
the estate is a masterwork of optimistic humanism.

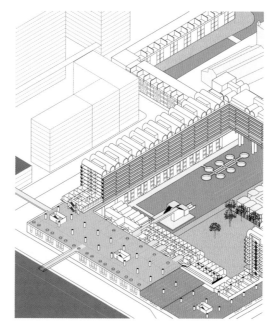

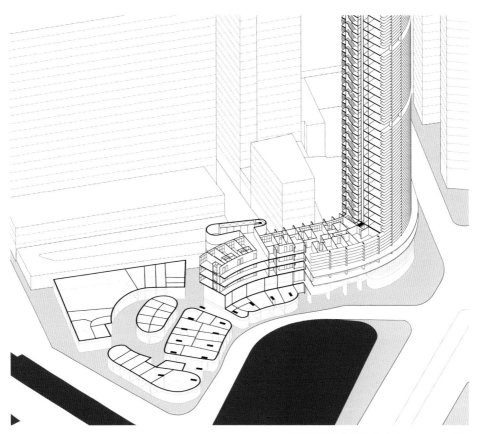

Edifício Copan
São Paulo, Brazil (1966)

No less ambitious than its London successor, but on a much more constrained parcel, Edifício Copan boasts 1,160 units and 72 commercial establishments packed into a single tower. Oscar Niemeyer's sinuous form gives the building its distinctive charisma relative to its brutalist counterparts while navigating its eccentric, undulating site. The building's signature frame unifies this gesture while colorful curtains break down the scale, as if alluding to the personalities of individual residents. The layer of shops that occupy the plinth also beautifully embed the tower into its urban context unlike most epic structures of this era, with a network of ramped passageways through the base that enmesh the commercial base with the surrounding neighborhood.

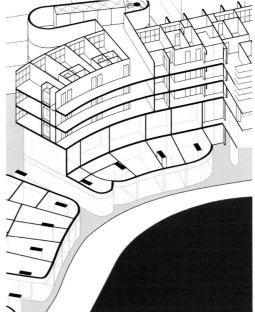

Barbican Estate
London, UK (1976)

Edifício Copan
São Paulo, Brazil (1966)

URBAN HOUSING

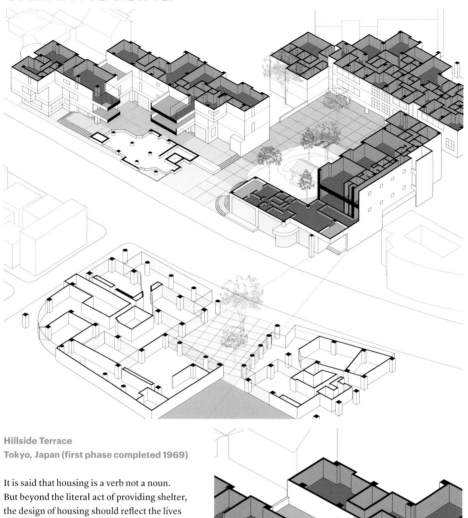

Hillside Terrace
Tokyo, Japan (first phase completed 1969)

It is said that housing is a verb not a noun.
But beyond the literal act of providing shelter,
the design of housing should reflect the lives
of its users, their customs and daily needs,
and common spaces for neighborly connection,
which in the case of Hillside Terrace includes
a Shinto shrine and burial mound that is over
1,300 years old. Fumihiko Maki's influential
housing project was built in phases, with each
segment designed in response to conversations
with the owners and residents about the
preceding stages. The project's second and
third phases define a series of courtyards
partially sheltered from the street around which
shops are arrayed with apartments above.

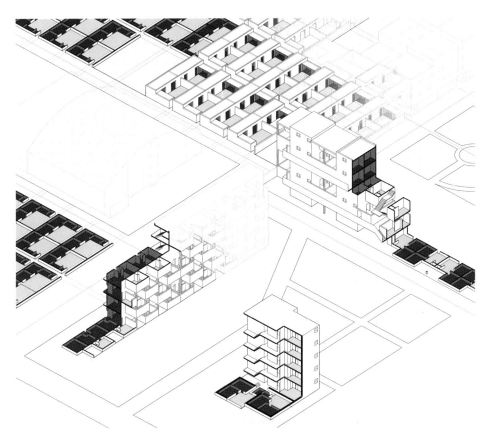

Carrières Centrales
Casablanca, Morocco (1952)

Fifteen years before Maki began Hillside
Terrace, Michel Écochard, the planning director
of French colonial Morocco, assigned Georges
Candilis, Shadrach Woods—future members of
Team 10—and Alexis Josic to design affordable
housing in response to the mass urban
in-migration caused by colonization. Using
cutting-edge sociological research methods,
the trio assessed the needs of potentially restive
colonial subjects. The project provided schools,
mosques, clinics, and shops but also catered to
Islamic cultural norms, arraying the housing
around networks of increasingly private nested
courts to shield the inhabitants from the prying
eyes of the street. Many of the courtyards have
since been filled in as the residents expanded
the units, even adding floors and partially
enclosing balconies as outdoor kitchens, to meet
their changing needs.

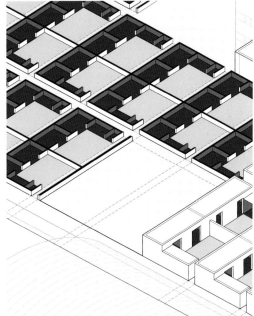

Hillside Terrace
Tokyo, Japan (first phase completed 1969)

PUBLIC SQUARES

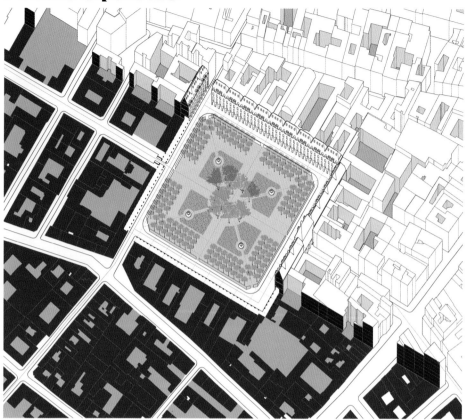

Place des Vosges
Paris, France (1605)

Public squares are among our most celebrated commons. Place des Vosges is an upscale neighborhood park, where the uniformity of surrounding facades and the regularity of platonic planting create a Cartesian outdoor room within the idiosyncrasies of otherwise irregular Parisian blocks. A continuous perimeter arcade creates intimacy and a porous relationship between the pedestrian realm of the city and the public space within.

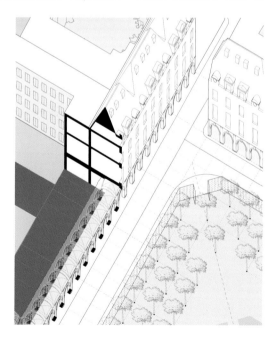

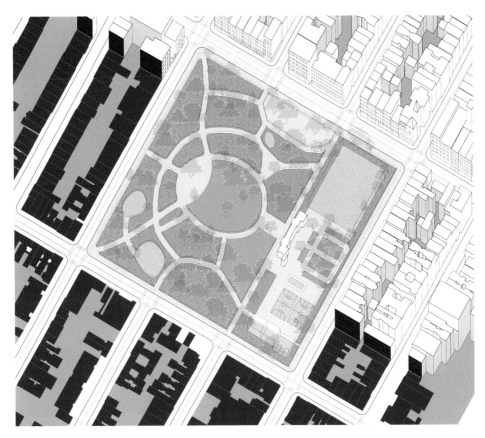

Tompkins Square Park
New York, USA (1834)

Much less formal than Place des Vosges, though
now gentrified as well, Tompkins Square Park
is no less of a prized neighborhood treasure
renowned as a platform for past protests.
With all four corners open, the park is tied
seamlessly into the grid. The irregular rhythm
of facades and staggered storefronts creates
a gritty resonance with the palimpsest of the
neighborhood's history, which is reinforced by
the Moses-era imposition of utilitarian playing
fields in the original pastoral plan for the park.

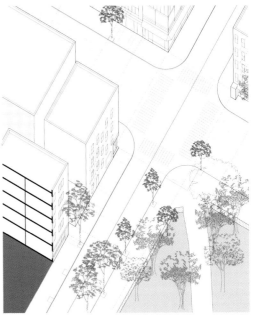

GRAND BOULEVARDS

Unter den Linden
Berlin, Germany (1647)

Berlin's Unter den Linden has undergone a
renaissance in the last three decades in the
aftermath of postwar East German austerity,
which was preceded by the clearing of trees to
make way for flags and parading Nazis. Despite
the return of the bustling café culture of its
early-twentieth-century heyday, the regular
formal planting of its wide central median,
flanked by several lanes of traffic on either side
and bookended by monuments to Prussian
generals, gives a staid, formal quality to the
boulevard's pedestrian experience.

Paseo de la Reforma
Mexico City, Mexico (1867)

A similarly formal and monument-studded
thoroughfare, Avenida Paseo de la Reforma
is one of Mexico City's main business and
tourist districts. In addition to its cultural and
economic gravitas, the design of la Reforma is
intimate for people. Through traffic is routed
down the center of the alignment, creating
two pedestrian aisles that are separated from
the restaurants and building entrances only by
small, slower-moving local access roads. Lush
and varied planting brings some of the tropical
mystique of the Bosque de Chapultepec to the
avenue, while the towering skyscrapers beyond
help frame each block as an outdoor room,
counterintuitively increasing the human scale
of la Reforma's public spaces.

Unter den Linden
Berlin, Germany (1647)

Paseo de la Reforma
Mexico City, Mexico (1867)

OLD WORKING STREETS

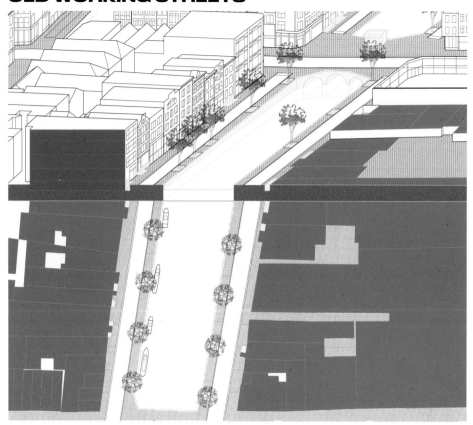

OZ Voorburgwal
Amsterdam, Netherlands
(first built in 1385)

Some smaller, old working streets—specialized
to the needs of their geography and the
industries of the people who built them—are
among the world's most beloved. Oudezijds
Voorburgwal is a typical Amsterdam canal
street, designed to serve as both flood
mitigation and freight artery. It is lined with
narrow, elegant canal houses, the homes of
the independent merchant class of the Dutch
Golden Age who used the canal for commerce.
Ground floors were raised a half story above
grade to protect against flooding and provide
easier passage from the barges to cellars, where
goods were stored. Bridges span the canal,
allowing pedestrians to navigate the tartan of
water and brick.

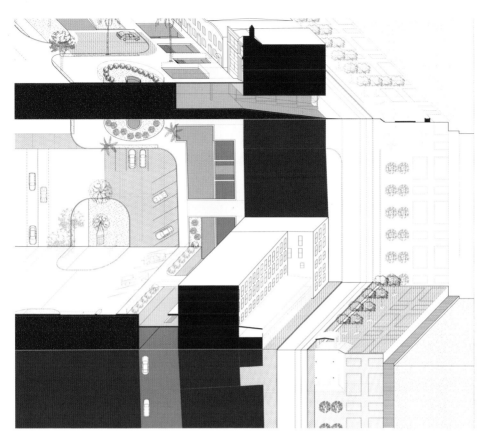

Bay and River Streets
Savannah, USA
(first built in 1700s; rebuilt in 1977)

In another city of barges, Savannah's Bay
and River Streets, along with the buildings of
Factors' Row that navigate the grade change
between them, speak to the physical hierarchies
of slavery. The warehouses of the Row had
offices on their upper floors—for the market
officials, known as "factors," who determined
the price of cotton—with bridges that tied their
offices directly to Bay Street and Savannah
society beyond. Beneath the bridges, a service
passage connects the back doors of the
storerooms at the quay level, allowing unseen
enslaved people to move inventory between
warehouses without disrupting the unloading
of barges along River Street. Like the canals in
Amsterdam, this area is now a thriving tourist
destination despite its troubling past.

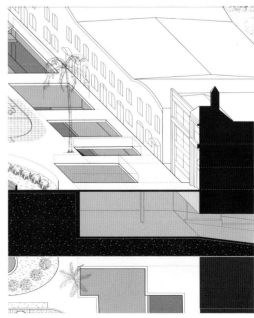

OZ Voorburgwal
Amsterdam, Netherlands (first built in 1385)

INSTITUTIONAL CAMPUSES

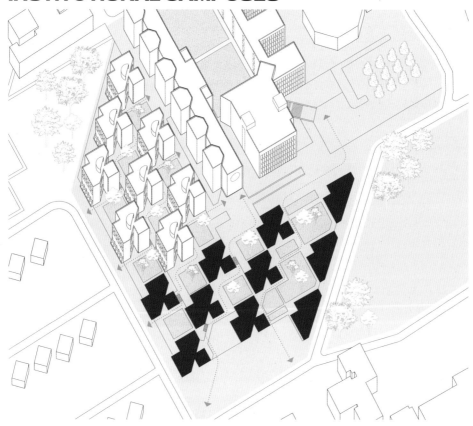

Indian Institute of Management
Ahmedabad, India (1974)

Campuses are defined by the relationship between buildings, circulation, and public space typically with the intention of creating serendipity among students, faculty, and staff. The repetitive patterning of buildings and spaces creates hierarchy at the landmark Indian Institute of Management (IIM) in Ahmedabad, with the smaller, more private spaces woven into the intricate lattice of dormitories, while larger public spaces adjoin either major buildings or clusters of smaller ones. As of this writing the IIM remains under threat by current administrators and a right-wing national government; international eyes must stay focused on the fate of Louis Kahn's masterpiece.

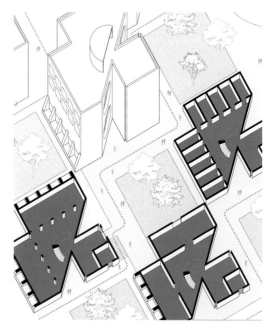

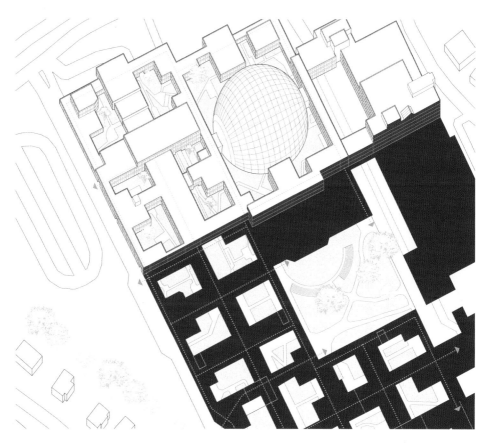

Freie Universität
Berlin, Germany (first phase, 1973)

The groundbreaking innovation of Berlin's
Freie Universität lies in its network of open
interior public circulation, in which the typical
relationship between buildings and landscape
is reversed. This move creates intimate
courtyard spaces that bring light into interior
circulation corridors and provide quiet places of
refuge. Larger public open spaces sit decisively
adjacent to the circulation network, analogous
to "quads" in campuses with open-air pathways.

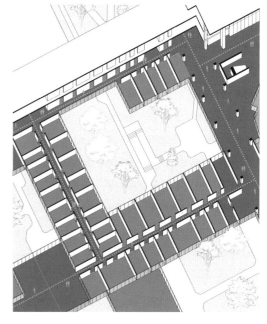

SELF-PLANNING AND DESIGN

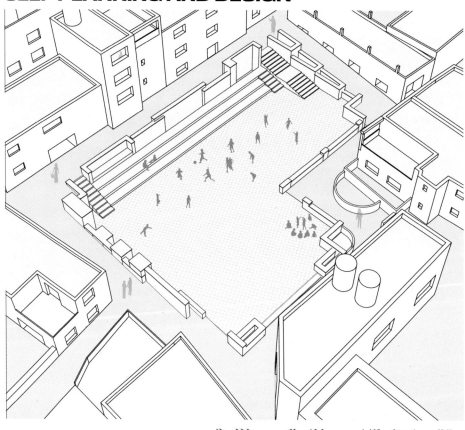

Saha Al Qassas
Al Fawwar, the West Bank (2014)

Refugee populations do not usually have the privilege of participating in planning their homes and neighborhoods. The aid workers who do this for them usually implement their camps with austere utilitarianism, both to maximize the number of displaced persons that can be housed and to avoid a sense of permanence that might jeopardize the political claims of refugees under international law. These factors make the case of Saha Al Qassas, a DIY plaza in the West Bank, particularly remarkable. Local residents worked with Campus in Camps (an education NGO) and the design firm DAAR to replace some of their dwellings in order to expand and formalize a small gathering space in their neighborhood.

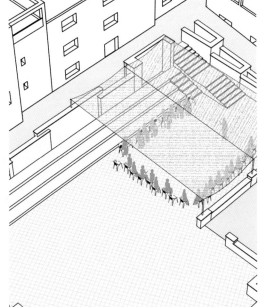

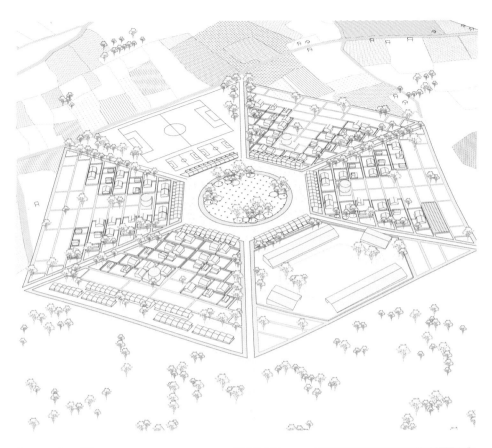

Opportunigee Village
Nakivale, Uganda
(ongoing; founded in 2016)

Refugees from the Rwandan genocide have
been living in Nakivale for so long that entire
generations have been born there. However,
Ugandan law does not grant them citizenship
nor any tenure to their land and forbids them
from constructing permanent buildings. In this
context, Opportunigee, a community-founded
and -led arts and technology incubator, has
developed a prototypical village, which it
plans to build in the surrounding countryside
to help the camp grow intentionally. Using
recycled materials that deliberately skirt
the legal definition of "permanence," the
scheme provides housing, education, food
production, and shops, all arranged around a
central community meeting area that forges
connections among the culturally diverse
individuals who call this place home.

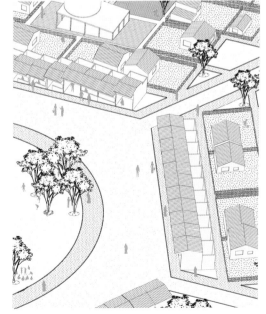

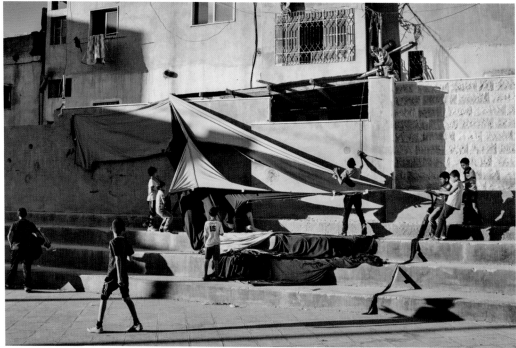

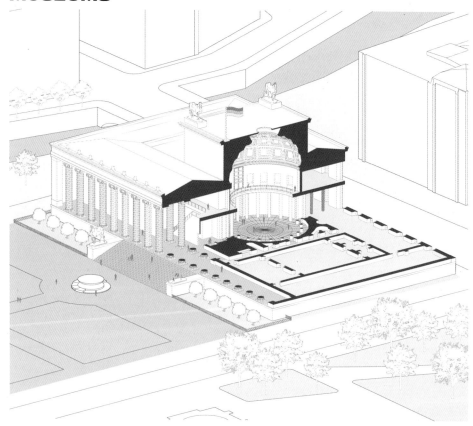

Altes Museum
Berlin, Germany (1830)

As archetypical civic institutions, many museums have a dual design ethos: they are a public forum that must be open and welcoming while serving as a sanctum for study and a secure repository for precious objects. Karl Friedrich Schinkel's Altes Museum provides a canonical response to this challenge. The grand entry stair and front portico evoke classical temple design but also serve to welcome the public, displaying statuary for the benefit of those who do not venture inside. The primary entry has visitors enter a grand rotunda, which immediately sets a somber, contemplative tone while shielding the circulation of the even quieter, more intimate galleries from the bustle outside.

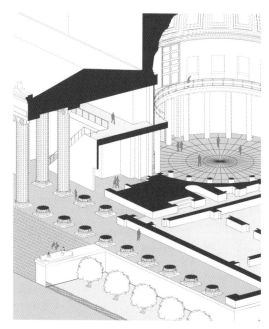

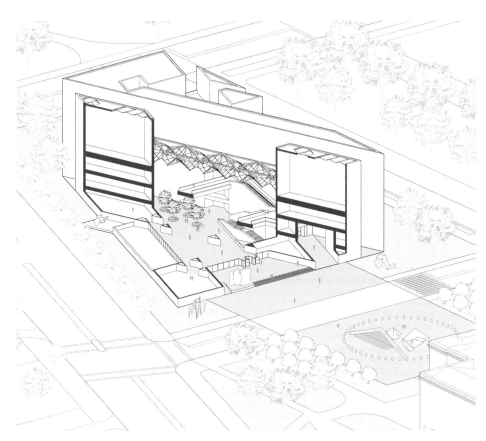

East Building, National Gallery
Washington, D.C., USA (1978)

Like the Altes Museum, I. M. Pei's addition to
the National Gallery is at once formally austere
while being a place of deep cultural connection
tied back to the original building by John
Russell Pope through its use of pink Tennessee
marble. Maintaining a palpable monumentality
while eschewing traditional forms, the
addition's triangular shape is a direct response
to its site, where Pennsylvania Avenue digs into
the National Mall. Rather than facing the mall
or the Capitol, the entrance portico is placed
off an intimate plaza opposite the original
building. Visitors enter an airy, skylit atrium,
not unlike Schinkel's rotunda, with quieter
galleries arrayed at its perimeter. The building's
main stair switchbacks up one edge, allowing
meandering visitors to explore the atrium in
section as well as plan.

PP
PP
T
RR TITI
RR
CC
CC
AA CC
AA CCE
CE
MAKES
PERTINENCE

THE WIDE-RANGING, LARGELY HISTORICAL

examples presented in the last chapter are but a taste of designs worldwide that ground our collective communities through their celebration of nature, culture, and joy and their implicit, mutual, idealistic desire to spur shared prosperity. For the layperson, especially one involved in government or science or economics, this may seem like a reach—how can architecture attempt to advance such lofty and elusive ambitions? Consider that whether designing a refugee camp or park or museum or streetscape or university or housing complex, accomplished designers of excellence bear the larger goals of social and ecological purpose with them silently but soulfully, similar to how a great, experienced physician embodies the Hippocratic oath with every action and decision. And like any other seasoned and well-meaning professional, those who intelligently work at our craft for decades know how to translate good intentions into great outcomes. Even if you are not a part of design endeavors, you should care about this work for the same reason you care about every undertaking that together will make or break the outcome of this crucial century in human history. As this book has already argued, fixing our built environment through advocacy and example is critical to the success and survival of our multitudes, but to better understand this one must understand not only what successes design professionals have had in the past but also the luminaries who are blazing a path toward an architecture of urbanity in the present and, finally, how new generations might be trained to follow in their footsteps in the future.

This chapter highlights select examples of innovative and affordable new forms of public housing and social infrastructure being built worldwide to promote economic and cultural mobility. For our distressed populations globally, as is well known by all those who study the plight of the poor, the lack of housing, health care, and education is central to their circumstances, and to this I would add the less tangible but no less pressing need for inspiration. In order to prosper, people across the world need the basic triumvirate of a stable home, secure health, and an education that advances their livelihoods, and these needs are better and more creatively met when the venerable work with the vulnerable. Much of the work that follows responds to the need for housing, health care, educational, and community facilities not only by implementing inspiring low-cost solutions but by enacting co-design processes with communities that build pride, resilience, agency, and a sense of collective ownership along with the new structures people need to better their lives.

If you are a decision maker, support these kinds of practitioners and projects while remaining wary of the many architects who claim to care about social impact but whose portfolios reveal otherwise. Instead seek out talents like those highlighted on these pages, demand the best of them, trust their instincts, treat them as equals, pay them fairly, then exalt their relevance from the rooftops. Do so because truly impactful designers of excellence, as discussed in this book's

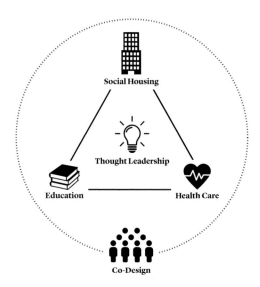

introduction, are much too scarce, which is true in part because great talent is a precious commodity, in part because those who possess it receive insufficient support from the widget-prone leadership of this world, but in largest measure because the design professions and the systems that sustain them, particularly in the West, remain largely out of sync with the planet and its people. To this we must respond "physician, heal thyself," and indeed, this chapter and the next discuss a mere fraction of us who are intent on course correction for our disciplines. Who are these trailblazers and what examples do they set for the next generations? What is a better notion of practice, why does it matter, and, as for students, how might we all, regardless of our professions, guide them toward a more mindful path in their careers?

The idea of practice is searingly beautiful, meaningful, and rare. While there are many jobs in the world—bank teller, garbage collector, coder, management consultant, tugboat captain, politician—few are described overtly as an asymptote, in which the repeated exercise of a skill set brings one ever closer, but never completely, to mastery of a complex discipline. In very few instances do we formally use the term "practice" to describe a profession because of its very specific connotations associated with training and, often, licensure. People are said to practice medicine, law, and architecture, and arguably a few other disciplines, but why do these differ from being a shop steward, tailor, accountant, or member of any other vocation that similarly requires years of experience to gain proficiency? Two excellent books, Dana Cuff's *Architecture: The Story of Practice* and Tom Fisher's *In the Scheme of Things*, outline to varying degrees the history of the profession of architecture.[1] The latter more specifically attributes the rise of public respect for doctors with the formalization of the medical internship and residency process in the late nineteenth and early twentieth centuries. Whereas in architecture we have legal structures around liability and nomenclature—in the United States one cannot legally call themselves an *architect* without passing the licensing exam—architects do not adhere to a training system anywhere near as rigorous as those of young doctors, despite the fact that the health and welfare of the public are similarly at stake, albeit in vastly differing ways. While some architecture practices take the professional training of young hires seriously, many firms seem to have no compunction about having bright young talent learn nothing other than how to create glossy renderings, as if that might advance their knowledge of this extraordinarily complex and important discipline.

Critics rightfully argue that licensure, despite the need to require training around public health and welfare, is purposefully exclusionary, particularly to women and people of color. The state of affairs is abysmal: in 2020 only 17 percent of registered architects in the United States were women—who typically represent half of architecture students in our schools today but leave the profession in droves after they graduate—and less than 5 percent of licensed architects in the United States are African American.[2] Architecture practice as originally conceived in the Western world, evolving as it did from the École des Beaux-Arts in France, is without question a bastion of privileged white men that persists openly today in the well-appointed conference rooms of our leading corporate firms. In March 2005—at the dawn of a new millennium—I was told point-blank by a partner of a much-heralded legacy architecture firm that I would never be promoted to partnership because I am not white.

Understandably, many feel that to advocate for the practice of architecture is to defend the indefensible. In the context of the United States, a pro-practice position becomes even harder to justify when the vast majority of architecture firms seem content to take almost any commission that comes their way, whether to foist another blue glass tower of arbitrary shape upon our cities or to blithely draw up execution chambers and exposed stainless-steel toilets in jail cells to build their "Justice" portfolio. Is it a wonder that idealistic young students fueled by caffeine and debt graduate from architecture programs uninspired by the commissions many practices see fit to accept? Add to this the widespread exploitation of young graduates asked to take internships or full-time employment without fair compensation, which is now more commonplace in adulated boutique design firms (imagine the nation's esteemed law firms barely paying hires fresh from the best schools)—not to mention the tragic ongoing sexual harassment scandals roiling the profession—and we have the perfect storm undergirding the calls from many to dismantle architecture practice as we know it.

Such calls are partially correct. Architecture practice as currently conceived, particularly in the United States, is hurtling toward disastrous irrelevance. For decades architects have retrenched from risk with the encouragement of professional organizations like the American Institute of Architects, which is hopefully rebooting with promising new leadership after decades of status quo stasis. Historically the contracts they have promulgated have encouraged developers, professional program managers, builders, and other consultants to take over such critical factors as programming, cost estimation, the means and methods of construction, and therefore the agency and major sources of revenue for architects. The thinking behind this retrenchment, which centers on the principle of taking lower fees in exchange for less liability, has been stunningly myopic because it has also led to less relevance in the eyes of the world's decision makers. After relegating ourselves to the kiddie table, we have the nerve to complain about the quality of the chicken nuggets.

As a consequence, there are constant and growing threats to the long-term health of the profession, with a significant portion of new construction occurring worldwide without any input from professional architects. Much of the Global South builds informally, without the involvement of the professions, and while in rural areas this may be fine, haphazard denser construction is worrisome as the world urbanizes in the midst of climate change—consider, for example, the death toll in the 2023 earthquake in western Turkey that was exacerbated by the poor regulation of design professionals. Most single-family homes in the United States are built and renovated by merchant builders and DIY Home Depot devotees with little regard for the quality of the built environment. At the broader scale, the tech world already has the computational ability to automate the cookie-cutter architecture many firms produce, which isn't surprising given how artificial the intelligence is that creates such work. These trends are becoming increasingly global; mass-produced suburban subdivisions and repetitive urban glass towers, all of little architectural merit and soon to be easily automated in their design, are subsuming the planet.

However, this automation hasn't yet taken hold. To the contrary, as the large economies of the world become more urban, formal, wealthy, litigious, environmentally conscientious, and politically complex, the demand for architectural services remains steady as of this writing, but that doesn't mean the real writing isn't on the wall. In the coming years, there likely will be widespread dislocation in our field. Given that our top architecture schools are reevaluating their own role due to their concerns about the profession, it is possible that in the foreseeable future there will be drastically reduced demand for architecture graduates in large-scale practices, or at least a need to redirect them to other disciplines where their skills are more valued, like software development, game design, real estate, or urban planning. The hard truth is that the world needs fewer automotive workers and mechanics than we did just decades ago due to automated manufacturing and electric drivetrains, and we may very well need fewer, but hopefully better, professional architects in the epoch to come.

Reimagining practice does not equate with its wholesale rejection. My opening assertion that practice is searingly beautiful, meaningful, and rare begins with the conviction that it entails far more than the technocratic strictures of licensure or the hard-core realities of professional practice in a capitalist context. Beyond professions, we as humans "practice" in both the arts and sciences, something I learned from having one parent in each realm. People of faith practice their religions, and ethicists speak of practice in a parallel manner. Malcolm Gladwell famously noted that successful practitioners pursue their disciplines for at least 10,000 hours to achieve mastery, a finding he puts forward to dispel the genius myth surrounding such figures, particularly artists.[3] Pianists, poets, chefs, and professional race car drivers all must work at their craft; few to none are born gifted beyond their capacity to build upon a passion to which they are inexorably, inexplicably called. Unlike in the finance and tech sectors, it is nearly impossible to become wildly successful at a young age in pursuits of practice. For what seems to be a waning few, the art and science of architecture holds this deep allure of personal commitment—ours is not a profession for the impatient—and for those of us who in tandem have a long-simmering, sensual love affair with the feline unknowns of the city, we could no more reject practice than could Tennessee Williams's Brick rebuff Maggie on her hot tin roof.

While urbanism demands a passion for places forged by connected human energy, it also offers architecture relevance at this precise moment of disciplinary crisis. Most major departments of architecture are co-located with the historically allied departments of urban planning, landscape architecture, and historic preservation, disciplines that have central roles to play in dealing with the enormous challenges of our era, from climate change to social fragmentation. Yet in our design and planning schools today, one rarely perceives any real impact from these adjacencies. The faculty, students, and curricula rarely interact across departments despite valiant but insufficient efforts toward the interdisciplinary. Consequently, well-intentioned architects often speak too simplistically about issues like gentrification and global warming without meaningful exchange, much less joint research, with their peers in urban planning and landscape architecture or other related fields like engineering, law, and business. I have experienced this phenomenon of disciplinary silos firsthand as an educator; as an architect also trained in urban planning, art history, and engineering; and as a professional schooled in the hard knocks of work across multiple sectors.

There are notable exceptions in academia and beyond, such as the extraordinarily well-informed social and artistic accomplishments of an advocacy studio like Forensic Architecture, which states as its mission "to develop, disseminate, and employ new techniques for evidence gathering and presentation in the service of human rights and environmental investigations and in support of communities exposed to state violence and persecution."[4] From their successful challenge to the board of the Whitney Museum of American Art, to their analysis of the Grenfell Tower disaster, to their unrelenting work in the Middle East and Ukraine, Forensic Architecture has offered a compelling new vision for what architecture advocacy can be. To this end, Forensic founder Eyal Weizman has explicitly stated:

> My desire to be an architect was to use architecture as a social and political tool, and I realized that **architecture is not about designing buildings**. Architecture is a way of seeing the spatial dimensions of relationships of people, of societies, and the way they exist in space. Architecture is a way to analyze a violation of human rights, to unpack the politics in a way that other frameworks are perhaps not.[5]

As laudable as such work is, I must ask if our strength as advocates and urbanists has to come at the expense of not designing buildings, the craft around which our entire educational and accreditation system remains focused. For some it is this very centering that is problematic and must be dismantled; many academics and activists believe the entire architectural endeavor must first confront its roots in colonialism and slavery. So be it: as a non-white practitioner born in an India that colonialism ravaged, and raised in an America where the N-word was continuously hurled at me throughout a bloody childhood, I couldn't agree more. But for those who suggest it, does such a recentering really mean we can no longer design buildings and urban environments? For those of us who still love architecture and believe in the humanist capacity of design to better society, this feels like a false choice. Can we not fight for a more equitable and ecological world while also, for example, admiring the extraordinary accomplishments of built works like those highlighted in the preceding chapter?

Beguiling as those projects might be, the closing assertions of chapters 3 and 4 bear repetition here not only for practitioners in architecture and urbanism but for anyone who cares about the relationship among our built environment, our global climate, and our fraying society. Those outside of these professions should care for the same reasons we who are outside of politics or journalism or environmental law care about the effectiveness, integrity, and relevance of those professions—because our collective future depends on it. Despite our flaws, I insist that practicing architects and urbanists *can* be indispensable partners in the fight against global warming and social segregation, and *can* gain societal relevance in doing so, but only if we use our disciplinary expertise to help envision and, yes, *build* a different, connective, urbane world—again, because our collective future depends on it.

As this chapter and the next demonstrate, practicing architects and urbanists must live with the myriad imperfections of the world as do so many upstanding civic leaders, government workers, journalists, cultural figures, community organizers, nonprofits, philanthropists, doctors, attorneys, and institutional actors, all of whom toil in the daily grind for societal betterment inch by inch, block by block. Like professional urban planners and preservationists, who are typically less perfectionist about the world's failings, design professionals must sully their hands with the dirt of the world beyond their sites and sights, including understanding the logic systems that drive land use and infrastructure policy, housing production, construction, technology, finance, and all the other systemic structures that we simultaneously know to be unjust. By saying this I am not suggesting a blind embrace of such systems or an inability to criticize them effectively as activists like Forensic and exhibitions like the Museum of Modern Art's *Reconstructions: Architecture and Blackness in America* have done so brilliantly, but it does mean a recognition that relevance also requires us to engage the world as it is, not only as we believe it should be.[6]

Imagine if all the other professions disassociated themselves from the world for similar reasons of disdain and distrust—doctors who stopped treating dying patients because of our broken health-care system, journalists who stopped reporting the news because of the corporate consolidation of media, congressional leaders who stopped investigating insurrections and kleptocracy because of our corrupt campaign finance system, or public defenders who stopped representing defendants because of the structural racism in our justice system. Such disengagement would not only be tantamount to acquiescence to the worst forces in the world; it would represent our failure to meet our own version of a Hippocratic oath as architects. As already noted, the world is careering toward a plateau of just over ten billion people, and since we are unable to house and provide social infrastructure for our existing population of eight billion, the notion that we should stop practicing, much less today's fashionable assertion that we should stop building altogether, is nonsensical. We have work to do.

If practice rebooted cannot be practice rejected, we must turn to new modalities that succumb to neither corporate drudgery nor academic paralysis. Today, we are living in a golden age in the reinvention, or actually the rediscovery, of the purpose of architecture. The Overton window—essentially, the window of discourse—around what constitutes meritorious practice has shifted dramatically. Despite all the headwinds for conventional practice, we have a new set of global examples to which we can aspire, including some that have been recognized by none other than the Pritzker Prize. The Pritzker is still considered by many to be the pinnacle of achievement in the architecture profession, despite substantial past controversies such as the ongoing exclusion of Robert Venturi's partner, Denise Scott Brown.[7] Critics may balk at the relevance of the Pritzker given its role in advancing only male and mainly Caucasian architects throughout the twentieth century: in 2004, Zaha Hadid was the first woman to receive the award, which was established in 1979. However, the significant course correction the Pritzker has made in the

The Late Twentieth Century:
More Is More
Pritzker Prize winners in the late
twentieth century: awarded to
Frank Gehry in 1989 (*top row*) and
awarded to Richard Meier in 1984
(*bottom row*).

A New Millennium
Defining moments shaping the
early years of the twenty-first
century: the September 11 attacks,
heightened natural disasters, the
Great Recession, and the Black
Lives Matter movement.

The Venerable Work
with the Vulnerable
The significant shift made by the
Pritzker committee in the twenty-
first century: Alejandro Aravena
in 2016, Balkrishna Doshi in 2018,
Anne Lacaton and Jean-Philippe
Vassal in 2021, and Francis Kéré in
2022 (*clockwise from top left*).

twenty-first century—in terms of not only the diversity of its recipients but also the nature and purpose of their work—contains lessons for the trajectory everyday practitioners could consider if societal relevance is important to them.

In the short window of time between the fall of the Berlin Wall and the rise of the new millennium, we moved from the irrational exuberance of the 1990s and the concomitant rise of "more is more" architecture to the thoughtful, constraint-driven, socially relevant, truly interdisciplinary design work that is now continually recognized by the Pritzker Prize in the aftermath of the third millennium's earth-shattering events like 9/11, the Great Recession, the murder of George Floyd, the pandemic, and the ferocious manifestations of climate change globally. Of course, environmentally driven architecture practice has always existed with legends like Norman Foster and Hassan Fathy, but under the weight of neoliberalism, the social movement in architecture arguably did not break into the mainstream until the award of the Pritzker Prize to the Chilean intellect Alejandro Aravena in 2016. Much to the chagrin of those who miss the "starchitecture" of the neoliberal era, the Pritzker Prize's movement toward socially minded design continues, with awardees including brilliant practitioners like Anne Lacaton and Jean-Philippe Vassal, Balkrishna Doshi, and Diébédo Francis Kéré. In honoring these talents, rather than think about them as celebrities, we should instead understand them for what they are: thought leaders who with counterparts across many disciplines work to address the biggest challenges our societies confront. Beyond architecture, there are innumerable landscape architects and other urbanists whose work deserves full-throated accolades for their many positive impacts, but for reasons of both space and focus limitations, this chapter centers primarily on the work of architects.

What these studios have in common is far more than the pursuit of socially responsible architectural practice as defined broadly through the well-known lenses of affordability, sustainability, equity, or participatory design with communities. While all such achievements are laudable, these projects and approaches exemplify varying forms of connective design that simultaneously promote nature, culture, and joy. Free of postmodern cynicism, these designers employ their extraordinary talents to design work that knits together communities brick by brick, block by block, public space by public space. Importantly, they are all pedestrian in their orientation, rejecting or at least ignoring the automobile unlike most of twentieth-century modernism. The morphologies they deploy celebrate rather than shun the street, exemplifying what chapter 8 will discuss further as an *arrière-garde* movement in architecture and urbanism intent upon building urbanity and encouraging the palimpsest of our world. None of this work is historicist, but in a wide variety of means associated with both local context and personal agency, these architects build upon and amplify the layers of the existing environment through volume, materials, tectonics, and the shaping of light.

Before digging into the merits of these projects, and given the call I am making for practice to embrace the world's messiness, it is critical to understand the broader social roles these architects play. Lacatoñ has become a global advocate for minimizing the demolition of existing buildings. Kéré has spoken eloquently about the co-design process he uses as he works with his community. And in arguably the best example of broader social and political engagement, Aravena in early 2020 was helping *to rewrite the Chilean constitution* in the fallout from that nation's riots in 2019 and 2020. Imagine, in a profession where one hears constant pining among architects for respect and relevance, that such a figure was asked to help draft his nation's defining document because it was the very nature of his practice at Elemental that led to his larger pertinence. Unlike the American tendency to silo disciplines in academia and society at large, which is predicated on the capitalist belief that we can only as professionals do one thing well, Elemental represents a "both-and" in architecture and urbanism, in which design is defined in the broadest sense. It is an understanding that enhances the firm's street cred as a model of both design intelligence and social impact.

These broader sociopolitical activities reveal the lineage these architects share. Repeatedly cited for their social advancements, both Aravena's "Half a Good House" (2013) in Chile and Doshi's Aranya Low-Cost Housing (1989) in India are clear offshoots of the structuralist tradition. These projects advance the ethos of the Dutch architect and theorist N. John Habraken and the subsequent 1970s *sites and services* approach to user-controlled housing on behalf of the poor— both of which advocated for providing the impoverished with a certain amount of fixed infrastructure upon which they could build as they desired.[8] Autonomy and accretion are essential to Aravena's approach in particular, allowing residents to alter and guide their surroundings as their circumstances change. Intended as low-cost residences drawing upon the vernacular, his project enables users to build out the second half of their home as they see fit, providing them a sense of ownership, belonging, and identity that is rare in social housing. By contrast, Doshi's Aranya project is designed to accommodate a range of incomes and family sizes, with semi-public zones shared by multiple families within a hierarchy of larger public spaces. In both cases, the housing is built with climatic sensitivity, using materials suitable for their environments while remaining low in maintenance costs.

In recent times, several groundbreaking social housing projects have emerged worldwide, particularly outside of the United States, that emulate these characteristics, especially in their desire to advance social mobility by providing stable, permanent housing in partnership with low-income residents. One example is the Ciudad Acuña Housing Project (2015) built by the architect Tatiana Bilbao for Mexican families whose homes were damaged in a devastating tornado. Also rooted in Habraken, Bilbao's houses are expandable and divisible to accommodate

Tatiana Bilbao, Ciudad Acuña Housing Project

Reflecting the scale of the surrounding buildings, Bilbao's houses showcase carefully composed facades and intimate open spaces, signifying an elevated form of vernacular design. The houses are designed to be expandable and divisible, allowing residents to adapt and modify their homes in various ways to meet changing needs.

multiple rooms all while embracing the streetscape and reflecting the scale of the surrounding context. Bilbao's diagrams explain the ability for residents to expand and change their homes in multiple ways as their needs change. While the architectural expression of the housing can be understood as regional, Bilbao's careful composition of the facades and the spaces they hold are indicative of an elevated vernacular that is also evident in Doshi's work. Both reject the notion that low-income housing must feel cheap or announce their social mission and instead grant dignity through the use of durable materials, elegant proportions, and unambiguously urban relationships to the street.

Among the most innovative social housing projects in the world is Lacaton and Vassal's 2011 Tour Bois le Prêtre renovation in Paris. Rather than demolishing an existing structure and building anew (as is sometimes but not always necessary), the architects, who collaborated with Frédéric Druot, took on a banal modernist tower and transformed it by layering a sequence of luminescent and liminal spaces at the exterior wall, changing the experiential and performance characteristics of the existing structure without squandering the considerable embodied energy that went into its construction. They successfully added outdoor space for residents, changed the bleak appearance of the original, and decreased power consumption by half, all in an effort conceived and implemented alongside the residents. This inventive, co-designed approach to both the space within dwelling units and the building's overall appearance is not only a tremendous advancement for residents; it speaks to a different kind of future for postwar public housing worldwide. Consider that across the Western world in particular, some of society's most vulnerable live in this type of housing, and as we witnessed during Superstorm Sandy in New York City, the combination of poverty, climate change, racism, and societal neglect has left these populations in ever more dire precarity. Unfortunately, far too many of us have become inured to these circumstances, watching tragedies like London's Grenfell fire and television shows

**Lacaton and Vassal,
Transformation of the
Tour Bois le Prêtre**
Working with the social-
housing residents, the architects
transformed a banal modernist
tower on the outskirts of Paris
by layering a sequence of
luminescent and liminal spaces
at the exterior wall. The addition
successfully adds outdoor space
for residents and decreased power
consumption by half.

**O'Donnell and Tuomey,
Timberyard Housing**
Both the scale and materiality of
this multifamily project weave it
into its Dublin context. Residents
are connected by means of a
dynamic courtyard animated by
balconies and doorways.

**Michael Maltzan,
Star Apartments**
The complexity in section enables
negative spaces that fully resonate
with the climate and culture of
Los Angeles. An elevated courtyard
frames views of the city.

like *The Wire* with discomfort from a comfortable distance, imagining that the situation has become too intractable in these public housing projects for anyone to do anything about.[9] Tour Bois le Prêtre should serve as a wake-up call to every mayor, governor, and national leader, particularly across Europe and the United States, that change undertaken in cooperation with residents is both possible and necessary. Because many of these projects were built around Le Corbusier's "tower in the park" framework, which more often than not became tower in the parking due to the suburban nature of this morphology, the rethinking of such projects includes the possibility of densifying the housing sites to introduce more mixed uses and incomes if existing residents agree. With most public housing worldwide facing immense budget shortfalls in the wake of neoliberalism, strategies that both urbanize and radically improve public housing must be considered.

One of the more urban social housing projects completed in recent memory is Sheila O'Donnell and John Tuomey's Timberyard Housing (2009) in Dublin, Ireland, which through its streetwall, material expression, and creation of intimate public space recalls the social imperatives of Team 10, the porous material gravity of Louis Kahn, and the scalar ambiguity of what William Wurster called "the large small house."[10] The project connects its residents in a dynamic courtyard animated by balconies and doorways. This semi-public space is cleverly situated just off the sidewalk at the narrowest point of the courtyard, providing the residents with both privacy and an openness to the city beyond. Both the scale and materiality of this project weave it into its context without any further nods to contextualism—the color of the brick alone resonates with neighboring buildings from eras past. From this perspective Timberyard is neither classically modern, in the sense that it embraces rather than rejects the street, nor postmodern in that it is not the slightest bit historicist or nostalgic. This "both-and" quality is indicative of a clear path forward for urban social housing in cities composed of tight-knit blocks and pedestrian-oriented streets, a path illuminated by innovative architecture that respects the city and its communities.

Within the United States, given the historic withdrawal of the federal government from social housing, far more limited examples are available. Among the best is the work of Los Angeles architect Michael Maltzan, whose 2013 Star Apartments possesses noteworthy sectional complexity while providing much-needed housing for the formerly unhoused. The project is unabashedly urban, with storefront glass facing the sidewalk and an elevated courtyard framing the skyline. Maltzan, who has completed a number of accomplished social housing projects across the city, has an uncanny ability to use low-cost materials in a way that feels rich, and while such expressions would never feel right in O'Donnell and Tuomey's Dublin, they exude the exuberant qualities of Los Angeles as extolled by Reyner Banham as the city's "freedom of movement." The negative spaces in

Maltzan's housing dance around and through their structures, creating a territorial ambiguity that fully resonates with the climate and culture of the city of angels.

California architect Deanna Van Buren, who insists upon the act of building through practice, creates racially progressive work in Oakland that speaks to restorative economics on behalf of communities in need—particularly the formerly incarcerated—in projects such as her Center for Restorative Justice and Restorative Economics (2013). In the mission statement for her nonprofit firm Designing Justice + Designing Spaces, Van Buren says, "Our bold idea is that by transforming the spaces and places where we do justice, we can help our society make the shift from a punitive justice system to a restorative justice system. We hope to see peacemaking centers in every community in this country and end the age of mass incarceration."[11] Occupying a humble corner retail location, the center is embedded in Oakland in a manner that helps reintegrate this often-shunned population back into the life of the city. The expression of Van Buren's work is as gritty as its surrounds, with a limited set of architectural moves that allow users and passersby to feel that her work shares a sense of neighborhood belonging.

The continent of Africa is increasingly the epicenter for a number of architects of significance, perhaps most notable among them Pritzker laureate Diébédo Francis Kéré, who hails from Burkina Faso. In its citation for his award the committee writes:

> Francis Kéré's work is, by its essence and its presence, fruit of its circumstances. In a world where architects are building projects in the most diverse contexts— not without controversies—Kéré contributes to the debate by incorporating local, national, regional and global dimensions in a very personal balance of grass roots experience, academic quality, low tech, high tech, and truly sophisticated multiculturalism. . . .
>
> He has developed a sensitive, bottom-up approach in its embrace of community participation. At the same time, he has no problem incorporating the best possible type of top-down process in his devotion to advanced architectural solutions. His simultaneously local and global perspective goes well beyond aesthetics and good intentions, allowing him to integrate the traditional with the contemporary.
>
> Francis Kéré's work also reminds us of the necessary struggle to change unsustainable patterns of production and consumption, as we strive to provide adequate buildings and infrastructure for billions in need. He raises fundamental questions of the meaning of permanence and durability of construction in a context of constant technological changes and of use and re-use of structures. At the same time his development of a contemporary humanism merges a deep respect for history, tradition, precision, written and unwritten rules. . . . **In a world in crisis, amidst changing values and**

generations, he reminds us of what has been, and will undoubtably continue to be a cornerstone of architectural practice: a sense of community and narrative quality, which he himself is so able to recount with compassion and pride. In this he provides a narrative in which architecture can become a source of continued and lasting happiness and joy.[12]

Among Kéré's most notable works is his Gando Teachers' Housing in rural Burkino Faso. As stated at this chapter's outset, the works we are examining here represent advancements in public housing and social infrastructure. In this case the project addresses both. It was devised to attract teachers into a rural area as educational infrastructure while providing much-needed attainable housing. Kéré's firm describes the project as a series of adaptable modules that compare in size to the huts of the region, but innovation lies in the ability to combine modules into larger units. The curvature of the plan is intended to echo traditional building compounds, and most of the materials are locally sourced. The walls, which are constructed of adobe resting on a foundation of cement and granite stones, are connected by tie beams that

**Patrick Muvunga,
Uhuru Amphitheater,
Nakivale Refugee Settlement**

The elegant amphitheater is built from low-cost found materials, including rocks and mud, with a deliberate focus on ensuring long-term durability for decades of use. The engaging public space within the Nakivale settlement—which is home to refugees from Burundi, DRC, Eritrea, Ethiopia, Rwanda, Somalia, South Sudan, and Sudan—has become a popular gathering spot for live performances by local artists and dancers.

**Marina Tabassum,
Bait Ur Rouf Mosque**

Set on a plinth to mitigate flood risk, the mosque doubles as a community center. Tabassum's design maintains a minimalist material palette and adheres to a limited budget. Brick is deployed with austerity and acumen, manifested in the celestial ceiling treatment and control of light in the stunning main prayer room.

support concrete barrel vaults poured in situ to avoid the waste of formwork. The roof is shielded with corrugated metal, which channels rainwater into storage tanks below. Furthermore, as the firm states: "The enthusiastic involvement of the people of Gando was the key to the success of this project. The villagers gained not only new skills but also a sense of responsibility, awareness and sensitivity to both the traditional and innovative aspects of building."[13]

Exciting connective design is also emerging from Africa's informal sector. Self-taught designer and artist Patrick Muvunga's elegant Uhuru Amphitheater (2018) in his multicultural refugee settlement in Nakivale, Uganda, like his rocket toilet and bottle house, is built from low-cost found materials and has created a place of gathering that is popular for live performances by local artists and dancers. Muvunga's purview extends into urban design as he works with his community to contend with the expansion of his ethnically diverse refugee camp; his constant emphasis on public space reminds us of the definition of urbanity established in the introduction to this book: *a community inhabited by people from many different cultures and classes who spatially interact*. Regardless of whether we are discussing Nakivale or New York, it is not the size or sponsorship that matters for our purposes; it is the emphasis on the positive social friction of communal and multicultural interaction that these works so brilliantly share.

A new generation of South Asian architects has created designs of exceptional urbanity and profound beauty in recent years. This work again advances the social infrastructure that is so critically needed by vulnerable populations worldwide, in this case through structures that serve as community and educational centers that build societal connection.

Aga Khan Award–winning Bangladeshi architect Marina Tabassum's urban Bait Ur Rouf Mosque (2012) is a tour de force of tectonics, light, and material play, culminating in a spiritual building that replaces overtly religious architectural gestures with public space in the heart of the dense city of Dhaka. Built to mitigate flood risk, the mosque essentially doubles as a community center, all while adhering to a highly limited budget and a refreshingly edited material palette. Like Timberyard Housing, but in Dhaka rather than Dublin, brick is used to connect to context, yet in a fundamentally different manner related to the specifics of her culture. Departing from the rough-and-tumble masonry found in the surrounding neighborhood, Tabassum deploys brick with austerity and acumen, particularly in the construction of contemporary jalis—the perforated or lattice screens known throughout traditional Islamic architecture—as a means to transmit light while shielding out heat. This is taken a step further with a celestial ceiling treatment and control of light in the stunning main prayer room that unequivocally establishes the mosque as a critical new piece of global architecture despite its respect for its local roots.

Completed in 2020, University of Liberal Arts Bangladesh (ULAB) by Aga Khan Award recipient Kashef Chowdhury, a former collaborator with Tabassum, shows a similar sense of constraint while relying on cross-ventilation and stack effect in a volumetric open floor plan that eschews climate control. Chowdhury's details, such as the non-faceted brick forming the rotunda, speak to the users about the building's construction and introduce a play of light and shadow specific to this river delta nation that borders my own home state of West Bengal. But despite this understanding of regional context and climate, the building's facade is unabashedly contemporary, with an expression reminiscent of Louis Kahn and Aldo Rossi.

A world away, Gurmeet Sian has accomplished a number of urban acupuncture projects such as the community-based Phoenix Garden (2017), which won him the RIBA London Project Architect of the Year. In the project, a new garden boundary wall is punctuated by an expansive arch that gives way to a community gathering space and garden beyond. While many of the works cited in this chapter are formed with brick, in part because this is a material we have used to build many of our great cities worldwide, the reader should note the wide variety of brick sizes and hues deployed by these architects: bricks are no more alike than windows or doors. In this case Sian deploys a pale orange brick that clearly echoes the streets of London, but he caps the structure with bold stone signage that, along with the oversized arch, demands that the modest community center be recognized in its significance. Much like London's traditional row house architecture, the rear of the building has a much more porous facade that opens with an array of doors into the uniquely wild garden. Sian cites an extensive process working with both the head gardener and the local community to design the project, which is simultaneously a humble and monumental addition to the streets of London.

Sharing this sense of intimate monumentality, but at a fundamentally different scale, Grafton Architects' new campus for UTEC, the University of Engineering and Technology (2015), in Lima, Peru, is among the most important works of architecture of our epoch due to its unabashed declaration of the significance of educational, geological, and cultural connection realized in a bold formal statement. Led by Pritzker laureates Yvonne Farrell and Shelley McNamara, Grafton has given us a design unprecedented in its form yet deeply reflective of climate, community, and context, all without resorting to pastiche, nostalgia, or overt historical reference. Of the new landmark, they write:

> The unique condition of Lima and its relationship to the Pacific, with cliffs defining the boundary between the city and the sea, was a starting point in the conception of this project. A green valley connects the site with the sea. The UTEC campus project is conceived as a "new cliff", continuing the sea edge, clearly stating and defining the University on its new ground. The northern

**Kashef Chowdhury,
University of Liberal Arts
Bangladesh**

The rotunda at the center of the building not only enhances natural lighting but also facilitates the upward escape of hot air. The open and permeable design responds to the hot and humid local climate, while the use of brick pays homage to the long-standing brick tradition in Bengal's building history.

**Office Sian,
Phoenix Garden**

The modest community center employs a reddish-beige brick, referencing the streets of London, with monumental stone signage and an oversized arch to underscore its significance.
At the rear of the structure, a much more porous facade opens with an array of doors into the garden, akin to many of the historic row houses in central London.

**Grafton Architects,
UTEC Campus, Lima**

The open plastic form enables the potential coexistence of varied uses, promoting a sense of diversity and pluralism. The epic section and scale of the work are a clear nod to Lima's dramatic cliffs.

boundary of the site contains a busy road network. We see this northern boundary as the main façade of the project, visible from passing traffic and it is the register of the new campus in the public mind. We have positioned the special rooms of the University: the auditorium, the conference rooms, the theatre/movie venue, at the base of the "cliff" face, marking the northern boundary to the highway, encouraging cultural interaction with the wider public.[14]

The fluid rhythms of the project's section, darting from outside to in, create microclimates and programmatic interventions in keeping with the university's stated public goals. The open plastic form continually suggests the potential for pluralism in inhabitation, channeling the ethos of structuralism without being beholden to stylistic gesture. The epic section and scale of the work, clearly a nod to Lima's cliffs, are more reminiscent of a sports stadium than a university, connoting perhaps the significance of education over entertainment. While some may criticize the expansive use of poured-in-place concrete due to its high embodied energy, sustainability here is about an approach that values the innovative dynamics of people and place. Of course, the sustainability of the building materials is of great significance, but arguably the greater climate change battle is to create a climate of urbanity, which UTEC unquestionably does by providing such an exuberant platform for positive social friction.

The inspirational design work presented in this chapter, whether from Pritzker Prize winners, new young talent, or self-taught refugees, highlights a change in the instrumentality of architecture to focus upon today's most pressing issues of global warming and social inequity through the voice and actions of practice, much as the humanist modernists imagined after World War II, but this time with leaders and agendas that both represent and collaborate with the rich diversity of our world. The settings for these projects are starkly different from one another, but the through line is the insistence that practice can create a more connected urbanity, whether at the scale of a small mosque or a nation's new constitution.

What do these works signify for society at large as an emergent and lasting movement? When aided and abetted by enlightened public and private sector leaders—as well as a galvanized public hungry for change—what role can be realized by architects, urbanists, and all those committed to the benefits of a more connected, socially mobile, ecologically resilient urbanity during this inflection point in human history? For younger professionals, and those who wish to support them in more meaningful careers, a series of choices seem evident that could, upon reflection of the scenarios below, help lead to a kind of Hippocratic oath for the design community.

1

We can imagine we have no voice in the power structure that guides the future of society, and as a consequence go into traditional practices while occasionally voting. For young designers taught that their professions could help reshape the world, this path will quickly lead to ennui.

2

We can join market-savvy, branded practices that design LEED Silver shopping malls, net-zero single-family houses, or CLT suburban office parks with the contention that such work has widespread impact. While we should of course limit the embodied energy of new construction, to do so while promoting sprawl with the rationalization that suburban green buildings are better for the environment than dense normative structures along a subway line is absurd. For young designers, this path will lead to ennui and confusion.

3

We can accept commissions from fascists and petro-dictators with the extraordinarily colonialist delusion that these projects will somehow change such societies from within, all with the full knowledge that these commissions will lead to fanciful forms that deliver enormous financial and branding benefits for their architects. These designers tend to blithely believe that their work is unaccountable "art" while being constructed by indentured labor. For young designers in such firms, this path will lead to ennui, confusion, anger, and, hopefully, a letter of resignation.

4

We can isolate ourselves in academia while railing against capitalism and encouraging students to do the same, all while they obtain debt-driven *professional* degrees. There are many merits to fighting social and environmental injustice, particularly through the specific lens of academic criticality, but how will students become professionally impactful and financially solvent if most forms of design practice are deemed unacceptable by the academy? Why should students pay for professional degrees to learn the *instrumentalities* of design and urbanism practice if we teach them that any form of practice in the current economic system is corrupt? For young designers, this path will lead to ennui, confusion, anger, and insurmountable levels of student debt.

5

Or, *we can pledge to use our specific instrumentalities of drawing, criticality, design, and advocacy to help society envision and build a connected, socially mobile, largely urban world in harmony with nature and the needs of our growing populace*. For young architects, this path, however challenging, can lead to instrumental practice and, if they intentionally seek out fair employers who treat and train them well, a way out of debt.

This means that we can all commit to a role in advancing better forms of practice that everyone, not just we in the professions, can celebrate as relevant. Society and the design professions should strike an explicit bargain as part of such an oath: society will value these professions when they build works that advance the needs of a climate and a culture in crisis. If the professions achieve this, they should of course be compensated on par with the other professions that provide society with a similar value proposition. But beyond money, such reform and commitment should land designers a seat at the adult dinner table where our most serious societal questions must be debated and decided.

The projects illustrated in this chapter exude this move toward pertinence, particularly those that were conceived and built in the Global South. Ironically it is in cultures with fewer resources that a more critical architecture of urbanity is emergent, which is not to say good examples cannot be found in the West, as well as important projects found throughout East Asia. Practices that build in deeply capitalist nations, particularly in the United States, must work within the limited framework described earlier in this chapter, and must therefore employ a more tactical set of architectural and planning strategies specific to their clients, communities, climates, and construction methods, but that makes them no less noteworthy in their efforts to advance urbanity. It is within this neoliberal context that PAU, the studio I founded, practices, which is where we turn next.

THE TAU OF PAU

AS STATED IN THE BOOK'S INTRODUCTION,

the means for the design professions to advance an architecture of urbanity are increasingly clear. To do so, much like the examples cited in chapters 6 and 7, architecture practices should strive to build an infrastructure of opportunity that expands urban affordability; fights global warming through what we do and don't construct; creates a magnetic public realm that connects people across their differences; advances pluralistic cultural, educational, and social institutions; reimagines urban mobility without the private automobile; and collaborates with partners in the public, private, nonprofit, and community sectors who share these aspirations. We must do this with impassioned teams of talented and dedicated designers and staff who are compensated fairly and treated with respect, are able to advance their own goals as professionals, and are given the credit they deserve. The nonnegotiable need for consummate design skills cannot be overlooked in the pursuit of a just built environment—to the contrary, as stated in the last chapter, a social impact practice must combine inspiration and perspiration to fulfill human need. It is not good enough, for example, to measure the health of a community's housing stock solely by how many affordable housing units it is producing. People are not widgets, and people's homes cannot be the formulaic outcome of mass production, no matter how affordable. We need an architecture of urbanity that fulfills the needs of our hearts as much as it does our pocketbooks, which, given the limited resources of the world, means that our architects must be of even greater talent in order to achieve more with less, as beautifully exemplified in the last chapter.

If practices are to be understood as relevant to society at large it is critical that they be discerning about their purpose, and it was this exact question that would undergird my lifelong desire to build an architecture of urbanity and instigate my founding of Practice for Architecture and Urbanism, which is abbreviated as PAU, is pronounced "Pow!" and unmistakably avoids conflating the firm's name with my own. PAU began with an explicit statement about what we would and wouldn't do, with the latter including anything we deemed to be unequivocally socially deleterious, from advancing suburban sprawl to working for dictators to designing prison cells. With our 2015 launch we declared that we would enthusiastically consider architecture and planning commissions that advanced urbanity, and would not pursue commissions that undermined it. Our enlightened self-interest in adopting such a mission is as clear as the mirror we confront when we arise each morning—it is to fulfill the affirmation of purpose we all seek as humans.

We question ourselves continually despite these shared values. We do find that such a forthright statement of convictions has been resonant with the clients we attract, the communities we serve, and the collaborators we treasure, including our own team. As Ned Cramer of *Architect* magazine wrote in an article about PAU soon after its founding titled "What Won't You Build?":

Saintliness isn't a requirement of licensure, and every project, no matter how well-intentioned, entails compromise. Still, who doesn't ask themselves, now and again, "Where should I draw the line?" Maybe we should ask ourselves that question more often, as individuals, as firms, and as a profession. Protecting the health, safety, and welfare of the public encompasses far more than preventing buildings from falling down. The social contract invests architects with responsibility for civilization itself.[1]

A number of our projects, which do attempt to propel communal civilization forward, are described below. While recognizing the perils of showing my own studio's work here, to be true to the book's call for instrumental, relevant, and ethical practice, I must provide the example of my attempts at the same no matter how often we fail. I leave the reader to judge whether the work meets the mark from either a design or social perspective—but as the introduction to the previous chapter explains, practice is an asymptote; we do it because we strive to fulfill our mission with what are hopefully the right questions, understanding that we arrive with the right answers only when we are at our best.

PAU began in New York, loosely using my first book, *A Country of Cities*, as a north star. Unabashedly committed to advancing urbanity, we set out on a journey free of a specific style or technological process, a journey that led us repeatedly to an architecture of human connection created through compositions of open, volumetric forms that invite serendipity and plural interpretation while reflecting the mass and materiality of the city. We approach every project, regardless of program or scale, as a community center that aspires to rebuild our fraying societal bonds. With democracy and our planet in peril, it is our minimal duty as urban architects to advance the physical agora because we believe that collective life is the last and best hope for humanity.

Our portfolio has formed around four major categories: cultural and educational institutions in cities and campuses; public infrastructure and planning; workspaces of the future; and multi-family social housing, all of which are intended to build an architecture of urbanity. Beyond each specific program and site, however, we dig like archaeologists, trying to find new public space wherever we can, researching the history of a place as we must, deploying a design language that is resonant with a place and its people through an expression of material, tectonics, volume, color, and light in ways we hope will be both fresh and familiar. We celebrate the lyricism of the existing, which is often expressed by adding layers to the palimpsest of the city and juxtaposing the new with the old. We believe architecture and urbanism are inextricably linked, which results in a scale-fluid approach in which buildings intensify cities and cities permeate buildings. For us a key litmus test is the specificity of place that a project conjures—if a design can be transported outside of its site and still make sense due only to its internal logic, we know we have failed.

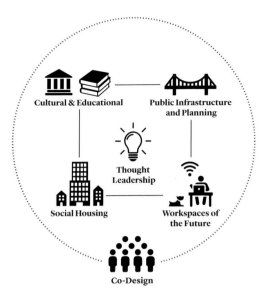

PAU only works in democracies, partially out of ethical concerns (we turned down working on Saudi's NEOM project three times) but also because we genuinely enjoy collaborating with communities, governments, and civic organizations to advance our collective work. We do not view these stakeholders as a bureaucracy to overcome, or as special interests who will compromise our artistic vision, because architecture is a public art form. We seek to build in people's neighborhoods, and it is only through some form of co-design that we can come to a collective vision that advances everyone's hopes and dreams, not just our own. Our profession will never achieve our own version of a Hippocratic oath unless and until we see ourselves as designers in the service of the public.

Propelled by these values and intentions, we collectively arrived at a design process we call Place | Needs | Connection. Rooted in Diana Agrest's admonition that we must read a place before we write in it with architecture we, like many firms, thoroughly investigate the nature of a place, its climate, construction techniques, and context.[2] Again, like most good architects and urbanists, we then turn to the needs statement, from not only our client but also the larger communities we serve. Unique are the specific formal tools we deploy in response to place and needs in an effort to forge human connection at the scale of the individual, the community, and the planet. This has culminated in what has become a firm motto, "place needs connection," a straightforward but often forgotten recognition that in a world divided by ideology and social media, physical place has the ability to provide a much-needed platform for positive, face-to-face social friction.

But to claim that this process is laudatory raises critical questions. The word "place" demands further investigation, given that its long history in our field has been co-opted by the forces of gentrification, nostalgia, and even racial hegemony.

PAU's design process forges human connection at the scale of the individual, the community, and the climate, in response to place and needs.

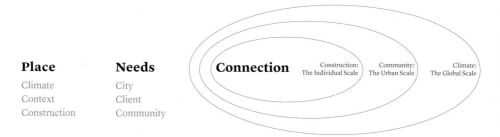

Place
Climate
Context
Construction

Needs
City
Client
Community

Connection

Construction:
The Individual Scale

Community:
The Urban Scale

Climate:
The Global Scale

When the term became common parlance in the lexicon of architecture, urban design, and city planning, it was a revolution that was contemporaneous with the societal transformations that arrived in the aftermath of World War II. The early modern movement, founded in the early 1900s, focused on the making of universal *space* as opposed to location-specific *place*. With the birth of Team 10 in 1953 and the subsequent dissolution of CIAM (Congrès Internationaux d'Architecture Moderne) at Otterloo in 1959, an international group of architects splintered from their elders by arguing for a place-based humanist modernism derived from local needs. Beyond architecture, this period also ushered in the term "urban design" with the work of Kevin Lynch, Gordon Cullen, Camillo Sitte, and others such as Giancarlo di Carlo, who would serve as bridge figures between the architects of Team 10 and the urban "placemakers" who followed. Much of this work stemmed from the writings of John Habraken, who as we have noted argued for an open-ended, structuralist approach to design that would allow for greater levels of community control and autonomy. In this paradigm the designer would create a flexible platform for inhabitation rather than a fixed solution. Humanist modernists like Alvar Aalto and Aldo van Eyck imagined an architecture centered not only on the user but also on the capacity of communities to change and reinterpret their own environments through the act of inhabitation, prompting one of van Eyck's most famous quotes: "Whatever space and time mean, place and occasion mean more."[3]

Unfortunately, the humanist modernism of that era, albeit driven largely by progressive white men, was no match for the neoliberalism that would soon follow—particularly given that the civil rights movement demanded that we all be counted as equals within the humanist frame, a prospect that remains anathema to many. So pervasive was the neoliberal agenda that modernism would be fully co-opted and commercialized to the point of corporate banality. Seizing on this failure, the tribal, cynical, fractious postmodern cartel, embodied by both historicism and deconstructivism, replaced the naivete of the flawed modern

"Whatever space and time mean, place and occasion mean more."
Aldo van Eyck

"Many have forgotten—or never knew—that modern architecture was once primarily concerned with social and civic improvement."
Catherine Bauer

"People have ideas about what a place should become, without any understanding of what's there. You hear people say 'placemaking,' which I really hate. It's this colonial attitude, versus going into a place and trying to cultivate what's there."
Walter Hood

project. Postmodernism has largely served to hurtle us toward oblivion, bringing with it the death of expertise and objective reality, and the consecration of individual opinion over verifiable fact.

Catherine Bauer, the prominent American "houser" who passed away well before the flowering of such cynicism, seemed prescient when she stated, "Many have forgotten— or never knew—that modern architecture was once primarily concerned with social and civic improvement."[4]

Urban design, while more consistently humanist in its rhetoric than architecture, would be no less co-opted by the neoliberal agenda, perhaps best exemplified in the racially homogeneous iconography of wealthy Seaside, Florida. With the advent of the Black Lives Matter movement and the increasing empowerment of marginalized communities, "placemaking" as a concept is receiving deserved critique by prominent scholars and practitioners as a means, intentional or not, to catalyze gentrification and privilege dominant cultures over the actual urbanity of a place. Walter Hood, the landscape architect, scholar, and MacArthur Fellow, has spoken out viscerally against the term:

People have ideas about what a place should become, without any understanding of what's there. You hear people say "placemaking," which I really hate. It's this colonial attitude, versus going into a place and trying to cultivate what's there. But it's hard to do because of aesthetics, and the ways that making landscapes are codified, bureaucratized, and maintained.[5]

Some have turned to the term "placekeeping" as an alternative, in which the existing characteristics of a place can be amplified or given greater significance through the act of design in concert with, not on behalf of, community stakeholders. While we will return to this broad theme of the archaeology of the existing—of the architecture of palimpsest—the previous chapter focused on global examples of Hood's call to "cultivate what's there." Fundamental to Hood's critique is his separation of "placemaking" from "place." For this author, Hood is not critiquing the importance of place over space as framed by van Eyck but is questioning the instrumentality of architects and urban designers as they graft their biases, which are often grounded in both white privilege and iconography, onto urbanity in the name of placemaking. In this way, and with great irony, the practice of urban design often yields retrograde results in which lived urbanity is replaced by a chain store–riven, capitalism-driven simulacrum of the city.

Hood's critique leads us back to the highly important framework of Critical Regionalism as originally put forth by Alexander Tzonis and Liane Lefaivre, but more famously championed and elucidated by the indefatigable architect and historian Kenneth Frampton in his famed article (1983) and subsequent landmark book *Toward a Critical Regionalism* (1993). A movement that questions both universal modernism and postmodern pastiche, Critical Regionalism argues instead for an insistent and intentional modern architecture that draws upon the characteristics of place to inform a contemporary but regionally influenced architecture, particularly in terms of *tectonics*, or the science and art of construction.[6] Although decades old, Frampton's influential work has regained significance with the growing awareness of climate change, late-stage globalization, and our search for pluralistic expression in the face of racial and social reckoning. In 2019, Léa-Catherine Szacka and Véronique Patteeuw, writing for the *Architectural Review*, argued for the relevance of Frampton's work on Critical Regionalism to our current cultural moment:

> It is our conviction that the text represents today much more than a historical artifact. While the work of Postmodern architects such as Aldo Rossi and Robert Venturi is rediscovered by younger generations, Frampton's text and the projects mentioned in his *Perspecta* article offer new perspectives on the heritage of Postmodern architecture. His "critique from within", arguing against ideas of sign, symbol or irony, brings about notions of authenticity, tactility, materiality and tectonics that are most valuable in light of the ecological, economical and political challenges the architectural profession is facing today. But beyond that, **Frampton's text has a compelling character: it frames new forms of practices and new imperatives linked to place and context.** While architects are faced with requirements of density to preserve open space for nature and agriculture, a certain sensibility to the qualities of the ground in which projects are embedded is imperative to rethink the concept of ground occupation. And while the current state of ecological transition confronts the profession with short cycles and economies of means, local materials, building knowledge and craftsmanship become more and more appealing if not necessary. As such, the text provides a framework for younger architectural practices aspiring to *a rearguard perspective* and aiming at keeping "a certain cultural ethic alive."[7]

Practices such as ours, embedded as PAU is in the commercial beehive that is New York City, work with a different set of reference points and ground rules than most of the examples cited in chapter 7. We certainly do not invite any comparisons to such global luminaries. We do, however, share as a framework a goal of regionally responsive architecture that connects people to their existing places, communities, and cultures—an architecture of the palimpsest. Most if not all of the projects cited in the previous chapter can be understood through the perspective of Critical Regionalism, reinforcing Szacka and Patteeuw's assertion that this frame is extraordinarily relevant to the challenges of our day.

In terms of New York, it is our "urban vernacular"—and by this I mean less the Beaux-Arts finery of McKim, Mead & White, the grand apartment houses of Rosario Candela, the tenements of the Lower East Side, Brownstone Brooklyn, or any of the edifices that are traditionally conceived as Gotham's built fabric but instead the city's public vernacular of subways, sidewalks, and squares— that often provides the central canvas for radical change. Metropoles like New York, Tokyo, Kolkata, or Dublin all offer a built fabric carved from the frontal rhythms and gravitational materiality of streetwall urbanity, and as such they together represent a somewhat immutable urban typology that is fundamentally different from the cliffs of Lima or the expanse of Nakivale. And while vast social inequities and solvable climate problems abound in streetwall cities, the reckonings they demand must, by zoning, manifest within and between their zero lot line boundary conditions—conditions which are often undergirded by a stubbornly commercial economic substrate. This is why in our architecture projects we tend to design buildings that reinforce, extend, and celebrate urban streets and public spaces.

Frustrated by such constraints, modernist architects often fight the streetwall, rarely with good outcomes for the street. Frank Lloyd Wright's Guggenheim Museum is a stunning piece of radical architecture, but it hardly meets the sidewalk in a manner that advances urbanity, perhaps reflecting Wright's infamous anti-urban philosophy. For many architects today—particularly those trying hard to be avant-garde—Le Corbusier's call to "kill the street" still resonates; fortunately the studios highlighted in the last chapter have ignored and even reversed this destructive call with projects like the Star Apartments and Timberyard Housing, perhaps because as architects focused on promoting urbanity, these practices are more grounded in Frampton's *arrière-garde* perspective, as opposed to those who fashion themselves as avant-garde.

In recent years, we have seen the emergence of hopeful cultural theories such as *meta-modernism*, which by sieving through the detritus of modernism and postmodernism to salvage their most useful seeds provides a much overdue focus on the narratives of lived experience. As PAU interprets it, meta-modernism is a movement of utopian pragmatists that embrace Frampton's notion of the rearguard. Much of the architecture focused upon in this book shares this utopian pragmatist ethos by eschewing the tired fights between the epistemological, centered on the intellectual theories of knowledge, and the ontological, centered on the nature of existence, with the understanding that any attempt at connective design must oscillate between and beyond both.

It is almost entirely with this meta-modern, rearguard perspective that we at PAU find ourselves aligned in the sense that we cannot believe in the new simply for the sake of newness. Such a stance will inevitably invite accusations of being reactionary, historicist, nostalgic, or even racially hegemonic, but we in the twenty-first century should learn to transcend such easy binaries. Architecture's avant-garde and Frampton's *arrière-garde* would probably agree, for instance, that the New Urbanist movement, much like the Moral Majority, is neither. That in no way undermines our unshakable belief in the street or the streetwalls that define them or the public spaces that they form.

PAU began its work with a highly limited number of clients. Our first built work was completed eight years after our founding, as a recipient of the Miller Prize in Columbus, Indiana, small-city home of renowned architecture famously sponsored by Irwin and Xenia Miller. We used the prize, which is awarded by Exhibit Columbus, to design and construct a pavilion meant to engage the public in the community. Our project, in the heart of downtown, recycles decommissioned existing light pole foundations at the city's main intersection to form an illuminated gateway, pavilion, and occasional dance floor at the main crossroads of Columbus. With much of the community expressing concern about downtown revitalization in the aftermath of the pandemic, and with local teens asking for a place to hang out, the gateway project serves as a reminder of the downtown's cultural significance in this small but diverse midwestern community.

Given our stated mission, we quickly realized that the work of the firm would become two-pronged, with work sponsored by clients that advanced urbanism and human connection at a variety of scales, and advocacy projects we sponsored ourselves in order to fight for urbanism and human connection. The inclusion of advocacy in our portfolio has proven to have an additional advantage: when client work ebbs, this type of self-paced work allows us to keep staff employed and engaged. We have titled this second category as PAU:SE, or PAU Special Editions, and in many ways, it has established our thought leadership reputation as assuredly as the work we perform on behalf of our clients.

For example, in 2017, soon after our founding, we formed a partnership with twelve civic organizations, including the American Civil Liberties Union, to draft a letter to Mayor Bill de Blasio in response to Donald Trump's undemocratic attempts against the First Amendment, recommending seven actions the city could take to support and encourage demonstrations, political speech, and other expressions of civic engagement in New York's public spaces. One of the actions proposed was the creation of a network of protest sites spanning all five boroughs. To support

PAU, InterOculus

The InterOculus—PAU's first built work in response to winning the Miller Prize—creates a cultural crossroads at the heart of downtown Columbus, drawing inspiration from the Roman Pantheon, the wigwams of the Shawnee and Miami people, and the entrance archways to the Indiana State Fair. Recycling decommissioned light pole foundations at the city's main intersection, the project forms an illuminated gateway and asks the community to celebrate a space normally reserved for cars.

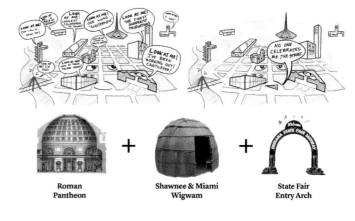

Roman
Pantheon

Shawnee & Miami
Wigwam

State Fair
Entry Arch

PAU with Twelve Civic Organizations, Public Space for Free Expression: A Letter to Mayor De Blasio

Analytical maps illustrate the expansive impact of the proposed network of protest sites across all five boroughs, particularly in marginalized communities.

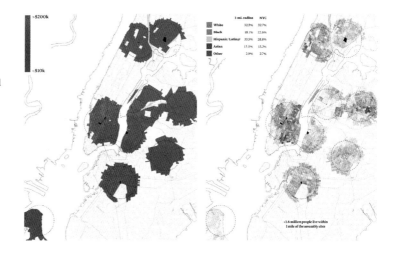

PAU with the *New York Times* and Buro Happold, N.Y.C.— Not Your Car

Originally an avenue centered on a park in the early twentieth century, Park Avenue lost much of its green space to roads for cars. A redesigned vision could restore its former glory with a spacious pedestrian promenade.

PAU with the *New York Times*, Penn Palimpsest

Recycling the superstructure and foundations of Madison Square Garden allows for the creation of a grand commuter pavilion at minimal public cost and disruption. The proposal sought to provide much-needed public space in the form of both a luminous new commuter station and a generous surrounding public realm that would complement the recently opened Moynihan Station.

this recommendation, we produced a series of analytical maps illustrating the potentially exponential impact of this action: a much broader cross-section of New Yorkers—in terms of income level, race, and ethnicity—could more easily participate in free expression. Instead of being held at single locations, marches and protests could be staged at multiple points across the city, facilitating larger turnout overall and enabling far more voices to be heard.

PAU also proposed three major urban advocacy projects in conjunction with the *New York Times*: N.Y.C.—Not Your Car and Penn Palimpsest, the ideas for which have gained validity in the post-pandemic context as cities fight to restore transit ridership while improving the local quality of life for all urban residents. Our third collaboration with the *Times*, regarding housing, is discussed in chapter 10.

In 2019, for N.Y.C.—Not Your Car, PAU and its partner Buro Happold, proposed a sweeping change: to ban all privately owned personal cars in Manhattan, leaving the streets for people, bikes, taxis, buses, emergency and freight vehicles, Access-A-Ride for the disabled, and ride-share services. This action would transform the spatial and social experience not only of Manhattan by upcycling its asphalt, which constitutes a staggering third of the island's land mass, but also all of the boroughs and regional neighborhoods that are forced to host Manhattan's inbound and outbound commuter traffic. Given the childhood asthma rates in the outer-ring neighborhoods of color around Manhattan, especially in the Bronx and parts of Brooklyn, suburban commuter traffic represents one of the most critical environmental justice issues the city and region face. Not Your Car would advance a vastly more equitable, ecological, and enjoyable region that would recover faster from its ongoing inequity crises. If adopted, New York's streets would engender fairer health outcomes, better climate resilience, greater accessibility for the disabled, enhanced homeless services, responsible waste management, and faster, more pleasant commutes for workers who today must compete for invaluable space on regional arterials clogged with those wealthy enough to drive into and within Manhattan. Because of the enormous amounts of space it would open up at little expense, the proposal would give Manhattan's communities an opportunity to reshape their own public realm in order to build human connection and, just as importantly, drastically reduce express bus commutation times across the tristate region. While intended as a provocation, it is conceivable that in the coming decades we will see the elimination of private cars from the congested centers of our big cities, given that our work became part of the advocacy to enact congestion pricing in New York City.

Penn Palimpsest was created in 2016 also in partnership with the *New York Times*, with subsequent support from the local community and the Ford Foundation. The project presented our vision to adaptively reuse and transform the existing structure of Madison Square Garden (MSG), which sits atop the transportation hub of Pennsylvania Station, into a new, safe, affordable, and spacious public gateway to serve all of the station's existing and anticipated commuters and straphangers as additional rail capacity is introduced. Rather than design a new station from scratch, which would cost untold billions in construction and disruption, this design would recycle the foundations, structure, and roof of the arena to both save money and highlight the complex history of the site. The proposal sought to provide much-needed public space in the form of both a luminous new commuter station and a generous surrounding public realm that would complement the recently opened Moynihan Station, which primarily serves Amtrak. This project spurred the creation of a new 501(c)(3), Public for Penn, as well as ongoing efforts within the public sector regarding how to best address the challenges of Penn Station, its rail capacity issues, and its neighborhood environment. More recently, as we will discuss in detail at the conclusion of this chapter, PAU's Penn Palimpsest inspired an actual commission to fix Pennsylvania Station, an extraordinary fact that is only possible because of the advocacy work in which we have continually invested.

These advocacy proposals would drastically improve equity and quality of life for Gotham's residents by enhancing our sense of connectedness. They would also help the region respond to the competitive threat proposed by remote work by enhancing workers' commutes, which would in turn set an example for other global metropoles to ban private cars, enhance mass transit, and enable public space for free speech and positive social friction.

In addition to advocacy, PAU has undertaken substantial architectural research projects tied to the mixing of uses within buildings. Inspired by warehouses like the one in which our studio is located, we investigated what it would take within the context of today's building codes to create contemporary lofts that could flexibly mix residential and commercial uses, or in some cases have the ability to mix more intensive activities such as light manufacturing and laboratories. This inquiry led to a three-scale project we call "The Bears," with Baby and Mama Bear allowing for mixed residential and commercial, and Papa Bear having enough infrastructure to accommodate everything from industrial to academic uses.

Along these same lines, in the aftermath of the pandemic, we have been actively studying the conversion of obsolete mid-century office buildings into affordable residential buildings with ample space for working from home. Such conversions are difficult and expensive, but could provide much-needed housing with minimal new amounts of embodied energy. They could also help revitalize central business districts—a term we should replace with the idea of "community business districts"— with vibrant retail and public space that would serve new residents, who would in turn reactivate local retail and mass transit.

Despite our passion for advocacy and research, constructing projects centered on nature, culture, and joy is at the core of PAU's architecture practice. When possible, such building is about adaptive reuse, as with our second built design,

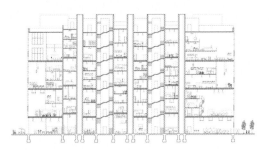

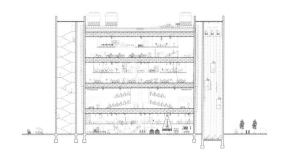

PAU, "The Bears"

Baby Bear: a horizontal mixture of residential and commercial uses (*top left*). Mama Bear: a vertical mixture of residential and commercial uses (*top right*). Papa Bear: an infrastructure-rich prototype for commercial, industrial, and academic uses (*bottom right*).

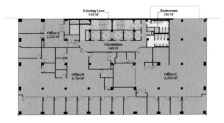

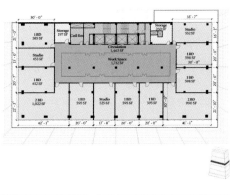

PAU,
Office-to-Live | Work Conversion
The study investigates the conversion of an existing office building in midtown Manhattan (*left*) into affordable residential buildings with ample shared space for working from home (*right*).

the Domino Sugar Refinery, where we inserted a new barrel-vaulted curtain-wall structure into an existing landmark, resulting in an interstitial gap between the two that will let light, rain, snow, and vegetation inhabit this breathing facade. This porosity is especially operative at the ground floor, something that is true with all of our projects. In this case we transformed the barrel-vaulted ground floor windows into an enfilade of doors at the building's perimeter in order to engage the public spaces surrounding the building, a master plan created in collaboration with Field Operations.

For the Domino Sugar Refinery, we completed the construction documents for the curtain wall, a critical learning process for our team. Like many firms, we have chosen to collaborate with executive architects who complete the construction documentation for most of our other work. I mention this highly practical internal issue because it directly bears on the culture and size of our studio, which we believe functions most effectively as a smaller practice, one in which we all know each other and learn together. Furthermore, like most architecture firms, we are also a business enterprise, and as such we have discovered that this structure allows us to optimize staff compensation, benefits, and training while being investment-forward about future projects, PAU:SE initiatives, and our work with nonprofits to advance issues like race and gender diversity in the profession.

One of the unique aspects of Domino is that the project is inexorably tied to its surroundings: it is of, by, and for its neighborhood along the Brooklyn waterfront. We strive for this rootedness, this palimpsest, in all of our architecture, even if the project is all new construction. We've enacted this approach in the use of red polychromatic metal on the facade of our Schuylkill Yards tower, which echoes the tones of the brick and terra cotta of Philadelphia; in our brick and timber building, known as Hobson College, at the heart of Princeton University's campus, which helps form a spatial sequence of exciting new courtyards; and in the branched structural form of our Wave Bridge in Indianapolis—designed in concert with the structural engineers at Schlaich Bergermann Partners—which intentionally echoes trees on the surrounding embankments and for the first time in Indy's history offers a bridge that is more pedestrian than vehicular. We strongly believe that human cultural connection is forged through these interpretive acts of design. They serve as a balm against the relentless placelessness people encounter daily in new construction, all without resorting to historicism or pastiche.

One of our most challenging undertakings in this effort to "placekeep" came with our commission to design a twelve-acre walkable village in the heart of Mongolia's capital, Ulaanbaatar. For this project, our response to culture and climate seeks greater degrees of expression by channeling local methods of construction and coloration. Perhaps most significantly, our client asked us to reflect upon the loss of rural nomadic life felt by the capital's residents. The site plan that we presented celebrates the nomad embedded in the city, where there

PAU, JFK Towers at Schuylkill Yards

The red polychromatic metal and terra cotta on the facade of the Schuylkill Yards east tower echoes the tones of the brick and terra cotta of Philadelphia.

PAU, Hobson College, Princeton University

The brick and timber building forms a spatial sequence of exciting new courtyards, envisioning the new college as both a thoroughfare and a destination.

PAU, Wave Bridge

The branched structural form of the bridge echoes the organic lines of the trees on the embankments below.

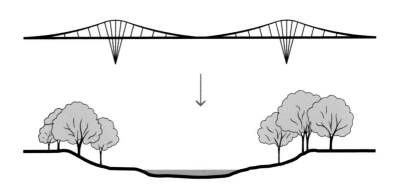

PAU, Domino Sugar Refinery

The historic refinery was built as three conjoined structures with misaligned brick fenestration that enclosed enormous equipment. PAU's design inserted a brand-new building into the existing volume, creating a dialogue between history and the future. The adapted structure features porosity at the ground floor and engages with the public spaces surrounding the building, while the glass barrel vault above echoes the American Round Arch Style of the original facade. The ten- to twelve-foot gap between the new and the old envelopes allows for ideal and standardized floor heights, light penetration, and vegetation to inhabit this breathing facade.

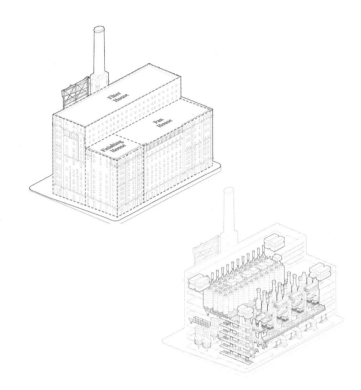

PAU, Ulaanbaatar Village

The nonlinear and non-gridded site plan celebrates a centuries-old nomadic culture in largely rural Mongolia. The village responds to its natural surroundings in a multitude of ways. The undulating, angled rooftops and the warm colors of stained concrete and stone echo the majestic mountains nearby. People are encouraged to wander through the buildings and plazas as *flâneurs*, following meandering paths that embody the ideals of both urban and nomadic life: autonomy and discovery.

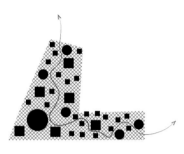

PAU, Attainable New York

The eleven-acre parking lot will be reconceived, with a performing arts center, day-care facility, and trade school joining the existing Christian Cultural Center to form the heart of the campus. The interior streets connect to the surrounding street grid, tying the development to its context. The development will provide approximately 2,050 income-based apartments, including transitional supportive housing and round-the-clock, on-site social services, with space for a host of community facilities at the ground level.

PAU, Rock and Roll Hall of Fame and Museum

The expansion celebrates the original I. M. Pei pyramid, the city of Cleveland, and Lake Erie. At the heart of the expansion is a dynamic new lobby and pre-exhibition space situated among the platonic solids, reverberating with energy, lighting, and sound. As visitors pass through to the interior, they will be immersed in the visceral, gritty quality that has always defined spaces for rock music.

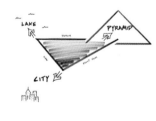

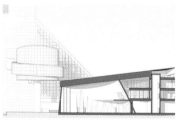

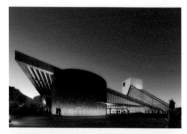

are no axial views and one can get lost in urbanity only to find oneself anew. The project includes everything from a 250-seat folk theater to a haunted house, as well as residences, live/work lofts for local craftspeople, and an array of public spaces including "campfire" moments with pavilions designed by our friend and collaborator, James Carpenter.

A site in Brooklyn's East New York, similar in size to Ulaanbaatar Village, also required architecture and urban design skills, in this case in the service of a 100 percent low- to middle-income housing project, including transitional supportive housing and round-the-clock, on-site social services. The project was commissioned by the Christian Cultural Center, a pillar of the neighborhood led by the Reverend A. R. Bernard. Budget constraints limit the form of the housing to a normative double-loaded corridor typology in which highly regulated affordable housing units are organized around hallways. The residential buildings are rendered in the varying brick facades sought by the local community, but the site plan, a community center, a school, and the addition of a 300-seat performing arts center provide further opportunities for design and innovation in one of the lowest-income yet extraordinarily vibrant communities of color in New York City.

As we entered our fifth year of practice, nothing short of a miracle transpired. Short-listed among some of the world's greatest architectural talents, PAU successfully won three global competitions, for the aforementioned Hobson College at Princeton University and Wave Bridge in Indianapolis, as well as an extraordinary commission to ambitiously expand I. M. Pei's Rock and Roll Hall of Fame and Museum in Cleveland alongside talents such as LERA as structural engineers, Jaffe Holden on acoustics, and L'Observatoire International for lighting. With construction underway, we are committed to a Rock Hall expansion that celebrates the original Pei pyramid, the city of Cleveland—for which this is a critically important urban institution— and Lake Erie, on the shores of which the project is situated. As a series of platonic volumes echoing the original Pei structure, the expansion creates new public space both in and outside of Rock Hall with the hopes of engaging tomorrow's youth in this ever-evolving musical genre. At the heart of the expansion is a dynamic new lobby and pre-exhibition space situated among the platonic solids, reverberating with energy, lighting, and sound as it navigates the section from Pei's plaza down to the lakefront. As with all such institutions, the project will play an outsized role as a mirror and window into our cultural condition in terms of race, gender, and physical abilities, particularly in this gritty industrial hub that has seen its share of economic and environmental challenges. The defiant spirit rock and roll conjures as the intransigent voice of the young must pulse through the project, including its dynamic spaces, raw material expression, and urban connections.

While the Rock Hall expansion, Hobson College, and the Wave Bridge were invited competitions, we won a fourth, open competition to design the nation's next generation of regional, modular, and sustainable air traffic control towers.

PAU normally doesn't enter open competitions as they tend to be exploitative, but this was different because it was sponsored by the Federal Aviation Administration (FAA), which broke the competition into phases such that the initial cost of entry was low, leading to a compensated short list for the final phase. This same competition was won by I. M. Pei in 1962, but in the ensuing decades funding to create a state-of-the-art air traffic control system fell short until President Biden's bipartisan infrastructure bill was passed in 2021. The short list for the new towers came down to us and some of the world's foremost aviation architects; when we were notified about our win, we were thrilled to receive an FAA report card explaining that we had the highest technical and aesthetic scores with our "F4 Tower," which stands for Form Follows Function with Flair. These towers will be deployed in smaller communities throughout the United States, and as such may well be the tallest things in town, akin to local water towers and lighthouses. In addition to these industrial inspirations, we drew from the thinking of Bertram Goodhue—who through projects like the Nebraska State Capitol understood the impact of verticality on the American plains—and the functionality of R2D2, who like our tower has the ability to telescope to differing heights. This project for PAU is a classic example of why urbanity need not be about big cities; we see these petite towers as community beacons, small reminders of the aspirations we share, including travel. The towers are almost purely about engineering as illustrated in our collaboration with Thornton Tomasetti and Jaros, Baum & Bolles, both of which are leading sustainability firms in their respective disciplines. Some may balk at the idea of "sustainable" air traffic control towers given the emissions problems with the aviation industry, but it is critical to note that these towers are part of Transportation Secretary Pete Buttigieg's plan to decarbonize the American aviation industry by 2050.

These competition successes signal the same type of sea change discussed in chapter 7 as a shift in the Overton window delineating an evolving, back-to-the-future role for architecture. The world is finally moving away from the object-based architecture of the late twentieth century and toward practices and processes that fully engage the communities, climates, and constraints in which an architecture of urbanity is by definition situated. Interestingly, when asked why these prominent and diverse clients chose a firm as young as PAU for such complex, difficult to obtain, and challenging commissions, the clients uniformly responded that it was our credibility in dealing with urban and community forces that led them to us, despite the fact that their sites vary from inner city to campus settings to small airports. As stated earlier, we view every project as a community center, and increasingly this is what our clients want, too. For us, this is a validation of the idea that urbanity is far more about human connectedness and the desire for positive social friction than the simple calling of the big metropolis. It also confirms the conviction that the practice of architecture becomes relevant when you make it so.

PAU, F4 Towers

The air traffic control prototype drew inspiration from lighthouses, state capitol buildings, and water towers that dot the horizon of the American landscape, as well as the functionality of R2D2's ability to telescope to differing heights. The tower is designed equally to support the specialized mechanical equipment it houses and the operators themselves, providing an environment with optimal conditions for both the systems and the humans who run them.

Circulation   Structure   MEP/FP   Program

Many of our projects are not in New York or other wealthy mega-cities but actually represent interventions in rising cities like Newark, Cleveland, Detroit, and the City of Niagara Falls, several of which surround the Great Lakes. Whether in big cities or beyond, many of our current projects are in communities still recovering from deindustrialization. For example, our urban design work around Michigan Central Station in downtown Detroit is a collaboration with local communities and the Ford Motor Company, with the goal of helping to establish a district centered on the future of mobility and society in a city still filled with the "maker" culture of the Motor City.

Similarly, for the State of New York we were commissioned to create a plan to help entice the eight million annual visitors to Niagara Falls into the adjacent downtown. Working with the local community, often on Zoom during the pandemic, we framed a proposal that includes a Heritage Trail that highlights the extraordinary history of the city, punctuated by new open spaces including an overlook we are designing over the Niagara River, as well as a new public park being designed by Hargreaves Jones. This work led to yet another extraordinary planning exercise, a memorial to Freedom Seekers who came to Niagara as the last stop on their journey on the Underground Railroad through a former hotel called Cataract House, where a network of African American waiters aided the formerly enslaved in reaching Canada across treacherous waters. Our hope is that this small, powerful, and well-located memorial will engage not just those who are destination visitors but the millions who come to visit Niagara Falls each year only to encounter this extraordinary history serendipitously, which will hopefully entice them to visit the excellent heritage center located nearby. Of particular poignance is the fact that well after the Emancipation Proclamation, people were trying to escape our country across our international border to the north, perhaps reminding us to have more compassion for those attempting to cross into our nation from the south.

While this chapter has covered numerous projects that exemplify our attempts at building an infrastructure of opportunity through connective design, no one project grounds the firm like our advocacy and architecture for Pennsylvania Station. As discussed in chapter 5, the replacement of the original McKim, Mead & White station with private development signified a national inflection point from city to suburb, from train to plane, from rail stock to gridlock, from urban might to white flight, from a symphony of we to a cacophony of me. This author's lifelong obsession with Penn is only in part about questions of a rail station, safe and dignified architecture, or even its vital neighborhood—it is a question of whether we still care about ourselves as a society. Will all things civic continue to be relegated to the bean-counting world of green eyeshades, the craven sensibility that says today's unthinkable status quo is good enough for one of the world's great cities? Or can we, once again, excel?

Penn Palimpsest not only posed that question in 2016 but inspired an actual bid to fix the station by a public-private partnership that has become PAU's client. Unlike Palimpsest, this far more developed design keeps Madison Square Garden in place above the station because no one in government has the interest to relocate it. Our team's plan would remove MSG's enormous theater complex and still allow for a relocation of the entire arena someday. In the interim the plan creates improvements that start at the track level in terms of fire safety, passenger egress, and train capacity by working with the transportation architects at HOK. PAU became the lead architectural designer in mid-2023, utilizing much of the historical and track research done for the 2016 proposal with the *New York Times*. A few months later we revealed a contemporary stone building we refer to as "the mirror of a mirror of a ghost," which refers to the fact that McKim designed the Farley Building, now Moynihan Station, across the street as a mirror of the original Penn,

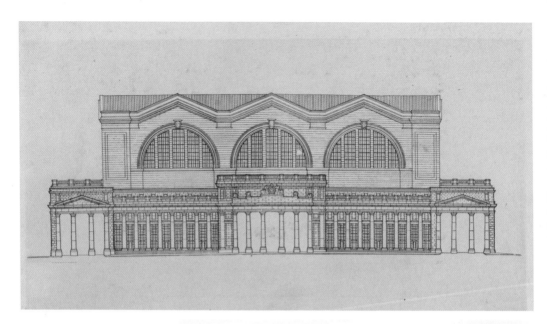

PAU, New New York Penn

The proposal reimagines the current cramped and disjointed, split-level concourses as a seamless, single-level station, with an improved public realm around the entire block at the street level. The proposed facade (*top right*) is a mirror of a mirror of the historic Penn Station (*top left*). The proposal returns a sense of civic grandeur to the station by circumscribing Madison Square Garden within a new podium that fills out the streetwalls of the block. A soaring Eighth Avenue entrance will restore the civic gravitas, dignity, and public safety that have been absent since the 1963 demolition of the historic Penn Station.

Existing

Proposed

Existing

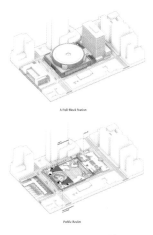

A Full-Block Station

Public Realm

Concourse Level

Platform Level

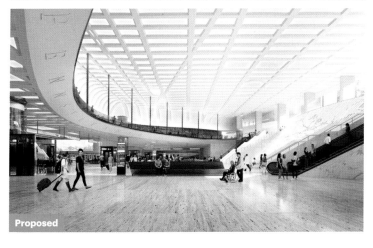

Proposed

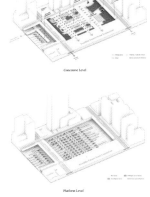

which is now an apparition. Our project mirrors both Farley and that apparition in terms of their cadence, materiality, and the facade depth we associate with neoclassical architecture, dating back to precedents like Schinkel's Altes Museum. The design still reaches for a palimpsest by reusing McKim's original foundations and echoing some of his language, albeit in a much more porous and public manner than the foreboding beauty of the original. MSG is incorporated above in a unified structural and design approach, while the below-grade is vastly improved by the removal of the theater and the vast improvement of the passenger experience in one intuitive concourse level with high ceilings and without dead ends. As a public-private partnership, the restrooms, elevators, and escalators must all be maintained properly including two ADA elevators for each platform, which would receive daylight under our proposal. The retail proposal is the furthest thing from a mall, with an emphasis on food and beverage, including new public porches at the corners of Eighth Avenue.

Some of the best opportunities to create an architecture of urbanity in our cities have come when we have been able to proactively propose the introduction of public spaces, regardless of whether they were in our original project brief, particularly when we hear the call for them from the local community. At PAU we find that we must continually fight for pedestrian space where clients may want to place vehicular or other private needs. Per Walter Hood's critique, such public space, once proposed, should not represent an urban design that engages in placemaking solely for the dominant culture but rather as a platform for existing and new subcultures to express themselves and where serendipities may occur.

To this end, we now depart from the discussion of PAU's work and the formal work of architecture practices more generally, turning instead to some of the best public spaces in our cities, designed with a welcome minimalism. For example, near our studio at the northern end of Manhattan's Union Square Park is one of our favorite urban spaces, a refreshingly undifferentiated flat paved hardscape designed by landscape architect Michael Van Valkenburgh Associates that is, depending on the moment, home to farmer's markets, BLM protests, punk skateboarders, headphone dance parties, composting stations, a rather comical anti-circumcision group, and of course the enduring aroma of pot. In landscape architecture, too, less can indeed be more, especially if we want to encourage the quality that seems most endangered in our big cities today: iconoclasm.

Cities increasingly feel homogeneous not only due to gentrification but also because of the convergence of our global culture into a monolith that makes our individual communities feel increasingly the same. As discussed in the introduction, planners may rightfully fight for transit-oriented density, but if experientially we can only reproduce banality, we are lost, not only because the results are so boring but because we lose the iconoclastic spirit that draws us to urbanity in the first place. Perhaps the most famous lyric from the Talking Heads classic "This Must Be the Place" is "I'm just an animal looking for a home."[8] Who among us hasn't felt that sense of isolation and concomitant desire for community at some point in our lives, especially as young adults? Iconoclasm isn't only about individuals being different to be different but about how difference spreads to become the social progress that ultimately forms new norms. Urbane sights that we have come to value as normal or necessary, such as people of the same gender kissing in public, interracial couples walking hand in hand, people with green hair, people wearing sneakers with suits, a young Kevin Bacon dancing in public, or the Pussyhat march on the National Mall— it all had to happen somewhere, because after all what's a rebel without a stage?

THIS IS A BOOK ABOUT DESIGN IN CITIES

and the design of cities. However, much of the way cities are inhabited—what people do with the space after the initial architecture and planning work is done—complicates our linear understanding of how the design professions impact the built environment. Something about cities, and more specifically urbane cities as defined in this book, engenders iconoclasm in a way that suburbs and more homogeneous cities typically do not. Both architecture and the design of public space and infrastructure when more broadly conceived can spark the unexpected. The dimensions and characteristics of a dynamic commons—generous outdoor rooms, lots of spectators and performers, spectators acting as performers, cross-traffic created by the mixing uses and multiple modes of transit, the intersection of different and plural neighborhoods—all conspire to bring our favorite urban public spaces to life as places of unorthodox exchange. This is not design determinism; it is celebratory, open, non-deterministic design that can be co-opted and defined by the public. This is the subtlety of designing spaces of connective potential that build on the richness of their surroundings.

To approach it differently, let's look at sidewalks. Most cities, and even many suburbs, have sidewalks. They are all made of roughly the same material and are usually built in the same dimensional range, and yet do they offer the same platform for iconoclasm? Of course not, because such a platform is fully contingent on who and what goes on around it. This is neither a determinist nor a neutral stance about the importance of design; the truth lies in between. Urban public space, which is sometimes successfully advanced by architecture, has the potential to be a stage for transgressive or countercultural behaviors in a way that architecture conceived in a vacuum simply can't, which in turn connects us to the unexpected—connects us to nature, culture, and joy.

As David Byrne has described, the German poet Hugo Ball in his *Dada Manifesto* of 1916 declared that Dadaism was striving "to remind the world that there are people of independent minds—beyond war and nationalism—who live for different ideals."[1] Ball's poem "Gadji beri bimba," like the Talking Heads song "I Zimbra" it inspired, used nonsense to make sense of a world that didn't make sense.[2] Both Byrne's and Ball's pieces utilize abstract language to deal with the darkness of the world. In the spirit of the Dadaist tradition, they do so in a way that is more celebratory than the nihilism sometimes found in Surrealism or Abstract Expressionism. This is the spirit that separates Dalí from De Chirico or Miró from Munch. In such works we are reminded that humans and the cultures we create are messy, leading us from Ball to Byrne to Bowie: "Rebel rebel, this *place* is a mess."[3] The following illustrations embrace that cheery defiance, celebrating those who joyously appropriate urban space despite the challenges cities and their residents face alongside the exemplary urban spaces that uplift and connect those who appropriate them. Hopefully, they exclaim to their respective subjects, "Hot tramp, I love you so."

34th Street / Herald Square Station, New York

Chicano Park, Barrio Logan, San Diego

Place Georges Pompidou, Paris

HSBC Plaza, Hong Kong

McCarren Park "Pool," Brooklyn

Puente Viaducto, Cochabamba

LOVE Park, Philadelphia

Washington Square, New York

Black Lives Matter Plaza, Washington, D.C.

The LA River, Los Angeles

THE URBAN GARDEN

WE HAVE TAKEN A JOURNEY TOGETHER

through some of the lows of human settlements as they exist today to the highs of the life we could achieve if we connected the collective. As this journey closes, let's return to the question posed at the outset of this book:

What could a global population of ten billion living in harmony with our planet look like by 2100?

Given our limited resources and the need to heal our divisions, it is clear that we must reconceive human habitation around collective communities. I am not advocating for everyone to live in a city; I mean no such thing. Individuals must of course have the inalienable right to live as they please, but the decision to live in sprawl must reflect its true cost to society in terms of pollution, congestion, and land degradation. Would people more easily and more sustainably opt out of suburban life if the monies for free highway networks and great public schools and concentrated mortgage benefits were diverted back to cities, where most people live, and to rural areas, where most of our food is produced? As described in chapter 3, there are equally low carbon emissions per person in our farmland as there are in our big cities—the problem centers on the fully auto-dependent, often segregated, largely subsidized, overly landscaped suburbs that sit between the rural and the urban. By contrast we have seen how rural villages, small townships, academic campuses, and even refugee camps share urbane characteristics with many big cities, a way of living that represents not only a smaller carbon footprint but a larger communal imprint.

The preceding chapters have illustrated specific buildings and territories that invite this broader communal imprint. Some are examples designed by architects at the height of their professions, while others are redefined by everyday people in ways their designers never imagined. For readers it may be difficult to extrapolate these select examples to the larger world. It is wonderful to examine a thriving social housing project or a successful public space as singular highlights, but what could such small glimmers of sun possibly mean for our vast tempest-tossed planet?

Rest assured that larger-scale examples of progressive urban interventions also abound. In the 1990s in Berlin, the Internationale Bau-Ausstellung (IBA) extended the tradition of German social housing exhibitions from suburban sites into inner-city affordable residential with great success.[1] In the year 2000 Bogotá, Colombia, launched the famed TransMilenio, building upon the concept of Bus Rapid Transit (BRT) in dedicated lanes that despite some growing pains has now been emulated worldwide as a model for fast, frugal, and flexible mass transit. For the past several decades forward-thinking Vienna, which by law can operate as an independent political entity from the rest of conservative Austria, has created some of the best and most integrated social housing in the world tied to both affordable transit and culture.[2] Paris is also advancing social housing in its historic core, and, under the leadership of the brilliant and brave Mayor Anne Hidalgo, the city of lights has become the city of bikes, with widespread pedestrianization greening the shores of the Seine. Dallas has built a park and cultural center over one of its freeways, while Madrid has replaced a highway with a linear park. Los Angeles is looking to do the same with its storied riverbed on the heels of one of the biggest subway expansions in the country. London, Stockholm, and New York City charge private vehicles for inner-city use during rush hour. These and many other examples, which together impact the lives of billions, should fuel hope, particularly if they can be better tied to the goals of an architecture of urbanity.

We defined urbanity as a community in which people from many different cultures and classes spatially interact, a condition necessary to promote positive social friction. While many of the interventions above are laudable, most of them are occurring in the wealthiest and least diverse cities on earth, with few reaching a broad span of cultures, classes, and colors. Conversely, mass transit like the TransMilenio, extraordinary as it is, tends not to be patronized by the wealthy, who consequently drive to all of our detriment. (It was the groundbreaking mayor of Bogotá, Enrique Peñalosa, who said "an advanced city is not one where even the poor use cars, but rather one where even the rich use public transport, or bicycles.")[3] All of the projects above speak to building place and honoring planet, but many do not sufficiently encourage pluralistic exchange to the point of engendering shared prosperity.

This is especially problematic not just due to population growth but to mass migrations that will continue to occur as a result of wars, climate change, and poverty. Can the laudable social housing policies of Western European cities hold up under increased immigration from the Global South, or will the pressure to extend those benefits to non-white newcomers trigger the kind of reactionary fascistic reactions we are already witnessing in Italy, France, Germany, and elsewhere on the Continent? Did we all notice the difference in the welcome Ukrainian refugees received versus Syrians in Europe or Venezuelans in the United States? This is precisely why the notion of urbanity, as opposed to the wonderful but limited act of providing benefits to one's existing metropolitan residents and those who look like them, is so crucial in a more populous and multicultural world. It means we must build better cities that are welcoming to all.

The city is narrative, the city is artifact, and in the weaving of the two, the city is transcendent. An architecture of urbanity forged by connective design must channel and be a platform for interaction and desegregation. We rely on this friction, however uncomfortable it may be, to engender a better understanding of one another, of the planet and its ecosystems, of this floating rock that is our one and only home.

Strangers from differing walks of life becoming cognizant of one another in physical space is much like the pulsing of blood cells through the body; it is paramount to what gives our society color and cadence. Just as medical vaccines

Schlangenbader Straße, Berlin; IBA Wien, Vienna; Madrid Rio, Madrid;
Klyde Warren Park, Dallas, Texas (*clockwise from top left*).

Parc Rives de Seine, Paris; TransMilenio BRT System, Bogotá; Metrocable, Medellín;
Citi Bike, New York City (*clockwise from top left*).

paved the path of recovery from the pandemic, we must consider the social vaccines that will allow us to recover culturally from our divisions and regain positive social friction despite the shallow attractions of remote work, which will only serve to segregate and suburbanize us further. But should cities return to the polluted, unequal, segregated, gentrified, infrastructure-impoverished heat islands we called cities prior to 2020? Or should we strive for something better?

In the foregoing pages, I have argued for a different urban future than our immediate past. We have looked to cities dating back to antiquity, cities that existed prior to the automobile, to understand how preindustrial urban morphologies catalyzed human connection and exchange, and we simultaneously must look forward to cities without private automobiles, highways, and the single-occupant vehicle congestion that has partitioned our populations and bathed us in banality. We have focused on examples that have helped us embrace the informal city—not as slums and temporary refugee settlements but as vibrant economies and cultures, in many respects more laudable than the auto-oriented, gentrified, predictable cities we have created as part of the formal economy.

In such a world, we can imagine a relationship between the urban and rural that avoids the hackneyed Machine in the Garden binary of technology versus nature, which culture tends to imagine as our own biblical devolution at the hands of science.[4] Instead, imagine technology and nature as inseparable and co-dependent, such that we allow ourselves to press for our own necessary evolution. In such an evolution, could much-needed investments in infrastructure, social housing, education, and public health systems spawn a concomitant revival of urban and rural economies, systems, and cultures? Could prefabricated timber urbanism, metropolitan agriculture, urban manufacturing, regional logistics, density imbued with biophilia, and ecosystem-based resource management all create equitable urban and rural prosperity such that both emerge stronger? While limited examples of this exist to date, through the lens of Raworth's *Doughnut Economics*, could we imagine a symbiotic rural and urban landscape, a "both-and" dialectic, understood as "rurbanity"? In this construct, the city is not the invader of the so-called natural world but is inextricable from the world a priori—the machine is the garden and the garden is the machine. Envisioned as such, both urban and rural life are the wellsprings of nature, culture, and joy, tributaries to a distant but visible sea of shared global prosperity.

By now, we know the statistics, know the majority of the world lives in urbanized areas, and know there are far more people migrating to cities due to a lack of rural opportunities. But instead of simply knowing and fearing such trends, can we embrace their possibilities, lessons, and cures? Cities and rural areas must not only survive, they must evolve together to achieve both mutual dependence and respect. There never was a Garden of Eden, but could an evolution of "rurbanity" lead us to a Garden of Urban?

The projects highlighted in this volume are not intended to provide a fully resolved view of what such a future, what a *garden of urban*, might offer. They are instead presented as seeds that might grow to inspire a harvest of hope. Absent a comprehensive vision for a sustainable and harmonious planet, we remain hungry. Given that the world indeed feels like it is disintegrating into factions, expansive positive visions of the future are a critical antidote to cynicism and despair. This is true if you are a meta-modernist but also if you are just a normal human being. Positive but not positivist visions of the future give us hope, give us optimism for what our society could become. But in attempting to provide optimistic visions of the future, architects and urbanists must be careful. By calling for such conjectures, I don't refer to absurd propositions like "master" plans for the planet, or what's become known as "PRarchitecture," in which firms posit big global visions for the sake of a public relations boost, most of which offer glossy renderings of tech-built societies that imagine a frictionless, homogenized world. Cities built from scratch are an oxymoron; no matter the quality of the underlying intentions, urbanity is impossible without the accretive nature of time, which is why we have focused on an architecture of urbanity that builds a sense of palimpsest rather than the novelty of the new.

Such are the responsibilities of our endeavors, and we should be humble in the face of them.

This is where narrative, where movies, novels, poems, and video games can also play an outsized role. They can free themselves, and in doing so free us, from the important but constraining exigencies of architecture and urbanism through the generous yet credible use of artistic license. While dystopian visions depicting the future of our planet abound, few pop culture visions offer us a hopeful view of the future in which millions of humans cohabitate in a garden of urban like *Black Panther* (2018) and its sequel, *Wakanda Forever* (2022).[5] Critics Mark Lamster and Alexandra Lange wrote of the story's physical and spiritual center, Wakanda, as they awarded 2018 Urbanist of the Year to its visionary creative force, Hannah Beachler:

> Who built our dream city with shiny, swooping public transportation, a walkable core, and skyscrapers made of brick, concrete and vibranium? Production designer Hannah Beachler, whose Wakandan capital combined Afrofuturism with Zahaphilia. ... A wish for urban planning in the 2020s: that the richness of reference and diversity of experience required to create the fictional Wakanda be reflected in this planning our cities IRL.[6]

For those unfamiliar with the films, it is critical to understand that the Wakandan utopia is fueled by a fictional extraterrestrial element called *vibranium*, which gives its residents unlimited clean energy. Critics could claim that such a vision is unrealistic. Yet given the advances in solar and wind power we have discussed,

as well as the potential for clean nuclear fusion, this feels less fantastical by the day. We have already discovered unlimited clean energy; we are in fact surrounded by vibranium.

But the pull of Wakanda goes well beyond vibranium. The vision is dependent on a healthy society in which differences are celebrated, urban and rural cultures respectfully exist adjacent to one another without a suburban layer between— this was one of the more fascinating urban design juxtapositions in the Wakanda vision—and we live in balanced harmony with the resources of the planet.

Wakanda imagines nature and city woven into a Garden of Urban, but it also conjures a joyous culture that embraces the "both-and" of rurbanity. It is this communal yet frictional spirit—not the vibranium that fuels it—that beckons cross-chested: "Wakanda Forever!"

The enormous hunger for this type of imagination is precisely why the dream of Wakanda's capital created such a stir within and beyond the design and planning disciplines, which is also why this book attempts to speak to readers within and beyond these disciplines. Our society at times feels as though it is on the brink of dystopia. Our world is desperate for the optimism of utopian pragmatists, activist professionals who dream big while sweating the details, who create art that transcends the tired gestalt of the self-absorbed, who go beyond our established notions of diversity by embracing a myriad of mindsets, who dare to design with full knowledge of the problems of the world without succumbing to the cynicism they engender.

Let's maintain this spirit of utopian pragmatism but leave Wakanda, returning our focus to the troubled world we actually inhabit. We know that by 2100 we must design for a world in which ten billion people can live in harmony with the resources of the planet *and* one another.[7] While the good news is that population growth is projected to decelerate substantially by the close of this century due to advances in global prosperity, this outcome still requires that we provide housing supply to meet the demands of two billion additional individuals, as well as those the planet so poorly houses today. Given that the dual forces of global warming and segregationist fascism are already upon us, how can we offer high-quality housing to these billions while advancing the health and pluralism of the planet and its existing populace?

To ask this question is not to be pro-growth or anti-growth—significant population increases are coming regardless of where we stand politically and philosophically; it is not about growth for growth's sake. To house these coming billions, estimates indicate that we will need to construct over 2.4 trillion square feet of new space, which is the equivalent of building an additional New York City every month for the next forty years, although more immigration from the growing Global South to the shrinking Global North would clearly reduce some pressure to build anew. The prospect of so much construction no doubt incenses those concerned with the embodied energy, and to be sure, we should put every effort into adaptively reusing our existing building stock—including reimagining our quickly degrading but largely occupied public housing—wherever possible to accommodate these needs. Obsolete urban office buildings around the world, many of which have reduced demand due to remote work, can be adaptively reused as discussed in chapter 8, but only at considerable expense.

But given the already high levels of housing scarcity for our existing population, in addition to our coming housing needs, it is clear that adaptive reuse will barely make a dent in the supply we require. As discussed in previous chapters, these facts will cause considerable consternation across the political spectrum, but none of us—particularly Westerners, who have so disproportionately used the world's resources—have the right to deny these newcomers the housing, food, clean water, and energy they need to live fulfilling, dignified lives. To the contrary, if we are to stem unbridled global population growth even by 2100, it is in all of our best interests to provide every human with the opportunity to thrive. If we don't, it will be this precise lack of opportunity that will incentivize the poor in agrarian societies with high infant mortality rates and limited women's rights to have more and more children in order to maintain sufficient farmhands. (My family is from a rural village; I am deeply familiar with this tragic dynamic.) A fairer economy that provides social mobility through the aforementioned infrastructure of opportunity is our best hope to break this vicious cycle of unsustainable growth. For architects and urbanists and the decision makers and communities with whom they collaborate, this effort should center on creating attainable social housing and its associated physical, economic, and cultural infrastructure.

So, if we can agree on this set of facts, let's stipulate that we will need to build substantial amounts of new and affordable homes. The question for this author, and really the world, becomes how this new housing can be part of the solution to our global problems rather than exacerbate our immense existing challenges. If these challenges can be vastly oversimplified into two broad categories—global warming and social division—what if new housing could be both carbon negative and socially positive? What if residents could offset the carbon they use while living in a connected manner that is conducive to positive social friction? Furthermore, given the urgency of our challenges, what if we could accomplish these goals through the use of today's technologies, with the vibranium we have at hand?

For example, we already have the means to build carbon-negative housing in terms of offsetting "operational" residential energy needs. Dwellings both

Green Single-Family Home
A single-family home can be
made to be operationally carbon
negative, but in most cases
remain car-dependent.

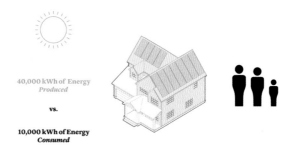

40,000 kWh of Energy
Produced

vs.

10,000 kWh of Energy
Consumed

**Carbon-Negative Towers,
a Dream for Now**
The technologies needed to make
towers fully carbon negative are years
away from widespread adoption,
particularly in the urbanizing parts
of the Global South.

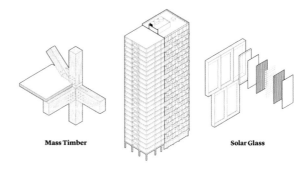

Mass Timber   **Solar Glass**

passively use and actively produce carbon: they contain the *embedded* carbon that
was emitted in the production of their homes and the contents within them,
and they *emit* carbon associated with the power consumption needed for heating,
cooling, and daily operations. (We also emit greenhouse gases in areas unrelated
to energy, particularly the methane associated with the consumption of red meat.
While this is a somewhat separate topic, eat less red meat, people.) In most sunny
climates—and remember, the world is getting hotter and therefore has increased
solar exposure even in more northern latitudes—a single-family home can be made
to be operationally carbon negative in the sense that the energy used by that home's
residents can be supplied, and in many locations surpassed, by readily available
but, ideally, ethically sourced solar power and battery storage. This is possible
because the roof area of most single-family homes is large enough to produce more
energy with solar cells than its residents can consume.

But single-family homes, even if they are green, offer no hope for our
current and future housing challenges. We need policies and design that provide
permanent, dignified dwellings for billions. If we built billions of single-family
homes in response, the resulting sprawl would be horrifying, regardless of how
"sustainable" we make the individual houses. First, the vast majority of single-
family homes are auto-centric, and as we saw in chapter 2—cars, even electric and
autonomous cars—lead us on a road to nowhere due to the space and infrastructure

they demand. Second, even green-washed sprawl leads to a loss of farms, forests, and wetlands, as chapter 3 illustrates. One cannot be pro-suburban and pro-rural at the same time. We have to recognize that suburban is not only different from rural, it is the far greater enemy of the rural than the urban because of its voracious appetite for land. Finally, in terms of the loss of community, a loss of density tends to lead to the social segregation, racial and economic divisions, and social-media bubbles that have brought our societies to the brink of ruination. So while the technologies used to make single-family homes more sustainable offer clues to a better future, our answers clearly lie in a different scale of intervention.

Any good urbanist might surmise that the right answer to housing our coming multitudes is to build towers, but this would be an oversimplification. I love beautiful towers in dense cities—we try to design them at PAU, and I have even been called "Professor Skyscraper." Pioneering architecture and engineering technologies have enabled massive advances in sustainable tower design. Without question, a longer-term sustainable future must include electrified towers built from sustainable materials that rely on clean-energy grids in our existing cities. It is important to continue to build better towers that are transit oriented, socially urban, and technological harbingers of a more sustainable future. As an act of full disclosure, I serve on the board of a start-up company that is making low-emissions concrete using algae, which would allow us to build towers with much lower embodied energy in the future and therefore could be one of many breakthroughs that could lead us to carbon-negative towers someday.

But the challenge for our moment, again returning to the tyranny of today, is that we are decades away from clean grids powered by renewable energy in most of our cities, especially in the very cities where the world's anticipated population growth will take place. Similarly, the much-discussed technologies needed to make our towers more sustainable, such as cross-laminated timber, bio-concrete, and glazing that doubles as solar panels, all represent huge leaps forward that we must continue to explore. They also remain years away from widespread adoption, particularly in the more impoverished but growing regions of our world. At some point our grids will be clean, our building materials will be sustainable, and the investments and investigations we are making in the future of carbon-negative towers today will pay off tomorrow, but we must recognize that they remain a distant dream. In the interim we need more immediate carbon-negative, socially positive solutions to bridge our housing supply needs—particularly in developing nations where most urban growth is happening in the lower-density urban outskirts.

The answer is hiding in plain sight, at a scale that is the sweet spot between houses and towers, a "Goldilocks" density at which we have already built some of the most cherished and joyous parts of our world. From the brownstones of Boston to the hutongs of Beijing, some of our most revered urban housing has been built at a scale of about three stories. At almost fifty units per acre, this size and scale is dense enough to create urban neighborhoods that support light rail or express bus demand, but straightforward enough for almost every society in the world, including our developing nations, to build inexpensively out of local, relatively low embodied-energy materials such as basic wood or brick, all using indigenous labor.

There are taller and denser versions of this typology at five to eight stories tall—Paris and Barcelona offer some of the densest low-rise, high-density housing in the world. However, it is critical to note the shortcomings of this beautiful but outdated form of inner-city European urbanity. Most of that housing is not compliant with existing codes for wheelchair accessibility or modern light and air standards. Modern, code-compliant, shorter versions of this typology exist, particularly in growing cities like Los Angeles and Austin, where we see what is known as "four plus one" housing: four-story, stick-frame residences are built above a concrete plinth that often houses retail and parking. But this housing is actually too dense to be operationally carbon negative using today's technology—there simply isn't enough roof area for the solar panels needed to provide all those residents with the energy they need. Furthermore, such housing demands lots of unsustainable concrete in terms of the plinth, the elevators, and the multiple fire stairs code requires.

By contrast, the Goldilocks scale of three stories can be designed for both operational carbon negativity and low embodied energy at affordable construction costs while offering the social positive friction of connective, transit-based urbanity. Research PAU has conducted with the renowned global engineering firm Thornton Tomasetti clearly indicates that in most sunny climates, solar panels on housing of this scale provide more energy than its residents require, unlike five- to eight-story apartment buildings, which house far more residents than its limited amount of rooftop solar can support. When equipped with today's batteries, electric heat pumps and passive measures for climate control, and composting facilities, such a framework can provide a prototype for dense, equitable, and generous housing for rural main streets, villages in developed and developing nations, and infill sites in cities. As a prototype, this housing can be designed with communities to respond to local climate and character using readily available materials and tectonics that are regionally recognizable. At three stories, but again, no higher, international building code allows housing to be designed with a single communal stair as long as wheelchair-accessible units are provided on the ground floor, alongside retail and other social uses. Elevator shafts and enclosed fire stairs can be eliminated if a building is three stories or fewer, dramatically decreasing the need for our two highest embodied-energy materials: concrete and steel.

In addition to providing much-needed affordable housing, Goldilocks would provide the urbane, connected communities in rural and urban settings that this book has advocated. As stated earlier, such housing is dense enough to activate mass transit such as buses, light rail, bikes, and walking, but even more important than that technocratic performance benefit is the joy of community experience.

Beloved Urban Density

A "Goldilocks" density is evident in some of the most cherished and joyous parts of our world: Center City, Philadelphia, Pennsylvania; Nanluoguxiang Hutong, Beijing, China; Old Havana, Havana, Cuba; Lapa District, Rio de Janeiro, Brazil (*clockwise from top left*).

Hitting the Sweet Spot

Between the House and Tower, the Goldilocks scale—at almost fifty units per acre—enables both carbon-negative and socially positive outcomes, all while using today's technologies and local construction methods.

130,000 kWh of Energy
Produced

vs.

120,000 kWh of Energy
Consumed

Local Materials

Buildings of this scale can be constructed inexpensively out of local, relatively low-embodied-energy materials such as basic wood or brick.

Taller Is Not Always Better
Seven-story housing in Paris does not comply with existing codes for wheelchair accessibility and modern light and air standards, while code-compliant five-story housing in Los Angeles faces challenges in achieving operational carbon negativity.

The Three-Story Advantage
Five-story housing requires large quantities of unsustainable concrete to build the plinth, the elevator shafts, and the multiple fire stairs prescribed by international code, whereas three-story housing can be designed with a single communal stair, as long as the ground floor units are accessible to wheelchairs.

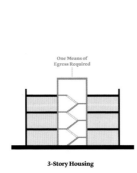

One Means of
Egress Required

3-Story Housing

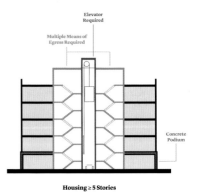

Elevator
Required

Multiple Means of
Egress Required

Concrete
Podium

Housing ≥ 5 Stories

This is a housing prototype that if designed properly, with and in community, can reflect and retain the stories of place, helping to "placekeep" as opposed to "placemake," in the words of Walter Hood. This scale could work equally well in the context of single-family neighborhoods in search of transit-based density (for example, in rail-accessible suburbs seeking to densify) and on the outskirts of big cities.

The opportunities for regional variations abound. For instance, if deployed in the growing outskirts of my home city of Kolkata, where the Metro has already been extended, Goldilocks would likely be designed with brick and limited glazing. The housing would form courtyards that would expel heat, would expand airflow, and would be resplendent with long grasses, lazy cows, cricket-crazed kids, and vendors hawking their wares. But if deployed in the outer boroughs of my other home city of New York, say, in eastern Queens or southeastern Brooklyn, Goldilocks would more likely be built as infill housing out of light-gauge steel and weather-tight windows, forming streetwalls along a city of sidewalks festooned with hot dog carts, hydrants, and hip-hop. In both cases, residents would meet up on that single staircase, and act on concern if they hadn't recently seen an elderly neighbor. Goldilocks is not really new, except for its potential to be carbon negative—a big exception! For decades, many architects and urbanists have

A Climate Asset

The three-story model could become a climate asset, with state-of-the-art battery systems that balance out peaks in solar supply and user demand, electric heat pumps for climate control, and composting facilities.

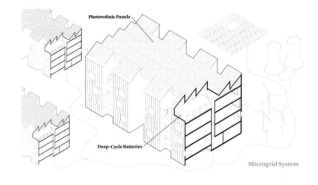

Spacious, Communal, and Equitable

Goldilocks is a flexible transformer with the potential to be collaboratively designed with communities, adapting to local climate and character.

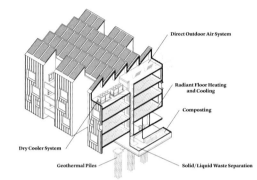

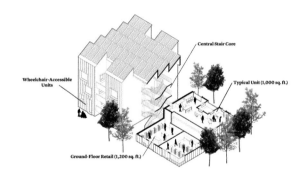

Integration into Existing Communities

It can also serve as the building block for urban sustainability because it is dense enough to support mass transit. Goldilocks can be integrated into the outskirts of cities or in denser rail-based suburbs, with workplaces, parks, schools, and other social infrastructure.

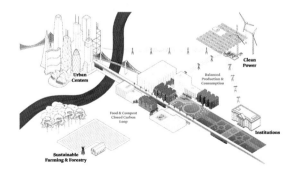

Walkable and Carbon Negative
Goldilocks can house the same number of residents in a walkable and carbon-negative manner, outperforming sprawl and towers.

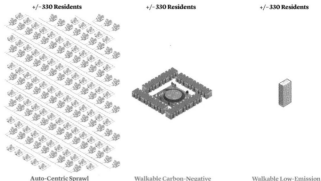

+/- 330 Residents   +/- 330 Residents   +/- 330 Residents

Auto-Centric Sprawl   Walkable Carbon-Negative   Walkable Low-Emission

Climate Responsive
In New York, the three-story model would likely be constructed as infill outer borough housing using lightweight steel studs and weather-tight windows, whereas in Kolkata, it might be designed with brick and limited glazing.

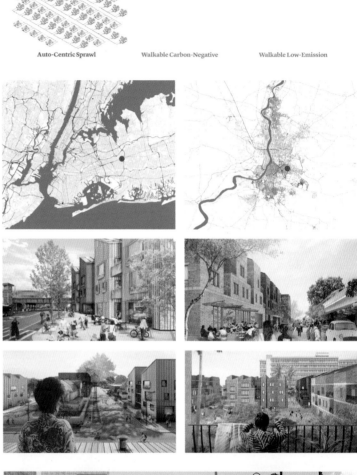

A Better Long Island
In small towns like Bellport, Long Island, Goldilocks could densify areas near commuter stations with simple wood construction.

advocated the value of low-rise, high-density urbanism, but what Goldilocks adds to this somewhat forgotten advocacy is an achievable means to address today's threats to planet and pluralism while amplifying, rather than re-creating, place. If this scale feels too small to you, consider that if all ten billion of us lived like this, we could offset all the carbon emissions of the cars operating today, and we would do so while leaving over 99.5 percent of the world's area for nature, farming, and water.

Interestingly, since we first announced this prototype at a TED conference focused on climate change, we have had innumerable inquiries and possibilities to deploy it in places as far-reaching as western India, Buffalo, New York, and Houston, Texas. We have even proposed it near commuter stations such as in Bellport, New York, a lovely Long Island town served by mass transit but in dire need of density and diversification.

The Goldilocks prototype played a significant role in our third and most recent collaboration with the *New York Times* Opinion section titled "How to Make Room for One Million New Yorkers," which was published in December 2023. New York City is experiencing a severe housing shortage, with residents often spending more than a third of their paychecks on rent, approximately 100,000 (including families and small children) living unhoused on our streets, and a heart-wrenching influx of foreign migrants that sadly has overwhelmed the shelter system. Given the magnitude of the need for affordable and dignified housing for all of these populations, New Yorkers conjure fears of having to live in a forest of skyscrapers to meet the demand. Such concerns freeze the debate and polarize opposing camps, resulting in democratic gridlock and an ever-dwindling housing supply. The two sides in such debates used to be characterized by big developers versus historic preservationists, but thankfully a new progressive youth movement has organized around the need for new homes given the precarity in which they find themselves, which has forged their common cause with the unhoused and international migrants. For most people in our cities today, from nurses and firefighters to former convicts to young college graduates to those who braved the Darién Gap, the rent is just too damn high.

In response to this crisis, the *Times* asked PAU to analyze and imagine how and where to build desperately needed homes across all five boroughs. As urbanist architects, we felt it paramount to do so without substantially altering the character of New York City's neighborhoods or its landmark districts. Using both data analysis and the specific tools of architectural visualization, we were able to prove that New York could add over 520,000 homes—enough to shelter more than 1.3 million new residents—without changing the look and feel of the city. We published a transparent methodology for our work: we excluded land far from mass transit or in flood zones and despite these restrictions found more than 10,000 parcels across 1,700 acres that were either vacant or occupied by single-story retail.

PAU with the *New York Times*, How to Make Room for One Million New Yorkers

Increased height and density are particularly appropriate when commensurate with a neighborhood's existing character. Goldilocks built on an existing vacant lot can house more people than single-family homes in low-rise neighborhoods near mass transit (*top row*). A mid-rise apartment building with a replacement grocery store at the ground floor can add density while preserving neighborhood retail (*middle row*). Strategically placed high-rise apartment buildings would integrate seamlessly into already dense neighborhoods (*third row*). Implementing these strategies citywide, in combination with office-to-residential conversions, could add over 500,000 homes on available parcels that are transit-adjacent and situated outside of future flood zones.

Getting to 500,000
How many housing units our proposed buildings would add.

Mid-rises	336,551
High-rises	93,331
Low-rises	55,056
Office conversions	35,307
Total	**520,245**

Mid-rises wouldn't feel out of place in many parts of the Bronx and Queens.

Almost all of the office conversions we're proposing are in Manhattan.

Residents of high-rises along Atlantic Avenue could easily take the subway to work.

Low-rises near the Staten Island Railway could house thousands more New Yorkers.

Of the half million new homes that could be built on these parcels, over 80 percent were envisioned as low-rise structures akin to Goldilocks or mid-rise apartment buildings. Most of these were located in areas where land cost less and would have the additional advantage of lower construction costs due to their reduced scale, meaning that basic market-based affordability could be achieved for transit-oriented, climate-resilient, middle-class homes with limited government subsidy. Additional public subsidy could be utilized to transform a number of these homes into transitional and supportive housing for the unhoused, the mentally ill, or migrants, including the necessary social services. While we also considered both high-rise construction and office-to-residential conversions that seemed feasible, we found that these together only provided about 20 percent of our housing total. The response to our work from multiple news outlets and civic organizations was tremendous and largely positive, including from community groups often stereotyped as anti-development. The strongest negative reaction came from big New York real estate because of their tendency to focus only on large, lucrative, lobotomized towers.

The positive global response we received indicated not just the strength of the argument but the hunger for design professionals to speak to the issues of our day in collaboration with policymakers, economists, community organizers, and journalists. As discussed earlier, our professions cannot pine for relevance while focusing on the irrelevant—design professionals bring critical expertise to our social and climate challenges, meaning we can lead communities toward an architecture of urbanity if we have the chutzpah to communicate using both sides of our brains.

The architecture of urbanity is social, cultural, and emotional, weaving together our material understanding of the world with its human narratives, advancing a more equitable world for which most of us yearn today, one that reflects the past as it lurches, however imperfectly, forward. Our work is not a panacea; it is just one example of what connective architecture and urban design could be and do for a world in need of social mobility and ecological stewardship, an idea of architecture not as a singular, static object but plural, dynamic seeds in the Garden of Urban.

The art of urban architecture embodies a trajectory in which each artistic invention is built upon the shoulders of the people, places, and cultural advancements that came before it. This archaeological approach to the future is essential to an architecture of urbanity—to celebrating and elevating communities inhabited by people from many different cultures and classes who spatially interact. Otherwise, the elite novelty of object architecture tends to reject rather than embrace communities, causing our fragile world to break through fracture rather than bond through friction.

If the twentieth century was about reinventing the world from scratch, the twenty-first is about reimagining our relationship with the existing world—its climate, its species, its communities, its narratives, its cultures. If the twentieth century was the era of a clean slate that was never clean, the twenty-first is the century of the palimpsest, of the complex layers of history, race, and gender that form the story of our relationships with the natural world, with the past, and with each other as we imagine our collective, connected future.

Yuval Noah Harari tells us that the art of narrative is what distinguishes us as a species.[8] For an architecture of urbanity, narrative—as clearly distinct from historicism, tribalism, or nostalgia—is the through line binding the past, present, and future of the communities that we must together construct. Without a built environment that inspirationally embodies urban narrative through lived experience, we will never achieve the data-driven, technocratic desires to advance equity, the environment, and the economy that are so often voiced.

We should be guardians of the palimpsest, acting as thought partners with the communities and climate we treasure. The allied disciplines of the built environment, including all of us who demand more from our banal physical surroundings, are at the tip of the spear in the fight for an urbane planet imbued with sustainability, social mobility, human agency, pluralistic belonging, and civic delight. Our mission is to create new daily experiences that unearth and amplify the rich wonders of the world's existing tableau, that fill the cultural empathy void we all sense, that generate a connected society and awaken a global calling for planetary stewardship and shared prosperity. It is only then that we can bear the fruits of utopian pragmatism in our garden of urban, with cities and rural life working in harmony in an allied rurbanity, yielding the nature, culture, and joy that can unite and inspire ten billion people on this warm, sweet earth.

The Garden of Urban
Ten billion people can live in harmony
with the planet and each other.

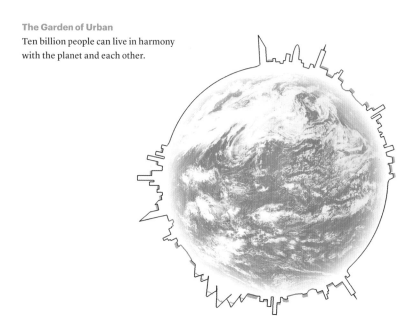

ACKNOWLEDGMENTS

As these pages have, I hope, made clear, architecture is a collaborative discipline requiring the work of many. Writing a book may seem like a more individual endeavor, but it too demands the labor of an expansive collective, particularly when it entails such a wide array of research, viewpoints, and graphics as this project has.

The publishing team at Princeton University Press, led by Michelle Komie, has been nothing short of extraordinary. Michelle believed in this project from the outset and has steadfastly stood by it through pandemics and insurrections, never wavering in her confidence in the long-term merits of these ideas regardless of the turmoil continually presented by global events. Our trust in one another would not have been possible without an introduction arranged by Diana Murphy, my publisher for *A Country of Cities* while she was at Metropolis Books, my friend, and my trusted advisor on this project since its inception. Diana helped form the core proposal for this book, advised on its key concepts, read and edited every word, and has tirelessly worked with my team at PAU to ensure the quality, veracity, and relevance of each concept and image presented herein. Every author should be so lucky as to have the dynamic duo of Michelle and Diana pushing them forward and sticking with them to the finish line.

Pentagram, the esteemed graphic design firm, led by the legendary Michael Bierut and his brilliant colleague Britt Cobb, have given this book energy, beauty, and visual rigor. This same team defined much of the graphic palette for *A Country of Cities* but for this book had the ability to work with complete freedom from cover to cover. Michael and Britt are also responsible for PAU's graphic language—it is a joy to see that language find a through line in this publication. Pentagram's contributions to our firm and my life have been manifold, for which I will forever be grateful.

At PAU we took on this work as we would any project in our office, yet another testament to the "Swiss Army knives" who form our team given their professional dexterity ranging from architecture to research to academic and journalistic publications. In addition to years of my personal time, our team logged over 2,500 hours of work in the creation of this volume—for us, the equivalent of a small architecture project. Beyond the hours, though, was the team's constant thoughtfulness about what content would be the most relevant and impactful. Key to this has been the intensive work of Skylar Bisom-Rapp, our second employee at PAU, a former student of mine, and my teaching and research assistant at Columbia University as we taught Theories of Urban Form together. Skylar is a true genius, and his contributions to this book are too voluminous to outline here; to him, however, I owe a special thanks for helping me formulate the narrative of the book's first chapter, a history we once taught together with glee. Junxi Wu spent, in aggregate, well over twenty weeks of full-time work on the drawings and images in this book—Junxi is as meticulous as he is artistic, creating imagery that is both informative and beguiling, and working tirelessly on all aspects of the book's completion. Maria Lucia Morelli's hours of toil included research verification, translation, and a triple-check of narrative logic. One of our most senior team members, Mark Faulkner, is the author of the explosive color hand sketches that constitute chapter 9; designing with Mark has been one of the great pleasures of my life, and I am forever grateful for his innumerable talents. Past team members and interns who contributed to this publication include Mahdi Sabbagh, Fani Christina Papadopoulou, Fernando Canteli de Castro, Vinayak Portonovo, Caroline Chen, Bennett Adamson, and Will Suzuki. Bryan Dorsey, who has been with me as my right hand since the inception of PAU, has been an extraordinary organizational and steadying force for both our firm and this project. And, finally, nothing our office does, this book included, would be possible without our senior principal, the person who runs our studio day-to-day, Ruchika Modi. Ruchi is the most talented architect with whom I have ever worked, and to her PAU owes so much of its success.

Of course, every PAU team member, past and present, deserves thanks for our studio's work as presented in chapter 8, and to this we must add our gratitude to our collaborators and clients.

I close this book as I opened it, with a dedication to my family. Architecture and writing share certain characteristics, chief among them the gnawing sense that neither is ever complete. My family puts up with my absences, both physical and mental, to do this seemingly endless labor with love, humor, and enthusiasm. May the hopes and dreams this book presents for the world extend to all of our children, for whom we should work harder to bequeath a better planet.

Notes and Illustration Sources

Author's Note

Notes

1 Research from *The Good Life: Lessons from the World's Longest Scientific Study of Happiness* (Simon & Schuster, 2023), Harvard University's Robert Waldinger, MD, and Marc Schulz, PhD, page 29 and page 47. While social connections are clearly possible anywhere, does it not follow that the physical proximity of urbanity—whether in cities or villages—engenders lasting relationships better than the tenuous likes of social media? The research regarding a correlation between improved social connections and urban density is mixed, however the question above pertains to urbanity as defined in this book as opposed to just density.

Introduction: The Excellence of Relevance

Notes

1 United Nations Department of Economic and Social Affairs, *The 2019 Revision of World Population Prospects*, https://www.un.org/en/desa/world-population-projected -reach-98-billion-2050-and-112-billion-2100.

2 United Nations Department of Economic and Social Affairs, Population Division, *World Urbanization Prospects: The 2018 Revision* (New York: United Nations, 2019), https:// population.un.org/wup/publications/Files/WUP2018 -Report.pdf.

3 See, for example, Kevin Lynch, *The Image of the City* (Cambridge, MA: MIT Press, 1960); Kenneth Frampton, "Towards a Critical Regionalism: Six Points for an Architecture of Resistance," in *The Anti-Aesthetic: Essays on Postmodern Culture*, ed. Hal Foster (Port Townsend, WA: Bay Press, 1983), 16–30; Aldo Rossi, *The Architecture of the City* (Cambridge, MA: MIT Press, 1984); and Dolores Hayden, *The Power of Place: Urban Landscapes was Public History* (Cambridge, MA: MIT Press, 1995).

4 See, for example, Jane Jacobs, *The Death and Life of Great American Cities* (New York: Random House, 1961); and Rem Koolhaas, *Delirious New York: A Retroactive Manifesto for Manhattan* (New York: Monacelli Press, 1994).

5 See, for example, Alvin H. Hansen, "The Theory of Technological Progress and the Dislocation of Employment," *American Economic Review* 22, no. 1 (1932): 25–31.

6 See, for example, Edward L. Glaeser, "Sprawl and Urban Growth," in *Handbook of Regional and Urban Economics*, vol. 4, *Cities and Geography*, ed. J. V. Henderson and J. F. Thisse (Amsterdam: North-Holland, 2004), 2481–527, https://doi .org/10.1016/s1574-0080(04)80013-0; Dolores Hayden, *Building Suburbia: Green Fields and Urban Growth, 1820–2000* (New York: Vintage Books, 2003); Ta-Nehisi Coates, "The Case for Reparations," *The Atlantic*, June 2014, https://www .theatlantic.com/magazine/archive/2014/06/the-case-for -reparations/361631/; and Joe T. Darden, Richard Child Hill, June Thomas, and Richard Thomas, *Detroit: Race and Uneven Development* (Philadelphia: Temple University Press, 1987).

7 Daniel Hoornweg, Lorraine Sugar, and Claudia Lorena Trejos Gómez, "Cities and Greenhouse Gas Emissions: Moving Forward," *Environment and Urbanization* 23, no. 1 (April 2011): 207–27.

8 See, for example, David Harvey, *Rebel Cities: From the Right to the City to the Urban Revolution* (London: Verso, 2012); Richard Sennett, "Capitalism and the City," in *The City Reader*, ed. Richard T. LeGates and Frederic Stout (Abingdon: Routledge, 2019), 92–104; and James O'Connor, "On the Two Contradictions of Capitalism," *Capitalism, Nature, Socialism* 2, no. 3 (1991): 11–28.

9 Vishaan Chakrabarti, *A Country of Cities: A Manifesto for an Urban America* (New York: Metropolis Books, 2013).

10 Christian Parreno, *Boredom, Architecture, and Spatial Experience* (London: Bloomsbury, 2021), 13.

11 Peggy Lee, "Is That All There Is?," 1969, track 1 on *Is That All There Is?*, Capitol Records, 1969, LP.

12 See, for example, Ezra Klein, "All Biden Has to Do Now Is Change the Way We Live," *New York Times*, September 11, 2022, https://www.nytimes.com/2022/09/11/opinion /biden-climate-congress-infrastructure.html; Thomas L. Friedman, *Hot, Flat, and Crowded: Why We Need a Green Revolution—and How It Can Renew America* (New York: Farrar, Straus and Giroux, 2008); and Nick Danlag, "Christine Todd Whitman Talks Acting Anew to Confront Climate Change," *Chautauquan Daily*, June 30, 2020, https://chqdaily.com /2020/06/christine-todd-whitman-talks-acting-anew-to -confront-climate-change/.

13 David Ackerly, in discussion with the author, 2020.

14 According to *Merriam-Webster's Dictionary*, "urbanity" is a fifteenth-century term synonymous with "sophistication" and "cosmopolitanism." According to the *Oxford English Dictionary*, "urbanity," a mid-sixteenth-century term of French or Latin origin, can mean either a "courteousness and refinement of manner" or "urban life." According to a 2004 entry in the Urban Dictionary, "urbanity" means "urban lifestyle, attitude."

15 Donald J. Trump, "Inaugural Address," delivered January 20, 2017, U.S. Capitol, Washington, D.C.

16 "Cosmopolis," Oxford Lexico, https://www.dictionary .com/browse/cosmopolis.

17 Global travel was obviously possible prior to capitalism and colonialism, simply not in a manner that was widespread or easily accessible. It is notable, however, that prior to the depredations of the British, Bengal developed one of the largest shipbuilding industries in the world, which along with textiles and trade undergirded South Asia's 27 percent share of global GDP in the 1700s.

18 Kathleen James-Chakraborty, "Beyond Postcolonialism: New Directions for the History of Nonwestern Architecture," *Frontiers of Architectural Research* 3, no. 1 (2014): 1–9.

19 See, for example, Thomas Stackpole, "Content Moderation Is Terrible by Design," *Harvard Business Review*,

November 9, 2022, https://hbr.org/2022/11/content
-moderation-is-terrible-by-design; and Jeremy Merrill and
Will Oremus, "Five Points for Anger, One for a 'Like': How
Facebook's Formula Fostered Rage and Misinformation,"
Washington Post, October 26, 2021, https://www
.washingtonpost.com/technology/2021/10/26/facebook
-angry-emoji-algorithm/.

20 *Schitt's Creek*, created by Dan Levy and Eugene Levy,
aired January 13, 2015, to April 7, 2020, on CBC Television.

21 Angelos Theodorou Angelopoulos, *The Third World and
the Rich Countries: Prospects for the Year 2000* (New York:
Praeger, 1972), 9.

22 Emma Bubola, "Denmark Aims a Wrecking Ball at 'Non-
Western' Neighborhoods," *New York Times*, October 26, 2023,
https://www.nytimes.com/2023/10/26/world/europe
/denmark-housing.html?searchResultPosition=8.

23 See Office of the Federal Register, "Promoting Beautiful
Federal Civic Architecture," Administration of Donald J.
Trump, Executive Order 13967, Office of the Press Secretary:
Federal Register, December 23, 2020; William Hauptman,
"The Suppression of Art in the McCarthy Decade," *Artforum*,
October 1973, https://www.artforum.com/print/197308
/the-suppression-of-art-in-the-mccarthy-decade-37985;
and Greg Barnhisel, ed., *Cold War Modernists: Art, Literature,
and American Cultural Diplomacy* (New York: Columbia
University Press, 2015).

24 Walt Whitman, *Leaves of Grass* (Brooklyn, NY: Self-
published, 1855); Barack Obama, "Remarks by the President
at the Dedication of the National Museum of African
American History and Culture," transcript of speech
delivered at the National Mall, Washington, D.C., September
24, 2016, https://obamawhitehouse.archives.gov/the-press
-office/2016/09/24/remarks-president-dedication-national
-museum-african-american-history.

Illustrations

P. 2 A World of Ten Billion
Data from United Nations, Department of Economic
and Social Affairs, Population Division, *World Population
Prospects 2022, Online Edition*, https://population.un.org
/wpp/, and *World Urbanization Prospects 2022, Online
Edition*, https://population.un.org/wup/

P. 2 A Tale of Two Trends
Data from United Nations, Department of Economic
and Social Affairs, Population Division, *World Population
Prospects 2022, Online Edition*, https://population.un.org
/wpp/

**P. 6 Is that all there is? —Homogeneous Suburbs across
Six Continents**
Google Earth

**P. 6 Is that all there is? —Homogeneous Suburbs across
Six Continents**
Top: panoramarx / Deposit Photos
Top: © Angela Perryman/Dreamstime.com

Top: imagecom/123RF
Bottom left: Kim Petersen/Alamy Stock Photo
Bottom center: mors74/Deposit Photos
Bottom right: MJ_Prototype/iStock

P. 9 Anti-Urbanism in Western Culture
Top: Wiki/Daderot, https://en.m.wikipedia.org/wiki
/File:Sodom_and_Gomorrah_afire,_by_Jacob_Jacobsz
._de_Wet_d._J.,_probably_Köln,_c._1680,_oil_on_canvas
_-_Hessisches_Landesmuseum_Darmstadt_-_Darmstadt
,_Germany_-_DSC01149.jpg, CC0 1.0
Bottom: World History Archive/Alamy Stock Photo

P. 10 The Urbanity of Rural Villages in India
Hari Mahidhar/Dreamstime.com

P. 11 Urbanity Advances Culture
Diagram based on Kōnstantinos Apostolou Doxiadēs,
"The Increasing Problems," in "The Inevitable City," in
Anthropopolis: City for Human Development (New York: W. W.
Norton, 1975), 34–41

P. 12 Small-Town Urbanity
Top: Greater Patchogue Chamber of Commerce
Center: © Bobhilscher/Dreamstime.com
Bottom: Serhii Chrucky/Dreamstime.com

Chapter 1: From Here to Banality
Notes

1 Maya Angelou, "One of the Most Important Lessons Dr.
Maya Angelou Ever Taught Oprah," interview by Oprah
Winfrey, *The Oprah Winfrey Show*, May 19, 2014, https://
www.youtube.com/watch?v=nJgmaHkcFP8.

2 The roots of this chapter lie in Theories of Urban Form, a
course I developed and taught with my PAU colleague Skylar
Bisom-Rapp at Columbia University's Graduate School for
Architecture, Planning, and Preservation between 2016 and
2019. That class owed a great debt to a similar course, offered
at MIT, originally taught by Kevin Lynch, which I took as a
graduate student with Professor Julian Beinart, as well as
a course titled The City, taught by Professor Ananya Roy,
which Skylar took with her at the University of California,
Berkeley. The historic arc outlined in the following pages
is built on the foundation provided by Professors Lynch,
Beinart, and Roy, as well as the lively discussion and
participation of the students who took our iteration of the
class, with particular acknowledgments owed to Michael
(Jong Won) Choi, Julie Pedtke, Leonardo Tamargo Niebla,
Britta Ritter-Armour, Mayrah Udvardi, and Luis Sebastián
Ugás for their contributions.

3 Renia Ehrenfeucht and Anastasia Loukaitou-Sideris,
Sidewalks: Conflict and Negotiation over Public Space
(Cambridge, MA: MIT Press, 2009), 15.

4 George Dalton, "A Note of Clarification on Economic
Surplus," *American Anthropologist* 62, no. 3 (1960): 483–90.

5 Thomas B. Edsall, "How a 'Golden Era for Large Cities'
Might Be Turning into an 'Urban Doom Loop,'" *New York
Times*, November 30, 2022, https://www.nytimes.com

/2022/11/30/opinion/covid-pandemic-cities-future
.html.

6 CBRE, "Covid-19 Impact on Resident Migration Patterns" (CBRE, 2021), 5, https://www.cbre.com/insights/reports /covid-19-impact-on-migration-patterns.

7 See, for example, Joseph Rykwert, *The Idea of a Town: The Anthropology of Urban Form in Rome, Italy, and the Ancient World* (Princeton: Princeton University Press, 1986); Kevin Lynch, *A Theory of Good City Form* (Cambridge, MA: MIT Press, 1981); Spiro Kostof, *The City Shaped: Urban Patterns and Meanings through History* (Boston: Bulfinch Press, 1991); and Richard Sennett, *The Conscience of the Eye: The Design and Social Life of Cities* (New York: W. W. Norton, 1990).

8 Julian Beinart, "Normative Theory II: The City as Machine," Lecture 3, MIT 4.241J Theory of City Form, Spring 2013, YouTube MIT OpenCourseWare, June 30, 2014, https://www.youtube.com/playlist?list =PLUl4u3cNGP63hVXZEMszpS_CWvUFsURr6.

9 Stanford Anderson, "The Plan of Savannah and Changes of Occupancy during Its Early Years: City Plan as Resource," *Harvard Architecture Review* 2 (Spring 1981): 60–67.

10 Mabel O. Wilson, "Notes on the Virginia Capitol: Nation, Race, and Slavery in Jefferson's America," in *Race and Modern Architecture: A Critical History from the Enlightenment to the Present*, ed. Irene Cheng, Charles L. Davis II, and Mabel O. Wilson (Pittsburgh: University of Pittsburgh Press, 2020), 37.

11 David Harvey, "The Organization of Space Relations," in *Paris, Capital of Modernity* (New York: Routledge, 2003), 102–12.

12 Eduardo Aibar and Wiebe E. Bijker, "Constructing a City: The Cerdà Plan for the Extension of Barcelona," *Science, Technology, & Human Values* 22, no. 1 (1997): 3–30, http:// www.jstor.org/stable/689964.

13 Montserrat Pallares-Barbera, Anna Badia, and Jordi Duch, "The Need for a New City and Service Provision," *Urbani Izziv* 22, no. 2 (December 2011): 122–36.

14 David Roberts, "Barcelona's Superblocks Are a New Model for 'Post-Car' Urban Living," *Vox*, April 11, 2019, https://www.vox.com/energy-and-environment/2019 /4/11/18273896/barcelona-spain-politics-superblocks.

15 *The Age of Innocence*, dir. Martin Scorsese (Columbia Pictures, 1993).

16 Rem Koolhaas, *Delirious New York: A Retroactive Manifesto for Manhattan* (New York: Monacelli Press, 2014), 21.

17 Richard Howe, "Notes on 19th Century Lot Sizes," *Built Environment* (blog), Gotham Center for New York City History, November 15, 2012, https://www.gothamcenter .org/blog/notes-on-19th-century-lot-sizes.

18 Donald L. Miller, *City of the Century: The Epic of Chicago and the Making of America* (Chicago: Simon & Schuster, 1996).

19 Curbed Staff, "The Equitable Building and the Birth of NYC Zoning Law," *Curbed New York*, March 13, 2013, https:// ny.curbed.com/2013/3/15/10263912/the-equitable -building-and-the-birth-of-nyc-zoning-law.

20 Le Corbusier, *When the Cathedrals Were White*, trans. Francis E. Hyslop Jr. (New York: McGraw-Hill, 1964), 90.

21 Le Corbusier, *The Athens Charter*, trans. Anthony Eardley (New York: Grossman Publishers, 1973).

22 Le Corbusier and Pierre Jeanneret, *Le Corbusier and Pierre Jeanneret, Oeuvre complète*, vol. 1, *1910–1929*, ed. Oscar Stonorov and Willy Boesiger (Basel: Birkhäuser, 2013), 109–17.

23 Ibid., 118–19.

24 Le Corbusier, *When the Cathedrals Were White*, 37.

25 See, for example, Jane Jacobs, *The Death and Life of Great American Cities* (New York: Vintage Books, 1992); and Jane Jacobs, *The Economy of Cities* (New York: Vintage Books, 1970).

26 Saskia Sassen, *The Global City: New York, London, Tokyo* (Princeton: Princeton University Press, 2001).

27 North Carolina State University, "Mayday 23: World Population Becomes More Urban than Rural," *ScienceDaily*, May 25, 2007, http://www.sciencedaily.com/releases/2007 /05/070525000642.htm.

28 See, for example, Will Dunham and Jonathan Oatis, "Despite Recent Uptick, New York City Crime Down in the Past Decades," Reuters, April 13, 2022, https://www.reuters .com/world/us/despite-recent-uptick-new-york-city-crime -down-past-decades-2022-04-12/.

29 CBRE, "Covid-19 Impact on Resident Migration Patterns," 5.

30 Krittivas Mukherjee, "Massive Migration Pushes India's Cities to the Brink," Reuters, January 20, 2007, https://www .reuters.com/article/uk-cities-india-mumbai /massive-migration-pushes-indias-cities-to-the-brink -idUKDEL28784020061211.

31 *Parasite*, dir. Bong Joon-Ho (CJ Entertainment, 2019).

32 David W. Dunlap, "Blocks: Unheard Voices on Planning New Trade Center," *New York Times*, October 16, 2003, https://www.nytimes.com/2003/10/16/nyregion/blocks -unheard-voices-on-planning-new-trade-center.html.

33 Laurie Anderson, "The Dream Before," 1989, track 8 on *Strange Angels*, Warner Brothers Records, 1989, CD.

34 Shane O'Mara, *In Praise of Walking* (San Francisco: W. W. Norton, 1942).

Illustrations

P. 21 The Century Begins
Wiki/Unesco, https://commons.wikimedia.org/wiki /File:Smaller-Buddha-of-Bamiyan-before-and-after-3.jpg, CC BY-SA 3.0 IGO. Left image: Hackin M., Godard A., and Godard Y. Right image: Alessandro Balsamo of UNESCO, edits by User:BevinKacon

P. 22 Streets Predate Cars
Wiki/Dvortygirl, https://commons.wikimedia.org/wiki /File:Wheel_ruts_Pompeii.JPG, CC BY-SA 4.0

P. 22 This Is Not a Street
Wiki/U, https://commons.wikimedia.org/wiki/File:Bus _Hwy_121_south_from_IH35E_south.jpg, CC BY-SA 2.5

P. 24–25 A Select History of Urban Morphology
Top row, left to right: "Form and Meaning in the Earliest Cities: A New Approach to Ancient Urban Planning," Michael E. Smith, *Journal of Planning History* (2007) 6: 3, DOI : 10.1177/1538513206293713, https://faculty.washington.edu /plape/citiesaut11/readings/Journal of Planning History -2007-Smith-3-47.pdf; Wellcome Collection; https://doi .org/10.1371/journal.pone.0231529.g003; Figure from Representation of the spatio-temporal narrative of *The Tale of Li Wa*, April 2020, PLoS ONE 15(4):e0231529 DOI:10.1371 /journal.pone.0231529, License CC BY; Wiki/H. Ling Roth, https://commons.wikimedia.org/wiki/File:H._Ling_Roth _-_Benin_City_1897.pn; Rainer Zenz/Wiki, https://commons .wikimedia.org/wiki/File:Idealstadt.jpg; Wiki https:// commons.wikimedia.org/wiki/File:Giovanni_Battista_Nolli -Nuova_Pianta_di_Roma_%281748%29_05-12.JPG; Wiki /Andriveau-Goujon, David Rumsey Historical Map Collection, https://commons.wikimedia.org/wiki /File:Andriveau-Goujon,_Plan_d%27ensemble_des_travaux _de_Paris,_1868_-_David_Rumsey.jpg; Wiki, https:// commons.wikimedia.org/wiki/File:Garden_Cities _of_Tomorrow,_No._2.jpg; https://archimaps.tumblr .com/post/7539129658/tony-garniers-sketch-for-his -cit%C3%A9-industrielle.; Radburn Association, https:// peregrinenationdotcom.files.wordpress.com/2015/12/site .jpg; © The Frank Lloyd Wright Fdn, AZ / Art Resource, NY © 2024 Frank Lloyd Wright Foundation. All Rights Reserved. Licensed by Artists Rights Society; Duany Plater-Zyberk and Company (DPZ) and Arquitectonica; Courtesy SOM
Bottom row, left to right: Reproduced with permission of The Licensor through PLSCLear; Frederik Pöll; Jesper Nielsen and Christophe Helmke, "Reinterpreting the Plaza de los Glifos, La Ventilla, Teotihuacan," *Ancient Mesoamerica*, December 2011 © Cambridge University Press, reproduced with permission; Tracy Miller, *Of Palaces and Pagodas: Palatial Symbolism in the Buddhist Architecture of Early Medieval China*, Frontiers of History in China, 2015; Wiki/Guillermo Ramos Flamerich, https://commons.wikimedia.org/wiki/File:First _Map_of_Caracas_1578.jpg; Wiki/Moss Eng. Co., NY, https:// commons.wikimedia.org/wiki/File:Savannah_cityplan_1818 .jpg; https://commons.wikimedia.org/wiki/File :NYCGRID-1811.png; VM/BT / Alamy Stock Photo; Wiki, https://ca.wikipedia.org/wiki/Fitxer:PlaCerda1859b.jpg; © F.L.C. / ADAGP, Paris / Artists Rights Society (ARS), New York 2024; New York (N.Y.). Department of Parks. https:// commons.wikimedia.org/wiki/File:30_years_of _progress,_1934-1964_-_Department_of_Parks_-_300th _anniversary_of_the_City_of_New_York_-_New_York_World's _Fair._(1964)_(16478136350).jpg; © 1975 John Portman and Associates. All rights reserved; Foster + Partners; courtesy SCAPE

P. 27 Homo Sapiens Generated Material Surplus
Christian Jegou/Science Photo Library

P. 28 The Cardo and Decumanus Unify an Empire

Top left: *The Augustan Temple and Forum of the Colony of Barcino: A 90 Degree Turn*, Author: Ada Cortés, Hector A. Orengo Publication: *Oxford Journal of Archaeology* Publisher: John Wiley and Sons Date: Jan 8, 2014 © 2014 The Authors. *Oxford Journal of Archaeology* published by John Wiley & Sons Ltd.
Top right: Bibliothèque nationale de France
Bottom left: Private Collection Look and Learn/Peter Jackson Collection/Bridgeman Images
Bottom right: Wiki/Frederik Pöll, https://commons .wikimedia.org/wiki/File:Timgad_-_Expansion_in_2nd_and _3rd_Century.jpg, CC BY-SA 3.0

P. 29 East Facade of the Louvre (1667–74)
Jean-Pierre Dalbéra/Flickr, https://www.flickr.com/photos/ dalbera/4793076608/, https://creativecommons.org /licenses/by/2.0/

P.29 Jacques-Louis David, *Oath of the Horatii* (1784)
Wiki, https://commons.wikimedia.org/wiki /File:Jacques-Louis_David,_Le_Serment_des_Horaces.jpg

P. 30 The Oglethorpe Plan for Savannah, Georgia (1733)
National Gallery of Art, Washington

P. 30 The Jeffersonian Grid Unifies a Nation
Top: Wiki/NASA, https://commons.wikimedia.org/wiki /File:Crops_Kansas_AST_20010624.jpg
Bottom: Wiki/US Interior Bureau of Land Management, https://commons.wikimedia.org/wiki /File:Theoreticaltownshipmap.gif

P. 32 Cerdà's Studies of Block Chamfers
Wiki https://commons.wikimedia.org/wiki /File:CruillesCerda.jpg

P. 34 The Logic of Nineteenth-Century New York City
Bottom Left: Tetra Images/Alamy Stock Photo
Bottom right: https://commons.wikimedia.org/wiki /File:NYC-GRID-1811.png

P. 35 The Industrial Era Trifecta That Transformed the World
Left: Historical Society of Greenfield, Ohio
Center: The Reading Room/Alamy Stock Photo
Right: Wiki, https://commons.wikimedia.org/wiki /File:Framework_of_Flatiron_Building.jpg

P. 36 The Chicago School
Left: Library of Congress Prints and Photographs Division Washington, D.C.: HABS ILL,16-CHIG,65—1
Center: Library of Congress Prints and Photographs Division Washington, D.C.: HABS ILL,16-CHIG,88—1
Right: Library of Congress Prints and Photographs Division Washington, D.C.:HABS ILL,16-CHIG,30—3

P. 36 Chicago's "Goldilocks" Block Size Compared to Those of Other Cities
Diagram based on imagery and data from Google Maps

P. 37 The Equitable Building and the Origins of U.S. Zoning
Left: Library of Congress Prints and Photographs Division

Washington, D.C. 20540, U.S. GEOG FILE—New York—New York City—Equitable Building

Right: Wiki, https://commons.wikimedia.org/wiki /File:Drawing,_Study_for_Maximum_Mass_Permitted _by_the_1916_New_York_Zoning_Law,_Stage_1,_1922 _(CH_18468711).jpg, Used with permission from Ropes & Gray LLP

P. 38 Twentieth-Century Buildings Crowbarred into Small Nineteenth-Century Blocks

Illustrations based on imagery from Google Earth

P. 39 "Death Avenue"

New York Central photo, Kalmbach Media collection

P. 39 Le Corbusier on New York

© F.L.C./ ADAGP, Paris/Artists Rights Society (ARS), New York, 2024

P. 39 The Modernist Movement in the Machine Age

Top left: © akg-images/arkivi

Top right: Wiki/Arturdiasr, https://commons.wikimedia .org/wiki/File:Planalto_Central_(cropped).jpg, CC BY-SA 4.0

Bottom: Wiki/Museum of Fine Arts Lyon, https://commons .wikimedia.org/wiki/File:Garnier-Tony,_Cité _industrielle,_usine_métallurgique.jpg, CC BY-SA 4.0

P. 40 Le Corbusier, Plan Voisin

© F.L.C./ ADAGP, Paris/Artists Rights Society (ARS), New York, 2024

P. 40 Le Corbusier, Plan Obus

© F.L.C./ ADAGP, Paris/Artists Rights Society (ARS), New York, 2024

P. 40 Gustav Klimt, Beethoven Frieze (1902)

Ian Dagnall Computing/Alamy Stock Photo

P. 41 "Ornament Is Crime"

Top: Wiki/Museum of Fine Arts Lyon, https://commons .wikimedia.org/wiki/File:Garnier-Tony,_Cité_industrielle, _usine_métallurgique.jpg, CC BY-SA 4.0 39 bottom; Wiki/© C.Stadler/Bwag, or © C.Stadler/Bwag, https://commons .wikimedia.org/wiki/File:Wien_-_Österreichische _Postsparkasse,_Georg-Coch-Platz.JPG, CC-BY-SA-4.0

Upper center: Granger Archive

Bottom: eSeL.at/Harald Gögele

P. 41 Berlin of "Germania"

Bundesarchiv, Bild 146III-373

P. 42 Urbanity Strikes Back

Composite image left to right: Library of Congress, Reproduction number LC-USZ62-42768; Wiki/Bibliothèque nationale de France, https://commons.wikimedia.org /wiki/File:Georges-Eugène_Haussmann_-_BNF_Gallica .jpg; Nationaal Archief, CC0, 916-9288; Everett Collection Inc / Alamy Stock Photo; Library of Congress Prints and Photographs Division Washington, D.C., 20540, LC-USZ-62-137838; MediaPunch Inc/Alamy Stock Photo

P. 42 Saskia Sassen and the Global City

Left: Wiki/Luckycolours, https://en.wikipedia.org /wiki/File:Jamestown_harbour_canary_view.jpg

Center: Wiki/Shampoorobot, https://commons.wikimedia

.org/wiki/File:Roppongi_Hills_2013-12-01.jpg, CC BY-SA 3.0

Right: Bill Benzon

P. 43 (Sub)urbanization

Top: RoschetzkyIstockPhoto/iStock

Center: Jan-Otto/iStock

Bottom: Ranimiro Lotufo Neto/iStock

P. 44 The Demand for Space

Diagram based on apartment floor plans of Liberty View, New York, NY, and 15 Hudson Yards, New York, NY

P. 45 The Wealth Gap of Mumbai

Dmitry Rukhlenko—Photos of India/Alamy Stock Photo

P. 45 *Parasite*

© 2019 CJ ENM Corporation, Barunson E&A, all rights reserved

P. 46 Homogenized Cities Formed by Well-Intentioned Codes

Top left: Wiki, https://commons.wikimedia.org/wiki /File:Antiguo_ascensor_presidencial,_Casa_Rosada_03.jpg, CC BY 2.5 AR

Top middle: Yadid Levy/Alamy Stock Photo

Top right: corinnetje/Pixabay

Upper center left: jewhyte/Deposit Photos

Upper center right: Crater Valley/Deposit Photos

Lower center left: Phillip Minnis/Deposit Photos

Lower center right: Chunyip Wong/iStock

Bottom left: Andrey Khrobostov/Alamy Stock Photo

Bottom right: Wiki / Epizentrum, https://commons .wikimedia.org/wiki/File:Frankfurt_Hainer _Weg_24.20130512.jpg, CC BY-SA 3.0

P. 47 This Is Not the Density We Are Looking For

Wiki/Godsfriendchuck, https://commons.wikimedia.org /wiki/File:Madison_Square_Park_Tower_February_2017.jpg, CC BY-SA 4.0

P. 48 Building Codes: The Wrong Tools for the Right Battles

Top right: Scewo

Top left, bottom left: Image from K. E. Hedges, *Architectural Graphic Standards*, Wiley 2017. Used with permission

Bottom right: Maxim Zmeyev/Reuters

P. 49 J. Max Bond Jr.

Todd France

P. 49 Paul Klee, *Angelus Novus* (1920)

Heritage Image Partnership Ltd./Alamy Stock Photo

Chapter 2: Rage against the Machine Illustrations

PP. 52–53 Car Commuting Kills

Top left: Data from World Health Organization, *Global Health Estimates 2020: Deaths by Cause, Age, Sex, by Country and by Region, 2000-2019* (Geneva: World Health Organization, 2020), https://www.who.int/data/gho/data /themes/mortality-and-global-health-estimates/ghe -leading-causes-of-death

Bottom left: Data from World Health Organization, *Global*

Health Estimates 2020: Deaths by Cause, Age, Sex, by Country and by Region, 2000–2019 (Geneva: World Health Organization, 2020), https://www.who.int/data/gho /data/themes/mortality-and-global-health-estimates/ghe -leading-causes-of-death; and Dong E, Du H, Gardner L, "An Interactive Web-based Dashboard to Track COVID-19 in Real Time," *Lancet Inf Dis*, 20, no. 5 (May 2020): 533–34
Top right: Data from Christine M. Hoehner, Carolyn E. Barlow, Peg Allen, Mario Schootman, "Commuting Distance, Cardiorespiratory Fitness, and Metabolic Risk," *American Journal of Preventive Medicine*, 42, no. 6 (June 2012): 571–78
Bottom right: Data from Erika Sandow, "Til Work Do Us Part: The Social Fallacy of Long-Distance Commuting," *Urban Studies*, vol. 51, no. 3 (February 2014): 526–43

PP. 54–55 Correlation between Traffic and Health Hazards
Data from U.S. Environmental Protection Agency, *EJScreen, 2019 Version* (Washington, DC: U.S. Environmental Protection Agency, 2023), https://www.epa.gov/ejscreen /download-ejscreen-data

P. 56 Hastings Street/Chrysler Freeway
Top, center: Detroit Historical Society
Bottom: © Jacques Demêtre and Marcel Chauvard/Soul Bag Archives

P. 57 Cypress Street/Cypress Freeway
Top: KK Levine
Center: Oakland Tribune/Oakland Museum
Bottom: Oakland Tribune/Oakland Museum

PP. 58–59 Induced Demand and Car's Erasure of City Fabric
Left: Adapted from June Manning Thomas, et al. *Mapping Detroit: Land, Community, and Shaping a City* (Detroit, MI: Wayne State University Press, 2015)
Right: Diagram based on aerial imagery from Google Maps and data from Max Brantley, "Freeways: Widen Them and Traffic Moves Slower," *Arkansas Times*, January 5, 2016, https://arktimes.com/arkansas-blog/2016/01/05/freeways -widen-them-and-traffic-moves-slower

PP. 60–61 Negative Impacts of Daily Car Use
Top left: Data from Intergovernmental Panel on Climate Change, *Climate Change 2014: Mitigation of Climate Change. Contribution of Working Group III to the Fifth Assessment Report of the Intergovernmental Panel on Climate Change* (Cambridge, UK, and New York, NY: Cambridge University Press, 2014), https://www.ipcc.ch/site/assets/uploads/2018 /02/ipcc_wg3_ar5_full.pdf
Bottom left: Data from U.S. Environmental Protection Agency, "Sources of Greenhouse Gas Emissions," November 2023, https://www.epa.gov/ghgemissions/sources -greenhouse-gas-emissions; and U.S. Environmental Protection Agency, "Fast Facts on Transportation Greenhouse Gas Emissions," October 2023, https://www .epa.gov/greenvehicles/fast-facts-transportation -greenhouse-gas-emissions

Top right: Data from Bushman, Barbara A., "FACSM, ACSM -CEP, ACSM-EP, ACSM-CPT Metabolic Calculations in Action: Part 1", *ACSM's Health & Fitness Journal*, 5/6, volume 24, issue 3 (2020): 6-10; European Cyclists' Federation, "Cycle More Often 2 Cool Down Planet: Quantifying CO2 Savings from Cycling," November 2011, https://www .ecf.com/groups/cycle-more-often-2-cool-down-planet -quantifying-co2-savings-cycling; Chester Mikhail and Arpad Horvath, *Life-cycle Energy and Emissions Inventories for Motorcycles, Diesel Automobiles, School Buses, Electric Buses, Chicago Rail, and New York City Rail* (United States: UC Berkeley Center for Future Urban Transport, 2009); and U.S. Department of Transportation, Federal Transit Administration, "Public Transportation's Role in Responding to Climate Change," January 2010,https://www.transit.dot. gov/sites/fta.dot.gov/files/docs/PublicTransportationsRole InRespondingToClimateChange2010.pdf
Bottom right: Data from Intergovernmental Panel on Climate Change, *Climate Change 2014: Mitigation of Climate Change. Contribution of Working Group III to the Fifth Assessment Report of the Intergovernmental Panel on Climate Change* (Cambridge, UK, and New York, NY: Cambridge University Press, 2014), https://www.ipcc.ch/site/assets /uploads/2018/02/ipcc_wg3_ar5_full.pdf; and Susan E. Williams, Stacy Cagle Davis, and Robert Gary Boundy, *Transportation Energy Data Book*, Edition 36, (United States: Oak Ridge National Laboratory [ORNL], 2017)

PP. 62–63 New Mobility Technologies
Left: Data from Union of Concerned Scientists, "Ride-Hailing Climate Risks," https://www.ucsusa.org/resources /ride-hailing-climate-risks; Irene Michelle Berry, "The Effects of Driving Style and Vehicle Performance on the Real-World Fuel Consumption of U.S. Light-Duty Vehicles," graduate thesis, Massachusetts Institute of Technology, 2010, https://web.mit.edu/sloan-auto-lab/research /beforeh2/files/IreneBerry_Thesis_February2010.pdf; Commute Seattle, "Commute Seattle Toolkit: Chapter 1," 2017, https://www.commuteseattle.com/wp-content /uploads/2017/03/CSToolkit_TBT_Ch1.pdf; Cooney & Conway, "Advantages and Disadvantages of Ridesharing," https://www.cooneyconway.com/blog/advantages-and -disadvantages-ridesharing; Kevin Luttrell, Michael Weaver, and Mitchel Harris, "The Effect of Autonomous Vehicles on Trauma and Health Care," *Journal of Trauma and Acute Care Surgery*, 79, no. 4 (October 2015): 678-82; Aggelos Soteropoulos, Martin Berger, and Francesco Ciari, "Impacts of Automated Vehicles on Travel Behaviour and Land Use: An International Review of Modelling Studies," *Transport Reviews*, 39 (2019): 29-49; and International Energy Agency, *Global EV Outlook 2020* (Paris: IEA, 2020), https://www.iea .org/reports/global-ev-outlook-2020
Right: Ride-hailing data from Schaller Consulting, "Unsustainable? The Growth of App-Based Ride Services and Traffic, Travel and the Future of New York City,"

February 27, 2017, http://schallerconsult.com/rideservices/unsustainable.pdf

PP. 64–65 Life-cycle Carbon Comparison between Private Car and Subway
Data from Chester Mikhail and Arpad Horvath, *Life-cycle Energy and Emissions Inventories for Motorcycles, Diesel Automobiles, School Buses, Electric Buses, Chicago Rail, and New York City Rail* (Berkeley, CA: UC Berkeley Center for Future Urban Transport, 2009), https://escholarship.org/uc/item/6z37f2jr; and International Council on Clean Transportation (ICCT), "Global LCA Passenger Cars," July, 2021, https://theicct.org/wp-content/uploads/2022/01/Global-LCA-passenger-cars-FS-EN-jul2021.pdf

P. 66 "Gehzeug" or "Walkmobile" Used at a Protest in Thailand
Guenter Emberger/TU Institute, courtesy of Hermann Knoflacher

P. 68 Pregerson Interchange Los Angeles, CA
Google Earth

P. 69 Centro Storico Florence, Italy
Google Earth

PP. 70–71 New York City's Space Dedicated to Cars
Diagram based on aerial imagery from Google Earth and data from New York City Department of City Planning, "PLUTO: MapPLUTO," 2020, https://www1.nyc.gov/site/planning/data-maps/open-data/dwn-pluto-mappluto.page

P. 72 Re-imagining FDR Dr. New York, USA
Renderings by PAU based on imagery from Google Earth

P. 73 Re-imagining 46th St. New York, USA
Renderings by PAU based on imagery from Google Earth

Chapter 3: As the World Burns
Notes
1 Sabrina Zwick, "Suburban Living Really Is the Absolute Worst for Carbon Emissions," *Fast Company*, July 8, 2021, https://www.fastcompany.com/90652943/suburban-living-really-is-the-absolute-worst-for-carbon-emissions; and Robert Sanders, "Suburban Sprawl Cancels Carbon-Footprint Savings of Dense Urban Cores," *Berkeley News*, January 6, 2014, https://news.berkeley.edu/2014/01/06/suburban-sprawl-cancels-carbon-footprint-savings-of-dense-urban-cores.
2 Yuval N. Harari, *Sapiens: A Brief History of Humankind* (New York: Harper, 2014).
3 James Irungu Mwangi, "Africa's Great Carbon Valley—and How to End Energy Poverty," video recording of talk delivered at TED Countdown Talk New York Session, June 14, 2022, https://www.ted.com/talks/james_irungu_mwangi_africa_s_great_carbon_valley_and_how_to_end_energy_poverty.
4 Jeffrey D. Sachs, *The End of Poverty: Economic Possibilities for Our Time* (London: Penguin Books, 2005).
5 Kate Raworth, *Doughnut Economics: Seven Ways to Think Like a 21st-Century Economist* (White River Junction, VT:

Chelsea Green Publishing, 2017), 254.
6 Albert Arnold Gore Jr. (former vice president), in discussion with the author, April 13, 2018.
7 Denise Lu and Christopher Flavelle, "Rising Seas Will Erase More Cities by 2050, New Research Shows," *New York Times*, October 29, 2019, https://www.nytimes.com/interactive/2019/10/29/climate/coastal-cities-underwater.html.
8 Olivia Lazard, "The Green Sport of the Green Energy Transition," video recording of talk delivered at TED Countdown Talk New York Session, June 14, 2022, https://www.ted.com/talks/olivia_lazard_the_blind_spots_of_the_green_energy_transition.
9 Steven Pinker, "Wealth," in *Enlightenment Now: The Case for Reason, Science, Humanism, and Progress* (New York: Penguin Books, 2018), note 18.
10 David Wallace-Wells, "The Uninhabitable Earth," *New York Magazine*, July 10, 2017, https://nymag.com/intelligencer/2017/07/climate-change-earth-too-hot-for-humans.html.
11 Tess Riley, "Just 100 Companies Responsible for 71% of Global Emissions, Study Says," *The Guardian*, July 10, 2017, https://www.theguardian.com/sustainable-business/2017/jul/10/100-fossil-fuel-companies-investors-responsible-71-global-emissions-cdp-study-climate-change.
12 Sandra Laville, "Top Oil Firms Spending Millions Lobbying to Block Climate Change Policies, Says Report," *The Guardian*, March 22, 2019, https://www.theguardian.com/business/2019/mar/22/top-oil-firms-spending-millions-lobbying-to-block-climate-change-policies-says-report.

Illustrations
P. 76 Humankind's Greenest Invention
Top left: Wiki/Estial, https://commons.wikimedia.org/wiki/File:Hong_Kong_Skyscrapers.jpg, CC BY-SA 4.0
Top right: Wiki/Yodalica, https://commons.wikimedia.org/wiki/File:Tokyo_from_the_top_of_the_SkyTree.JPG, CC BY-SA 4.0
Bottom left: RoschetzkyIstockPhoto/iStock
Bottom right: Rovshan Aghayev/iStock
P. 76 Average Household Carbon Footprint in Eastern United States
© 2013 American Chemical Society: https://pubs.acs.org/doi/10.1021/es4034364
P. 76 The Predicament of Suburban Living
MattGush/iStock
P. 79 Stop the Subsidies
Top left: Library of Congress Prints and Photographs Division Washington, D.C.: HABS MD-1257-1
Top right: irina88w/iStock
Bottom left: Wiki/nakhon100, https://commons.wikimedia.org/wiki/File:Ford_Falcon_1968_(7811027052).jpg, CC 2.0
Bottom right: Wiki/Kevauto, https://commons.wikimedia

.org/wiki/File:2004_Ford_Excursion_Limited,_front_11.4.19
.jpg, CC BY-SA 4.0

P. 79 Polluters vs. Population

Data from Global Carbon Project, "Carbon Emissions," https://globalcarbonatlas.org/emissions/carbon-emissions/; and United Nations, Department of Economic and Social Affairs, Population Division, *World Population Prospects 2022, Online Edition*, https://population.un.org/wpp/

P. 80 A Suburban Lot Larger than an Entire African Village

Left: © Bonandbon Dw/Dreamstime.com
Right: Westend61/Veam

P. 80 Africa Could Become the World's First Net Negative Continent

Data from International Energy Agency, "Power Generation Capacity Additions in Africa in the Sustainable Africa Scenario (2011-2030)," June 20, 2022, https://www.iea.org/data-and-statistics/charts/power-generation-capacity-additions-in-africa-in-the-sustainable-africa-scenario-2011-2030

P. 81 Raworth's *Doughnut Economics*

Kate Raworth and Christian Guthier. CC-BY-SA 4.0. K. Raworth, *Doughnut Economics: Seven Ways to Think Like a 21st Century Economist*. London: Penguin Random House, 2017

P. 84 Disparity in Responses to Environmental Tragedies

Top left: Gibson Outdoor Photography/Alamy Stock Photo
Top right: Agencja Fotograficzna Caro/Alamy Stock Photo
Bottom left: Spencer Grant/Alamy Stock Photo
Bottom right: Wiki/U.S. Air Force, photo by Master Sgt. Mark C. Olsen, https://commons.wikimedia.org/wiki/File:121030-F-AL508-081c_Aerial_views_during_an_Army_search_and_rescue_mission_show_damage_from_Hurricane_Sandy_to_the_New_Jersey_coast,_Oct._30,_2012.jpg

P. 85 Carbon Emissions Dominated by 100 Corporations

Data from Paul Griffin, *Carbon Majors Report 2017* (London: Carbon Disclosure Project (CDP), 2017), https://cdn.cdp.net/cdp-production/cms/reports/documents/000/002/327/original/Carbon-Majors-Report-2017.pdf?1501833772

Chapter 4: Mister Robinson's Neighborhood

Notes

1 *Saturday Night Live*, season 45, episode 10, "Mr. Robinson's Neighborhood," hosted by Eddie Murphy, aired December 21, 2019, NBC, https://www.youtube.com/watch?v=whfQf3Pd5bU.

2 Heather McGhee, *The Sum of Us: What Racism Costs Everyone and How We Can Prosper Together* (New York: Random House, 2021).

3 Kōnstantinos Apostolou Doxiadēs, "The Increasing Problems," in "The Inevitable City," in *Anthropopolis: City for Human Development* (New York: W. W. Norton, 1975), 34-41.

4 See *Get Out*, dir. Jordan Peele (Universal Pictures, 2017),

and *Stepford Wives*, dir. Frank Oz (Paramount Pictures, 2004).

5 Julian Beinart, "Spatial & Social Structure II: Bipolarity," Lecture 17, MIT 4.241J Theory of City Form, Spring 2013, YouTube MIT OpenCourseWare, March 6, 2014, https://www.youtube.com/watch?v=1Aj6M4peeGw.

6 Michael Kimmelman, "How Houston Moved 25,000 People from the Streets into Homes of Their Own," *New York Times*, June 14, 2022, https://www.nytimes.com/2022/06/14/headway/houston-homeless-people.html.

7 Ezra Klein, "What America Needs Is a Liberalism That Builds," *New York Times*, May 29, 2022, https://www.nytimes.com/2022/05/29/opinion/biden-liberalism-infrastructure-building.html.

Illustrations

P. 87 Doxiades: Cities as Catalysts for Social Change

Diagram based on Kōnstantinos Apostolou Doxiadēs, "The Increasing Problems," in "The Inevitable City," in *Anthropopolis: City for Human Development* (New York: W. W. Norton, 1975), 34-41

P. 88 Upper East Side versus Williamsburg

Top: Cecile Marion/Alamy Stock Photo
Bottom: LWYang/Wiki, https://commons.wikimedia.org/wiki/File:Williamsburg-cheese-shop.jpg, CC BY 2.0

P. 90 Extreme Right: "The Country Is Full"

https://www.reddit.com/r/trashy/comments/9xfe3a/f_off_were_full/

P. 90 Extreme Left: "The City Is Full"

Rick Mohler

P. 92 Positive Social Friction versus Unsocial Frictionless Transactions

Left: Peter Forsberg/Shopping/Alamy Stock Photo
Right: Scharfsinn/Alamy Stock Photo

Chapter 5: For Whom the Dole Tolls

Notes

1 Ella Howard, "Rise of Conservatism in the 1980s," Digital Public Library of America, http://dp.la/primary-source-sets/rise-of-conservatism-in-the-1980s.

2 *Wall Street*, dir. Oliver Stone (20th Century Studios, 1987).

3 *The Big Chill*, dir. Lawrence Kasdan (Carson Productions, 1983).

4 Martha S. Jones, *Vanguard: How Black Women Broke Barriers, Won the Vote, and Insisted on Equality for All* (New York: Basic Books, 2020), 8.

5 Congressional Research Service, *The U.S. Land-Grant University System: An Overview*, https://crsreports.congress.gov/product/pdf/R/R45897.

6 H. Peter Oberlander and Eva M. Newbrun, *Houser: The Life and Work of Catherine Bauer, 1905-64* (Vancouver: University of British Columbia Press, 2011), 156.

7 Congress of the United States of America, *An act to amend*

and supplement the Federal-Aid Road Act approved July 11, 1916, to authorize appropriations for continuing the construction of highways; to amend the Internal Revenue Code of 1954 to provide additional revenue from the taxes on motor fuel, tires and trucks and buses; and for other purposes, Enrolled Acts and Resolutions of Congress, 1789–1996, General Records of the United States Government, Record Group 11, National Archives, Washington, D.C., June 29, 1956.

8 Randall Bennett Woods, "LBJ, Politics, and 1968," *South Central Review* 16/17 (1999): 17.

9 See, for example, Kriston Caps, "How the Federal Government Built White Suburbia," *City Lab*, September 2, 2015, https://www.bloomberg.com/news/articles /2015-09-02/how-the-federal-government-built -white-suburbia; and Matthew Desmond, *Poverty, by America* (New York: Crown Publishing Group, 2023).

10 See, for example, Sanford F. Schram, Joe Soss, and Richard C. Fording, eds., *Race and the Politics of Welfare Reform* (Ann Arbor: University of Michigan Press, 2003); and Bruce Bartlett, *Starve the Beast* (New York: Vintage Books, 2008).

11 *The Pruitt-Igoe Myth*, dir. Chad Freidrichs (First Run Films, 2011).

12 Danielle Aubert, Lana Cavar, and Natasha Chandani, *Thanks for the View, Mr. Mies: Lafayette Park, Detroit* (New York: Metropolis Books, 2019).

13 Congress of the United States of America, *Guidance on Complying with the Maximum Number of Units Eligible for Operating Subsidy Pursuant to Section 9(g)(3)(A) of the Housing Act of 1937 (aka the Faircloth Limit)*, October 1999, https:// www.hud.gov/sites/documents/FRCLTH-LMT.PDF.

14 Elon Musk, Twitter post, December 28, 2019, archived at https://twitter.com/drmistercody/status /1211500119935176704/photo/1.

15 Vishaan Chakrabarti, *A Country of Cities: A Manifesto for an Urban America* (New York: Metropolis Books, 2013), 155.

16 Winnie Hu, "Major Traffic Experiment in NYC: Cars All but Banned on Major Street," *New York Times*, August 8, 2019, https://www.nytimes.com/2019/08/08/nyregion/14th -street-busway.html.

17 Shelly Tan, Youjin Shin, and Danielle Rindler, "How One of America's Ugliest Days Unraveled inside and outside the Capitol," *Washington Post*, January 9, 2021, https://www .washingtonpost.com/nation/interactive/2021/capitol -insurrection-visual-timeline/.

18 Matthew Desmond, *Poverty, by America* (New York: Crown, 2023), 95.

19 See Vishaan Chakrabarti, "America's Urban Future," *New York Times*, April 16, 2014, https://www.nytimes. com/2014/04/17/opinion/americas-urban-future.html; and Dallas News Administrator, "Q&A: Urban Planner Vishaan Chakrabarti Urges Dallas to Chart Its Own Course," *Dallas Morning News*, January 24, 2015, https://www.dallasnews .com/arts-entertainment/architecture/2015/01/25/qa

-urban-planner-vishaan-chakrabarti-urges-dallas-to-chart -its-own-course/.

20 "The Pandemic Has Made Homelessness More Visible in Many American Cities," *The Economist*, August 5, 2021, https://www.economist.com/united-states/2021/08/02 /the-pandemic-has-made-homelessness-more-visible-in -many-american-cities.

21 "Why Is This Happening? Why America Is So Polarized with Ezra Klein: Podcast and Transcript," NBC News, February 4, 2020, https://www.nbcnews.com/think /opinion/why-america-so-polarized-ezra-klein-podcast -transcript-ncna1126481.

22 Steven Pinker, *Enlightenment Now: The Case for Reason, Science, Humanism, and Progress* (New York: Penguin Books, 2018).

23 Raymond Zhong, "How to Save a Forest by Burning It," *New York Times*, September 7, 2022, https://www.nytimes .com/2022/09/07/climate/california-wildfire-prescribed -burn.html.

24 Chakrabarti, *A Country of Cities*, 177.

25 California State Senate, *Planning and Zoning: Housing Development: Streamlined Approval: Incentives*, California Legislature—2019–2020 Regular Session, Senator Wiener, SB-50, Sacramento, December 3, 2018, https://leginfo .legislature.ca.gov/faces/billStatusClient.xhtml?bill _id=201920200SB50.

26 Talking Heads, "Don't Worry about the Government," 1977, track 8 on *Talking Heads: 77*, Sire Records, 1977, LP.

Illustrations
P. 95 Neoliberal Icons
Top: MediaPunch Inc./Alamy Stock Photo
Center: The Shock Doctrine, documentary, https://www .researchgate.net/figure/Pinochet-meets-Milton-Friedman -Source-The-shock-doctrine-documentary_fig2_338630726
P. 95 The United States of Tax Cuts
Adapted from Steve Sims, "Electoral College 1984," June 14, 2008, https://en.wikipedia.org/wiki/File :ElectoralCollege1984.svg
P. 96 The Reagan Coalition
Top: Allstar Picture Library Ltd./Alamy Stock Photo
Bottom: Moviestore Collection Ltd./Alamy Stock Photo
P. 97 The "Again" in MAGA: 1950s Welfare for Whites
Archive PL/Alamy Stock Photo
P. 98 Neoliberalism Made Manifest: The Detritus of the Historic Pennsylvania Station
Bob Koller/NY Daily News Archive/ Getty Images
P. 100 Private Defeats Public
Top: Wiki/United States Department of Housing and Urban Development, https://commons.wikimedia.org/wiki/File :Pruitt-Igoe-collapses.jpg
Bottom left: Chad Freidrichs
Bottom right: Adapted from Vishaan Chakrabarti, *A Country of Cities: A Manifesto for an Urban America* (New York:

Metropolis Books, 2013)

P. 102 The Fight over the 14th Street Bus Lanes
Left: Wiki/Tdorante10, https://commons.wikimedia.org
/wiki/File:14th_St_Bway_td_(2019-10-28)_22.jpg, CC BY-SA
4.0
Bottom: Liam Quigley, https://www.amny.com/transit/14th
-street-bus-service-1-35017117/

P. 102 An Infrastructure of Opportunity
Adapted from Chakrabarti, *A Country of Cities*

P. 102 Polling in Online Public Meetings
Screenshot by PAU from the Advisory Group Meeting 02 for
Downtown Niagara Falls Development Strategy, Dec. 10,
2020, and the engagement session for PAU's 2023 Miller
Prize entry, Dec. 12, 2022

**P. 104 The Culture Wars of " Guns, God, and Gays"
Now Includes Gas Guzzlers**
Top: Francisco Blanco/Alamy Stock Photo
Center: Alyson McClaran/Reuters
Bottom: https://www.teslarati.com/tesla-supercharger-solo
-mass-iceing-photo/

P. 106 Suburban Poverty on the Rise
Data from Brookings Institution, "The Changing Geography
of U.S. Poverty," February 15, 2017, https://www.brookings
.edu/articles/the-changing-geography-of-us-poverty/

P. 107 Population without Representation
Data from University of Virginia Weldon Cooper Center,
"National Population Projections," 2018, https://
coopercenter.org/national-population-projections

**PP. 110–11 American Smart Infrastructure Act (from *A
Country of Cities*)**
Adapted from Chakrabarti, *A Country of Cities*

Chapter 6: Here! Here!
Notes
1 Gertrude Stein, *Everybody's Autobiography* (New York:
Random House, 1937).

Illustrations
**P. 120 Dupont Circle Metro Washington, D.C., USA
(1977)**
Top: Eric Kilbey/Wiki, https://commons.wikimedia.org
/wiki/File:Dupont_Circle_Metro_station.jpg, CC BY-SA 2.0
Bottom: Alan Wolf/Flickr, https://www.flickr.com/photos
/alumroot/6016889922 https://creativecommons.org
/licenses/by/2.0/

**P. 121 Central–Mid-Levels Escalator System
Hong Kong (1993)**
Top: Ian Dagnall/Alamy Stock Photo
Bottom: Wiki/Wanmtamgoi, https://commons.wikimedia
.org/wiki/File:HK_Central_Escalators_interior_visitors_Oct
-013_(2).JPG, CC BY-SA 3.0

P. 124 Barbican Estate London, UK (1976)
Top: Chris Harris/Alamy Stock Photo
Bottom: Greg Balfour Evans/Alamy Stock Photo

P. 125 Edifício Copan São Paulo, Brazil (1966)
Top: Richard Sowersby/Alamy Stock Photo
Bottom: Gabriel Cabral

**P. 128 Hillside Terrace Tokyo, Japan (first phase
completed 1969)**
Top: XIAZHi Pictures
Bottom: PIXTA:IDEA

P. 129 Carrières Centrales Casablanca, Morocco (1952)
Top: © Avery, Columbia University, New York, https://www
.flickr.com/photos/desingel/21431608358
Bottom: ETH Zurich/Andre Studer

P. 132 Place des Vosges Paris, France (1605)
Top: Pexels
Bottom: lillisphotography/iStock

P. 133 Tompkins Square Park New York, USA (1834)
Top: James/Adobe Stock
Bottom: Deberarr/Adobe Stock

P. 136 Unter den Linden Berlin, Germany (1647)
Top: Alexey_Fedoren/iStock
Bottom: mistervlad/Bigstock

P. 137 Paseo de la Reforma Mexico City, Mexico (1867)
Top: Orbon Alija/iStock
Bottom: agcuesta1/Deposit Photos

**P. 140 OZ Voorburgwal Amsterdam, Netherlands (first
built in 1385)**
Top: Lex Schruijer
Bottom: Wiki/Remi Mathis, https://commons.wikimedia
.org/wiki/File:Amsterdam_-_Koninginnedag_2012_-_Boats
_Oudezijds_voorburgwal.JPG, CC BY-SA 3.0

**P. 141 Bay and River Streets Savannah, USA (first built
in 1700s; rebuilt in 1977)**
Top: John Wollwerth/Alamy Stock Photo
Bottom: RiverNorthPhotography/iStock

**P. 144 Indian Institute of Management Ahmedabad,
India (1974)**
Top: HCP Design, Planning and Management Pvt. Ltd.
Bottom: Laurian Ghinitoiu

**P. 145 Freie Universität Berlin, Germany (first phase,
1973)**
Top: Dirk Laubner
Bottom: Trevor Patt

P. 148 Saha Al Qassas Al Fawwar, Palestine (2014)
Top: Curry Stone Foundation/Decolonizing Architecture Art
Residency (DAAR)
Bottom: Adam Ferguson

**P. 149 Opportunigee Village Nakivale, Uganda
(ongoing; founded in 2016)**
Top, bottom: Patrick Muvunga

P. 152 Altes Museum Berlin, Germany (1830)
Top: Juergen Henkelmann Photography/Alamy Stock Photo
Bottom: Agencja Fotograficzna Caro/Alamy Stock Photo

**P. 153 East Building, National Gallery Washington, D.C.,
USA (1978)**
Top: Wiki/The National Gallery of Art, https://commons

.wikimedia.org/wiki/File:National_Gallery_of_Art%2C_East
_Building.jpg, CC BY-SA 4.0
Bottom: Wiki/Difference engine, https://commons
.wikimedia.org/wiki/File:East_Building_of_the_National
_Gallery_of_Art,_atrium.jpg, CC BY-SA 4.0

Chapter 7: Practice Makes Pertinence
Notes

1 Dana Cuff, *Architecture: The Story of Practice* (Cambridge, MA: MIT Press, 1992); Tom Fisher, *In the Scheme of Things* (Minneapolis: University of Minnesota Press, 2000).
2 See "Women in Architecture," American Institute of Architects, January 6, 2020, https://www.aia.org /articles/6252982-women-in-architecture; and Despina Stratigakos, *Where Are the Women Architects?* (Princeton: Princeton University Press, 2016), 21.
3 Malcolm Gladwell, "10000 Hour Rule," in *Outliers: The Story of Success* (New York: Little, Brown, 2008), 35–68.
4 "About: Agency," Forensic Architecture, https://forensic -architecture.org/about/agency.
5 David Freedlander, "Forensic Architecture, the Artists Who Blew Up the Whitney Biennial," *Daily Beast*, August 8, 2019, https://www.thedailybeast.com/forensic -architecture-the-artists-who-blew-up-the-whitney -biennial?utm_source=Breakfast+with+ARTnews&utm _campaign=dbf7f18c65-EMAILCAMPAIGN_2019_08_08_06 _41&utm_medium=email&utm_term=0_c5d7f10ceb -dbf7f18c65-293940819, emphasis mine.
6 Sean Anderson and Mabel O. Wilson, eds., *Reconstructions: Architecture and Blackness in America*, exhibition catalogue (New York: Museum of Modern Art, 2021).
7 Karissa Rosenfield, "Pritzker Responds to Denise Scott Brown Controversy," *ArchDaily*, April 1, 2013, https://www .archdaily.com/353219/pritzker-responds-to-denise-scott -brown-controversy.
8 N. John Habraken, *Variations: The Systematic Design of Supports* (Cambridge, MA: MIT Press, 1976), 10.
9 *The Wire*, created by David Simon, aired June 2, 2002, to March 9, 2008, on HBO Entertainment.
10 R. Thomas Hille and William Wurster, *Inside the Large Small House: The Residential Design Legacy of William W. Wurster* (Princeton: Princeton Architectural Press, 1994).
11 "About," Designing Justice, https://designingjustice.org /about/.
12 "Jury Citation," Pritzker Architecture Prize, 2022, https:// www.pritzkerprize.com/laureates/diebedo-francis -kere#laureate-page-2441, emphasis mine.
13 "Gando Teachers' Housing/Kéré Architecture," *ArchDaily*, April 25, 2016, https://www.archdaily .com/785956/gando-teachers-housing-kere-architecture.
14 "University Campus UTEC Lima: Grafton Architects," Grafton Architects, https://www.graftonarchitects.ie /University-Campus-UTEC-Lima.

Illustrations
P. 162 The Late Twentieth Century: More Is More
Top left: Sandra Cohen-Rose and Colin Rose/Flickr, https:// www.flickr.com/photos/73416633@N00/291171517
Top right: © Frank O. Gehry. Courtesy of Getty Research Institute, Los Angeles (2017.M.66)
Bottom left: J. Paul Getty Trust
Bottom right: Roland Halbe

P. 162 A New Millennium
Top left: Wiki/rds323, https://commons.wikimedia .org/wiki/File:Explosion_following_the_plane_impact_into _the_South_Tower_(WTC_2)_-_B6019-11.jpg
Top right: NASA
Bottom left: Feverpitch/Deposit Photos
Bottom right: Wiki/GoToVan from Vancouver, Canada, https://commons.wikimedia.org/wiki/File:Black_Lives _Matter,_Anti-racism_rally_at_Vancouver_Art_Gallery _(49957865853).jpg

P. 162 The Venerable Work with the Vulnerable
Top left: Suyin Chia/Elemental Architecture
Top right: Balkrishna Doshi Archives, Vastushilpa Foundation, Ahmedabad, India
Bottom left: Photo: Simeon Duchoud, 2006. Courtesy Kéré Architecture
Bottom right: Philippe Ruault

P. 165 Tatiana Bilbao, Ciudad Acuña Housing Project
Left: Tatiana Bilbao Estudio
Right: Iwan Baan

P. 166 Lacaton and Vassal, Transformation of the Tour Bois le Prêtre
Top left: © Druot, Lacaton Vassal
Bottom left: © Philippe Ruault. Courtesy Druot, Lacaton & Vassal
Right: © Druot, Lacaton Vassal

P. 166 O'Donnell and Tuomey, Timberyard Housing
Left, right: Dennis Gilbert-VIEW/Alamy Stock Photo

P. 166 Michael Maltzan, Star Apartments
Left: Gabor Ekecs
Right: Photo: Iwan Baan

P. 169 Francis Kéré, Gando Teachers' Housing
Top: Erik-Jan Ouwerkerk, 2009
Bottom: Kéré Architecture

P. 170 Patrick Muvunga, Uhuru Amphitheater, Nakivale Refugee Settlement
Top, right: Patrick Muvunga

P. 170 Marina Tabassum, Bait Ur Rouf Mosque
Top: Marina Tabassum Architects/Sandro Di Carlo Darsa
Bottom: Marina Tabassum Architects/Rajesh Vora

P. 173 Kashef Chowdhury, University of Liberal Arts Bangladesh
Left, right: Shakil Ibne Hai

P. 173 Office Sian, Phoenix Garden
Left, right: Office Sian

P. 173 Grafton Architects, UTEC Campus, Lima

Left: Iwan Baan
Right: Section © Grafton Architects

Chapter 8: The TAU of PAU
Notes

1 Ned Cramer, "What Won't You Build?" *Architect Magazine*, April 5, 2017, https://www.architectmagazine.com/design /editorial/what-wont-you-build_o.
2 Diana Agrest, "The City as the Place of Representation," *Design Quarterly*, no. 113/114 (1980): 8, https://doi .org/10.2307/4091024.
3 Aldo van Eyck, "Team 10 Primer," in *Theories and Manifestoes of Contemporary Architecture*, ed. Charles Jencks and Karl Kropf (Chichester, NY: Wiley-Academy, 1997), 27.
4 Catherine Bauer, "The Social Front of Modern Architecture in the 1930s," J*ournal of the Society of Architectural Historians* 24, no. 1 (1965): 50.
5 Cathleen McGuigan, "Interview with Walter Hood on History and Race in Landscape Design," *Architectural Record*, August 4, 2020, https://artsdesign.berkeley.edu/design /news/interview-with-walter-hood-on-history-and-race-in -landscape-design.
6 Kenneth Frampton, "Towards a Critical Regionalism: Six Points for an Architecture of Resistance," in *The Anti-Aesthetic, Essays on Postmodern Culture*, ed. Hal Foster (Port Townsend, WA: Bay Press, 1983), 20–21.
7 Léa-Catherine Szacka and Véronique Patteeuw, "Critical Regionalism for Our Time," *Architectural Review*, November 22, 2019, https://www.architectural-review.com/essays /critical-regionalism-for-our-time, emphasis mine.
8 The Talking Heads, "This Must Be the Place (Naive Melody)," 1982, track 9 on *Speaking in Tongues*, Sire, 1983, LP.

Illustrations
P. 181 Aldo van Eyck
RIBA Collections
P. 181 Catherine Bauer
Environmental Design Archives, UC Berkeley: CED Records
P. 181 Walter Hood
Wiki/GSAPPstudent, https://commons.wikimedia .org/wiki/File:Walter_Hood_at_Columbia_GSAPP.jpg, CC BY-SA 4.0
P. 185 PAU, InterOculus
Bottom left, right: Hadley Fruits for Landmark Columbus Foundation
P. 186 PAU with the *New York Times* and Buro Happold, N.Y.C.—Not Your Car
Top left: The Reading Room/Alamy Stock Photo
Top right, bottom: Renderings by PAU based on imagery from Google Earth
P. 186 PAU with the *New York Times*, Penn Palimpsest
Top left: Collage by PAU with image from javimax/Flickr
P. 189 PAU, Office-to-Live/Work Conversion
Bottom left, right: Renderings by PAU based on imagery

from Google Earth
P. 193 PAU, Domino Sugar Refinery
Top right: Christopher Payne/Esto
Other: Max Touhey
P. 197 PAU, F4 Towers
Upper center left: Judy Lovell-Janthina Images/Alamy Stock Photo
Upper center second from left: traveler1116/iStock
Upper center second from right: RidingMetaphor/Alamy Stock Photo
Upper center right: Jake Ratz/Alamy Stock Photo
P. 198 PAU, Niagara Falls Heritage Gateways
Top: Diagram by PAU based on imagery from Google Earth
P. 200 PAU, New New York Penn
Top: Item no. 280, AA712 M195 FF, Page No. 209. Avery Architectural & Fine Arts Library, Columbia University, Gift of Amherst College Library

Chapter 9: Rebel Rebel
Notes

1 Oh No Compassion, "David Byrne's *American Utopia*: I Zimbra (Live on Colbert, 2021)," YouTube video, 3:59, May 21, 2021, https://www.youtube.com/watch?v =2kx03MYsKDY.
2 Gary M. Kramer, "David Byrne's *American Utopia* Is a Rousing, Vibrant Spectacular That Rivals *Stop Making Sense*," *Salon*, October 17, 2020, https://www.salon.com/2020 /10/17/david-byrnes-american-utopia-review-hbo/.
3 David Bowie, "Rebel Rebel," 1974, B-side track 1 on *Diamond Dogs*, RCA Records, 1974, LP.

Chapter 10: The Garden of Urban
Notes

1 Vishaan P. Chakrabarti, "Transforming the Siedlung: The IBA and Beyond," in "Rebuilding the Urban Margin and the Modern Ideal" (graduate thesis, Massachusetts Institute of Technology, 1993), 31–50, https://dspace.mit.edu /handle/1721.1/17326.
2 Francesca Mari, "Imagine a Renters' Utopia: It Might Look Like Vienna," *New York Times*, May 23, 2023, https://www .nytimes.com/2023/05/23/magazine/vienna-social -housing.html.
3 Enrique Peñalosa, "Por qué los autobuses representan la democracia en acción," video recording of talk delivered at TED, December 2023, https://www.ted.com/talks /enrique_penalosa_why_buses_represent_democracy_in _action?language=es.
4 See, for example, Leo Marx, *The Machine in the Garden: Technology and the Pastoral Ideal in America* (New York: Oxford University Press, 1964).
5 See *Black Panther*, dir. Ryan Coogler (Marvel Studios, 2018); and *Black Panther: Wakanda Forever*, dir. Ryan Coogler (Marvel Studios, 2022).
6 Mark Lamster and Alexandra Lange, "2018 in

Architecture: The Good, The Bad, and The Urbanism,"
Curbed, December 27, 2018, https://archive.curbed.
com/2018/12/27/18149185/architecture-awards-2018
-year-in-review.
7 International Energy Agency, *Credible Pathways to 1.5°C*
(IEA Publications, April 2023), https://www.iea.org/reports
/credible-pathways-to-150c.
8 Yuval N. Harari, *Sapiens: A Brief History of Humankind* (New
York: Harper, 2014).

Illustrations

P. 229 Social Housing and Urban Parks
Top left: gruppe F/Freiraum für alle GmbH (CC-BY-ND)
Top right: © IBA_Vienna-Ludwig Schedl
Bottom left: halbergman/iStock
Bottom right: Image rights granted by the Madrid City
Council, https://www.madrid.es/portales/munimadrid
/es/Inicio/El-Ayuntamiento/Arganzuela/Madrid-Rio
-Especial-Informativo/?vgnextfmt=default&vgnextoid=5acc
7f0917afc110VgnVCM2000000c205a0aRCRD&vgnextcha
nnel=e6f1ca5d5fb96010VgnVCM100000dc0ca8c0RCRD&
idCapitulo=5697990

P. 229 Reclaimed Streets and Public Transportation
Top left: Wiki/Guilhem Vellut, https://commons
.wikimedia.org/wiki/File:Parc_Rives_de_Seine_@_Pont
_Alexandre_III_@_Paris_(33517514834).jpg, CC BY 2.0
Top right: Claudio Olivares Medina
Bottom left: Wiki/Tdorante10, https://commons.wikimedia
.org/wiki/File:Bergen_St_Smith_St_td_(2019-09-23)_03
_-_Citi_Bike.jpg, CC BY-SA 4.0
Bottom right: La Secretaría de Movilidad de Medellín,
https://www.flickr.com/photos/transitomedellin
/31746210465 https://creativecommons.org/licenses/by
/2.0/

P. 232 We've Got the Power
Kenueone/Pixabay

P. 237 Beloved Urban Density
Top left: Jon Bilous/Alamy Stock Photo
Top right: Yuen Man Cheung/Alamy Stock Photo
Bottom left: mikolajn/Deposit Photos
Bottom right: diegograndi/Adobe Stock

P. 238 Taller Is Not Always Better
Left: Guilhem Vellut
Right: Wiki/Downtowngal, https://commons.wikimedia.org
/wiki/File:548_S_Normandie,_Los_Angeles.jpg, CC BY-SA
4.0

**P. 242 PAU with the *New York Times*, How to Make
Room for One Million New Yorkers**
Before-and-after renderings by PAU and the *New York Times*
based on photographs by Xizmo Media; illustrative map by
PAU and the *New York Times*

P. 245 Nature, Culture, and Joy
Hadley Fruits for Landmark Columbus Foundation

All other illustrations by PAU and Pentagram.

Index

Note: Page numbers in italic type indicate illustrations.

30

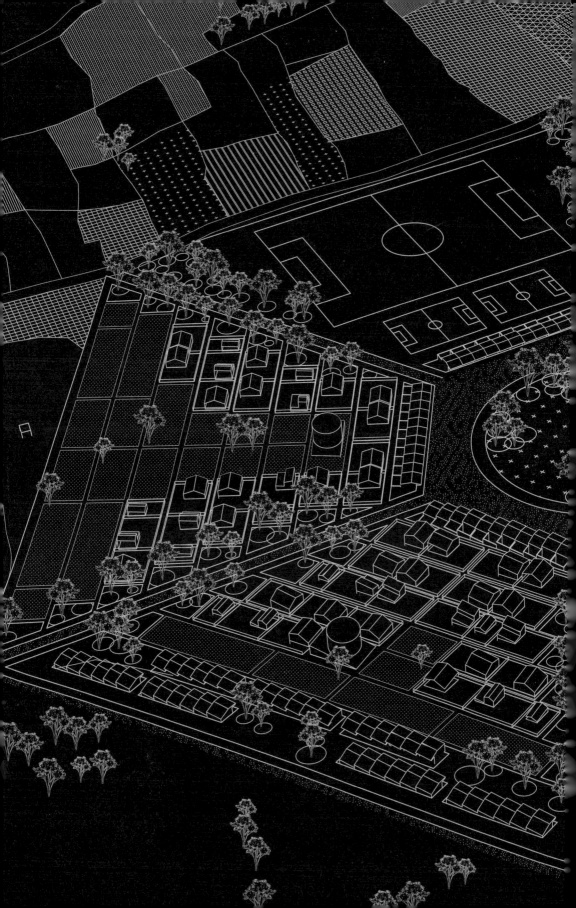